Analytical
Archaeology

Analytical Archaeology

David L. Clarke

SECOND EDITION

revised by
BOB CHAPMAN

METHUEN & CO LTD

First published in 1968 by Methuen & Co Ltd
11 New Fetter Lane London EC4P 4EE
This edition published 1978
© 1968, 1978 The estate of David L. Clarke
Printed in Great Britain by
J. W. Arrowsmith Ltd., Bristol

ISBN hardbound 0 416 85450 8
ISBN paperback 0 416 85460 5

To my wife, Stella

Contents

Foreword to the revised edition   xi
Preface   xv
Acknowledgements   xix

1 Introduction and polemic   1
   I The history of archaeology   2
   II The nature of archaeology   10
   III The nature of archaeological data   13
   IV The aims of archaeology   19
   V Terminology, definition and meaning   23
   VI Models   30

2 Culture systems – the model   42
   I Systems theory, an outline   42
   II A tentative general model   72
   III Discussion   77

**3 Cultural morphology and cultural
ecology – the setting**   84
   I The nature of cultural systems   85
   II Culture as an information system   88
   III Culture as a system with subsystems   101
   IV Environment as a system with subsystems   132

4 Material culture systems – attribute and artefact   149
   I Introduction   149
   II Attribute and artefact systems   152
   III Phase pattern regularities   162
   IV Time pattern regularities   180
   V System pattern regularities   195

5 Artefact and type   205
  I Introduction   205
  II Artefact-type systems   207
  III Phase pattern regularities   209
  IV Time pattern regularities   217
  V System pattern regularities   237

6 Assemblage and culture   245
  I Introduction   245
  II Cultural assemblage systems   249
  III Phase pattern regularities   261
  IV Time pattern regularities   272
  V System pattern regularities   285

7 Culture and culture group   299
  I Introduction   299
  II Culture group systems   302
  III Phase pattern regularities   305
  IV Time pattern regularities   315
  V System pattern regularities   324

8 Culture group and technocomplex   328
  I Introduction   328
  II Technocomplex systems   330
  III Phase pattern regularities   337
  IV Time pattern regularities   339
  V System pattern regularities   354

9 Group ethnology   363
  I Introduction   363
  II Internal evidence   367
  III Recent ethnographic evidence   370
  IV Historical ethnographic evidence   394

10 Entities and processes and procedure   409
  I Introduction   409
  II Entities   412
  III Processes   416
  IV Procedure   458

11 Discussion and speculation   465
   I Theoretical background   465
  II Disciplined procedure   471
 III Archaeological grammar   479
 IV Speculations   485

Definitions   489
Bibliography   497
Index   514

Foreword to the revised edition

During the early months of 1976 David Clarke began planning a second, revised edition of this book. By academic standards the first edition had been a great publishing success and all copies printed in Britain had been sold. But the demand for the book had continued, with second-hand copies fetching high prices. His intention was to reduce the volume by over 200 pages, remove outdated aspects and repetitive passages, summarize overlengthy sections, improve the prose style where it was obscure and write two new chapters. He agreed with the publishers that the revised edition would be submitted to them in the autumn and asked me to assist him with much of the preliminary work. We discussed the general areas of revision which were thought necessary and I started to work on the book after Easter.

After his death at the end of June 1976 I consulted both the publishers and Mrs Stella Clarke about the revision. Both agreed that they wished it to go ahead, although it could not be in exactly the same form as had been planned. David's own personal papers were of little help, since like with many other subjects he carried most of the ideas in his head and what was jotted down in note form was heavily condensed or illegible! The book clearly breaks down into two parts, theory and methods, and although both have been developed in the last ten years it has been the methods that have undergone the most drastic changes. There are important recent works on the use of computer and mathematical models (Doran and Hodson 1975) and on the application of quantitative techniques of spatial analysis derived from contemporary geography (Hodder and Orton 1975). Many of the suggestions and examples contained in chapters 11–13 of the first edition have been pursued by other archaeologists in different areas of the world and in order to do justice to this work at least two, if not three, new chapters would have had to be written. As far as I was concerned, this would have meant too great a personal intrusion into the publication of someone for whom I had the greatest admiration and respect.

The alternative plan, which I have adopted in this revision, is to retain the first part of the book with its basic structure intact. To this I have added the concluding chapter (chapter 14 in the first edition). Now of course theory is a constant source of debate within archaeology, and the thoughts expressed in *Analytical Archaeology* have been both welcomed and condemned, accepted and criticized. The concepts and language of systems theory are nowhere expressed in such detail in relation to archaeological entities and the argument for a more rigorous concern with theory has seldom been put more forcefully. Although some archaeologists may find the message rather baffling (because of its unfamiliar expression) or brash or think it irrelevant to their own detailed interests, the book remains popular and influential. As regards David Clarke's development of Gordon Childe's methodology (a hierarchical classification of archaeological entities, among which the culture is the central organizing unit), there are those who now argue that the interpretation of these entities in terms of social groups is unrealistic and helps to mask important variability in human behaviour in the past (see chapter 9, note 1). In the light of these gradual shifts in theoretical orientation, it would seem useful to have the classic statement of 'hierarchical' or 'culture' theory in archaeology available to both students and professionals alike.

Other justifications for the revised edition can be put forward. The discussion of systems theory remains both useful and stimulating. The condemnation of ambiguity, undisciplined procedure and lack of concern with theory are matters which the student of archaeology would benefit from reading. Finally, there is the more general value of a book which is openly outward-looking – exploring other areas of the disciplinary universe for methods and concepts which may be of use in our own subject. Students should be made aware of the 'frontiers' of their subject and there is no finer example of this attitude than *Analytical Archaeology*.

In line with the author's wishes I have tried to make the book more comprehensible without sacrificing the basic ideas in it. I have simplified some of the arguments and removed some of the more repetitive or confusing passages. New references and figures have been added. Wherever possible I have confined my intrusions into the text to notes at the end of each chapter. These are designed to comment on more recent developments in both methods and theory and will I hope lead the reader on to other sources. In one or two cases I have included material from the original Part II in this edition, and on two particular occasions I have rewritten more substantial parts of the text: on economic subsystems in chapter 3 and on diffusion models in chapter 10.

During the course of revising this book I have received welcome encouragement and professional assistance from Richard Bradley, David Coombs and Mike Fulford. I have also benefited from the patience of the publishers and the encouragement of Mrs Stella Clarke. My wife Jan has been of immeasurable help in the preparation of the typescript and her tolerance of a reviser working to an increasingly closer deadline. My greatest acknowledgement is to David Clarke himself. During the eight years in which I studied under him as both undergraduate and research student he was an unfailing source of stimulus and encouragement in my work and his personal kindnesses were too numerous to mention. Like others of my generation in Cambridge, I count myself fortunate to have known him and to have gained from his help and friendship. This revised edition has been produced in memory of a most exceptional man whose contribution to contemporary archaeology was outstanding.

Reading   Bob Chapman
September 1977

Preface

Archaeology is an undisciplined empirical discipline. A discipline lacking a scheme of systematic and ordered study based upon declared and clearly defined models and rules of procedure. It further lacks a body of central theory capable of synthesizing the general regularities within its data in such a way that the unique residuals distinguishing each particular case might be quickly isolated and easily assessed. Archaeologists do not agree upon central theory, although, regardless of place, period, and culture, they employ similar tacit models and procedures based upon similar and distinctive entities – the attributes, artefacts, types, assemblages, cultures and culture groups. Lacking an explicit theory defining these entities and their relationships and transformations in a viable form, archaeology has remained an intuitive skill – an inexplicit manipulative dexterity learned by rote.

It seems likely, however, that the second half of the twentieth century will retrospectively be seen to mark an important threshold in the development of archaeology – a phase of transition towards a new disciplinary configuration. Since the 1950s archaeologists have been made increasingly aware of the inadequacies of their own archaic formulations by the disjunctive comments of a whole new generation of techniques and procedures now widely used in the fields of inter-jacent social sciences. The adaptive repatterning of archaeology has been set in motion by the discipline's coupling with the study of systems, games theory, set and group theory, topology, information and communication theory, cultural ecology, locational analysis and analytical and inductive statistics powered by those key innovations – the digital and analogue computers. A whole array of new studies has developed whose implications have diffused piecemeal into archaeology and which increasingly permeate its fabric in a somewhat disconnected fashion. One response to these new developments has been to avoid them by a nostalgic retreat into historiography, another response has faced these innovations and initiated a period of groping experiment, inevitable error, and constructive feedback, whilst yet a third response awaits the outcome, inert within carefully encysted reputations – all of these reactions are concurrently in full development.

However, merely to add these new techniques to the existing structure of archaeology, like so many lean-to extensions of a shabby and already rambling edifice, is no solution to archaeological amorphism. The implications of these developments must be integrated within a fully congruent and re-designed discipline – the feedback in these new couplings is such that not only must these techniques be selectively modified to match archaeological dimensions but archaeology must itself adapt and change to gain the best advantage of this freshly emergent potential.

This book therefore follows Bacon's conception of the necessary development of scientific theory by 'anticipations, rash and premature' (*Novum Organum*, 1620). This book is a personal attempt towards the integration demanded by the events sketched above – it is a synthesis of many analyses in an attempt to trace system regularities. Above all else, this work is a temporary and tentative assessment of a complex theoretical development that must inevitably take one or two more generations to mature as a reasonably comprehensive and fairly viable set of disciplined procedure. The increasingly mathematical, statistical and computerized analysis of archaeological data will certainly ensure that the hitherto tacit and naive archaeological models will be made viable and explicit, or abandoned and replaced. These models will themselves escalate from iconic to analogue and then symbolic models of many kinds – ensuring an increasingly direct liaison with computer studies and a more powerful and general development of synthesizing axioms and principles within the discipline itself.

It is perhaps necessary to relate analytical archaeology to archaeological central theory and to other archaeological approaches. The contemporary study of sociocultural systems has emphasized that the analysis of ancient or modern human units and their products cannot be satisfactorily accomplished in terms of information from single network aspects of these complex systems. The social, psychological, linguistic, religious, economic and material attributes of hominid communities cannot be realistically studied if isolated from the integral context of the sociocultural and environmental system precipitating them in that particular mutually adjusted configuration. It may not be possible for the archaeologist to specify the exact values of these former factors but his analyses must at least take into account their interdependence, the probable range of their limited tolerance, and the compounded constraint imposed by such limitations.

It follows that since one may selectively trace an infinity of particular networks through sociocultural systems and their fossil remains, no single approach can have the sole prerogative of accuracy and informative utility. Consequently, there are as many competing opinions about the proper orientation and dimensions of archaeological analysis as there are archaeologists – thus even the domain of archaeology is partitioned into the overlapping fields of vigorous rival archaeologies (Chang 1967, p. 137) or 'paradigms' (Clarke 1972) upon which the progressive development of archaeology depends. Nevertheless, there is one critical subsystem within archaeological studies which may not claim pre-eminence in virtue but which may claim *droit de seigneur* in the whole domain – and that is archaeological central theory, the largely tacit procedures common to archaeology everywhere.

Almost every kind and class of archaeological study contributes something to our understanding of the domain of archaeology but all such studies, in their turn, depend upon the adequacy of the general theory which frames their analyses and which should unite studies within the discipline regardless of area, period, and culture. The introductory polemic of chapter 1 must be understood in this context as intended merely to redress the balance in which central theory has been neglected in the pursuit of narrative history and particularist analyses. There is certainly a valuable role for all the rival archaeologies but the central theory uniting analytical archaeology will remain central – however weak and inadequate its contemporary manifestations may be. Analytical archaeology is therefore primarily a syntactical approach to synthesis and central theory, a changing corpus of conceptual frameworks which emphasize that no archaeological study can be better than the ideological assumptions which underlie the development of its arguments.

It is with deep gratitude that I acknowledge the assistance and support which has been afforded me by colleagues in Europe, Africa and America. In particular I would mention the extensive and stimulating support of Professor J. G. D. Clark of Cambridge, at whose original request the course of lectures was written that have been recast in this volume. At the same time it is a great pleasure to acknowledge the impetus and direction imparted to this work by the friendship and kindness of Dr P. H. A. Sneath, a small side-effect of his dynamic impact upon British studies in numerical taxonomy. To my College, Peterhouse, I owe the academic frame which has enabled me to live in and exploit the atmosphere of opportunities which circulate in a great University; perhaps the most fundamental gift that I can acknowledge.

I would also like to mention the debts that I owe to certain contemporaries and colleagues, especially Glynn Isaac and David Pilbeam, Mike Jarman and Paul Wilkinson – a stimulating reservoir of provocative comment.

For invaluable help with all my work I would like to thank my wife, to whom this book is dedicated – Stella Clarke.

Peterhouse   D.L.C.
January 1968

Acknowledgements

The authors and publishers wish to thank the following for permission to reproduce figures from the sources given below:

A. P. Watt & Son for fig. 5 (fig. 4/11/1 from *An Introduction to Cybernetics* by W. Ross Ashby, published by Chapman & Hall Ltd); Association of American Geographers for fig. 17b (by P. R. Gould from *Annals of the Association of American Geographers*, 53); P. R. Gould for figs 17a and 17c; these figures reproduced in *Locational Analysis in Human Geography* by P. Haggett, published by Edward Arnold Ltd; the Editor, *Norsk Geografisk Tidsskrift*, for figs 18 and 19 (figs 1 and 2 by F. Barth from *Norsk Geografisk Tidsskrift*, 1959–60, Bind XVII); Academic Press Inc (London) Ltd for figs 20, 102 and 103 (figs 5 and 6 from *Hunter–Gatherer Subsistence and Settlement: A Predictive Model* by M. A. Jochim, and figs 24 and 25 from *Spatial Archaeology* edited by D. L. Clarke); the Prehistoric Society for figs 21, 30a, 30b, and 30d (figs 6, 7 and 9 by G. Barker from *Proceedings of the Prehistoric Society*, 1972, XXXVIII, figs 6 by L. Vertes and 7 by J. G. D. Clark from *Proceedings of the Prehistoric Society*, NS, XXVI, and fig. 5 by H. Case from *Proceedings of the Prehistoric Society*, NS, XXVII); Scottish Academic Press Ltd for fig. 25 (fig. 5 from *Calibration of Hominoid Evolution* edited by W. W. Bishop and J. A. Miller); the American Anthropological Association for fig. 27 (figs 3–5 by J. R. Sackett from *American Anthropologist*, 1966, 68, pt 2, no. 2); George Harrap & Co. Ltd for figs 28a, 28b and 89 (fig. 18 from *Anthropology* by A. L. Kroeber and fig. 1 from *Man and Culture* by C. Wissler); W. H. Freeman & Co. Ltd for figs 28c and 55 (figs 8.6 and 9.1 from *Principles of Numerical Taxonomy* by R. R. Sokal and P. H. A. Sneath); J. Briard and the Laboratoire d'Anthropologie, Rennes for fig. 30c (fig. 103 from *Les Dépôts Bretons et L'Age du Bronze*

Atlantique); the Macmillan Company for figs 31 and 32 (figs 13 and 14 from *Differential Psychology: Individual and Group Differences in Behaviour* by A. Anastasi); the Editor, *Acta Archaeologica Lundensia* for figs 33–5 (figs 81 and 83 by M. P. Malmer from *Acta Archaeologica Lundensia*, no. 2); the Editor, *World Archaeology* for figs 37, 92 and 93 (fig. 1 by G. Isaac from *World Archaeology*, 1969, 1, and figs 19 and 22 by I. Hodder from *World Archaeology*, 1974, 6); Country Life Ltd (the Hamlyn Publishing Group) for fig. 38 (pp. 56 and 58 from *The Country Life Collector's Pocket Book* by G. B. Hughes, illustrated by Therle Hughes); the Editor, *American Antiquity* for figs 39, 47, 108, 109 and 110 (figs 5 and 3 by E. Dethlefsen and J. Deetz from *American Antiquity*, 1966, 31, and figs 1, 2 and 3 by D. C. Roper from *American Antiquity*, 1976, 41); Penguin Books Ltd for figs 40a and 40b (figs 42 and 25 from *Facts from Figures* by M. J. Moroney); the University of California Press for figs 44, 45, 77 and 86 (figs 1 and 2 by A. L. Kroeber and J. Richardson from *Anthropological Records*, 1940, 5, no. 2, and p. 5 and diagram 4 by E. W. Gifford from *Anthropological Records*, 1940, 4, no. 1); Edinburgh University Press for figs 53, 65 and 91 (figs 9.17 and 9.25 from *Mathematics and Computers in Archaeology* by J. E. Doran and F. R. Hodson, and fig. 105 from *Ancient Europe* by S. Piggott); the Biometrika Trust for fig. 54 (fig. 6 by F. R. Hodson, P. H. A. Sneath and J. E. Doran from *Biometrika*, 1966, 53, nos 3, 4); the Editor, *Fieldiana: Anthropology* for fig. 57a (fig. 59 by A. Spoehr from *Fieldiana: Anthropology*, 48); the American Museum of Natural History for fig. 57b (fig. 24 by J. A. Ford and C. H. Webb from *Anthropological Papers of the American Museum of Natural History* 46, pt 1); W. Shawcross and the Polynesian Society for fig. 58a (fig. 7 from the *Journal of the Polynesian Society*, 73); the Editor, *Nature* for fig. 66 (fig. 1 by J. E. Doran and F. R. Hodson from *Nature*, 1966, vol. 210); Methuen & Co. Ltd for fig. 90 (figs 20.9, 20.10 and 20.12 from *The Emergence of Civilisation* by C. Renfrew); Gerald Duckworth & Co. Ltd for fig. 94 (fig. 1 by A. J. Ammerman and L. L. Cavalli-Sforza from *The Explanation of Culture Change* edited by C. Renfrew); the Royal Anthropological Institute of Great Britain and Ireland for fig. 95 (fig. 6 by A. J. Ammerman and L. L. Cavalli-Sforza from *Man*, NS, 6); the Editor, *Lund Studies in Geography*, and Lund Universitets Geografiska Institution for fig. 96 (p. 118 by W. Bunge from *Lund Studies in Geography*, Series C, General and Mathematical Geography 1, and by T. Hägerstrand from *Avhandlingar*, no. 25); Svenska Sällskapet för Antropologi och Geografi for fig. 97 (on p. 226

by E. Bylund from *Geografiska Annaler*, 42); the Editor, *Lund Studies in Geography* for fig. 98 (on p. 119 by R. L. Morrill from *Lund Studies in Geography, Series B, Human Geography 24*); Cambridge University Press for figs 99, 100 and 101 (figs 5.17, 5.18, 5.30 and 5.33 from *Spatial Analysis in Archaeology* by I. Hodder and C. Orton); the Editor, *Archaeology and Physical Anthropology in Oceania* and the University of Minnesota Press for fig. 104 (figs 1–4 by M. Levison, R. G. Ward and J. Webb in *Archaeology and Physical Anthropology in Oceania*, 1972, VIII, and figs 20, 26, 27, 28 from *The Settlement of Polynesia : A Computer Simulation* by the same authors); the Institute of British Geographers and the American Association of Petroleum Geologists for fig. 106 (by R. Chorley and P. Haggett in *Institute of British Geographers Publication*, no. 37, and by W. C. Krumbein in *Bulletin of the American Association of Petroleum Geologists*, 40); and Edward Arnold Ltd for fig. 107 (fig. 9.21 from *Locational Analysis in Human Geography* by P. Haggett).

1   Introduction and polemic

> Now, here, you see, it takes all the running you can do, to
> keep in the same place.
>
> The Queen to Alice, *Through the Looking-Glass*,
>   chapter 2,
> LEWIS CARROLL 1832–1898

Every year produces a fresh crop of archaeological excavations, a new
harvest of prehistoric artefacts. Every decade produces one or more
sites of outstanding importance and impact, that linger on in the
literature or sparkle briefly on the glossy pages of ephemeral publications. The archaeologists come and go, new names and sites
outshine the old, whilst hundreds of years of collected material
overflows and submerges our museum storerooms. At the same time a
relentless current of articles and books describe and label the new
material so that the intrepid archaeologist, by dint of furious activity,
can just maintain his *status quo* against the constant stream of data.
However, the nebulous doubt arises in our minds that a modern
empirical discipline ought to be able to aim at more rewarding results
than the maintenance of a relative *status quo* and a steady flow of
counterfeit history books.

The purpose of this work is to draw attention from specific
archaeological areas and periods to the general theory underlying
modern archaeology, to refocus this attention on the inconsistencies
and inadequacy of general archaeological theory, and to integrate
powerful new methods into our analytical armoury. To achieve these
ends we need some knowledge of the historical development of
modern archaeology, for we cannot fully comprehend contemporary
concepts and theories without knowing something of their origins. We
must understand how archaeology reached its present curious and
transient state, if only to emphasize that the views of our time have no
finality, and in order that we might assess the comparative development of prehistoric studies with that of related disciplines. When we
have outlined the historical background we can proceed with a deeper
understanding to investigate the nature of archaeology and its raw

material, and the nature of the subject's aims, ailments and potential
development.

1   The history of archaeology

The historical background of archaeology, like that of most modern
arts and sciences, takes us back to the Italian Renaissance and the
reawakening of philosophical curiosity. This extraordinary florescence
developed cumulatively upon the 'commercial revolution' which
revitalized certain of the Italo-Byzantine maritime cities in the twelfth,
thirteenth and fourteenth centuries of our era. In these centuries the
mercantile cities of Venice, Genoa, Pisa, Amalfi and Naples gradually
surpassed in wealth the greatest centres of the classical world, financ-
ing in their turn the rise of Rome, Florence, Milan and the cities of
northern Italy.

By the fifteenth century the commercial empires of Genoa and
Venice stretched from the Canaries to the Caspian Sea and from the
Netherlands to the river Niger in Africa. From their permanent
colonial bases around the Mediterranean and the Black Sea the
Venetians and Genoese established regular trade with China and the
Mongol hordes, with Arab and Negro Africa and with the Hanse cities
of north Germany. From the Orient came spices, precious metals,
silks, jewels, porcelain, paper for the bankers' notes and Renaissance
sketchpads, the printing press for learned works, the Chinese cross-
bow and gunpowder for the notorious Genoese mercenaries and above
all the compass, clock and astrolabe with their navigational potential
for the Voyages of Discovery across open seas. From Africa and the
markets of Timbuktu, Florentine and Genoese merchants bought
gold, ivory and slaves; from the northern trade came cloth, timber,
corn, iron, tin and copper. But beyond price were the myriad ideas,
innovations and inventions which this overall trade network focused
on the receptive cities of northern Italy.

Quite apart from our interest in the Renaissance as the germinal
background for archaeological curiosity, the whole phenomenon of
cultural florescence is one to which we will return in a later chapter
(chapter 6). Nevertheless, we can observe in this particular case that
the Renaissance florescence was based on the politically diverse urban
centres of northern Italy, followed a massive economic boom, grew by
cumulative integration of innovations – ransacked from neighbouring
cultures – and finally reached a threshold of expansion in the fifteenth

century. After culminating in an exponential burst of development in many interrelated fields the phenomenon subsided in Italy, only to be continued in a secondary form in France and the North.

Retrospectively, we see the many interrelated fields of development of the Renaissance 'super-nova' as the crucial formulation of the basic format of many contemporary arts and sciences. Nevertheless, in their Renaissance setting these diverse arts and sciences were integral aspects of the 'new philosophy' and later the 'experimental method'. The Renaissance scholar pursued a wide unitary spectrum of studies although we may now retrospectively label them for their contributions in single disciplines. Leonardo da Vinci was a painter, sculptor, engineer, architect, physicist, biologist and philosopher but to his contemporaries he was simply a scholar of the new philosophy, ending his days like so many of his countrymen in the service of the king of France, Francis I.

An early facet of the Renaissance was the literary revival and the search for ancient Latin texts of unimpeachable style urged by the Florentines Petrarch, Dante and Boccaccio. In these recovered classical volumes, in the results of the great Genoese inspired voyages of discovery and in the stirrings of Renaissance curiosity the components of archaeology slowly formed. In the same context the essentials of modern mathematics were being developed by Tartaglia and Cardano; natural history, medicine and chemistry by Salviani, Belon, Aldrovandi and Malpighi; anatomy by Vesalius and Fallopius; physics and astronomy by Galileo, Copernicus, Torricelli and Leonardo. Against this setting the first scientific societies were formed – at Naples in 1560 the Academia Secretorum Naturae, at Rome in 1600 the Academia dei Lincei and later others at Florence (1657), London (1660) and Paris (1666).

By the mid-sixteenth century the Italian scholars had made available most of the major works of the great classical authors, if only from Latin translations. These classical works preserved observations in Homer and Hesiod directly reflecting Greek life nine centuries before Christ and in Homer preserving earlier oral traditions of Sub-Mycenean times. These and other works preserved contemporary accounts of the transition from a bronze to an iron technology, together with ethnographic speculations about the former existence of an era of stone weapons and tools, such as were occasionally observed amongst neighbouring barbarians. However, no surviving classical work unequivocally connects these philosophical speculations with the stone, bronze and iron artefacts dug from the earth. In this lack of practical implementation we may detect a crucial difference between the Greek and the Renaissance attitude towards natural philosophy and the embryo sciences.

The Renaissance scholars of Italy were therefore able to read with interest the classical meditations upon a succession of ages in which the use of stone preceded that of bronze and iron. These ideas are found in varying forms in some dozen or more classical authors but are best summarized in the words of Lucretius, 95–53 BC. 'The earliest weapons were the hands, nails and teeth, as well as stones, pieces of wood, flames and fire as soon as they were known. Later the properties of iron and bronze were discovered, but bronze came first, the use of iron not being known until later . . . gradually the iron blade replaced the bronze sickle' (*De Natura Rerum*, verses 1283–1296: Cheynier 1936, p. 8). In such passages as this the classical authors preserved a clear and continuous tradition based on ancient memories and observation but increasingly philosophical and poetic and quite unconnected with the ancient artefacts in the soil. The peasant who dug up and preserved these artefacts believed that they were celestial thunderbolts with magical properties. With the medieval resurgence of European peasant traditions the celestial origin became the scholarly hypothesis, found in the literature from Marbodius (1035–1132) to Paracelsus (1493–1541).

The Renaissance immediately brought into conflict the classical interpretation of the artefacts as relics of former epochs and the folk interpretation of the artefacts as celestial objects of miraculous properties. In contrast to the Greek philosophical approach the Renaissance naturalists had early encountered ancient artefacts in the field and classed them with other interesting phenomena like the fossils. In this context several Renaissance naturalists expressed their firm belief in the human origin of these tools. The 'geologist' Agricola (1490–1555) dismissed the idea of celestial origin (Cheynier 1936, p. 9). The famous naturalist and 'anatomist' Ulysses Aldrovandi (1522–1607) asserted that these stone tools were used by ancient peoples before the use of metals, supporting his argument with quotations from Pliny. Finally, in a definitive work, Michael Mercati (1541–93) integrated the practical observations of the peasants, the knowledge of the classical authors and the fresh thought of the 'new philosophy'.

Michael Mercati is the archaeological counterpart of Cardano in mathematics, Vesalius in anatomy, Galileo in the physical sciences and

Copernicus in astronomy. Mercati can by no means be said to be an 'archaeologist' and yet his work is among the first to contain the elements from which the subject later emerged. Michael Mercati was primarily a naturalist, he was Superintendent of the Vatican Botanical Gardens, he kept a collection of minerals and fossils as well as acting as medical adviser to Pope Clement VIII. Being a field naturalist Mercati's attention was soon drawn to the problem of ancient stone implements and their origins. His Renaissance education gave him a sound acquaintance with the works of Pliny, Lucretius and Festus amongst others and made him aware of the classical tradition of the former existence of successive eras of stone, bronze and iron tools. As a pious Vatican official Mercati also drew from that other great compilation of ancient oral tradition – the Old Testament, which parallels Homer in its memories of stone and bronze implements and its historic account of the introduction of iron by the Philistines. The third component of Mercati's understanding was the growing collection of Asiatic and American Indian artefacts given to the Vatican by the Italian, Portuguese and Spanish explorers and voyagers. These three strands, comprising field observations, ancient tradition, and contemporary ethnology were the foundations of Mercati's interpretation and remain, in altered form, the foundations of modern archaeology.

The manuscript which Mercati prepared spoke of the credulity of the argument for celestial origin and quoted the summary of Lucretius, given earlier in this section. Mercati went on to explain how flint implements are made and illustrated polished stone axes, flint arrowheads and blades to point out the purpose of these artefacts. The manuscript as a whole was only part of Mercati's great work on minerals and fossils, the 'Metallotheca', which remained in the Vatican library until Pope Clement XI ordered its publication in 1717. Although unpublished until this late date the work was well known by the early seventeenth century and the same views appear in the works of several naturalists of this period. Together with Aldrovandi and others, Mercati had established that the artefacts excavated by the peasants were indeed humanly made tools from ancient times and directly related this material to the classical hypothesis of a stone, bronze and iron using succession of ages. The addition of contemporary accounts of primitive tools and weapons collected by the merchant explorers completed Mercati's observations (Cheynier 1936, pp. 8–10).

The seventeenth century saw the eclipse of the Italian Renaissance by its French satellite under the Italianate courts of the successive Louis, culminating in 'le Roi Soleil', Louis XIV. We may remember that Leonardo worked in France, as had Cellini and many other Italian artists and scholars. Seventeenth-century France was permeated with Italian art, science, mathematics, architecture, music and general fashion. In this context it is hardly surprising to find Mercati's ideas mirrored in French Jesuit authors of the period. The French countryside is especially rich in antiquities either as scattered artefacts or more strikingly in the great stone mounds and tombs. Here, as elsewhere in Europe, men had dug and pillaged with little further thought or curiosity about the curious tools of stone and bronze. It was not until the Renaissance ideas diffused French scholarship that useful developments ensued.

By 1685 the Jesuit Montfaucon had already published a paper on a megalithic tomb containing skeletons and stone axeheads, at Evreux in Normandy. However, by 1717 Mercati's great work was widely available in print. A little later, in 1721, Antoine de Jussieu read a paper at the Académie Royale des Sciences in which he refuted the celestial theory and compared the artefacts with American and Canadian Indian flint implements – formulating a Stone Age on this basis. Similarly, another French Jesuit, Lafitau, published two volumes on 'The customs of the American Indians, compared with the customs of early times', which appeared in 1724. In 1730, Mahudel read a paper to the Académie des Inscriptions quoting Mercati and confirming the idea of three successive ages or epochs. Montfaucon forcefully re-iterated the same ideas in an illustrated publication of a paper to the same society in 1734, postulating a Stone, Bronze and Iron Age. By 1758, Goguet, in a memoir on 'L'origine des Lois', could state that 'the use of bronze preceded that of iron . . . formerly stones, flint pebbles, bones, horn, fish-bones, shells, reeds, and thorns were used for everything for which civilized peoples use metal today. Primitive peoples give us a faithful picture of ancient societies' (Cheynier 1936, pp. 10–14).

In France Mercati's work was widely disseminated and appreciated. The idea of three successive ages using stone, bronze, and iron is specifically repeated by such authors as Montfaucon and Mahudel with prehistoric artefacts illustrated under these successive categories (Laming 1952, pp. 16–19). These ideas and their practical and stratigraphic implications were further developed in France in the work of men like Jouannet (1765–1845) and Boucher de Perthes (1788–1868). However, by a curious but not inexplicable chance, the full implications and explicit formulation of the 'three ages' system first appeared not in France – but in Denmark.

Historically, the fortunes of the tiny state of Denmark fluctuated throughout the seventeenth and eighteenth centuries from the role of a major Scandinavian power to bankrupt insignificance and back again. A small country buffeted back and forth between alternating alliances with various great European Powers, Denmark was beyond the ancient influence of Imperial Roman and early Renaissance literacy, with a written history shorter by more than 500 years as compared with its southern neighbours. The need to assert the country's ancient existence and respectable antiquity was certainly one significant factor in the national interest in its antiquities.

The most important cultural influence in Denmark between 1670–1870 was undoubtedly French. With the succession of Christian V (1670–99) Denmark threw off the narrower restraints of Protestant philosophy and remodelled its attitudes on those of the brilliant French court. Christian V deliberately reorganized his army, court and state along the lines of 'le Roi Soleil'. The Danish army adopted French styled uniforms, military formations and words of command. The Danish court and aristocracy spoke French, the royal household took over the procedure and French titles of Versailles, even the royal decrees were in French and Danish. Encouraged by gifts of money from the French king, Christian V and his aristocrats aped French fashions, built country houses in the château style and patronized numbers of French scholars and craftsmen. The first serious ripples of Renaissance learning were reaching Denmark from the secondary centre of France and continued to arrive until the disastrous Napoleonic alliance.

So we find sixteenth-century Italian learning permeating seventeenth-century France and finally reaching eighteenth- and nineteenth-century Denmark. Bobbing along with the literary current we find the ideas of Mercati, Mahudel and Montfaucon appearing in learned Danish circles, usually unacknowledged but betrayed by their precise form and sudden appearance. As early as 1655 an old Danish antiquarian, Olaf Worm, was proclaiming the human origin of the flint tools which he dug from ancient barrows (Cheynier 1936, p. 10). More specific references to the theory of successive ages using stone, bronze and iron appear sporadically in the Danish as in the French and

German literature of the eighteenth century. In Denmark these remarks, increasingly based on locally excavated collections, culminate in the works of Skuli Thorlacius (1802) and Vedel-Simonsen (1813) (Aarbøger 1953, p. 201). Nevertheless, despite the growing acceptance of the 'three ages' theory and its firm association with the artefacts dug from the ground in increasing numbers, there was up to this time little understanding of the implications and potential of Mercati's ideas.

In 1788 Christian Thomsen was born in Copenhagen, the first son of a wealthy Danish merchant-banker and ship-owner. The education that Christian received was primarily intended to equip him in the best possible manner to follow his father in the family business. He was given a thorough grounding in modern languages and literature with a significant emphasis on French thought and learning. Among the friends of the Thomsen family was another wealthy Danish merchant, recently Danish Consul-General in Paris – Consul-General Grove. During the French Revolution Grove had astutely bought-up quantities of French art treasures, including antiquities and coins. On his return from Paris in 1804 the young Thomsen helped arrange the Grove family treasures and was especially fired with enthusiasm for the collections of coins and antiquities. By 1807, the year in which the British fleet burned Copenhagen, Thomsen had developed his passion for coins and antiquities by establishing contact with Rasmus Nyerup, secretary of the Royal Commission for the Preservation of Danish Antiquities (Bibby 1962, pp. 22–8).

Christian Jürgensen Thomsen integrated in one personality a strong interest in antiquities, a thorough grounding in French antiquarian thought and a working experience of warehouse classification as applied to stockpiled merchandise. Whether Mercati's Renaissance ideas reached Thomsen through a knowledge of the French works of Montfaucon, Mahudel, Goguet and their many contemporaries, or whether they came from the same source via the assimilations of Skuli Thorlacius, Vedel-Simonsen and others remains unknown. However, the diffusion of ideas is a most complex business and Thomsen's work is hardly diminished in importance if we suspect that its stimuli had ancient and widespread sources.[1]

In 1816 the ageing Nyerup retired, overwhelmed with the burden of organizing the classification and display of the accumulated Danish antiquities and the Royal Commission appointed Thomsen to succeed him. Between 1816–19 he began to reorganize the growing collection of antiquities. He appears at first to have simply implemented his warehouse technique of classification under raw material and then subdivided according to probable usage. Nevertheless, the formal divisions stone, bronze and iron appear from the beginning and his purblind contemporary critics pointed out there were illogically no gold, silver, glass or bone age divisions. Clearly, Thomsen already believed in Mercati's 'three ages' system, at first merely as an obscure guide but later he increasingly perceived the classification as a conceptual model of considerable predictive value.

The first stages of this revelation were completed by 1819 when Thomsen opened his museum to the public with the 'three ages' demonstrated in three consecutive cases. The full awareness of the implications of the scheme then gradually accumulated and caused Thomsen to write his account of the system in 1836 in a 'Guide to Scandinavian Antiquities'. The later translation of this work into German, English and French, combined with Thomsen's industrious and kindly correspondence with other scholars, quickly spread the knowledge of the scheme throughout Europe.

It has now become rather fashionable to decry and minimize the importance of the 'three ages' scheme. Certainly it would be strange if a century and a half of archaeology had not modified and qualified some of Thomsen's ideas. Certainly Thomsen's hypothesis had precursors but this is the case with most great innovations. In fairness to Thomsen we must compare the information value of collections of prehistoric artefacts before his work and after it. Before Thomsen physically demonstrated his concept with a large prehistoric collection, the antiquarian was faced simply with heaps of incoherent data. After the development of the 'three ages' model and its later stratigraphic verification, the grouped artefacts revealed the key to cultural identity, exposed the sequential patterning of typological development and tacitly implied the cultural significance of technological and economic development. Crude though the 'three ages' model may have been it nevertheless proved to be the basis of cultural taxonomy, the typological method, and the economic approach to prehistory. We might care to learn from this example that the ancient artefacts only took meaning upon the framework of a model – the conceptual model of the 'three ages'. Archaeological 'facts' take their meaning from their conceptual arrangement and the adequacy or inadequacy of that arrangement, model, or hypothesis accounts for the amount of information made available to the archaeologist.

The 'three ages' system represents the development of the essential basis of modern analytical archaeology. Thomsen's work was continued by his colleague Worsaae (1821–85) and by the Swede Montelius (1843–1921) and in the overlapping lifetimes of these three great men the form of modern archaeology was established. Of course there were many other contributors and contributary streams but in the essential elements modern archaeology was born. Since those days we have really added very little of fundamental importance – excavation has become more precise, dating has been dramatically revised and the volume of material has swollen incredibly.[2] Nevertheless, most of these contributions are a matter of degree alone, an almost unavoidable consequence of passing time and hardly a justification for archaeological complacency. Even in 1847 the great Worsaae could put the beginning of the Danish Neolithic at c. 3000 BC and fully appreciated careful stratigraphic excavation as well as the aids and dangers of typological taxonomy.

We are forced to return to the point of the opening paragraphs that a modern empirical discipline ought to be able to aim at more rewarding results than the piling up of data and a steady output of imitation history books. The truth is that the existing interpretative machinery of archaeology – the general theory – is neglected and outmoded.[3] If archaeological 'facts' take meaning from their context, and a model or hypothesis of that context, then we may have more 'facts' but we are getting very little more information.

II   The nature of archaeology

Archaeology is the discipline concerned with the recovery, systematic description and study of material culture in the past; the archaeologist is the man responsible for these studies.[4] Another terminology currently favours the designation 'prehistoric studies' and calls its operators prehistorians. Strictly defined, prehistoric studies and the prehistorian operate only in those areas and periods which lack a contemporary written account of themselves. Archaeology and the archaeologist are definitions which contain prehistoric studies and the prehistorian. It follows that the prehistorian is always an archaeologist and prehistoric studies are always archaeological. Because archaeology contributes most heavily to our knowledge of societies without a written record, archaeology is often synonymous with prehistory and the archaeologist with the prehistorian, reflecting the common area of the two sets. Consequently in this work we will frequently alternate the terms archaeology and prehistory, archaeologist and pre-historian without implying any distinction other than that just noted. Important examples of the wider scope of archaeology stretching beyond the perimeter of prehistoric studies would include such aspects as classical, medieval, recent colonial and industrial archaeology.

However, despite the general acceptance of the boundaries and relative disposition of archaeology and prehistoric studies, recent works have inclined to distort these terms in a dangerous fashion. There is currently a tendency to take the term prehistorian as meaning 'a writer of history covering periods without written records', with the implication that the 'prehistorian' is an armchair synthesizer of the analytical work of the 'archaeologist'. Here the term archaeologist is warped to mean the unintelligent 'excavator' or the narrow-minded 'specialist' – the term prehistorian thus acquiring a rosy flush of dilettante virtue at the expense of the devalued archaeologist. It is this attempt to convey smooth historical narrative as the essence of pre-historic studies, in the total absence of the record appropriate to that art and in the presence of records of a quite peculiar and especial nature – the artefacts, which we may well view as 'counterfeit' history. The expression of archaeological results may call for nicely written historical narrative but this is a matter of choosing one particular vehicle to convey results obtained by quite alien methods. The danger of historical narrative as a vehicle for archaeological results is that it pleases by virtue of its smooth coverage and apparent finality, whilst the data on which it is based are never comprehensive, never capable of supporting but one interpretation and rest upon complex prob-abilities. Archaeological data are not historical data and consequently archaeology is not history.

The view taken in this work is that archaeology is archaeology is archaeology (with apologies to Gertrude Stein). Archaeology is a discipline in its own right, concerned with archaeological data which it clusters in archaeological entities displaying certain archaeological processes and studied in terms of archaeological aims, concepts and procedures. We fully appreciate that these entities and processes were once historical and social entities but the nature of the archaeological record is such that there is no simple way of equating our archaeolo-gical percepta with these lost events. We must certainly try to find out the social and historical equivalents of our archaeological entities and processes but we should not delude ourselves about the simplicity of these equivalents or our success in isolating them (chapter 9).

An archaeological culture is not a racial group, nor a historical tribe, nor a linguistic unit, it is simply an archaeological culture. Given great care, a large quantity of first class archaeological data, precise definition and rigorous use of terms, and a good archaeological model, then we may with a margin of error be able to identify an archaeological entity in approximate social and historical terms. But this is the best we can do and it is in any case only one of the aims of archaeological activity. The reconstruction of a historical or social picture of prehistoric cultures, written in historical narrative, is a valid but incidental and dangerous aspect of archaeology. Although aesthetically satisfying in the familiarity of its form of expression it is necessarily as ephemeral and as reliable as the facial expression reconstructed on the bones of a Neanderthal skull.

We can stress that archaeology is, among other things, the time dimension of anthropology and ethnology. In many parts of the world recorded ethnology is only a generation or so deep and beyond that lies only the archaeological record. With the current demise of ethnology in academic circles it is interesting to notice that archaeology is taking on many of the tasks and problems formerly left to the ethnologist ('ethnoarchaeology' – for a review see Stiles 1977). Indeed, the archaeologist might soberly reflect that any failure of archaeology to establish itself as more than a popular opiate will surely assign the discipline to the same limbo plumbed by museum ethnology.

To recapitulate, archaeology can be redefined as the discipline concerned with the recovery, systematic description and study of material culture in the past. Archaeology is a discipline in its own right, providing a framework within which the entities and processes of archaeology act one upon another. The entities, processes, aims, procedures and concepts of archaeology have a validity of their own in reference to the archaeological frame and despite their generation by – and partial correlation with – former social and historic entities.

Under this definition we may understand archaeology as having three interrelated spheres of activity (fig. 2). The sphere concentrating on data recovery – principally excavation, the sphere engaged in systematic description – taxonomy and classification, and finally the integrating, synthesizing study generating models, hypotheses and theories. Two of these spheres are concerned with genuine experimental data recovery and in their modern form represent the sensory organs of the discipline – these are (i) excavation and collection, (ii) analytical and statistical taxonomy. The third sphere should generate idealized models or hypotheses about the data received and retransmit these models to the experimental aspects for further testing and modification (fig. 2). By the continuous feedback cycle of observation, hypothesis, experiment and idealized model, the models and hypotheses gradually become more accurately adapted to the pattern of the observed data. Gradually the hypotheses may be elevated to theories and ultimately the theories elevated to synthesizing principles – if the results should happily warrant that step.

The sphere of activity undertaking data collection and excavation is largely outside the theoretical frame of reference of this work. It is the sphere of data analysis and the sphere of synthesis and theory which are our main concern. In the analysis aspect we now have a new experimental dimension of archaeology using powerful and incisive statistical and computer techniques (Doran and Hodson 1975). In the theoretical aspect we have the long neglected and festering field of general theory – assiduously avoided by all who wish to preserve their status by concealing their actual method of procedure and dubious mental concepts. If we intend to try to alter this latter situation then we must first prepare the foundation by carefully examining the nature of archaeological data or 'facts' in order that we might handle them in an appropriate and sensible manner.

III   The nature of archaeological data

If archaeology is the discipline concerned with the study of past material culture then artefacts are the archaeologist's main data even though other specialists may supply him with complementary evidence on fauna, flora, dating and the like. The archaeologist's facts are artefacts and the information observed about their contextual and specific attributes. The contextual attributes are the special concern of the experimental sphere of archaeology dealing with data recovery. The specific attributes are the main concern of the other experimental sphere of the discipline – the sphere of analysis and classification or taxonomy. The total information from these sensory spheres of activity feeds observations into the third sphere of synthesis and fits the best model or hypothesis to the observations for further testing. The fundamental property of the data is that it is observed or perceived information based on attributes of the artefacts.

In order to gauge the nature of archaeological data it is essential to analyse both the qualities of the 'observations', 'perceived facts', or 'perceived information' and the significance of artefact attributes. Briefly, it is imperative to realize that 'perceived facts' or attributes are necessarily facts and attributes selected from a vast range possessed by every artefact. We may choose to perceive the length, breadth, thickness and weight of a handaxe but we may not choose to perceive its chemical composition, its temperature, radioactivity, elasticity, refractive index and so on. Clearly, we do not observe these latter attributes because we think them 'archaeologically unimportant' – consequently, all observations, all perceived facts depend on the observer, his frame of reference and personal idiosyncrasies. The observer consciously or unconsciously selects the 'facts' to be perceived and recorded and no two observers need record the same perceptions about even a single artefact. Clearly, then, archaeological facts or data change in the changing light of what the archaeologist deems 'significant attributes'.

The attributes of most artefacts are almost infinite and to suggest that the objective archaeologist must analyse them all is unrealistic and in practice the attempt is never made. We restrict the archaeological observations to perceiving and noting those attributes which the observer believes to have been man-made or selected-for by man. This latter judgement is again arbitrary and dependent on the observer and his views or model of the mind of ancient man. We can guess that the handaxe pebble was not selected for radioactivity or its refractive index; we reasonably guess that size and weight were selected – for, probably the material also, but what about colour and all the other possible attributes? Clearly, some attributes were regularly and carefully selected-for and these give us archaeological 'information' or data, other attributes were not regularly selected-for and make up distracting 'noise' or 'non-information'. The separation between these classes of attributes ultimately and arbitrarily depends on the observer's guesses but the term 'regularly selected-for' reveals the statistical aid that can be sought when dealing with aggregates of similar artefacts. This incisive aid will help cut down the area of the individual's subjective judgement in this matter but can never entirely remove it. The observation and record of the specific and contextual attributes of archaeological artefacts is not a procedure capable of producing final lists of definitive, unimpeachable facts. Nevertheless, various aids and a measure of agreement based on a common discipline will enable archaeologists to decide which attributes are 'certainly' worth investigating and which can be discarded temporarily.

Which are the attributes 'certainly' worth investigating? Archaeologists agree that those attributes which can only have been produced on the raw material by human action are the attributes most worthy of careful study. On this basis archaeological attributes equal the results of human or hominid actions, or sequences of actions, and regularities amongst artefact attributes represent regularities of hominid behaviour. The archaeologist is therefore studying concealed and obscure facets of hominid behaviour through the peculiar medium of the fossilized and congealed results of this behaviour, imprisoned in the attributes of ancient artefacts. Archaeology is a discipline in its own right because it alone provides the conceptual apparatus for analysing these peculiar data; a different discipline and different conceptual apparatus from that required for the study of history in its limited sense.

Archaeological 'facts' or observations are for the most part of two kinds, either they claim that:

(a) These entities have these defined attributes. The attributes being specific, contextual or frequently both; or

(b) These entities have these defined attributes and by inference so do certain unobserved or untested entities of the same class. The entities in both examples can be artefacts, assemblages, cultures, sites, or any of the archaeological entities which we will later define.

The class (a) observation is the class of 'perceived facts' already discussed at length. The second kind, class (b), is the most useful, most frequent and most dangerous class of observation found in archaeological literature – the class of 'generalization', 'inferred facts' or 'induced facts'.

To generalize is to infer that what has been found true in observed cases of a class, is also true of certain unobserved cases of the same class, thus becoming a predictive proposition. Most scientific laws and principles are just such statistical generalizations of very high probability, asserting no more than the 'constant' conjunction of certain attributes. Other generalizations are equally respectable and are really 'low-level' laws or principles. Famous examples are Darwin's valid generalization that 'all white cats with blue eyes are deaf' or Cuvier's 'no animals with horns and hoofs habitually eat flesh' (Mander 1936, p.

72). One might compare with these such archaeological statements as 'all urban societies are food producing' or 'no mesolithic society used the wheel'. The difference between these low-level propositions and scientific laws resides principally in the degree of statistical reliance or tolerance that can be placed on the words 'all' or 'no'. If archaeology can come to terms with the complex problem of adequately defining the order of probability of such terms there is no inherent reason why its cumulative information could not be expressed in axiomatic form. Certainly modern anthropology is moving increasingly and successfully in this direction (e.g. Goody 1976).

Generalization and induction are one of the main routes by which new knowledge is revealed from accumulated data. Unfortunately, the borderline between valid and invalid generalization is such that philosophers have to fight hard to justify the inductive method at all. The degree of confidence that we are logically justified in placing in many archaeological generalizations is often undermined by failure to specify the proportion of observed cases, the variety of circumstances or the existence of conflicting examples. Despite these abuses most archaeological propositions are made by inference and induction rather than by classic deduction (but see Binford 1968a; Watson, LeBlanc and Redman 1971; and Hill 1972 in support of the 'hypothetico-deductive method'). In the process of deduction a conclusion follows as a logical consequence of certain premises and cannot be false while the premises remain true. Whereas in the process of induction an empirical generalization is inferred from its individual instances. Archaeological propositions are not only made by inference or induction, for the most part, but they also happen frequently to be rather special kinds of induced hypotheses, needing particular and careful handling in argument.

Archaeological observations are very rarely 'general propositions' of the kind 'all *A*s are *B*s' or 'all *A*s have *B*s'. The more common archaeological proposition takes the form 'some *A*s are *B*s' or 'some *A*s have *B*s', making the statement a statistical or probability proposition (Braithwaite 1960, p. 115). Thus, we might say that 'some Venus figurines are Gravettian', 'some Dimini pots have trichrome spirals', or 'some La Tène burials are Celtic'. It is these statistical or probability propositions that require careful handling and which must be carefully distinguished from the general propositions handled by deductive methods.

The special characteristics of probability propositions, including most archaeological propositions are:

(1) They are usually of the form 'some *A*s are *B*s' or 'some *A*s have *B*s' (where *B* may be an attribute).

(2) Their probability aspect can be of two quite different kinds.
   (a) An aspect of relative frequency – '90 per cent of handaxes are between 3–30 cms long'.
   (b) An aspect of reasonableness or credibility – 'no handaxe was used for metalworking'.

(3) Statistical or probability propositions have limits beyond which they are not necessarily true.

(4) Such propositions are not conclusively refutable by producing contrary examples. The rejection of a probability hypothesis rests on assessing the probability as being outside the limiting values – e.g. the proposition that 'most La Tène equipped graves are Celtic' is not necessarily refuted by proving that several such burials are Teutonic.

(5) Probability propositions are usefully integrated into hypotheses by inductive generalization – the inference of an empirical generalization from its instances, by the simple enumeration of 'n' positive instances without refutation and by eliminating every alternative hypothesis while not being refuted itself.

These special characteristics of statistical or probability propositions are elaborated by Braithwaite 1960 (p. 115).

We may illustrate these points with archaeological propositions. If we take the statement that 'the majority of burials with a La Tène metalwork assemblage occur in France and Germany and belong to Celtic aristocrats' – then this proposition may remain true even though La Tène graves also occur in Britain and Bulgaria, some Celtic areas have no La Tène burials at all, some La Tène burials belong to Teutons and so on. The original statement is in probability form, there are limits beyond which it is not true, there are contrary examples but most alternative hypotheses have been eliminated and the generalization remains valid.

On similar lines we may take the observation that 'some Mousterian industries were made by Neanderthal man'. This proposition is an inferred generalization based on a limited number of particular observations. However, the probability nature of the proposition by no means necessarily supports that 'all Mousterian industries are Neanderthal products' nor does it exclude the possibility that 'Neanderthal man made other industries' or that 'some Mousterian industries might be the work of Homo sapiens'. To conclude that all Mousterian artefacts were the work of Neanderthalers would be forcing the observation from a rather weak probability proposition to an untested and sweeping general proposition.

A summary of this overbrief outline of the nature of archaeological 'facts' suggests that the data take the form of observations based on the specific and contextual attributes of artefacts. These observations customarily escalate from 'perceived attributes' to 'inferred attributes'. Even physically perceived attributes are subject to personal bias and represent a partially agreed selection from an infinite variety – although this variety can usefully be limited by concentrating on humanly imposed traits of statistical significance. The inferred attributes or induced probability propositions are the most useful and the most dangerous and require special treatment and testing, especially in respect of negative evidence. Possibly the majority of archaeological statements are statistical or probability propositions with their own special characteristics and proper logical manipulation procedure.

The data studied by the archaeologist and the anthropologist are both aspects of the phenomenon of hominid 'culture'. In this sense 'culture' consists of learned modes of behaviour and its material manifestations, socially transmitted from one generation to the next and from one society or individual to another. It is customary to separate the material and tangible manifestations of hominid culture and classify it apart as 'material culture' as opposed to the intangible 'non-material culture'. However, this division is largely conceptual and there is no basic difference between the material manifestation of abstract concepts of form and function fossilized in the attributes of artefacts and the social manifestations of similar concepts ephemerally translated into social activities. Activities are sequences of partially preconceived actions, artefacts too are similar sequences of similar solidified actions as every attribute bears witness. As manifestations of hominid behaviour artefacts form a special case within the broader field of animal behaviour, in which many other species already demonstrate the use of implements (Lawick-Goodall 1971), the holding and defence of territory (e.g. Wynne-Edwards 1962), social hierarchy, leadership and social organization on a kinship basis (e.g.

H. and J. von Lawick-Goodall 1970). The specifically hominid feature remains the phenomenon of culture – learned as well as instinctive modes of behaviour, with its material implementation, and its acquisitive transmission from individual to individual and from group to group.

IV   The aims of archaeology

The aims of archaeology are of course the sum of the aims of archaeologists and prehistorians in general. Consequently, there are as many different aims in archaeology as there are archaeologists; some archaeologists see their role as historians, others consider themselves palaeoecologists. I have argued that in essence archaeology is uniquely itself, an immature discipline struggling to find its dimensions and assert its separate existence from bordering disciplines of greater maturity. It follows from this that the aims that I will choose are rather different from those of some of my colleagues but I would defend them as being central and not peripheral to the essential nature of the subject.

The reasons for defining our aims became apparent in our investigation of the nature of archaeological 'facts'. These 'facts' turn out to be observations in which the nature of the observer and his intentions play a large part in which 'facts' are observed and recorded. Different observers see the same 'facts' through differently tinted spectacles. If the aims of archaeologists vary then these differing aims and objectives will give varying direction and potential to the analysis of archaeological data and may account for differing views of the same 'facts', without necessarily invoking error on the part of any party (e.g. the Mousterian controversy – Binford and Binford 1966; Bordes and de Sonneville – Bordes 1970; Mellars 1970; Binford 1973). On some occasions this variety of aims and interpretations is a strength rather than a weakness in that no single view or interpretation of a set of data can ever be wholly comprehensive or 'true'. Indeed we should encourage the analysis of archaeological problems from as many differently based approaches as possible and integrate their overall consensus. On other occasions, the variety of aims and interpretations is a grave weakness based not on error, or personal idiosyncrasy but upon ambiguous and inexplicit terminology, differing use of the same terms by different individuals. This latter symptom is the single most damaging characteristic, isolating archaeology in an undisciplined fever from the calm status of a coherent discipline. This kind of ailment is not unknown in the case-histories of developing disciplines and we shall pay some attention to possible remedies in a later section. Unfortunately the infection is in an advanced state in archaeology because of the neglect shown to general theory and surgery will prove painful if the discipline is to survive.

The aims or objectives of archaeology are therefore of more than passing importance since they direct the overall strategy and modify the results. In the light of the earlier discussion about the nature of archaeology as a discipline and the nature of its data, three broad objectives seem to be of central importance:

(1) First, the definition of the fundamental entities that pervade the diverse material, their elements, structures and patterns, the processes that operate on them, and the effects of the processes on the entities in the dimensions of space and time. A study in statics and dynamics going beyond particular instances.

(2) Second, the search for repeated similarities or regularities in form, function, association, or developmental sequence amongst the particular entities from every area, period and environment.

(3) Third, the development of higher category knowledge or principles that synthesize and correlate the material at hand whilst possessing a high predictive value. The development of increasingly comprehensive and informative general models and hypotheses.

Archaeologists fall into three groups in relation to these aims. Those archaeologists who agree with most of these aims and believe their possible attainment; those who agree with some of the aims but believe the entity concepts merely abstractions, incapable of viable definition, and finally, those archaeologists who find these aims sterile, clinical, inhuman and devoid of the evocative glow and beauty of the material, whilst expressing disbelief in any synthesizing or predictive principles. It is tempting to label these first-class, second-class and third-class archaeologists but perhaps that would be unfair. This text is designed for the first two viewpoints, the latter will doubtless continue to cultivate the popular and lucrative fields of vulgarization or blinker themselves to narrow aspects of narrow problems without the comfort of knowing the value of their activities. The wise archaeologist must skilfully differentiate his discipline and role from that of entertainer and entertainment on one hand and the meaningless accumulation of data on the other. The undisciplined and questionless accumulation of data has in itself no more value than the collection of engine numbers or cheese labels, whilst the entertainer belongs to quite another profession with different allegiances and motives.

The cynical reader will be demanding to know what are these fundamental archaeological entities, these processes, patterns, regularities and principles? The fundamental entities are the attribute, artefact, the artefact-type, the assemblage, the culture and the culture group. The primary processes are those of inevitable variation, multilinear development, invention, diffusion and cultural selection. Combined in many permutations and circumstances these processes give rise to such complex processes as acculturation, and cultural growth, decay and disintegration. Each level of entity clearly has corresponding levels of process which are appropriate to that class of situation.

The repeated similarities or regularities are those systematically correlated attributes that give recognizable group identity to members of a given archaeological class or regularly follow membership of such a class, or sequence of classes. They may be regularities in material, social, economic or technological attributes and they may not necessarily be simple 'one to one' regularities any more than a regular physical wave need be a simple sine wave. In archaeology these 'regularities' follow from certain limiting conditions or constraints imposed on the material either by physical or social action. These limits or constraints may be so gross and obvious as to be uninformative, or so unexpected as to bring us new information – we may observe that the narrower the constraint the greater the predictive information we can get from it and the greater the degree of regularity. The great importance of these 'limiting conditions' or 'constraints' is this predictive advantage that can usually be taken of them. Indeed, our third aim depends on the existence of such constraints in archaeological and anthropological data (Ashby 1956, p. 127).

Synthesizing principles and informative models draw their predictive capacity from constraints which imply that the full range of possible variety is not exploited and that many variations are never found. Gross examples would be the absence of elaborate metallurgy amongst hunter–fisher–gatherers or the regularities that we see occurring independently in areas of Old and New World prehistory – the independent development of cereal farming, stock-breeding, pottery, copper and bronze metallurgy, cities and city-states, priests, specialists, temples, writing, the zero, mathematics, astronomy, calendars and so on. These regularities and the constraints which gave rise to them are precisely those which gave usefulness and predictive power to Thomsen's 'three ages' model of prehistory. The Thomsen model tacitly implied many intercorrelated technological, economic and social constraints and regularities which only subsequently became explicit. The best models are usually those that are more comprehensive and accurate than the model-maker first imagined.

If archaeology is a discipline in search of principles and predictive models then it is necessarily searching for regularities and the constraints which cause them. Since any particular culture is a peculiarly unique integration of components, the search for regularities revolves around the analysis and comparison of limited similarities and parallels within each multilinear development. The tracing of such regularities or repeated correlations that exist within our material and the definition of the constraints or 'limits' of the factors involved in producing these regularities emerges as a major aim in archaeological studies.

By this time I suspect that we have long ago lost our third class of semi-historical prehistorians – the historians without written records. Nevertheless, we still march in company with the second class who would refute any fundamental entities in archaeological data as abstractions of no reality, impossible to define in a form that can be used and leading to no useful general statements or principles. One answer to this criticism is that the function of the archaeologist is not to doubt well-tested propositions accepted by common sense, but to provide analysis or elucidations of them – the function of the modern philosopher since G. E. Moore expounded 'that it is futile to doubt, or to pretend to doubt, common-sense propositions' (Braithwaite 1960, p. 5).

It would seem that one hundred years of archaeology and anthropology have shown that the difficult concepts of 'type', 'culture', 'tribe', 'nation', 'family', 'kin' and other similar concepts are common-sense propositions and have a real existence even should we be unable to define them precisely. It would surely be futile to doubt these propositions merely because our notation is too primitive to define them adequately. However, immediate help is at hand in the form of developments in numerical taxonomy (Sokal and Sneath 1963; Doran and Hodson 1975) which now provide a basis for viable definitions for such entities as these. Whether or not any general principle or theory is possible on this fresh basis remains to be seen. It is sufficient that this excursion has probably finally reduced us to the first class of prehistorians and in this company we shall be happy to proceed to investigate these new developments and their implications.

v   Terminology, definition and meaning

In an earlier section it was suggested that the single most restricting factor in the development of archaeology as a discipline was the ambiguous and inexplicit terminology. It would be naive to suppose that defining our terms carefully and precisely would remove this barrier, although it would certainly contribute more than any other single action. A certain range of variation in the meaning of words is unavoidable and provides a welcome flexibility which in some cases can amount to predictive suggestion by inferring the unexpectedly wide but still valid scope of the terminology – even a word can be a predictive model! Nevertheless it is hardly sensible to worry about seepage in the terminological dam if great gaps exist in the retaining wall, allowing torrents of information to go to waste. Similarly, it would be naive to imagine that individual definitions will be immediately acclaimed and universally adopted – this has been tried and has failed and the long hours of impressive International Congresses have resulted apparently in nothing. But archaeology is not unique in having this kind of problem and we hinted earlier that it may well be the disease of immature and growing disciplines. If this be the case then we may find it worthwhile to compare the development of archaeological terminology with that of contemporary disciplines.

This chapter commenced with a section on the history of archaeology. One of the intentions of that essay was to provide an account for the subject as it stands and to give some impression of the study changing continuously through time. We can now use the same section to compare the development of archaeology in broad outline with that of some of the other Renaissance stimulated disciplines.

The natural philosophers of the Renaissance reopened areas of enquiry, speculated about almost everything and tested their speculations with probing experiments framed to try the predictive value of their new hypotheses; above all they collected data of all kinds – both observations and specimens. The cycle of the scientific method – systematic observations, preliminary hypothesis, testing experiments and tentative theory, then the reapplication of the model to reality – these techniques were implicit by the time of Leonardo and explicit in the works of Galileo (1564–1642). These newly diffused techniques and the great new tools of the Renaissance – the microscope (1590), the telescope (1609) and the thermometer (1609) – together flooded the seventeenth century with countless new observations or 'facts'.

The first result was growing bewilderment and confusion, furious debate and divisive contradiction. Various incompatible hypotheses jostled one with another and every authority used his own terms in his own way. Gradually, however, the philosophers began to specialize in particular activities and to use specially devised and defined terms converted from the handiest everyday equivalent. Fierce argument and sheer convenience gradually selected the most viable entities and definitions and imperceptibly these passed into disciplined usage as the field of furious argument shifted to newer foci. Old terms were defined and redefined whilst new terms were drawn into specific use. To this episode we owe the definitions of such concepts as – mass, force, velocity, acceleration and atom, element and compound, or acid, base and alkali.

The slowly condensing specialist studies were grouping and defining their basic entities in forms which made sense of the new observations and predicted further information about other members of the class; henceforward the classification of data began on a large scale. Many of the entities defined by the new disciplines were intangible and possibly 'unreal' outside their own frame of reference – atom, force, electricity – these are difficult conceptual entities to define. Nevertheless, such terms were defined and accepted because they proved useful approximations to a complex reality and they could also be used to build a calculus of internally consistent hypotheses of predictive value. The great taxonomic schemes of Linnaeus, Darwin, Mendeleef and others systematically organized classes of animals, plants, elements and physical particles which were painstakingly erected in the early frameworks of the great predictive theories of the scientific disciplines.

In the separate phases of their development these disciplines show certain sequential regularities regardless of their particular sphere of operation. Initially we have the awakening of organized curiosity, the collection of observational and material data – the piling up of miscellaneous 'facts'. The variety and confusion of this situation leads to repeated attempts to isolate from the mass of data various coherent and useful conceptual entities – albeit variously defined and differingly used. In this second phase some but not all of the concepts prove useful in synthesizing and subsuming the new information in hierarchies of hypotheses; the successful concepts are saved and fed back into the next development. In the third phase, large-scale classification and analysis in terms of the newly defined entities and concepts yields some comprehensive syntheses in which like entities are not only classified together but the overall relationships governing the scheme's regularities are 'explained'. The fourth and subsequent phases gradually see the refined discovery of observations inexplicable in terms of the old taxonomic syntheses – and the cycle begins yet again, with new theories subsuming old ones as particular cases.

If we compare the development of archaeology with these parallel developments of closely related Renaissance lines of enquiry it is difficult not to notice similar general patterning. Archaeology too passed from a phase of alchemical mysticism, with its thunderstones and elf-shot, to a phase of enlivened curiosity and the piling up of miscellaneous 'facts'. Nineteenth-century endeavours entered the second phase of defining entities and attempts at syntheses, with the inevitable variety of contradictory opinions and definitions. The twentieth century continues to pile up data and the attempts to grapple with it go on, at least in some quarters.

The beginning of some rough common agreement about the meaning and definition of entities has commenced in this century of archaeology but it is by no means satisfactorily completed – in main part by virtue of the disinclination of archaeologists to consider the inner core of their intuitive procedure. Not only is this reticence retarding the development of the discipline but it makes teaching by condensed instruction impossible and endangers the integrity of the subject. Archaeology is presently writhing in the 'natural history' or second phase of development – a frustrating time but not entirely without advantage when compared with the contemporary recasting of many of the more mature disciplines. It is characteristic of this state that variety and confusion of opinion and definition are accompanied by a complacent belief that we can do no more than collect data, whilst simultaneously the first usefully defined entities are recognized and attempts towards reformation and conceptual classification are being made.

From this preamble it would appear that the first task of the archaeologist interested in developing the power of his discipline is to concern himself with the careful definition of terms and the isolation of conceptual entities of value. Not in the naive hope that these definitions will be universally adopted, nor in the vain belief that his concepts alone are all equally correct, but in the firm conviction that only in such a way can order gradually be brought to a confused situation.

The problem of defining the most useful archaeological entities – attribute, artefact, type, assemblage, culture, culture group – is taken up in later chapters along with the inherent implications of these definitions (chapters 4–8). At this point we will concern ourselves with loose terminology and its results, without for one moment supposing that this book is in any way free of these perils.

The most frequent forms of dangerous terminology in archaeological discussion come under the three classes of 'value judgements', 'non-specific generalizations' and 'ambiguities'. The only remedy for these plagues is to avoid them oneself and to spot them in the argument of others. Value judgements involve the incorrect transference of the coloured opinions of the observer to the record of the observation. Such terms as 'primitive', 'crude', 'degenerate' and 'devolved' are particularly abused. One amusing example is the contrast between the Victorian and the modern opinion of British Neolithic pottery. The very ornate Peterborough Ware was just as highly regarded by Victorian excavators as the 'crude' plain Western Neolithic Wares. Subsequently the conviction arose that the Peterborough Ware was 'thick' (it has baroque rims), 'crude' (it is coil built as is Western Neolithic pottery) and 'degenerate' (it is often completely covered with profuse decoration resembling basketry). These grounds were used to substantiate a theory claiming that Peterborough Ware was made by primitive Mesolithic hunters copying the fine wares of the earliest Neolithic settlers. Developing research indicates that the Peterborough pottery is simply the later development of the early Neolithic pottery in a unified and continuous tradition (Smith 1974). The Victorian appraisal of Peterborough pottery was clearly in the light of the prevailing taste for ornate composition; the recent esteem of the austere undecorated, Western Neolithic pottery stemming from the modern 'Scandinavian' cult of austerity and simplicity in adornment. In a similar manner the isolated domestic aspects of pottery assemblages are frequently referred to as 'degenerate', with implications of temporal lateness, when compared with the finer vessels from the very same potter's hand. These simple examples are probably sufficient to illustrate the danger of such terms.

The field of 'non-specific generalizations' has already been briefly touched upon in the discussion of archaeological 'facts' as inferred generalizations especially of the kind known as probability propositions. Non-specific generalizations cover those terms which are used to support the case for a generalization from numbers of observations but which fail to define the proportion of instances. This kind of argument is frequently used when the bulk of the evidence is contrary to the hypothesis favoured by the manipulator. The words to watch in these cases are 'rare', 'common', 'frequent', 'most', 'some', 'few', 'many' and even unspecified measurements like 'long', 'short', 'thick', and 'thin', are meaningless without a comparative standard.

Generalization is a valid and useful procedure but a generalization can be invalid if there are not proportionately enough test cases, if the circumstances are not controlled and if conflicting cases are not considered. Most of the offending terms are relative and not absolute values and they do not say what sample they are of the whole. An occurrence of 100 observations of a particular correlation might be called 'frequent', 'common', 'typical', or 'characteristic', especially if only a total of 150 cases were known. However an occurrence of 100 observations could contrarily be called 'rare', 'atypical', or 'few', if the investigator had a sample of 100,000. We need to know 'how many cases were positive' out of 'how many cases were tested' and 'how many cases were not tested'. The degree of confidence that we are justified in placing in a generalization depends upon the answer to these questions and these can properly be expressed, if the data are numerical, in the form of a confidence statistic or by confidence intervals (Moroney 1957, p. 238).

This discussion brings us to the most interesting and exasperating class of malady – 'ambiguity'. This ailment has two common forms, the use of one and the same term for differing sets of phenomena or the use of the same term for quite different levels of a hierarchy of sets. An example of the first kind of ambiguity is often concealed in the most dangerous of all archaeological terms, the label 'typical' or 'type'. 'Typical' is sometimes used to denote the most common or frequent form of artefact within an assemblage – so that one might say that the handaxe is the 'typical' Acheulean artefact. Alternatively, the 'typical' artefact is used to denote an artefact form so rare and so peculiar as to be confined to this group and therefore to be used as a diagnostic 'type-fossil' for the group as a whole. In this latter sense the split-base bone point can be said to be a 'typical' Aurignacian artefact, although it is an absolutely rare item. At one and the same time, sometimes in the same piece of work, the label 'typical' can be applied to the most common and the most rare artefact in an assemblage. Great confusion arises when arguments proper to one sense of the term are transferred to the other, or what is worse, when attempting to define a population of assemblages one artefact type is arbitrarily defined as 'typical' thus prejudicing the definition and the content of the group as a whole.

A practical example of this latter class of ambiguity arises in the classification of British megalithic long barrows. In western Britain two major classes of tombs are defined by the Severn/Cotswold 'type' and the Clyde/Carlingford 'type' whilst peripheral to these groups and also running through them are various 'atypical' or 'degenerate' types (fig. 1). The 'typical' Severn/Cotswold tomb is defined as having a

Fig. 1 British megalithic tomb typology.

Severn Cotswold type

Clyde Carlingford type

Widespread unspecialized type

slightly trapezoidal long mound with a convex horned forecourt and a transepted megalithic gallery. The 'typical' Clyde/Carlingford tomb has a rounded rectangular mound with concave horned forecourt and a simple segmented gallery, without lateral transepts. These two tomb types seem nicely defined by this typology and neatly concentrated in two natural geographical areas. Attempts to trace continental counterparts for both tomb types have led to the definition of a small group of transepted tombs on the Loire estuary, taxonomically close to the Severn/Cotswold type from which it is suggested that the Clyde/Carlingford type can perhaps be derived as a secondary development (Daniel 1939).

However, close examination reveals a rather complex situation. Both of the 'typical' tomb forms are typical in the sense that they represent the integration of all those aspects peculiar to their area; thus, out of some eighty or so Severn/Cotswold tombs only about ten present all the 'typical' features, including the transepted chamber. Similarly, in the Clyde/Carlingford group of about one hundred and fifty tombs only fifty or so have all the typical features. It is quite clear that the sense of the word typical being used here is the sense emphasizing local peculiarities, the regional idiosyncrasies. If we take the opposite sense and take as typical the tomb plan most commonly found in the two areas we find a much more generalized form 'typical' not only of these two areas but also significantly comprising megaliths from the coasts of Cornwall, Devon, Dorset and Kent (Penwith and Medway groups). This most widespread and frequent 'typical' tomb form is the rather ovate mound with a flat or slightly indented façade with a single or multiple segmented chamber without transepts. If we took this latter form as 'typical' it would emphasize the common basis of the British regional megalithic long barrow groups and link them geographically and taxonomically with a very large class of simple tombs commonly found in Atlantic France. This view would provide an interesting alternative hypothesis opposed to, or subsuming, that deriving the whole phenomenon by unspecified developments from fourteen tombs on the Loire. The important point is the observation that two different usages of the term 'typical' can give rise to two opposed hypotheses for the same data. Which of these two hypotheses is correct we do not know without detailed research framed to test the hypothetical models against the data.

This example stresses the differing implications of the term 'typical', the one aspect emphasizing group idiosyncrasies and the other the group modal type. When it comes to discussing type origins based on diffusion then the modal or most common type is likely to be the most useful since the idiosyncratic type by definition must often reflect local lines of development. As an example of ambiguity arising from one term defining two different sets the term 'typical' should be avoided at all costs and a proper definition of artefact type and frequency used instead.

The alternative form of common ambiguity is the problem of one term being used for several levels of a hierarchy of sets – the problem of levels of meaning. The problem of one term being used to define entities of quite different levels of complexity is not easy to spot or to solve. Take, for example, the propositions that 'an axe is a type of artefact', 'a bronze axe is a type of axe', 'a palstave is a type of bronze axe'. This list covers a descending hierarchy of 'types' of varying complexity but each group on each level is called by an identical term – a 'type'. Difficulties arise when 'types' which refer to entities of different levels of complexity are being compared. The presence of one 'type' of palstave as opposed to another palstave 'type' would probably not be used to divide two assemblages which were similar in many other respects. However, the comparison between an assemblage with a palstave axe 'type' and another assemblage with a stone axe 'type' would probably be sufficient to attribute one to the Middle Bronze Age and the other to the Neolithic horizon. The same 'type' was present in both assemblages at one level – the axe 'type' level, but at a more complex level the axe 'types' were critically different.

In much the same way the older text-books describe Paleolithic entities as forming an Acheulean 'culture', a Mousterian 'culture' or an Aurignacian 'culture' and yet these levels of meaning for the word 'culture' are quite different from the entities intended by the same term in the Wessex 'culture' or the Aunjetitz 'culture'. The vital word 'culture' is here being used at quite different levels of complexity and meaning, linked only by being hierarchic classes of the same general categories, for all of which we are accustomed to use the same word – a 'culture'. If we recognize the different levels of meaning carried by certain group terms we not only avoid confusion but also reveal interesting information about the subtle nature of our intuitive entity concepts.

The common implication of this prolonged but not exhaustive discussion of definition and meaning is that the full potential of archaeology as a discipline can hardly be approached until a concise, incisive and defined terminology has become widely accepted and used. The preliminary steps towards this objective must involve the laborious and various definition of all uncertain terms of key importance in controversial debate, with the ultimate belief that the best terms will survive. In addition to this objective the plagues of value judgement, non-specific generalization and ambiguity must be cast out and where possible the observations should be treated numerically and statistically.

VI   Models

The birth of archaeology as a discipline dates from Thomsen's concept of three successive but overlapping technological eras. This replaced earlier chaotic ideas about ancient artefacts with a simple, largely accurate, predictive framework for structuring and investigating archaeological data. These latter qualities are characteristic of 'models'. Essentially, models are hypotheses or sets of hypotheses which simplify complex observations whilst offering a largely accurate predictive framework structuring these observations – usefully separating 'noise' from information. Which aspect is noise and which counts as information is solely dependent upon the frame of reference of the model.

Models and hypotheses succeed in simplifying complex situations by ignoring information outside their frame of reference and by accurate generalization within it. It has been suggested that our intuitive procedure in trying to make generalizing inferences about the unknown, based on accumulated observations, is usually formed upon imaginary models so constructed that the necessary consequences in thought of these mind-models are always the pictures of the necessary consequences in the real world (Braithwaite 1960, p. 91). When we have succeeded in constructing models based upon our accumulated experience, with the desired properties, we can quickly derive from them a prediction of the consequences which should follow from a certain set of facts fitting the model. Clearly, a great deal depends upon our conceptual models being well constructed and a close fit to reality.

There are a number of different kinds of model, some already recognizable in archaeological thinking, others are inexplicitly used and some remain undreamed of. In this section we will introduce the main kinds of model, outline some dangers of their employment and discuss three general models concerning archaeology (for a more detailed discussion of models see Clarke 1972).

Models can roughly be ordered in three levels of sophistication each with its appropriate procedure and field of application (Ackoff *et al.* 1962). As a discipline or study progresses it is usually the case that its models are being raised from the lowest class of iconic models to that of analogue models and finally to symbolic models or calculus (fig. 2). Iconic models represent observed attributes registered as iconic symbols – as a code; this lowest level of model frequently follows the need for condensed documentation. An archaeological distribution map and simple histograms or scatter diagrams rank as iconic models of archaeological situations – useful as concise documentation and for generalization purposes (fig. 2 model column 1). Analogue models represent observed attributes by substituting other kinds

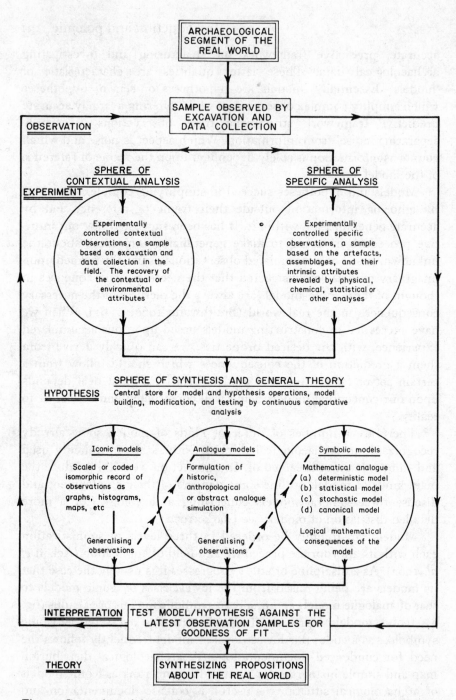

Fig. 2 General model (a) – A model for archaeological procedure. A model for the organization and relation of archaeological activities within a disciplined procedure.

Modified from the geographical model of Chorley 1964, p. 129.

of 'analogous' attributes whose consequences are congruent to those of the observed attributes. In archaeology analogue models are currently the most common and most tantalizingly dangerous form of model with historical, anthropological or abstract situations providing generalizations transferred to archaeological situations. The third and most sophisticated class of model is the symbolic model in which the observed attributes are represented by symbols which unlike iconic symbols are integrated in a specific calculus. The calculus of a symbolic model is usually a mathematical analogue of a deterministic, statistical or stochastic kind such that reality is approximated by the logical mathematical consequences of the model. Symbolic models of this kind have hardly been considered suitable for archaeological studies but in the light of the growing maturity of the discipline and its tools this kind of model should be increasingly developed.

The kinds of model ascend in power from the iconic through the analogue to the symbolic models because each higher rank of model requires a commensurately greater amount of condensed information and has a commensurately greater general scope. The most sophisticated models are usually mathematical or statistical because these vehicles allow the least biased and the most powerful pure deductive systems. An example of the independence of the hypothesis and its vehicle can be gauged from Einstein's adoption in 1915 of a completely abstract system of geometry developed by Riemann merely as an exercise in 1854; Einstein found that this piece of geometry provided a framework of wide predictive value in his theory of general relativity (Braithwaite 1960, p. 48).

However, at the moment most archaeological models are simple situation analogues based on history and anthropology or simple iconic documentations. These models provide different prehistorians with different conceptual frameworks over which they stretch the same facts but with differing results which can be compared and contrasted for their accuracy or inaccuracy in the light of accumulating evidence. The powers of numerical taxonomy promise faint hope that one day even archaeologists might be able to express their mind models in efficient abstract terms of high predictive value. In the meantime it is essential that we appreciate that consciously, or unconsciously, our minds erect models of archaeological situations based on our accumulated experience and breadth of vision. These latter are the features that pick out the skilful from the naive archaeologist and distinguish good and useful models from bad ones.

The topic of bad conceptual models reminds us that throughout this book the most useful and powerful techniques are also repeatedly the most difficult and dangerous to employ. In model building there are several inherent dangers. It is all too easy to mistakenly transfer too many attributes from the model to the theory – this is especially the case with historically based analogues or generalizations. Sometimes the model adopted is too limited in scope and may obscure actual relationships because it is insufficiently general. Ideally the limits of the model and the theory should be identical so that physical impossibility in the theory should correspond to logical impossibility in the model (Braithwaite 1960, p. 109). Despite these characteristics model making remains a most powerful procedure and the fitting of successively more accurate models to reality enlightens as much by the areas of poor fit as by those snugly accommodated. This is perhaps a suitable point at which to introduce three general models or frameworks which will be extensively developed throughout the rest of this book:

(a) A model for archaeological procedure – illustrating the three main spheres of archaeology as a discipline (fig. 2).
(b) A model for archaeological entities – the polythetic versus the monothetic entity (figs 3, 49).
(c) A model for archaeological processes – systems theory, the general model and its setting in archaeology (fig. 11).

(A) A MODEL FOR ARCHAEOLOGICAL PROCEDURE

This model is simply the development of the concepts sketched in the section on the nature of archaeology as a discipline (section II). In that section we defined three main spheres of archaeological activity, comprising observational data recovered by excavation and collection and falling into either the sphere of contextual attributes (location, stratification, association etc.) or the sphere of specific attributes (attributes present or absent amongst the artefacts or assemblages) these spheres together, or independently, contributing to the central sphere of synthesis and model building.

The model illustrating these spheres and their relationships is presented as a flowchart in fig. 2. The chart is drawn up in such a way as to emphasize the difference between the archaeological segment of the real world and the observations inevitably based upon a small

sample of that segment. The spheres of contextual and specific observations can be fully experimental if properly controlled excavation and
data analysis is used. The flow starts with the sample of observations
and passes on from the spheres concerned with experiment and data
recovery to the sphere of model and hypothesis operations. The three
parallel columns represent the alternative routes of analysis using
iconic, analogue or symbolic models. In reality, as we have noted
earlier, these routes are really alternatives of increasing sophistication.
These methods may be used in a cascade sequence in which an iconic
model is converted into an analogue and then a symbolic model –
either in one sequence of operations or gradually over generations as
the discipline and the data gradually improve in information content.
Finally, a feedback route compares the newly devised model or hypothesis with the latest state of the observational data and agreements
and discrepancies are filtered back into the system again, to provide
fresh modifications or new models. The continuous cycle ultimately
producing a distillate of synthesizing propositions, principles or
hypotheses (Chorley 1964, p. 129).

(B) A MODEL FOR ARCHAEOLOGICAL ENTITIES

Most archaeological entities consist of clusters or aggregates of entities
of lower taxonomic rank. We are concerned with groups, groups of
groups, and groups of groups of groups of attributes based on observational data. Culture groups are clusters of cultures, cultures are
clusters of assemblages, assemblages are clusters of types, types are
clusters of artefacts and artefacts are clusters of attributes or traits. To
the archaeologist the process of grouping objects into 'sensible'
groups, clusters, or sequences has been a normal activity for decades.
The nature of these groupings seemed quite clear; one made a list of
attributes intuitively prejudging that it would give the 'best' grouping
and then placed entities in the group if they possessed the attributes
and outside if they did not. The intended nature of these groups was
also transparently clear, they were solid and tangible defined entities
like an artefact type or a cultural assemblage, each possessed a necessary list of qualifying attributes and they could be handled like discrete and solid bricks. This class of group is well known to
taxonomists and is called a *monothetic* group – a group of entities so
defined that the possession of a unique set of attributes is both

sufficient and necessary for membership (fig. 3) (Sokal and Sneath 1963, p. 13). The model for archaeological entities was a monothetic model.

The monothetic box of bricks model is still the prevailing concept tacitly underlying the definition of most archaeological entities. Prehistorians still seem to think that in order to define groups it is necessary that every member within the group must have all the qualifying attributes. In practice this ideal has never been demonstrated in archaeology; no group of cultural assemblages from a single culture ever contains, nor ever did contain, all of the cultural artefacts (Childe 1956, p. 33; 1963, p. 41); no groups of artefacts within a single type population are ever identical in their lists of attributes. Instead, we are conscious that these groups are defined by a range of variation between defined limits, by populations of attributes or types of which a high proportion are variously shared between individual members of the group. This situation is not a monothetic grouping at all but belongs to the other great class of taxonomic groups – the *polythetic* groups (fig. 3) (Sokal and Sneath, 1963, pp. 13–15).[5]

Fig. 3   General model (b) – A model for archaeological entities. A model suggesting that archaeological entities are structured as polythetic group populations and may not be treated as monothetic group populations.

A polythetic group is – a group of entities such that each entity possesses a large number of the attributes of the group, each attribute is shared by large numbers of entities and no single attribute is both sufficient and necessary to the group membership. Whereas there is only one form of monothetic group there are many varieties of polythetic grouping according to the number of shared attributes, the maximum and minimum number of attributes shared between any pair, and the number of attributes possessed by each individual. One of the most important future tasks is going to be the definition of the precise nature of the polythetic groupings underlying archaeological taxonomy.

The fundamental implications of the realization that archaeological entities are polythetic, or partially polythetic groups of various kinds is beyond simple statement. For the first time we can honestly admit the wide variation in attributes defining artefact types, assemblages and cultures without having to abandon them as defined entities. The foolhardiness of emphasizing a single attribute or single type-fossil as the criterion for group membership can be recognized. For the first time it is possible to see that this awkward variety and range of variation of our entities and their attributes underlies their original potential to change by mosaic and multilinear development and not by an agreed mythology of simple unilinear typologies. We need no longer be ashamed of the obvious inadequacies of our theoretical concepts and definitions in the face of the actual complexities of the data. Viable definitions of archaeological entities can be produced and used as the incisive tools they should be, not consigned to unused primers or buried in glossaries. There is no longer any need to sweep the untidy and inexplicable fringe of peripheral forms into unrealistic 'hybrid' heaps with all the implications of that pseudogenetic term.

Archaeological theory and definition has rather dishonestly and inconsistently operated at two levels. A theoretical level of interpretation in terms of rigid monothetic groupings and a practical level of groupings by broad affinity or similarity assessed on an intuitive basis. This schizophrenic division has seriously impaired the development of prehistoric studies, in which lip-service has been paid to a theoretical model of demonstrable inadequacy whilst actual practical advance has been accomplished by rather furtive groping – with the results subsequently presented as having been achieved by intelligent theorizing.

In conclusion then, this work will proceed on the assumption that the best model for most archaeological entities is a polythetic model of some kind (also now advocated in social anthropology – Needham 1975). The later chapters will attempt to build up a soundly based hierarchy of defined entity concepts using this model and will pursue its far-reaching implications (chapters 4–8).[6]

(C) A MODEL FOR ARCHAEOLOGICAL PROCESSES

The cultures studied by the archaeologist once existed fully equipped and working within an ecological framework but now we have only a few broken cogs, springs and structured fragments from which the whole clockwork must be restored and the principles of mechanics induced. Here we have the model of culture as an elaborate machine with intermeshed working parts, with a measurable efficiency and inertia, with potential energy and driving forces, tensions and escape mechanisms, the whole lubricated with social oils. Then again we may take the model of culture as a superorganism, segmented by kinship, responding to stimulus, extracting a food supply, growing, reproducing and dying; a complex integration of many small units such that the aggregate has a much greater potential than the simple sum of the parts. Finally, we have thought of culture as a physical model in which constellations of elements are structured into clusters and the clusters integrated into greater patterns – the cultural galaxies, changing with time and gliding or colliding with yet other similar cultural galaxies. All of these models are valuable but not one of them is predictively useful, they are still at the stage of simple analogues.

A little thought about these favourite analogues for cultural entities will reveal that both they and individual cultures share certain essential characteristics – the very characteristics which give some power to the analogues but power which in each specific case is spoiled as a general model by having too limited a scope. If we can distil these quintessential characteristics we should be able to define a model of more general scope and utility. These shared characteristics would seem to be the essential aspects of being dynamic complex wholes, formed of intercommunicating networks of entities or attributes – they are all dynamic systems. The general and inherent properties of different kinds of systems are the field of cybernetics and it is clearly in aspects of this field that useful models for cultural entities can best be sought.

It would be all too easy at this stage to take systems theory as our model for archaeological processes and the cultural entities that generate them, without isolating precisely the kind of system these entities represent. This would simply extend systems theory and its terminology as yet another vague analogy of no practical potential. Consequently, although this section puts forward a dynamic system model as suitable for archaeological conceptualization it will take another two chapters to attempt to define the nature of such archaeological systems. We must try and understand what kinds of system exist in archaeology, what are their roles, limits and inherent properties as systems, how are they networked by subsystems and within what setting can these systems be conceived as existing? We cannot possibly be fully successful in these attempts, since anthropologists themselves are only just beginning to analyse social systems in these terms (e.g. Rappaport 1968). Given another generation of results from the analysis of the more fully documented anthropological data then the archaeologist may begin more fruitfully to scavenge archaeologically relevant facets. In the meantime, the archaeologist can start to explore the potential of the dynamic system models. We must try to find out which kinds of systems are relevant and which are irrelevant as archaeological process models and to elucidate the methods for investigating these very complex systems. Having established some idea of the kinds of system involved we can probe their inherent properties regardless of particular attribute values. In the light of all these investigations we may attempt to define a general system model best suited as a framework for archaeological analysis and hypothesis. These are the tasks pursued in the next chapter.

Briefly, we may anticipate that culture groups, cultures, assemblages, types and artefacts changing with time can be thought of as certain kinds of dynamic systems with certain inherent characteristics stemming from the general structure of the systems rather than from their specific attribute or entity values. Our aim is the isolation of archaeological entities as functional systems, the definition of the limiting values of the systems' states and the specification of the inherent properties of the systems as general systems. The first part will concern a general systems model for archaeological entities, the second part will apply this specifically to cultures, and the third part will apply the model to artefacts as systems. Much of the discussion of a general systems model must be conceived as applying simultaneously to these two levels – to cultures and to artefacts. The reasons why so much that is applicable to one level is also applicable to the other level of entity will gradually become apparent. In the chapters that follow we are primarily engaged in, first – the development of suitable general models of predictive value, second – the development of the setting for such models. At the culture level we can expect a model which will involve dynamic cultural systems of complex networked subsystems coupled with an environmental system setting of equal complexity (figs 22, 23). The study of whole sociocultural systems, the mutual relations between such systems and their environment, and the adaptive changes of these systems with passing time constitutes the study of cultural ecology and a topic of our third chapter. Having spent so much time generating models and settings for the models the rest of the text re-applies the implications of these concepts to our special field of archaeological entities and processes with particular examples (chapters 4–10).

Notes

(1) Daniel (1976) prefers to emphasize the distinction between the work of Thomsen and that of the earlier Italian, French, English and Danish scholars who 'engaged in general philosophical speculations' about technological ages in man's past. He argues that these speculations were *not* a general way of thinking in these countries and that Thomsen was unaffected 'in any very significant way' by the ideas of Mercati, Mahudel and others. Given the currently available evidence, it is difficult to decide between Daniel's views and the author's conclusion that the stimuli for Thomsen's work had 'ancient and widespread sources'. Klindt-Jensen's recent history of Scandinavian archaeology (1975) offers no help in resolving this problem.

(2) A notable omission in this discussion is the work of V. Gordon Childe, and in particular his development of the concept of archaeological 'cultures' (e.g. 1929). After the earlier preoccupation with chronological sequences through the use of stratigraphy and Montelius' typological method, Childe stimulated a new systemization of European prehistory by using the culture as a temporal *and* a spatial unit of analysis.

(3) As an example of the neglect of general theory and methodology, it is worth noting that before the publication of Childe's *Piecing Together the Past* (1956) there was no book in Britain which discussed methodology in an *explicit* way. This neglect was also visible in America, with the works of Taylor (1948) and Willey and Phillips (1958) being rare exceptions.

(4) The phrase 'material culture in the past' is here substituted for 'antiquities', which seemed an unfortunate choice of word in the first publication of this volume. Although the study of material culture *in the past* is widely associated with the discipline of archaeology, this is not universally the case at present. For example Schiffer (1976, p. 4) argues that 'the subject matter of archaeology is the relationships between human behaviour and material culture *in all times* and places' (my emphasis). According to this definition the discipline includes 'traditional' archaeology as well as studies of material culture in both ethnographic and industrial societies (e.g. Schiffer 1976, pp. 188–93).

(5) Doran and Hodson (1975, pp. 161–7) have noted how some archaeologists (e.g. Childe, Bordes, Krieger) have *hinted* at the use of a polythetic model for archaeological entities such as types and cultures. But there was no explicit development of this concept and they point out that Childe's classification of types ('the individual members . . . exhibit certain common features, repeated . . . *in all members of the class*': Childe 1956, pp. 5–6, my emphasis) was what we would now call monothetic.

(6) While the polythetic classification of archaeological entities has been strongly supported and developed within British archaeology (e.g. Doran and Hodson 1975), some workers in America have taken a different point of view. Thomas (1970) argues that the author fails to distinguish *two* important meanings of 'classification': the first concerns the act of forming groups of archaeological entities, which Thomas agrees is where the polythetic concept is vital; the second concerns the *identification* of new specimens so that they can be allotted to existing taxa. In the latter case the archaeologist is concerned with a smaller number of criteria which discriminate between taxa, and Thomas claims that this is a monothetic procedure. Whallon (1971, 1972) goes further than this in maintaining that a monothetic approach, as practised in plant ecology, gives a more meaningful classification into types of his own data (Owasco period pottery from central and eastern New York State) than either polythetic methods or Spaulding's (1953) method for attribute analysis. For example when he used Spaulding's method of testing for significant, non-random associations between attributes by use of the Chi-square statistic, he found he could only define *two* pottery types, compared with the traditional *sixteen* established by Ritchie and MacNeish. This divergence of opinion over the use of polythetic classifications in archaeology can be seen further in Doran and Hodson's (1975, pp. 177–80) criticisms of the Whallon method, which they claim does not deal with quantitative attributes and requires a full comparative test on the same data with a polythetic cluster analysis, as has been done in plant ecology.

2 Culture systems – the model

Culture is . . . the system of the total extrasomatic means of
adaptation. Such a system involves complex sets of
relationships among people, places, and things whose
matrix may be understood in multivariate terms,
LEWIS R. BINFORD, 1965, p. 209

1 Systems theory, an outline

Cybernetics, or systems theory, is a complex and rapidly expanding
discipline which it would be quite impossible to condense into this
short section. The excellent elementary textbooks by Ashby (1956)
and by Wiener (1948) describe the basis which we need for our
purposes and this sketch amounts to no more than an imperfect
outline intended to acquaint the reader with this kind of approach. An
exhortation to go first to these and other primary sources (e.g.
Bertalanffy 1950, 1969; Hall and Fagan 1956; Miller 1965; Buckley
1967, 1968) cannot be emphasized too strongly.

Nevertheless, our intention is to use this developing and potentially fundamental craft to help construct a model for archaeological
processes. This will inevitably be an inadequate model but still one
which may summarize our information and promise some capacity for
further development.

Briefly, the tentative general model that we are about to develop
arises from the assumption that cultural systems are integral whole
units. Material culture, economic structure, religious dogma, and
social organization are on this hypothesis merely subsystems arbitrarily extracted from their coupled context by the specialist academic.
The sociocultural system is a unit system in which all the cultural
information is a stabilized but constantly changing network of intercommunicating attributes forming a complex whole – a dynamic
system. An extension of this assumption would suggest that material
culture can only be properly studied if its former coupling within a
sociocultural system is taken into account.

A general system model on this basis should be representative of cultural processes at several levels within a sociocultural unit. The designation 'general' model is thus intended to convey the erstwhile hope that the model will relate the effect of change upon cultural entities – processes, in fact – from the level of attributes within artefacts to that of artefacts within cultures, or kinship attributes within social structure, or religious tenets within a dogma system. The immediate purpose is therefore to give an introductory outline of the necessary procedure, to create a tentative general system model and to develop the preliminary implications of the general model for cultural data.

It would perhaps be best to start by considering the great variety of kinds of system that exist in the world and then to take a brief look at some of their inherent properties or regularities. It is these inherent properties of various kinds of system which are of particular interest to us in our pursuit of a model that tells us something about the general behaviour of particular classes of very complex systems, regardless of the specific state of their particular attributes. These inherent characteristics of systems of the same class arise from common features in the structure of the individual systems, the aspect commonly referred to as 'pattern' in static concepts and which is best transformed into 'system' in dynamic situations changing with space and time. The term system is here taken to embrace any 'intercommunicating network of attributes or entities forming a complex whole'. We are thus constructing a mind-model in which we have systems of intercommunicating attributes or entities such that the components' states or values change sequentially with space, time, or both and consequently the overall system state changes with their complex integration. The component attributes or entities are said to be 'intercommunicating' in that changes in the values or states of some of these components can be shown to alter with the value or state of some of their neighbours. Any such change in value or state is customarily called a *transformation* and a sequence of transformations following a particular course is then called a *trajectory*.

It follows from this model that any particular system state can be shown either to be a time or space transformation of another specific and different system state, or it can be shown that the one system cannot be a transformation of the other – however prolonged the operation. Archaeology revolves about numbers of decisions grouping some sets of systems – artefacts, assemblages, cultures – as transformations one of another and differentiating them from other sets of systems which are claimed as quite separate but parallel transformation sets. The problems of sensibly clustering related time and space transformations and of aligning such clusters to those respective axes are two of the main problems of archaeology.

To complete this elementary picture of a system we must then add that most systems can be acted upon by various external conditions and can themselves act upon such conditions. The varying external conditions acting upon the system are called its *input* and the varying actions of the system upon its environment are called the system's *output* (which output is simultaneously the environment's input and vice versa) (figs 11, 23).

The organic and inorganic objects of the world provide a very large number, possibly an infinity of classes of system. It follows that in calling attention to the system aspect of archaeological entities we are only drawing attention to a single part of this infinity and in doing so we gain very little new information about these entities. In order to progress we must specify more and more closely what special categories of system we are considering and thus define their inherent properties. Are archaeological entities open systems, closed systems, plastic systems, determinate or indeterminate systems, 'Black Box' systems, Markovian systems – and so on? One answer is that we do not yet know what sort of system we are dealing with, we know a little about which kinds of system are not represented and we know little bits of these archaeological systems' behaviour that we can roughly match in other kinds of system. What we require is a carefully built and fitted model integrating these bits of knowledge and closely approaching our total knowledge of archaeological systems. A comprehensive form of such a model, capable of generating each parameter and property at any given moment and capable of generating its progressive sequences of transformations is called a *canonical* model (Ashby 1956, p. 29). A canonical representation or model embodies the transformation trajectories of a system and this makes it a powerful and useful model.

We have not the space in this preamble to attempt a comprehensive survey of the main kinds of system but let us instead take a look at an arbitrary set of properties commonly found in several classes of system and possibly related to our search for a model. Perhaps from these bits and pieces we can construct some temporary framework.

CONTINUITY

First of all, we are certainly dealing with systems that change as some complex integration of their changing attribute or entity components. This characteristic capacity for change or transformation is most often demonstrated as a process of continuous though not necessarily regular change – overall change brought about by successive, infinitesimal transformations, individually imperceptible but quite apparent in cumulative result. The importance of conceptualizing our archaeological systems as dynamic and continuous systems lies in the special properties of continuous systems.

One might take an aircraft flying across the sky as an example of a continuous system, in that its course can be expressed as a cumulative sequence of successive positions. Now, if we were intent on shooting down this aircraft we would align our missile just ahead of the aircraft on its present course, knowing that although certain deflecting evasive action was possible on the part of the aircraft, nevertheless it could not precipitately change its position in the sky without describing a continuous course between its former and future position. The gun-layer is using the property of constraint which confines the variety of activities of a continuous system and gives rise to a certain amount of behavioural regularity, predictable within certain limits; in the case of the radar tracked aircraft this may be a fatal regularity. Consequently, the characterization of our archaeological systems as continuous systems increases the expectation of detecting constraints and resultant regularities in the trajectory of such systems. The power of this constraint lies in the inability of a continuous function to change other than from one state or value to an immediately neighbouring value (Ashby 1956, p. 133). Our first proposition towards a general model system is therefore: that the system is dynamic and continuous, with the attributes or entities having specific values or states which vary by successive transformations.

FEEDBACK

We have described the kind of system that we are trying to model as an 'intercommunicating network of attributes or entities forming a complex whole' so that changes in some of these components may give rise to correlated changes in some of the other system components. This concept allows us to visualize the components as having communicating channels between them, even though these remain as intangible as the magnetic field linking a moving magnet with a changing pattern of iron filings. This connection can be symbolized by a line joining the particular attributes or entities, with an arrow representing the direction of connection, from the source of stimulus to the receiving attribute or entity acted upon (fig. 4i).

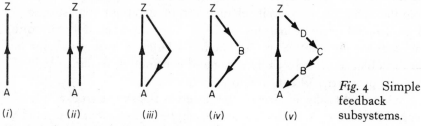

Fig. 4   Simple feedback subsystems.

(i)   (ii)   (iii)   (iv)   (v)

(i) *single channel, no feedback*
(ii)–(v) *looped channels, feedback subsystems*

However, it is more frequently the case that the attribute or entity values are coupled 'or connected in such a manner that a change or transformation in either one may produce a corresponding trans-formation in the value of the other. In such a case a connecting line and arrow must be shown in both directions constituting a 'loop' line which may run direct (fig. 4i, ii) or it may run via another attribute, entity, or a set of such components (fig. 4iv, v); in all these cases there is a functional loop feeding back information from the recipient to the stimulator. Such a connection or loop constitutes a 'feedback loop' and the recycling of information in this way constitutes *feedback* in which the stimulator may be modified by the return of some of its emitted information. Any two-way arrow in a systems diagram constitutes a feedback subsystem although it may take various forms (fig. 4i–v).

Since feedback subsystems will operate wherever and whenever such a connecting 'loop' can be traced through the connections of networks of nodes in a system, then it follows that a richly networked system will usually integrate many such local feedback subsystems. The special characteristics of such subsystems will then immeasurably enrich and complicate the properties of the system as a whole – providing it with great flexibility of response. Even with only four attributes or entities, each one affecting the other three, then twenty separate circuits can be traced through them (fig. 5). Knowing the properties of all the twenty circuits does not give complete informa-tion about the system. 'Such complex systems cannot be treated as an interlaced set of more or less independent feedback circuits, but only

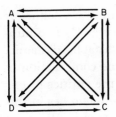

Fig. 5 A simple example of a complex system; twenty circuits may be traced through this simple network.
Source: Ashby 1956, p. 54.

as a whole. What is important is that complex systems, richly cross-connected internally, have complex '"behaviours", and that these "behaviours" can be goal-seeking in complex patterns' (Ashby 1956, p. 54).

For our purposes it is sufficient to recognize that many of the special qualities that sometimes appear to endow complex entities and systems with intelligence – goal-seeking, adaptation, response to stimulus, behaviour, self-regulation, memory, foresight – stem from an anthropomorphic view of these kinds of feedback subsystems and this kind of richly networked system. One must be careful not to attribute the individual human capacity for reasoned thought to the material systems generated by human societies – they share certain similar properties by virtue of being complex systems, these properties are inherent in all such kinds of system.

We can conclude this brief glance at feedback couplings by discussing the two alternative forms of information feedback – negative feedback and positive feedback. Negative feedback is said to be operating if the outgoing information (fig. 4 A to Z) comes back round the loop (from Z to A, fig. 4) to its source, with a size or sign such as to diminish the source's output. This kind of feedback may repeatedly recycle around the feedback loop and cumulatively diminish the source output to zero. Alternatively, the feedback information returning down the loop may add to the source's output, cumulatively pushing it up as it recycles; this is positive feedback. Both kinds of feedback are important in their respective capacities for bringing systems up to, or away from, states of *equilibrium* or stability.

EQUILIBRIUM OR STABILITY

The vague and undefined usages of the terms 'system' and 'equilibrium' are responsible for more 'unreal' problems and have obscured useful model building more than any other pair of abused terms. Having said that an entity is a system and that it has states of equilibrium or stability we have said nothing at all until we define, or try to define, precisely what kind of system and what kind of equilibrium we are considering. Do we mean stable, metastable, dynamic, steady state, unstable or statistical equilibrium, some combination of these, or some new form of equilibrium special to the entities of our study? It is easy to see that one of the keys to our problem lies in this simple challenge, it is less easy to provide a simple answer. We must try to be more specific about the forms of equilibrium involved although we are sure to be guilty of some ambiguity in so fundamental a field.

(1) *Stable equilibrium*

A system is said to be in stable equilibrium if a small displacement from the equilibrium state gives rise to a return to that state in due course. If we consider a large horizontal concave mirror with a ball-bearing at rest in the depressed centre of the mirror – then a displacement of the ball-bearing away from the centre will only result in the ball oscillating about the centre and gradually reassuming its original state. The centre of the horizontal concave mirror is the stable equilibrium point for this system. Since the state of stable equilibrium is restored by cumulatively diminishing the disturbing displacement it follows that such systems may frequently but not exclusively be returned to stable equilibrium by means of the 'regulating' effect of a negative feedback subsystem. This capacity for feedback subsystems to act as 'regulators' will be discussed at some length later in this section.

(2) *Unstable equilibrium*

A system is said to be in unstable equilibrium if a small displacement from the equilibrium state gives rise to a cumulatively greater displacement from that specific state – usually towards some alternative and fresh equilibrium state. If we balanced our ball-bearing on the domed centre of a convex mirror – then any slight displacement would cause the ball-bearing to roll down the dome and away to some new equilibrium point. Since the state of unstable equilibrium, when displaced, gives rise to cumulatively greater displacement, it follows that regulating subsystems may often but not exclusively incorporate positive feedback outputs to produce this property.

(3) *Metastable equilibrium*

A system is said to be in metastable equilibrium if its state is only stable in the absence of a suitable catalyst, which if introduced into the system would immediately initiate displacement away from the equilibrium state. The potential energy of such a system although minimum is not vanishingly small (Lotka 1925, p. 143). Examples of metastable systems are super-saturated salt solutions prior to crystal seeding or explosive mixtures before detonation. Such systems commonly involve cumulative change building up to a threshold beyond which the system cannot continue unchanged. The thresholds can be regarded as temporarily separating one system state from a successive sequence of system states, each separated from the other by a threshold requiring specific 'catalytic' states or values to be introduced, possibly in a particular order, before the system's trajectory can pass from one state to another. The number and order of the 'essential' or 'catalytic' values that must be introduced into the system before a particular transition will take place is some measure of the 'height' of this threshold.

(4) *Steady state equilibrium*

A system is said to be in steady state equilibrium if its state is only stable in the presence of certain constantly maintained variables, attribute states, or values. If we imagine a system in which a vibrationless helicopter hovers motionless at a fixed point in the air, containing in its cabin the concave mirror with the ball-bearing motionless at its central equilibrium point – then in this case the ball-bearing is in a steady state equilibrium. The ball-bearing will remain in equilibrium in this system only so long as the helicopter is maintained 'motionless' by the vigorous expenditure of energy by its engines and rotors.

(5) *Dynamic equilibrium*

A system is said to be in dynamic equilibrium if, in spite of the continuously changing values of its components, at successive points in time these components closely approximate to a stable state. Coupled systems are often said to be in dynamic equilibrium one with another and in such cases although each system is changing, they are jointly changing in such a way as to trace a path through successive equilibrium points. One may imagine a giant and a man playing a game in which a pair of scales is continuously kept in balance although the giant successively alters the weights on his side, causing imbalance, and the man must quickly rebalance the scale by altering the weights on his side; every day the scales are in equilibrium, but every day the state of equilibrium is changed – thus we have a dynamic equilibrium with a moving balance point or value. This allusion to a giant and a man playing a game can be compared with the relationship between culture systems and their coupled environment systems (for Game Theory, see below pp. 66–72).

(6) *Statistical equilibrium*

Systems are said to be in statistical equilibrium if the frequency of occurrence of the component populations continues to remain proportionately allocated according to certain probabilities, regardless of the vagaries of individual elements. It might be the case, for example, that the populations of the three Benelux countries remain distributed in the relative proportions of $3 : 3\frac{1}{2} : 1$ respectively, even though all the populations are constantly changing in numbers and people are going to and fro across the borders. In an archaeological context one might say that the hunting sites of a certain culture over a certain time are characterized by populations of artefacts distributed according to the ratio of five arrowheads, to every three scrapers, for every single burin – even though individual sites in the class have different absolute numbers of these artefacts (cf. different Mousterian variants in South West France). If such observations record very large numbers of attributes or entities and their relative frequency of occurrence then this kind of equilibrium may well be sought for.

(7) *Equilibrium basin, area, or set*

A system is said to have an equilibrium basin, area, or a stable set of states or values, when under a certain set of conditions the transformations of these values continue to remain within a limited set constituting the 'basin' or stable region. In the preceding examples of different classes of equilibria each case referred to the maintenance of equilibrium existing at any one of a limited set of states or values. It follows that an equilibrium basin or stable region can be formulated for any class of equilibrium – stable, unstable, dynamic, and so on.

This brief survey sketches some of the different meanings that can lie behind the term equilibrium when applied to a system. It should be apparent that the various forms of equilibrium are not necessarily mutually exclusive, so that a particular system may illustrate an equilibrium that is both dynamic and statistical in its properties. Furthermore, we can see that any of these equilibria may refer to attribute or entity values and states or they may refer to vectors, sequences of values, or rates of change. This flexibility of the equilibrium concept constitutes its greatest asset, since if it is possible to fit some kind of equilibrium model to our changing entities' 'behaviour' then it is usually possible to begin some form of canonical or symbolic representation. A final observation upon this topic might usefully re-emphasize the need to specify the qualities of the particular breed of equilibrium under consideration and for the realization that even within a single system different kinds of equilibrium 'behaviour' may be illustrated, possibly relevant to the different levels of the system and its subsystems.

GOAL-SEEKING OR HOMEOSTASIS

Many kinds of system, especially complex richly networked systems, may appear to have the capacity for searching-out and converging upon 'desirable' goals or states. The continually self-regulating guidance system of a ballistic missile is an example of such a goal-seeking system, another is the robot fire-extinguisher which seeks out, approaches and puts out fires. It is important to differentiate two properties of these systems – first, that they converge upon some state – secondly, that the state is customarily described as a 'desirable' one, a goal. In humanly made systems the goal usually coincides with the end desired by the manufacturer and can hardly imply 'desire' on the part of the system especially when, in such cases as the ballistic missile, the system has a trajectory ending in the system's own destruction.

It is apparent that goal-seeking 'behaviour' in systems is an anthropomorphic interpretation of – first, that a system's trajectories converge upon states of equilibrium – secondly, that some components of such systems act as regulators and can restrict the variety of possible outcomes. We will discuss the aspect of regulation and control in the next section but simple regulation is quite apparent in such systems as the guided missile, thermostats and mechanical governors of various kinds. Goal-seeking 'behaviour' is largely an extension of a human interpretation to systems running towards equilibrium states or regions, states that may be desirable or undesirable according to the point of view. Such equilibrium-seeking is characteristic of complex systems and it frequently arises from positive or negative feedback loops which occasion oscillating convergence upon a stable state. These oscillations about an equilibrium state are also anthropomorphized as 'searching', 'scanning the set of possibilities for a suitable state', 'trial and error', or 'hunt and stick' (Ashby 1956, p. 230).

Whether a humanly made system, such as a cultural system or an artefact system, has a time-trajectory running from equilibrium to equilibrium, each preselected and preconceived by its makers, or whether such systems are stochastically running to successive equilibria poses an interesting question. However, what the use of such anthropomorphic terms implies is that the appropriate model may be the same − it does not matter that the multilinear transformations of the handaxe system were not 'scanning' the variety of alternative forms for successively more effective variants − the system behaves 'as if' this did take place. The 'adaptation', 'regulation', 'goal-seeking', 'memory capacity', 'foresight' and 'evolution' of such systems have comparable results for the systems as the related human capacities have for human beings.

REGULATION AND CONTROL

Another inherent capacity of certain kinds of complex system is the capacity to act 'as if' capable of self-control by self-regulation. When a cold draft blows upon a thermostatically controlled oven the temperature of the oven drops, the thermostat comes into operation and increases the temperature, the oven gets too hot and the thermostat cuts out allowing the temperature to fall. Here we have an error-controlled regulator oscillating about a set temperature. There are many different ways of constructing such a regulator and conversely many different forms that the regulation can take in a system which is manifestly controlling its own table of 'responses' to 'stimulus'. The principle behind most of these regulators is the same category of feedback loop responsible for such other 'behavioural' characteristics as goal-seeking. We can understand that if such complex consequences follow upon so simple a kind of circuit connection as this 'loop', then almost any complex system is going to manifest this kind of 'behaviour'.

As a general example let us take a particular environmental disturbance 'E' acting upon – and therefore coupled to – an entity possessing as part of its system, a subsystem 'R', through which the input disturbance from 'E' must pass. The resulting state or 'response' of the entity 'S' is a limited set out of the total table of possible states 'T', as restricted or constrained by the necessity of being compatible with the output from 'R'. The looped subsystem through 'R' is acting as a constraint which reduces the total possible number of outcomes to a restricted set according to the conditions – 'R' is acting as a control and regulator to the system (fig. 6).

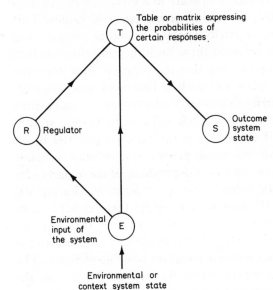

Table or matrix expressing the probabilities of certain responses

T

R) Regulator

S) Outcome system state

Environmental input of the system

E

Environmental or context system state

Fig. 6   A simple system with a controlling regulator 'R'.

The importance of regulating and controlling subsystems of this kind is their capacity for acting as an 'insulating' medium between the system and its environment or context. The regulator blocks and filters the extreme range of external fluctuations by constraining their variety and maintaining the essential system parameters within certain limits. From the point of view of survival, systems integrating good regulating subsystems are better able to survive unchanged than similar systems with less efficient 'insulation'. Regulation controls the flow of variety from the environment to the system coupled to it. Much of social and material culture can be seen as in part exercising a regulating control over the effect of external and internal variations upon the system outcomes. The law of requisite variety suggests that only variety can modulate or destroy variety (Ashby 1956, p. 207). Only variety or sophistication in a culture system's components can force down the variety in the system's final states and keep them within tolerable limits. We will return to the role of culture as a regulator on several occasions.

LIMITS AND NETWORKS

We have been repeatedly stating that certain propositions or certain conditions are true, or are found to operate in a system, when certain other conditions are fulfilled, or hold a certain range of values. This proposition, or that system, or attribute state, is said to remain valid within certain limits. If the range of these limiting conditions shrinks to a single point or state, then we say that the proposition is 'the case' or the system state will be 'such and such' if this condition is operating. When the system or attribute state in such conditions has become not a possible range of values but a single value – the system state is determinate. Conversely, if the single point expands and the limits become infinitely wide and the same proposition or state remains valid, then the proposition or state is 'independent' of these particular conditions, which may vary at will without necessarily altering the state under consideration. We may then consider these conditions so permissive in respect of this state or trajectory that they are not 'essential variables' in the sense that they provide no constraint to the particular state – they tell us nothing about its possible changes. The situation becomes more complex when we not only say that the limiting conditions have such and such a range but that the accompanying state may also have a range of probable values within limits. The system is no longer fully determinate but nevertheless its states are limited in a way that can be expressed in terms of probabilities (fig. 10). We will shortly consider the effect of this complication upon the amount we can say about the 'behaviour' of such a system.

The discovery of the limits which constrain the variety of states of an attribute or system enables us to understand the regularity in the 'behaviour' of the system or attribute. Such limits are sometimes observed in relation to human activities or their products but there is often reticence about expressing these limits on the grounds that they are 'hopelessly broad'. This observation is generally an accurate recognition of the large range of viable or acceptable states but the epithet 'hopelessly' broad requires modification. The point here is that although the limits brought about by any one condition may be broad, nevertheless the final effect of compounding numbers or relevantly operating broad limits may still constrain the outcome quite tightly – as in fig. 7. We should not abandon attempts to investigate and define the limits operating in a certain study simply because each individual set of limits is rather broad.

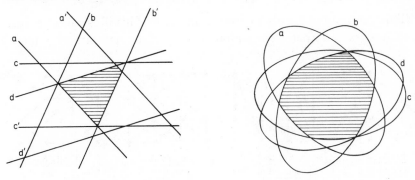

Fig. 7   Compounded constraints – although the limiting conditions of each particular constraint may be broad a–a', b–b', c–c', d–d', or sets a, b, c, d, nevertheless their joint operation narrowly constrains the stable area illustrated by the hatched regions.

The diagram of constraint brought about by compounded limiting conditions (fig. 7) also enables us to make another observation. If we think of our limits as operating at certain points on a linear scale of values then we tend to draw the limits as though they were two parallel lines drawn through the operating boundaries (fig. 7). However, we can also think of these same limits as defining the boundary of a 'set' of values, reflecting stable areas or regions whose intersecting boundaries define the constrained equilibrium area (fig. 7). This latter modification gives us a timely reminder that we are consciously or unconsciously working within the field of set and group theory with its well developed theorems about intersecting sets and subsets, and their properties. Once again we catch a glimpse of a potentially valuable array of techniques with a symbolic calculus quite relevant to our ascent from iconic, through analogue to symbolic models (Green 1965).[1]

Systems can be visualized and depicted as interlinked networks of attributes or entities forming a complex whole, a concept which gives rise to the static impression of structure and pattern within various entities. One consequence of the networked nature of such complex systems is the inherent capacity for the system to have more properties than simply the sum of those of its components (fig. 5). Another property worthy of our attention involves the infinite number of system circuits that can be recognized as operating as networks through the attribute nodes of any complex entity, for example the twenty alternative circuits linking the four attributes of the entity in fig. 5.

This property is simply expressed in fig. 8. This illustration helps us to understand that any person, attribute, or activity may be a

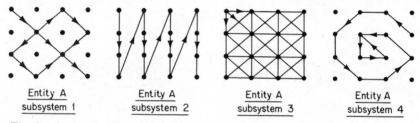

| Entity A | Entity A | Entity A | Entity A |
| subsystem 1 | subsystem 2 | subsystem 3 | subsystem 4 |

Fig. 8   A simple illustration of the vast number of network subsystems which may simultaneously or sequentially operate through the nodes of a system.

simultaneous member of hundreds of 'independent' systems or subsystems, each operating for quite different purposes and at quite different levels. One example would be the man who at one and the same time belonged to a football team, a political party, a family, a military unit, a working party and so on – the man is a single node through which many different systems operate. Another example is that of most human actions and activities. An archaeologist may appear on television because the act simultaneously satisfies personal systems designed to earn money, to inform an audience, to satisfy a psychological need, for propaganda purposes, to increase status and to fulfil some obligation. In these examples the node uniting these various systems may also be usefully thought of as a vector of the many systems acting through it.

This example helps to point out that according to the particular system and network under study some nodes will be relevant or activated and others may not (fig. 8). This is yet another way of looking at the 'essential variables' taking part in some system trajectory and differentiating them from similar but inactive nodes loosely belonging to the same entity but not actively involved in the particular system development under investigation. The essential variables are the attributes which are relevant to the frame of reference of the study – they are the attributes connected within the system of interest. A point which should recall the 'artificial' selection of attributes for study in connection with particular problems.

ADAPTATION AND DIRECTIVE CORRELATION

In any coupled systems or subsystems, a change in attribute states in one system may frequently occasion similar changes in the coupled partner, especially if the systems are jointly in equilibrium. When an observer notices that a change in an environment system is connected with accompanying changes in a coupled culture system, then he anthropomorphizes this change as an 'adaptation' by the one system to changes in the other. We see that this adaptive response is merely a particular case of jointly correlated transformations in coupled systems, to be found in any such systems of more than a very simple structure. There are scarcely any cases of coupled complex systems that do not manifest such 'response' by one partner to 'stimulus' by the other, or the successive sequence of 'adaptation' that follows series of such changes. Adaptation is an anthropomorphic label for a commonplace property inherent in most coupled complex systems.

Further consideration of adaptive changes with changing conditions leads us to realize that only certain attributes in either system need change in such situations. The attribute states or values that do change are those 'essential variables' whose stability limits are exceeded by the particular transitions under consideration. Other attribute states or values will remain unchanged in the system because their 'tolerance' is greater than that of the other 'essential variables'; that is to say the set of stable values within their threshold basin is sufficient to contain the fresh disturbances without transformation. The key 'essential variables' will consequently be different attributes according to the nature and extent of the particular changes being considered in the coupled system.

In anthropology and archaeology it is usually the case that the systems have a past condition, a present condition and a future condition, or overall state. In most of these systems the future condition or state is some function of not only the present condition of the system but also of a whole sequence of 'essential' variables in past states of the system. Whether Britain should declare war on Germany over the Polish issue, in 1939, depended not only on the then condition of Britain but also upon the whole sequence of alliance conditions leading up to that time. What happened in this case was some function of those relevant past and contemporary conditions and the causally relevant field conditions of the European environment at the time. In every system changing or 'adapting' with time there is a certain limited set of attributes or entities whose past and present variation is essentially relevant to some future condition of the system – following Sommerhoff we will call this limited set 'directively correlated' towards this future condition (Sommerhoff 1950, pp. 37–110).

A specific future condition is attainable only if the system's attribute states fall within a particular sequence of sets defining the variety of possible trajectories to that future condition. The range of permissible variation in the set of past and present states in order to attain the future condition may be taken as a measure of the degree of the directive correlation. The number of correlated variables involved in any directive correlation may be taken as the order of the correlation. This concept, expressing the degree and order of directive correlation within a systems time-trajectory, is closely connected with the concept of the degree of 'coherence', the strength or degree of 'integral definition' of a cultural tradition and we shall later attempt to use this measure (chapter 5). We may hope to distinguish between those attributes of a system which are directively correlated towards some future condition, the essential variables framed in reference to the future condition, and those attributes which are not correlated towards this condition and which may thus vary within less constrained limits, with less regularity (fig. 11). A distinction once again reminiscent of that between 'information' and 'noise' in communication systems.

THE PROBLEM OF THE INCOMPLETE AND VERY LARGE
BLACK BOX

This analogy represents the archaeologist and anthropologist as investigators attempting to analyse very complex and incompletely observable systems whose internal mechanisms and subsystems are never fully available for inspection. The analogy stresses that the approach to the problems of cultural analysis must be made in the light of the nature of the data and the probes available to the analyst. In particular the analogy raises the whole problem of how the analyst can proceed when faced with such severe handicaps, what properties are and are not discoverable in this context and what are the most efficient methods to use? The terms of this analogy subsume the classic systems problems of the Black Box, the Very Large Box and the Incompletely Observable Box (Ashby 1956, pp. 86–117).

The problem of the Black Box arises in theoretical and practical terms when the investigator is faced with a complex system, completely concealed but for an input terminal and an output terminal. The only information available about the system within the box must come from observing the changing relationships between varying values at the input and output terminals. Consequently the investigation of Black Box systems depends upon the tabulation of as many varied input states and sequences of states as is possible together with a record of the corresponding output states. The investigator will primarily look for any evidence for constraint in the variety of states and for regularities in states or sequences of states, such regularities as we can often observe in archaeological and anthropological data. Above all, the investigator will be trying to make the system determinate so that the consequences of a given input are known and can be expressed as a limited set of output states. This output set may be a single state or a large number of states or values, the set may merely encompass a variety of probabilities for outcomes – a stochastic table, or a sequence of possible states, but essentially the set and the possible variety of outcome is limited, however broad the limits, however complex the limitation.

On the basis of such observations the investigator should be able to draw up a canonical model representing the transformation pattern of the Black Box and capable of expression as an isomorphic system. That is to say representation by a system 'with the same pattern' of behaviour as far as the frame of reference of the observations go – the greater the variety of observed data incorporated the closer the isomorphic model comes to the 'real' system within the box. In this sense a map can be understood as an isomorphic model of the countryside and most models may be conceived as diagrammatic, iconic, symbolic, electrical or mechanical isomorphs of their particular problem 'boxes'. The analog computer and the digital computer can act as precisely such kinds of isomorphic models and their output may be made to represent the 'behaviour of the problem box under investigation.

These brief observations on Black Box problems show that it is theoretically possible to produce a very accurate and powerful model of such obscure systems in spite of their shroud, if the correct investigating procedure is adopted. The crucial part of this procedure is the attempt to organize, rewrite, rearrange or relabel the observed transformations in such a way as to make them determinate. In this crucial activity intelligent juggling and particularly the arbitrary choice of variables play a central role.

If we take our Black Box and make it a very large box, with room for an enormously large and richly networked system then a new aspect arises. We may have accumulated quite a set of data about the properties of the individual components of the system before it was assembled in the secrecy of the box, or conversely after it has been excavated in fragments, and we may hope to integrate these observations in a comprehensive model of the new system. However, our elementary study warned us that the properties of systems are not simply the aggregate of the properties of their component subsystems. It is an important property of such systems and populations that their properties are more complex than the simple sum of the properties of the components. The reason for this we have seen to be the exponentially increasing number of alternative circuits and subsystems that result from the introduction of just one new node and some channels (fig. 5). The overall result is that when we test the 'behaviour' of the newly assembled very large Black Box we will often find that unexpected and newly 'emergent' properties appear – sometimes very important and surprising ones. As an example one might take the 'emergent' property of television pictures as a surprising result of networking some valves, an amplifier and a tube in a certain way with other components – none of which independently produces pictures.

The cultural importance of very large box systems is that the archaeologist and anthropologist ought not to be surprised when systems networking the same components show discrepant properties. Furthermore, it seems that the 'invention' or development of new properties and 'behaviour', sometimes of a dramatically important kind, frequently follows the insignificant rearrangement of otherwise well-tested components.

The last modification of the box in order to make it more like our complex systems, has stipulated that it has been incompletely recovered and therefore incompletely observed. The archaeologist has only a fragmentary and partially studied segment of the real systems, and even the anthropologist has a similarly biased and limited set of information about his systems. It is important to note at this point that a complex entity contains a great number of connected but separate circuits of systems and specialists studying the same entity may often be studying quite different circuit systems of the one entity (fig. 8). The anthropologist looks at aspects of the social system of cultures, archaeologists and ethnologists look at the material system of the same cultures – the systems are not the same and yet neither are they unconnected. Serious dangers await those who transfer observations about the one class of system to the other (Allen and Richardson 1971) and yet it is important that the coupling between the different systems and their attributes should be explored and made explicit (chapter 9).

The incompletely recovered or observed system can often be made determinate by considering the sequences of attribute states or values in the table of known variation and by expressing these sequences as vectors. This assumes that any state of the system can be expressed 'in the light of' its preceding sequences of states and their attribute trajectories. This hindsight on the part of the investigator is the device which enables him to talk of directive correlation towards future conditions of the system and enables him to restore some predictability. Nevertheless, this hindsight and the observer are alone responsible for the system appearing to have 'a memory' and to be moving towards a known 'goal', providing another anthropomorphic view of a lifeless system.

We can summarize by suggesting that archaeological and anthropological systems present the classic problems of the Black Box, the Very Large Box, and the Incompletely Observable Box. This section has described the special problems of these kinds of system and the special measures necessary to get them into a determinate form. The greatest difficulty resides in the selection and definition of the 'essential variables' among the vast numbers and levels of variables that could be considered – especially since these 'essential variables' may turn out to be such vectors as 'sequences of states' or 'rates of change'. Many archaeologists and anthropologists would deny the possibility of ever getting their systems into a determinate form but fortunately, with the increasing acknowledgement of the complexity of such systems there has come increasing success in their useful

manipulation; initial oversimplification has always been the biggest
barrier to progressive research (Murdock 1949; Steward 1955).

CHANGE IN THE SIMPLE SYSTEM

To conclude these observations on some of the inherent properties of
certain kinds of system we should consider the aspect of continuous
change. If we take a simple system with four attribute states or values
a, b, c, d, or similarly if we take four systems a, b, c, d, we may imagine
that there might be three alternative changes or transformations of
these states according to the specific conditions of the system at the
time – let us call these alternative conditions R1, R2, R3. Under
conditions R1 the transformation functions so that a changes to c, b to
d, c to d, and d to b; this transformation would usually be written:

$$\text{R1:}\downarrow \begin{array}{cccc} a & b & c & d \\ c & d & d & b \end{array}$$

with the arrow giving the direction of the transformation. Under other
conditions, R2, R3, other transformations would operate with
different results, let us say:

$$\text{R2:}\downarrow \begin{array}{cccc} a & b & c & d \\ b & a & d & c \end{array} \quad \text{and} \quad \text{R3:}\downarrow \begin{array}{cccc} a & b & c & d \\ d & c & d & b \end{array}$$

The point of this arbitrary example is that all of this cumbersome
information can be succintly expressed as a table or matrix of transformations, thus:

Transformations of system(s) a, b, c, d, under conditions	$\downarrow$	a	b	c	d
	R1	c	d	d	b
	R2	b	a	d	c
	R3	d	c	d	b

Archaeological and anthropological data is frequently of this cumbersome form, with many alternative transformation values according to
the conditions and consequently this kind of table or matrix is a
convenient device for portraying these observations (fig. 16).

The table just illustrated depicts only transformations that are
closed and single-valued. That is to say, the results of the transformations R1, R2, R3, do not create any new states, no x or y appear,
only combinations of a, b, c, d; under such conditions the transformations are said to be 'closed'. Similarly, the term 'single-valued'

restricts these observations to cases where the given transformation of a particular state has only one possible result – thus, $a \rightarrow b$. Clearly, there are many real cases where the transformation of a could give either b, or c, or d, with equal probability, or with more sophistication we can imagine a system in which the single transformations of a might not only be a large number of alternative states but they might well have varying probabilities according to the conditions. This latter elaboration is only a moderate one and yet it will obviously produce a bewildering degree of complication. Furthermore, experience would seem to suggest that archaeological and anthropological transformations are rarely closed and single-valued but, on the contrary, they are usually many-valued on a probability basis dependent upon the conditions. We have therefore developed a model transformation table of the right general order but not of the right specific level.

It would seem that archaeological systems are unlikely to involve only closed or single-valued transformations and they are unlikely to be simply 'determinate'. That is to say that the 'behaviour' of the system is unlikely to be predictable on the basis of single chains or trajectories of transformations. Nevertheless, we intuitively gather that the frequencies or probabilities of a limited set of derivative transformations might be susceptible to definition on the basis of the acknowledged constraint and regularities in the observable data. A culture and its artefacts are as incapable of immediate and complete transformation as the example of the flying aeroplane or any other continuous system. We appear to be looking for a system which may or may not be determinate, single-valued, or closed and which operates as if on a probability basis, with the transformations dependent upon certain limiting conditions. Conveniently, Ross Ashby develops such a model system – the Markovian system, which we can use as a basis for further modifications (Ashby 1956, p. 225).

Now any process which may be described in terms of probabilities can be correctly called a 'stochastic process' (Cherry 1957, pp. 38–9, 306). It would seem that our desired canonical model might be a system with transformations that can be summarized as a stochastic table or matrix of probable outcomes. One example of such a stochastic sequence or chain is called the Markov chain after its discoverer A. A. Markov, who in 1913 published a statistical study of Pushkin's novel *Eugène Onĕgin*. The Markov chain originally implied any process generating a stochastic series, the adjacent terms of which are related by given transition probabilities. Ross Ashby develops his

Markovian system by considering a system whose 'behaviour' can be summarized by a matrix or table of probabilities such that the probabilities of transition from one value or state to another do not depend on any earlier states of the attributes or systems. In other words if *a* goes to *b* in 60 per cent of the cases then it must do so regardless of whether it is an *a* transformed from a former state *d* or an *a* that was formerly of state *c*; its present transformation must take no account of the former trajectory of the state *a*. Such a system constitutes a Markovian system which can then be expressed canonically as a matrix with entities expressing the frequency or probability of that particular state or value being transformed to some other state, under the conditions specified for that transformation, thus:

	↓	*a*	*b*	*c*	*d*
Transformations of system(s) *a, b, c, d*, under conditions R1	*a*	0·0	0·1	0·0	1·0
	b	0·3	0·4	0·2	0·0
	c	0·6	0·2	0·1	0·0
	d	0·1	0·3	0·7	0·0

This matrix, for example, expresses the observations that state *d* will only change to state *a*, whereas state *c* may go with varying frequency to states *b, c, d* and state *c* cannot be transformed into state *a* – given conditions R1 for this system.

However, our real situations still differ from this strict Markov system in that the transformations of our entities are likely to have probabilities of transition that do depend on the previous states or trajectory of the component attributes or systems. Furthermore, the matrix of transition probabilities should ideally vary with varying conditions and we cannot guarantee that the ratio expressing the relative proportion of alternative transformations is exactly constant. Our problem systems are apparently stochastic but not fully Markovian in expression; let us therefore call them Semi-Markovian for the moment.

Now, fortunately it is possible to modify the strict Markovian model to accommodate most of these peculiar requirements. In the first place it is usually possible to re-code such a Semi-Markovian system in a Markov form by treating each state not as a single value but as a vector expressing that state's previous change trajectory. Instead of individual states *a, b, c, d*, we can take the transition sequences as our entities, thus: (*a–b*), (*b–c*), (*c–d*), etc., and providing the system is found to produce trajectories in which some transition probabilities depend on what states preceded the present ones, then although not Markovian in its original form it can often be re-written in vector form as a Semi-Markovian system (Ashby 1956, p. 171).

When such Semi-Markovian systems have transformations linked or limited by preceding sequences of transformations the whole system appears to be acting 'in the light of' its previous history – such systems are said to appear to have a 'memory' (fig. 9, left). This again amounts to an anthropomorphic view of systems. In order to express this capacity of our systems to have modified outcomes according to past trajectories we can integrate some of the observations scattered in the preceding text. The matrix of possible transformations or 'responses' expresses the limits of the set of possible outcomes under varying conditions (fig. 10) – it is a summary of observable data. This table is the same table of possible outcomes or responses that we portrayed in the section on regulation and control as 'T' (fig. 6). In that section we saw how the actual outcome of the table could be modified or controlled by subsystem 'R' which regulated the eventual state of the system 'S' in the light of the operating conditions 'E'. If in

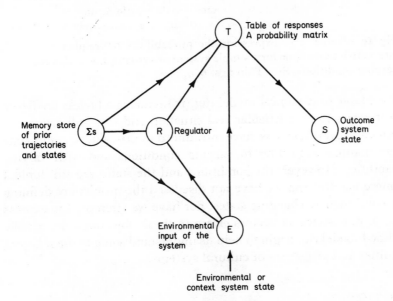

Fig. 9 A simple system with a controlling 'R' and a controlling 'memory' store 'Σs' – the future transformations of the system will be limited by the previous trajectory of the system.

addition we now feed stored information on the systems' past trajectory 'Σs' into the regulator then that aspect will also be expected to further constrain the particular outcome from the table of possible outcomes 'T' (fig. 9).

Transformations of system(s) a, b, c, d, under conditions		↓	a	b	c	d
R1	a		0·0	0·1	0·0	1·0
	b		0·3	0·4	0·2	0·0
	c		0·6	0·2	0·1	0·0
	d		0·1	0·3	0·7	0·0
R2	b		0·5	0·1	1·0	0·1
	c		0·3	0·3	0·0	0·5
	d		0·1	0·4	0·0	0·4
	e		0·1	0·2	0·0	0·0
R3	c		0·9	0·1	0·0	0·3
	d		0·0	0·4	0·2	0·7
	e		0·1	0·4	0·7	0·0
	f		0·0	0·1	0·1	0·0
R4	d		0·0	0·0	0·0	0·0
	e		0·2	0·3	0·4	0·0
	f		0·3	0·4	0·5	0·6
	g		0·5	0·3	0·1	0·4

Assume that the transformations of
e, f, g, remain e, f, g, respectively.

Fig. 10 Table 'T' – expressing the probabilities or frequencies of alternative transitions for a simple system or systems a, b, c, d, under varying conditions. See 'T' in figs. 6, 9, 11.

This table or canonical model (fig. 10) remains a lifeless lay-figure since it refers to no particular real situation and it is still arbitrarily simplified. Nevertheless we have introduced multi-value or multi-state transformations according to varying conditions and with varying probabilities. However, the conditions and the states are still limited to a mere handful and we have not discussed the problem of defining these continuously changing states, nor have we attempted to express the a, b, c, d states as vectors. Despite these objections the grossly simplified model can begin to help us understand some of the inherent difficulties and properties of cultural systems.

GAME THEORY

One development of this model is that we can resume our analogy between 'cultural systems' and their 'environmental context' as complex two-player games with various strategies and equilibrium trajectories (Neumann and Morgenstern 1947). The table of transformations (fig. 10), does not refer to a real system nor the conditions R1–R4 to real conditions – they have been constructed as a temporary and simple analogue model. Taken in this light we can use the canonical table as though it were the list of permitted moves in a game between system or systems a, b, c, d, and changing conditions R1, R2, R3, R4 – conditions which we can either consider changing in geographical space, R1 in this area, R2 in that, or we can consider them changing sequentially in time R1 to R4. This dimensionless approach to system transformations helps to underline the characteristics of system variation in space shared with system variation in time. We can now play through a few transformations and consider the possible outcome of real and more complex situations. In the next chapter game theory will provide us with real and predictive models for real situations.

Let us first of all play through the most probable and the least probable outcomes starting in each case with two identical systems a, b, c, d, and with conditions changing successively from R1 to R2 to R3 to R4 as though these conditions were a time sequence, then according to our model, fig. 10:

Example (1)	↓	a	b	c	d	Initial system
						state
Most probable outcome system	R1	c	b	d	a	
a, b, c, d, under conditions	R2	b	d	c	b	
	R3	d	d	e	d	
	R4	f	f	e	f	

Example (2)	↓	a	b	c	d	Initial system
Least probable outcome system						state
a, b, c, d, under conditions	R1	d	a	c	a	
	R2	b	e	b	d	
From model	R3	f	e	c	c	
table, fig. 10	R4	f	e	g	g	

These two examples show how very diverse are the multilinear trajectories and system states that can develop from identical systems changing under identical conditions. If left to these transformations all examples of the system a, b, c, d would eventually yield systems composed entirely of combinations of e, f, g, since we stipulated that the transformation of these would give themselves (e to e, f to f, g to g). The system would in this sense ultimately change into another system or systems, from one formerly composed of a, b, c, ds to others composed of e, f, gs – new states which successively and cumulatively appear under the sequence of conditions. These systems of e, f, gs are immutable under the rules stipulated here and therefore constitute stable equilibria for this system. From an examination of just these two possible trajectories of the changing system a, b, c, d we can understand that the development of classes of such systems must always be multilinear with some particular trajectories diverging towards novel patterns and others converging upon stable equilibrium basins, often by oscillating trajectories (column trajectories c-d-c-e and c-b-c-g in each example under attribute c).

The transformation of system a, b, c, d into another, e, f, g, also draws our attention to the 'birth' and 'death' of systems. We see that the cumulative and successive introduction of new states or attributes can gradually transform the whole system. In our two examples the first glimpse of the new e, f, g pattern appears under R2 with b, e, b, d in trajectory (2) and under R3 with d, d, e, d in (1). Although this so-called system 'death'/'birth' transition may be abrupt, nevertheless in the majority of cases it will be gradually accomplished by the cumulative and successive introduction of new states. A process which illustrates the polythetic nature of this kind of system and its changing forms – for example, the transition from a basically a, b, c, d system to an e, f, g system may be judged to have occurred when more than 50 per cent (or some other percentage) of the elements have reached values typical of the new system; this occurs in both examples in the transformation R3 to R4 but in other trajectories of this same system could occur R2 to R3 – multilinear change across a threshold is not usually sudden or contemporaneous.

Another aspect of this same polythetic process reproduces the 'threshold' phenomenon discussed earlier under kinds of equilibria. The 50 per cent threshold separating system a, b, c, d from new system e, f, g is approached under trajectory (1) by transition from 0–25–100 per cent (R2–R3–R4) of new elements, and in trajectory (2) by transition from 0–25–50–100 per cent (R1–R2–R3–R4). Here we are observing the cumulative and successive introduction of new states which do not change the overall system network immediately and independently but which build up by cumulative effect to a threshold of metastable equilibrium. At this crucial point the introduction of a single new element precipitates the system into a new pattern and in this case a new stable equilibrium region. We can understand that cumulative effect building up to a threshold is especially characteristic of our sorts of polythetic system. The 'death' and 'birth' of our systems is no more than their reformation by cumulative transformation.

In a final look at our canonical model (fig. 10) we might usefully consider the three following trajectories of three a, b, c, d, systems, leading from identical state (a, b, c, d) to another identical state (g, g, g, g) under identical conditions (R1, R2, R3, R4) but by very different trajectories:

			Trajectories											
Example nos			(3)					(4)					(5)	
	↓	a	b	c	d	↓	a	b	c	d	↓	a	b	c	d
Various possible outcomes of system *a, b, c, d,* under conditions	R1	d	a	c	a		c	b	d	a		b	a	b	a
	R2	d	c	b	c		b	d	b	b		d	c	d	b
From model	R3	c	d	d	d		d	d	d	d		c	d	c	d
table, fig. 10	R4	g	g	g	g		g	g	g	g		g	g	g	g

These trajectories remind us that regularities in our changing systems can be caused by correlated constraint in a variety of initial states, terminal states, field conditions, or trajectories, and they can arise from any one or any combination of these four classes of variety. In this particular example we have a regularity involving the same initial states (a, b, c, d), terminal states (g, g, g, g) and the same field conditions (R1–R4) but brought about by differing individual trajectories (Examples (3) (4) (5)). If we take the R1 stage of these three systems – (3) d, a, c, a (4) c, b, d, a (5) b, a, b, a and imagine that we knew only these phases as the 'initial states' then the example equally shows how three different systems can run to the same terminal state. If, as we assert, regularities arise as the noticeable association of constraint in one variety of attribute with constraint in another variety of attribute, then with four classes of variety – initial state, terminal state, field conditions, and trajectories (sequences) – we have in outline at least eleven kinds of regularity linking correlated constraint in sets of:

(1) initial states/terminal states
(2) initial states/field conditions
(3) initial states/trajectories
(4) terminal states/field conditions
(5) terminal states/trajectories
(6) field conditions/trajectories
(7) initial states/terminal states/field conditions
(8) initial states/terminal states/trajectories

    (9) terminal states/field conditions/trajectories
    (10) field conditions/trajectories/initial states
    (11) initial states/terminal states/field conditions/trajectories.

This list emphasizes the number of different kinds of regularity which might exist in data documenting systems of the kind under investigation. The difficulties involved in isolating and defining suitable 'essential variables' and their relevant states together with the difficulty of deciding upon the class of regularity operating – coincide with the difficulty of expressing cultural data in determinate models.

We have noted that the three system trajectories (3), (4), (5), in the last examples share their initial states and their directive correlation towards the stable equilibrium state g, g, g, g. The number of possible trajectories taking systems a, b, c, d, to state g, g, g, g, is the measure of this directive correlation and can be expressed as the number of routes that can be traced from a, b, c, d, to g, g, g, g, through the lattice given below, from our arbitrary table of possibilities (fig. 10).

At each stage of the system trajectories a, b, c, d to g, g, g, g, the states of the systems must fall within a limited set in order to reach their ultimate 'goal' (fig. 10a). It is the size of these successive sets that determines the degree of directive correlation and defines the essential variables for the changes being studied. When such a set is closely constrained, allowing very few routes through the set, then the set amounts to a threshold which the various system states must approach and enter before moving on into the stable region of the 'goal'. Such a constrained set is Set 4 in the lattice (fig. 10a), with only two possible states c and d admitting access to a final state of g – the most constrained set may of course come at any point in the trajectory. This form of constraint in the transformations of a set or of a single attribute acts as a funnel – channelling and constricting the trajectories of change. Such a constraint is illustrated not only by Set 4 in our example but also by the effect of the single-value transformation of state d under $R1$ in which d can only go to a.

These observations allow us to think of the attributes of the changing systems as roughly belonging to three categories, according to the frame of reference of the study:

    (i) Inessential attributes (variables, parameters, etc.)
    (ii) Essential attributes (variables, parameters, etc.)
    (iii) Key attributes (variables, parameters, etc.)

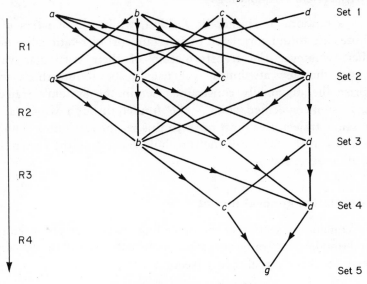

a, b, c, d, g, —system entity states
R1, R2, R3, R4—successive field conditions
Fig. 10a.

Inessential attributes include those which are not relevant to the study in hand and which consequently do not figure in the system as defined, and those attributes which are constant throughout. The essential attributes are those 'essential variables' which are part of the system and whose values may change as part of the changing system. These essential variables express the 'survival' or 'continuity' of the system as the same system format rather than as a transmutation; it is these essential variables which an efficient regulator R must protect from transformation by blocking the flow of variety from disturbances E, if the system is to survive in its present form (fig. 9).

Finally, the key attributes may be regarded as those essential attributes in the system whose successive transformation values are covarying in some specific relationship with successive values of other similar attributes. The values or states of key attributes not only change as part of the changing system but change in a correlated and non-random fashion – either as successive transitions in a continuous trend or covarying in specific correlation with a cluster of similar attributes. The continued joint covariation of these key attributes expresses the survival of a particular inner 'pattern' or 'structure' peculiar to this system format and part of its identity. In contrast, some essential attributes may vary quite independently of one another and in a random or spasmodic fashion, whilst the clusters of key attributes are found correlated in a certain sort of relationship one to another, whatever the transformation of their particular values. Amongst the key attributes will usually be found those which comprise the maximally constrained set in the system's trajectory towards some specified state – the funnel through which all the permissible trajectories must pass. In this set the attributes define the threshold and the height of the threshold separating the system from some alternative state.

II   A tentative general model

In the concluding section of the preceding chapter we proposed three general models or frameworks as potentially useful in developing neglected archaeological theory (section VI):

(a) A model for archaeological procedure (fig. 2).
(b) A polythetic model for archaeological entities (fig. 3).
(c) A systems model for archaeological processes.

The systems model for archaeological processes was not further developed in that chapter. The reasons for this rest upon the observation that such a model should preferably be of greater power than merely another vague analogy of no predictive value, the model should be a general model of cultural dynamics in an attempt to carry validity at several cultural levels and as compatible with modern anthropological thought as possible. In order to accommodate these ambitious aims the construction of the model has been deferred so that this preparatory outline sketch of systems theory could be attempted.

We have now reached the state where a general model for analysing archaeological processes on a systems framework can be diffidently approached. It would be naive to pretend that the model that we are going to develop fulfils our high intentions but, however inadequate it may prove, in attempting the problem, it may make somewhat clearer the areas of imprecision, as well as raising hope that such an approach may one day be successfully accomplished.

The model is expressed in two parts. One part, the diagram fig. 11, is an endeavour to represent the organizational categories of 'essential variables' coupled together both inside and outside our entities or systems. It is important to realize that this is not yet an attempt to analyse and express the internal components within a particular

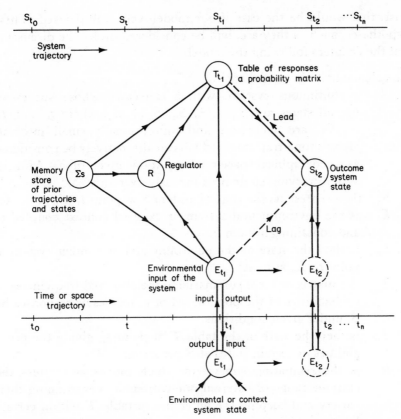

S_{t_0} S_t S_{t_1} S_{t_2} $\cdots S_{t_n}$

System trajectory →

Table of responses a probability matrix

T_{t_1}

Lead

Memory store of prior trajectories and states Σs R   Regulator S_{t_2} Outcome system state

Lag

Environmental input of the system E_{t_1} → E_{t_2}

Time or space trajectory →

input   output

t_0 t t_1 t_2 $\cdots$ t_n

output   input

E_{t_1} → E_{t_2}

Environmental or context system state

Fig. 11   General model (c) – A model for archaeological processes. A model suggesting that archaeological entities, at several levels, change as special kinds of dynamic systems coupled with environing or contextual systems.

system and their networked relationship. The sketch merely tries to approach an isomorphic representation connecting some aspects of some of the variables concerned, in order to explain some of the relationships noted in the second part of the model. The structure of the system in the figure can recognizably be seen to integrate as components some of the various kinds of subsystem whose 'behaviour' has been sketched earlier (fig. 11, compare figs 4, 5, 6, 9). The second part of the model comprises a tentative summary of the inherent 'behaviour' of the system in the diagram under a series of condensed observations. These observations amount to very tentative postulates on which depend some hypotheses of predictive value – at least, that would be the case if our model were well devised. These hypotheses, such as they are, will be considered under the discussion and the chapters following the model.

The elements in the model are:

S a continuous system, with a trajectory whose successive overall states are $S_{t_0} \ldots S_t, S_{t_1}, S_{t_2} \ldots S_{t_n}$, where $t_0 \ldots t, t_1, t_2 \ldots t_n$ are successive and infinitesimally small intervals along a time-trajectory (which can alternatively be considered as a geographical space territory at one given time – with the system varying contemporaneously over an area).

S_{t_1} then represents the state of system S at point t_1; S_{t_2} at t_2, etc.

E is the environmental system or external context coupled to and containing system S.

E_{t_1} is then the state of the environmental or context system at point t_1; E_{t_2} at t_2, etc.

T is a matrix or table summarizing the observed frequencies or probabilities of the possible set of outcomes or responses by S, under given conditions.

T_{t_1} is then the state of the table T at point t_1, giving the probabilities of certain states of S occurring.

R is the regulating subsystem which blocks and filters the extreme range of external fluctuations by constraining their variety and keeping the outcomes in table T within certain limits.

Σs expresses the set of past conditions or prior states of the essential variables, through which the trajectory of the system has passed, up to the point in question – the 'memory' store.

The diagram (fig. 11) is intended to convey the relationship between these organizational elements as it would operate in defining the state of the system at point t_2, state S_{t_2}. The state of the system S_{t_2} being the outcome of the elements operating on the table T_{t_1} at point t_1, an infinitely small time (or distance) antecedent to t_2.

THE TENTATIVE GENERAL MODEL (fig. 11)

Consider a class of Semi-Markovian system S (fig. 11), comprising an incompletely recorded and only partially observable network of attributes or entities forming subsystems within a complex whole. This general class of system is coupled to an external system E (an environment or context) so that the input of the general system is the output of the external system and vice versa.

POSTULATES

(1) *Continuously changing system.* The system S is dynamic and continuous, with the attributes or entities having specific values or states which change by infinitesimal transformations.

(2) *Constraint of variety hence regularities.* The variety of known states or values of the system's components is limited functionally and idiosyncratically. Functionally, by the limited set of stable or dynamic equilibrium states for the system as a whole. Idiosyncratically, by virtue of the selective choice of the system's generators.

(3) *Inessential, essential, and key attributes or components.* It is convenient to distinguish between inessential, essential and key attributes or variables within the changing system S:

> *Inessential* attributes or variables – those which are not relevant to the study in hand and which consequently do not figure in the system as defined, and those attributes which remain unchanged throughout.
> *Essential* attributes or variables – those whose values or states change as part of the changing system.
> *Key* attributes or components – those whose values or states not only change as part of the changing system but which change in a correlated and non-random fashion – either as successive transitions in a continuous trend or covarying in specific correlation with a cluster of similar attributes.

The inessential, essential and key attributes or components in a changing system depend upon the frame of reference of the study and upon the trajectories of the attributes within the changing system; they do *not* necessarily apply to other studies of the same entity in which the same attributes may be networked in alternative systems (fig. 8).

(4) *Format stability – the state of equilibrium.* This particular class of system has a limited but very large set of equilibrium states (basins) in which the state of the system as a whole may remain unchanged in spite of some transformations affecting some component attributes or entities.

(5) *Dynamic equilibrium.* Since the input from the external coupled system, environment or context E is continuously changing, then the

accompanying continuously changing, successively measurable states of S will constitute a dynamic equilibrium.

(6) *Adaptive response*. Change in the coupled system E may lead to new states in the component attributes or entities of system S, or correspondingly modify the transition probabilities T of future transformations or sequences of transformations (trajectories). Such a change, in that it represents a system 'response' to an external stimulus, may be designated an 'adaptive response' by the system S.

(7) *Displacement of equilibrium*. If the equilibrium of such a system S is dislocated, it adapts itself to the stimulus which causes the dislocation, in such a manner that the said stimulus continually diminishes in effect until finally the *original* or a *new* equilibrium is again established.

(8) *Cumulative effect displacing metastable equilibrium at a threshold*. New states or values successively introduced into the system S may cumulatively approach a threshold beyond which the system cannot continue unchanged.

(9) *Control and regulation based on feedback*. The states of the components in S, change not by single-valued closed transformations alone, but by a limited matrix of transition probabilities T whose values vary partly as a function of the past and present states of the system, and its context E – thus constituting a *feedback loop*. Every event in the system S is thus controlled by the whole previous state of the system together with the causally relevant factors in the system's environment or field E.

(10) *Homeostasis – oscillation around and towards stable states (goals)*. Since the feedback loop regulates the matrix of transition probabilities T and controls future states of the system S, and since the set of stable system states is limited – the system will tend to oscillate around (hunt) and converge upon (seek) successive stable states.

(11) *Oscillation*. Oscillation is a common phenomenon in systems and components of this class of system S. Oscillations may occur:

(a) as oscillations induced by oscillations in the coupled environment or context system (lag and lead phenomena),

(b) as oscillations towards or away from stable equilibria (hunt and seek),

(c) as oscillations within the permissive boundaries of a stable set or basin, allowing many trajectories (multilinear stochastic development).

Furthermore, oscillations may occur at any or all of three network levels:

(i) between system S and containing environment or context E,
(ii) Between system S and a component subsystem,
(iii) between component subsystems within S.

(12) *Directive correlation.* Such systems S have a sequence of past states, a present state, and a future state; in that we believe the future state to be a function of the past and present states and the causally relevant external field conditions E, the system can be said to be directively correlated in respect of a future state.

(13) *Regularities due to constraint in possible trajectories.* Given a present state S_t and a future state S_{t_2} of the system S, there are a limited set of field conditions E that will produce S_{t_2} from state S_t. The range or set of field conditions will limit and constrain any particular causal chain $S_t \rightarrow S_{t_2}$ but several alternative trajectories or chains may link $S_t \rightarrow S_{t_2}$, each trajectory having its specific constraining conditions; although in the limiting case there may be only one possible trajectory or sequence of transformations leading $S_t \rightarrow S_{t_2}$.

(14) *Constrained sets and directive correlation.* The future state S_{t_2} of system S is attainable only if some of the system's component attribute or entity states fall within a particular set in the past, set t_0, and in the present set t, in which respect the sets at t_0 and t can be said to be directively correlated toward future state S_{t_2}.

(15) *Degree and order of directive correlation.* The range of permissible variation in the set of past and present states set t_0 and set t, to attain the future state S_{t_2} may be taken as a measure of the degree of the directive correlation. The number of permissible trajectories or routes through these sets may be taken as the order of that correlation.

(16) *Correlated regularities and predictive capacity.* Regularities consequent upon constraint in the variety in the system states and trajectories should allow low-level predictive synthesis in which observed correlations between constraints in initial states, terminal states, field conditions, and trajectories can be expressed.

III   **Discussion**

We have already observed that these tentative postulates amount to a set of low-level predictive hypotheses about how systems of this particular kind S can 'behave'. One could, if one wished, rewrite these postulates as a list of hypotheses to be tested against the real 'behaviour' of real systems and certainly such a testing of the postulates is highly desirable. However, some of the postulates are still so general in scope as to tell us very little about how to tackle real systems of this class. Some of the other more promising postulates are correspondingly vague about the essential terms which give them predictive power – such terms as equilibrium again fall within this category. Rather than enumerate all the hypotheses with specific instances it may be more useful to select and discuss the more promising postulates and develop their potential as hypotheses for practical application.

The first group of postulates we can consider are those that suggest that cultural systems and their components are in dynamic equilibrium and will proceed from one equilibrium state to another. Surely, if we know a great deal about a system and its conditions we ought by these means to be able to say which particular equilibrium state it will next run to? The problem here is to define the relevant aspects of the entity's systems – at which level one is working, and then to define what is meant by equilibrium in terms of those kinds of attribute. How does one define equilibrium amongst social, religious, economic or psychological attributes? Clearly, we have the old problem of there being many sorts of subsystem, each with its own kind of equilibria, each operating in different networks of the same overall system and variously in equilibrium one with another (fig. 8). It is apparent that this problem cannot be approached at so general a level, one must take specific cases and explain what is meant. Consequently, all that we can do at this stage is to reiterate these equilibrium postulates ((2), (4), (5), (7), (10)) until we have elaborated the equilibrium concept and in the meanwhile to speculate that our various kinds of equilibrium occur when certain functions of the variable factors in the system are jointly minimized. We have yet to define in each case which variable factors are jointly minimized, how this is brought about, and how this information can be used.

Let us quickly move to some more easily developed postulates and try and show some positive rewards for these efforts. We can perhaps make some immediate progress with multiple causes and cumulative effect (8) and in later chapters with directive correlation and essential variables (14) and (15), and with correlation between regularities (16).

It appears that new states, or values, successively introduced into a system of this kind (S), may cumulatively approach a threshold beyond which the system cannot continue unchanged (consider trajectory examples nos (1) (2) system a, b, c, d, to systems of e, f, g). This observation suggests that many cultural system changes cannot be considered as the consequence of a single attribute or entity transformation, or of a single environmental change; it does not rule out that this may be so but makes it a limiting case. This might lead us to specify that 'neither too few, nor simply single factor causes are to be assumed to be necessary to account for single cultural system transformations'. This hypothesis is deliberately phrased to point out that it surprisingly appears to contradict William of Occam's famous axiom that 'neither more, nor more complex, causes are to be assumed than are necessary to account for the phenomena'. The more surprising since Occam's Razor – 'entia non sunt multiplicanda praeter necessitatem' is the foundation for many important systems of hypotheses and his work as a whole, 1280–1349, part of the kindling Renaissance.

However, a brief consideration of the Occam and the Converse-Occam axioms will show that they are not only compatible but jointly powerful in a helpful way which sharpens the original postulate (8). One can see that Occam's Razor encompasses both approaches by the use of the word 'necessitatem' but the Razor is intent upon taking a multiplicity of possible causes and whittling them down to the fewest necessary, comprehensive, key components (fig. 12). However, with situations in which a few key components may well outline 'most' of the system behaviour it is still desirable to search for the minor but essential components that specify the residual system characteristics. Occam already assumes that more than enough factors have already been cited and that reduction is the prime requirement.

The Converse-Occam is developed here as a consequence of the behaviour of the complex systems which we are investigating. It is simply a control procedure to prevent the over-vigorous use of the Razor. The Converse-Occam simply suggests that it is sometimes useful as a procedure to take the suggested causes or factors, to think hard and add to them any additional factors which might be operable until a network of interacting factors has been devised which does account for the situation under investigation. The Converse-Occam suggests that large numbers of complex factors may well be involved in changes in cultural systems and that to invoke barely sufficient or single causes may be mistaken.

However, from the kinematic graph of these two procedures in action (fig. 12) we can see that there will usually be a saddle-point at

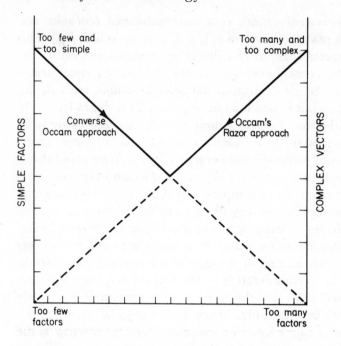

Fig. 12   The hypothesis of multiple factors and cumulative effect for changes in complex systems, as controlled by the Occam's Razor and Converse Occam qualifications.

which both lines of argument are satisfied. It follows that we should use these two approaches jointly to try and arrive at a more accurate understanding of the nature of change in the kinds of system that we are studying.

Nevertheless, it is not sufficient to say simply that such an event had 'many contributory causes' as a replacement for 'this factor caused that event'. The point of jointly harnessing both approaches to the saddle-point is to enumerate, define, test and assess the relevance, power and range of the factors involved. This having been done, the network of cumulative interaction between these factors should be made explicit and their joint trajectory towards the threshold carefully defined in terms of the system as a whole.

One of the purposes of a general model is to employ its predictive framework to simulate developmental change at the many different levels of cultural process. The system *S* that we have discussed in abstract can be materialized as a system of attributes within a population of artefacts, a system of artefacts within a changing cultural assemblage, or a system of social attributes within a changing society and so on. If the general model has any validity it is to these kinds of system and their problems that hypotheses based on the model should be applied – such problems as the transformations which bring about the 'birth' or 'death' of an artefact type, a cultural assemblage, a social system, a kinship system, or an economic system. If we are asked to account for the 'death' or transmutation of the Roman Empire in the West in terms of climatic decline, increased barbarian invasion, overstretched military commitments, monetary devaluation, agricultural decline, decrease in birth-rate, over-taxation, waste, shrinking resources, and so forth, one might usefully employ the methods sketched above, which depend on general observations about change in complex systems of this kind.

If such a general model can be made substantially adequate, then hypotheses developed from its postulates should be helpful. The first tentative development from this basis is the hypothesis of multiple factors and cumulative effect, as controlled by the Occam and Converse-Occam qualifications.

HYPOTHESIS OF MULTIPLE FACTORS, AND CUMULATIVE EFFECT

(1) Single attributes or factors, successively introduced into a system, may cumulatively approach a threshold beyond which the system cannot survive unchanged.

(2) Neither more, nor more complex, attributes or factors are to be assumed than are necessary to account for the phenomena.

(3) Neither too few, nor simply single-component, attributes or factors are to be assumed than are necessary to account for the phenomena.

This hypothesis is intended for application in situations in which many variables are, or are said to be operating, in order that the essential variables directively correlated towards some event may be defined and their cumulative interaction within the system evaluated.

Notes

(1) Regularities in distribution areas occur at every level of archaeological organization from attribute to artefact-type, assemblage, culture, culture-group and technocomplex. In all these cases, the analyst is concerned with an entity area, apparently a solid natural unit, but in fact usually an area defined by a polythetic array of intersecting *sets*, whilst it is itself a composite mosaic of principal component sets and their intersection (fig. 13). The factors defining these intersecting sets may be ecological, sociocultural, or indeed any

VENNLAND

(*i*) Vennland as an entity

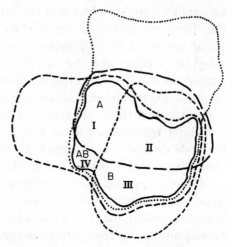

(*ii*) As an entity defined by a polythetic array of intersecting sets

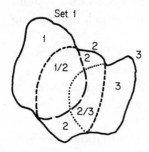

Set 1

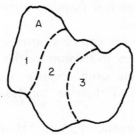

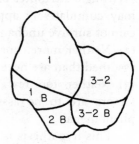

(*iii*) As an entity composed of intersecting sets in three principal components 1, 2, 3

(*iv*) Lathe-form, an historical subdivision of Vennland in which boundaries reflect the descending hierarchy of sets 3, 2, 1 and wherein distribution 'A' was critical.

(*v*) Quadrat-form, an historic subdivision of Vennland in which distribution 'B' was critical and in which sets 1 and 3 were principal components.

Fig. 13 Vennland – a schematic illustration of a Culture Area as the product of intersecting sets (ecological or otherwise) and their fluctuating relative significance for the Culture in occupation – where the area whole is both an idiosyncratic subset of larger sets and the sum of selected parts within that subset.

combination of factors relevant to the system represented by the distribution area vector for the particular entity. It is the persistence of these intersecting sets of factors which provide the continuing, although modifying constraint which gives rise to the sporadic reappearance of former territorial patterns.

The mathematical study of sets and their intersection and partition developments is clearly relevant to these practical problems (Green 1965; Haggett 1965, pp. 243–4). This same approach is also pertinent to the abstract problems of the kinds of archaeological entities defined by polythetic sets of components (chapter 1, VI; B and figs 67, 72) as well as to the correlation and intersection of the various levels of the hierarchical sets defining social, linguistic, racial and archaeological classifications (figs 75, 76).

The basic procedure in set theory uses symbolic models of the concepts and distributions under investigation – these models are sometimes known as Venn diagrams and are discussed in terms of an axiomatic and symbolic calculus (Green 1965). In fig. 13i an imaginary culture occupies an area which we will call 'Vennland'. A close scrutiny of Vennlandish culture reveals that the cultural assemblage is a polythetic set of elements with overlapping but differently orientated distribution areas (fig. 13ii). At the same time it is noted that although Vennland is a 'natural area' bounded by 'natural' boundaries, its existence is really defined by the intersection pattern of a number of environmental sets (fig. 13ii) and by the identity given this intersect by its own characteristic compound of yet smaller sets (fig. 13iii). By using a single diagram to express both environmental and cultural polythetic sets, we are also reminded that their distribution patterns may in fact be partly intercorrelated.

Vennland is also compounded of three principal components represented by the intersecting sets 1, 2, 3 (fig. 13iii), which may be either environmental subdivisions or sociocultural subcultures, or a combination of both. Apparently the history of Vennland over the last thousand years has shown a tendency towards the reappearance of two modal kinds of pattern, the latheform (fig. 13iv) and the quadrat-form (fig. 13v). This would have involved various integrations and reintegrations of both macro- (fig. 13ii) and microdivisions (fig. 13iii) of Vennland. In these historical fluctuations it is likely that the distributions of factor A (fig. 13ii, A is I plus IV) and factor B (ii, IV plus III) were important elements, possibly representing certain resources or sociocultural groups or both, whose significance was a variable through time. The complexity of this oversimplified example reminds us that practical complexity need not mean chaotic lack of order and that order and regularity do not necessarily imply simplicity.

Practical examples of the application of set theory to archaeological data have been limited in number, but a good introduction is given by Litvak King and García Moll (1972) and a further study by Serra Puche (1976).

3 Cultural morphology and cultural ecology – the setting

Communication is the discriminatory response of an
organism to stimulus,
S. S. STEVENS 1950,
'Introduction: A Definition of Communication',
                    J. Acoust, Soc. Am., 22, no. 6
... communities are composed of recognizable population
elements and evolutionary ecology depends upon
population systems, since population systems become
adapted to their environments to a greater degree than the
individual,
                                ALLEE *et al.* 1950, p. 6

One of the main reasons for the premature attempt at a general model
for cultural processes is the need to emphasize that the systems of
relationships investigated by archaeologists are but special manifestations of much more comprehensive systems that once existed. The
striking similarities in the structure, complexity, and inherent
'behaviour' of archaeological and anthropological data stems from
their joint generation as products of the same kinds of system – human
societies. One of the distinctive attributes of such societies is culture –
the communication system of acquired beliefs which increasingly
supplements instinctive behaviour in man. Regardless of their specific
outward form, all cultural systems consist of learned modes of
behaviour and its material manifestations, socially transmitted from
one society or individual to another. A cultural system is therefore an
organized structure integrating amongst others, social, religious, psychological, linguistic, economic and material culture subsystems.
These subsystems are the equilibrium networks within any particular
cultural system, coupled one with another and with the external
environing system. In order to understand the many possible meanings of the regularities that he discovers, the archaeologist must be
aware of the complex connections between his subsystem's input and
output and that of the other interconnected subsystems networking
the overall system. How else can the archaeologist hope to interpret

the social, religious, economic, and other kindred aspects of his material?

After a preliminary look at the essential nature of cultural systems it is our intention to analyse briefly the coupling and connections of the various subsystems within the general system S – thus providing the beginnings of a setting within which to examine particular archaeological cultures. The internal setting of subsystems within the system constitutes what we intend by 'cultural morphology'; the external setting of the integrated system then comprises 'cultural ecology' – the mutual relationships between such systems and their environment, and the adaptive changes of these systems with time and space. The time has also come when we must be more specific about the nature and mechanisms of the cultural system as an entity and of the component subsystems, if we are usefully to develop the equilibrium postulates and hypotheses promised by the general model. Unfortunately, this must mean the repeated reiteration in particular contexts and levels of the relationships observed as inherent in culture systems in general, as integrated in the general model.

1   The nature of cultural systems

Archaeologists and anthropologists are most often dealing with cultural data relating either to artefacts or to activities and there is a tendency to regard these aspects as the fundamental elements of culture systems. In an earlier discussion on artefacts however, it was pointed out that every attribute on an artefact is equivalent to a fossilized action, every artefact is a solidified sequence of actions or activities, and whole assemblages of artefacts are tantamount to whole patterns of behaviour. If we disregard the material or non-material implementation of the acts then we can understand artefacts as simply 'solid' behaviour, in which a rough equivalence can be struck between:

Action	Anthropology	Archaeology
an action	an attribute	an attribute
a cluster of actions	an activity	an artefact
repeated clusters of actions	behaviour	assemblages of artefacts

This remains meaningful so long as care is taken to keep the terminology defined and in use at the same level – as long as a social 'activity' is not confused with its basic 'attributes'. If the levels are to be maintained for comparative purposes and interpretation then the 'sun dance' or the 'initiation ceremony' are cultural artefacts or assemblages of artefacts, not attributes. In essence, it seems that both artefacts and activities can be reduced to behaviour composed of actions on the part of the system's generators.

This argument might lead to the assumption that cultural systems are behaviour systems which can be completely described in terms of the behaviour observed. However, the elementary discussion of simple systems illustrated just how much system 'behaviour' may be inherent in the structure of the system and in any case this discussion of cultural artefacts and activities has neglected to deal with the even more fundamental aspect of cultural 'beliefs'. Living societies are represented by corporate groups of people, and their culture systems by the relationships explicitly or tacitly inferred by their repeated patterns of activities, artefacts, and beliefs. The basic attributes of such culture systems are consequently activities, artefacts, and beliefs, not in their own guise but as 'information' controlling and regulating these three derivative expressions of cultural tradition. Culture is an information system, wherein the messages are accumulated survival information plus miscellaneous and random noise peculiar to each system and its past trajectory (Σs in fig. 11).

Now, it has been suggested that the significant difference between the ape-like ancestors of man and the ape-like ancestors of the modern apes lay in the difference between strongly social large 'apes' and the less social large pongid 'apes'. The early hominids were social animals before they were bearers of material or non-material culture. It was possibly this social and co-operative behaviour of 'man' the bipedal ground-ape that led to the early hominid preservation of an unspecialized physique, a decreasing level of instinctive behaviour and the advantageous development of elaborate intercommunication by speech and other means. Whereas the survival of other species centred around the inheritance of a large body of instinctive behaviour, the survival of the early hominids is likely to have been increasingly dependent upon their co-operative activities in social groups. In this sense, then, co-operative social activities in the early hominids were a partial alternative to increasingly specialized instinctive behaviour. Consequently, man is unusually dependent on behaviour information communicated by seniors and contemporaries in his social group; one of the prime functions of that clustered group being to 'inform' the young hominid how to survive in the given conditions.

Before speech had fully developed man had a social organization and probably simple artefacts, and at this stage the material and non-material culture of the group may have played the vital role in transmitting and communicating survival information to the immature and defenceless hominid. In an important sense cultural systems are the continuous transmission systems of cumulatively acquired information, supplementing instinctive behaviour in man. They are information systems of signs and symbols of great advantage in the face of natural selection and perhaps even the coded forerunners of true speech. In any event, the efficiency of the particular culture system clearly depends on the amount of information that it can store and convey, by whatever means, at a conscious or unconscious level.

Elaborate formal teaching in the modern sense is usually but slightly developed in primitive societies, although by no means entirely absent. Such teaching is essentially supplementary to the information received by the individual from the earliest days of infancy in the various codes of artefacts and their attributes, speech and signs, activities and ceremonies. The mere recognition and definition of an activity by the production of a concomitant set of artefacts constitutes the transmission of information or a message – the ordered selection of a set of attributes from amongst the infinite variety of possible cultural expressions. A child brought up amongst motor-cars and skyscrapers is differently informed to another child born amongst stone axes and pig hunts – irrespective of any qualifying verbal elaboration.

The young learn to survive first of all within their particular culture system and later within its external environment, by the conscious and subconscious assimilation of the social, religious, economic, artefactual, and psychological patterns of their culture. These patterns of behaviour are the code for survival imprinted on the individual by his growing-up within and through them, as surely as an external pattern is imprinted on a substance expanding within a mould. That imprint is not the infinitely complex impression of the 'real and total' environment but that intermediate approximation selectively perceived and reflected in the particular social tradition.

Survival is all that really matters to a species and this means survival of the fittest species. The fittest are biologically defined as those with an increasing rate of progeny survival, as opposed to a static or declining rate. Consequently, any system that can continuously convey complex survival information, based on many experiences of many past environments, to very young progeny, teaching them to survive by subconscious imprint even before they are capable of conscious comprehension, any such system must be of infinite value in increasing the biological 'fitness' of the species. As cumulative systems, culture systems have become cumulatively more efficient in their role of enabling the hominid species to survive, multiply and spread across the globe. As survival information systems they have become cumulatively more efficient in transmitting information – speech has been perfected, international languages and communications fostered, writing and printing developed, wireless and television flourish. It follows that there is an accompanying increase in the scope for the transmission of misleading, mistaken or mutually contradictory information with a concurrent increase in the social ambiguity and dislocation that this must cause.

II   Culture as an information system

If cultural systems are information systems carrying information on cultural values and cultural norms in terms of cross-referencing images, codes, beliefs, fables and myths then how do they work and how can their anomalies be explained?

The transmission of information is essentially brought about whenever constraint restricts the variety of outcomes in a coupled system – when only a limited set of variety is transmitted. A message in these terms constitutes an ordered selection from an agreed set of selected variety. Disturbances which do not represent any part of the 'essential message' from the source are termed 'noise' in information theory. This concept of 'noise' is very useful in the analysis of information systems – the relationship between 'noise' and 'information' is simply that they are in no way intrinsically distinguishable one from the other as categories of variety – except that noise is the variety not essential to the source's message. One can see that this relationship is closely similar to that between the inessential and essential attributes or variables in a system. Now that we understand our cultural systems as in essence kinds of information systems, then the 'essential attributes' are the 'information' in the system and the inessential attributes are the 'noise' – much of it introduced by the nature of the system and its past trajectory (Ashby 1956, pp. 121–60; Cherry 1957, pp. 303–7).

This outlines the background of the earlier statement that culture is an information system, where the messages are accumulated survival information, plus miscellaneous and idiosyncratic noise peculiar to each system and its past trajectory (Σs in fig. 11). As we shall see, this concept is applicable to real data and enables the analyst to separate the essential and key variables from the inessential variables in artefact assemblages.

Information enters cultural systems either as the communication of constraint in the variety of outcomes with external systems (fig. 11, $E \rightarrow S$) including other cultural systems, or as a similar set of selected variety generated within the internal subsystems of S. The first category of information corresponds to the 'adaptive' and discriminatory response of the culture system to its environment, including the capacity to accept information diffused by communication from other cultural systems, thereby increasing the system's own information variety from external sources. The second category of internally generated variety corresponds to internal invention or innovation – usually as part of the minor re-networking of components producing surprising, newly 'emergent' variety in component properties (see above p. 60).

By and large fresh information or new variety affects the cultural information system in a limited number of ways. The system may either accept or reject the new set of variety – where the conditions for acceptance or rejection will be discussed shortly. If the message or set of variety is accepted, then it will be in one of four relationships to existing variety in the attributes of the culture system: the new variety will be wholly new, or it may be additional but alternative to that already existing in the system, or it may flatly contradict and destroy existing system information, or finally it may confirm and be identical with existing information. This flow of kinds of new information and their effects can be displayed as follows:

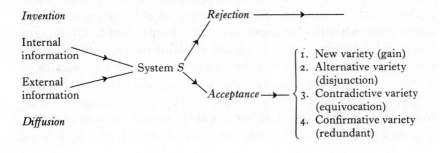

The terms in brackets express the nearest information theory equivalents to our terms 1–4 (Cherry 1957, pp. 303–7).

It is important to grasp that the variety in information which we are discussing in general terms can be quite specifically demonstrated as new, alternative, contradictive, or confirmative in the spheres of the material culture, social, religious, psychological, linguistic or economic value subsystems. The significance of these concepts is that they enable us to come to grips with the meaning of equilibrium in cultural system contexts, other than at the gross level of numerical or mechanical equilibrium.

As a dangerous but ultimately advantageous move it may be helpful to use the information theory version of the terms 1–4 – gain, disjunction, equivocation and redundancy – whilst fully realizing that these terms are rather more narrowly constrained than accurately fits our purpose. Gain can be defined as the increase in system information resulting from the receipt of a message (Ashby 1956, p. 178). Disjunction occurs when information presents alternative variety to the set already held – presenting various alternative choices and trajectories. Equivocation occurs when the incoming information presents a partially or totally contradictory and therefore mutually incompatible set of variety to that already held; since only variety can destroy variety, some of the system's variety in information will then be destroyed and produce uncertainty about the information as a whole. Redundancy occurs when the incoming information presents the identical set of variety to that already held by the system – thereby confirming that set and increasing consistency but not increasing the system's information variety.

It will be noticed that gain and disjunction will increase the variety of information in the system and therefore the new variety they provide increases the regulatory capacity of the system in that it now holds larger reserves of variety at R to counter variety from the environment E (figs 6, 9, 11). Consequently, we can define a more 'sophisticated' or complex culture system, or subsystem, as one in which more activities or more artefacts are produced, implying a greater information content or variety available for regulatory 'insulation'. One is reminded here of the information system implications of Steward's comparison between the 500,000 different artefact-types landed by the United States military forces at Casablanca during World War II and the 3,000–6,000 total variety of artefact-types produced by Californian Indian tribes (Steward 1955, p. 81). Here we have a clear measure of the comparative regulatory or insulatory capacity of two culture systems based on artefact-type counts and underlying information theory – a technique which we will explore later (fig. 24).

Even at this stage it would seem likely that a culture system's capacity as a regulator or insulator cannot exceed its capacity as a communication system, since only variety in culture can force down variety in the outcomes. Information cannot be transmitted in larger quantity than the system's variety allows and the greater the number of connecting channels or networks, the greater the number of coded means of intercommunication (artefacts, activities, speech, writing, etc.), the greater the regulatory potential of the system as a whole.

Redundancy, on the other hand, is not accompanied by any change in the system's variety. Redundant information confirms the existing consensus of the system's communication channels, strengthening the system in its existing state in spite of all the factors of uncertainty acting against its continuity – noise, disjunction, equivocation and so on. The capacity of a system transmitting information to continue or survive as the same system depends on the maintenance of the essential attributes or information being conveyed. However, the fluctuating variety within the system is not inviolate, the greater the changes in variety introduced, the greater the number of possible trajectories and the lower the chances of the consistent communication of the system's syntax in the same general format. The complex syntactical rules of culture systems represent a set of constraints marking the thresholds defining the systems as individual entities. There exist, therefore, thresholds marking the survival capacity of that particular information system beyond which it becomes transformed into other systems (trajectory examples (1)–(5), chapter 2). Redundancy is the vital factor which makes for consistency and continuity, preserving the system in its present general format. Redundancy is tantamount to conformity of behaviour information, a high rate of redundancy from all the channels in a culture system means little or no change. In this way redundancy can help to combat noise or other kinds of variety tending to distort the system's distinctive information format.

The three broad categories of oscillation postulated as inherent in cultural systems are significantly connected with the transmission of information (postulate 11, general model p. 76). Information feedback exists whenever the system or subsystem to which the culture system is coupled gives rise to an output which causes the culture system to modify its own output – either positively or negatively – thereby influencing the other system's transformations (fig. 4). Oscillations in the environing system will therefore bring about oscillations in the coupled cultural system (postulate 11a). Alternatively, internal oscillations towards stable equilibria often occur amongst the system's subsystems, usually with lag and lead phenomena and by the same feedback process (postulate 11b). Time lag arises when information bringing about a transformation takes a definable time after its appearance and before the consequent system change. Time lead occurs when a system's past trajectory is such that certain future transformations can be anticipated and give rise to other prescient changes.

In the general model diagram (fig. 11) 'lag' is illustrated by the time taken for the environmental conditions E_{t_1} at time t_1 to affect the system S, not as S_{t_1} but as S_{t_2}. In the same figure, 'lead' is illustrated by the constrained set of possible system outcomes under conditions E_{t_2} influencing the table of probable responses at t_1. A culture system demonstrates 'lag' when, for example, centuries of increasing deforestation finally brings about a reluctant change in hunting techniques. Such a culture system shows 'lead' when it acts in the light of religious beliefs forecasting the end of the world, or when it shifts its fields in order not to exhaust the fertility of the land. Given a high gain in information variety, alternative variety based on disjunctions, or uncertainty stemming from equivocations, then oscillation amongst the system attributes or components must often occur. Especially if these increases in variety are part of lag or lead situations when the present or retrospective changes may turn out to be over-drastic or underestimated and need compensation in the manner of the error-controlled regulator. Even amongst coupled systems in dynamic equilibrium, stability is never completely achieved because the environment is continually changing and integration takes time. Consequently, there is always a lag in the implementation of regulated control transformations and the feedback will set up oscillations 'hunting' about a satisfactory strategy (fig. 11, circuit E, R, T, S, E).

The third kind of oscillation is not connected directly with movement towards a stable consensus but is the aimless stochastic oscillation that can occur when the permissive boundaries of the stable sets of component values allow many equally probable trajectories (postulate 11c). This aimless wandering among attribute values may be advantageous to the system in that the multiplicity of aimlessly oscillating aspects may chance upon an arrangement with emergent and latent potentialities. This leads to exploitative development by retaining the advantageous changes and oscillating neutral ones; fashion fluctuations of this kind may be thought of as 'scanning' through variety 'in search of' useful transformations – an efficient inherent tendency in this kind of system, maximizing random discovery (figs 44, 45).

Earlier in this chapter the three major levels of dynamic equilibrium within cultural systems were noted as actively moving towards:

(i) equilibrium within each subsystem – including the social, economic, religious subsystems, etc.,

(ii) equilibrium between the outputs of the various component subsystems,

(iii) equilibrium between the system as a whole and its environment.

This activity has been portrayed as a continuous three level game, or a ceaseless three level 'debate'. This arises from the moves to reconcile the variety of information flowing through the system. By these means the information reaching any single node in the generating network from the various systems and subsystems is made less mutually contradictory and self-destructive so as not to imperil the consistent communication of the system's syntactical format. If the information variety is contradictory, then some variety is destroyed and beyond a certain threshold the capacity of the system to continue in its existing format is unavoidably impaired.

Now one way of reconciling mutually contradictory information, or destructive variety following equivocation, is to generate fresh variety making both sets mutually tolerable and thus not reducing the valuable variety in the system as a whole. This 'blending' strategy subsumes and reconciles the two former sets of contradictory variety within a new and more comprehensive set. This is a procedure often observed in 'new' economic strategies blending formerly independent components, in 'new' mythologies or religions blending formerly alien components, and in 'new' social patterns integrating components from several sources. This blending strategy as a move towards maintaining equilibrium is therefore revealed as a very important stimulus for the production of 'new' patterns in sociocultural subsystems.

The three level debate, or equilibrium game, ceaselessly presents the sociocultural system with a limited variety of alternative transitions in its component values and attributes. We have already seen how these alternative transitions can be treated 'as if' the culture is selecting certain strategies in order to satisfy the limiting conditions of the transformations and to ensure an equilibrium outcome; in this context we have noted the mixed or randomizing strategy advantageously underlying multilinear development and now a mixed strategy creatively blending components in 'new' patterns. In order to appreciate the many different kinds of strategy which might be sought for in cultural system trajectories and in order to state in general terms much of specific value to us later on we might briefly look at the concept of strategy in game theory (Braithwaite 1960, pp. 200–50).

The first point to emphasize is that of course the culture systems are not choosing strategies and playing games but on the contrary we are trying to closely approximate the observed input/output regularities of these Black Box systems by fitting or comparing them with homomorphic models based on game theory. Bearing this in mind it is convenient to divide strategies into two classes – the optimizer strategies and the satisficer strategies (Simon 1957, pp. 195–200). Crudely speaking the optimizer strategies include all strategies which attempt to optimize the desirable outcomes in a series of situations involving alternative trajectories – optimizer strategies try to get the best possible results given the conditions. Satisficer strategies, on the contrary, rank all the relevant alternative trajectories in order of preference and then select from this set a prudent trajectory that satisfies the system's tolerances without it being the best possible – satisficer strategies are satisfactory and safe, without being optimal. In the light of hindsight and fully documented conditions it is often difficult to understand why certain systems did not take the optimal trajectories but in real life it is rarely the case that complete information is available to the system before the alternative transitions must occur. Rather than risk all on an optimizer strategy societies often follow some kind of satisficer strategy – usually of the mixed kind.

Wolpert (1964) has used linear programming and regression analysis to contrast the actual productivity of the Swedish Mellansverige district and the potential optimum productivity estimated for the area. Less than half the district had outputs of more than 70 per cent of the optimum and in some cases the output was regularly as low as 40 per cent of the possible optimum. The local Swedish farmer was not aiming at optimum productivity, but rather at a safe, low risk, satisficer yield. In addition it appeared that one factor in this particular case was a regional 'uncertainty' about the most prudent live-stock and cereal mixes in the face of the contemporary fluctuations in local conditions, market prices, crop and stock diseases and other changing factors. This situation can be interpreted as part of an oscillating trajectory moving away from a former metastable state, towards some new future equilibrium strategy suitable for the temporarily stabilized conditions of that future time.

Two kinds of strategy are frequently employed as satisficer strategies when optimizer versions seem too risky, these are the mixed or randomized strategy and the minimax strategy. We have already encountered the mixed strategy in which a number of different specific strategies are blended according to the prevailing conditions, and the randomized version where the blending of the basic strategies is stochastically arranged to 'search' the outcomes for advantages. The mixed or randomized strategy rests on the assumption that it might be better not to employ the same strategy all the time but sometimes to use one and sometimes another in succession – or alternatively, to use a single simultaneous blend of strategies.

The minimax, maximin, or 'most prudent' kind of strategy, aims at maximizing the minimum outcome (maximin), or put another way, on minimizing the maximum risk (minimax). Now the system or subsystem's ultimate trajectory depends on the successive values of a table of transformations expressing the distribution of probabilities around the various alternative transitions. Therefore in order to pursue a prudential or minimax policy the system must take those successive values which are the most 'prudent' of the non-optimal outcomes in the light of possible countermoves (lead). In this way the prudential trajectory takes successive values such that whatever the subsequent alternatives in the successive stages of the developing situation, the system always takes those values which will ensure the best of the non-optimum outcomes that can be forced upon it. This strategy ensures that however well the 'opponent' plays, however bad conditions may become, the outcome is the best that could be achieved in the circumstances (Braithwaite 1960, pp. 238–46). The drawback of this policy being that frequently conditions turn out not to be as bad as they might have been and yet the system is already committed to a non-optimal stance – prepared to make the best of the worst situation.

In the context in which we are examining these various kinds of strategy, the 'prudent' outcome is that state or value which most satisfactorily approaches dynamic equilibrium in terms of total information variety. We can venture to suggest that in such a system (S), pursuing such a strategy (minimax), those successive transitions, and that trajectory will be adopted which minimize the maximum amount of information variety destroyed by contradiction and dislocation within the system. The principle of minimizing the maximum amount of change necessary for survival, in the light of the systems' past and present values, suggests a means for defining the concept of equilibrium in such information systems which we will now pursue.

Let us take the commonly used term 'dislocation' and define it as meaning, for our purposes – the relationship existing between coupled systems or subsystems when their information variety outputs are in some part mutually contradictory, thereby destroying variety in the system as a whole and ultimately imperilling the survival of that system in that form. The state of equilibrium in such systems and subsystems then becomes the state in which dislocation is jointly minimized – or the state in which the rate of destruction of information variety is minimized. This is the vital meaning of equilibrium in the original postulates 1–16 of the general model and this meaning now enables us to give those postulates predictive 'teeth'. It is very important in this context not to confuse the term 'dislocation' with the earlier term 'disjunction' expressing alternative variety; especially since it is not 'disjunction' but 'equivocation' – contradictive and therefore destructive variety which is most frequently involved in system dislocation.

This concept of dislocation enables us to grasp a fresh comprehension not only of the equilibrium postulates but also of such other aspects as the acceptance or rejection of information by culture systems, the nature of the thresholds defining the survival capacity of such systems, and the focusing of innovation in successive areas of the cultural system network. This fresh approach can best be made clear from a consideration of the role of the individual in the sociocultural system – an approach which has been unavoidably postponed until this late stage.

Every man is part of a society, a generator and a receiver, and is influenced by his society's sociocultural system in many subtle and constraining ways. Every activity of such a man is a vector of several simultaneous factors (biological, psychological, religious, social, economic or other components). The act may not be uniquely 'determined' but it will be very closely 'constrained'. The act is a node at which the network of cultural and personal subsystems converge with information on the set of variety allowed the act – some actions having few relevant components and great freedom of variation, others may have many bonds and the more components there are, the more restricted the prescribed resultant (fig. 7). A so-called simple culture may not itself recognize or designate these component subsystems bearing on the act but this does not mean that the subsystems are not acting – just as they are in more elaborate cultures which have arbitrarily formalized and recognized their own social, religious, and economic spheres.

The ideal is for the man to act without dislocation because dislocation, as opposed to permissive disjunction, results in an act which communicates a set of contradictory values – capable of causing confusion, loss of cohesion and ultimately social anarchy. Such an act may be accepted only if dislocation is minimal, only if it can be accommodated as a valid alternative, as a disjunction within the tolerance thresholds of the system. This immediately brings us to a fresh view of the process of diffusion of material and non-material artefacts – both representing messages with information.

Diffusion has three phases: (1) the presentation of the new element; (2) the acceptance; (3) the integration and frequently the modification of the element. The optimal presentation of new variety may be gained by increasing the number and capacity of outside communication channels, which if maximized will maximize in turn the input of new variety advantageous to the system regulation and control – one may recollect for example, the rise of the Renaissance in the wake of the fresh channels developed by the Venetian, Pisan, Genoan and Florentine merchant explorers. However, the crucial phase is acceptance, for if rejected the information is as if it had never existed as far as that culture is concerned. Why do some cultural systems accept some diffusing innovations and yet reject others? The answer can only be proposed in detail for each specific case but the general syntax is the same. New variety will not be accepted if its concomitant dislocation cannot be minimized to vanishing point – it must be variety which does not contradict and destroy any of the essential attributes concerned with the continuity of the system.

This tells us why such new information variety may be rejected but what causes acceptance? In the same manner, parts of the system or subsystems may be oscillating in an unstable equilibrium or in minor dislocation, consequently any convenient new variety communicated to the system and capable of bringing this localized disequilibrium to stability will immediately be accepted and integrated. Since the systems and subsystems are dynamic, there is constant disequilibrium or dislocation of a minor kind but quite sufficient to attract new variety and its unforeseen consequences. Here again we have lag and lead, oscillation towards equilibrium and apparent goal-seeking in our systems. In such circumstances a diffusing attribute may be accepted and integrated if its immediate capacity for diminishing serious dislocations already existing in the system are greater than any small dislocations which its integration may cause.

Culture systems continuously vary in their complexity and in their stability or lack of dislocation. Consequently, the network of converging information bearing on a given act will vary from culture to culture in the number of channels involved and in the 'tolerance' within the boundaries of the set of stable variants. In a highly institutionalized system with rather rigid and narrow limits defining stable transformations the ability to assimilate and integrate diffusing variety will be impaired; the system has become in certain respects 'non-adaptive' and may ultimately collapse if the tolerance threshold of the system as a whole is overwhelmed by severe contradiction and dislocation. This situation reveals the dangers of certain kinds of over-elaborate cultural complexity (cf. Flannery 1972, p. 423), possibly over-adapted to peculiar contexts and unable to cope with fresh variety of a different kind. In contrast, a less specialized culture system although lacking such large resources of system variety, may be less vulnerable in the broader limits of the stable sets comprising its essential variables.

It seems that overspecialization is another phenomenon shared by cultural and organic living systems, with cultural dinosaurs just as vulnerable as animal ones. As an example one might reflect on the accumulating evidence that the incipient food producing cultures appear not out of the ranks of the most sophisticated hunter–fisher–gatherers but from the not so complex and rather unspecialized peripheral systems in more marginal and increasingly trying environments (e.g. Binford 1968b) – environments stimulating increasing disjunction and equivocation – demanding 'new' variety development.

A combination of flexibility and sufficient complexity seems to be the requirement best able to maintain a given system intact in a great variety of contexts or environments. The collapse of such a sociocultural system does not usually or necessarily depend on or coincide with, the wholesale destruction of the system's generators or their entire way of life. The 'death' of a sociocultural system is usually the 'birth' of a new alternative, quite irrespective of the generator's population fluctuation. The 'death' of the system amounts to no more than the collapse of the syntax defining the format of the essential attributes and the bursting of the thresholds of the key sets of constrained variety. The 'birth' of a new system is usually accompanied by the survival of large parts of the old subsystems' values which are re-networked in novel ways, with newly 'emergent' potential consequent upon this change, together with the integration of fresh variety in attributes diffused from without. Similarly, the 'death' or collapse of such systems can result from serious dislocation within or between subsystems, or between the system as a whole and its environment. The great inherent tolerance of such systems has already suggested that, with rare exceptions, such apparently dramatic transformations are most often gradual, cumulative, and multifocused.

An earlier part of this discussion described the concept of distinct and definable development foci within particular systems at particular times, located in particular parts of the system's networked components – foci for innovation and the acceptance of fresh variety. The archaeologist detects such foci in aspects of changing artefact-types and material culture assemblages, the anthropologist recognizes similar foci in changing aspects of social structure and in both cases the distinctive mark is the greatly accelerated rate of change in these foci as opposed to the steadier rate of change elsewhere in the systems. An important development of this concept is the bite which it can be given by taxonomic methods capable of measuring 'rate of change'.

At any one time there usually appears to be one or more major foci of accelerated change in the subsystems of sociocultural systems. These foci will often tend to be areas focusing the variety of effects of multiple environmental stimuli new to the culture upon incompatible variety in the existing system. It follows that these foci of development will tend to move around and through the different subsystem networks in a continuous cycle of growth and renewal. On occasions the foci will shift away from areas of once intense development to new fields, old foci may partially revert to a simple or generalized pattern last seen in a pre-elaboration phase providing an interesting sequence of apparently cyclical oscillation from simple to complex to simple forms again (fig. 38). This oscillation is found in material and non-material culture but we will be particularly interested in its material artefact manifestations. As brief examples one might cite the return of some Late African Acheulean and Sangoan handaxe types to forms closely resembling Early Acheulean simple forms; or the Neolithic shift of focus from many aspects of the flint assemblages to other areas such as pottery elaboration, with a concomitant reversion of burin and scraper types to 'early' simple and unelaborate forms in many instances. Of course this reversion or 'dis-elaboration' inevitably reflects changes in connected aspects of the societies' other subsystems; in these examples and in the main such changes in material culture are usually correlated with economic and environmental fluctuations, although religious and social foci are almost as frequently so reflected. One aspect which can be informative is the correlation between reversion or dis-elaboration in one locus and the shift of the foci or change to new fields of concentration, thus pointing out the successive sequence of areas of system dislocation and perhaps suggesting their causes.

The fundamental elements of sociocultural systems – activities, artefacts, and traditions – are all in essence forms of information. The continuous rhythm of repeated activity sequences, day by day, month by month, season by season, and year by year generate a distinctive information code idiosyncratic to that particular cultural system. The continuous output of solid activities – the artefacts – convey discriminatory response and intention; not a response to everything but a peculiarly discrete response to the partial environment perceived through the cultural system's 'sensory' organs. This constrained and continuous response embodies in material artefact form, sets of transformations converting information from one representation into another – an ordered selection from a limited set of signs – in short, a coded message. The conversation, beliefs, legends, myths, fables and traditions are even more directly comprehended as coded information on socially acceptable norms, their boundaries and the consequent taboos. The individuals generating the changing sociocultural information system move through their personal cycles of age- and sex-graded activities – the individual's actions vary irregularly, but overall the continuous, redundant rhythm of patterned activity continues, changing slowly but perceptibly in a man's lifetime. A rhythmic intimation of survival information and idiosyncratic noise on a comprehensive scale, ensuring the survival of the young within the group and the group within its changing environment, with the minimum of disruption. The accumulative continuity of the cultural information system represents the aspect most advantageous to its generators.

III   Culture as a system with subsystems

The internal setting of subsystems within the general system constitutes 'cultural morphology' as opposed to the external setting of the system in its environment, comprising 'cultural ecology'. Both of these fields are sufficient to fill several books with discussion and elaboration but the intention here is merely to sketch in two successive sections the implications of the developing general model for these specialist fields. If the model is well constructed it should be possible to say succinctly and in general what should prove to be the case in particular instances. Since the subsystems within culture are the subject of highly-specialized studies we are here only interested in seeing them in a particular light in preparation for their use as a setting for archaeological data.

It is, of course, quite as arbitrary and dangerous to describe a sociocultural system as having component subsystems as to describe any unitary and highly complex system in terms of a number of its component circuits, for the self-same reasons (fig. 5). Not only are the subsystems really different aspects of the same system (fig. 8) but even could we define them adequately in terms of content and boundaries one would still not have defined the system containing them. Such complex systems cannot be treated as an interlaced set of more or less independent subsystems since, as we have seen, the 'behaviour' of such a unit is more complex than simply the expression of the sum of its components' 'behaviours' (fig. 5). Nevertheless, as long as we continue to realize the arbitrary nature of this kind of component description it will perhaps serve to partially describe an otherwise extremely complex reality. In the full realization that where we arbitrarily describe say five component subsystems the system generators may have conceptualized only one, or possibly three, or perhaps sixty – but as long as we are consistent this arbitrariness will temporarily serve our purpose.

In the arbitrary setting devised here it is intended to distinguish five subsystems within which we will imagine the information in sociocultural systems to be more richly interconnected than externally networked within the system as a whole:

(1) *Social subsystem.* The hierarchical network of inferred personal relationships, including kinship and rank status.

(2) *Religious subsystem.* The structure of mutually adjusted beliefs relating to the supernatural, as expressed in a body of doctrine and a sequence of rituals, which together interpret the environment to the society in terms of its own percepta.

(3) *Psychological subsystem.* The integrated system of supra-personal subconscious beliefs induced upon the individuals in a society by their culture, their environment and their language; essentially the subconscious system of comparative values.

(4) *Economic subsystem.* The integrated strategy of component subsistence methods and extraction processes which feed and equip the society.

(5) *Material culture subsystem.* The patterned constellations of artefacts which outline the behaviour patterns of the system as a whole and embody that system's technology.

These five subsystem headings are transparently based on the prejudices of current opinion, underlining their arbitrary nature. Even by the standards of this biased basis, many will find them unsatisfactory and will wish to reorganize them accordingly (e.g. Renfrew (1972) distinguishes 'social', 'projective/symbolic', 'subsistence', 'technological' and 'trade and communications' subsystems). However, we will arbitrarily conceptualize cultural systems as integrating these five main information subsystems as a coherent ensemble in dynamic equilibrium at the three levels:

(i) within each subsystem,
(ii) between the subsystem outputs,
(iii) between the whole system and its environment (fig. 14).

Equilibrium being defined in terms of the information concepts earlier discussed – minimizing immediate system dislocation. These relationships can be crudely summed up in a diagram, first in a static background (fig. 14), and then against a changing background (fig. 15). In these diagrams the entity simply labelled system S or S_t in previous figures is expanded in terms of these arbitrary components (figs 9, 11). This setting will now enable us to discuss very briefly the relevance of the earlier postulates and the general model to these particular subsystem spheres.

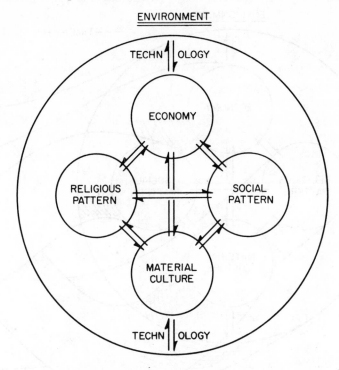

Fig. 14   A static model representing the dynamic equilibrium between the subsystem networks of a sociocultural system and its environment. The psychological subsystem may be envisaged as centrally encased by the other subsystems – a genetic inheritance modified by an induced field; see fig. 23.

SOCIAL SUBSYSTEM

The attributes integrated in this subsystem are conceptual ideas or information about the relationships between the individuals within a system. Although these concepts and this information may be partially equated with lines of genetic relationship this is by no means the rule of organization for social subsystems. Rank, status and obligation often operate on other bases than genetic relationship (e.g. Service 1962; Fried 1967) and even kinship itself is an arbitrary concept which may ignore one side of the family completely for some purposes and yet link remarkably distant blood relations in some other direction. The social subsystem 'does not consist of the objective ties by descent or consanguinity that obtain among individuals; it exists only in

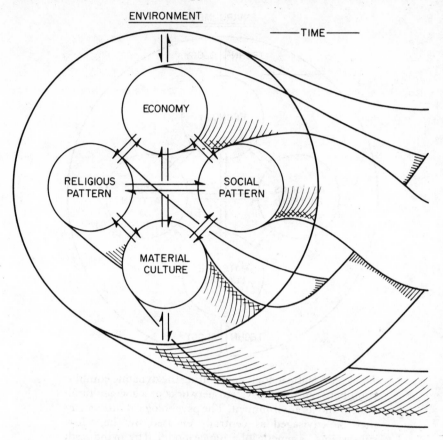

Fig. 15   A schematic model suggesting the oscillating subsystem states and values in the networks of a sociocultural system in dynamic equilibrium with the oscillating states of its coupled environment.

human consciousness, it is an arbitrary system of ideas, not the spontaneous development of a factual situation' (Lévi-Strauss 1945). This commonly held information causes the individuals in a group to repeatedly act according to an explicit or tacit pattern. On the basis of these ideational patterns human groups are everywhere networked by an intersecting web of exclusive or non-exclusive divisions which are orientated towards proscribed sets of activities within the system. These segments include such sets as elite groups, education groups, age groups, ceremonial, military, recreational, religious and political groupings. Within these groupings different individuals are variously linked with various neighbours in a great intercommunicating network (fig. 8). The social cohesion of a group depends on the intensity of internal reticulation within this network, as opposed to the comparatively sparse connections running beyond the society to other societies. The social subsystem is an idiosyncratic and multipurpose network generated by a set of acquired ideas or information. The successive replication of itself, by conscious and subconscious imprint, is not the least function of the social subsystem – continuity is overwhelmingly advantageous in the maintenance of variety.

The information in the social subsystem, as in the other subsystems, seems mainly concerned with expressing the accepted rules of behaviour and their range of tolerance as comprehensive sets. When the observed social norm differs from the socially communicated conceptual rule, as is often the case, then disjunction or equivocation results, usually followed by oscillation around a 'new' rule subsuming the former aberrations. This lag or lead in social norms reaching compatible equilibrium with the existing social rule constitutes an unstable feedback system depending on the perceptible time that values and attitudes take to diffuse throughout the social network – the resulting oscillation is often characterized as action/reaction within the system.

This latter class of oscillation represents oscillation towards stable equilibrium within the subsystem (postulate 11b). The two other general classes of oscillation are also detectable in changing social subsystem values – oscillation induced by coupled contextual oscillation (11a), and oscillation within the sets of alternative stable values (11c). Oscillation induced by fluctuations in coupled systems or subsystems may be illustrated by the centuries of oscillation in European moral codes between the puritan and the liberal ideals or the interesting social reversion to nuclear family units in modern urban societies – both oscillations being coupled with fluctuations in other cultural subsystems. Oscillation within the sets of stable values is everywhere demonstrated by the multilinear trajectories and values of the dispersed component groups within the same broad, polythetic, sociocultural system.

Similarly, new states or values successively introduced into the social subsystem do cumulatively approach a threshold beyond which the system cannot continue unchanged (postulate 8). The contemporary fluctuation of many African social subsystems and their gradual transmutation to newly emergent formats reflects the transitions across the thresholds of the old tribal patterns. The former

106 Analytical Archaeology

systems could no longer function without serious dislocation by reason of the growing number of incompatible European ideals steadily integrated within them. Very similar processes operated in the accelerated detribalization of Europe between AD 500 and 1000 and the rise of emergent and more complex social and political units. Acculturation, or saturating diffusion brought about by the intricate interpenetration of different cultural systems is repeatedly but not invariably followed by cumulative integration and eventually system transmutation. In all these social processes detailed study reveals certain essential attributes involved in the subsystem's trajectory and amongst these the key attributes which express the characteristic syntax of that system; these are the attributes cumulatively contradicted by the successively accepted external variety. If several loosely related sociocultural systems are cumulatively integrating the same set of diffusing attributes these systems may become convergently similar and represent a gross entity closely related to the archaeological culture group (chapter 7).

An important claim made in the postulates of the general model was that the states of the components in the subsystem change not by single-valued, closed transformations alone, but as a limited matrix of transitions whose probabilities vary partly as a function of the past and the present state of the system as a whole (postulate 9). Because these systems have this Semi-Markovian form it was claimed that there are usually several trajectories by which any given state may be reached (postulate 13). Modern studies in social subsystems illustrate these points particularly well, especially the analytical cross-cultural studies of Murdock based upon a statistical analysis of hundreds of societies and their social structures (Murdock 1949).

It is impossible to discuss the full scope and relevance of Murdock's work in such a confined context but it is hoped that some of its implications can be usefully conveyed. In the section that best illustrates this discussion Murdock takes two hundred and fifty societies from around the world and on the basis of his analyses describes forty-seven main structural sub-types – claimed as cross-cultural regularities in social subsystem structure. A study of the evidence suggested the probable and possible trajectories by means of which each particular structural sub-type could be attained, thus:

Structural sub-type	Probable and possible derivations
Normal Eskimo ←	Patri-Eskimo, Neo-Yuman, Neo-Fox, Neo-Hawaiian, (Neo-Guinea), (Neo-Nankanse), (Matri-Eskimo), (Bi-Eskimo)

– the order of the possible derivations indicating the rough order of probability, the improbable but possible derivations in parentheses (Murdock 1949, pp. 323–6).

The source of Murdock's sample, his methods of analysis and his resulting typology may of course be held in question[1] but that the results obtained indicate the general nature of the data can hardly be doubted. In short, Murdock's table of social structure derivations amounts to the construction of a model matrix of transition probabilities for social subsystems – a real example of the arbitrary Table 'T' used in our earlier general discussion (figs 9, 10, 11). In order to convey an impression of this attempt at a canonical representation of social-subsystem trajectories Murdock's table is schematically reproduced here in matrix form (fig. 16).

The salient points emerging from this and similar analyses are the presence of constraint in social variety and therefore discernible regularities in cross-cultural social structure – the clues resting in the comprehensive analysis of large quantities of examples of input/output data and its sifting for directively correlated essential variables – a classic Black Box operation. The analysis clearly shows that unique trajectories leading to particular social structures are very unusual but on the other hand the number of viable trajectories directively correlated to one state is severely limited – between one and nine trajectories linking any pair of states (fig. 16). The constraining or 'funnelling' role of some social structures as opposed to the axial and 'radiating' role of others is repeatedly emphasized in trajectories traced through this table (fig. 16). The shifting foci of dislocation and consequent change within social subsystems are particularly well brought out by Murdock's investigations – which quite apart from specific reservations is an excellent example of the powerful new developments in the experimental spheres of both archaeology and anthropology (fig. 2) (Murdock 1949, chapters 8, 9, 10, 11).

An equally perceptive study of the correlated constraint in variety and the consequent regularities in social subsystems is developed in the work of Steward (1955, pp. 101–72). In a search for cross-cultural regularities linking ecology and social structure Steward convincingly demonstrates several striking modes of clustering social and economic subsystem components. In one example a clear relationship is demonstrated between patrilineal, patrilocal, exogamous multifamily band organization and the constraint imposed by territories with limited and scattered food resources, mainly small game in very small

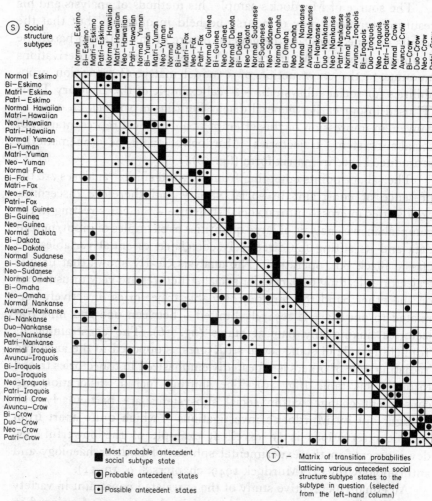

Fig. 16 The social structure game. A schematic representation of Murdock's table of social structure derivations (1949, pp. 324–6) as a retrospective matrix of transition probabilities 'T' for tracing the past trajectories of particular social subtypes. To play, select any subtype 'S' in the left-hand column, trace most probable and probable antecedent states in its horizontal row, then repeat this procedure for the antecedent states of each antecedent and so on. Note that some structures allow many possible antecedent trajectories (nine for normal Dakota type) and provide 'radiating' nodes in the lattice, whilst others offer constraint and allow only one or two approach lines (two for Neo-Sudanese).

groups, and a hunting–gathering economy based on simple tech-nology. In another case the correlation between hunting–gathering economies based on large migratory herds of big herbivores is linked with more complex societies organized in composite bands. In no case does the environment and its resources force a single variety of viable economic sub-system strategy or a single variety of coupled social subsystem but varying degrees of constraint to restrict the variety of subsystem but varying degrees of constraint do restrict the variety of ted in detail. Such limiting regularities linking social organization, economy and environment are particularly vital for the archaeologist who wishes to know something of the possible range of social organizations behind his data. The real data and the general model show that, given the detailed economic and ecological background, the archaeologist cannot reconstruct the social subsystem pattern behind his material but it becomes increasingly possible for him to narrowly define the limited range of possible variety this pattern might have taken.[2]

Perhaps the most significant results of these and other studies are their implications for the selection and analysis of the varying input-output attributes in the search for correlated regularities. All these studies are unanimous in emphasizing that it is not possible, with precision, to separate out the inessential, essential and key attributes *before* the analysis; which attributes fall in which category depends on the particular study and on the results *following* the analysis. Other-wise, circularity may be introduced by the acceptance of intuitive 'type-markers' or 'type-fossils' said to be 'typical(?)' of the set and thus prejudicing its definition, boundaries and contents – a point already elaborated in chapter 1.

The same studies raise again the problem of seeking the relevant level for characterizing the components amongst which correlated regularities are believed to exist. If we take the Steward analysis of hunting tribes it can be seen that no significant correlation would probably result from the sifting of hundreds of social structures shar-ing economies based on specifically hunting, say – kangaroo, or gazelle, or wild goat, or buffalo, for example. However, if these traits had been tested for under societies based on hunting migratory large herd herbivores as one category, and dispersed small game as another, the useful regularity might be observed. Characterized as sharing 'hunting game' is too general, characterized as 'hunting kangaroo' is too specific – 'hunting dispersed small game' and 'hunting large herd herbivores' is the characterization which is most informative. This specification problem is the single greatest barrier in detecting significant correlations between regularities in archaeological and anthropological analyses – every entity and even a given attribute has many levels of characterization and can take a Protean variety of forms.

RELIGIOUS SUBSYSTEM

The artificial separation of the religious from the psychological subsystem merely underlines the essentially arbitrary nature of this scheme. Under the definition followed here this is a device to isolate the body of information forming 'the structure of mutually adjusted beliefs relating to the supernatural, as expressed in a body of doctrine and a sequence of rituals which together interpret the environment to the society in terms of its own percepta'. We are intent mainly on showing in the briefest way that this subsystem is also an information variety system with many of the general characteristics already discussed (postulates 1–16, chapter 2).

It is commonplace to observe that religious concepts, in the broadest sense, play an active part in constraining the activities of individuals in most societies. Religious beliefs are usually expressed as a body of doctrine communicated by stories, parables, myths, legends, or fables expressing the 'ideal' rules for certain behaviour. Religious rituals provide a further communication system redundantly reinforcing the channels for passing religious information – this time in the coded form of celebrations, feasts, holy days, dances, games and ceremonies of all kinds.

Information circulates within the subsystem, with continuous readjustment attempting to minimize dislocation which would impair the continuity of the system. The collapse of such a religious subsystem and its subsequent transmutation is aptly reflected in the European Reformation. The cumulative build-up of alternative and contradictive information breached the threshold defining the Old Catholicism of parts of sixteenth-century Europe – but significantly not in other parts. Most of this contradictive and alternative variety clearly arose from the rapidly 'modernizing' technology and economy of north-west Europe in the period c. 1500–1600. The need to establish equilibrium between the tenets of the expanding capitalist economy and the Catholic 'rule' condemning usury is well documented in the development of capitalism and the rise of the Protestant religion (Green 1959). Even at the present time we can observe the oscillations of the Catholic Dogma in the face of the contradictory information about birth control – a momentary dislocation which will doubtless be neutralized by a comprehensive 'new' doctrine, establishing equilibrium over this matter as over so many others in the past. These equivocations and dislocations are not confined to any one religious subsystem or to any one period, they are a continuous process in all such systems.

The cumulative encrustation and elaboration of the cycles of religious myths provide yet more excellent examples of the continuously moving equilibrium process of minimizing the maximum religious dislocation by the generation or acceptance of 'new' doctrine adjusting the old and the new information. The ramifications of the changing relationships of the Graeco-Roman gods and goddesses effectively express a coded fossil of the states of belief at successive intervals in space and time. The same cumulative complexity is found in similar systems from the changing Norse pantheon to the accretions of the Old Testament. These religious cycles share this continuous readjustment to minimize dislocation within the religious subsystem and between that subsystem and its context, frequently with the three kinds of oscillating variation already noted (postulate 11). Cumulative change to thresholds, transmutation to new syntactical formats, foci of rapid and concentrated change, dynamic equilibrium in information variety – these are all general characteristics of religious subsystems.

If we wish to speculate how knowledge of these inherent characteristics can help the archaeologist in reconstruction we can see that, as with the other subsystems, observed constraint and correlated regularity can help to limit the possible interpretations. With historical aid, for example, one can observe the subtle cumulative changes in the religious doctrine of the patriarchal tribes of nomad Hebrew pastoralists from the third millennium BC onwards. The oscillating transition from a primitive and comprehensive monotheism under a tribal Baal, with standing stone altars, sheep sacrifices and the tented Ark, to the culminating complex Judaism of a sophisticated urban society with far-flung commercial connections communicating a great variety of new information – splendidly assimilated in the continuing simple format. In such a case sufficient data survives to trace the changing trajectory of the religious subsystem in terms of the constraints and variety associated with its successive transitions.

In purely archaeological contexts the interpretation of religious data must be more speculative and broad by the very nature of the paucity and complexity of the surviving record (e.g. Flannery's attempt (1976, pp. 333–45) to distinguish public, household/sodality and personal rituals in Formative villages in the Oaxaca valley, Mexico; Gimbutas' (1974) interpretation of the religious beliefs expressed in figurines, models etc. in south-east Europe from 7000 to 3500 BC). Indeed it is for this reason that a general inductive model sketching the general relationships between religious subsystems and the other more tangible subsystems may help to throw light upon how the archaeologist might converge upon some interpretation of religious artefacts. The general model suggests that sociocultural systems tend to preserve vestigial 'memories' of their former trajectories and environments in both material and social configurations, as well as in oral traditions (Σs and Lag, fig. 11).

Long after the situations that prompted specific adaptations have passed they may survive in such systems – especially embalmed within the conservative memory of the religious subsystem. It is very tempting to suspect that the Minoan Cretan fixation with the wild bull and his horns represents a 'memory' of a time and place when the herds of giant wild cattle were an integrated and living part of an economic and religious equilibrium. It is tempting to see the later Minoan idealized bull cult and related components, as a relic of a long and multilinear history of development centred around the massive wild cattle of the Western Anatolian grasslands. Cattle, which together with their leopard predators, were of fundamental contemporary significance to the early Neolithic cultures of that area (Mellaart 1967). The fossilized vestiges from the continuous, complex and dynamic interaction of the economic, religious, and artistic subsystems in former system states are firmly portrayed in many prehistoric cultures.[3]

PSYCHOLOGICAL SUBSYSTEM

Anthropologists, sociologists and psychologists agree that the differing kinds, quantity, reticulation and organization of information variety within sociocultural systems forms one important component imprinted on the individual personality. These four dimensions of variety are differently filled in different cultures whilst being largely shared within each culture. Consequently, it is hardly surprising that populations of sufficient multitude polythetically share certain general personality attributes which are intuitively summed-up, with varying accuracy, in 'national character' and even in attempts at the psychological taxonomy of 'tribal character' (Kroeber 1948, pp. 321–6, 594–7). It would seem that cultures induce a broad psychological pattern on their generators, with considerable personal variation and are extremely difficult to express in a rigorous fashion. The pattern takes the form of a subsystem of supra-personal subconscious concepts and values induced upon the individuals in society by their culture, their environment but above all by their language – the channel linking the immature mind, almost from birth, with adult minds and the cumulative coded information of former generations (Σs, fig. 11).

Language has emotive as well as symbolic power and the act of learning a language which may recognize and differentiate one hundred categories of seal or six thousand attributes of camels, or twenty categories of greenstone for axes – differently orientates the perception of the immature Eskimo, Arab and Maori. The differing emphasis and the comparative scale of values underlying the variety of information circulating within the system, from every form of communication, constitutes the culture's psychological subsystem. In an important sense this induced system of values and orientation, the psychological subsystem, represents a canonical model of the sociocultural system as a whole, in that it is capable of generating the transformations characterizing that system if communicated to that system's individuals from birth. It is on the basis of constraint and regularity in the environment that constraint and regularity appear in the variety of cultural systems – and it is this quality which makes such systems highly efficient teaching devices capable of communicating survival information and noise to individuals within the group, from the individual's earliest hours, by a multiplicity of coded channels (Ashby 1956, pp. 130–4).

The psychological subsystem as defined here equates roughly with the 'psychological field space' of the psychologists, the psychological environment within which the individual personality must operate. The psychologist is primarily interested in the dynamic equilibrium at this lowest level, between the individual personality and the psychological subsystem of his sociocultural system (Lewin 1936, p. 6). However, the subsystem must equally maintain stability with the information in the other cultural subsystems and with the whole system and its environment – the three general levels of dynamic equilibrium, oscillation and 'debate' minimizing dislocation.

Dislocation or disequilibrium at the lowest level represents the personal stresses, strains and conflicts arising from contradictory information at the interface between the individual personality and the psychological subsystem of the culture – frequently the outcome of contradiction between personal instinctive behaviour and the socializing process. The general terms alternative, contradictive and redundant variety equate with the psychologist's low conflict, high conflict and neutral stimuli – their disequilibria and barriers equating roughly with our dislocations and thresholds. Against this background it is interesting to note that at the lowest level contradictive information may initiate discordant and mutually interfering processes in the central nervous system – and thus that dislocation or disequilibrium arising from the integration of inconsistent information is now judged the main factor in stimulating the learning process to nullify and stabilize the system. In other words, such dislocation in the individual's subsystem must be minimized by the acquisition or generation of new and comprehensive variety – by learning (Berlyne 1966, pp. 82–7).

ECONOMIC SUBSYSTEM

At first sight the fundamental attributes of a culture's economic subsystem might be assumed to be a set of artefacts and a set of resources and indeed this is the case at a superficial level. However, a very brief acquaintance with the economic patterns of prehistoric and historic societies quickly reveals that these subsystems do not exploit all the varied resources of their environment, but on the contrary are marked by idiosyncratic selections of favourite staples – even failing to gain an optimal yield on occasions when this is possible. Among hunter–fisher–gatherer societies we may note the examples of the Tuluaqmiut band of the Nunamiut Eskimos, to whom only 12 out of 149 edible plant species are of dietary importance (Campbell 1968). The satisficer strategies employed by Swedish farmers in obtaining outputs of 40–70 per cent of optimal yields have already been demonstrated by Wolpert (above pp. 94–5). Furthermore taboos and religious constraint arbitrarily reduce the variety of resources, sometimes even engendering unnecessary death and starvation – the Arabs will not eat pork, the aboriginal Tasmanians would not eat scaled fish, the Chinese will not drink milk and the English will not eat horse.

Thus it seems that a society's economy is a highly peculiar, selective and apparently irrational compound of extractive processes from within the broad variety of possible stable subsistence techniques. The economic subsystem comprises a set of information about the resources of a territory and conveys a strategy indicating, within broad limits, an arbitrary scale of importance of the various resources, as well as apportioning and co-ordinating the amount of time devoted to each process and deciding the organization and distribution of the output.

The economic subsystem provides information patterned in an elaborate mixture of strategies based on the cumulative register of past conditions and upon an extrapolated estimation of future contingencies (Σs and lead, fig. 11). The more complex or sophisticated the culture, the greater the variety of strategies in its economic array. The strategy of this subsystem, as in other subsystems, rests on the continuous effort of the generators to maintain the format and syntax of the subsystem by continually minimizing serious dislocation between all the varying component states in its trajectory. Strategy is our formal recognition of the subsystem's continuous co-ordination of fluctuating, new, alternative, contradictive and confirmative information variety concerning resources and their exploitation.

Once again the subsystem illustrates three basic levels of dynamic equilibrium:

    (i) within the subsystem, between its attributes,
    (ii) between this subsystem and the other subsystem components,
    (iii) between this part of the whole system and the environment.

At the lowest level stability must be maintained between the competing demands of the subsystem's attributes, in this case the *perceived* resources. These are simply those resources which the system's technology is capable of recognizing, thus making clear the 'sensory' role of the material culture subsystem. The strategy at this level is concerned with the division of time and labour, the allocation of roles, resources, distribution, control and regulation. The quality of 'lead' or 'foresight' is all-important; the estimation of future contingencies includes such vital and mundane things as how much seed to reserve, how many domestic animals to keep or slaughter, how much output to trade as surplus, how effort should be apportioned between hunting, fishing or gathering and which combinations of species are to be exploited. All these decisions are made in advance, in the light of past experience and they affect the system before the events they cater for have occurred ('T' affected by Σs and S_{t_2} at $_{t_1}$, fig. 11). Thomas (1972, p. 691) has noted the possibility that the prehistoric Shoshoneans could have predicted the relative yields of piñon nuts two years before the actual crop by simple macroscopic inspection. Strategies for resource exploitation and population distribution could then have been planned in advance, especially in the event of a predicted crop failure.

The dynamic equilibrium between the economic subsystem and the other subsystems is stabilized by continually adjusting the mutual values and states of these networks. The economy must be kept as nearly as possible in equilibrium with the information on and constraint from taboos, social organization and division of labour by age and sex, individual personalities, and the available capacity or range of variety of material culture. 'Lag' can be seen in the response of the economic subsystem to changes in demography and settlement patterns (e.g. Washburn 1974, p. 325; Brose 1976, p. 18).

At the highest level the economic subsystem must keep the whole system in a stable relationship with the environment. Resources must not be over-exploited, changing combinations of crops and animals must be tried in the face of changing conditions, new variety from penetrating the thresholds of new ecological niches (e.g. desert and steppe fringes) can be exploited and must be accommodated. Among hunter–fisher–gatherers resource scheduling and seasonal site occupation are important factors, whilst among agricultural communities, crop rotation, manuring, length of fallow periods and settlement rotation may be crucial factors in maintaining this stable relationship with the environment. Where economic crisis threatens the survival of the system as a whole, then regulatory control or fresh and powerful variety must be interposed ('R' in fig. 11), or the system as a whole must change.

At each of these three levels of 'continuous debate' between coupled systems, an adequate blend of information variety (i.e. an adequate mixed strategy) must be pursued. New, contradictive, alternative and confirmative economic variety must be balanced in a moving and frequently oscillating equilibrium, minimizing the maximum immediate dislocation in the system's trajectory. The three general categories of system oscillation are particularly marked in economic subsystems and have been the subject of intensive modern research (Tustin 1954). Oscillation induced in the equilibrium of the subsystem as a whole is found in the 'trial and error' adjustment of primitive economies as well as in modern business cycles, wheat price fluctuations and pig-iron output oscillations (Ellsworth Huntington 1964, pp. 466–73). Internal oscillation readjusting the attributes within the subsystem frequently occurs when new information, resources or techniques are developed or introduced: the dislocations caused by the new variety are gradually countered by error-controlled regulation. The third class of 'aimless' oscillation, within the boundaries of broad, permissive sets, is often detectable in the fluctuating 'fashions' in the blends of secondary economic processes – the staple processes continuing in broader oscillations of lower frequency.

The concepts of moving foci of development and directive correlation are particularly useful in the analysis of economic subsystem trajectories. Areas within the economic structure are continually in the process of readjustment and the inevitable dislocations are the foci for minimizing action by the development or acquisition of new variety. The artefacts in the archaeological record provide an invaluable trace of the foci of accelerated development to meet the new economic contingencies successively affecting ancient cultures. Directive correlation enables one to isolate early on in the multilinear sequences those key attributes which subsequently integrate into crucial new system formats with dramatic emergent properties. In this manner the directive correlation of such features as plant and animal domestication, polished stone axes, pottery, 'permanent' settlement can be studied converging and coalescing in a stable and coherent 'new' economy of immense potential (cf. fig. 68).

Enough has probably been covered to sketch the relevance of the general model to economic subsystems (postulates 1–16 and fig. 11, chapter 2). The strategy concept has been used increasingly in anthropological and archaeological analysis of subsistence, especially in tracing the trajectory of the successive equilibria of economic subsystems. The archaeologist can isolate and model the two main, related categories of strategy (i.e. subsistence organization and site location) within economic subsystems and it is to examples of these that we now turn.

(1) Subsistence organization strategies

Economic subsystems are characterized by the particular way in which combinations of resource staples are integrated in a stable mixed strategy. As an example of this from a contemporary society we may take Gould's (1963) study of the village of Jantilla in western Ghana. The local climate fluctuates between very wet and very dry years and the yields of the five staple crops (yams, maize, cassava, millet and

(a) Crop yields under alternative environmental strategies

Environmental strategies:	Wet year	Dry year
Crop yields per unit of area:		
Yams	82	11
Maize	61	49
Cassava	12	38
Millet	43	32
Hill-rice	30	71

(b) Stages in the determination of the optimum crop mix for a Ghanaian village by game-theory analysis

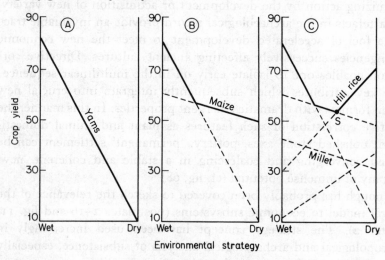

Environmental strategy

(c) Computation of optimum counter strategy.

Alternative crops:	Maize	Hill-rice
Yield under alternative environmental strategy:		
Wet year	61	30
Dry year	49	71
Difference in yield	12	41
Proportional difference	$\left\lvert \dfrac{41}{12-41} \right\rvert = 1 \cdot 4$	$\left\lvert \dfrac{12}{12-41} \right\rvert = 0 \cdot 4$
Optimum counter-strategy	77%	23%

Fig. 17a, b, c An analysis and model of the subsistence strategy of the Ghanaian village of Jantilla.
Source: Haggett, after Gould 1963, p. 293.

hill-rice) vary accordingly (fig. 17a). The problem faced by the villagers, as in all economies is

(a) whether to pursue a mainly high-yield but high-risk mixture of staples,

(b) whether to pursue a safe, low-risk but low-yield mixture,

(c) whether to pursue a prudential, intermediate strategy using the culture store of information on probable events and conditions (fig. 11).

First, given the two by five variables, Gould estimated the most prudential mixed crop strategy in the light of the conditions. A graph of crop yield was plotted for each crop against a scale running from extremely wet to extremely dry conditions – the resulting line sloping according to the trend of the crop towards high output in either wet or dry conditions. The superimposed output lines for the various crops intersect at several points but by following the highest-yield intersections, which form a concave curve (fig. 17b), it is possible to locate the saddle-point 'S' representing the best crop combination. This crop strategy gives that combination of staples which will yield on average the highest returns in a sequence of good and bad years – this is a prudent and minimax solution.

The proportional share of each crop in the minimax strategy is computed by comparing the yields of the crops in pairs of wet and dry years; then the wet and dry year difference for each crop is transferred to the other, which divided by the comparative difference between the crop pair gives indices (1·4 and 0·4) representing the proportional share of each crop in the array of crops (fig. 17c). In the Jantilla experiment the comparison of maize and hill-rice planting suggested a minimax strategy using 77 per cent maize and 23 per cent hill-rice which approximates the actual planting strategy used by the villagers. This example produced a hypothetical model for the most prudent agrarian strategy and then showed that this closely fitted the strategy in use – thus confirming our understanding of the basis of this mixture of crops and illustrating a case of a prudent satisficer strategy pursued when risky optimal, or less effective, satisficer blends might have been used. This raises the question of how such a mixed strategy would arise without a knowledge of calculation and minimax theory? Here again we have a clear indication of the decades of oscillating multilinear trial and error combinations, with a continuous feedback of output observations which have gradually converged upon the most practical solution (fig. 11) (Gould 1963; Haggett 1965, pp. 173–4).

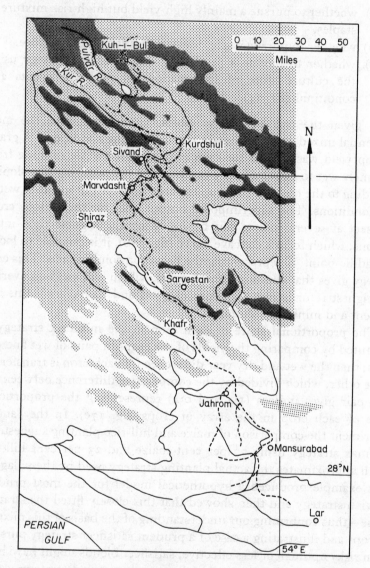

Fig. 18 The part of Fars province, South Persia, in which the
Basseri tribe migrates. Route shown by dotted line. Lighter
shading – above 5,000 ft; darker shading – above 8,000 ft
altitude.
Source: Barth 1959, p. 4.

Studies of other contemporary small-scale agricultural communities illustrate some of the general points already made about economic subsystems. These include the three basic levels of dynamic equilibrium (e.g. Freeman 1955; Conklin 1957) and the occurrence of annual oscillation in crop yields, which among slash-and-burn agricultural tribes can be quite drastic in effect (e.g. yields down by 50 per cent per acre among the Iban of Sarawak – Freeman 1955).

Another good example of a minimax strategy can be seen in the migratory cycle of the Arab pastoral nomads in South Persia (Barth 1959). This cycle of successive occupation of different pastures through an area of the greatest possible ecological diversity enables the Arabs to compensate for the poor resources of the desert and to avoid the extreme range of climatic variation found in that area. The markedly seasonal pastures are successively exploited by the nomads' flocks in a strict but flexible rotation – each tribe moving through a series of territories in its 'il-rah', or 'tribal road', covering a continuous strip from the low deserts in the south to the high mountains in the north (fig. 18). In any one locality there is a succession of occupants through the seasons and very few areas are ever unoccupied by anyone (fig. 19). The individual il-rah is therefore a rota or schedule of traditional rights to resources at certain places and times and the successive occupation of a given area by different tribes allows the full exploitation of the scanty resources, with short periods of rejuvenation and fallow in between. By this means the population capacity of the area as a whole may approach the carrying capacity of the individual component areas at the season of maximum, not minimum, productivity, a result of the rotational strategy which would be quite impossible if one tribe stayed at one locus for most of the year. Similar reasoning may be applied to agricultural economies which contain a mobile element associated with stock-breeding, particularly in areas of marked ecological diversity and constraints such as the Mediterranean (e.g. Barker 1972).

Mobility among extant hunter–fisher–gatherers is inextricably interrelated with the uneven distribution of economic resources through the year and across individual territories. Population aggregation and dispersion vary in frequency, range and scale in different societies but the most prudent general strategy is to maintain population levels below those supportable by optimal yields of food resources. This seems to be the long-term result of the need to maintain the equilibrium between the economic subsystem and the

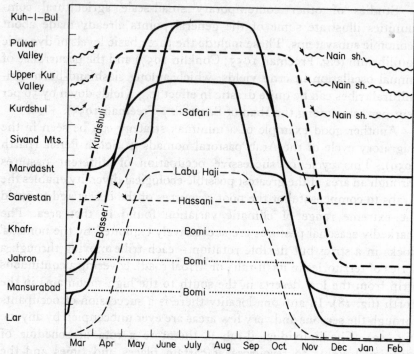

Fig. 19   An analysis and model of the subsistence strategy of the Basseri nomads over an annual cycle in which a succession of different tribal groups sequentially occupy the same chain of pastures; for localities see fig. 18. Solid line – schedule and route of the Basseri; heavy dashed line – Kurdshuli tribe; thin dashed lines – Arab tribes; wavy lines – other shepherds; small arrows – place and time where other tribes enter or leave the Basseri strip.
Source: Barth 1959, p. 6.

environment in the face of resource oscillations, especially those unpredictable periods of minimal, disastrous yields which last for more than a season or a single year (cf. Clarke 1972, fig. 1.15). Two contrasting studies of resource types and distribution, population aggregation and seasonal mobility may be seen in those of the Tulu-aqmiut Eskimos (Campbell 1968) and the Dobe !Kung Bushmen (Lee 1969).

Perhaps the nearest archaeological study comparable to Gould's game theory analysis of a subsistence strategy is by Jochim (1976), who attempts to derive a predictive model of hunter–fisher–gatherer economies from generalizations based on ethnographic data. The

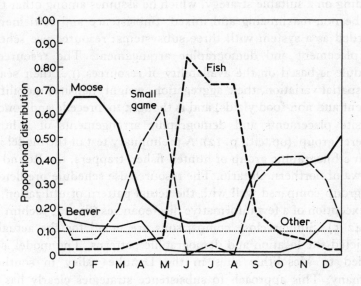

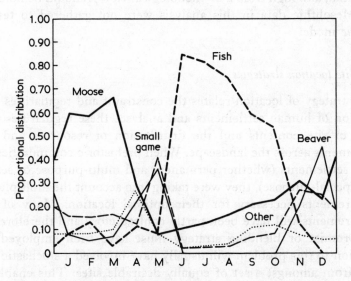

Fig. 20 A comparison of the predicted (top) and actual (bottom) resource use schedule of the Round Lake Ojibwa hunter–fisher–trappers of northern Ontario.
Source: Jochim 1976, pp. 43, 44.

author is trying to model the decision-making processes involved in deciding on a suitable strategy, which he assumes among other things will be non-maximizing and mixed. Subsistence and settlement are regarded as a system with three subsystems: resource use schedule, site placement and demographic arrangement. The resource use schedule is based on the availability of resources (i.e. their seasonal and spatial variation, their aggregation, weight, density, mobility, fat content and non-food yields) and is thought to 'precede and condition the site placements and demographic arrangements of a hunter–gatherer group' (op. cit., p. 12). A preliminary test of the model is run on an ethnographic group of hunter–fisher–trappers, the Round Lake Ojibwa of northern Ontario. The resource use schedule predicted for this group compared well with the actual pattern of utilization, with the exception of a few informative discrepancies (fig. 20; Jochim 1976, pp. 42–5). Similar close comparisons are noted for the actual and predicted site location and demographic patterns. The model is then applied to Mesolithic sites in the Danube valley in south-west Germany. This approach to subsistence strategies clearly has great potential, although from a methodological view it should be noted that the Mesolithic data in this analysis were not gathered to test this *specific* model.

(2) *Site location strategies*

The strategy of location relates the constraint and regularities in the location of human settlements and analyses these regularities in the light of site contents and the distribution of resources and other settlements across the landscape. When prehistoric communities sited their settlements (whether permanent and multi-purpose or seasonal and special-purpose), they were taking into account the multiplicity of requirements necessary for their optimal location. Many of these requirements will have been partly contradictory and therefore some compromise or blending strategy must have been employed. The solution to this problem will usually have involved a stochastic selection from amongst a set of equally desirable sites. This enables the archaeologist to study the regularity of site distribution and to try and define the particular constraints operating and their correlation with the sites.

This approach opens up such problems as the location of Neolithic sites in relation to soils, water, woodland and other resources, the dispersion of hunting camps at different seasons within limited territories, the relationships between open sites and cave sites – these are all susceptible to analysis in terms of a mixed strategy locational model. At the level of the individual site, the method of 'site-catchment analysis' has been developed to relate the subsistence practised to the resources available within an exploitable distance from the site. Vita-Finzi and Higgs (1970, p. 7) argue that 'the further the area is from the site, the less it is likely to be exploited, and the less rewarding is its exploitation (unless it is peculiarly productive) since the energy consumed in movement to and from the site will tend to cancel out that derived from the resource'. This principle is derived ultimately from the concentric ring model of land use developed by von Thünen in the last century and pursued in more detail over wider areas by Chisholm (1962). Chisholm's conclusions, as well as a number of ethnographic observations, lead Vita-Finzi and Higgs to propose that the exploitation territories of sedentary communities will lie within 5 km or an hour's walk from their sites and those of mobile hunter–gatherers within 10 km or two hours' walking distance (see also Higgs and Vita-Finzi 1972). Within these territories the resources available to prehistoric communities are defined in terms of land use categories (fig. 21), whose relative importance is taken as evidence for the subsistence strategy practised from individual sites. The analysis is then taken a step further in the reconstruction of economic exploitation systems linking a number of seasonally occupied sites (fig. 21; Barker 1972).

This method for the analysis of site location strategies has not escaped criticism of its basic assumptions and procedures. It would be useful to present a short summary of these to put the method into perspective.

(a) The basic von Thünen/Chisholm model of concentric exploitation zones needs further testing in the light of contemporary observations from rural Africa (Hodder and Orton 1976, p. 233).

(b) Changes in the local environment (e.g. deforestation, erosion, lowering of the water-table) over hundreds or, more often, thousands of years may negate the use of modern land use categories in the analysis of site territories (Hodder and Orton 1976, p. 233). A more optimistic method could be to reconstruct the prehistoric environment as fully as possible and still hope to identify economic constraints on site location (Flannery 1976, p. 95).

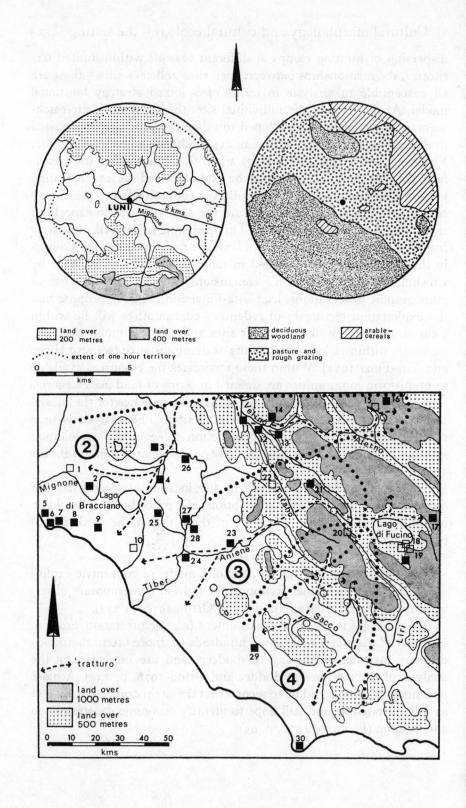

land over 200 metres   land over 400 metres   deciduous woodland   arable–cereals

••••• extent of one hour territory   pasture and rough grazing

0   5
kms

'tratturo'

land over 1000 metres

land over 500 metres

0   10   20   30   40   50
kms

(c) The relative importance of land use categories within a site territory does not necessarily correlate directly with the importance of animal or cereal exploitation at a particular site. If 'arable' land constitutes less than 10 per cent of the site territory, does this mean that the subsistence was *non*-agricultural? Flannery (1976, pp. 92–4) points out that many agricultural Pueblo sites in the American south-west have less than 10 per cent arable land within their 5 km territories. Given modern cereal yields in both Mesoamerica and the Near East, communities of up to fifty families could support themselves on the harvests from only 1 per cent of their total territories. Flannery argues that we should always consider the population which could have been supported at a specific site and that estimates should be made of the frequency of arable land *within* a site territory compared with that in the region as a whole. This last point has been developed by Zarky (1976) and Green (1973) who both use statistical (i.e. Chi-square, binomial and 't') tests to assess the significance of site location in relation to resource distribution. In this context the locations which were not chosen for settlement may provide the archaeologist with important 'negative' evidence.

(d) Related to (c) is the fact that different resource areas may have wide variations in productivity (Cassels 1972a). Site catchment analysis provides 'a qualitative description of arbitrary habitat *types* that are available around the site' but does not attempt to measure their 'extractive value' in terms of the relationship between primary and secondary productivity and the 'extractive efficiency' of the human cultural system (Foley 1977, p. 164).

(e) The specific location of individual sites may be determined by the relative mobility and security of resources rather than by those resources which are most important to the occupants of these sites

---

Fig. 21   An example of site catchment analysis. *Top.* Topography and modern land use plotted for the one hour and 5 km territories of the Eneolithic and Bronze Age site of Luni sul Mignone in central Etruria. *Bottom.* A reconstruction of three of the economic exploitation systems in the Bronze Age of southern Etruria and the Upper Velino, marked as (2), (3) and (4). Each consists of complementary resources in the coastal zone and the Apennine mountains, which are linked together by modern droveroads ('tratturo').
Open circles – Eneolithic burials; open squares – Eneolithic and Bronze Age settlement sites; closed squares – Bronze Age settlement sites. Number 1 is the site of Luni sul Mignone.
Source: Barker 1972, pp. 186, 194.

(Cassels 1972b, pp. 218–19; Jochim 1976, pp. 52–60). Generalizations from ethnography suggest that there may be three 'levels' or 'zones' of spatial organization around a hunter–gatherer site, a one-mile territory of non-mobile resources (e.g. water, wood, shelter, view), a five-mile territory of low mobility and relatively high security resources (e.g. vegetal foods, small game) and a fifteen-mile territory of high mobility resources (i.e. big game), so that while big game may be the most important resource to a site it will not determine its specific location (Jochim op. cit.).

(f) Lastly, site catchment analysis disregards the importance of non-subsistence factors in site location. Even considering subsistence it can be objected that published studies place too much emphasis on land use categories and not enough on such factors as shelter, topography and water supply (see Sullivan 1976): the last factor may be critical in agriculturally-marginal areas. The significance of rivers and streams for transport should not be underestimated (Cassels 1972b; Green 1973) and the availability of resources such as clays for pottery, salt, ores, flint and igneous stone is often neglected (but see Clarke 1972a, fig. 21.7; Flannery 1976, fig. 4.6). What also of the social ties between communities? In areas where there is regularity in site spacing but an *irregular* distribution of resources between the sites, one might argue for the greater importance of social factors in site location (Flannery 1976, p. 177 and fig. 6.9). If we accept the basic point outlined above that site location should be analysed in terms of mixed strategy models, then clearly site catchment analysis as originally conceived gives us only a partial insight into the general problem of settlement location and distribution.

This last point leads us conveniently into the analysis of settlement patterns and site location strategies in terms of factors such as markets, transport and administration – in short the provision of *services*. This is a field of archaeological analysis which has been revolutionized by the introduction of methods and concepts from plant ecology and geography. This involves the archaeologist in the analysis of settlement distributions to *define* different types of patterns (e.g. nearest-neighbour analysis) and then the application of models (e.g. Central-Place theory) in order to *interpret* these patterns. In this way the archaeologist can hope to relate site location to such factors as social and political hierarchies, trade and markets and resource localization (see Hodder and Orton 1976 for a full discussion and illustration of these studies). Only when we can interpret site location strategies within this broad framework, as well as in terms of specific resource constraints, will our understanding of the economic subsystem increase to a more productive level.

MATERIAL CULTURE SUBSYSTEM

Material culture constitutes an information subsystem of patterned constellations of artefacts which outline the behaviour patterns of a sociocultural system and embody that system's technology. It is pattern, or coherent structure, which passes the information and pattern is synonymous with correlated attributes.

The complexity of material culture as an information subsystem stems from its hierarchy of entities and their variety of information. It is helpful to think in terms of new, alternative, contradictive and redundant attributes, artefacts, assemblages and cultures, when focusing a study on any of these equilibrium interfaces involving any of these coupled entities. Attributes may be mutually incompatible, or alternatives, or redundant when clustered in certain artefacts. The functional cutting blade of a bronze dagger is incompatible with plastic ornament along its edge, but the dagger may have either punched or alternatively incised blade ornament, and its hilt may redundantly show rivets and binding notches. Similarly, at the artefact-type/artefact-type level it is apparent that the six-inch dagger is incompatible against the contradictive variety of the three-foot long rapier, or clothing pins may contradict fibulae and both may contradict buttons, the musket contradicts the variety of armour and so on. This essential need to reconcile conflicting variety is usually characterized by the analogy of stimulus and response – particularly well demonstrated in the moving equilibrium between offensive and defensive weapons, as studied, for example, by Yadin in Palestinian warfare from 3000–500 BC (Yadin 1963, pp. 1–31). This oscillating equilibrium is a fine example of an unstable dynamic equilibrium based on a feedback circuit connecting the aggressor and defender. Sometimes a stable equilibrium basin is reached even in armament – the armoured chariot and warrior of the Palestinian Bronze Age could only be countered by a similar array, likewise for a while the medieval knight and the World War II battle-tank could best be countered only by the same equipment. Noticeably, such saddle-points or metastable equilibria persist only as long as developing technology will allow. Quite apart from armament studies, the analysis of subsystems of coupled artefacts or attributes can best be set out in terms of the interaction of variety.

Feedback in the material culture subsystem usually results from the coupling existing within sociocultural systems and, like the other subsystems, feedback and complex feedback 'behaviour' is consequently inherent in the system and subsystems. The artefact population or population of types which one generation of a system used is its output and the input fed back into the phenotypic constitution of the next generation. In this way the attributes of the type population constantly adjust to the environment over successive generations – in the light of, or on the basis of, the former system trajectory (Σs, fig. 11). This inherent property accounts for the 'memory-like' capacity of sociocultural systems.

The material culture subsystem operates at the same three general levels and with the same variety of oscillating 'behaviour' as the other subsystems in the network. Dislocation between the subsystem and the environing system, between the various component subsystems, and between the attributes in the artefact subsystem is kept within the 'tolerance' of the whole sociocultural system by taking those transitions which appear to minimize the maximum amount of immediate contradiction and dislocation. Oscillating equilibrium at the highest level – between the whole material culture subsystem and the environing system – is often associated with 'response' to coupled climatic or similar environmental oscillations. The glacial/interglacial and tundra/forest oscillations of prehistory provide numerous examples of correlated changes in the material culture of the coupled cultural systems. At the middle level, oscillating equilibrium between the artefact subsystem and other subsystems occurs as induced feedback 'response' to fluctuations in the religious, psychological, social and economic subsystems. For example the 'trial and error' or 'hunt and seek' oscillations set up by the trajectory of the economic subsystem towards a suitable minimax strategy will often be accompanied by oscillating manifestations amongst the material culture. At the lowest level, the continuous stochastic fashion oscillations within the margins of the successive stable sets of transition possibilities is a very familiar quality found in most artefact-types, from women's fashions to grandfather clocks and gravestones (figs 38, 39, 47). The important role of all these oscillations 'scanning and searching' for advantageous variety and its subsequent incorporation in innovating and emergent arrangements has already been stressed.

Invention or innovation appears as the deliberate or accidental integration of networks of attributes exhibiting 'new' emergent properties, often by simply re-networking long existing system attributes. An alternative way of generating new variety capable of reconciling contradictive variety and dislocation is to borrow from the constant flow of diffusing variety reaching the system from without. Since the pooled innovation output of groups of cultures is correspondingly greater than the invention rate of an individual culture it follows that integration and modification of new variety from diffusion provides the great bulk of a culture system's variety, cumulatively gathered to minimize dislocations. In terms of strategy we can view the number of artefact-types and the relative percentage of each type produced as marking a particular mixed strategy blend to meet the total system requirements. To characterize a culture's sites by the constant recurrence of an assemblage varying around – 10 per cent burins, 20 per cent scrapers, 30 per cent blades, 30 per cent points and 10 per cent microliths – reflects a strategy adopted by that system in a given situation and reached by a limited but multilinear bundle of trajectories.

In the more detailed studies that follow the continuous movement and cycle of foci of accelerated change through the cultural subsystems will be confirmed in the preserved form of the material culture subsystem. These fossilized foci, or grouped foci forming nodes of change, are particularly important in defining the boundary or threshold between one type and another – at the artefact, assemblage and culture level. Thresholds separating one polythetic type from another polythetic type are cumulatively reached in the characteristic way by successively supplanting the essential and key attributes by newly integrated variants (examples (1) and (2), chapter 2). Birth and death in artefact-type systems, assemblage systems and culture systems amounts to no more than the anthropocentric view of cumulative change to successive thresholds separating polythetic systems of successive 'types' or syntactical formats. It is not possible to characterize whole cultures as inherently 'innovating' or 'conserving' when the foci of development in all cultural systems are constantly moving through some aspects of their framework. However, the concept of directive correlation enables us with hindsight to isolate those essential variables concerned in a system and more particularly those key variables that subsequently integrate from converging trajectories cumulatively to form a network of important emergent properties and potential (figs 26, 68).

IV   Environment as a system with subsystems

The aim of this final section is to continue the perspective view of the material culture subsystem as merely one network aspect, or component, within sociocultural systems coupled with environing systems. Once again, a study of environment as a system with subsystems would be sufficient to fill many individual works but here we are interested simply in showing that environment is a system with subsystems and relating our special archaeological interest to it. Our particular interest is centred around the concept of environment and culture as systems with inherent properties and particularly with the model portraying this relationship as a complex two-player game with inherent rules and permitting a variety of strategies.

Throughout the general discussion and the framing of the general model and its postulates we have used the term 'environment' in its broadest sense – sometimes amplified a little by coupling with it the term 'context'. The intention has been to convey simultaneously, in single statements, observations about systems within and coupled with environments, whether they be sociocultural systems and the enveloping physical environment, or artefacts and their assemblage context. The special case of artefact systems within material culture subsystem contexts is the special obsession of the archaeologist and is further developed in the chapters that follow, but it should not be forgotten that this is a special case within the general model. Similarly, the external environment of cultural systems is taken as including other cultural systems besides the category under study and in addition to the flora, fauna, geology and climate. Our use of the term environment implies total environment, including other sociocultural systems and also including those segments of reality not perceived or understood by the culture englobed. We are concerned therefore, with 'open' systems in which matter, energy and/or information is exchanged with the environment (Hall and Fagan 1956; Trigger 1971).

A great deal of space has so far been allocated to the discussion of cultural morphology and the sociocultural subsystems. However, in the earlier discussion of the three basic levels of equilibrium and oscillation found in the subsystems, the highest level was that between the subsystems and the environing system – that sector of the outer face of the whole system which especially communicated variety affecting particular subsystems. Remember, of course, that our divided model is an arbitrary view of particular aspects or circuit networks connecting a unitary entity (fig. 8). It therefore turns out that the highest level equilibrium in each subsystem is merely a particular aspect of the dynamic equilibrium coupling the whole system and the environing system – merely aspects of cultural ecology. Cultural ecology forms a useful frame for the study of whole sociocultural systems, the mutual relations between such systems and their environments, and the 'adaptive' changes of these systems; nevertheless, cultural ecology is inseparable from cultural morphology and the study of the subsystem attributes. Cultural ecology and cultural morphology are the outer and inner surfaces of the same sphere and constraint and regularity in the structure of one will be coupled with constraint and regularity in the other.

The environment of a culture system expresses the attributes external to that system and their varying and successive states in time and space. These environmental attributes may be partly perceived by the enclosed culture and partly not; from the culture's point of view some environmental attributes are inessential, some essential, and some are key attributes for that culture system. Conventionally, we organize the external environment under many headings but these can be roughly subsumed under – other sociocultural systems, fauna, flora, climate and geology; taking these terms in their broadest sense so that for example geography and topography are mere manifes-

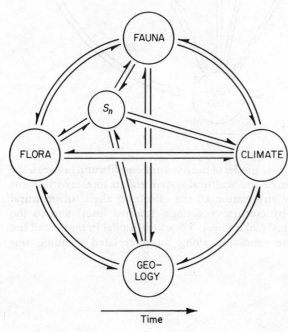

Fig. 22   A static and schematic model of the 'environmental system' of a sociocultural system which is excluded from the diagram. S_n here represents the summation of the effects of *other* alien sociocultural systems within the same interconnected territory.

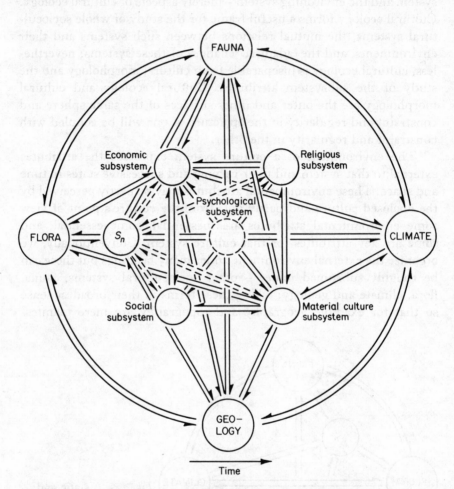

Fig. 23 A static and schematic model of the dynamic equilibrium between the subsystem networks of a single sociocultural system and its total environment system. S_n represents the summation of the effects of alien sociocultural systems connected to S by cultural 'coactions' (dashed lines) and to the environment by 'interactions' (solid lines). To set the model in motion all the components must oscillate randomly along intercorrelated trending trajectories.

tations of geology. These five subsystems are taken as interconnected networks of attributes forming complex wholes and themselves an ensemble within the environmental system (fig. 22). If we were to approach a rigorous treatment of the environmental system then each subsystem would merit a section portraying the nature of its attributes, the networking of those elements, the inherent properties of each subsystem and more besides; this task will not be attempted here.

So far we have artificially conceptualized sociocultural systems as five component subsystems coupled in a moving equilibrium with a five component environmental system (fig. 23). One way of crudely summing-up the dynamic equilibrium between sociocultural system S and environmental system E would be to express one as a function of the other 'buffered' by some expression (k) – S being a function of E if a change in E may produce a change in S and vice versa. This might simply be expressed as

$$E \rightleftharpoons (k) . S$$

The 'buffer' (k) in this expression would then represent the degree to which S is 'insulated' from changes in E, and conversely E from S. Now, in an earlier section it was suggested that the regulatory or insulatory capacity of a culture system is proportional to its variety and its capacity as a communication system – since only variety in cultural attributes can force down variety in outcomes in the environmental 'game'. It was therefore further suggested that a rough relative measure of the regulatory or insulatory control capacity of a culture system would be the number of differentiable artefact-types made by that system. Of course, allowances would have to be made for the archaeological loss of the organic artefacts and great care taken to use justifiable samples. Nevertheless, if the variety of types produced is a crude measure of the degree to which S is insulated from E then it is crudely an expression of (k) – which can now be conceptualized as a rough indicator of the 'degree of insulation' or 'degree of sophistication' based on a culture's technological level and variety in artefact-types. Thus (k) is related to the interposed regulator R and the size of the set of transition probabilities or degrees of freedom of the table of outcomes T (figs 6, 9, 11). Making allowances for the percentage of lost organic artefact-types, the archaeologist can still construct a very approximate picture of the cumulative increase in (k) – albeit by a fluctuating trajectory of which we are selecting only the successively most complex cultures (fig. 24).

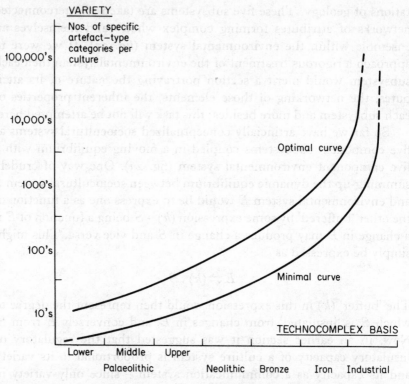

VARIETY

Nos. of specific
artefact−type
categories per
culture

100,000's

10,000's

1000's

100's

10's

Optimal curve

Minimal curve

TECHNOCOMPLEX BASIS

Lower   Middle   Upper
Palaeolithic   Neolithic   Bronze   Iron   Industrial

Fig. 24   A schematic diagram of the increased regulatory capacity 'R' of successively later culture systems, where 'R' is proportional to the cultures' variety content. The area between the two curves suggests the range of variety variation that might be expected in different examples of a given technocomplex configuration.

A more detailed version of the Palaeolithic parts of the curves in fig. 18 has been published by Isaac (1972a) and is reproduced here in fig. 25. It shows the increase in artefact-type categories used to characterize Palaeolithic stone industries in Atlantic Europe and Sub-Saharan Africa. Isaac also notes an increase in standardization of tool forms and in the numbers of distinct stone industries during the Pleistocene (e.g. 1972a, fig. 6 for African industries). Putting these observations together, he draws the following conclusion about regulation and communication in Palaeolithic cultural systems:

It is suspected that the acceleration in the rate of change, the extent of local differentiation and the degree of artefact standardization can be considered together as symptomatic of a great increase in

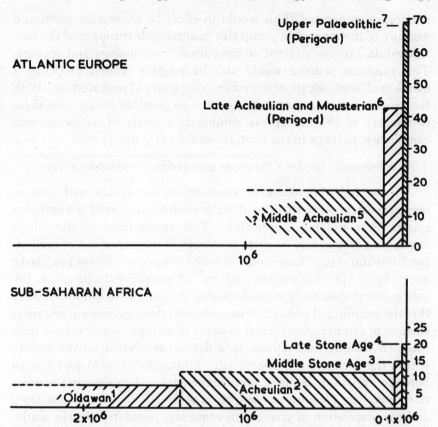

Fig. 25 The increased regularity capacity 'R' of successively later culture systems – a practical example. The increase in categories of artefact-types during the Palaeolithic in Atlantic Europe and Sub-Saharan Africa. Source: Isaac 1972a, p. 394.

the complexity of cultural rule systems, and since the complexity of rule systems is liable to have been limited in large measure by the efficacy of the communication system, these changes imply that during the Upper Pleistocene, language crossed a critical threshold in its information capacity and precision of expression (1972a, pp. 395–6).

Another statistic which may become available from the great increase in archaeological data is some approximate estimate of the average number of individuals maintained in a culture's dispersed components throughout most of the year – excluding special and temporary gatherings. This would in effect be an average minimum measure of the maximum group size maintainable throughout the year and would express a vector of the cultural morphology and ecology. This minimax statistic would also be roughly related to (k) as a measure of 'sophistication' or rather 'complexity of organization'. With the great increase in data it might even be possible to combine these two facets of (k) to express comparative levels of socioeconomic complexity, perhaps in the form (Steward 1955, pp. 43–63)

$$\text{Socioeconomic level} = \sqrt{\text{Minimax group size. Artefact-type variety}}$$

To conclude this section on environment as a system with subsystems, we can observe that the physical environment itself is a complex system in a moving equilibrium. The equilibrium of the whole environing system and its parts is subject to the same kind of oscillating fluctuations (e.g. for a model of food resource oscillation see Clarke 1972, fig. 1.15), dislocations and foci of accelerated change as the sociocultural systems that reside within it. Indeed we can understand that the coupling of cultural systems within their environing system is such as to require the cultural systems to change in accordance with these environing fluctuations, to a degree dependent on the variety within the sociocultural system (e.g. McBurney's (1968) correlations between variations in stone tool frequencies and in animal resources during the late Pleistocene occupation of the Ali Tappeh cave in Iran; and the association of changes in economy, population levels, settlement patterns and social integration with climatic and vegetational change and soil erosion in the American south-west c. AD 1100–1300, summarized in Hill 1970, pp. 82–96). Thus in so far as a culture is an adaptation to a specific environment, a change in the environment may produce changes in the culture to maintain equilibrium inversely proportional to the culture's technological level.[4]

Notes

(1) Needham (1975, pp. 359–60) accepts the *possibility* of the evolution of social subsystems by regular transformations, as in the Semi-Markovian model developed here by the author. But in considering Murdock's methods of analysis, Needham notes that 'by the introduction of an additional discriminating feature (viz. prescriptive alliance) that Murdock did not take into account, it can be shown that a number of societies in the sample can be placed in quite different relative positions from those which they occupy on Murdock's premises'.

(2) An influential study of regularities in social organization, which became more popular after the first publication of this volume, was Service's *Primitive Social Organisation* (1962). In this he defined an evolutionary sequence of increasingly complex types of social organization, from the hunting-and-gathering 'band' through the agricultural 'tribe' and 'chiefdom' to the 'state'. Although Service later recanted on this general model of social organization (1971), it has been applied in both the New World (e.g. Sanders and Price 1968) and the Old World (e.g. Renfrew 1972). Chiefdoms have attracted particular attention and Renfrew has attempted to identify the main features of this model in Neolithic Wessex (1973a), prehistoric Malta (1973b) and Mycenaean Greece (1972). He has even recognized a distinction between 'group-oriented' (Wessex, Malta) and 'individualizing' (e.g. Greece, Bronze Age Central Europe) chiefdoms (1974). Critics of this approach to prehistoric social organization (e.g. Tringham in Renfrew 1974) have emphasized the disparity between the model itself and the archaeological contexts to which it has been applied and the apparent 'invisibility' of many traits of anthropological chiefdoms in the archaeological record. In its defence it can be argued that, like Fried's (1967) study, it does enable the archaeologist to think about 'the possible range of social organizations behind his data' (above, p. 109). After all the 'correlated constraint in variety' (p. 107) which led to regularities in contemporary small-scale societies may have led also to analogous regularities in the past.

In addition to this analogue model, archaeologists have attempted to analyse prehistoric social organization by using two complementary data-sets. First a number of American archaeologists have been instrumental in analysing settlements and trying to test models of residence and descent patterns derived from anthropological studies. The basic assumption involved is that patterning in human behaviour which results from the existence of residence, descent or other special purpose groups, will be reflected in the patterning which the archaeologist can detect in the artefacts he studies from excavated settlements (Deetz 1968). Given this position, the appropriate analyses have to be computer-processed and statistically tested in order to define patterns of association (e.g. use of the Chi-square statistic) and covariation (use of factor analysis) among the artefacts. The resulting artefactual patterns are then assessed, residence units isolated and sometimes even descent groups inferred. Such analyses have been pursued *between* phases of a site's occupation (Deetz 1965), within occupation phases (Longacre 1968, 1970; Hill 1968, 1970) and through time between different sites in a localized area (Whallon 1968).

While these studies have been cumulatively stimulating, their underlying theory has been open to increasing criticism. As far as residence and descent groups are concerned, Allen and Richardson (1971) stress the difference between the 'ideal' rules and the actual operation of societies: thus choices are made by individuals as to where they wish to reside after marriage and these choices may be influenced by such variables as economics and property ownership. Similarly they doubt whether completely *discrete* descent groups can be recognized. On these grounds the interpretations of two localized matrilineal descent groups at the Carter Ranch Pueblo (Longacre, see above) and five localized uxorilocal residence units at Broken K Pueblo (Hill, see above) can be laid open to doubt. The effect of rebuilding, rubbish disposal, complex patterns of ceramic motif transmission between communities and generations and social mobility upon within-site artefact patterning has been discussed by Stanislawski (1973, 1974). He argues that 'the localization of ceramic types in prehistoric and modern Pueblos is more likely to be a matter of the localization of "ad hoc" work groups of neighbours and friends, including both kin and non-kin, than clan residences or descent localization' (1973, p. 121). Taking all these criticisms into consideration, it seems clear that the assumptions and theory underlying 'social' analyses of prehistoric and historic settlements need rethinking and further testing if the stimulus of the original pioneering studies is to be fulfilled.

The second broad approach to social organization in the past has been by the analysis of patterning in burial practices. The assumption which is basic to this approach is that a society will practise several different methods of disposing of its dead and that the forms which these methods take will be correlated, in some measurable way, with the status of the deceased individuals. This assumption is derived from cross-cultural anthropological observations (Saxe 1970; Binford 1971) and focuses attention upon the covariation of such features as population structure (e.g. age and sex distributions), grave goods (e.g. spatial variability in deposition of 'exotic' raw materials) and burial methods (e.g. relative energy expenditure, spatial patterning). A review of examples of this approach can be found in Chapman (1977). Recent studies have also introduced a more complex systemic approach to the use of burial data for measuring changes in social structure and organization in the past (Tainter 1977).

As with 'social' studies of settlements, this is another expanding research area within archaeology and as such it has again attracted criticism. The confidence with which archaeologists can associate burial practices with social status has been attacked on ethnographic grounds (Ucko 1969). Clearly also the interpretation of complex patterns of association and covariation within burial data in terms of particular anthropologically-recorded patterns of social organization is a field mined with potentially circular arguments. But coupled with data derived from settlement excavation, there seems room for optimism that the social analysis of burial data will expand into productive new areas within the next decade. In this context it would seem that the *spatial* analysis of burials within cemeteries and cemeteries related to settlements and other variables (e.g. topography, economy) is an open research field.

(3) In this discussion the author followed the predominant thought of the time in equating religion solely with 'beliefs relating to the supernatural'.

However, more recent anthropological research by Rappaport (1968, 1971a, 1971b) among the Tsembaga group of the Maring speaking peoples of New Guinea has stressed the relationship of religion and ritual in general to other subsystems and the local environment. Rappaport does not argue against the partly psychological or sociological functions of rituals in giving security to human populations who are unable to control all the events and processes of their environment (1968, p. 2). Like the author he also views rituals in terms of information communication and in this respect there is a great similarity between animal and human behaviour: rituals, after all, are only 'conventionalized acts of display' (1971a, p. 63). But where he differs is in his interpretation of rituals as *regulating mechanisms* (chapter 2, pp. 52–4) within an ecosystem. Thus he argues that among other things the ritual cycles of the Tsembaga help to distribute surpluses of pork through local and regional populations, to regulate the consumption of non-domesticated animals, to enable inter-group trading or exchange, to maintain the local environment and to regulate the frequency of local fighting or warfare (e.g. 1968, pp. 3–4; 1971a).

Rappaport notes an alternating cycle of periods of local warfare and peace, with the latter being marked by a ritual ('Kaiko') in which the ancestors are thanked for their aid during the fighting. While the Tsembaga themselves may see these rituals solely in terms of the propitiation of their ancestors' spirits, their function as regulatory mechanisms is also argued by Rappaport. Fighting is forbidden during these rituals, so in this way the frequency of warfare is controlled. Furthermore the slaughter of pigs which takes place during the ritual period (ten years on average) helps to regulate the size of pig populations, reduce local tension (caused by the damage done by increasing numbers of pigs to fences, gardens etc.), preserve the local environment, distribute food supplies and reduce population pressure and competition for land (cf. Reichel–Dolmatoff's (1976) study of spirits and cosmology among the Tukano Indians of Columbia: note especially the belief that the spirits of game animals cause sickness – another example of a regulator acting on the exploitation of local fauna).

In discussing communication, Rappaport also distinguishes religious from other types of ritual. The essential distinction as he sees it, is that religious rituals are endowed with *sanctity*: 'the quality of unquestionable truthfulness imputed by the faithful to unverifiable propositions' (1971a, p. 69). To put it another way 'to sanctify sentences is to certify them' (1971b, p. 29). Since religious messages are accepted as 'true', they contribute to the maintenance of order within human societies (1971a, p. 69), especially by reducing the conflict between the needs and desires of the individual and those of society (1971b, p. 36).

Attempts to apply Rappaport's theoretical framework to the analysis of religion in prehistoric societies have so far been rare. In one study Drennan (1976) has linked the development of religious rituals as a mechanism for securing the acceptance of social conventions with the evolution of complex societies in Formative Mesoamerica.

At the same time it should be noted that Rappaport has been criticized by other anthropologists for being too 'materialistic' or 'functionalist' in his interpretations. Friedman (1974, pp. 459–60) doubts whether the Tsembaga ritual cycle acts as a regulator since both human and pig populations were well below carrying capacity when Rappaport studied the 'Kaiko'. Friedman prefers to emphasize the part played by social relationships (e.g. prestigious exchange) in the frequency and scale of pig sacrifices. Similarly McArthur (1974) views the pig sacrifices in terms of the prestige gained by the possession of large herds which can be given to other individuals or groups to cancel existing exchange obligations. As for Rappaport's interpretation of the ritual being a means of preventing pigs from damaging the local environment and increasing tension between social groups, McArthur points out that it is the *deliberate accumulation* of the pig herds during the years leading up to the 'Kaiko' ceremony that creates this situation. Indeed large amounts of pork consumed at the ritual are nutritionally wasted and thus the redistribution function seems less convincing. Finally it is noted that in cases where fighting has led to refugee groups arriving in a new area soon after the beginning of a ritual cycle, there may be 10–20 years of over-population and possible environmental damage in that area. This is one example of a disadvantageous result of the ritual. In spite of these criticisms, Rappaport's study still offers the archaeologist a source of stimulus in his study of prehistoric societies in terms of dynamic systems, with all the characteristics given in chapter 2.

(4) The 'systemic approach' to cultural change has enjoyed special popularity among American archaeologists during the last decade. The comparative lack of systemic studies and the more hostile reception within British archaeology may be explained partly in terms of the different ways in which the concepts of systems theory and cybernetics have been introduced into the subject. In America the main impetus was provided by Lewis Binford (e.g. 1962, 1965), who developed the view that culture should be studied as a whole system and that its primary function was an adaptive one:

> ... as archaeologists we are faced with the methodological task of isolating extinct sociocultural systems as the most appropriate unit for the study of the evolutionary processes which result in cultural similarities and differences. If we view culture as man's extrasomatic means of adaptation, we must isolate and define the ecological setting of any given sociocultural system, not only with respect to the points of articulation with the physical and biological environment, but also with the points of articulation with the sociocultural environment. It is suggested that changes in the ecological setting of any given systems are the prime causative situations activating processes of cultural change (Binford 1964, reprinted in Binford 1972, pp. 159–60).

The main roots of this approach lay in the evolutionary anthropology of Leslie White, as Binford has acknowledged (1972). The increasing popularity of Whitean anthropology, to which archaeological students were exposed as part of their university education, coupled with Binford's dynamic impact in the 1960s has ensured the 'success' of the systemic approach within American archaeology. In Britain, the anthropological perspective has been largely absent from general archaeological work and university syllabus. It can be argued that the more abstract presentation of systems theory given by David Clarke in 1968, with its detailed discussion of concepts such as equilibrium, homeostasis and adaptation (chapters 2 and 3), was less well received in Britain because of the lack of this reinforcing anthropological theory: without it the systems approach may have seemed too 'distant' from the archaeologist's concern with the study of human behaviour in the past.

One soon becomes aware of this differential popularity and application of systems theory in America and Britain when examining the results of a decade of research within archaeology. We must ask how concepts and models derived from systems theory and cybernetics have been applied to archaeological problems. At the same time criticisms of specific applications or concepts (e.g. homeostasis, adaptation), or indeed of the general concept of systems analysis, must be considered so that the subject may be put in perspective. The remaining part of this note will illustrate and discuss these issues, so that the theory and concepts presented in chapters 2 and 3 can be considered within the context of subsequent research.

In a recent review article, Plog (1975) has discussed five ways in which systems theory has been used in archaeology: as a theory of archaeology, as a source of concepts, models and propositions/principles and as an approach to explanation. It is instructive to use this framework and consider each of these ways in turn, along with reference to specific examples of research (not all of which are present in Plog's publication).

(a) *A theory of archaeology*. The need for a central theory of archaeology, expressed in systemic terms and concerned with isolating regularities in archaeological data, is the aim of *Analytical Archaeology* (e.g. see above pp. xv–xvii).

(b) *A source of concepts*. As Plog indicates (1975, p. 213) the use of concepts such as homeostasis, feedback and adaptation in archaeological research has been associated with an underlying concern to isolate *processes* of change in the past. The emphasis is now on generalizing rather than particularistic studies and on relationships between important variables rather than simply their individual attributes. In this context systems analysis has enabled archaeologists to reconceptualize old problems and look at them in new ways (cf. Doran 1970, p. 294). Increasing familiarity with demographic, ethnographic, ethnological and agricultural studies has led the archaeologist to become more aware of the role of population as an important variable in cultural change. Homeostatic controls on the size of animal populations in relation to the local carrying capacity of resources are already widely known (Wynne-Edwards 1962). Studies of hunter–gatherer groups have extended our knowledge of *cultural* means of regulating population sizes (Hayden 1972) and Boserup's (1965) study of agricultural growth has established the view that population acts as an independent variable, rather than one which is dependent on developments in agricultural techniques. This new perspective on population was one of the bases of Binford's (1968b) reanalysis of the origins of food production in the Near East. In this he argued that population growth occurred in that area as a by-product of increased sedentism based on the exploitation of more nucleated animal resources. Sedentism was held to be responsible for the reduced necessity for cultural means of regulating population size. Thus the regulatory controls had broken down and the population-natural resources equilibrium was disturbed. Excess population from sedentary areas would 'bud off' into more marginal zones with less favourable resources, thus maintaining equilibrium in the optimal areas but creating population pressure beyond them. The result of this pressure was the emergence of methods of food production which would raise the carrying capacity of the marginal areas and enable them to support the higher population levels. In a more recent paper Binford and Chasko (1976) have examined the relationship of increased fertility, sedentism and dietary changes among the Nunamiut Eskimos.

In another study of the development of food production, this time in Mesoamerica, Flannery (1968) has used the concept of positive feedback, or more specifically 'deviation-amplifying mutual causal processes', to explain the emergence of maize and bean cultivation. The same author (1972) has also analysed the evolution of civilizations, and more particularly the state, in terms of two systemic processes: *segregation* (i.e. differentiation and specialization of subsystems) and *centralization* (i.e. the degree of linkage between subsystems). These processes are argued to be universal in state evolution, as are the mechanisms by which they take place (i.e. 'promotion' and 'linearization'), but the actual socio-environmental stresses (e.g. warfare, trade, population growth, irrigation) that set these mechanisms in action are held to be local in origin. Once again emphasis has been placed on general processes rather than particular developments in an attempt to understand regularities in cultural change.

The concepts of information theory which David Clarke derived from Ashby's work (1956) and applied in his model of culture as a system have been little developed in subsequent research. However the concepts of 'variety' and 'constraint' have been used by Rathje (1973) in analysing Lowland Classic Maya cultural change.

(c) *A source of models*. Under this heading Plog (1975, pp. 216–18) includes the use of flow charts and simulation models, whose usage has accompanied systems theory into archaeological research. Flow charts are, of course, a by-product of the impact of computers on archaeology. They represent sets of relationships between different variables and can be used at various scales, with varying degrees of specificity and with a range of qualitative to fully quantitative data. In addition they can be efficient methods of reducing a vast amount of information or a complicated interpretation into a readily comprehensible form. Excellent examples of this quality can be found in Newcomb's model of a Danish medieval parish, Kemp's chart showing the quantified flow of energy in an Eskimo hunting society (both reproduced in Clarke 1972, figs 1.10 and 1.11) and Thomas's (1972, fig. 17.3) model of the Shoshonean economic cycle based upon data derived from earlier work by Julian Steward. In the terminology of Chorley and Kennedy (1971) Newcomb's work is an example of a *morphological* system (i.e. specifying the structural relationships between the different components/variables) while Kemp's flow chàrt represents a *cascading* system (i.e. a quantitative analysis of energy exchanges or the flow of information). Archaeologists have also used flow charts to represent processes of classification or interpretation, for example Clarke's (1972, fig. 1.14) model for his classification of British beaker pottery and Schiffer's (1976, figs 9.4–9.8) models for his classification of chipped stone artefacts from the Joint site in Hay Hollow valley, Arizona. In addition Schiffer (1976, figs. 4.1–4.2) has used flow charts to represent the general processes through which material culture is incorporated in the archaeological record.

Thomas' (1972) model of the Shoshonean economic cycle leads us conveniently into the field of simulation studies. These form a growing research area in which certain variables (e.g. economy, population statistics) are specified in a computer programme which produces a simulated behavioural pattern to be compared with actual archaeological data. Thomas states that his model, BASIN I, is 'designed to simulate deposition of archaeological artefacts resulting from a posited ethnographic pattern'. He views the Shoshonean settlement pattern as a system which has two properties: *structure* and *behaviour*. The structure is represented in the flow chart mentioned above as a 'functioning system in statistical equilibrium'. In considering the system's behaviour, Thomas follows David Clarke's distinction (this volume, pp. 70–2) between 'inessential', 'essential' and 'key' attributes or variables in looking at different resource subsystems (e.g. piñon nuts, jack rabbits, antelope) and uses a Markov chain model (this volume pp. 63–6) to simulate temporal and spatial variation in the yields of piñon nuts. This variation is then related to variation in Shoshonean subsistence strategies. The simulation was found to compare well with Steward's previously untested model of the Shoshonean economic cycle. A Markovian model has also been used by Reynolds (1976) in studying Pre-Classic settlements in a 40-mile stretch of the Upper Grijalva River in Chiapas state, Mexico. A more ambitious simulation study within a fully systemic framework has been published by Wobst (1974): in this he uses Monte Carlo techniques to analyse Pleistocene population units, simulating up to 400 years of population variation by means of specified age, sex, fertility and mortality variation. In particular he is interested in the effects of such factors as monogamy, polygyny, incest taboos and exogamy on equilibrium sizes in Palaeolithic human populations. The ultimate aim of this study is to predict the size and longevity of Palaeolithic social units and to develop appropriate sampling models for the archaeological investigation of Palaeolithic sites in given areas. Finally Plog (1975, pp.

217–18) outlines Zubrow's simulation model relating population and carrying capacity, which are used in his research in the Hay Hollow valley, Arizona (e.g. Zubrow 1971, 1975; see below pp. 444–6).

Markovian simulations are, of course, part of a wider series of *stochastic* models (Clarke 1972, pp. 19–29; Doran and Hodson 1975, pp. 295–8) which do not necessarily have to be explicitly formulated within a systemic framework. We will return to these types of simulation when considering artefact/settlement distribution patterns in chapter 10.

(d) *A source of propositions/principles.* Some archaeologists have preferred to look at archaeological problems from a general systemic perspective: instead of breaking their systems down into analytical subsystems ('economic', 'social' etc.) they have analysed their data in terms of general propositions or principles. Thus Flannery (1972) has looked at the origins of the state in terms of segregation and centralization processes and Plog (1974) has constructed a dynamic equilibrium model of cultural growth in the Basketmaker–Pueblo transition in Arizona in terms of changes in the relationships between population, system differentiation and integration (cf. Flannery) and energy exchanges. Tainter (1977) has also recently applied general systemic principles in the analysis of Woodland burial practices.

(e) *An approach to explanation.* This last category of systemic research in archaeology overlaps with (b) the use of systems concepts. Both the Binford (1968b) and Flannery (1968, 1972) papers mentioned above are attempts to explain such complex problems as the origins of agriculture and civilization in terms of systemic processes. Similarly Renfrew (1972) has used the concepts of systems theory to construct an explanation for the local development of the Bronze Age civilization in the Aegean. After presenting the main cultural sequences in each local area he analyses changes from *c.* 6000–1000 BC in terms of five subsystems (subsistence, technological, social, projective/symbolic and trade/communication – 1972, pp. 225–475). Interactions *between* these subsystems are then specified and the emergence of civilization explained in terms of the operation of the 'multiplier effect', a special type of positive feedback (1972, pp. 476–504).

The range of systemic applications in archaeology which have been presented here should not be allowed to obscure disagreement over their current success and potential. The more realistic proponents of the systemic approach themselves recognize that much of the research outlined above is still at a preliminary, experimental stage (Plog 1975, p. 220). Even among those researching in general systems theory there are reservations about the practicality of its application in other subjects, as it is claimed that there is still much intensive research to be undertaken (Klir, quoted in Doran and Hodson 1975, p. 337). Critics within archaeology have argued that systemic concepts are not as revolutionary as has been claimed (Higgs and Jarman 1975, p. 3) and that there is a disparity between these concepts and the empirical data of archaeology. Either there is supposed to be insufficient data to reconstruct, for example, social organization or religious subsystems or, to put it another way, 'archaeological data are insufficient for the mathematics of systems theory to be made to work' (Doran and Hodson 1975, p. 339; cf. Steiger 1971, p. 69). This then reduces systems theory to the status of a general analogy, a method for clearer thinking rather than an incisive analytical tool (cf. von Bertalanffy's (1962) criticism of systemic research in biology and psychology). On the other hand it cannot be denied that the systemic approach has enabled archaeologists to reconceptualize old problems and in particular to emphasize relationships and processes of change rather than preoccupying themselves with linear causality and particularistic artefactual studies.

The two concepts in systemic archaeological research which have been most criticized are homeostasis and adaptation. Wood and Matson (1973) have distinguished two models of sociocultural systems, the *homeostatic* and *complex adaptive* systems. The latter is derived from such systems theorists as Buckley (1967), von Bertalanffy (1962) and Maruyama (1963). It is defined as an open system exhibiting continuous (though varying rates of) change, the source of which may be both within and outside the system as a whole. This change may not only be counteracted by negative feedback mechanisms, thus restoring the system's equilibrium, but it may also be *amplified* by positive feedback (e.g. Flannery 1968; Renfrew 1972). In contrast the homeostatic model (Ashby 1956) emphasizes the part played by regulatory mechanisms (i.e. negative feedback) in maintaining system stability. Positive feedback will only occur when these regulatory mechanisms fail and a new equilibrium level will be reached. Thus periods of change alternate with periods of stability (the latter being the 'normal' condition) and the source of change is held to be *external* to the system (see Hill 1971). Wood and Matson comment that this homeostatic model is functionalist in origin, unsuitable in dealing with positive feedback processes and 'if we insist that change comes from outside of the system, we then run the risk of a self-fulfilling prophecy; that is, if we look hard enough for a changing environmental variable, we shall surely find one' (1973, pp. 681–2).

In a similar vein, Bennett (1975, 1976) has argued that the homeostatic model is inappropriate for sociocultural systems characterized by long-term and sometimes more dynamic changes. Thus he writes that

the persistent developmental or exponential tendency in human behaviour, visible wherever the time span observed is long enough, should be evidence that the regularity and return to preexisting states characteristic of homeostatic movement are temporary phenomena that are useful in analysing limited sequences but not for understanding the basics of species behaviour (1976, p. 848).

The homeostatic model has been based, Bennett argues, on short-term observation by anthropologists among 'the relatively isolated, relatively slow to change, low-energy society' (1975, p. 296) and is an inappropriate model for periods of more rapid and complex cultural changes. However, current archaeological thinking (e.g. Isaac 1972b, p. 186) would seem to support the existence of fairly stable cultural traditions associated with low population densities and a low frequency of social interaction over much of the early Pleistocene period. In this case the application of a homeostatic model seems to be supported by the archaeological evidence. Indeed it could be suggested that the homeostatic model is more appropriate to studies of early Pleistocene cultural evolution and the complex adaptive model of greater relevance to the rapid increase in social and cultural complexity of the late and post-Pleistocene periods.

Adaptation has been a key concept in archaeological and anthropological systemic research. Binford (1962), following Leslie White, defined culture as 'man's extrasomatic means of adaptation' and most systemic archaeologists have used the concept, either specifically or loosely in their work. More recently, doubts have been raised about its usage. For example, Burnham (1973) supports the general point that culture can be adaptive, citing the case of the Eskimos, but he then raises a number of important questions:

> It is only at a finer level of analysis that difficulties arise in discussing culture as man's adaptive dimension. Is all of culture positively adaptive or are there maladaptive traits? How would one assess and measure the adaptive advantages and disadvantages of a particular trait in a particular culture? (1973, p. 93)

He further argues that in order for the concept of adaptation to be meaningful, it is the responsibility of archaeologists and anthropologists to specify the exact cultural mechanism(s) which are 'realistic "equivalent(s) of natural selection" or, for that matter, equivalents to any of the other key components of the biological evolutionary process' (1973, p. 94; cf. Plog 1974, p. 48).

The questions asked of the use of concepts such as homeostasis and adaptation in cultural studies will undoubtedly continue, as will the debate over the types of systems model which best approximate our archaeological data. This is a healthy debate and archaeologists' own knowledge of systems theory has been greatly extended since the first publication of this volume. As I have tried to illustrate above, the range of systemic studies has increased, but the key problem which faces workers in this field at the present is whether they can, or need to, extend systems theory beyond the stage of being a useful vehicle for reconceptualizing archaeological problems. With its emphasis on processes and complex interrelationships it has enabled archaeologists to postulate mechanisms of change which no longer rely upon single explanations such as 'invasion' or 'diffusion'. But is this sufficient for significant progress to be made in our knowledge of human behaviour in the past? This is the challenge facing proponents of systems theory in contemporary archaeology.

4 Material culture systems
– attribute and artefact

> The classes or sets of attributes that are employed in cluster
> analysis to codify formal variation within a specific group of
> artefacts constitute what is here termed an attribute system,
> JAMES R. SACKETT 1966, p. 359

I Introduction

The preceding chapters have attempted to introduce some ideas and
models which might be advantageously integrated in the discipline of
analytical archaeology. The annual output of archaeological data and
the advent of techniques with novel and fundamental incisive powers
make it quite apparent that archaeological interpretation is entering
new, exciting and difficult dimensions. It is equally apparent that the
use of these new techniques demands a more coherent and rigorous
framework of general conceptual scaffolding than that which the
archaeologist has hitherto bothered to erect. This contemporary situation healthily forces the archaeologist's attention to focus on the
neglected general theory that underlies his discipline and its procedures. It is time for archaeology to move from the status of an
intuitively acquired craft towards that of an explicit discipline.

The brief scrutiny of the history of archaeology introduced many
of the elementary plagues which still beset the struggles of the embryo
discipline – the diversity of opinions, aims, definitions, and
terminology, and the pseudo-problems which arise from these ailments. In an attempt to remedy this situation and at the same time to
rise to the challenge of the new methodology we have spent some time
developing general models – including a model for archaeological procedure (fig. 2), a polythetic model for archaeological entities (fig. 3),
and a system model for archaeological processes (fig. 11). In particular, emphasis has been centred upon cultural systems as quite
specific and peculiar kinds of system with certain inherent qualities
and innate 'behaviour' dependent upon their common structure,
rather than the customary emphasis upon particular cultures with

particular attribute values. Part of this procedure has involved a conception of sociocultural systems as elaborate behavioural information systems.

Since each sociocultural system is a unitary whole, and because the sub-division of such an entity into component subsystems is merely an arbitrary conceptualization of different aspects of the same network, it appears that the same set of general postulates may be relevant in each arbitrary subsystem. Material culture as a structured hierarchy of micro-systems is merely one such arbitrary aspect or subsystem, and it therefore displays the same set of inherent qualities. Archaeology, as a discipline concerned with the recovery, systematic description and study of ancient material culture can accordingly be expected to detect traces of this same inherent 'behaviour' defined in the postulates of the general model (postulates 1–16, chapter 2). It was the intention of the preceding chapters to attempt an outline of this 'behaviour' in order that we might now proceed to investigate its archaeological counterpart and its capacity for the analysis of data, the synthesis of information, and the prediction of results.

The succeeding chapters extend the archaeological part of the earlier general discussion. In each chapter that follows, successively higher levels of archaeological entities are defined in terms of the lower level components already isolated. This will enable us to gradually erect a developing series of definitions and a hierarchy of archaeological entities defined by archaeological attributes in archaeological material. Every one of these archaeological entities is composed of aggregates of lower-level components and as such they can be treated as micro-systems coupled within particular sociocultural systems.

One important corollary of the aggregate or composite nature of archaeological entities is that such populations exhibit their own specific 'behavioural' characteristics which are more complex than the simple sum of the characteristics of the components and more predictable than that of the individual components. One of the main tasks therefore, is to detect and trace these persistent regularity patterns in archaeological data and to use these predictable regularities as tests for real data. If the real data displays the regularity predicted then it should fulfil some already established conditions. If the real data departs from the predicted pattern then some conditions are not fulfilled and the nature of the discrepancy may suggest the divergent conditions responsible for the anomaly.

In the preliminary discussion of the aims of archaeology a set of tentative objectives was put forward as being compatible with the

nature of archaeological data and the nature of the discipline (chapter
1, section IV). These objectives suggested that there were fundamental
entities and processes that pervade the diverse material and that these
must be defined and explored before any of the higher aims could be
approached legitimately. These entities exist at increasingly higher
levels of organization, with an increasing value in terms of the
information that they can predict about the items put in them. We will
start, therefore, with the definition of an archaeological attribute and
then proceed to integrate that in the higher concept of the artefact.
The successive stages will take us from the attribute to the artefact, the
type, the assemblage, the culture, the culture group and the technocomplex. At each level we must define the entity involved and
laboriously investigate the implications of the definitions. With the
entities thus defined one can investigate the main processes which act
upon them and their resulting transformation patterns. In this way we
can hope to gain some knowledge of the general 'behaviour' of our
material in order both to be able to predict general patterning and to
learn from significant deviations from that patterning.

Although the various entities include such diverse categories as
artefacts at one level and culture groups at another, it will increasingly
emerge that the relationships between adjacent entity levels are strikingly regular. This regularity in the syntax of entity relationships
arises partly from the unity of material culture systems as mere aspects
of sociocultural systems and partly from the aggregate or population
quality of entities clustering lower-level components.

It will be found that entities composed of populations of
components exhibit general properties shared by many other population systems, including:

(1) The population entity is a unit system of components coupled
    in some environmental context.
(2) Emergent characteristics may appear in the overall system
    which are not found in the individual components forming the
    population.
(3) A definite structure and composition, stipulated for a given
    moment but varying with changing space and time.
(4) The population entity is ontogenetic. It may exhibit –
    (i) the quantitative growth and oscillation in numbers of
        components, from a few into myriads, ultimately followed
        by a decline in numbers to disappearance – giving the
        analogy of birth, maturity and death;

(ii) the quantitative growth and oscillation in numbers of the entity itself – again giving the impression of the birth, maturity and death of a population;

(iii) the entity system may manifest a quite different, qualitative ontogeny in terms of a change trajectory in which the components are successively replaced in such a way as to eventually transform the whole system from state to state – suggesting the birth, maturity and death of a given system state with limiting thresholds.

(5) The population entity has a 'heredity' – an antecedent trajectory. We may distinguish between the trajectory of the whole, fully coherent entity and the pre-existing bundle of trajectories of the components directively correlated towards the subsequent formation of the entity.

(6) An important characteristic of the population entity, as opposed to a single element, is that of numerical distribution in space and time – dispersion. Dispersion and the pattern of the dispersion is a group attribute of very great importance, since by altering the network of dispersed components the inherent characteristics of the whole system may be modified. Dispersion may affect the population of the entity itself, or the components within the entity, or both (Allee *et al.* 1950).

II   Attribute and artefact systems

Our immediate concern is directed towards the definition and investigation of the lowest levels of entity recognized by the archaeologist – the attribute and the artefact. The most tangible product of hominid behaviour is the material artefact – any object modified by a set of humanly imposed attributes. This gives us our first archaeological definition and brings us face to face with the raw material underlying the study of prehistory – the artefacts. However, the definition has already introduced us to an even more fundamental or lower-level entity – the set of attributes, traits, or characteristics that represent the particular modification imposed by hominid action. Although the artefact is the most common form in which the solid results of hominid activity are fossilized it is itself a compound of lower-level entities – the attributes, in this respect resembling the structure of everyday substances – elaborate chemical compounds the elements of which rarely, if ever, occur naturally in an independent state.

The behavioural significance of artefacts and their attributes can be appreciated if we conceptualize the individual artefact as occupying the common focus of two cones of directed activities or behaviour (fig. 26). In this figure the artefact is the focused result, directively cor-

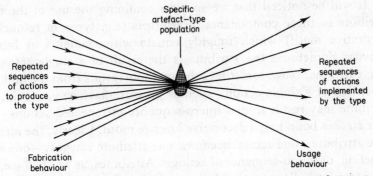

Fig. 26 The behavioural significance of specific artefact-type populations as the sum of a specific set of fabrication behaviour and of a specific usage behaviour implied by the design. The fabrication behaviour selectively and directively correlates the set of attributes and their ranges which together define the artefact-type.

relating a whole set of actions, sequences of actions, or behaviour necessary to materialize the abstract conception in the maker's mind. The very manufacture of the artefact directively correlates sets of actions and their resultant attributes and these complexes of attributes will remain so correlated as long as the artefact survives intact (Sommerhoff 1950, p. 187). At the same time, the artefact and its attributes are so constituted by the maker that they are patterned to perform and consequently imply yet another sequence of intended behaviour, integrating the artefact in other repeated actions and sequences of actions.

Each and every artefact therefore embodies a set of behaviour necessary for its fabrication and another set of behaviour implied by its fabrication – its usage. The artefact's attribute variety is consequently severely constrained by these percepta in the maker's mind and populations of the same kinds of artefact necessarily exhibit the regularities of repeatedly correlated clusters of attributes. Such clusters of selected and correlated attributes constitute a 'message' which still conveys information about the intentions of the fabricator.[1] The 'noise' is apparent in those uncorrelated attributes not essential to the purposes of the artefact maker and which consequently vary in an irregular and uncoordinated manner within that artefact population (fig. 62). Once again we recognize the hierarchy of inessential, essential and key attributes which partly depend on the reference frame of the study and to which we must repeatedly return.

It will be noticed that we are now confining the use of the term attribute to those components of artefacts (e.g. types of retouch or decorative motif) which roughly equate with elements of human activity. Sometimes the attribute is the result of a single action – a single hammer blow, sometimes the attribute results from the multiple repetition of a single action – such as pressure-flaking; yet again, the attribute may result from a micro-sequence of repeated actions – the four strokes bounding a decorative lozenge motif. Clearly, the ideal of 'one attribute – one action' becomes 'one attribute category – one kind of action, or micro-sequence of actions'. Attributes, as we shall see, are not of precisely the same level of complexity when compared one with another; they are not quite such elementally pure units as one would like.

However, what we are attempting to do is to define attribute entities in such a way that they are analytically useful and equate *roughly* at the same broad level of implied behaviour complexity. The real basis of objectivity is to be arbitrary in a narrowly confined and defined manner; to restrict the inevitable error to a finer range than will imperil the desired accuracy of the analysis. Our attributes may not be entities of precisely the same level of complexity one with another but they will all congregate about a mean level of complexity quite unlike the level implied for such entities as 'artefact-types'. From this point onwards we will restrict the use of the term 'attribute' to fossil behavioural elements of the level of single kinds of actions, or micro-sequences of actions. Henceforth such 'attributes' are the basis for our arbitrarily defined entity – the 'archaeological attribute', shortened to 'attribute' for convenience, with the wider use of the term attribute as a system component at any level replaced by such terms as 'trait' or 'character'.

In this gradual construction of a viable definition for archaeological attributes we have still some elements to bond together. For if we are to construct our hierarchy of definitions with care and precision we must not fail to secure this foundation. Fortunately, most of the necessary components have been discussed at length in earlier sections. These earlier sections have already pointed out that:

(1) Every artefact, indeed every material object, contains an infinity of attributes or variables and therefore of possible systems networking these attributes (Ashby 1956, p. 39).

(2) It is therefore necessary to select the particular attributes and the particular system that we wish to study – given the problem that we are investigating.

(3) Our definitions of 'artefact' and 'archaeology' tell us that the archaeologist is primarily concerned with those specific and contextual attributes imposed or selected-for by hominid action (see above pp. 14–15). On occasions only an unbiased analysis will show whether border-line attributes were selected-for but the majority of relevant attributes will be obvious.

(4) In order to avoid confusion and to maintain an homogeneous level of complexity the relevant attributes should be broken down into logically irreducible and independent variables. These attributes should be 'epistemically independent' (Sommerhoff 1950, p. 86).

(5) Preliminary analysis will separate the artefact attributes into:

   (a) inessential attributes – those which are not relevant to the study in hand and which consequently do not figure in the system as defined, and those attributes which are constant throughout;

   (b) essential attributes – those variables which are part of the relevant system and whose values or states may change as part of the changing system. Detailed analysis of the essential or relevant attributes may then isolate certain –

   (c) key attributes – those correlated clusters of attributes in the system whose successive values or states co-vary in some specific relationship with successive values of other similar attributes.

It is crucial to observe that the selection of attributes is to some extent arbitrary, that at least a preliminary analysis is needed to determine which are the essential and inessential attributes, and above all, that the key attributes cannot be accurately defined until after detailed analysis of the data. The intuitive and arbitrary 'spotting' of key attributes in a system, before proper analysis, leads to the arbitrary definition of group boundaries based on 'type-fossils'. Such set markers may be ultimately established but the 'typical' or the key attributes must be the terminal result of the analysis – not the premise of the opening gambit.[2]

Given the restricted level at which we wish to use the entity we can now approximately define an archaeological attribute as – *a logically irreducible character of two or more states, acting as an independent variable within a specific frame of reference*. The frame of reference being in this case an arbitrarily specified system of artefact characters. Such a definition includes all the behavioural attributes of an artefact whether they are specific or contextual, natural or artificial. The specific attributes refer to physical qualities of the artefact and the contextual attributes to the artefact's stratigraphic and geographic location and associations – in so far as these may have been humanly imposed. It must be remembered however, that a behavioural attribute can be imposed as much by the careful selection of natural raw material as by direct hominid alteration. The preferential selection of certain limited pebble sizes, shapes, and materials for the manufacture of handaxes and the deliberately selective preservation of the natural cortex on the butts of some of these tools – all of these attributes reflect hominid behaviour but themselves remain natural features.

Each attribute then is equivalent to a piece of premeditated and deliberate hominid behaviour – the behaviour being deliberate even should the attribute or the artefact be an accidental by-product.

It is important that our properly defined attribute should be 'logically irreducible' since this precaution ensures that we are comparing entities of a similar level of complexity and that our so-called attribute is not simply a manifestation of several component characters subsumed within it.[3] In this respect it would be incorrect to register as fundamental attributes the shape, size, volume, weight, and material of handaxes say, since the volume is a function of the size and shape, and the weight a function of the volume and material. This case is absurdly obvious but such errors may more easily creep in if quantitative ratios are being used and the denominator or numerator are unwittingly repeated (Roe 1964, fig. 15). The attributes should be independent variables and not varying as the direct mathematical function of other attributes already noted. Similarly, when analysing the decorative art styles of pottery, metalwork, or other materials one must be careful to separate the essential motif attributes from other attributes noting the relative positions of the motifs; otherwise one would fail to note that two different art styles might have a similar range of motifs but quite different systems of arranging them.

The second feature of the definition of an archaeological attribute emphasized that it should be a character of two or more states in relation to the artefact system under analysis. Most attributes can be reduced to characters of two states in relation to their system – the attribute may be either present or absent. However, archaeologists do not generally recognize that there are several other varieties of attribute and attribute state, which must vitally affect the comparison of artefacts and the assessment of their degree of similarity. If one artefact is imperfect, or damaged in such a way as to remove an attribute then this artefact must be noted for comparative purposes as having a state of No Comparison (NC) for this character; it must be realized that is not the same state as either the attribute being absent or present but rather a special state of its own – with different implications (Sokal and Sneath 1963, p. 74).

The attribute definition also caters specifically for an attribute having 'two or more' states. Two states are immediately necessary to allow for presence/absence comparisons but the 'or more' aspect reveals that attributes may sometimes be treated as loci at which several alternative attribute-states may be found. This may occur if the attribute is a size dimension and the measurement – say the artefact length – can be given as falling within any bracket, each bracket forming a possible state at that locus. This means that the particular artefact can have a variety of particular attribute states within the entity of that attribute, as though the attribute itself was composed of alternative sub-characters. This kind of attribute is referred to as a *multistate attribute* or character and if measurement is involved it becomes a *quantitative multistate attribute*. Alternatively, there also exist *qualitative multistate characters* such that several alternative qualitative states of the same attribute could be present. It could be noted, for example, that retouch was present or absent from a certain artefact locus; if retouch was present it could be coarse retouch, soft-hammer retouch, pressure-flake retouch, scraper retouch, blunting retouch and so on – these would all constitute possible states of the multistate attribute 'retouch at locus X' of which only one state can be present at the locus X of each artefact. Examples of quantitative multistate attributes include measurements like – handaxe length, flint blade thickness, the height of a pot, or the length of a sword blade. Qualitative multistate attributes include the categories of flint retouch, the permissible shapes of an artefact edge, the location of decoration on artefacts, or the catalogue of alternative motifs used in a given art-style. Quantitative and qualitative attributes also raise the difficult problem of the correct statistical procedure for handling 'discrete variables' with quite separate and distinct value categories, like the number of rivets in a sword hilt, as opposed to 'continuous variables' which may take any mathematical value, including a fractional one, such as the length of an artefact. There is thus a basic difference between discrete and continuous attributes but for many purposes this can be avoided by chopping the continuous attribute range into discrete sub-ranges.

Examples. An attribute list for Aurignacian flint blade end-scrapers from an assemblage in the Abri Castanet (Dordogne) has been published by Sackett (1966), who defined eight multistate attributes, both quantitative and qualitative, discrete and continuous (fig. 27). In dealing with British Beaker pottery Clarke (1962) compiled an attribute list of twenty-one multistate attribute headings, containing a total of thirty-nine attributes, as the basis for a computer classification into chronological and regional types.

The main work of an archaeologist hinges on his ability to compare numbers of artefacts or assemblages and to assess their relative degrees of similarity one with another. In this work the artefact attributes are of fundamental importance. We now see that when comparing one artefact with another the archaeologist is intuitively comparing their respective attribute assemblages; we further realize that this is not simply a presence/absence matter. The attribute can be absent from artefact *A* and present in artefact *B*, or vice-versa, or it can be present in both *A* and *B*, or absent in both *A* and *B*. Alternatively, the attribute can be Not Comparable in *A*, in *B*, or in both, because of damage or loss. Yet again, the attribute may take a multiplicity of states within a quantitative or qualitative multistate range – taking one alternative state in *A* and the same attribute but a different state in *B*. Altogether it can be appreciated that there are not only a great variety of kinds of attribute state but that these can be combined to give a confusingly large range of kinds of similarity, even between pairs of artefacts. This same problem recurs at every level of our hierarchy of entities, from the comparison of type with type, assemblage with assemblage, culture with culture, and so on; at all these levels we must seek solutions in the explicit methods of numerical taxonomy which underlie the intuitive methods that archaeologists usually apply.

Clusters of repeatedly and closely intercorrelated attributes can often be noted as recurrent 'attribute complexes'. These attribute complexes form an entity of a higher level of complexity than the

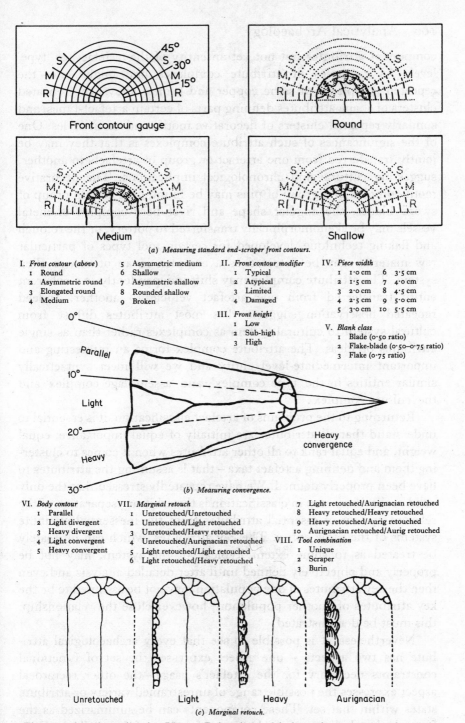

I. Front contour (above)
1. Round
2. Asymmetric round
3. Elongated round
4. Medium
5. Asymmetric medium
6. Shallow
7. Asymmetric shallow
8. Rounded shallow
9. Broken

II. Front contour modifier
1. Typical
2. Atypical
3. Limited
4. Damaged

III. Front height
1. Low
2. Sub-high
3. High

IV. Piece width
1. 1·0 cm
2. 1·5 cm
3. 2·0 cm
4. 2·5 cm
5. 3·0 cm
6. 3·5 cm
7. 4·0 cm
8. 4·5 cm
9. 5·0 cm
10. 5·5 cm

V. Blank class
1. Blade (0·50 ratio)
2. Flake-blade (0·50–0·75 ratio)
3. Flake (0·75 ratio)

(a) Measuring standard end-scraper front contours.

(b) Measuring convergence.

VI. Body contour
1. Parallel
2. Light divergent
3. Heavy divergent
4. Light convergent
5. Heavy convergent

VII. Marginal retouch
1. Unretouched/Unretouched
2. Unretouched/Light retouched
3. Unretouched/Heavy retouched
4. Unretouched/Aurignacian retouched
5. Light retouched/Light retouched
6. Light retouched/Heavy retouched
7. Light retouched/Aurignacian retouched
8. Heavy retouched/Heavy retouched
9. Heavy retouched/Aurig retouched
10. Aurignacian retouched/Aurig retouched

VIII. Tool combination
1. Unique
2. Scraper
3. Burin

(c) Marginal retouch.

Fig. 27 Attribute list for Upper Palaeolithic blade end-scrapers under eight multistate headings.

Source: Sackett 1966, pp. 362–4.

component attributes but not yet an entity of the 'artefact' or 'type' level. As examples of attribute complexes one might cite – the repeated complexes of some copper and bronze alloys, the repeated clusters of shape attributes defining parts of certain artefact-types, and similarly repeated clusters of decorative motifs and motif styles. One of the significances of such attribute complexes is that they may be jointly transferred from one artefact or group of artefacts to another, suggesting cultural and chronological implications. The decorative motif complex of a group of pins may be found on a certain group of sword blades, the angular shape and rivet boss complex of metal vessels may be skeuomorphically transferred to pottery, or the retouch and flaking technique developed for certain tool types of particular raw material may be detected as a complex in an otherwise alien system. The attribute complex may shift independently as a coherent entity transferred from one artefact vehicle to another. Indeed repeated observation suggests that most attributes diffuse from cultural system to cultural system as complexes rather than as single attributes or ideas. The attribute complex forms an interesting and important intermediate-level entity and we will meet syntactically similar entities in the 'type complex', and 'assemblage complex' and the 'culture complex'.

Returning to the problems of artefact classification, it is essential to understand that all attributes are initially of equal importance, equal weight, and equal rank to all other attributes when it comes to clustering them and defining artefact taxa – that is assuming the attributes to have been properly defined. We have repeatedly stressed that the only valid preliminary step in classification is the arbitrary separation of the relevant system of essential attributes from the inessential attribute systems of the same entity. The key attributes, which can ultimately be treated as to some extent 'typical' of the system, may not be properly and objectively defined until after detailed analysis and even then the key attributes of one population may not be assumed to be the key attributes of another population; however close the relationship, this must be demonstrated.

Nevertheless, it is possible to see that every archaeological attribute has two aspects – one aspect expresses the set of functional constraints necessary for the artefact's usage – the other reciprocal aspect expresses the possible range of unrestrained variety or attribute states within that set. These components can be summarized as the functional and idiosyncratic degrees of freedom of the attribute. Even the most functional attribute has some idiosyncratic degree of freedom; an axe blade must vary between certain limits in respect of its length, breadth, thickness, and weight attributes, but within these limits there is freedom of choice. Likewise, even the most idiosyncratic attribute has some functional restrictions; the decoration on pottery provides a very wide field for idiosyncratic choice but still falls within functional limits. We can, if we wish, simplify the real situation and polarize our attributes between functional attributes at one extreme and idiosyncratic attributes at the other; this would be a dangerous procedure but it may on occasions serve as a shorthand notation for the real position (compare Isaac's (1972b, pp. 176–7) distinction between the roles of 'function' and 'tradition' in stone tool production). The great importance of these attribute aspects for the prehistorian is the different quality of information provided by clusterings of functional attributes on one hand and clusterings of idiosyncratic attributes on another. The accuracy and incisiveness of the archaeologist's interpretation of artefact patterns in social terms depends on a proper understanding of this partial polarity.

At the moment we must concern ourselves with the fact that attributes have no existence independent of the artefact and always exist in correlated clusters. This clustered nature of the attributes defining artefacts provides us with an important analytical tool-kit, a methodology not only useful at this level, but at every succeeding level in the entity hierarchy outlined in this volume. The opening section of this chapter showed that an important characteristic of population entities is the numerical distribution in space and time of their components – their dispersion pattern (section 1, 6). The proper technique for the analysis of populations and their numerical distribution is of course statistical methodology (Doran and Hodson 1975).

The main concern of this section has been directed towards the definition and investigation of the lowest levels of entity recognized by the archaeologist – the attribute and the artefact. It has emerged that we can usefully define and visualize four successively more complex entity levels: the attribute state, attribute, attribute complex and artefact. These entities will now enable us to integrate populations of such units in the meaningful definition of yet higher level entities, each successive level disclosing more emergent information about the inherent 'behaviour' and implications of such entity systems. At the low level at which we have been currently working, the return in terms of unexpected information or patterning must be expected to be equally low – but more will follow. For the moment we will turn to the 'behaviour' of artefact attribute systems from homogeneous and contemporary spatial phases and then to the 'behaviour' of the same systems in time-depth trajectories.

III   Phase pattern regularities

The archaeologist can rarely, if ever, date excavated strata and their assemblages to precise points in time – all archaeological dates are relative, even the so-called absolute isotope decay datings. Not only are these archaeological dates relative but they also have variable probability ranges and even these loose 'fixed points' are not widely available to locate most artefact assemblages securely in time. To add to these complications, there is also rarely any possibility for discriminating between an assemblage laid down in a six-inch stratum over fifty years and an assemblage laid down in another six-inch stratum over three hundred years – without circularly appealing to the taxonomy of the artefacts themselves.

It follows from these observations that a spatially contemporaneous assemblage is very rare in archaeology – the excavated assemblage unit is almost always a time-trajectory segment in which time change is always a contaminating factor (fig. 61). The nearest approach to a unit segment that can be achieved is to take the set of taxonomically near-homogeneous assemblage states which have a higher mutual affinity within the unit than with any one assemblage beyond that cluster's borders. This arbitrary and unequal unit represents the thinnest recognizable slice of an artefact or assemblage time-trajectory, a compressed and distorted unit which we will call a 'phase' (Willey and Phillips 1958, p. 22).

A phase within an artefact or assemblage time-trajectory is thus an archaeological unit constituting the smallest taxonomically homogeneous set of entity states which may be distinguished within a minimal time-slice of that entity's system continuum. The key and essential variable states will distinguish such a unit from earlier and later manifestations of that entity's system trajectory and from those of other similar systems. The phase unit is applicable to the system trajectory of every level of archaeological entity – from the attribute to the culture group – representing as it does a space of even rate of change between nodes of accelerated change in the system variables. Entity time-depth trajectories will then be composed of stacked and multilinear phase units – most of which will be unknown and where the units themselves must be assumed to be tilted time plane discs rather than the horizontal discs that we usually conceptualize (fig. 61). This has the important corollary that the phase population will be graded fractions of successive horizon populations drawn unequally from the entity continuum, with some elements from early horizons, many from a contemporary set and a few from late horizons – a sampling factor which may account for some skew distribution curves for phase assemblage elements (fig. 30).

In this study we will therefore recognize two major archaeological dimensions – the phase and the tradition; these dimensions are the nearest archaeological equivalents to contemporary space and time respectively but they are not identical equivalents and may not be interchanged without considerable care. The tradition unit is the multilinear time-trajectory of any level of archaeological entity system and is not here restricted to the time depth of cultural assemblages. The phase and tradition units may be applied to the attribute, artefact, type, assemblage, culture, culture group and technocomplex entity levels.

It can be assumed, then, that in any analysis of archaeological entities the dimensions of time and space will both be present, with their differing implications for the orientation of the data. For this reason horizontal or contemporary spatial classification in prehistoric cultural situations is often an illusory aim, except in so far as one can attempt to take a negligibly thick horizon or an infinitely small time segment – and in most cases this is likely to reflect a century or more of compressed development. The idea of primarily classifying the data in different vertical traditions seems a more appropriate primary aim, although secondarily these traditions may be internally sub-divided into oblique phases of changing levels of similarity. The archaeological entity should first of all be attributed by the affinity of its essential format to a particular vertical time-trajectory or tradition – and then to a particular phase, on the joint basis of chronology and internal affinity.

From the point of view of the archaeologist the classification of the changing phenomena would therefore seem best expressed by a vertical time-depth classification, based on an objectively established chronological and affinity framework. Otherwise the archaeologist tends to forget that his distribution maps of artefacts and cultures represent fragmentary and distorted palimpsests of hundreds of years

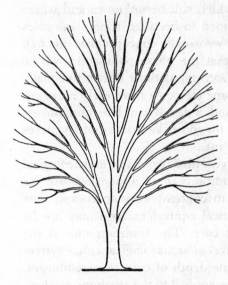

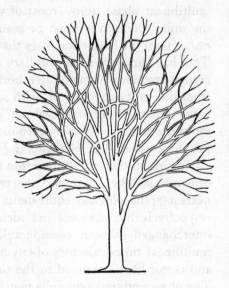

Fig. 28a The tree of organic phylogeny with its characteristic forking
branch pattern.
Source: Kroeber 1948, p. 260.

Fig. 28b The tree of cultural phylogeny with *its* characteristic reticulated branch pattern.
Source: Kroeber 1948, p. 260.

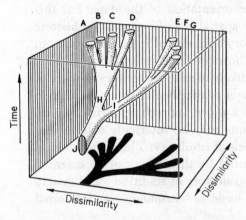

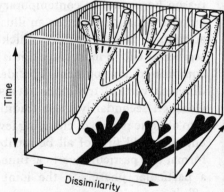

Fig. 28c A section of an organic phylogenetic tree in three dimensions, one of
time and two of phenetic dissimilarity.
The 'shadow' of the tree on the base
indicates the purely phenetic relationships
of the branches.
Source: Sokal and Sneath 1963, p. 234.

Fig. 28d A section of a cultural phylogenetic tree in three dimensions, one
of time and two of phenetic dissimilarity. The 'shadow' of the tree on
the base indicates the purely phenetic
relationships of the branches.

of successively changing distribution areas – histograms and distribution maps are time-compressed composites; indeed some Palaeolithic distributions are probably composites of tens of thousands of years.

The taxonomic assessment of affinity between entities will suggest the limited number of possible transformation trajectories which might link the network of particular entities in passing time. Great care must then be taken to avoid the danger of interpreting affinity relationships simply as descent relationships – a condition further complicated by the peculiar nature of branch convergence and fusion found in cultural phylogeny (fig. 28). This problem can only be controlled by providing an adequate chronological frame and by postulating multiple alternative hypotheses of development to link the established degree of affinity between sets of the entities under investigation (chapter 11, II).

Having established that what we mean by phase is in reality space with a little bit of time, as opposed to space with a great deal of successive time – we may return to the problem of how attributes behave in large numbers in a given phase population. If we take a large number of artefacts of one type from one homogeneous assemblage, limited in time and space, and if we study the pattern of dispersion of individual attributes in that series of artefacts, we usually find a skew, or normal, unimodal scatter pattern (figs 29, 30). The pattern is unimodal because there were repeated attempts to reproduce a commonly-held concept of a desired artefact form. Because these attempted facsimiles were randomly deflected in various attribute values by a large number of divergent factors, e.g. intractability of the raw material, its lack of homogeneity, the distributions should in theory express normal probability curves, and in practice approximations to the normal curve do occur (fig. 30). However, there are a number of overriding factors which individually, or as a group, conspire to make skew curves more frequent in 'real' data and this raises certain problems in interpretation and analytical treatment (fig. 30).

Distribution curves may vary from the 'normal curve' in three main features – skewness, kurtosis, and multimodality. A skew curve is one in which the peak, or mode, is displaced to right or left of the centre, piling-up the values at one end of the scale and thus modifying the bilateral symmetry of the normal curve (fig. 29). Kurtosis occurs when the curve is excessively flattened, depressing the curve from the normal distribution pattern. Finally, a multimodal curve simply has

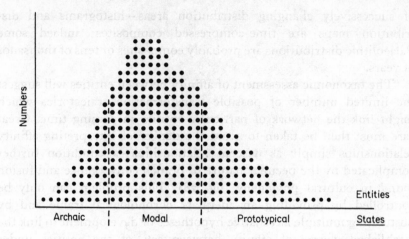

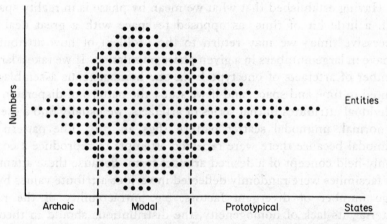

Fig. 29   A unimodal skew distribution of artefact or attribute states within a phase assemblage – two alternative portrayals of the same data. The subdivision of the distribution into archaic, modal, prototypical sections is only valid in cases where a moving mode may be traced; see figs 41, 47.

many separate peaks, from two upwards, and usually indicates the presence of more than one population of attributes each with its own mode (fig. 32). Distribution curves that differ significantly from the 'normal probability curve' occur quite frequently in archaeological studies under certain conditions. An understanding of these conditions will therefore help reveal or predict the particular factors operating in a particular case. At the moment we are preoccupied with the conditions which give rise to skew curves instead of normal ones in the problem already cited (fig. 30).

There are four factors that may singly or jointly give rise to a skew curve for an homogeneous population of a given attribute.

Illusory skewness – sometimes the initial and intuitive assessment of a curve's skew shape may be modified when careful testing shows that its departure from the 'normal' is not statistically significant. This happens most frequently with curves having too few class intervals or from a false impression of skewness induced by the stepped histogram, or angular polygon outline. Many archaeological skew curves may be found not to depart significantly from the normal distribution upon adequate testing (fig. 30).

Sampling errors arise very frequently and from various causes. The obvious sampling errors are: too small a sample, a non-random sample accidentally emphasizing some population aspect too strongly, a non-homogeneous sample accidentally drawing from more than one

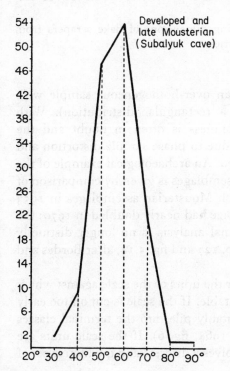

Developed and late Mousterian (Subalyuk cave)

Fig. 30a   Diagram plotting the dispersion of Hungarian Mousterian flint leaf-points in terms of the angle of the edge retouch. Source: Vertes 1960, p. 42.

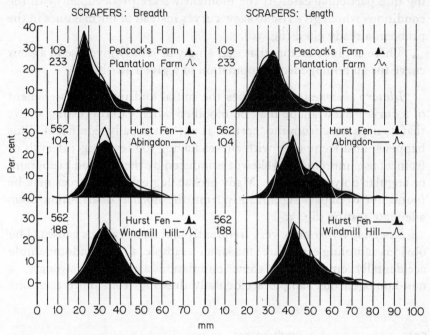

Fig. 30b   Diagram illustrating varying dimensions of flake scrapers from different British Neolithic flint industries.
Source: Clark 1960, p. 219.

discrete population (fig. 31), or an over-homogeneous sample with identical values (approximating a rectangular distribution). With archaeological samples the randomness is often in doubt and the unavoidable lack of homogeneity due to phase sample distortion and compression has already been noted. An archaeological example of the effect of sample size on artefact assemblages is given by comparison of the frequency of racloirs in French Mousterian assemblages in 1953 and when the assemblage sample size had nearly doubled in 1970: the suggested bimodality in the original analysis is no longer distinctly visible (Doran and Hodson 1975, p. 127 and fig. 5.14, after Bordes and de Sonneville-Bordes).

Scale errors arise if the range or the units of the scale against which the population is plotted are unsuitable. If the scale is cut off too early at either end the values will inevitably pile into the terminal classes with a resulting asymmetry (Roe 1964, fig. 6). If the scale units are unequal or if the scale of units involves a discrete and qualitative set of

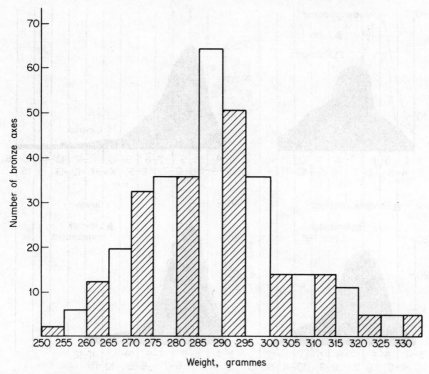

Fig. 30c Diagram plotting the dispersion of 320 Breton Late Bronze Age socketed axes from two hoards (la Bellière and Saint-Bugan) in terms of their weight.
Source: Briard 1965, p. 273.

attributes, skewness may arise from the unit inequality or from unsuitable scale sequences of qualitative values.

Special factors arise from conditions that peculiarly affect the attribute population in question. It has been suggested, for example, that human error may repeatedly stray in one direction rather than in a truly random fashion. For instance, populations of pressure-flaked projectile heads often show a larger number of points thicker than the mean rather than thinner – possibly suggesting that there might be a better accidental probability of making the points too thick than too thin – when they would break-up in manufacture. Alternatively it is conceivable that a craftsman may skew his error in the more desirable of two directions – it often being preferable to make things too thick, too strong, or too large rather than the converse.

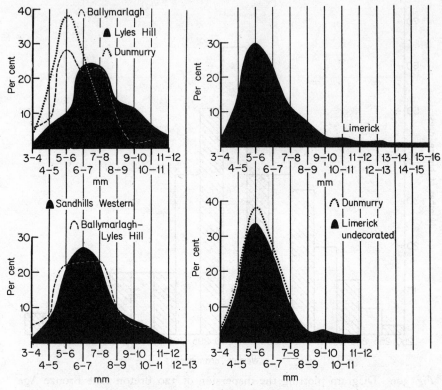

Fig. 30d   Thickness ranges and frequencies: Rim-sherds in various styles of Irish Neolithic pottery.
Source: Case 1961, p. 179.

Since any one, or combinations, of these error categories may affect the archaeological sample it is hardly surprising that many examples are skew (figs 30, 34). However, skew curves can be transformed to fit a normal distribution – by plotting on logarithmic scales and by similar devices (e.g. Vertes 1965) – or the skew curve can be approximated by one of the many other distribution curves with known properties such as – Gamma, Chi-square, Student's *t*, Snedecor's *F*, Binomial, or Poisson distributions. These curves are suitable for very specific cases, some for discrete attributes and others for continuous attributes and this must be kept in mind (Krumbein and Graybill 1965, pp. 61–115). But quite apart from these devices to express the population's qualities it is important to differentiate between 'skew distributions that would have been normal but for handling errors' i.e. whose original population was normal in distribution, as opposed to 'skew distributions deriving from distinctly non-normal attribute distributions' due to special factors (fig. 31). At the moment we will concern ourselves with the former cases.

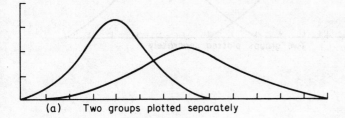

(a)   Two groups plotted separately

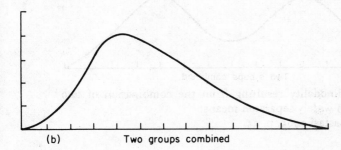

(b)   Two groups combined

Fig. 31
Skewness
resulting from
the combination
of groups with
different means
and ranges.
Source: Anastasi
1965, p. 35.

To reiterate our original finding then, if we take a large number of artefacts of one type, from one homogeneous assemblage, limited in time and space and if we study the distribution of individual attributes in that assemblage we usually find a unimodal pattern approximating to a normal probability distribution – or capable of being made to fit that model. This simple observation about the distribution curves produced by attributes clustering about a mean is really a very fundamental regularity – our first step towards a simple predictive principle. Given the specified conditions of large numbers of a single artefact-type from one cultural assemblage, limited in time and space, one would now expect an attribute by attribute analysis to produce in every case a unimodal curve approximating the normal distribution. When the reality departs from this model we know that the specified conditions are not being fulfilled by this particular sample. In other words we can detect the interfering influence of a sample mistakenly embracing several concealed artefact-types or populations, possibly from several unrelated assemblages, or possibly from populations too widely separated in space and time to share a common mean, mode and median. Minor humps and bumps may well be attributable to the

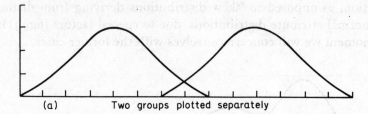

(a)   Two groups plotted separately

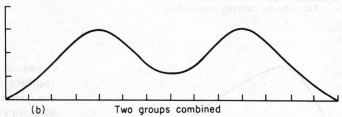

(b)   Two groups combined

Fig. 32   Bimodality resulting from the combination of two groups with widely separated means.
Source: Anastasi 1965, p. 35.

nature and size of the sample and whether these can be ignored or not can be tested for by simple statistical techniques. If these extra peaks cannot be disregarded then we can predict that the sample departs from the basic conditions and probably conceals a mixture of populations or entities.

Example. The data in this case was a quantitative and qualitative study of the attributes defining 192 flint axes from the graves of the Swedish Neolithic 'Battle-Axe' culture of around the end of the third millennium BC (Malmer 1962, pp. 351–71). The sample is rather small, but Malmer found that the histogram of the range of variation of the tapering butt angle gave an asymmetric and bimodal distribution curve (fig. 33). The distribution differed sufficiently from the normal as to suggest the possible presence of two axe 'populations' – one with practically parallel sides and the other form with acutely tapering sides converging towards the butt. In the study of the other attributes of the same axe sample Malmer discovered that the distribution of the axes' greatest width also exhibited a bimodal distribution (fig. 34). Here again there seemed to be two populations of axe forms, one with a range of cutting-edge of small dimensions and another centre of dispersion around a markedly broader cutting edge mean. Naturally, Malmer guessed that these bimodal distributions in the attributes of the same axe sample might be connected and in order to test this a correlation diagram was prepared plotting the butt angle of each axe against the greatest blade breadth (fig. 35). This correlation diagram immediately shows that indeed it is the flint axes with nearly parallel sides that also have the narrower blades and conversely, the axes with tapering sides that have the broader blades. In fact the same appears to show a bimodal division into chisel-like implements and heavier, wedge-shaped axes; this would accord with the woodworking requirements of the Neolithic economy. The correlation

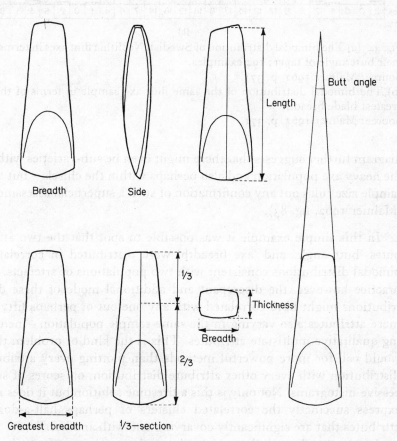

Fig. 33   The basic proportions of flint axes from the Swedish Battle-Axe culture; see figs 34, 35.
Source: Malmer 1962, p. 360.

BUTT ANGLE

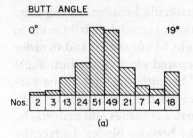

Nos.	2	3	13	24	51	49	21	7	4	18

(a)

GREATEST BREADTH

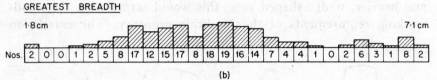

1·8cm   7·1cm

Nos.	2	0	0	1	2	5	8	17	12	15	17	8	18	19	16	14	7	4	4	1	0	2	6	3	1	8	2

(b)

Fig. 34 (a) The bimodal distribution of Swedish Neolithic flint axes in terms of their butt angle of taper; 192 examples.
Source: Malmer 1962, p. 371.
(b) The bimodal distribution of the same flint axe sample in terms of their greatest blade breadth.
Source: Malmer 1962, p. 371.

diagram further suggests that there might even be sub-varieties within the heavy axe population and also perhaps within the chisels – but the sample size rules out any confirmation of such a superficial assessment (Malmer 1962, fig. 83).

In this simple example it was possible to spot that the two attributes 'butt angle' and 'axe breadth' were distributed in correlated bimodal distributions consistent with two populations of artefacts. In practice however, the discrepant and additional mode of these distributions might have correlated with any one out of perhaps fifty or more attributes also varying in the same sample population – including qualitative multistate attributes. This is the kind of problem that would call for more powerful methods than plotting every attribute distribution with every other attribute distribution, on scores of successive histograms. Not only is this a tiresome solution but it does not express succinctly the correlated clusters of perhaps half-a-dozen attributes that are significantly covarying one with another.

In the condensed discussion about the variation of attributes within artefacts we have considered only one of four classes of variation:

(1) Populations of one attribute in one artefact-type population.
(2) Populations of several different attributes in one artefact-type population.

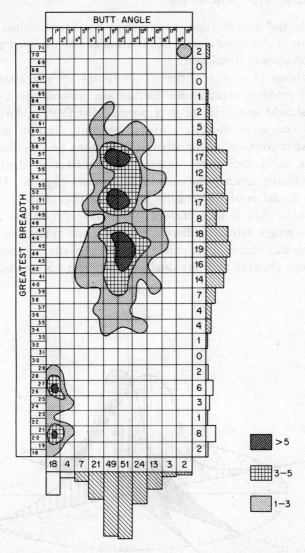

Fig. 35 Isarithmic correlation diagram of the greatest blade breadth and butt angle measurements from 192 flint axes of the Swedish Neolithic Battle-Axe culture.
Source: Malmer 1962, p. 371.

(3) Populations of one attribute in several different artefact-type populations.

(4) Populations of several different attributes in several different artefact-type populations.

So far only the first of these possibilities has been probed but the implications of the other classes of variation can be assessed using the information already developed.

Populations of several different attributes in one artefact-type present the problem noted under the flint axe example. Each different attribute should approximate to a normal distribution curve if the sample is homogeneous. An artificial conceptualization of all the normal distributions of all the attributes can then be visualized in the form of a solid bell curve integrating intersecting distributions arranged radially around the centralizing values (fig. 36). However, this latter model is of little utility since it is impossible to locate a single point within it to represent simultaneously all the attribute values of a single artefact – there are insufficient dimensions. If one can imagine an n-dimensional model to express n-attribute scales then the attribute clusters of individual artefacts can be located in this

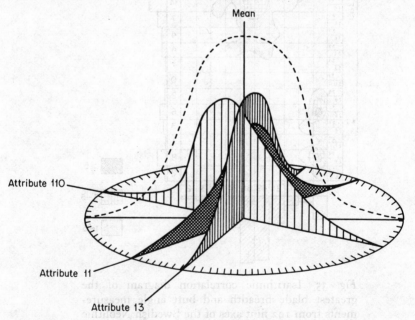

Fig. 36 The artificial conceptualization of a specific artefact-type population as the intersecting distributions of all its attributes.

multidimensional hyper-space – with relative distance measuring the degree of correlation; the clusters of attributes representing the correlated and covarying galaxies of attributes will express the overall dispersion and patterning of attribute complexes within the sample. It may be impossible to draw an undistorted model of these conceptual distribution diagrams but it is now within the capacity of modern methodology to analyse data in terms of these dimensions and to express the results in a comprehensive manner (figs 51, 53, 54).

To return from what is methodologically possible, to what is possibly required, brings us back to populations of one attribute in several different artefact-type populations. Distribution curves for such an attribute should show each artefact-type population with its own normal dispersion centred around its own mean values – probably in the form of a row of adjacent normal curves with their skirts overlapping to some extent to produce a multimodal curve (fig. 32). It should be pointed out however, that it is not impossible for otherwise quite dissimilar artefact populations to share a mean, mode and median for the distribution of one or more attributes – their differences as populations lying in all the other unplotted attribute distributions. Consequently, the proof of identity in attribute distribution in individual attribute cases does not serve to prove the identity of the populations from which they have been drawn – not, at least, until all or most of the other attribute distributions have been matched. This may seem quite obvious yet archaeological literature has produced cases where the matching distribution of single attributes in several artefact populations has been used as the sole support for claiming their virtual identity – despite the possibility of the samples being totally unalike in every respect other than the one tested.

Finally, there is the case of populations of several different attributes in several different artefact-types. Here again one would expect a multimodal distribution of each attribute in turn but the warning expressed in the previous case applies once more. Several different artefact-type populations may turn out to share identical distributions and centres of distribution in respect of particular attributes. Indeed, if the artefact-types happen to share a common attribute complex as part of their format then the distribution of attributes in this complex may well be identical, although serious artefact-type differences may reside in the remaining attributes. As a practical example, one might expect that several different types of Bronze Age sword, with quite different blade attributes, may nevertheless share a closely similar range of hilt attributes and values, which may form part of an independent attribute complex found from type to type.

Thus far the investigation has dealt with the first part of our project – with attributes and their behaviour in large numbers in artefact populations from a narrow and homogeneous time horizon or phase. Several widely applicable and useful observations and regularities have emerged from this study:

(1) Variation is inevitable, even amongst the most uniform arte-fact-types and their attributes. This variation stems partly from human whim and partly from human inability to reproduce repeatedly and exactly a given set of conditions, even when exact replication is strongly desired. As a further revealing example we might note Isaac's (1969, p. 19) analysis of variation in artefact morphology at the Acheulean sites of Isimila and Olorgesailie (East Africa), where 'individual tradi-tions may have oscillated at random within certain limits, giving innumerable minor but real variants of artefact assem-blages' (fig. 37). This stochastic variation should not be con-fused with activity/functional variation (Isaac 1972b, pp. 177–8) and through time it may produce the apparently aimless fluctuations in artefact-types which are mentioned below (chapter 4, IV; cf. Binford 1963; White and Thomas 1972, pp. 299–304).

(2) This inevitable population variation is the basis of develop-mental change, providing the mechanism by means of which one artefact-type or assemblage develops into another.

(3) It appears that within the homogeneous population of a single artefact-type, from a short phase in time, that the variable multistate attributes each cluster in a unimodal dispersion approximated by a curve varying between the normal and a skew distribution (fig. 30).

(4) It is the correlation between the dispersion patterns of the attributes within each artefact-type population which jointly express the 'personality' of that particular artefact-type.

This inquiry has given us a static impression of attribute variation within artefact populations. Now, it is time to pursue the dynamic 'behaviour' of these entities in passing time-depth. Once again our purpose is the isolation of generally applicable observations and

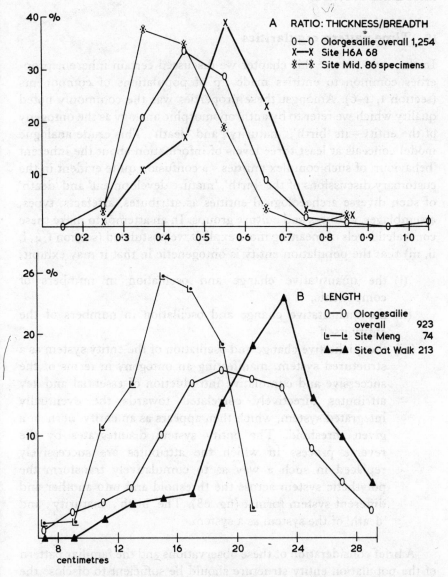

Fig. 37 Examples of stochastic variation in all the bifacial tools (A) and the handaxes alone (B) from penecontemporaneous sites at Olorgesailie (East Africa).
Source: Isaac 1969, p. 14.

regularities which depend upon the severe constraints operating in these kinds of system.

IV   Time pattern regularities

In the early part of this chapter we discussed certain inherent properties common to entities made up of populations of components (section I, 1–6). Amongst these properties was the commonly noted quality which we refer to by anthropomorphic analogy as the ontogeny of the entity – its 'birth', 'maturity', and 'death'. This crude analogue model conceals at least three levels of information about the inherent 'behaviour' of such complex entities – a confusion quite evident in the customary discussions of the 'birth', 'mature development' and 'death' of such diverse archaeological entities as attributes, artefacts, types, assemblages, cultures and culture groups. In an attempt to make these concealed levels of meaning more explicit we postulated (section I, 4, i, ii, iii) that the population entity is ontogenetic in that it may exhibit:

(i) the quantitative change and oscillation in numbers of components,

(ii) the quantitative change and oscillation in numbers of the entity itself –

(iii) the qualitative change and oscillation of the entity system as a structured system, manifesting an ontogeny in terms of the successive and cumulative introduction of essential and key attributes directively correlated towards the eventually integrated system, which then appears as an entity 'born' at a given threshold. The entity system disintegrates by the reverse process in which the attributes are successively replaced in such a way as to cumulatively transform the polythetic system across the threshold and into another and different system format (fig. 68). The 'birth', 'maturity', and 'death' of the system as a system.

A brief consideration of these observations and the familiar pattern of the population entity structure should be sufficient to disclose the identity with our general model structure and its three general levels of equilibrium oscillation (postulate 11):

(i) equilibrium oscillation within the subsystem components;

(ii) equilibrium oscillation between the subsystems in the system;

(iii) equilibrium oscillation of the whole system as an integrated system.

At the specific plane of this chapter we can equate the 'system' with an homogeneous artefact-type population, the 'subsystems' with the artefacts in these populations, and the subsystem 'components' with the attributes networked within each artefact. Rewritten at this level the immediate problem is to discover any time pattern regularities expressed in the ontogeny or time-depth trajectory generated by:

(i) the quantitative growth and oscillation in kind and numbers of attributes within homogeneous artefact populations (types) changing with time.

(ii) the quantitative growth and oscillation in kind and number of artefact-types within diverse artefact populations (assemblages) changing with time.

(iii) the qualitative growth and oscillation of the artefact-type population system as a structured system of inessential, essential and key attributes – the directive correlation of successively introduced attributes towards the formative threshold, mature coherence, and ultimately the disintegrating transformation of the artefact-type.

Since the level of this chapter is arbitrarily restricted to the regularities shown in the relationships between attributes within general artefact systems, only the first of the listed aspects will be covered in this section. The other aspects, (ii) and (iii), involve the characteristics of artefact-types and assemblages, higher level entities that we have not yet defined and which must therefore be left over for the next stage of the hierarchical model (chapter 5, IV). The time patterning of these various oscillating and multilinear system trajectories tends to be artificially complicated by the confusion of their several levels of operation. It is in order to try and avoid this complication that we will treat each level independently, beginning with the lowest, (i).

First let us clarify our intentions – our purpose is to discuss this level of time change and then on this basis to propose models which might be predictively used in relation to real data. The problem has already been defined as the nature of the quantitative growth and oscillation in kind and numbers of attributes within artefact-type populations changing with time. The problem then immediately presents two separate but not uncorrelated aspects – the distribution or dispersion of the attributes in terms of each artefact, and the distribution or dispersion of the artefact population in terms of each attribute.

The attributes found on artefacts within a certain population can be expressed as a polythetic list or set within which the attributes of every artefact in that population may be noted. Quantitatively, the system can change by increasing or decreasing the number of attributes in the polythetic set, by fluctuating the number of attributes per artefact, or by both processes jointly. The additional problem of an increasing or decreasing output of artefacts during the system's time-trajectory is a separate aspect at a separate level (ii).

If the number of attributes in the polythetic set defining the population is increasing or decreasing but the number of attributes per artefact remains roughly constant – then the only change is in the dispersion or distribution of the population about the range of attributes (fig. 41). However, it is also possible for the system to acquire and integrate new attributes in such a way as to change the size of the polythetic set and also to change the number of attributes to be found on each artefact in the population. The artefacts may become increasingly or decreasingly elaborate in terms of the number of modifying attributes that they carry – a change in the 'sophistication' of the artefacts. It is important to differentiate the implications of quantitatively changing the polythetic set of the system's attributes, changing the number of attributes per artefact, or changing both simultaneously. To return to the case of a quantitative increase or decrease in attributes per artefact it is apparent that this reflects the cumulative increase or decrease in the attribute variety, or the degree of elaboration of the artefact-type. This change may or may not be accompanied by an increase or decrease in the number of attributes in the overall polythetic set and the relationship operating between these separate trends may reveal considerable information about the circumstances of the changes.

One kind of quantitative change that may be expected in an artefact system time-trajectory is therefore equivalent to a changing degree of artefact elaboration within successive phases – and this may or may not co-ordinate with an increasing or decreasing range of attribute variation within the successive populations. There are broadly speaking four categories of quantitative attribute change on this basis:

Nos of different attributes in population's polythetic set	Nos of different attributes per artefact in the population	Implications
(1) Decrease	Increase	Increasing artefact elaboration with a decreasing range of artefact variation
(2) Increase	Increase	Increasing artefact elaboration with an increasing range of artefact variation
(3) Decrease	Decrease	Decreasing artefact elaboration with a decreasing range of artefact variation
(4) Increase	Decrease	Decreasing artefact elaboration with an increasing range of artefact variation

The detailed implications of these categories of change depend a great deal upon the particular kinds of functional or idiosyncratic attributes that are quantitatively changing with time, as well as depending upon the numbers changing, the rate of change, and above all the degree of correlation between the changes in the individual attribute trajectories. Nevertheless, it appears that the successive transformation of an artefact-type from threshold to threshold and from type-state to type-state has many of the characteristics of the sequence roughly sketched by the transitions given above as: . . . 4/1-2-3-4/1-2 . . . and so on. These changes are not themselves responsible for separating one artefact state from another but it does seem that they accompany such changes somewhat in the manner suggested.

Phase (0) – pre-formative threshold, decreasing artefact elaboration with an increasing range of artefact variation within the population of type S_0 with key attributes A_0.

Phase (1) – formative, increasing elaboration of each artefact but a decreasing range of variation within the population of new formative types S_1 – the new format becoming coherent with key attributes A_1.

Phase (2) – coherent, increasing artefact elaboration with an increasing range of artefact variation – a great regional variety of artefacts and attributes within the population of type S_1.

Phase (3) – post-coherent, decreasing artefact elaboration, a decreasing range of artefact variety within the population of type S_1.

Phase (o) – pre-formative threshold, decreasing artefact elaboration – an increasing range of variation, allowing great freedom for individual divergence within the population of type S_1/S_2. The phase in which the attribute format A_2 of type S_2 first becomes apparent in the increasing directive correlation of certain new key attribute trajectories.

It must be very strongly emphasized that these are not the changes which are responsible for forming and defining the thresholds between type-states but merely changes which frequently combine with the threshold changes. Neither is this cycle of change the simple sequence just expressed – the number of attributes defining the population, and each artefact in it, are capriciously oscillating with time – but it is the broad correlation of the separate trends and their correlation in turn with yet other trends, which together mark the thresholds.

The increasing or decreasing numbers of attributes per artefact in the trajectory of a type population changing with time may take the form of steadily trending gradients towards the poles of elaboration or simplicity, or they may exhibit irregular oscillation from one pole to another (figs 38, 39). This oscillation in the degree of artefact elaboration may be connected with functional development and foci of innovation in the system, or it may equally frequently exist as the apparently aimless fluctuation in numbers of decorative or idiosyncratic attributes within the stable set of possibilities. However, there is usually a cumulative and overall trend towards the increasing physical elaboration of the artefact-type up to a certain point, beyond which the trend towards simplicity and fewer attributes sets in (figs 38, 39). Only an examination of the attributes and the system would reveal the particular operating circumstances – but the idiosyncratic and least constrained attributes, such as decorative motifs, are particularly susceptible to this kind of cumulative development, as many prehistoric sequences show. Good examples of this kind of trajectory are the oscillating fluctuations in attributes per artefact – from austere simplicity, to baroque elaboration, and back again – that we can

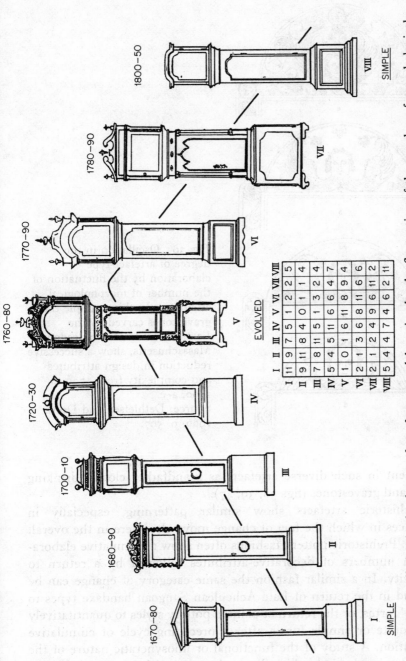

1670-80 1680-90 1700-10 1720-30 1760-80 1770-90 1780-90 1800-50

I II III IV V VI VII VIII

SIMPLE EVOLVED SIMPLE

	I	II	III	IV	V	VI	VII	VIII
I	11	9	7	5	1	2	1	5
II	9	11	8	4	0	2	1	4
III	7	8	11	5	1	4	3	4
IV	5	4	5	11	6	8	6	7
V	1	0	1	6	11	8	9	4
VI	2	2	4	8	8	11	6	6
VII	1	1	3	6	9	6	11	2
VIII	5	4	4	7	4	6	2	11

Fig. 38 Oscillation in the degree of artefact-type elaboration by the fluctuation of the number of morphological attributes. In this example the cases of English grandfather clocks c. 1670–1850. The matrix table lists the number of case attributes shared between every pair of type-states – the reversal of the fashion trend and convergent simplicity would probably mistakenly seriate examples VI, VII, VIII between I–V.
Source: Hughes 1963.

Fig. 39   Oscillation in the
degree of artefact-type
elaboration by the fluctuation of
the number of morphological
attributes. In this example the
gravestones carved by the
Lamson family of Charlesdown,
Massachusetts, show a successive
reduction in design attributes
and complexity from 1720 to
1760, a–c.
Source: Dethlefsen and Deetz
1966, p. 507.

document in such diverse artefacts as grandfather clocks, drinking
mugs, and gravestones (figs 38, 39, 47).

Prehistoric artefacts show similar patterning, especially in
sequences in which the foci of change move elsewhere in the overall
system. Prehistoric pottery fashions often show a cumulative elaboration in numbers of decorative-attributes followed by a return to
simplicity. In a similar fashion the same category of change can be
detected in the return of Late Acheulean Sangoan handaxe types to
'simple' forms, or the return of painted pottery styles to quantitatively
unelaborate or simple forms after a preceding cycle of cumulative
elaboration. A study of the functional or idiosyncratic nature of the
attributes involved should indicate the nature of the stimuli behind
such changes.

So far we have considered the time pattern regularities of the quantitative changes in numbers of attributes in the time-trajectory of an artefact-type population – the distribution or dispersion of the attributes in terms of the population and the artefact. We have been careful to separate the implications resulting from fluctuations in the polythetic set of the population's attributes and fluctuations in the numbers of attributes per artefact. The result of these speculations has been to confirm the oscillating nature of these variables and to suggest a connection between their broad and combined trends and the thresholds between successive artefact-type states. We must now turn to another aspect of the same kind of population trajectory and examine its implications – the time changes in the distribution or dispersion of the artefact population in terms of each attribute. Our objective, as before is the search for an 'organization' of the data that will consistently yield a definable regularity, which in turn may then be used as a controlled model for real data organized in the same arbitrary way.

The distribution of the successive phase populations of an artefact-type in terms of each attribute is the converse of the aspect just completed. This kind of fluctuation need reflect no change in the absolute numbers of attributes per artefact – no necessary change in the total variety of the polythetic attribute list. Instead there may be oscillations or trends in the successive states of the population distribution within the existing range of states in multistate attributes – successive changes in the artefact population dispersion in respect of an individual or several attributes (fig. 42). On many occasions all of these three separate categories of change may be operating – change in the polythetic attribute set, change in the numbers of attributes per artefact, and change in the distribution of the artefact population in terms of its component attributes. For the time being we will consider these changes independently and the last category in particular.

In order to elaborate this model we must return to the unimodal distribution expressing the centralizing values or states within a population exhibiting a given range of states at a particular population phase in time (fig. 29). Now, a population and consequently its distribution curve may not only change its mean, mode and median values with changing time but it may also change its standard deviation and its range spread, separately or jointly (figs 40, 41, 42). Whereas the standard deviation measures the degree of the centralizing tendency, the 'peakedness' of the curve, and the number of artefacts piled on the central values, the spread of the curve expresses the permissible range of states or values of a particular attribute found in a particular artefact population.

On the basis of our earlier static phase model of the distribution of an artefact type population in respect of a given attribute we can now

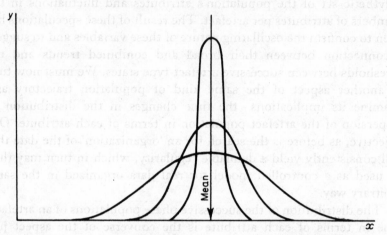

Fig. 40a Distributions with the same mean, but different standard deviations.
Source: Moroney 1957, p. 112.

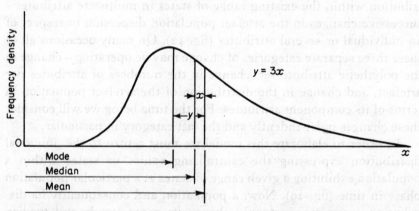

Fig. 40b Mean, Median and Mode in moderately skew cases. For moderately skew distributions we have the simple approximate relation: Mean − Mode = 3(Mean − Median). For a perfectly symmetrical distribution they all coincide.
Source: Moroney 1957, p. 48.

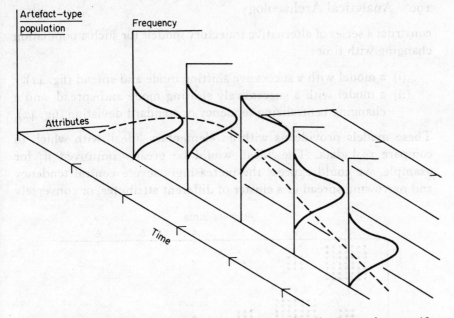

Fig. 41 A schematic model of the successive distributions of a specific artefact-type population in respect of a given attribute – with a shifting mode and spread.

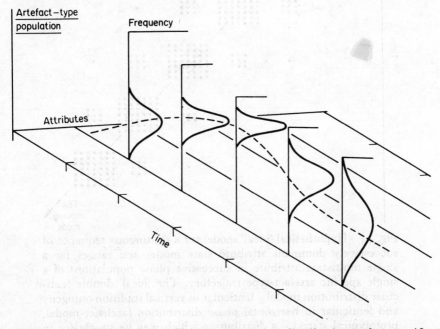

Fig. 42 A schematic model of the successive distributions of a specific artefact-type population in respect of a given attribute – with a shifting mode and spread, and a changing centralizing tendency or standard deviation.

construct a series of alternative trajectory models for such a population changing with time:

  (i) a model with a successive shifting mode and spread (fig. 41).
  (ii) a model with a successively shifting mode and spread, and a changing centralizing tendency or standard deviation (fig. 42).

These models provide us with an elementary 'ideal' with which to compare real data. The 'ideal' would be greatly improved if, for example, we could express the increasingly severe central tendency and narrowing spread of a cluster of different attributes, or conversely

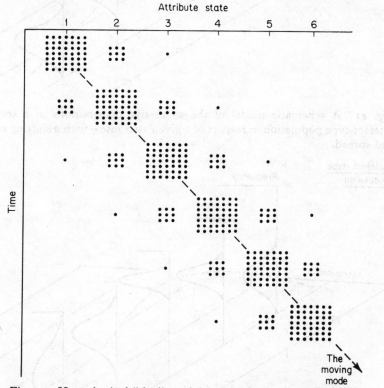

Fig. 43 Hypothetical 'ideal' model for a continuous sequence of successively dominant attribute state modes and ranges for a single multistate attribute in successive phase populations of a single specific artefact-type trajectory. The 'ideal' double lenticular distribution model – lenticular in vertical tradition ontogeny and lenticular in horizontal phase distribution (archaic, modal, prototypical states) – a distribution which may be sought-for in suitable data (see figs 46, 47).

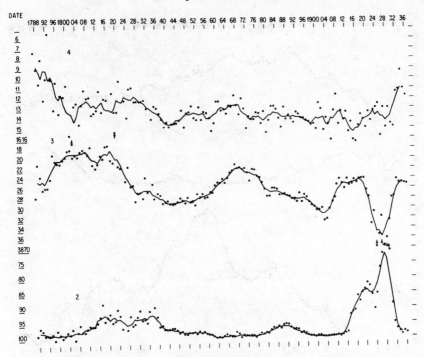

Fig. 44   The oscillating modal state of multistate attributes within successive phase populations of an artefact-type – women's day dresses 1788–1936, length of skirt (graph 2), height of waist (graph 3), height of décolletage (graph 4). Lines, five-year moving averages; dots means for years.
Source: Kroeber and Richardson 1940, p. 114.

the increasing slackness and increasingly wide dispersion and spreading range of a changing artefact-type – concepts that have a great deal in common with the intuitive ideas of artefact-types growing in coherence and definition and artefact-types slackening and losing their distinct format.

Now we must turn to the time-trajectories of real artefact populations and see how they match the regularities of our models. One well-documented example is the oscillating trajectory of dress attributes in women's fashions – an example that has extended the term 'fashion changes' to the general category of oscillating change trajectories (figs 44, 45). Fashion oscillations in this sense represent the sequence of successively dominant modes and ranges in attribute distributions which trend between the arbitrary or functional

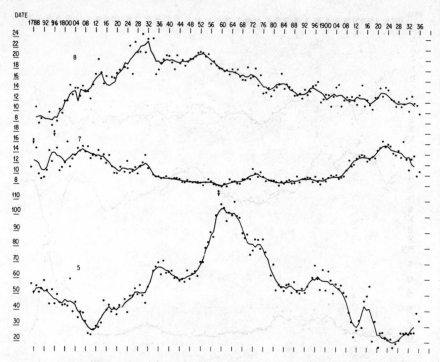

Fig. 45   The oscillating modal state of multistate attributes within successive phase populations of an artefact-type – women's day dresses 1788–1936, width of skirt (graph 5), width of waist (graph 7), width of décolletage (graph 8). Lines, five-year moving averages; dots means for years.
Source: Kroeber and Richardson 1940, p. 115.

boundaries of their stable sets of values. Such stochastic fashion oscillations have been very well documented from historic and pre-historic artefact trajectories through time (fig. 47). We may compare with the models, for example, the marked double lenticular trend in vertical traditions and horizontal phase populations of the beaker example – with an overall diagonal trend of modal values in decorative styles (fig. 46).

A brief evaluation would suggest that the two simplified models of the way in which attribute populations in artefact-types change with time are reasonably useful and predictive of an expected pattern. Deviations from such a pattern are to be anticipated in practice and emphasized by fitting to the expected curve. Common deviations from this pattern could be minor irregularities caused by too small samples, by sequences that were not homogeneous or continuous and other customary statistical requirements which if not fulfilled may serve to obliterate or fragment the patterning. Larger and more deliberate deviations are the kind that this technique is designed to highlight and isolate for their information value. The trajectory may perhaps show discrepancies caused by divergent multilinear development giving rise to two or more isolated and divergent contemporary populations, stemming from a common basis. Just such a divergence is illustrated by the beaker diagram (fig. 46) where the separate development of contemporary Northern British (N1, N2, N3, N4) and Southern British (S1, S2, S3, S4) beaker subcultures is neatly shown by the dislocation and overlapping symmetry of the diagram (S1, S2, S3, stylistically equate with N2, N3, N4). This is the kind of discrepancy which a prognosticated model can powerfully illuminate despite the necessarily simple form the model might take. Such models can be made increasingly close approximations to a specific patterning, until the data are fully 'explained' in the terms of the model.

Retrospectively, it seems that we can conceptually divide the unimodal attribute dispersion of a phase population into three sub-ranges in respect of each attribute – an 'archaic', 'modal' or 'typical', and a 'prototypical' range (figs 29, 46). The archaic range represents the continuity in an artefact population of some of the attribute values or states that were once modal in earlier population states in the trajectory – a conservative minority preserving a 'memory' of previous system states (Σs, fig. 9). However, the great bulk of the artefacts in a phase sample will be exhibiting a distinctive contemporary set of values for this attribute – the modal or 'typical' values for that population at that phase in time – values developed from among the 'prototypical' fringe of earlier states. Even this sample will itself have an extreme set of 'prototypical' values, *some* of which express the values to be developed as modal or 'typical' in the succeeding phase states of the population trajectory (figs 43, 46).

In this way the time-trajectory of the modal values or states expresses a kind of progressive cycle in which attribute states move from prototypical to typical and to archaic frequencies in time, whilst they are simultaneously part of successive phase populations in which the other prototypical, typical or archaic values are also reflected – a double lenticular pattern of population distribution (fig. 46). However, the complications arise when it is realized that the artefacts in a phase population are never uniformly prototypical, typical or archaic in all their attribute states. The polythetic reality shows that

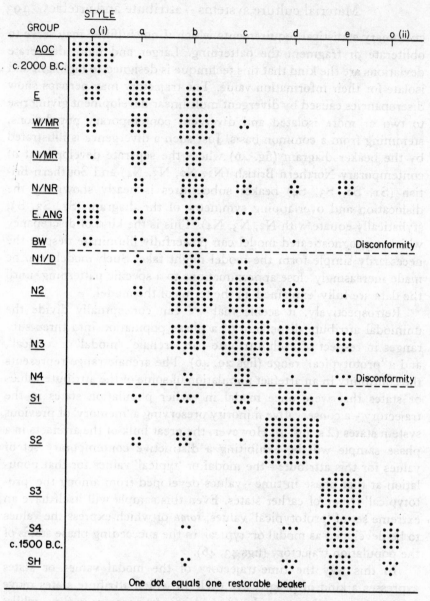

Fig. 46 The double lenticular attribute trend in vertical style traditions and horizontal phase populations of an artefact-type; in this example, the successive phase populations of British Late Neolithic beaker pottery in terms of their distribution across seven successive 'position-of-decoration' styles (o(*i*)–o(*ii*)). The disconformities represent departures from the 'ideal' model and confirm the regional nature of the development – thus the Northern British groups overlap the Southern British groups chronologically (N2, N3, N4 equate with S1, S2, S3, S4).

most artefacts have prototypical values for some of their attributes, modal values for others, and archaic values for the remainder.

In conclusion it appears that artefact-type populations of attributes produce four repeatedly recognizable regularities in their time-trajectories:

(i) an oscillating variation in the numbers of different attributes defining the polythetic set of each successive population phase;

(ii) an oscillating variation in the numbers of different attributes per artefact in the successive population phases;

(iii) a tentative impression that correlations between these two irregularly oscillating variations may jointly co-vary with other factors to define the boundaries or thresholds between one artefact-type state and another;

(iv) an oscillating variation in the successive modes that rise to prominence in an interesting double lenticular pattern:
Lenticular in horizontal population distribution – with archaic, modal and prototypical attribute states.
Lenticular in vertical distribution – with the successive introduction, modal dominance, archaic decline and disappearance of each attribute state in the time-trajectory of the type.

These regularities provide some useful models of expected time change patterns which can be cautiously used to illuminate real data – providing the necessary statistical safeguards are observed. The regularities in entity 'behaviour' allow the development of prediction from discrepancies.

v System pattern regularities

The main text of this discussion about artefacts in terms of their component attributes has made little reference to the general model earlier proposed for archaeological processes (fig. 11, postulates 1–16, chapter 2). This omission was deliberately permitted in order that the particular changes, processes and regularities being studied might independently verify in detail much that the model had covered in general. However, it is the intention of this section to draw attention to the particular ways in which the system model applies to this particular level of entity – attributes within artefacts.

We have identified the system that this chapter has been discussing as the system of attributes within artefacts – which themselves are merely subsystems of the cultural assemblage system and ultimately of the sociocultural system and its environmental setting. At the lower level the artefact system is set in the immediate context of an assemblage of other artefact systems – the artefact system is immediately coupled as a component in the assemblage system. Fluctuations in the assemblage system may therefore be expected to correlate with changes in particular artefact systems on occasions.

In the analysis of any artefact-type it is always useful to sketch the specific categories of attributes and the system networking their interconnection. The system model must be given the structure of the particular artefact under investigation. Not only does this express the obvious relationships between the artefact's attributes but it may draw attention to surprising connections and it will certainly clarify the processes of the artefact system's possible trajectories. The system model for a particular artefact, or indeed for any archaeological entity, emphasizes the interconnected and highly integrated nature of cultural entities and their change processes. Such models prevent the undiscerning concentration on variation in a single aspect which can never be unconnected with variation in many other system aspects (fig. 5).

The preliminary outline of material culture as merely one sociocultural aspect or subsystem has already anticipated the view that the analysis of systems of networked artefacts or attributes can best be set out in terms of the interaction of variety (chapter 3, III). Variety under the relative categories of new variety (gain), alternative variety (disjunction), contradictive variety (equivocation) and confirmative variety (redundant) – variety which at this level means variety in attributes. We have already noted that new attribute variety can only impinge on an artefact/attribute system as external variety diffused from neighbouring systems of all levels, or as internal variety generated within the same sociocultural system by innovating accident, play, or invention – with the chance development of emergent qualities which may appear simply on re-networking old components. Invention and diffusion provide two of the major processes relevant to this level of archaeological entity but neither can be manifested without the third process of acceptance and integration. Integration of new variety depends on the system being able to 'reconcile' all the myriad coupled values in the gross system by minimizing the maximum amount of system dislocation, in order to ensure continuity.

Against this background new attribute variety may take the form of a new kind of flint retouch, the idea of a tool-kit made on blades instead of flakes, or simply the idea of putting a notch or a rivet where there had never been one before. Most of this new variety will simply be alternative or disjunctive and the new attribute may be assimilated in the artefact population as an alternative state under a multistate attribute – a quantitative increase in the number of attribute states. Indeed, all the states of a multistate attribute are simply alternative or disjunctive variety. Sometimes of course, the 'new' variety diffusing to the system through its coupling channels will merely be redundant or confirmative in that the particular system already has that particular attribute.

The more interesting variety is contradictive variety, when equivocation may give rise to oscillating instability. Contradictive attributes take the form of attributes that conflict with some of the previously existing variety of attributes in the artefact structure. The normal course is for the sociocultural system to reject such contradictive variety in which case no change or problem arises, but on occasions it sometimes occurs that one piece of contradictive variety may minimize a whole group of serious dislocations pre-existing in the system. In which case a minor equivocation and dislocation will be acceptable as a solution to a major disconformity – thus minimizing the maximum amount of system dislocation. It follows that the integration of contradictive variety must be accompanied by other system repercussions and readjustments – often generating a comprehensive new set of variety for this purpose – sometimes with unforeseen and subsequently emergent results.

Contradictive attribute variety could arise from the need to integrate the attributes of a slashing sword-edge with the shape and capacity for rapier thrusting. These contradictive requirements were settled in the Bronze Age Keszthely-Boiu rapier (Cowen 1966) and the Carp's-tongue sword (Hencken 1956) by 'new' and comprehensive blade shapes offering a compromise or blending strategy. The halberd is just such a 'new' artefact variety arising from the attempt to employ a dagger-blade at long-range and in a battle-axe manner; the spear presents an alternative solution to the same problem compatible with a rapier thrusting technique. Artefact hafting has always been a major source of contradictive variety and its reconciliation. A stone missile head must be thin and unobstructed for maximal penetration, and yet it must be rigidly held in the end of a relatively thick shaft: a tang is clearly one of the best solutions.

Contradictive attribute variety is particularly important to the archaeologist because it is often instrumental in the generation of 'new' varieties of artefact and attribute, these may frequently be unstable and short-lived compromise solutions with oscillating states or values, but equally some of the new variety may have significant emergent potential. In all these cases a strategy combining the attributes in the system may adopt a mixed, random, optimizer, satisficer, or minimax solution. The strategy of attribute blending adopted throws additional light on the dislocations and their foci within the artefact system, as well as helping to define the key attributes.

Equilibrium in an artefact system is therefore largely a matter of keeping all the variations in all the attributes in the system compatible with the purposes for which the artefact was intended and with the sociocultural system that made it. Equilibrium occurs at the charac-teristic three levels – between the attributes, between the attributes and the artefact, and between the artefact system and its total context. Unstable oscillation and aimless stochastic oscillation within stable multistate attribute sets occur normally and we have illustrated several actual examples of such oscillating change trajectories (figs 44–7). The role of oscillating and aimless 'random walk' variation in invention and the chance production of emergent system qualities should not be overlooked (Isaac 1969, p.19). Needless to say, as in all these entity systems it is the human generators who fulfil the inter-connecting loops and channels by means of which attribute is linked with attribute and artefact with artefact (fig. 48). It is the artefact maker who feeds back into the phenotypic constitution of the next generation of artefacts the modified characteristics of the preceding populations of artefacts (Σs, fig. 9), and it is in this way that the artefact population has continuity in its trajectory and yet is continu-ously shifting its attribute format and dispersion (figs 46, 48).

The phenomenon of lag is represented by the gap between the eventual artefact population being modified and the first appearance of the dislocation requiring the change; the lead is the gap between the modifications which anticipate certain events and the time when the events would have occurred – the anticipation commonly removing the danger of the events. A long time lag or lead are often pre-conditions for oscillating instability in an artefact system causing the

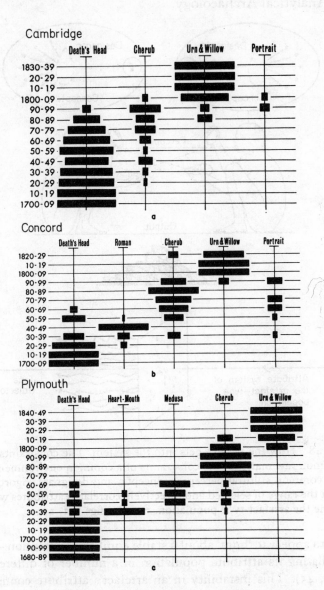

Fig. 47 The double lenticular attribute trend in vertical style traditions (infrequent, frequent, infrequent) and horizontal phase populations (archaic, modal, prototypical) of an artefact-type; in this case New England gravestones from three areas in terms of seven motif attributes. Note the moving mode, from bottom left to top right 1700–1830, in each case.
Source: Dethlefsen and Deetz 1966, p. 505.

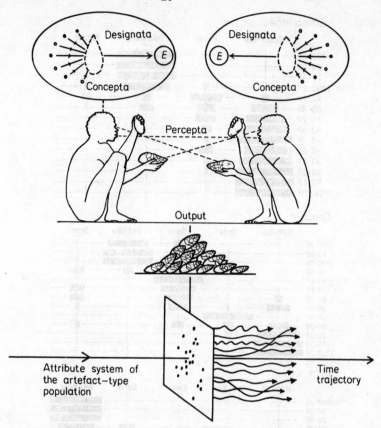

Fig. 48   How the pattern gets into the system. The constraints of a common raw material, the constraints of a common environment 'E' and common cultural percepta, concepta, and designata, rigorously limit the range of selected and directively correlated attributes which define the artefact-type population. See also figs 111, 112.

system to appear to 'hunt' about a stable equilibrium solution – usually by oscillating its attribute population in a number of different ways (figs 44, 45). This instability in an artefact's attribute configuration frequently characterizes 'new' comprehensive formats attempting to blend contradictive variety within the system. The early developments of a new artefact-type consequently often display a wide variety of short-lived variants which steadily die away leaving one or two stable variants as modal forms. This initial variety within a single artefact-type in a single assemblage should not be confused with the subsequent variety in the same type based on contemporary regional variants – each of which is modal and stable for its own territory and assemblage.

Any population of artefacts can be defined by the systemic structure of the polythetic set listing their attributes. Any artefact within such a population will have a particular subset of attributes from within the range of the polythetic set. We have already seen the several different ways in which the subset of attributes defining an artefact may fluctuate both quantitatively and qualitatively, both absolutely and relatively to the overall polythetic set. Every artefact is in a sense the embodiment of a small-scale strategy devised by its fabricator in order to satisfy and blend the requirements of its fabrication, its context and its intended usage. The particular artefact therefore represents a particular micro-strategy expressed as a particular mixture and proportion of specific attributes and attribute states – a population of such artefacts represents a set of similar strategies or minimax solutions to a particular array of competing and even conflicting environmental problems. The analysis of a population of artefacts within a single type category can usefully be set up to investigate the artefacts as attribute systems adopting a certain strategy in relation to their fabrication and usage.

The identification and role of inessential, essential and key attributes within an artefact-type's attribute system and its trajectory has already been discussed at length. In broad outline we have seen that it is the essential attributes which map the format of the relevant system, distinguishing the artefact's 'archaeological' system from its natural characteristics. It is the essential attributes that express the 'continuity' of the system as the same system rather than as a transmutation. The key attributes are detectable as those essential attributes that not only change with the changing system but which change in a tightly correlated and covarying pattern of relationships. It is this pattern of relationships that give that particular artefact-type its coherent identity despite its range of variation in component attributes and their states. The inessential, essential and key attributes within an artefact population depend on the frame of reference of the enquiry but once this is established the particular category of particular attributes within the system may be statistically defined (e.g. Judge, 1970).

It is the successive and cumulative introduction of the key and essential attributes into the system's time-trajectory that define the thresholds at which the specific artefact format is first recognizable as an integral whole, and the terminal threshold when it is last identifiable within the limits of this same format. Retrospectively, and in light of a specific attribute format, these essential and key attributes can be viewed as directively correlated towards the formation and subsequently the successive transformation of the particular artefact system of attributes. This apparent 'birth' and 'death' of an artefact format is one of the system qualities anthropomorphized under those ontogenetic terms. The concept of artefact 'birth', 'maturity' and 'death' confuses the three levels of – the changing degree of artefact elaboration, the changing numbers of artefact produced, and the changing artefact format and its transformation from state to state. Thus the 'death' of an artefact population may reflect simply its return to a simple, unelaborate format, the total cessation of its production by a given culture, or its continuation in a transformation state radically different from that arbitrary range of states regarded as limiting the 'type' format. The same confusion operates in relation to higher system entities with the same and increasingly serious consequences for analysis and interpretation.

In conclusion we may perceive that the postulates of the general model suggest that archaeological entities can be viewed as dynamic systems of attributes. The equilibrium or stability of such systems seem best set out in terms of the interaction of attribute variety – whether new, alternative, contradictive, or redundant to the system format. This kind of system should show oscillating equilibrium at the three main levels of coupling – between attributes, between subsystems of attributes and between the system and its context. The concepts of inessential, essential and key attributes, directive correlation, cumulative approach to thresholds, and apparent ontogeny should also be demonstrated by the kind of system modelled in the postulates. In this chapter we have attempted to show that just these very aspects can be found in the 'behaviour' of attributes within artefact populations and their trajectories. The general model may well be imperfect in a number of features but it appears to promise a capacity for more powerful development and at least a temporary utility.

Notes

(1) The author's concept of the relationship between 'percepta in the maker's mind' and the artefact and its attributes is one example of the metaphysical position whereby the archaeologist gears his typological

methods to the definition of 'real' artefact-types. These are thought to have been those specifically produced by their makers with a clear function in mind ('each attribute ... is equivalent to a piece of premeditated and deliberate hominid behaviour', above p. 156). The regularities observed by the archaeologist in artefact-types (e.g. size, shape) are the direct result of 'mental templates' or 'type concepts' among the historic or prehistoric population that fabricated them. This model for typology is referred to as 'empiricist' by Hill and Evans (1972) in a provocative study containing many useful examples of archaeologists' approaches to 'types' and typology. They argue that types *are* real (i.e. non-random clusters of attributes) but that a variety of these may be defined according to the problem or hypothesis under investigation. Furthermore the people that produced these types need not necessarily have been aware of them. The pottery types defined by Longacre (1970) and Hill (1970) in their analyses of social organization in Pueblo settlements are a case in point: 'although the individual manufacturers of the pottery undoubtedly had things in mind, and knew what they were trying to paint on the vessels, they were not necessarily aware of the minute attribute differences taken into consideration in these studies' (Hill and Evans 1972, pp. 256–7). The existence of distinctions between 'folk taxonomies' and archaeological classifications has been rarely studied. Birmingham (1975) and Gould (1974) both note the existence of native classifications of pottery and flint tools based upon *function* rather than form, while White and Thomas (1972) have concluded that the New Guinea highlanders today 'do not regard their flaked stone tools as a series of formal or single-functional types, but as pieces of stone, parts of which may be used to perform certain activities' (p. 278). Their observations on inter-community variation of type sizes suggest the existence of a 'template' or 'type concept', although it is *not explicitly recognized* by the local population. This is an important point and supports the argument that there may be archaeologically detectable regularity in artefact 'types' which was the result of 'covert' rather than consciously 'cognized' constraints among prehistoric populations (White and Thomas 1972, p. 298).

(2) Doran and Hodson (1975, pp. 161–2) follow Childe in distinguishing the types that *comprise* an assemblage or culture and those that *distinguish* this entity from others of a similar rank. These latter types were referred to by Childe as 'type-fossils' and are presumably to be recognized, as Clarke argues here, after a full analysis. However, this does not remove the need for caution in using the word 'typical' in this sense, as its ambiguity (e.g. when non-quantified) can lead to confusion and misinterpretation (see above, chapter 1, v).

(3) The argument that the attribute is 'logically irreducible' is disputed by Steiger (1971, p. 67), who claims that if taken literally this definition would restrict the attribute to the world's four major dimensions: length, time, mass and electric charge. In a similar vein, Hill and Evans (1972, p. 265) write that *all* attributes are divisible and are not 'immutable natural

units of observation'. There is an element of semantic quibbling in Steiger's criticism, but it can be argued that there are 'levels' of attribute definition, the lowest most general and least archaeologically useful of which would be the 'logically irreducible' one defined in this chapter (Doran and Hodson 1975, pp. 101–2). At the same time Hill and Evans take no note of the flexibility inherent in the author's distinction of quantitative and qualitative attribute *states* (see above pp. 156–8).

5 Artefact and type

Archaeological phenomena can be grouped together as
types just because results of private experience, of
individual trial and error, have been communicated to
other members of a society and adopted and replicated by
them,
V. GORDON CHILDE 1956, p. 8

1 Introduction

Using the broad foundations outlined in the preceding chapters it is
now possible to clamber a little higher up the framework of our
hierarchical model of archaeological entities (fig. 49). Archaeological
attributes exist in clusters as components of artefacts. The archaeologist and prehistorian usually subdivide the vast array of artefacts into
'artefact-types' or 'families' on an intuitive basis that subtly blends an
unconscious assessment of similarities in sets of attributes with a swift
guess at a common usage pattern for the artefacts as a group. It is this
unspecified blending of empirical observation with intuitive
experience which has given rise to so much debate about the real or
imaginary nature of the 'type' concept. Clearly, we must pause to
analyse the basis of the 'type' concept in terms of our existing
definitions and in the ultimate hope of producing a viable definition
for this fundamental entity.

The importance of developing an adequate definition for artefact-
types and then applying the definition with all possible rigour cannot
be overestimated. Many contemporary studies, particularly in the
Palaeolithic field, make great play about variations from artefact
assemblage to assemblage of the relative percentages of given artefact-
types. Some of the most elegant and powerful of modern methods
such as factor analysis and principal component analysis have been
applied to this kind of data (Binford and Binford 1966; Doran and
Hodson 1966). However, hardly any of these studies define their unit
artefact-types on other than an intuitive and arbitrary basis of very
debatable adequacy, and one which is certainly not sufficiently

CULTURE
A polythetic set of specific and comprehensive artefact-type categories which consistently recur together in *assemblages* within a limited geographical area. Levels: culture group, culture, subculture.

CULTURE GROUP
A family of transform cultures; collateral cultures characterized by sharing a polythetic range but differing states of the same *specific multistate artefact-types*.

ASSEMBLAGE
An associated set of contemporary artefact-*types*.

TYPE
Specific artefact-type; an homogeneous population of *artefacts* which share a consistently recurrent range of attribute states within a given polythetic set. Levels: type group, specific type, subtype.

TECHNOCOMPLEX
A group of cultures characterized by assemblages sharing a polythetic range but differing specific types of the same *general families of artefact-types*, shared as a widely diffused and interlinked response to common factors in environment, economy and technology. The material manifestation of cultural convergence within a common stable environmental strategy.

ARTEFACT
Any object modified by a set of humanly imposed *attributes*.

ATTRIBUTE
A logically irreducible character of two or more states, acting as an independent *variable* within a specific artefact system. An epistemically independent variable.

Fig. 49   A schematic hierarchical model of the major archaeological entities arranged in ascending order of system complexity. The higher the entity in the classificatory scheme, the greater its predictive information content.

comprehensive in application or accurately defined in terms of attributes. The consequent danger is that an alternative or conflicting definition of the artefact-types within such assemblages would radically alter the much discussed relative percentages and correspondingly alter their meaningful interpretation. Such a procedure immediately undermines the power and elegance of the techniques used in the analysis and most of the objective virtues of the histograms and cumulative curves of such intuitive types.[1]

Surely, it is incongruous to use powerful and modern techniques to build up an impression of the upper levels of prehistoric entities when the lower levels and foundations are certainly inadequate and unsafe – one cannot build sound structures from shoddy components. If elaborate techniques are to be used in the higher levels of interpretation then the entities of the lowest level must be similarly defined. The distaste generated by the thought of having to so define each of the main type categories must be swallowed if undue haste is not to spoil the quality of the results of much time-consuming and expensive analysis.

II   Artefact-type systems

It is frequently assumed that artefact-types are self-evident groups of artefacts intended for a specific usage (e.g. projectile points, axes, swords, burins or scrapers). Now although it is clear that the concept of an artefact-type often coincides with a group of artefacts sharing a common purpose this does not necessarily mean that usage pattern is both the sufficient and necessary feature for the definition of artefact-types. On the contrary, there are many different types of artefact which share a common usage and many single artefact-types which have multiple and diverse purposes in different sociocultural contexts. Furthermore, prehistorians are often completely at a loss to define the precise use of many artefacts but this does not prevent artefacts of unknown purpose being sorted into types. The linkage between arte-fact usage and artefact type is simply that artefacts intended for a given purpose will also necessarily possess a large number of functional attributes and constraints in common.

Analysis would seem to show that artefact-types are conceived in terms of detailed sets of similarities between numbers of artefacts such that the degree of similarity between artefacts within the type group is greater than any similarity between artefacts in separate type groups. One can imagine a similarity gradient falling-off exponentially towards yet other groups of internally similar type groups. Evidently the boundary between type clusters conceived in this way will be rather arbitrary in precise location. Furthermore, the type concept seems to express some relationship linking a population of artefacts with a structured or patterned population of attributes.

Under the older, tacit models of the type entity, the sceptics were quick to notice that unfortunately no two artefacts, even within the same artefact-type, ever possess completely identical attribute assemblages or sets. This would seem to prevent the archaeologist from usefully defining the type categories simply as those separate populations of artefacts respectively carrying attributes 1–50–type 1, 51–100 – type 2, 101–150 – type 3, and so on in neat, rigid, mutually exclusive attribute clusters. Unfortunately instead of openly recognizing the fact that archaeological groups are not of this nature, most prehistorians have continued to pretend that the concepts of types, cultures, and culture groups were monothetic in nature. This violence to the real situation has served to obscure one of the most interesting and significant characteristics of archaeological group concepts – namely, that most of these groupings are polythetic (fig. 3).

No single property or attribute is necessary for the membership of a polythetic group, although nothing denies or warrants the possibility that some property in the set may be sufficient for membership within the aggregate. As it turns out, both natural taxa and archaeological taxa are not always fully polythetic since some attributes may be common to all members of the taxon. For example – all flint scrapers have retouch, all burins have burin-blow scars, all pottery is made of clay and so on. It has already been observed that one of the vital aspects to be investigated in the future should be the definition of the different structural categories of polythetic groups found amongst the particular levels of archaeological entities and the investigation of precisely how this structure influences their 'behaviour' characteristics. Such an investigation must clearly await the accumulation of analysed instances.

To return to the immediate problem, we appear to have accumulated a certain amount of data about the necessary properties of an archaeological artefact-type. So far it has been noted that artefacts are defined by their component clusters of attributes. These attributes are of all kinds and states, reflecting aspects of raw material, shape, size, detail, and location of detail. We are now concerned not with the static phase pattern of a single attribute within a population but with the clusters of tens or hundreds of different attributes that integrate to define artefacts as complete entities. It would seem that artefact-types are populations of artefacts that are richly cross-connected amongst themselves in terms of affinity between their sets of attributes. The artefact-type cluster represents a comprehensive population of artefacts internally bound by a high level of similarity between the individual sets of attributes, even though these sets may share attributes with other type clusters and even though the artefacts within the population vary amongst themselves within a polythetic pattern. Artefact-types, so it appears, are not usually fully polythetic, because certain attributes may be shared by all members of the group.

The problem is to attempt to distil from all these preceding observations a concise and viable definition of an artefact-type or 'type'. As a tentative attempt along these lines it may be suggested that an artefact-type is – *an homogeneous population of artefacts which share a consistently recurrent range of attribute states within a given polythetic set.*

III Phase pattern regularities

One curious corollary of the type concept is that the term 'type' is a collective noun expressing the attributes of a population of artefacts varying between certain limits, although the word 'type' may sometimes be used in a singular sense for a hypothetical 'mean' artefact-type about which the population of artefacts can be said to vary. If this latter sense of the word 'type' is understood merely as a symbolic shorthand for the defined population of artefacts and their constellation of dispersed attributes then this usage is acceptable but dangerous. Very few real artefacts in such a population will closely resemble the hypothetical 'mean artefact' incorporating all the mean or modal attributes – the majority of the artefacts display some archaic, some prototypical and only a proportion of modal or mean attribute values. Any archaeologist who has faced the task of attempting to select one real artefact from a sample population to illustrate all the 'typical' characteristics of that population has realized how atypical such an artefact is.

It would seem worthwhile to investigate the patterning of the constellations of different attributes that cluster to define an artefact-type under our definition. This approach, however, is made difficult by the absence of any number of exhaustive analyses of prehistoric artefact-types in terms of their component attributes. Indeed, all the properties of the higher archaeological entities, from types to cultures and culture groups, are artificially clouded by the absence of sufficiently detailed analyses or experiments. Prehistorians all too often fall back upon a few vague and undefined opinions expressed in an expansive way over a pipe of tobacco, with the warm conviction that these concepts will always remain elusive wraiths – which of course they will unless they do something about it. One suspects that the drudgery of an attribute by attribute analysis of hundreds of artefacts is the thought which really deters the intrepid prehistorian. In such a situation one can at the moment do no more than make the most of the few available analyses and combine these with speculative and necessarily dangerous hypotheses.

From analyses, it appears that amongst the set of attributes combined to define a population of artefacts some few attributes may be present on every example – these we have noted as inessential attributes in the sense of being inessential to the changing system, although they may be far from inessential to the artefact-type's function. These inessential system attributes are for example the characteristics that all handaxes are made of stone, all daggers or swords of a certain type have riveted hilts, all pots of a certain type may have the same form of rim, and so on. These very few inessential attributes shared by all the examples of the type are usually the nucleus of mainly functional attributes which prevent the attribute set for the population being fully polythetic. Since they are present in every example of the population it is clear that such attributes would have a 100 per cent coefficient of correlation within the type, each of these attributes always occurring with the others. Such universal attributes are obviously exceptional in comparison with their less universal attribute associates; most of the other attributes in the population will occur together frequently, but not on 100 per cent of the artefacts. These latter form the majority of the system's essential attributes with usually a more balanced functional and idiosyncratic aspect, perhaps having an optimum correlation of 60 per cent or so with some other attributes in the type population. Finally, there is the extreme fringe or penumbra of the range of attributes, characters which do occur together on this type of artefact but only at a mutually sporadic level. Many attributes with a high idiosyncratic and low functional aspect fall into this general category of exotic and occasional characters. Such attributes may have less than a 10 per cent level of correlation with any other attributes in the artefact-type population.

It is particularly important to grasp that we are discussing the structuring of the population's attributes in terms of the correlation or frequency of mutual occurrence one with another and not simply their individual frequency in the population. An attribute may be absolutely rare in overall occurrence within the population – perhaps only occurring ten times in ten thousand artefacts – but on every artefact that this attribute does appear, it may always be joined by another equally rare attribute. In such a case the frequency of these attributes' occurrences in the artefact population may only be of the order of 10/10,000 but their mutual correlation would be 100 per cent. Nevertheless, since they are so infrequent in overall occurrence their correlation with other more numerous and common attributes would be very low – in fact, 0·1 per cent with any attribute occurring on all of the 10,000 artefacts. We can expect therefore a constellation of

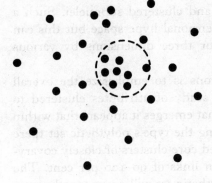

Fig. 50 Hypothetical 'ideal' model representing a single specific artefact-type population as the nucleated constellation of its intercorrelated attributes. Each dot represents an attribute, the encircled nucleus reflecting the essential multistate attributes of the system; the whole distorted from multidimensional to two dimensional space.

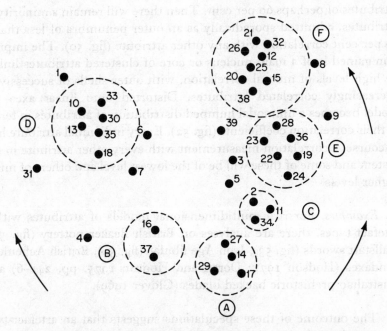

Fig. 51 A practical analysis computing a two-dimensional configuration of attribute intercorrelations from a multidimensional scaling procedure. The population in this example – a multi-subtype specific artefact-type population (760 pots) over *c.* 500 years – British Beaker pottery defined by thirty-nine basic attributes. External evidence shows the developmental trajectories proceeding A–B–D (AOC,E,W/MR,BW,E.Ang) and A–C–E–F (E,N1–4,S1–4) in parallel in different regions.

attributes with distances proportional to the correlation between pairs of attributes to have several clustered nuclei but probably with one major nucleus of jointly correlated and clustered subnuclei. Such a model would clearly need multidimensional hyperspace but this can be reduced and distorted to two or three dimensions by various practical techniques (fig. 51).

The purpose of these observations is to emphasize the overall impression that develops from the study of attributes clustered to define artefact-types. In the model that emerges it appears that within the constellation of attributes defining the type's polythetic set there may be one or more tightly correlated core clusters of closely covarying attributes, with some correlation links of 90–100 per cent. The majority of the attributes in the polythetic set will occur together at a less pronounced level, with some correlations with the core cluster attributes of perhaps 60 per cent. Then there will remain a minority of attributes, admitted sporadically as an outer penumbra of less than a 10 per cent correlation with any other attribute (fig. 50). The impression gained is of a main nucleus or core of clustered attributes linked by high levels of mutual correlation, with outer shells of successively decreasingly correlated attributes. Distorted onto linear axes the model becomes a unimodal humped distribution of attributes in terms of their correlation coefficients (fig. 52). Every individual attribute has, of course, a correlation measurement with every other attribute in the system and some of these will be of the lowest level and others of much higher levels.

Examples. For real multidimensional models of attributes within artefact-types, there are analyses on British Beaker pottery (fig. 51), Hallstatt swords (fig. 53), Iron Age fibulae (fig. 54), British Acheulean handaxes (Hodson 1971; Doran and Hodson 1975, pp. 241–6) and Australian prehistoric backed blades (Glover 1969).

The outcome of these speculations suggests that an artefact-type has a reality which resides in a highly correlated inner core of attributes within an outer group of attributes of decreasing levels of correlation. Each type may be represented by a nucleus cluster and its penumbra although closely related types will inevitably share attributes in their constellation shells whilst retaining distinctive and peculiar nucleus clusters and overall correlation structuring. In an analysis of the relationships between several different but related type

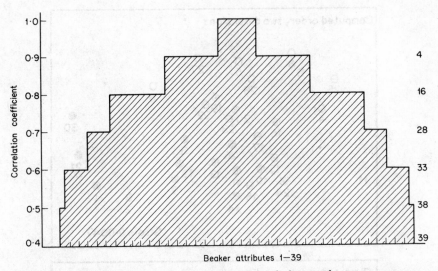

Fig. 52 A representation of the distribution of the product-moment correlation coefficients between 39 ceramic attributes in a population (760) of British Late Neolithic Beaker vessels (*c.* 2000–1400 BC). A multi-subtype specific artefact-type population.

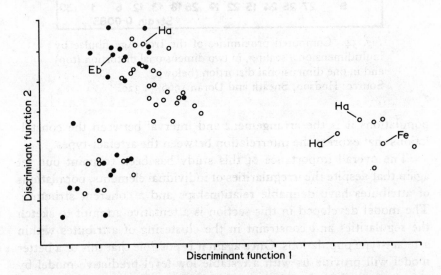

Fig. 53 A k = cluster analysis of sixty-five Hallstatt C swords described by 19 attributes and plotted on a two-dimensional scatter diagram. Open circles – continental swords; filled circles – British swords; Ha = Hallstatt; Eb = Ebberston, Yorks; Fe = iron sword from Court-St-Etienne, Belgium.
Source: Doran and Hodson 1975, p. 241.

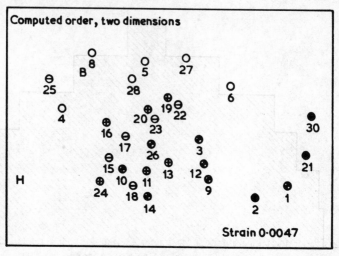

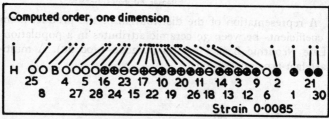

Fig. 54   Computed proximities of the Iron Age fibulae by multidimensional scaling, in two dimensional distortion (top) and in one dimensional distortion (below).
Source: Hodson, Sneath and Doran 1966, p. 320.

populations it is the arrangement and interval between the constellations that express the interrelation between the artefact-types.

The overall importance of this study has been to point out yet again that despite the irregularities of individual elements, populations of attributes have definable relationships and a coherent structure. The model developed in this section is a tentative attempt to sketch the regularities and constraint in the clustering of attributes within artefact-type populations. Once again it is possible that this or a better model will provide us with a testable low-level predictive model by means of which we can detect and isolate artefact-types or investigate the pattern of their deviation from the expected ideal.

One side-effect of this analysis throws some light on the confusion arising from the use of the term 'type' at different levels of complexity and meaning (see above, pp. 27–30). Take the statements:

a flint scraper is an artefact-type
a flint scraper flake is an artefact-type
a flint flake side-scraper is an artefact-type

and as a parallel example:

a bronze sword is an artefact-type
a bronze flange-tanged sword is an artefact-type
a bronze flange-tanged Erbenheim sword is an artefact-type.

In these successive statements it is apparent that the word 'type' is being used at quite different levels of complexity, linked only by being hierarchic levels of the same general set. In these examples there are three separate levels – the level of *artefact-type group*, or general family of function and material – such as flint scrapers and bronze swords; the level of *specific artefact-types* – such as flint flake scrapers and bronze flange-tanged swords; and finally the level of the variant or *subtype* – the flint flake side-scraper and the bronze Erbenheim sword.

However, the problem then arises – which arbitrary level in the hierarchy is to be designated subtype, which a type, and which a type group or family? Do types in such diverse artefact populations as flint scrapers, bronze swords, cooking pots and microliths represent taxa of precisely equivalent rank? The number of levels for attaching the subtype, type, or type group labels is almost infinite and archaeologists are completely inconsistent in their usage of the term 'type' and of the level of entity complexity to which they attach it. The arbitrary nature of the subtype, type, and type group levels is at once admitted but confusion must result if this arbitrariness is not at least consistent.

If we think back to our correlation model of the multidimensional attribute constellation we can begin to understand the basis and difficulty of the problem. The nuclei or core of highly correlated and frequently recurring attributes will include many of the highly functional attributes common to a utilitarian family of artefact-types and defining their essential 'axe-ness', 'scraper-ness' and 'sword-ness'. These structured attribute complexes will be found in the same general form in quite different artefact-type or specific type constellations – usually in the highly correlated core. However, if we take the outer shell of attributes, say with at best a 60 per cent correlation with the core attributes, then these will include many of the less-general and more-specific and idiosyncratic attributes of the artefact-type – it is this middle level which equates best with the artefact-type, specific type, or simply the type level of common terminology. In the outermost shell of a maximal correlation of 10 per cent the transect embraces most of the minor attributes and attribute complexes that define the whole range of subtypes or variants within the main type population.

One of the more important contributions of numerical taxonomy has been to suggest that the various internal levels of affinity and correlation diagrams may be used as a comparative measure of the rank of the groups at particular transects – using a unit called the phenon (Sokal and Sneath 1963) (fig. 55). Such a technique would

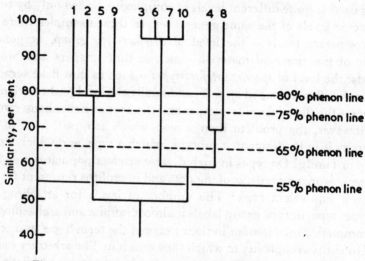

Fig. 55   Dendrogram to show the formation of phenons.
Source: Sokal and Sneath 1963, p. 252.

enable the archaeologist to compare the rank of artefact-types and subtypes in a more objective way and provide a basis for a gradually more standardized terminology. Using this kind of subdivision the 80 per cent level of the affinity or correlation diagram would be the 80 phenon level, the 60 per cent the 60 phenon, and the 10 per cent the 10 phenon level. It would seem ultimately possible on the basis of a large number of detailed studies of this kind to gradually establish the best arbitrary levels for the comparative ranks of the subtype, type and type group labels. Until such a time arrives some effort should be made to keep the use of these terms, with their differing implications, to consistent levels of complexity and content.

At this point some attempt may be made to gather together the general information about the artefact-type concept as an entity.

(1) Artefacts belong at one and the same time to three broad categories or intersecting sets – to a type group, a specific type, and a subtype.

(2) *Type group* – the artefact-type group or family; a group of affinally related, collateral artefact-types characterized by a common component subset of attributes which define a complex constraining functional usage and raw material. A low-level affinity, perhaps less than 30 per cent, uniting the group as a whole.

(3) *Type* – specific artefact-type; an homogeneous population of artefacts which share a consistently recurrent range of attribute states within a given polythetic set. No two artefacts within the type need be exactly alike in any single attribute and no artefact need possess all of the attributes in the set – an intermediate-level affinity or perhaps 30–60 per cent uniting the population as a whole.

(4) *Subtype* – artefact subtype or variant; an homogeneous sub-population of artefacts which share a given subset within an artefact-type's polythetic set of attributes. A sub-population with a high-level of affinity, perhaps 60–90 per cent, uniting the individuals within the whole.

(5) The artefact-type can be represented in terms of a nucleated constellation of attributes defining the polythetic set and arranged in terms of their correlation one with another in multidimensional space.

(6) The artefact subtype populations should be represented as secondary nuclei or clusters of highly correlated attributes within the overall constellation of the artefact-type.

(7) The presence of several distinct artefact-type populations within a sample population should be represented by multiple and separate nuclei within the overall galaxy of attributes.

IV Time pattern regularities

An earlier section of the preceding chapter briefly discussed the three main categories of change within changing artefact-type populations and proceeded to elaborate the simplest of these (chapter 4, IV i). To recapitulate, the three categories included

(i) the quantitative change and oscillation in numbers of attributes,

> (a) as variation in the number of different attributes defining the polythetic set of successive population phases;
>
> (b) as variation in the number of different attributes per artefact in successive phases;
>
> (c) as variations in both of the above aspects jointly, in a variety of combining trends;
>
> (ii) the quantitative change and oscillation in numbers of the artefact-type population itself, in successive phases,
>
> (iii) the qualitative change and oscillation of the artefact-type system as a structured system.

The more complex aspects (ii) and (iii) were deliberately left-over until this section since they are intimately bound-up with the ontogeny of artefact-types. It will be remembered that the organic and ontogenetic analogue of birth, growth, maturity, and death, appeared to confuse or remain inexplicit about the levels of change involved and the meaning of the analogy. We can now resume the study of these remaining processes and pursue the implications of the analogy.

Once again the main purpose is to scan the time-trajectory of these general categories of change for any useful regularities that might be employed in analysis. The grossest change and oscillation involving artefacts and attributes is change in the relative numbers of an artefact-type being made in the successive phases of the type's time-trajectory. This quantitative change and oscillation is gross because it overshadows and cuts across all other attribute fluctuations – a given attribute cannot exist and fluctuate independently if it is unique to an artefact-type no longer in production.

The output of a given artefact-type at successive intervals in time is usually expressed in relation to the output of other types in each sample – artefact-type A formed 25 per cent of a sample assemblage. Obviously this expression must be made in the light of proper sample precautions and sampling procedures. However, given these precautions the relative output of particular artefact-types within a cultural assemblage reflects a particular strategy on the part of the society reconciling the competing demands for working time and its deployment against the anticipated dislocating variety of the environment (lead, fig. 11). In this sense the percentages of different artefact-types in an assemblage represent the partial expression of a blending or mixed strategy towards aspects of the environmental and sociocultural situation. Particular sociocultural systems are characterized by particular overall strategies and consequently by their physical implementation in artefact form.

Quantitative oscillation in the relative output of given artefact-types therefore represents successive readjustments or changes in a cultural strategy – some insignificant and others dramatic. Nevertheless, although these gross oscillations cut across and perhaps terminate some attribute trends they do not necessarily co-ordinate in a simple way with one the function of the other. It is conceivable that a given artefact-type may have an increasing number of attributes per artefact and in its overall set whilst the artefact system is gradually transforming from one homeomorphic type-state to another – yet simultaneously the culture may suddenly cease the manufacture of the type. An artefact-type may be in the middle of a development towards an increasingly sophisticated and elaborate form and yet at the same time the culture may decide to cease its manufacture. The trend in numbers of attributes and attribute states may operate independently of the trend in total output and overall-system state. For obvious reasons it would be unusual for a culture to be systematically developing the elaboration of an artefact's format at the same time as it was decreasing its production. Accordingly, the three separate trends frequently, but not universally, reinforce one another with a decline in production accompanying a decline in elaboration and system state development.

Once again we have a situation in which three broad groups of trends may operate in various relationships one to another and assuming that each trend has the alternative states – increase, steady, decrease – these offer a bewildering variety of twenty-seven crude trend combinations in practice. An archaeological analysis of these three aspects of an artefact-type changing with time may be particularly informative if these three trends are isolated and then studied in relation to one another.

The quantitative increase or decrease in absolute numbers of an artefact-type may be part of a fashion oscillation but rather more frequently it reflects changes in the sociocultural system and especially, but not uniquely, changes in the economic strategy. The manner in which particular artefact-types oscillate in numbers with passing time often takes a familiar pattern – the double-lenticular pattern already seen in the modal trends of attribute states (fig. 56). Just as one particular attribute state is increasingly selected, becoming a modal state, only to be gradually replaced by another attribute state of

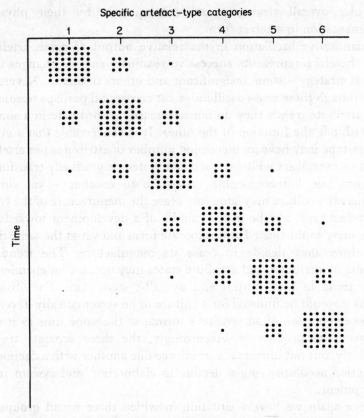

Fig. 56 Hypothetical 'ideal' model for a continuous sequence of successively dominant specific artefact-type states (1–6) and ranges for a single multistate artefact-type in successive phase populations of a single cultural assemblage trajectory. The 'ideal' double lenticular distribution model – lenticular in vertical tradition ontogeny and lenticular in horizontal phase distribution (archaic, modal, prototypical states) – a distribution which may be sought-for in suitable data (see figs 57–60).

formerly infrequent occurrence – so we find artefact-types appearing for the first time, becoming quantitatively common and widespread, until eventually replaced by a more efficient artefact, or itself developing into a more efficient artefact, or until the purpose for which it was employed is abandoned (fig. 57). It is important to grasp that this familiar pattern occurs for largely independent but similar reasons in both attributes within artefact-types and in artefact-types within assemblages. The pattern in not the same in both cases simply because the artefact-type is an integration of attributes changing in this way, but because artefact-types and attributes oscillate in the same way for closely similar reasons – namely, the continuous cultural process of selecting and developing successive aspects from the inevitable and broad range of attributes and artefact-types available. Nevertheless, the importance of this double-lenticular dispersion and its moving mode is the same for assemblage/type studies as for artefact-type/attribute studies – the pattern provides a crude predictive

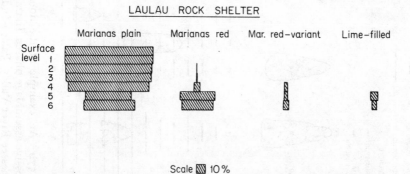

Fig. 57a Examples of the double lenticular ontogeny curves for specific artefact-types within successive assemblage phases. In this case pottery types stratified in rock shelters in the Mariana Islands, Micronesia. *c.* AD 800–1400.
Source: Spoehr 1957, p. 123.

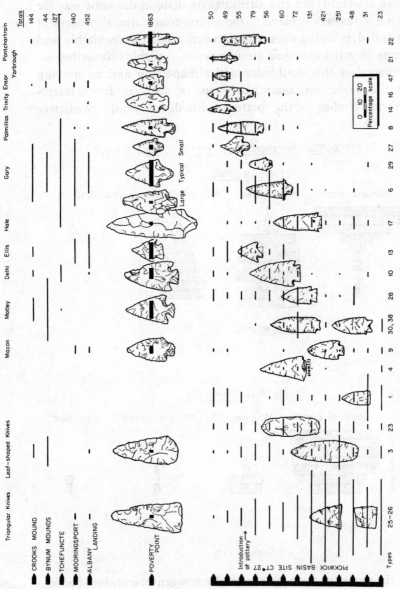

Fig. 57b An example of the double lenticular ontogeny curves for specific artefact-types within successive assemblage phases. In this case projectile point types stratified at Site Ct. 27, Pickwick Basin, Tennessee River Valley, Palaeo-Indian *c.* 800–2000 BC – compared with phase assemblages from other sites (note the transition from javelin-type points to arrow-type points about the time of the introduction of pottery).

principle or model such that agreement with, or deviation from the model will provide information about the situation being examined.

As evidence for the real nature of this patterning and in order to show how it may be sought for and used we can take several practical examples. It is essential to distinguish between actual stratified examples of this double-lenticular pattern (figs 57–9) and those examples of material which have been ordered using this model and its assumptions (fig. 60). The kinds of information that can be looked for in such studies are the phases in which whole groups of artefact-types show terminal or initial appearances, grouped nodes of change which often mark the replacement of one assemblage or type complex by another. On occasions it is sometimes possible to separate the smoothly trending patterns of whole groups of indigenous artefact-types from the fragmentary and irregular patterns sometimes associated with sporadically imported or traded items.

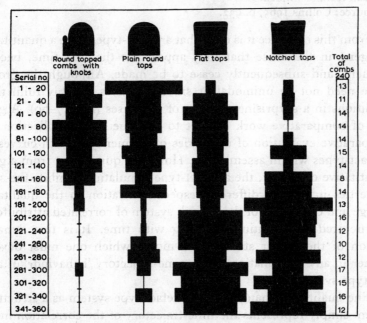

Fig. 58   An example of the double lenticular ontogeny curves for specific artefact-types within successive assemblage phases. In this case carved wooden Maori combs stratified at Kauri Point, New Zealand *c.* AD 1600–1800 (the curve irregularities in this case are largely due to the imposition of an arbitrary depth stratigraphy in a strata-less swamp). Source: Shawcross 1964, p. 391.

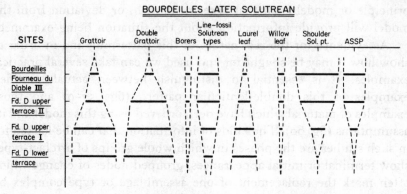

Fig. 59   An example of the lenticular ontogeny curves for specific artefact-types within successive assemblage phases. In this case flint artefact-types are stratified at the Fourneau du Diable shelter in the Bourdeilles region of France – an Upper Palaeolithic site of the Solutrean technocomplex.

Source: Collins 1965, p. 932.

From this evidence it is clear that artefact-types have a quantitative ontogeny in the sense that they appear for the first time, become frequent, and subsequently cease to be made. Although the growth curve need not be unimodal or smooth it does roughly fulfil these conditions in a surprising number of test cases (figs 57–60). A great deal of comparative work has yet to be done on the collection and comparative evaluation of categories of frequency growth curves for artefact-types within assemblages. However, quite apart from a gross quantitative ontogeny, the artefact-type population exhibits the same properties in a quite different respect in relation to the qualitative change and oscillation of the entity's system of correlated attributes as a structured constellation changing with time. It is this dynamic version of the earlier static phase model which one must develop further in any examination of the time-trajectory 'behaviour' of artefact-type systems.

The qualitative change of the artefact-type system as a structured system simply represents the time-trajectory of the correlation model and another way of looking at the manifestation of the kinds of changes already discussed. It is often useful to use several alternative models of even a single dynamic process in order that their useful regularities might supplement one another and in this case because the several models are tacitly employed with some confusion in studies of artefact and assemblage ontogeny.

Thus far we have a static model expressing the structure of an artefact-type population as a nucleated constellation of attributes arranged in clustered complexes and secondary nuclei in terms of the attribute intercorrelation in n-dimensional space (see above, pp. 210 ff). We now wish to develop some model of the 'behaviour' of successive generations or phase populations of these artefacts – the phenetic output of one phase being the input of the succeeding phase. In reality, of course, the successive developments of an artefact-type take place in many dispersed but interlinked settlement sites, with differing yet related sequences and lines of development. Nevertheless, the dynamic system trajectory of the developing artefact-type population may be arbitrarily expressed as a single overall integration of such subsystems and lineages within a single multilinear and mosaic

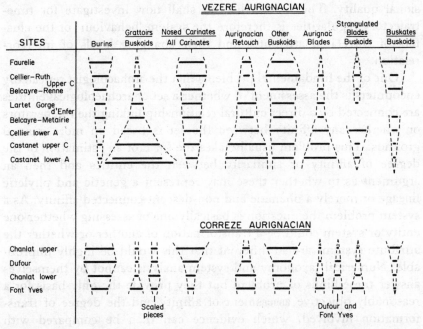

Fig. 60   Two examples of the lenticular ontogeny curves for specific artefact-types within successive assemblage phases. In these examples flint artefact-types, or their relative frequencies, are seriated for sites in very restricted territories – Aurignacian sites in the Vézère valley and Correze valley, Dordogne, France. Although the assemblages are from the Aurignacian technocomplex these regional seriation lines provide evidence of component cultural entities.

Source: Collins 1965, p. 932.

development. The archaeological record provides sporadic and successive sections of strands within this continuous cable of development and it is the relative ordering of these sample phase sections in relation to the orientation of the tradition cable that most exercises the archaeologist's researches.

In the dynamic model the nucleated constellation of attributes is continuously changing. New attributes join the system, old ones leave; attributes move from outer correlation shells into positions within the nuclei; new secondary nuclei slowly emerge as correlated attribute complexes and former secondary nuclei defining innovating subtypes within the type may move into central prominence as the modal type expression. Although the cosmological analogy is immediately apparent, it is the quite real and measurable intercorrelation of the attributes within the population which give the model this dimensional quality. The model that we shall now investigate for time-trajectory regularities is therefore the system 'behaviour' of the clusters of correlated attributes and their changing levels of intercorrelation.

One of the fundamental problems that the archaeologist repeatedly encounters is the assessment of whether a set of archaeological entities are connected by a direct cultural relationship linking their generators or whether any affinity between the set is based on more general grounds. This problem usually takes the form of an estimation of the degree of affinity or similarity between the entities and then an argument as to whether these may represent a genetic and phyletic lineage or merely a phenetic and non-descent connected affinity. As a system problem the question is basically one of assessing whether one entity or system could be a transformation of another or whether the attribute systems are so different that this would be highly improbable. Numerical taxonomy and system analysis cannot by themselves answer these kinds of problem but they provide the only basis for a reasonably objective assessment of affinity and the degree of transformation involved, which evidence can then be compared with control cases and with the time factor and other factors involved. If the entities can be shown to have a high level of affinity and perhaps to have polythetic sets with a large common intersect, then at least the possibility of phyletic connection can be entertained. Furthermore, if an analysis of the attribute correlation structures reveals common complexes or patterns of attribute relationships, especially between

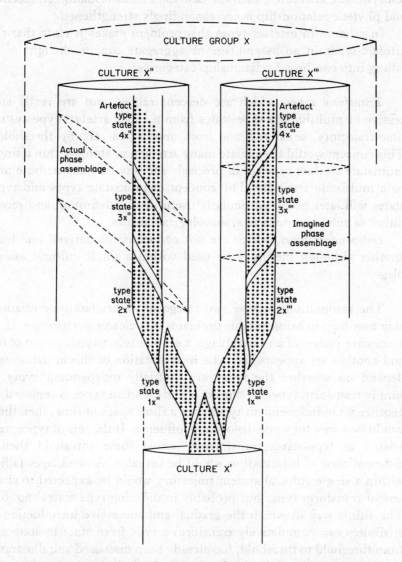

Fig. 61 A schematic illustration of the relationship uniting a group of cultural assemblages X', X'', X''' within a single culture group X by virtue of their polythetically shared assemblages of transform states of the same specific artefact-types, transform types x', x'', x''' in various phase states (1–4). The trajectory may be imagined as moving from bottom to top, or vice versa, and the divergence/convergence attributed to ecological or other field constraints.

idiosyncratic attributes, then the case for a transformation connection and phyletic relationship is correspondingly strengthened.

In relation to artefact-types this problem makes it clear that the artefact-types in an assemblage or aggregate can be thought of as falling into two broad relationship categories:

Transform types, which are descent related and are really successive or multilineage type-states from a single artefact-type system time-trajectory, separated one from another merely· by thresholds. This concept would then relate many artefacts as states within a single multistate artefact-type set in precisely the way that an attribute may be a multistate attribute. The concept of multistate types and type-states will later prove particularly useful in the definition and recognition of culture groups as archaeological entities.

Independent types, which are not connected or derived one from another although they may be used within a single cultural assemblage.

The recognition of these two categories of artefact-type relationship may help to bring various problems into clearer perspective. If, in successive phases of an assemblage, a set of artefact-types go out of use and another set appears then the interpretation of this situation will depend on whether the types are mutually independent types or simply transform types. If one set of independent types is replaced by another set of independent types over a short space of time, then there would be a case for some dislocating influence. If the sets of types were related as type-states transformed across some threshold then a different class of information would be revealed. Assemblages falling within a single cultural system trajectory would be expected to share sets of transform types but probably in differing type-states (fig. 61). The subtle way in which the gradual and successive introduction of attributes can cumulatively transform a type from state to state and from threshold to threshold, has already been discussed and illustrated in general terms in the hypothesis of multiple factors and cumulative effect (chapter 2, III).

It is time to return from general speculation to the field in which these kinds of change can best be studied. We now require a model of the time-trajectory of an artefact type which is dynamic (fig. 62) rather than static (fig. 50). Such a model can be conceptualized as a series of successive system states at infinitesimally small intervals along a time-

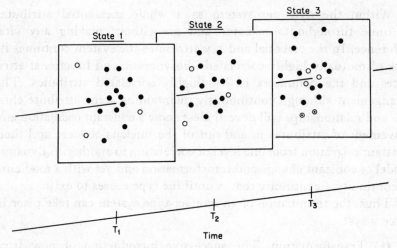

Fig. 62   A schematic model of the time-trajectory of an archaeological system in which successive population states are represented by the varyingly intercorrelated trajectories of the components comprising and defining the system. The model represents a series of successive system states, each expressed as the two-dimensional distortion of the inter-correlation diagram of the properties of the respective phase population (see figs 53, 54, 66). The system and components may be attributes within an artefact-type, or specific artefact-types within a changing cultural assemblage, or other archaeological entities.

trajectory – thus not only does the system as a whole have a time-trajectory but so also do the attributes within the system.

The dynamic artefact-type system as a system may first come into detectable existence as the successive and cumulative integration of a set of directively correlated essential and key attributes eventually crossing a definable threshold marking the first integrated appearance of a specific type format. Subsequently, the system will transform continuously from type-state to type-state and from threshold to threshold – the successive states all being transform types within the multi-state type. Although the model represents a unilinear system trajectory it is of course generated by the interconnected multilinear developments within the dispersed centres of production, a composite of individual site trajectories of very complex inter-reticulation. In the course of the whole system trajectory some component attributes will fluctuate more than others; the idiosyncratic attributes will be especially variable and the functional attributes much less so.

Within the dynamic system as a whole inessential attributes continue throughout, or come and go without making any vital difference. In the essential and key attributes the system continues its core of mutually highly-correlated idiosyncratic and functional attributes and the penumbra of less highly correlated attributes. The arrangement although continuously maintaining some attribute clusters and relationships will nevertheless show a constant oscillation and movement of attributes in and out of the nucleus clusters and their constant migration from one level of correlation to another. A dynamic model of constant change and transformation and yet with a modicum of continuity – continuity that is until the type ceases to exist.

Thus, the termination of an artefact-type system can take place in three ways:

(1) Transformation. The successive introduction of new attributes or attribute states to form a cumulatively new artefact format; simultaneously accompanied by the gradual loss of the key attribute syntax by the reverse process of directive correlation. If this transformation is severe and the threshold of the key format broken, then the transform may constitute a 'new' type. If the transformation remains within the key format threshold – then we have simply a new type-state or variant.

(2) Displacement. The physical displacement of one artefact-type from an assemblage or locus and its replacement by a new alternative – the outcome of competitive disjunction or equivocation.

(3) Cessation. The termination of the production of an artefact-type – its complete discontinuation without replacement, usually on grounds of redundancy.

The phenomena of transformation and displacement will also be discovered in the systems of the higher archaeological entities – in assemblages, cultures, culture groups, and technocomplexes. But the absolute and complete termination of production is characteristic only of the lower entity systems – attributes and artefact-types; continuity may only be simply severed at these lower levels. If transformation is sufficiently drastic and thereby modifies the existing key attribute format, then the artefact population may develop freshly emergent qualities precipitating a new type format and new key variables, constituting a genuine invention.

So far we have set up a system model and tried to understand in general terms how it might begin, develop, and end. Particularly important in these fluctuating changes are those that involve changes in the correlation values relating attribute clusters or complexes within the type – especially those relating the key attributes. The time-trajectory model of the static attribute cluster can perhaps be conceptualized as a bundle of attribute trajectories with continuously varying degrees of correlation between the component strands. If one attribute in the artefact population is always accompanied by another attribute, then together they form the basis of a tightly correlated bundle of trajectories within the changing artefact system. If, on the other hand, one of the attributes is accompanied by another within the complex at some lower level of frequency – say, only once in five cases – then this represents a trajectory less closely correlated within the bundle. There are descending degrees of correlation from complete correlation down to vanishing correlation and the total absence of interdependent variation. During the type system's time-trajectory the attributes within the complexes and clusters will move into and out of various levels of mutual correlation, continuously varying the degrees of correlation between the component strands, thereby altering the characterization of the type with passing time.

A very significant impression in this context is the concept of the 'coherence' or the overall degree of integration, or mutual intercorrelation, of attributes within types and types within cultural assemblages. If in successive phase populations of an artefact-type tradition it is found that the nucleus of highly correlated attributes are steadily decreasing their level of mutual intercorrelation then this change may be conceptualized as a decrease in the 'coherence' of the artefact format – possibly loosening into 'incoherence'. Conversely, increasing levels of intercorrelation between the attributes defining an artefact-type, in successive phases of its time-trajectory, increasingly define the format of the type – increasing the 'coherence' of that type.

The importance of the concept of 'coherence' as an expression of the changing levels of attribute correlation within a system is that it may be equally applied to the 'coherence' of types in terms of attributes and cultural assemblages or cultures in terms of artefact-types. The implications of these separate levels of organization must be considered independently but the concept operating is the same in both cases – another example of the same syntax operating at different hierarchical levels. In principle it is perfectly feasible to devise a taxonomic measure of the 'coherence', or the level of attribute inter-correlation, of successive artefact-type populations from a single type. Such a measure might be in some form of geometric mean for each population phase:

$$\text{geometric mean} = \sqrt[n]{(x_1 \times x_2 \times x_3 \times \ldots \times x_n)}$$

where x_1 is the product of all the positive correlation values of attribute one and where n is the number of attributes in the system aspect under study. Alternatively, the overall level of intercorrelation of 'coherence' might be better expressed by calculating the moment of inertia of the correlation network. It may require a certain amount of experiment to arrive at the most practicable measure of 'coherence' but there can be little doubt that this conceptual characteristic of successive phases of such a system trajectory can be measured on a relative scale.

Against this background of successive type populations with measured levels of attribute intercorrelation, or coherence, it is possible to think in terms of measuring the fluctuating 'strength' of artefact-type and assemblage traditions, varying from formative incoherence to stable coherence. The 'strength' of the system increasing with the increasing correlation between attributes and their decreasing deviation from increasingly well-defined modes. The 'birth' of an artefact-type then represents the successive introduction and growing coherence of a nucleus of directively correlated key attributes within the polythetic set defining the system. In this sense, the type becomes more and more coherent or integrated, more and more clearly defined, until such time as it should be totally discontinued or the process reverses and rapid change should shift the key attribute set to a new format and the system to a new system-state – the 'birth' of a new transform type. Clearly, the fluctuating levels of correlation between the components represents one of the crucial aspects behind the ontogenetic analogy of system 'birth', 'maturity', and 'death'.

To make this process more understandable it is perhaps worth-while to speculate about a practical example. Let us imagine the situation in beds I–II in Olduvai Gorge. The particular transition and transformation that interests us here is the hypothetical case of the first piriform handaxe types developing out of the earlier varieties of chopper-chopping tools. In this situation we can imagine millenia of development in which chopper-chopping tools continued in daily use but attribute by attribute inevitable variation and experimental modifications successively introduced new characters into the polythetic set defining chopper tools. The attributes that retrospectively we recognize as those that become directively correlated towards the piriform handaxe type are thus cumulatively introduced into the range of variation.

At first, it may be an increasing tendency to lateral flattening to better accommodate the chopper to the palm, then someone else may accentuate the secondary working around the radial edge except at the butt, other specimens may increasingly develop a pointed shape for particular functional requirements, and so on. Gradually, within the polythetic constellation of the ancestral artefact-type a new and growing nucleus appears, steadily increasing in content and intercorrelation level – a consistent variant is developing. The polythetic set defining the chopper-chopping tool type is consequently extended by new attributes in novel and increasingly recurrent clusterings. Eventually the extended set will divide on functional lines as the emergent properties of the new artefact format are increasingly appreciated, leading to the deliberate formalization, increasing differentiation and the specialized development of divergent artefact usage patterns. The chopper-chopping tool type continues but a pointed and increasingly preferred piriform variant has been precipitated in response to functional requirements. This process may perhaps represent the kind of cumulative development by means of which the handaxe type gradually came into being.[2]

The process just sketched remains purely hypothetical but it illustrates the general idea of the steadily growing coherence of the type and the steadily growing formation of a secondary nucleus of clustered attributes within a population's polythetic constellation of attributes. We know that this idea of increasing coherence reflects a quite tangible and objective process – the increasing degree of mutual correlation between certain attributes which were previously either absent from the system or at best were within the low correlation level penumbra. The overall importance of this model is the realization that it is perfectly feasible to estimate and express the correlation level of attributes within a system at successive phases in a development sequence. As a practical example illustrating the necessary methodology we may note the changing coherence of three successive phases of a pottery tradition from a stratified Arikara Indian site analysed by Deetz (1965).[3] By such techniques as these the actual process of the 'birth' and 'death' of artefact-types can be minutely investigated.

It emerges that one of the most important factors involved in defining archaeological entities and their ontogeny may be seen to be the changing correlation relationships of the system components – relationships that can be measured or estimated by the use of suitable techniques. Another factor of parallel importance is the rate of change of the system components. Between them these two factors help to define the thresholds separating system-state from system-state and transform type from transform type.

If we postulate an artefact-type slowly changing as the expression of its fluctuating attribute components over hundreds of years of steady development, then although the dissimilarity between the earliest examples of the type and the latest will be very considerable, the development will have been so gradual and by such infinitesimally small steps that the whole sequence will appear as an homogeneous time and space artefact population, based on a single polythetic set – it will appear as one type. Something approaching this very unusual situation is to be seen in the one million years of development in the homogeneous handaxe type or type family (Isaac 1972b, fig. 4.3 and p. 181). However, in the developmental sequence of most artefact-types this gradual and steady development is broken-up by phases of greatly accelerated change interspersed with longer phases of slower paced change and development. The exceptionally rapid change of particular attributes or attribute complexes within artefact-type systems is usually to be associated with sociocultural or environmental changes which produce momentary dislocation foci in respect of the artefact and the variety of its attributes. Retrospectively, these spurts of development divide up the time trajectory of the artefact-type and since they result in a rapid shift to new modes of attribute characterization they conveniently register the development of 'new' transform types, type-states, or subtypes. It would appear that the identity of new types sometimes rests on homogeneous development sequences separated by nodes of maximized change.

One of the problems which is raised is how different any type must be before it can be labelled 'new' – the problem of defining the clustered nodes of accelerated change. Unfortunately practical studies indicate that the nodal point for one attribute changing from modal state to modal state need not be correlated with the nodal points of change in the other attributes. It is very rare to find a case in which all the attributes of a system rapidly change together – rather more commonly they change in a staggered sequence (fig. 63). It seems sensible to take these clustered but staggered sequences of nodes of change as representing some major response to some significant stimulus and together capable of characterizing a new entity state with some validity. Consequently, in an artefact-type changing with time

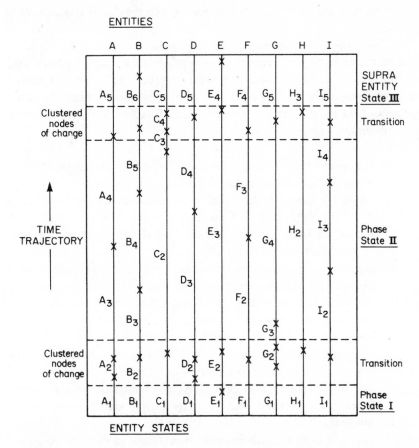

Fig. 63   The time-trajectory of a supra-entity defined by a system of component entities or characters A–I. The successive phase states of the supra-entity are separated one from another by transition thresholds of correlated changes amongst the system components – clustered nodes of change. The supra-entity and component entities might be an artefact-type and its attributes, or a cultural assemblage and its site assemblages.

the attribute trajectory bundles can be defined at either end by clustered nodes of maximal change – without ignoring the fact that all
attributes will display sporadically isolated nodes at several points
within the trajectory. The definition of these clustered nodes of
maximal rate of change in numbers of correlated attributes is
clearly once again a matter for careful investigation using taxonomic
methods. In practice this problem is often arbitrarily solved for the
archaeologist by the discontinuous and fragmentary samples at
his disposal – these give a false sense of 'obvious' and disconnected
type-states.

It may help to summarize at this stage the main features of
artefact-types changing with time – repeating the earlier points and
adding those just discussed. The three broad and interconnected
levels of change within the population time-trajectory remain the same
but now some supplementary details can be filled in. The artefact-type
time-trajectory can be seen to show:

(i) the quantitative change and oscillation in numbers of attributes within the system;
    (a) as variation in the number of different attributes defining
the polythetic set of successive population phases,
    (b) as variation in the number of different attributes per
artefact in successive phases,
    (c) as variations in both of the above aspects jointly, in a
variety of combining trends.
(ii) the quantitative change and oscillation in numbers of the
artefact-type population itself, in successive phases – the
horizontal and vertical double lenticular patterns.
(iii) the qualitative change and oscillation of the artefact-type
systems as a structured system – in which individual low-level
attribute changes may cumulatively change the whole system
from state to state and perhaps into a quite 'new' system
altogether;
    (a) it is useful to distinguish transform types from indepen-
dent types,
    (b) variation in correlation levels between attributes and
within attribute complexes (system coherence) appears to
be one of the main changes capable of altering the whole
system state,

(c) variation in rates of change introduces the factor capable of marking-out and defining those phases in which unusually large numbers of attributes change their modal characterization in a staggered and connected sequence – phases of accelerated change.

The analogy of ontogenetic 'birth', 'growth', and 'death' can be applied with different meanings at any of these three broad levels of change (i)–(iii) above. It now becomes apparent that these terms refer either to quantitative changes in numbers of attributes or artefacts, or they may refer to qualitative changes in an overall system state – these various implications usually being inexplicit and jointly confused. With respect to qualitative system changes and system ontogeny the two most important factors involved are first, the changing intercorrelation of attributes and second, the rate of change. It is particularly significant that these factors are relative and not absolute factors. There are many indications that archaeological data is on the whole quite unsuitable for the arrival at valid conclusions about absolute values but that it is suitable for assessing relative factors such as correlated covariance and rates of change. Indeed, in so far as the ontogenetic terms – birth, growth, maturity, and death – have any archaeological or cultural meaning at all, they seem to represent an intuitive recognition of analogies between the rates of change and changing coherence in organic systems and sociocultural systems.

v   System pattern regularities

Once again, the main purpose of this section is to underline and bring together the general system 'behaviour' scattered throughout this discussion of the artefact-type concept. The system which forms the bulk of this chapter is the system of attributes within changing artefact-types. Most of the regularities in the 'behaviour' of attribute systems have already been outlined in general terms in connection with attributes within artefacts in chapter 4 (section V).

Previous discussion has emphasized the utility of thinking of attribute variety in terms of new, alternative, contradictive and redundant values in relation to particular artefact systems, requiring the constant mutual readjustment of the components in order to minimize the dislocation of the whole. Dislocation and disequilibrium occur from time to time in the relationships between attributes within specific attribute complexes, between complexes within the type, and between the artefact-type and its sociocultural context. In any one artefact-type tradition, at any one time, there are usually several interrelated foci, detectable in successive phase populations, at which rapid change and adjustment is being made to accommodate certain contingencies. Such changes in attributes and attribute complexes often take the form of oscillating instability in which the type populations show a wide range of very diverse and short-lived solutions gradually moving towards a more stable consensus and a relatively stable attribute format. In general it is typical of the rich interconnection of material culture that the matrix of transitions allows and expresses interlinked multilinear developments of a most complex kind – there is usually no unique and homogeneous trajectory in the development of artefact-types.

If the circumstances are such that there are a large number of foci of accelerated change, involving most of the key attributes of the artefact-type system, then these correlated and accelerated changes are likely to transform the whole system format from one type-state to another – or even into an emergent or altogether new type system. This process involves the successive and cumulative integration of a new set of directively correlated attributes, which imperceptibly diversify the variety of the system until a certain threshold is reached and an effectively different artefact format is produced. The definition of such thresholds depends on recognizing and measuring the correlated quantitative and qualitative changes in attributes and their dispersion amongst the artefact population, combined with the recognition of the short phases of unusually rapid rates of attribute change. These grouped nodes of change mark out the thresholds and provide some basis for the subdivision of the continuing sequence of artefact-type states. The various type-states of a multistate type will represent both successive states from the sequence and contemporary states or variants from within the multilineage of the type trajectory.

Changes in type-state and format raise the whole problem of artefact-type ontogeny. We have already devoted some space to this complicated concept and have moved towards the impression that combinations of reinforcing and correlated trends coincide to mark the flux from format to format. These trends may equally be detected in space, where they reflect contemporary subtypes and variants, or in time where they reflect successive subtypes – the subtype being merely one type-state. Although the trends may act separately from one another they are nonetheless closely interrelated and achieve their effects by the cumulative interaction of their superimposed tendencies.

The transition from system-state to system-state is an elusive change which can only be mapped with great difficulty in terms of a number of arbitrary aspects. However, these changes are so important that it is perhaps worthwhile to try and model the kinds of trend involved in system 'birth', 'maturity', and 'death' – not only at this level of attributes within types but later for types within cultures and so on. This is a particularly hazardous and precarious speculation because of the already mourned absence of suitable studies on detailed data, although experiments are beginning to fill this gap (Clarke 1962). It therefore follows that the model outlined here is merely intended to sketch the variables involved and to provoke more realistic modifications.

The principal trends that we have been discussing include :

changes in numbers of attribute states defining the overall polythetic set,

changes in numbers of attributes per artefact (on average),

changes in numbers of artefacts per attribute state (location of the central tendency),

changes in the level of overall attribute intercorrelation (coherence),

changes in the rates of change of attributes from modal state to modal state.

These are some of the oscillating trends that may mutually reinforce one another in an almost infinite variety of patterns of change. It is tentatively suggested that these fluctuating changes may mark the thresholds in the system's time-trajectory somewhat in the following way:

(0) *Threshold – 'death/birth'*

Successive populations of an artefact-type exhibiting – increasing numbers of attribute states in successive polythetic sets,

decreasing numbers of attributes per artefact (population average),

decreasing numbers of artefacts with modal attribute states – slackening central tendency,

decreasing levels of overall intercorrelation between attributes,
increasing rates of change of attributes from state to state.

(1) *Formative – 'growth'*

Successive populations of an artefact-type exhibiting –
   decreasing numbers of attribute states in successive polythetic sets,
increasing numbers of attributes per artefact,
increasing numbers of artefacts with certain key attribute
   states – an increasing and new central tendency,
increasing level of overall intercorrelation between certain key
   attributes,
decreasing rates of change of essential attributes from state to
   state.

(2) *Coherent – 'maturity'*

Successive populations of an artefact-type exhibiting –
   increasing numbers of attribute states in successive polythetic sets,
increasing numbers of attributes per artefact,
maximal central tendency of artefacts around key attribute
   states,
maximal level of overall intercorrelation between certain
   attributes,
minimal rates of change from state to state.

(3) *Post-coherent – 'decline'*

Successive populations of an artefact-type exhibiting – decreasing numbers of attribute states in successive polythetic sets,
decreasing numbers of attributes per artefact,
decreasing central tendency of artefacts around former key
   attribute states,
decreasing level of overall intercorrelation between certain
   essential attributes,
increasing rates of change from state to state.

(0) *Threshold – 'death/birth'*

Successive populations of an artefact-type exhibiting –
   increasing numbers of attribute states in successive polythetic sets,
decreasing numbers of attributes per artefact,
decreasing central tendency of artefacts around formerly
   modal attribute states,

decreasing level of overall intercorrelation between attributes, increasing rates of change of attributes from state to state.

This outline emphasizes the point made earlier, that the onto-genetic terms only take archaeological and cultural meaning from certain repeated patterns of change found both in organic systems and sociocultural systems. Where possible, we should strive to replace such intuitive analogies by explicit details of the common basis – this is the vital process by which an intuitive skill may be gradually transformed into a discipline. The price that must be paid is the repeated trials and repeated errors in the successively less naive attempts upon these complex problems.

It is to be assumed that the model change process sketched under the ontogenetic headings is both highly idealized and only crudely meaningful. That there are many other combinations and permu-tations of the various fluctuating trends has already been admitted – other trends have probably been mistakenly omitted and some others naively treated. For example, we have omitted to include in this summary that gross trend which must cut across the continuous fluctuations of the system format – the absolute quantitative pro-duction of the artefact-type generating the system. It has already been noted that a culture may abruptly cease to manufacture a given artefact-type even at the very moment of increasingly developing its attribute elaboration and coherent format – some contemporary mili-tary aircraft have had time-trajectories of this unusual kind. In addi-tion there are other ways of combining the trends already noted, both one with another and with gross fluctuations in the type output. The model sequence as sketched is purely a hypothetical ideal but nonetheless remains a useful model against which the population trajectory of say an artefact-type from a stratified site of many levels might usefully be contrasted.

Even with great care and much ingenuity it proves impossible to discuss material culture changes without recourse to conceptually 'charged' terms. If we avoid the unsatisfactory extension of such organic terms as – birth, growth, maturity, florescence, death – we still encounter the only slightly less loaded terminology of – integration, disintegration, transformation and so on. In using such terms to describe material culture it is important to emphasize that these terms carry no simple implications outside their specific frame of reference amongst material artefacts. We are not suggesting that these changes and processes take place in isolation, of their own accord, or that they reflect identical changes in the non-material aspects of the cultures concerned. On the contrary, we are studying the manner in which changes having their origins in unknown developments and stimuli within the social, religious, psychological, and economic subsystems of a society are implemented in changing the material culture exoskeleton. We are simply analysing the external processes by means of which a culture changes its skin; why a culture should drastically change its external manifestation is another matter. What matters most at this moment in the development of archaeology is that for the first time it is not only possible to conceptualize these changes but also to measure and express them in relative terms.

Notes

(1) See Binford (1972, p. 248) for a reply to this criticism.

(2) This particular example requires revision in the light of the work of Mary Leakey and others in Olduvai Gorge (summarized, for example, in Isaac 1969, pp. 13–15). During at least half a million years the Oldowan industry shows no radical changes in tool typology and morphology, though among two new tool types which appear at the top of Bed I in Olduvai is the 'proto-biface'. But it is *not* possible to recognize the local step-by-step development from the Oldowan chopper tool to the handaxe which these proto-bifaces might suggest and which traditional typologies have proposed. On the contrary, handaxe assemblages appear suddenly in Bed II and almost complete Oldowan assemblages continue alongside them.

The reasons for this seemingly abrupt technological change have been postulated by different authors. Mary Leakey argues that the Acheulean handaxe assemblages at Olduvai must be intrusive and the result of more gradual development from Oldowan assemblages elsewhere. This interpretation, along with David Clarke's general model of gradual systemic change approaching important thresholds (e.g. 'a series of successive system states at infinitesimally small intervals along a time-trajectory') has been vigorously criticized by Binford (1972, pp. 244–94). His concern with the the Oldowan–Acheulean transition is with *one* example where the 'traditional' archaeologist's expectations about cultural change are not met. Thus he summarizes the traditional model of cultural change in terms of eight statements and three expectations:

Statements
'(1) *Culture is localized in individual human beings* . . .
(2) *Culture is transmitted among human beings* – through learning individuals assimilate culture from other persons.

(3) *Culture is shared* ...
(4) *Culture derives from humans* – it may be generated only by human acts of intervention.
(5) *Culture is cumulative* ...
(6) *Culture is a continuum* ... because the succession of individuals in generational succession is a continuum ...
(7) *Culture is continuously changing.*
(8) *Culture changes gradually* ... because individuals are replaced gradually in human populations.'

Expectations
'(1) ... a continuous sequence of variability, patterning as gradual directional changes in the relative frequencies of recognized artefact taxa ...
(2) A gradual increase in the numbers of artefact taxa recognizable if the isolated part of the archaeological record spans a 'sufficient' period of time.
(3) Transformational sequences showing a 'development' of artefact forms from antecedent forms.'

(1972, pp. 251–2)

Given this model of change, Binford argues that the traditional archaeologist is forced to conclude that 'breaks in continuity of cultural patterning must derive from breaks in the continuity of human populations in the area' (1972, p. 252). His counter-argument to this is that variability in stone tool assemblages does not necessarily reflect the degree of cultural or social interaction and/or continuity, but that it should reflect different activities carried out within the community (cf. Binford and Binford 1966). He also proposes that variability in assemblage composition should be inversely related to the degree that the stone tools were used for more than one purpose (cf. White and Thomas 1972, p. 278) and/or carried around from site to site rather than thrown away after usage. The effect of this 'curation' on assemblage composition has only been postulated in recent years (e.g. Binford 1973, 1976) and is clearly of great importance.

Isaac's (1969, 1976) views on the Oldowan–Acheulean transition and on cultural change in general seem to lie somewhere between those expressed by David Clarke in this volume and by Binford above. Thus he proposes that there may be important 'thresholds' in stone technology 'so that certain techniques are either present or absent and intermediate expressions are virtually non-existent' (1969, p. 16). As an example he cites the striking of large flakes from which handaxes and cleavers could be produced after minimal retouch (1969, p. 16) and man's discovery of the conchoidal fracture of flint, leading to the first Oldowan flake tools (1976, p. 41). But while Isaac proposes these threshold models, he suggests that gradual development also occurred over long periods of time (e.g. the Oldowan) and that these two types of interpretation are simply the extremes in a continuum.

Thus it can be seen that the problem of the Oldowan–Acheulean transition, which in 1968 was a good example of David Clarke's general systemic model for culture change, has now served to bring its *universal* application into question and open up an important area of debate.

(3) But for criticism of Deetz's methods, see Doran and Hodson 1975, p. 150.

6 Assemblage and culture

> The culture is not an *a priori* category elaborated in the
> studies of philosophers and then imposed from outside
> upon working archaeologists. Cultures are observed facts,
> 'Changing methods and aims in prehistory',
> *Proceedings of the Prehistoric Society for 1936*, p. 3.
> V. GORDON CHILDE 1936

1 Introduction

Thus far the discussion has slowly traversed the lower levels of the
hierarchy of archaeological entities, carefully defining the terms as
they were encountered. This ascent has involved an investigation of
the nature of archaeological attributes, their combination in particular
artefacts and in the populations of artefacts called artefact-types. The
next stage of the climb must negotiate the difficult and obscure
formations of the *assemblage* and the *culture* (fig. 49).

Let us start with the concept of an archaeological 'assemblage' –
one of the few entities which together with the 'artefact' shares a
reasonably established and accepted definition. This does not prevent
the disturbing abuse and misuse of both terms. Archaeological usage
has established an archaeological assemblage as – *an associated set of
contemporary artefact-types*. The important aspects of an artefact
assemblage under this definition are that the artefacts may belong to
more than one type and that they occur together in definite contemporary association with one another. The occurrence of several artefact-types of uncertain chronology, within the same limited geographical area, does not constitute an assemblage in the sense defined
here but rather constitutes an 'aggregate' of lesser significance and
information value (Childe 1956, p. 31). Many problems of interpretation have arisen in the past through the careless extension of the
name and implications of the term 'assemblage' to loose aggregates of
the latter kind. False assemblages compounded of artefact-types never
found in contemporary association but loosely occurring in one area
and convincingly expressed by palimpsest distribution mapping have

erroneously characterized quite illusory cultures from time to time. The first questions to be asked of any distribution map of several different artefact-types is how many of the types occur together in contemporary association, in what combinations, and on how many occasions?

Assemblages occur dispersed over geographical areas and these areas can be defined by limits if assemblages containing specific types are mapped. Taking the time dimension, we have already seen that assemblages of artefact-types will vary according to the varying numbers of the component artefact-types and that these types in turn will be changing as the integral of their oscillating attribute states.

A study of particular assemblages from particular areas of space and time rapidly brings us into contact with another entity: the 'cultural assemblage' or simply the 'culture' – probably the most important single concept in prehistoric studies. An archaeological culture is expressed by a set of specific artefact-types and represented by a group of assemblages containing some of those artefact-types. The special nature of the culture is embodied in the precise relationship between the group of assemblages and the comprehensive set of types which they exhibit.

The characteristics of the assemblages grouped into cultures are:

(1) The component assemblages share a large number of specific artefact-types one with another, although each assemblage need not contain all the types in the shared set.
(2) The artefact-types represented in the assemblages comprise a comprehensive selection of types from most of the material spheres of cultural activity.
(3) The same specific artefact-types occur together repeatedly in those component assemblages, albeit in varying combinations.
(4) Finally, the component assemblages must come from a limited, defined and continuous geographical area and period of time.

These are the four main characteristics that have to be compressed into any attempt at a definition of an archaeological culture as an entity. It would seem that two of these crucial conditions are fulfilled, indeed can only be fulfilled, if the cultural assemblage is regarded as a polythetic set of artefact-types. These necessary conditions are the ones that stipulate that the various component assemblages defining the culture must share a number of specific artefact-types from a larger set such that no assemblage need contain all the types, although the same artefact-types must repeatedly occur together in varying combinations (fig. 3).

The remaining characteristics or conditions emphasize that the artefacts in the assemblages must be matched as specific types or subtypes – it is not sufficient that they merely share a low-level affinity within a type group or family. In addition there should be numbers of different artefact-type categories involved and these should represent as many material aspects of cultural activity as survive – not simply a sample from a single sociocultural aspect like weapon assemblages, bronze artefact assemblages, or pottery assemblages. These latter assemblages are complexes of artefact-types related to special sub-cultures within the sociocultural system and we will deal later on with their special treatment (section II). The final condition, stipulating that the assemblages must have a coherent and homogeneous time and space distribution, is designed to ensure the reality of the group of assemblages as the material products of a single cultural tradition or phase.

It is rather difficult to condense and distil these vital conditions into a concise definition – a difficulty which has given rise to the repeated misuse of the culture concept and a mistaken impression that the concept has no tangible reality. An attempt at a working definition might perhaps run as follows: *an archaeological culture is a polythetic set of specific and comprehensive artefact-types which consistently recur together in assemblages within a limited geographic area.* The subsidiary conditions about contemporaneity and physical association are conveniently contained within the definition of the term 'assemblage' developed earlier on.

The information value of the archaeological culture concept as a high-level predictive category has been very seriously impaired by the repeated misuse of the term and its confusion with other entities with the same name in other disciplines. The persistent manipulation and expression of archaeological cultures as rigid, mutually exclusive, monothetic sets of artefacts has rightly failed to impress generations of students. So-called cultures composed almost entirely from single aspects of material culture have added to this disrepute. Ill-defined and widespread methods of flint tool technology have been persistently elevated to cultural status in a manner overruling the affinities and dissimilarities of the total artefact assemblages involved. Gross manufacturing techniques based upon core tools, flake tools, blade tools, prepared core tools, pressure flaked tools, and others have from time to time appeared in the literature as reflecting a core tool culture, a flake tool culture, a blade tool culture, a Levallois culture, or a Solutrean culture respectively, with unenlightening results. In a complementary fashion, assemblages from Britain to China and from Poland to Roumania have been designated part of a Tardenoisian culture, virtually on the basis of certain geometrical microliths which merely reflect a common technological background in a shared environment – namely post-glacial hunting cultures using the bow in pursuit of temperate forest game. This entity may be a valid and interesting entity to define but it is simpler in content and larger in dimension than a true culture (see Technocomplex, chapter 8).

The later periods of prehistory have similarly contributed to the confusion. There have been cultures defined by single pottery types in such a manner that the domestic heavy-duty pottery has been put in one culture and the finer wares put in another – even in the face of persistent physical association. Witness the artificial separation of the Bell Beaker culture from its Rusticated or Plain domestic wares, the Corded Ware culture from its domestic Globular Amphorae, the Proto-Sesklo painted ware from its domestic Pre-Sesklo impressed ware, and so on. In the same way the products of segments or classes of societies have often been elevated to full cultural status, so that a hundred rich graves distinguished entirely by a small set of rank and prestige weapons, trinkets, and gew-gaws has given us a Wessex culture whose domestic pottery and other cultural equipment belong within the British Collared Urn culture. Perhaps the worst abuse has arisen from the attempts to extend groupings based upon hoards of widely traded and industrially mass-produced bronze artefacts to cultural assemblages with which they do not entirely coincide. This conspires to conceal the interesting and important information that the European Middle and Late Bronze Age metal trade and its distribution pattern was often supra-cultural in a significant and informative way.[1]

This disturbing list of various and undefined usages of the term 'culture' could be endlessly extended without even having the merit of consistency under particular authors. Although the continuing misuse of a fundamental concept must seriously damage its residual information value we should not fall into the error of supposing that the entity fails to remain a fundamental entity, or that it is impossible to define it adequately. We cannot hope for agreement between archaeologists about the definition of particular terms but at least we can insist that they define what they mean by a term before using it.

II   Cultural assemblage systems

Some of the mystery and confusion surrounding the concept of an archaeological 'culture' is immediately dispelled by giving the entity its full title – an archaeological 'cultural assemblage'. Such a cultural assemblage we have already discovered to be a polythetic set of arte-fact-types variously represented in component assemblages which share a high-level mutual affinity one with another and with the cultural assemblage. Clearly, one of the more variable factors in the relationship between the component assemblages is their actual and precise level of similarity. On a previous occasion it appeared that the isolation of several broad levels of similarity, from 100 to 0 per cent, tended to help avoid confusion between the different extent and implications of the stacked sets of individuals – leading us to dis-tinguish the type group, type, and subtype levels of artefact sets. Now we are encountering a precisely similar situation with a similar basis for confusion, only this time the affinity relationship is between assemblages within a culture or cultural assemblage. Once again the repetitive syntax of the relationships between the entities in the archaeological hierarchy becomes apparent – attributes within types being congruent to types within cultures.

It is at this stage that contention is joined by intuitive practice, for archaeologists have long toyed with higher-level entities than the culture and ethnologists at least have drawn attention to the material equipment of the lower-level sub-cultural segments outlined by sociology. Once again a varied terminology has been inconsistently applied and rarely defined, but here largely for reasons of tradition and symmetry the arbitrary terms culture group, culture, and subculture will be used in further discussion. The symmetry in the nomenclature is a deliberate attempt to draw attention to the symmetry in the affinity relationships relating these parallel entities:

type group (or family)	culture group (or family)
type (specific type)	culture (specific culture)
subtype (variant)	subculture (segment)

The further elaboration of this comparison and the full definition of the archaeological culture group must await the next chapter.

Meanwhile, we may mark the parallel in structuring and the parallel basis of this formation in the levels of affinity of sets of items. Since the culture group concept must await our gradual approach and the culture concept has been outlined, it remains to debate the important and archaeologically neglected role of the subculture in material culture.

To place the subculture in its setting we can observe that archaeological cultures and their component assemblages display several kinds of variety and each category will herein be discussed in a relevant section:

> variety in polythetic structures of the component assemblages (section I),
>
> variety in artefact-type subsystems of the component assemblages (section II),
>
> variety in the dispersion pattern of the component assemblages (section III),
>
> variety in the numbers of the component assemblages (section IV).

Our interest at this point is focused upon subcultures as exhibiting variety and regularity in the subsystems of type complexes within cultural assemblages. The subculture has a number of different forms and roles but all of them are represented by type complexes. This latter intermediate level entity can be defined as a *specific artefact-type complex – a polythetic set of different specific artefact-types repeatedly found together in assemblages within a population of assemblages*; a definition that should be compared with that relating attributes and attribute complexes (chapter 4). The detection of the component type complexes within cultural assemblages should play an important part in sociocultural analysis and the assessment of the roles played in various social segments and activity groups. To some extent a sociocultural system can be viewed as a system of interacting subcultures or subsystems – made apparent in material culture as correlated and covarying type complexes within cultural assemblages.

An archaeological subculture might therefore be defined as – *an infra-cultural segment or activity alignment characterized by a specific type complex*. Such subcultures and their type complexes are particularly interesting both as analytical concepts and by virtue of their variety and semi-independent existence. Some subcultures are non-exclusive social fractions, others are rigidly exclusive in the sense that an individual may not belong to this segment and to certain others at the same time. Some subcultures are interchangeable and transferable from culture to culture; some appear to be economically parasitic and others symbiotic with their parent sociocultural system; some subcultures are marked by material equipment but many are not. As a broad scheme one might isolate five varieties of subculture which register in the archaeological record:

ethnic subcultures
regional subcultures
occupational subcultures
social subcultures
sex subcultures

Each subculture format may have a type complex of its own, under certain conditions. The artefact-type complex of such subcultures may also include a distinctive linguistic vocabulary, habits, customs, clothing, art styles, as well as a specific set of material equipment.

Ethnic subcultures are genetically related and discrete minorities existing within an 'alien' culture. Such ethnic subcultures are usually readily distinguished for a while by their traditional attributes and artefacts but eventually lose coherence as an identifiable entity. This loss of identity is a particularly significant process, it depends upon the rate of interaction and the critical mass of the group – the latter expression denoting the population size and its dispersion pattern. Archaeologically such ethnic groups are important in that they frequently represent the gradual termination or 'death' of a cultural assemblage; both the concept of critical mass and cultural disintegration will be pursued later on (fig. 64). Whether the minority is a powerful and intrusive caste or an engulfed aboriginal group does not alter the inevitable process of integration and transformation – witness the Norman subculture in medieval England and conversely the various American Indian subcultures of the present day. One interesting and additional feature is the capacity for almost obliterated subcultural distribution patterns to reassert themselves in a new guise in subsequent area developments. This suggests that long after any visible material trace of an ethnic subculture has disappeared from the archaeological record there may continue to remain vestigial social alignments and orientations which may later fracture along primeval lines of cleavage; a concept that we will also meet in connection with the repeated area formats that constitute the geographical 'personality' of a territory.

Example. As an archaeological example of ethnic subcultures one might note one interpretation of the Beaker culture enclaves of Late Neolithic Britain as intrusive immigrant minorities maintaining a full cultural identity from *c.* 2000–1500 BC only to be engulfed, isolated, and absorbed by the indigenous majority cultures (Clarke 1967, 1970).

Regional subcultures are genetically related, semi-discrete but continuous branches of a single culture which by virtue of poor intercommunication and growing isolation gradually develops distinctive subcultures by divergent development pooled over local territories. Regional divergence is the clue to regional subculture development – frequently on the basis of spatial, topographic, genetic, ecological and communication isolation. Sometimes this divergence expresses a straightforward subculture specialization in the economic exploitation of a local ecological niche; at other times the divergence may be subtly developed by localized idiosyncratic changes in seasonal cyclical behaviour, leading to increasing isolation and special adaptation. Such cyclic isolation seems to have operated amongst the later Neolithic and Bronze Age cultures of Alpine Europe in which some cultures developed seasonal transhumance with subcultures appropriate to the successive ecological zones and their cyclical exploitation; later some of these subcultures seem to have branched off and developed an agrarian strategy intimately integrated to single zonal habitats – the grass pastures above the tree-line for example. This process simultaneously illustrates the regional subculture as a potential embryo culture and the significance of ecological zonation in separating and isolating regional subculture strategies. Just as ethnic subcultures may on occasion reflect the 'death' of former cultural assemblages so regional subcultures have the potential to give 'birth' to new and emergent assemblage formats of type complexes. Once again the optimal conditions for such cultural 'birth' depend on the critical mass – in this case a large and expanding culture area, divided into many local groups exploiting divergent ecological niches and almost but not quite isolated from each other (fig. 64). Such a dispersion pattern maximizes regional subcultural variation in an increasingly divergent manner until the subcultural units fall below the affinity threshold emphasizing their former uniformity and the units cease to orientate intercommunication and development on the old basis.

Example. Regional subcultures are found in every large archaeological culture and the development of groups of regional subcultures

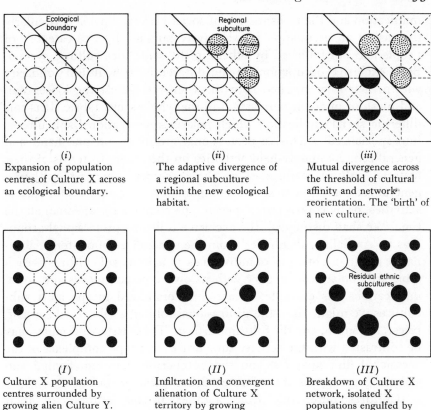

(i)	(ii)	(iii)
Expansion of population centres of Culture X across an ecological boundary.	The adaptive divergence of a regional subculture within the new ecological habitat.	Mutual divergence across the threshold of cultural affinity and network reorientation. The 'birth' of a new culture.

(I)	(II)	(III)
Culture X population centres surrounded by growing alien Culture Y.	Infiltration and convergent alienation of Culture X territory by growing Culture Y.	Breakdown of Culture X network, isolated X populations engulfed by growing Y populations. The 'death' of Culture X.

Fig. 64   Two schematic models illustrating the role of the cultural network in the maintenance of cultural identity. Model (*i*)–(*iii*) – the 'birth' of a new cultural assemblage by divergence under differential conditions. Model (*I*)– (*III*) – the 'death' of a cultural assemblage by network dislocation and subsequent isolation and loss of coherence.

within a former culture distribution area forms the basis of embryonic culture group development – as one possible but not the exclusive development trajectory. Interesting examples of regional subcultures are provided by the local artefact, ceramic, dialect and architecture groupings of Medieval Britain (Jope 1963) and by the regional group- ings within the European Neolithic Michelsberg culture (Scollar 1959).

Occupational subcultures. The activities that groups of people pursue together necessarily affects the network of social intercommunication and the transmission of social variety. This is particularly the case if an occupation is exclusively pursued by one category of people and not followed by others in the same sociocultural system. Such exclusive occupations create differential subcultural solidarity within their micromeshed network when set against the looser web and mesh of intercommunication in the whole social fabric. It is this differing social implication which polarizes occupational subcultures into specialized, exclusive professional groupings on one hand and generalized, commonly-held activities on the other. In terms of their material culture manifestations these segments generate either a generalized tool-kit with special component type complexes for special activities, or by contrast, one special type complex for one man all the time. We shall distinguish the exclusive full-time professional groupings as 'specialist subcultures' from the generalized short-term, alternative group orientations of individuals as 'activity subcultures' – each arbitrarily polarized category with its own type complexes and social implications. As examples of activities organized in specialist subcultures we might cite – the professional soldier, scribe, civil servant, priest, the smith, and the full-time artisan. These latter specialists may be contrasted with the activity subcultures and type complexes of the occasional flint knapper, and the butchering, hunting, fishing and gathering complexes of the hunter–fisher–gatherer societies.

Cultures differ one from another in the number of their component specialist and activity subcultural groupings, and particularly in the activities which they choose to arrange under these respective patterns of organization. Growing specialization and numbers of specialist subcultures will often mean decreasing homogeneity in the particular social system, thus allowing a greater variety of localized social action and stimulating subcultural segmentation around the specialist activities. When most men hunted or worked the soil the limiting factors were in common; when some men specialized in other full-time activities not only were the broadly uniform constraints removed but quite new and diverse ones were substituted. It is for these reasons that the economic surplus consequent upon an advantageous economic strategy has often reinforced this kind of growth in infracultural segments and greatly increased the variety in material culture that we see for example in post-Neolithic times.

Example. Archaeological examples of type complexes associated with activity subcultures are plentifully illustrated by the hunting, butchering, food-preparation, and manufacturing kits which form such a distinctive part of Palaeolithic assemblages (Binford and Binford 1966). Examples of activity or specialist subcultures and their kits can be documented from the personal hoards and burials of the Bronze Age smiths and artisans (e.g. Rowlands 1971, p. 216), as well as by the equipment of warriors, priests, and urban scribes.

Social subcultures. This rather unsatisfactory term is intended to imply the particular subcultures and type complexes emphasizing the various sections of particular social hierarchies – the subcultures of the ranks, classes and elites of societies, from the lowest to the highest. The very wealth and variety of elite and aristocratic subcultures tends to obscure the inevitably less elaborate but equally distinctive equipment of less fortunate and powerful subcultures, down to and including the lowest conditions of poverty. Habits and customs, together with their material implementation, gravitate up through social strata almost as often as they diffuse down – we simply note the latter more frequently.

It seems that under certain conditions the various strata of particular societies deliberately develop the idiosyncratic insignia of their various social classes – emphasizing and re-emphasizing their separate corporate existence. Material artefact-type complexes and their attributes then become favourite vehicles for this emphasis, arranged in complex scales of graded prestige. In many cases the more idiosyncratic, the less functional and the more condensed the 'wasted' time that an artefact conveys, the better prestige symbol it becomes. In many Neolithic cultures elaborate ceramics mark this prestige, but in most Bronze Age societies expensive weaponry replaces ceramics in this role, with a subsequent widespread decline or shift of focus resulting in merely adequate potting standards (Clarke 1976, especially p. 471). Clearly, one of the least functional and most idiosyncratic means of emphasis was and is the elaboration of motifs and art styles. In many societies various motifs and styles are exclusively reserved to mark and emphasize the symbols and insignia of particular social ranks, or religious regalia. The motifs may very well have no sensible meaning in themselves but organized and structured in a particular code they symbolize certain abstract notations intelligible to their fabricators. Perhaps one archaeological example of such a notation is marked by the approximate restriction of early La Tène art in Iron Age Europe to the equipment and insignia of an aristocratic subculture within the Celtic tribes. Certainly such decorative art often serves to convey current ethical and psychological interpretations in a multifacetted and ambiguous symbolism directly meaningful only to the society producing the code.

One particularly interesting feature of social subcultures is their capacity for semi-independent existence and their consequent transferability from sociocultural superstructure to superstructure – once again this is most frequently noted for aristocratic subcultures by virtue of their more obviously extravagant trappings and political importance. The Norman invasion of Saxon England truncated the existing social hierarchy and substituted an aristocratic subculture with its own language, religion, customs, laws, and material culture – meanwhile the peasant continued to develop his subordinate Saxo-Danish subculture without serious interference. The palace aristocrats of Mycenaean Greece developed a palace subculture quite different from that of their village-living, sheep-rearing subordinates, and the insignia of their rank and prestige survive to mark this social interface. In general therefore, social subcultures are particularly important because they introduce new units and fields for sociocultural process – the displacement, truncation and substitution interchange of largely intact subcultural units between alien systems (Steward 1955).

Example. One classic example of social subculture, other than the many historically documented examples, seems to be illustrated by the so-called Wessex 'culture' of Early Bronze Age England. The assemblages defining this entity are quite apparently not full cultural assemblages – on the contrary we are dealing with a hundred or so wealthy burials marked mainly by their wealth and the particular prestige system of expressing this wealth – gold, amber, bronze display weapons, trinkets, gew-gaws, and various clothing idiosyncrasies (Piggott 1938). The absence of a distinctive and full cultural equipment plus the exotic and imported nature of much of the finery and its peculiar distribution pattern together help to deny a cultural status to this elite subculture. The assemblage has been interpreted as showing the intrusive substitution of a small aristocratic subculture, complete with dependent artificers and trade connections (Piggott 1938, Burgess 1974).

Sex subcultures. Physique and anatomy provide a fundamental division between males and females and most societies recognize this polarity and organize the division of labour, activities, and roles in the light of this division. Nevertheless, sociocultural systems differ markedly in the degree and extent to which this sexual dimorphism is emphasized and expressed in terms of cultural dimorphism. The archaeologist can, if he wishes, compare and contrast the degree to which this dimorphism is recognized in terms of male and female artefact-type complexes in a number of cultural assemblages – usually relying on funerary equipment for evidence (Shennan 1975). Such sex subcultures or type complexes normally contain items reflecting differences in dress and different complexes of artefacts associated with different activities, the dimorphism may be even more elaborately developed in differing art styles and insignia as well as differing burial ritual and etiquette. Sociologically speaking such differences in sex subcultures should reflect important differences in the status of the sexes and this may be particularly enlightening when compared with the evidence from religious and secular represen-tational art, as well as that suggesting the economic roles within the particular system. Unfortunately, the archaeologist is still far too prone to extrapolate the cultural pattern of his own society in these respects when interpreting his alien evidence. Despite repeated warn-ings and contrary to much ethnographic data the archaeological lit-erature is still inclined to see pottery-making, jewellery and trinket wearing, hoe agriculture, seed-gathering and other miscellaneous attributes as necessarily feminine, and all tool-making, building, fighting and hunting as necessarily masculine. There is, of course, a probability assessment in these interpretations and although contrary examples may be rare and 'unusual' in the estimation of the archaeologist the mere fact that they have existed is sufficient to remove the basis for any simple conclusions – except perhaps in so far as repeated associations with large samples of properly sexed skeletons is concerned. Once again it is apparent that the processes generating fluctuations in sex subcultures and their type complexes must be rather different from those operating on the other categories of sub-culture.

Example. The best examples of cultural dimorphism along the lines of sex subcultures inevitably come from cemeteries and their grave goods – in Late Bronze Age and Iron Age Europe there is a marked contrast in many cultures between the fibulae, bracelets, chain girdles, knives and pottery services of female graves as opposed to the sword, dagger, axe and tool assemblages from the male graves. In the Wessex subculture there has been claimed to be a difference in burial rite and barrow form as well – female burials under disc barrows and male burials under bell barrows.

The analysis of a full cultural assemblage into its component subcultural segments is one of the most enlightening probes into cultural structure – the parsing of the system into its component subsystems. Sociocultural systems differ considerably in their degree of subcultural segmentation and its material implementation, thus providing a rich field for cross cultural studies. The various sub-cultures may be mutually exclusive or non-exclusive categories and it therefore follows that many groups in history and prehistory represent multiple subcultural aspects – the English Normans and the Conquis-tador Spaniards being simultaneously ethnic, regional, occupational and social subcultures. In the same manner the type complexes expressing subcultures form a polythetic whole, with many artefacts at one and the same time part of the paraphernalia of several subcultural assemblages. The constellation of artefact-types defining the full cultural assemblage thus reflecting an integrated artefact kit with many crosscutting and intersecting subcultural kits. Some resourceful and ingenious attempts have been made to analyse the principal subcultural components in Palaeolithic assemblages on the basis of the intercorrelation of artefact-types in the archaeological record (Binford and Binford 1966). In addition there is a developing programme of research into the cluster and multidimensional analysis of inter-assemblage relationships, whether within successive levels of a single site (fig. 65) or between contemporary site assemblages (fig. 66 and Frankel 1974). One interesting result of Azoury and Hodson's (1973) study of Upper Palaeolithic assemblages from Ksar Akil (Lebanon) is their observation that the two-dimensional constellation analysis of fifty-three types (fig. 65, C3) gave no advantage in pattern detection over that of only seventeen types (fig. 65, C1).

The nature and degree of subcultural segmentation within a given sociocultural system appears to mark a significant variable quality for comparative study. From the archaeological point of view the sub-cultural type complexes provide important information about former sociocultural structuring and make analytical interpretation more comprehensible. The archaeological subcultural assemblages must be carefully distinguished from the full cultural assemblage of which they

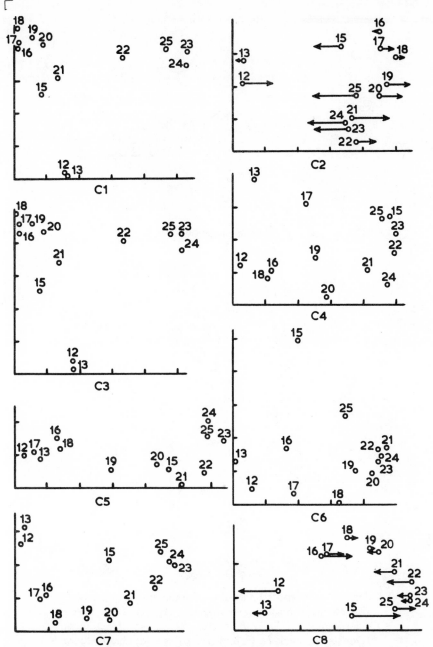

Fig. 65   A constellation analysis of the Upper Palaeolithic levels 25–12 of the rock shelter of Ksar Akil (Lebanon). Eight constellations are shown here (C1–8), with special interest centred on the close similarity between C1 ('short' type list of seventeen artefact-types used to characterize each level's assemblage) and C3 ('long' type test of fifty-three artefact-types).

Source: Doran and Hodson 1975, p. 262.

Data *A* (essential, modified)

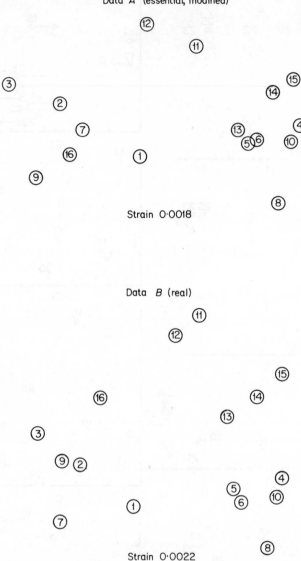

Strain 0·0018

Data *B* (real)

Strain 0·0022

Fig. 66 Computed two-dimensional configurations of sixteen Mousterian assemblages: (1)–(3) Pech d'Azé (Dordogne) levels 4, *B*, 7 (ref. 8); (4)–(7) Chadourne (Dordogne) levels *D, C, B, A* (ref. 9); (8)–(9) Haute-Roche (Charente), lower and middle levels (ref. 10); (10) l'Ermitage (Vienne) (ref. 11); (11) Oissel (Seine-Inf.) (ref. 12); (12) Houppeville (Seine-Inf.), série claire (ref. 12); (13) Rigabe (Var) level *G* (ref. 13); (14) Prince (Grimaldi) foyer *E* (ref. 14); (15) Kokkinopilos (Greece), surface finds (ref. 15); (16) Romani (Barcelona), levels 9/9*a*/9*b* (ref. 16). Source: Doran and Hodson 1966, p. 3.

will only represent a fraction; in several cases in the past subcultural complexes have been mistakenly given full cultural status with confusing results (e.g. the Wessex culture). Similarly, although all subcultural assemblages are recurrent type complexes, not all type complexes are necessarily full subcultures – the bit, stirrup, saddle, complex represents an activity which may be part of any subcultural assemblage which includes horses. Perhaps the most significant development that follows from the isolation of the various subculture entities is the full realization that the processes that act upon such varied units are specific and peculiar to their level of complexity and should not be confused with those other processes operating on systems of full cultural status. For example, ethnic and regional subcultures will often play very significant roles in the process of cultural ontogeny. Occupational subcultures express the degree and nature of the division of time and labour within the cultural strategy, where the increase in the number of full-time specialist subcultures is intimately connected with the growth of cultural variety. Social subcultures are especially relevant because of their comparative independence and interchangeability as units – the process of truncation and substitution, or even interpolation. Similarly sex subcultures reflect quite another factor with their own process dimensions – changes in marriage and kinship arrangements, cross subcultural marriage between intrusive male elites and female indigenes, and so on. The recognition and definition of a polythetic set of consistently recurrent artefact-types in a group of assemblages represents only a preliminary discovery – it must then be determined whether the set expresses a full culture or some kind of subculture – when this has been determined then the 'behaviour' and the processes acting upon the entity can be predictively modelled.

III   Phase pattern regularities

By definition a culture is represented by a scatter of component assemblages dispersed over space and through time. These assemblages tend, in practice, to share a few artefact-types which may occur in every assemblage in the set and thus prevent the cultural list being fully polythetic. The cultural list of component artefact-types is polythetic partly for reasons of differential and accidental preservation but mainly because no single assemblage from any culture ever contains, nor ever did contain, all the artefact-types produced by that culture, even at the time it was in use. Nevertheless, the few unchanging and invariable components, constant throughout, will constitute inessential types from the system standpoint. More important from the point of view of system analysis are the essential types which are part of the system being studied and whose quantitative and qualitative states change as part of the changing system. These essential and multistate types express the 'survival' or 'continuity' of the system as one system with a series of system states, rather than as a complete transmutation into a different system format. It is these essential and key artefact-types which express and form an efficient insulating regulator (R) preserving the existing sociocultural system variety from transformation by blocking the flow of variety from environing fluctuations (E) – up to certain threshold levels that is (figs 6, 11). Finally, the key artefact-types are distinguishable as those types in the culture system whose successive transformation states are covarying in some specific trend relationship with the successive states of other similar key artefact-types. The quantitative and qualitative states of the key artefact-types not only change as part of the changing system but they change together in a correlated and non-random fashion – preserving the pattern, structure, or format peculiar to this system and hence its quintessential identity. In contrast, the remaining essential types may vary quite independently of one another in a stochastic and spasmodic manner.

As an entity changing through time, the component assemblages of a culture together move through successive phases distinguished by the type-states of their component artefact-types – the phases being defined by nodes of co-ordinated change which transform the state of the system as a whole, the successive phases then being successive system-states. At any one time, in any one phase, such a cultural assemblage can be conceived as a multidimensional constellation of artefact-types, of varying levels of mutual intercorrelation, concentrated around nuclei of highly correlated type clusters. Ultimately it may perhaps be possible to study the comparative structure of attribute constellations defining types and type constellations defining cultures – perhaps it may even prove possible to develop a classification of categories of artefact-type and culture-type correlation constellations. Artefact-types and cultures may prove to be more directly comparable in terms of their system structure and pattern than in terms of the specific elements patterned or structured. In any event, the most satisfactory phase model for an archaeological culture seems to be a constellation model expressing the intercorrelation of the component type-states characteristic of that particular system-state. This is closely comparable with the pattern by which attributes are integrated within artefact-types (chapter 5, III).

DISTRIBUTION MODELS

Before moving on to the time dimension of this static constellation model it would be as well to spend a little time investigating the various alternative interpretations of cultural artefacts dispersed in space and their meaning in human terms. The first difficulty involves the full appreciation of the simple observation that no single site assemblage ever contains, nor ever did contain, all the artefact-types produced by its parent culture – the basis of the polythetic nature of cultural assemblages. Up to the present time two alternative concepts have held the field as models of cultural assemblage distribution patterns – one clearly untenable but nevertheless tacitly applied, the other explicitly put forward in honest attempts on the problem but remaining unsatisfactory in detail. These alternative concepts can be loosely labelled the 'cultural brick theory' and the 'radial contour theory'.

The cultural brick theory is the most disreputable and yet remains the model most often tacitly employed by prehistorians. This theory implies that cultural assemblages are rigid monothetic groups of arte-facts with identically shared distributions, cutting-off sharply at the cultural boundaries contiguous with other cultures. The model thus suggesting that cultures can be represented as rather solid entities with clear boundaries such that each culture can be conceived as a block or brick surrounded by other neighbouring bricks (fig. 67).

The second theory, the radial contour theory, was developed by ethnologists in the 1920s, principally by Wissler and by Dixon, in the light of the considerable body of real ethnological data accumulated by that time (Wissler 1923, Dixon 1928). This radial contour theory pointed out that if all the artefacts of a contemporary and well-studied culture are plotted one type at a time on a distribution map they rather surprisingly do not share identical distributions although they neces-sarily overlap. The outcome that was, and is, indisputably clear is that the component artefact-types *do not* share an identical and sharp cut-out boundary. The model of this situation was largely developed by Wissler in connection with the prevailing ideas on diffusion as a process by means of which series of concentric ripples of diffusing artefacts spread out into peripheral regions from a central 'cultural hearth' or 'kernel'. This radial contour theory suggested that there would be a cultural 'core area' in which all the cultural artefacts are found and that this core is surrounded by roughly concentric contours reflecting the differential distributions of the diffused artefact-types (fig. 67).

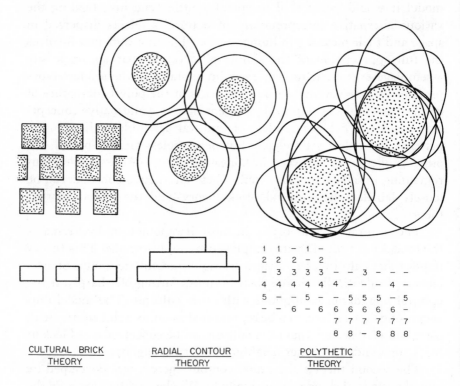

CULTURAL BRICK
THEORY

RADIAL CONTOUR
THEORY

POLYTHETIC
THEORY

Fig. 67 Three alternative schematic, conceptual models expressing the relationship between the distribution boundaries of the sets of cultural assemblage artefact-types and the boundary of the culture entity so defined.

These two models could be discussed at very great length. However, all that we have space to emphasize here is that the partial failure of the second more honest and sophisticated theory has led to the tacit use by prehistorians of the first and much more disreputable hypothesis. The 'cultural brick theory' necessarily assumes that cultural assemblages are monothetic sets of types, that all the components occur at all the sites, and that they all share identical distribution boundaries. These premises are without exception false.

The radial contour theory falls down on the grounds that artefact-type distribution is not entirely a matter of diffusion, that diffusion although irregularly radial is not truly concentric nor from a single centre, and finally there are no cultural hearths or nuclear areas in which all the types in the cultural assemblage occur together – just as there are no peripheral settlements with only half a cultural assemblage. The reality caricatured in this model is by no means easy to isolate and define. The relevant facts seem to be that the nucleus or the distribution mean, mode, and median region for one artefact-type is rarely the nucleus for another. Consequently, any nuclear region is not so much the area within which the original inventions and development took place, as rather the geographical and social focus where elements originating in various parts of the territory were co-ordinated and integrated. In addition, the polythetic selection of types in each site assemblage makes it almost impossible to sustain a radial and concentric distribution for all of them.

The realization of the polythetic nature of the cultural assemblage in terms of component artefact-types allows us to make some advance on these earlier hypotheses of assemblage patterning within cultural boundaries. The available evidence suggests that the individual distributions of the specific artefact-types from one culture extend in irregular lobes in various differing directions, many types also occurring as components in other cultural assemblages in neighbouring areas, and vice versa. However, the respective irregular distribution areas overlap to varying degrees in such a way that an area exists within which more than 50 per cent of the total number of types occur together in polythetic assemblages associating various sets of the cultural artefact-types. The boundaries of this culture area only occasionally coincide with the boundaries of any specific artefact-type or group of artefact-types (fig. 67). Nevertheless, the distribution pattern is not without regularity since the density of the type distributions do fall away rapidly in frequency of occurrence towards the boundaries of the dispersion area. However, because this gradation is more an exponential than a steady gradient, even the boundary assemblages of very intermixed neighbouring cultures will necessarily contain a greater number of types from one cultural set and lesser numbers from others (figs 79, 80, 83, 85). A situation which once again emphasizes the need for methods capable of assessing the degree of similarity of given assemblages with one cultural array or another, a need satisfied only by the methods of numerical taxonomy.

The outcome of this discussion has been the development of an alternative 'polythetic model' to the existing 'cultural brick model' and 'radial contour model' of assemblage patterning within culture areas. This of course is only a crude beginning – for more precise purposes an elaborate comparative cross-cultural distribution study is needed to gradually develop some idea of the range of variation and general categories of the composite distributions of the many different kinds of polythetic cultural assemblages. On such a basis it might be possible from an established polythetic format – number of types in the total set, range of types shared, number of types in component assemblages etc. – to predict and model an expected form of distribution category. In most practical examples of cultural artefact-type distribution patterns it will be found that since the cultural assemblage is imperfectly polythetic and since the culture is a manifestation of an internally intercommunicating social network – the number of specific types shared with other individual cultures will be small and the mutual boundaries fairly well defined by a band of exponential gradients marking the zones of 'most rapid fall-off' for the cultural artefacts in the boundary assemblages (fig. 80). The central zone or irregular plateau in which the mutual affinity between the polythetic assemblages remains high and roughly constant will then define the essential archaeological 'culture area' – how such a concept accords with linguistic, tribal and social areas we shall see later on (figs 79–85).

GEOGRAPHICAL MODELS

Geographical areas can be recognizably analysed into 'natural areas' and 'natural routes'. However, these routes and areas are always conceived in relation to a specific and idiosyncratic cultural outlook – the areas and routes are 'natural' given the technology, desired resources, social organization and political situation of the culture concerned. There are no absolute forever-established 'natural areas' and 'natural routes' – we have observed once already that the environment looks different to different cultures and cultures react purely in terms of their percepta, the environment as they understand it. The Palaeolithic hunter camping on top of the world's largest iron ore deposit does not 'perceive' this resource because his technological 'eye' is otherwise orientated.

It follows that a geographical territory can be divided and sub-divided into a number of different area formats based on routes, resources and barriers, taking into account how these would affect a given series of cultures with a given technology, desired resources, social organization and political situation – assuming that accurate palaeoecological knowledge is available. However, in a given geo-graphical area the number of alternative networks and formats is probably limited – to conceive an area as having one immutable breakdown is clearly wrong but to conceive an area as having principal format components – reflecting the least changing routes, resources and barriers – seems highly reasonable. Any particular cultural situa-tion will be unique in such an area but nevertheless it will be a specific blend or strategy integrating some out of the limited set of probable area component formats – the blend may be unique but the basic components should be limited in variety on the basis of the geo-graphical constraint (fig. 13). The greater the available information about the culture, the greater the information that can be established about the geographical constraints operating and the greater the pre-dictable regularities in the culture area's blend of principal format components. The compounds and fractions of the routes and areas fluctuate and alternate in the prehistoric and historic record – disap-pearing and reappearing as ghosts of former patterns. The constantly changing aspects of this cultural kaleidoscope reflect the constantly changing specific conditions but the constantly repetitive mosaic fragments of routes and areas reflect the continuity of the geographi-cal constraints operating in the area.

Geographical culture areas and their particular combination of the local principal format components are closely allied to the ecological concept of habitat niches and their structure – not surprisingly since the geography of an area embraces the surface topography, soil and rock geology, climate, fauna and vegetation. Any specific culture area or territory will necessarily include several interlaced ecological niches and microenvironments each with their own fluctuating boundaries. Culture areas, and the niches whose resources they tap, occupy coherent territories usually bounded by obvious environmental limits but although at any given time the equilibrium boundaries of these areas can be shown to be 'natural' these boundaries are never constant. If we view the problem from the ecological niche approach it will be found that ecological niches are not separate and discrete box entities but often cross-cut one another in a polythetic nested array. A particular river may be the boundary of one niche and simultaneously the very central spine of another; a particular plant species will occur simultaneously in several otherwise quite distinct niche formats in one area. Sociocultural systems exploit particular idiosyncratic combinations or strategic blends of territorial niches and their resources – farming the valleys, hunting the woodland slopes and grazing on the pastures above the mountain tree-line and so on. The succession of cultures occupying a given area are to be compared most significantly in the differing strategy adopted in the exploitation of the various niches of the territory. Specialized and highly-adapted social segments and their subcultures may become increasingly tied to one nest of niches and their peculiar exploitation pattern – possibly leading to divergent cultural developments. The complex and multi-level intersection of niches in a single area often allows the simultaneous and different exploitation of these resources by cultures sharing the same area at different 'levels' – for example, the Navaho horse nomads in and around the Pueblo farmers, or the Scythian horse nomads and the Slav farmers provide interesting examples of the unstable pattern often associated with nomad/agrarian system coupling, oscillating from symbiosis to outright parasitism.

If we summarize the evidence about cultural areas then we must emphasize their constant fluctuation and the futility of dividing a given territory into a hard and fast set of natural areas. In cultural studies of South America the territory has been variously divided into twenty-four areas by Murdock, eleven by Stout, five by Wissler, four by Kroeber, and three by Cooper – all to some degree useful and relevant to particular studies but all equally invalid as natural areas established for all time. A study of a similar nature attempted to force a network of 'naturally' defined areas on the whole prehistory of the British Iron Age with equally regrettable results (Hawkes 1959). Culture areas fluctuate constantly, their borders are always 'natural' but never constant and the areas often cross-cut one another if superimposed through time. It is quite proper to illuminate and analyse regularities in the distribution formats of the successive cultural occupations of a given territory by distribution mapping the associated specific artefact-types. But it is quite circular to force culture areas into a preconceived territorial format, unless this pro-cedure is used as a model to be rigorously tested by distribution mapping to frame hypotheses by the method of residues (chapter 11, II).

Nevertheless, geographical areas do display various regular prin-cipal format components which may recur in varying combinations to make a composite culture area habitat. The recurrent 'personality' of an area in Fox's (1932) sense therefore represents this recurrent and limited set of possible area components based upon the combinations of possible natural boundaries surrounding and intersecting the area and the natural routes giving access to it. In this way an area can have a variety of personalities, albeit a limited and repeated variety, depending on the limitations of the cultures concerned. The sporadic reappearance of familiar area patterns in specific territories provides one of the more interesting examples of regularities in history and prehistory (e.g. Neolithic and Bronze Age cultures in the Middle Danube Basin).

SOCIAL MODELS

This discussion of the essential nature of an archaeological culture has so far been primarily concerned with the cultural assemblage as a complex material phenomenon. This approach must never allow us to forget that the phenomenon was generated by groups of people occu-pying territorial areas through time and that it is a product of social behaviour. The reality and importance of the properly defined archaeological culture is its apparent but intricate relationship with ancient societies which once formed coherent areas of homogeneous behaviour patterning in which the attributes, artefact-types, the sets of types and the cultural assemblages were material elements. The cultural assemblage is the product of a social group of a certain com-plexity and dimension – what particular limits we would attach to the dimensions of the social groups responsible for prehistoric cultures is a matter which must be considered in a subsequent chapter (chapter 9).

The social basis of material cultures is not difficult to follow in general terms. The individual in the society is located in a web of kinship relations stretching beyond the family group. This web of kinship relations does not simply consist of an objective set of ties by descent or consanguinity among individuals, but exists only as an idiosyncratic and arbitrary system of ideas – often ignoring one side of the family completely for particular though not for all purposes. Within the society the different sets of kinsmen join together variously and co-operatively for producing, distributing and consuming; they are linked across kin boundaries by the mesh of educational, age-group, recreational, ceremonial, religious, political and military groupings and subcultures. The society is given cohesiveness by this cross-cutting web of obligations extending from group to group within certain geographical limits. The diffusion of artefacts, customs, games, ideas, religions, folk-lore, and techniques cannot occur without human activity – and this takes place consciously or unconsciously through this social network. It follows that items are most widely and homogeneously diffused over areas having good and regular intercommunication, common kinship, common language and common institutions – an area of optimal internal diffusion. Of course artefacts and ideas do travel beyond individual social networks but these diffusions are sporadic when compared with the continuously reinforcing and repeatedly sustained interchange circulating within the multiple linked nodes of the unit society – the area of primary diffusion.

A common cultural assemblage is thus the material manifestation of an area of maximized group intercommunication. The social network precipitates and maintains the culture area and the boundaries of the two should be broadly concurrent. A series of adjoining but largely discrete sociocultural networks can therefore be compared with a series of adjacent saucers each holding a specific artefact-type pool, linked only with difficulty across the watersheds between the network areas.

The development of these cultural assemblages and their sociocultural systems is therefore intimately connected with the mechanisms of population isolation both in terms of intercommunication and in differential adaptation to differing regional conditions. It is likely that many new cultural taxa develop as the result of the invasion of fresh ecological niches with the consequent rapid rate of change yielding a new configuration. This branching development conjures the impression of cultural configurations in phenetic space continuously developing to fit and penetrate the patterns of ecological space (Sokal and Sneath 1963, p. 219).

The accumulation of idiosyncratic traits as the result of change and selection further increases the effect of such divergent drift, especially where different sociological and environmental pressures are operating. As this cumulative change progresses the possible developmental trajectories and formats become increasingly restricted as the traits are highly integrated within a functional whole. The more moderate and slow rate of linguistic divergence would continue for a much longer period to preserve the original ancestry of the group and the possibility for renewed and efficient cultural interchange if conditions so demanded. In the light of this predisposition it is particularly interesting to observe the way in which divergent cultures of the same culture group often selectively expand within the pre-existing network of related populations (chapter 7, III, IV).

Culture differences can be seen to be based on largely cumulative systems of multiple factors, which are built up by the occurrence and integration of large numbers of independent developments. Hence, the probability that two isolated cultural assemblages will evolve in exactly the same way in all of their characteristics is astronomically low, and the convergence in every respect of previously dissimilar cultural assemblages is even less probable (Sokal and Sneath 1963, p. 218, after Stebbins). However, since cultures are rarely completely isolated from diffusing variety and since they may solve in the same way the similar problems facing them in similar environmental contexts – then a certain level of assemblage convergence within unit areas of this kind may be expected. Such convergence should induce supracultural material culture units with certain common configurations and a low-level mutual affinity which itself would make such an entity prone to certain selective development processes (Technocomplexes, chapter 8).

This brief discussion of the social basis of material culture units may help us to conceptualize the sociocultural convulsions which underlie the complex systematic changes that we can perceive in the superficial crust of material culture. However, as archaeologists we are more interested in classifying the systematic regularities of this crust and then correlating these with groups of probable social phenomena than with the converse procedure which constitutes the field of the anthropologist. This syntactic procedure should provide a framework for the detection of archaeological regularities and the construction of a certain amount of synthesizing theoretical superstructure on that basis. As part of this procedure we can now move on to examine the time pattern regularities which suggest themselves in the trajectories and traditions of many quite different cultures, not forgetting their social generation.

IV   Time pattern regularities

From our earlier statements about artefacts and assemblages changing with time it appears that cultural assemblages will change according to the varying numbers of the artefact-types and their distribution across the component assemblages and that these types will themselves be changing as the sum of their fluctuating attributes. These categories of change may act independently and in unco-ordinated and divergent trends or on occasions they jointly correlate and together move to mark significant nodes in the system's time-trajectory. In order to examine the complex interaction of these separate trends the cultural assemblage system and its changes can be laid out in the three familiar levels (see above pp. 180–1, 217–18):

   (i) The quantitative change and oscillation in numbers of arte-fact-types
       (a) as variation in the number of different specific artefact-type categories defining the cultural polythetic set in successive phases,
       (b) as variation in the number of different specific artefact-type categories per assemblage in successive phases,
       (c) as variations in both of the above aspects jointly, in a variety of combining trends.
   (ii) The quantitative change and oscillation in numbers of the population of component assemblages forming the cultural assemblage in successive phases.
   (iii) The qualitative change and oscillation of the overall cultural assemblage system as a structured system.

   Once again the consideration of these changes involves the concept of ontogeny and the culture entity. The culture as a population has various kinds of ontogeny, like the artefact-type population, and in the same way some confusion exists about the planes of 'birth, growth, maturity, and death' involved. Cultural ontogeny has the same general syntax as that of the artefact-type – the analogue resting on the same population trajectory basis, with a similar confusion of levels of meaning, but with one fundamental difference that will gradually emerge.

In addition we have the intuitive but tenacious concept of cultural florescence and climax, a concept which must be examined for its reality and basis.

(i) Taking the separate trends in cultural assemblage time-trajectories one by one, we start with the problem of the quantitative change and oscillation in the number of different artefact-types through time. The changing absolute or relative numbers of artefacts within successive phases of a type population has already been considered at length as a gross fluctuation cutting across attribute oscillations (chapter 5, IV(ii)). Fluctuations in individual artefact-type output tend to vary according to the well known double lenticular trend model (figs 56–60). However, we are now immediately concerned with the alternative changing aspects of quantities of artefact-types within assemblages as variations of the kinds (a), (b) and (c) mentioned above. The problem is essentially one of ascertaining the relationship between the distribution of the artefact-types in terms of each assemblage component and the distribution of the assemblage population in terms of each artefact-type.

In each case the variation in numbers can be crudely reduced to the relative basis of numerical increase, decrease, or stability in frequency in successive phases of the system trajectory. In this particular class of variation – (a) the number of different artefact-types found in each successive phase of a cultural assemblage system may increase, decrease or remain stable, representing an increasing, decreasing, or stable polythetic set of types in the cultural equipment. It is assumed that sampling precautions have been taken and that this is a 'real' fluctuation.

Similarly under class (b) the average number of different artefact-types per component assemblage may be increasing, decreasing, or remaining stable – subject to the same precautions. Now the interpretation of these trends depends very much on the relationship and synchronization between the two classes or aspects of change (a and b). Taken separately variation in the number of different artefact-types defining the overall cultural polythetic set can be represented as fluctuating the possible range of assemblage variation within the set (a). Variation in the average number of different artefact-type categories per assemblage reflects a fluctuating degree of assemblage variety and assemblage elaboration – fluctuation in the technological sophistication of the culture (b) (fig. 24). The joint effect and complex interaction of these trends can be glimpsed from the following combinations:

Nos different specific artefact-types in cultural polythetic set	Nos different specific artefact-types per assemblage in the cultural population	Implications
(1) Decrease	Increase	Increasing assemblage elaboration with a decreasing range of cultural variation
(2) Increase	Increase	Increasing assemblage elaboration with an increasing range of cultural variation
(3) Decrease	Decrease	Decreasing assemblage elaboration with a decreasing range of cultural variation
(4) Increase	Decrease	Decreasing assemblage elaboration with an increasing range of cultural variation

This model is of course highly simplified – in the first place only two variations have been combined for each factor – increase or decrease. If the three variations increase, decrease, and stability had been used this would allow not four categories of change but nine. The precise implications of these categories of change would depend upon the kinds of artefact-types involved in the changes, as well as upon the numbers fluctuating, the rate of change, and in particular the degree of correlation between the changes in the individual artefact-type trajectories. Nevertheless, it would appear that the rough sequence sketched in the model would have much in common with the characteristics of the sequence of development of a cultural assemblage through time:

Phase (o) – pre-formative, decreasing assemblage elaboration with an increasing range of cultural assemblage variation within the components of culture S_0.

Phase (1) – formative, increasing assemblage elaboration with a decreasing range of cultural assemblage variation within the components of formative cultural assemblage S_1 – the new culture becoming coherent.

Phase (2) – coherent, increasing assemblage elaboration with an increasing range of cultural assemblage variation – a great variety of types and assemblages within the local population of culture S_1.

Phase (3) – post-coherent, decreasing assemblage elaboration with a decreasing range of cultural assemblage variation – a simpler cultural assemblage with fewer types per assemblage component in culture S_1.

Phase (0) – pre-formative, decreasing assemblage elaboration with an increasing range of cultural assemblage variation – the assemblages become very diverse in their content accompanied by fewer S_1 artefacts per assemblage. The phase in which the assemblage format of cultural assemblage S_2 first becomes apparent in the increasing directive correlation of certain artefact-type trajectories.

It is not suggested that this sequence expresses the real characteristics of a developing cultural assemblage but merely that this model does suggest the general way in which the broad correlation of separate trends may combine to define and emphasize the threshold changes from one system state to another. This feature in turn raises the consideration of successive culture-states and the distinction between independent cultural assemblages and transform cultural assemblages related by phylogeny (see below, pp. 279–80).

The increasing or decreasing numbers of different artefact-types in successive cultural sets and numbers of different types per assemblage component also seem to trend in steady gradients or oscillate between poles. Unfortunately it is very difficult to find data recording both forms of variation although both categories are always present in some degree.

Example. In nine successive cultural assemblage phases from North Georgia, USA, a carefully recorded study established a steady change in the number of different specific ceramic types in the successive cultural assemblage polythetic sets. The average number of different ceramic types per component assemblage in the successive cultural populations was consistently less than the possible polythetic total for each cultural assemblage phase (Wauchope 1966, p. 24, table 4).

Cultural assemblage phases	Nos different ceramic artefact-types in cultural polythetic set	
Advanced phase	7 types	
Lamar phase	11	Late
Savannah phase	10	
Etowah phase	13	*Woodland*
Woodstock phase	8	*tradition*
Napier phase	5	*of North*
Swift Creek phase	5	*Georgia*
Deptford phase	4	Early
Fabric phase	1	

There remain two further aspects of quantitative change and oscillation in numbers of artefact-types within cultural assemblages. One aspect is the logical extension of the trends just discussed – the replacement of one set of fluctuating artefact-types by another – cultural substitution. In a complete stratigraphic record this process will usually appear as the truncation and discontinuity of one set of types and their replacement by a new set. However, since the assemblages are likely to have a polythetic overlap in types, even though they may be from differing cultures, then some few artefact-types will show an apparently continuous record although usually marked at the cultural interface by disconformity in the quantitative trends (fig. 46). Such disconformities in the record plus a large scale replacement of types is sufficient to mark a cultural change.

The remaining aspect is the converse of the variation patterns already examined – that is to say the consideration of the distribution of the total cultural assemblage of each successive phase over the range of artefact-types. This kind of fluctuation need reflect no change in the absolute numbers of specific types per phase assemblage and no necessary change in the total variety of the polythetic cultural assemblages. Instead there may be oscillations or trends in the successive states of the assemblage population distribution over the existing range of artefact-types – successive changes in the relative percentages of the particular types present. This of course reflects changes in the stance but not the content of the cultural assemblages and may often be connected with subcultural reorganization.

(ii) The quantitative study of the numbers of component assemblages forming the cultural assemblage in successive phases has received very little attention. The reasons for this omission partly arise from the difficulty of establishing accurate relative chronologies on other than the taxonomic grounds being researched and partly from the embarrassment of having to display the paucity of assemblages representing successive archaeological phases. Nevertheless, the numbers of assemblages representing each cultural phase should be in part a function of the population size and dispersion and in part a function of the steady displacement of one cultural assemblage state by another. Complications arise from the interaction of these two factors and the interference from sampling problems – the population of assemblages per phase is a complex vector of these components.

In practice, the number of assemblages per phase from a given culture tend to form the familiar and roughly lenticular frequency distribution through time – a few assemblages of the new culture appear initially, then there is positive sigmoid growth in assemblage numbers – a period of decreased growth rate as the asymptote is reached, followed by negative growth and the final disappearance of the culture in terms of its distinctive assemblage.

Example. The following example is based upon two regional sub-cultures of the British Early Bronze Age Beaker culture. In temporal and distribution terms an earlier and northerly subculture, the Northern British group, is being displaced by a related and southerly subculture, the Southern British group, which is itself finally engulfed by larger autochthonous cultures (fig. 46; Clarke 1967, 1970).

Culture phase		Nos of assemblages	Culture phase		Nos of assemblages
		–			
Primary Northern	N1	17			–
Developed Northern	N2	154	Primary Southern	S1	54
Late Northern	N3	157	Developed Southern	S2	158
Final Northern	N4	17	Late Southern	S3	66
		–	Final Southern	S4	76
					–

Assemblage trends of this kind suggest that the main factor detected in these samples is the gradual appearance, fluctuation, and disappearance of a particular set of equipment – the corres- ponding population of people continuing throughout, with unknown fluctuations. We should not imagine that a human population is appearing, fluctuating and disappearing in a simply correlated fashion – indeed exactly how demographic fluctuations affect assemblage trends is not clear; that they do affect them however is certain. The factor that may be relevant in the latter problem is the nature of the archaeological sample. Since the trends in the frequency of archaeological phase assemblages closely resemble historic and documented changes in recent cultural assemblages some degree of confidence is induced for the usefulness of archaeological data for further analysis. The nature and problems of the archaeological sample however, clearly demand close attention (e.g. Mueller, 1975).

If the quantitative ontogeny curves for artefact-types and assemblages may not be so simply related to human population fluctuations, is there any possibility of estimating demographic fluctuations from the information concealed in artefact assemblage trends? This problem has scarcely been investigated, although carefully controlled experiments with suitable modern hand-made artefacts would certainly prove enlightening. One interesting possibility is that given a growing human population, in which a roughly constant proportion of individuals are hand-producing standardized artefact-types, then one might imagine that the 'variance' of the attributes within particular artefact-type populations could be affected to a measurable degree. If this was indeed so, then in these very specific circumstances the role of population growth in increasing 'the rate of innovation' and 'integrative invention' may prove to be significant. However, this hypothetical model relationship remains for the moment untested but suggests the possibility of a number of interesting analyses of variance experiments.

(iii) The fluctuations and oscillations in the quantitative ontogeny of numbers and combinations of artefact-types and assemblages may be viewed as only part of the qualitative change and oscillation of the system of intercorrelated types as a structured constellation changing with time. In this dynamic version the earlier static phase model of the overall cultural assemblage develops a time-trajectory in which types come and go, change from state to state and move from correlation level to correlation level in reference to the other artefact-types in the cultural set. We start, then, with a polythetically generated constellation of artefact-types with varying levels of mutual intercorrelation, distributed around nuclei of key artefact-types. Subcultural kits or type complexes may appear as nuclei of covarying and correlated types but equally such nuclei may include key types from independent but related complexes which happen to covary. It is dangerous to assume that a correlated complex of artefact-types equates simply with a subcultural kit; there are several other ways in which such nuclei may arise (Binford and Binford 1966).

In the dynamic model of the cultural assemblage time-trajectory we are tracing the culture system from state to state throughout its recognizable history as a given system format. The system is of course generated by the integrated pattern of numbers of dispersed but interconnected assemblage trajectories united by continuing bonds of mutual affinity in terms of artefact-types and their succession of type-states. The system model represents the overall compounded 'behaviour' of these artefact-type relationships within the multilinear and mosaic developments of the many separate assemblages and their complex reticulation.

It follows from this dynamic model that any cultural system format will go through a series of successive format-states or culture-states differentiated one from another by quantitative fluctuations in inessential and essential types and by the particular phase states of the multistate artefact-types. Conversely, the successive system states will be unified by a common subset of key artefact-types and by common and continuing aspects of correlation structure. The culture entity, like the artefact-type, is a continuous and multistate system and once again it is useful to distinguish between those assemblages which may be related as transform cultural assemblages within a single system as opposed to assemblages from quite different and independent cultural assemblage systems.

Transform cultures. Cultural assemblages which are collaterally or descent related and represent simply different culture-states or formats from the time-trajectory of a single cultural system. Many cultural assemblages scattered in time and space may then be understood simply as culture-states from a common multistate culture system. Such homeomorphic assemblages are to be distinguished by their polythetic affinity one with another and by their continuation of transformations of at least the key artefact-types in a common arrangement – the majority of types in the assemblages can be shown simply to be different states of shared groups of multistate artefact-types. Having established a cluster of assemblages as transforms from a single cultural system the problem is then to distinguish the contemporary spatial transforms from the time transforms.

Independent cultures. Independent cultural assemblages or cultures are not connected or derived from a common system at the level being discussed here. Independent assemblages may share certain artefact-types but the level of affinity between the assemblages is low and the majority of artefact-types cannot be related as different states of single specific types. The essential and key artefact-types are different and their interrelationship in numbers of assemblages remains distinct. Nevertheless, independent cultures are transforms in some system, somewhere.

A particular cultural assemblage system will first emerge in an identifiable format as the successive and cumulative introduction of a growing set of directively correlated essential and key artefact-types – eventually crossing a threshold marking the first coherent and integrated appearance of the specific culture format (fig. 68). Previous to this threshold the individual essential artefact-types were simply appearing independently and sporadically in the assemblages of other systems, or in an ancestral system which is gradually so modified as to no longer represent simply a system state of the preceding trajectory. The difference between system state and system state within a single system as opposed to the difference between two transform systems is simply a matter of degree and threshold height. The difference between system states in the same cultural system is mainly a matter of differing artefact-type states and their manner of association. The difference between transform cultures is a much greater difference in artefact-type arrays and their association pattern – including a much lower level of affinity and differing essential artefact-types.

Once formed, the culture system format will move continuously from state to state marked by the continuous fluctuations in modal artefact-type states and the varying correlation between types within the system. The essential artefact-types mark those multistate types which are present in some state in every phase of the trajectory of the specific culture – expressing the continuity and survival of the system as that system. The key artefact-types are a subset of the essential types which are distinguished by a jointly maintained pattern of covariation and correlation within the system – types which occur in assemblages in repeated and specific relationship. Such key artefact-types and their transforms are largely responsible for the continuing identity of the cultural assemblage throughout its successive states.

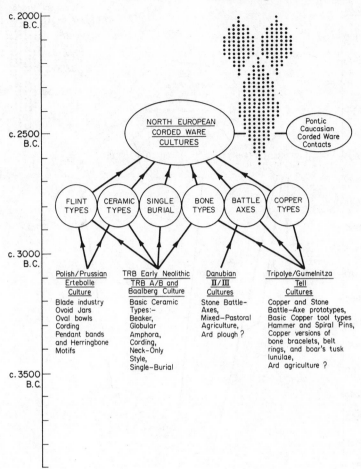

Fig. 68a   Directive correlation between artefact-types within an emergent culture or culture group. A schematic outline of the successive introduction and cumulative integration of essential and key artefact-types within the cultural system of the emergent Corded Ware/Battle-Axe cultures of northern Europe *c.* 2700–2500 BC.

Outside these regularities and constraints the inessential types will constantly come and go from the system and the remaining types will show a constant oscillation in state and correlation levels one with another.

The termination of such a cultural system trajectory can take place in two main ways:

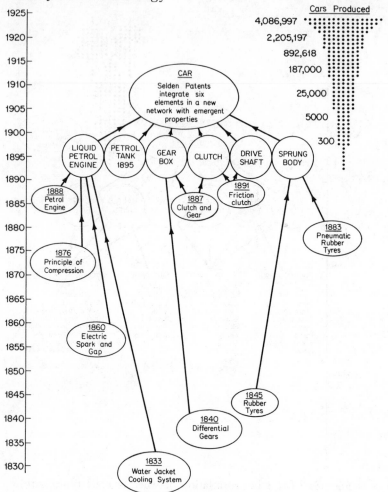

Fig. 68b   Directive correlation between attributes and artefact-types within an emergent artefact-type – the motor car in the USA – the threshold, 1895.
Modified from Broom and Selznick 1958, p. 65, after F. Stuart Chapin.

(1) The successive and cumulative introduction of new artefact-types until the old format loses coherence and a new format emerges integrating the novel artefact-types in an increasingly standardized arrangement – the development of one transform culture from another.

(2) The displacement and substitution of one cultural system by another independent system at a given locus.

The termination process is to be distinguished from the parallel case involving artefact-type systems and provides the fundamental difference between two otherwise closely congruent patterns of system 'behaviour'. In an artefact-type system the particular type may simply go out of production, cease to exist and disappear from the cultural range. In a cultural assemblage system the system and its population may be displaced by another independent system but the culture can rarely if ever, cease to exist, although continuing in increasingly divergent transformations. It is conceivable that on very rare occasions the complete population producing a particular sociocultural system might be completely wiped out by war, disease, or famine – but these occasions are of the highest rarity. Either the culture system is displaced and simply shifts its territory elsewhere, or the mutual impact of one or more culture systems in a restricted locus will give rise to a newly 'emergent' cultural assemblage on the lines already suggested (see (1) above). The emergent culture may have several 'ancestors' which may briefly survive within its format as vestigial ethnic or regional sub-cultures. The new cultural assemblage cannot be regarded as a trans-form of any one system but rather as a complex conjunct with an individual and unique format with emergent characteristics. It is this particular kind of new identity and this particular process which mark the 'independent culture' and its 'birth'. It is worth noting that such a process can have its possible occurrence optimized by taking a locus with several neighbouring, different, yet interacting cultures; it goes without saying that such a factor is not sufficient in itself to bring about this process but may provide one of several possible and cumulative causes.

CORRELATION AND CULTURAL COHERENCE

In the terms of the dynamic model that we are developing the time-trajectory of a cultural assemblage system resembles bundles of vary-ing intercorrelated artefact-type trajectories – with types appearing and disappearing, moving from state to state, and fluctuating in degree of correlation with other types. The level of correlation between the types within the changing constellation-trace expresses the inter-dependence between these variables such that when one changes so does the other, in some way similar to that represented by a mathema-tical function but not in such a completely dependent fashion. It is particularly important to realize that two variables – whether they are attribute trajectories or type trajectories – may be correlated one with the other without there necessarily being a simple direct connection between them. The intercorrelation may suggest a cause and effect relationship between the changing elements but equally the correlation may very often reflect a complex relationship shared by two or more variables being modified by the effects of a common cause linked with some other variable. There may be no significant connection between two type trajectories which exhibit correlation other than through their separate relationships to some third variable. It is a dangerous over-simplification to interpret clusters of correlated artefact-types simply as associated subculture artefact kits varying through time (Binford and Binford 1966). Once again statistical considerations provide a basis for interpretation but they do not provide unique and simple solutions to archaeological problems.

For the present it suffices that correlation measurements can express the interdependence between covarying artefact-types through the cultural system's time-trajectories. This correlation is n-dimensional where n is the number of artefact-types in the system – each type is in some sort of relationship with every other type in the system at every stage.

Successive system states in the trajectory of the changing cultural assemblage will necessarily show changes in the mutual intercorrelation of the artefact-types within the constellation – both individually between pairs of types and overall as the population of types is increasingly or decreasingly intercorrelated. We have previously suggested that this overall degree of system integration or component intercorrelation is the vector behind the intuitive impression of the degree of 'coherence' of a cultural assemblage. Increasing levels of overall intercorrelation between the artefact-types defining a culture's time-trajectory suggest an increasingly defined cultural format conceptualized as an increase in the cultural format coherence – the upshot of directive correlation. Conversely, decreasing overall intercorrelation linking the successive constellation of artefact-types would invoke a decreasingly defined cultural format – a decreasing cultural coherence. The significance of the 'coherence' concept is that it is capable of further definition and in theory at least it is a measurable and quantifiable factor, either in some form of geometric mean or perhaps as the moment of inertia of successive system states expressed as correlation values (chapter 6, IV).

RATES-OF-CHANGE AND THRESHOLDS

If the level of artefact-type intercorrelation is an important factor in cultural ontogeny then so is the correlation between the rates of change of the system components. The pattern of change and the rates of change of these components together help to define the thresholds separating culture state from culture state and transform culture from transform culture. In a very substantial way it is the accelerated rate of increase in new variety which marks the growth of a new cultural format – the greatly accelerated rate of increase in new artefact-type states and attribute states. These are the spurts of creative development which divide up the otherwise sporadically fluctuating cultural time-trajectory and it is these jointly correlated and rapid shifts to new modes of artefact-type characterization which conveniently register the development of new transform cultures, culture states, or subcultures – according to the degree and nature of the changes.

This model of a continuous time-trajectory for cultural assemblages raises the familiar problem of the differentiation of culture state from culture state and culture from culture in the sequence. Basically the thresholds separating culture state from culture state are slight and insignificant compared with those separating transform culture from transform culture. The thresholds between culture states or phases can be visualized as reflecting correlated changes in small numbers of essential artefact-types taking them from one modal state to another and from one intercorrelation locus to another within the system as a whole. At the same time some inessential artefact-types may help mark the phase by appearing or disappearing from the system. By comparison the thresholds marking the formation and reformation of the cultural format display correlated changes in most of the essential and key artefact-types, a great variability in all the system components, a greatly increased rate of change of types from state to state and the cumulative introduction of an increasingly coherent set of new key artefact-types replacing the old ones. Consequently, the time-trajectory of the cultural assemblage is segmented by clustered nodes of maximized change markedly more emphatic than the inevitable and sporadically continuous changes in between.

v System pattern regularities

Most of the regularities of assemblages and artefact-types within the culture system have been itemized in connection with the system's space and time-trajectories (section III–IV). There remain those inherent system regularities which depend upon the system as a fragment of a sociocultural information system with the usual moving and dynamic equilibrium between all the multifarious variety circulated as coded behavioural information from the cultural subsystems.

Given a particular cultural assemblage subsystem from a sociocultural system it is possible to see specific artefact-types as representing new, alternative, contradictive, or redundant variety in relation to the whole system and its material aspect. The constantly changing sociocultural system equilibrium is maintained by repeatedly minimizing the maximum amount of immediate system dislocation. It is this latter process which determines whether a particular piece of diffusing variety is suitable for integration or is to be rejected and similarly stimulates or fails to stimulate the internal integrative invention of 'new' variety by re-networking old components. Because the system is dynamic and coupled with a dynamic environing system sociocultural equilibrium is never fully achieved and consequently the equilibrium format is always changing. In any cultural assemblage trajectory, at any one time, there are several foci within the system requiring suitable variety to diminish the existing contradictory and disjunctive variety focused at these points in the system's structure. These foci fluctuate and move through the system forming loci of accelerated change constantly minimizing the amount of fresh system dislocation brought about by fresh developments at all levels within the system and within the coupled environment.

Against this background a particular artefact-type may appear within the communication network of a culture and may represent a totally new variety – if the new type minimizes some existing system dislocation in any subsystem then it will be accepted and integrated as a gain in system variety. The new type may well serve to stabilize a religious or psychological subsystem inconsistency as much as a material culture or economic subsystem dislocation. Many diffusing artefact-types will simply represent alternative forms to those already existing in the cultural format – simply differing states of multistate types generating no system inconsistencies or dislocation. A far larger class of artefact-types circulating and recirculating throughout the system will be simply redundant – that is to say that these are the modal types for this culture and their circulation effects no change in variety, they convey no 'new' behavioural information.

However, the most significant category of artefact-type variety will be those types which contradict sections of the system's behavioural code and its stabilized variety. The contradictive variety might be presented by swine-herding and its artefacts to a Jewish community, or by anthropomorphic sculpture to Moslems, or even the constant military equivocation between the developing artefacts of armour and those of mobility and fire power. In the face of contradictive variety the sociocultural system in most cases simply rejects or refuses to accept such diffusing variety and any internal integrative invention of the kind is neglected by the system, though it may be avidly borrowed by another. Nevertheless, it may be immediately advantageous to accept and integrate one piece of contradictive variety in order to stabilize an existing major dislocation at the expense of creating a new minor one. Since sociocultural systems are not altogether intelligent and forward looking organisms, such changes often subsequently lead to serious and unforeseen consequences – especially on the basis of the piecemeal integration of cumulative variety leading to an unforeseen threshold. The short term strategy seems always to be one of minimizing the maximum amount of immediate system dislocation and its dependent social ambiguity.

The culture system therefore displays all the system regularities expected of an arbitrary material subsystem within the sociocultural whole – those regularities pointed out in the general model. These regularities include the general categories of variety just discussed, the principle of dynamic adjustment to a moving equilibrium, system oscillation at several levels, feedback, foci of accelerated change, the operation of multiple factors and cumulative effect to thresholds, directive correlation and the many other points of the general model for cultural processes (fig. 11 and postulates 1–16, chapter 2).

The ontogeny of a specific culture or cultural assemblage has been outlined in terms of the successive introduction and cumulative integration of an emergent set of directively correlated essential and key artefact-types. The 'new' cultural format thus emerges for the first time as an integrated system at a major threshold (fig. 68), thereafter moving from system state to system state in space and time until the same process of cumulative change brings about the transmutation of the system into yet another major transform. These transitions, as we have repeatedly stressed, do not come about of their own accord or stem from innate qualities of the artefacts – we need only recognize that whatever the complex causes generating the changes may be, this is the way in which such changes occur. The principal manifestations of such transitions are marked by the cumulative interaction of the superimposed tendencies of reinforcing trends. These grouped trends

mark the thresholds and segment the continuous process of transformation, suggesting the 'birth, growth, death' analogy of the organic
world. We must now try and model in a tentative and crude manner
some of the trends generated by societies and responsible for the
apparent ontogeny of their material exoskeleton.

TENTATIVE MODEL OF MATERIAL CULTURE SYSTEM
ONTOGENY

The main trends thought to be involved, at varying levels of
importance, have been discussed in detail in earlier sections of this
chapter. These trends include:

> changes in numbers of specific artefact-type categories defining the
> culture's polythetic set,
> changes in numbers of specific artefact-type categories per
> component assemblage (average),
> changes in numbers of artefacts per specific artefact-type state
> (location and degree of central tendency),
> changes in numbers of component assemblages per culture phase
> or state,
> changes in the level of overall intercorrelation between specific
> artefact-types (coherence),
> changes in the rates of change, especially of types from type state
> to type state.

Each of these changes may be broadly divided into increasing, stable,
or decreasing attitudes or trends and therefore once again we have six
trending variables, each with three crude attitudes – allowing a possible 3^6 or 729 broad combinations or kinds of joint change. Taken
together, the interdependence of some of the variables, the crude
expression of their trends, and the number of possible permutations
all combine to make any simple model on this basis merely schematic.
However, it is suggested that it is these mutually fluctuating trends
which are responsible for defining cultural assemblage ontogeny,
somewhat in the following way:

> (o) *Threshold – 'birth/death'*
> > Successive phases of a cultural assemblage or culture exhibit-
> > ing:
> > > increasing numbers of type categories defining the cultural
> > > polythetic set,

decreasing numbers of type categories per component assemblage,

decreasing numbers of artefacts in previously modal states (Kurtosis),

decreasing numbers of component assemblages per phase,

decreasing level of overall intercorrelation between type categories,

increasing rates of change, especially of types from state to state.

(1) *Formative – 'growth'*

Successive phases of a cultural assemblage or culture exhibiting:

decreasing numbers of type categories defining the cultural polythetic set,

increasing numbers of type categories per component assemblage,

increasing numbers of artefacts in newly centred central tendency,

increasing numbers of component assemblages of the new format,

increasing level of overall intercorrelation between type categories,

decreasing rates of change, especially of types from state to state.

(2) *Coherent – 'maturity'*

Successive phases of a cultural assemblage or culture exhibiting:

increasing numbers of type categories defining the cultural polythetic set,

increasing numbers of type categories per component assemblage,

maximal central tendency of artefacts in new key type states,

maximal numbers of component assemblages of the new format,

maximal level of intercorrelation between essential artefact-types,

minimal rates of change, especially of types from state to state.

(3) *Post-Coherent – 'decline'*

Successive phases of a cultural assemblage or culture exhibiting:

decreasing numbers of type categories defining the cultural polythetic set,

decreasing numbers of type categories per component assemblage,

decreasing central tendency of artefacts around former modal states,

decreasing numbers of component assemblages,

decreasing level of overall intercorrelation between artefact-types,

increasing rates of change, especially of types from state to state.

(o) *Threshold – 'death/birth'*

Successive phases of a cultural assemblage or culture exhibiting:

increasing numbers of type categories defining the cultural polythetic set,

decreasing numbers of type categories per component assemblage,

decreasing numbers of artefacts in previously modal type states,

decreasing numbers of component assemblages per phase,

decreasing level of overall intercorrelation between artefact-types,

increasing rates of change, especially of types from state to state.

The scheme outlined above is intended as no more than a suggestion of the nature of some of the changes which suggest cultural system ontogeny – as a model the scheme is highly idealized and completely hypothetical. Nevertheless, the sequence does help to frame the processes involved in a way which emphasizes the complex interaction of trends in the system and despite its weakness the model provides a basis for the comparison of 'coherence' with the phenomenon of cultural 'climax'.

CULTURE CLIMAX

The schematic cultural system ontogeny just outlined has been defined purely in terms of variety and patterned changes in variety – there has been no mention of the economic or technological state of the system involved. Quite correctly so, since we recognize that this general ontogenetic pattern – 'birth, growth, death' – is displayed by Palaeolithic and by Iron Age cultures, by hunter–fisher–gatherer material cultures and by urban material cultures. We recognize that in terms of their material culture subsystem or specific cultural assemblage these entities are at one time non-existent, then they appear for the first time, become widespread, only to finally disappear from the scene again. This is the general case irrespective of the specific sociocultural form or complexity.

Now, sociocultural systems vary enormously in their technological content, micro-structure, economic organization and environmental conditions. It follows that the detailed development pattern of individual categories of sociocultural system will vary according to the characteristic constraints operating in that system category. Steward (1955), for example, has distinguished the pattern and pattern-potential of several levels of sociocultural integration based on taxa sharing certain social, economic, technological, territorial and population dispersion attributes. Sociocultural systems like machines extract energy from their environment and expend it in a variety of activities preconstrained by the system format and directed towards system continuity. Like machines, cultural systems may either extract energy steadily and release it gradually in a steady but small output of sociocultural variety, or at the other extreme, some highly organized and sophisticated cultural systems may extract energy from their resources in great quantities and by concentrating it enormously amplify the output of variety. The former strategy is a non-climax satisficer system and the latter strategy a climax and optimizer system – both systems have risks and advantages.

Since the economic subsystem is the extractive source of system energy, the more successful the particular economic strategy the greater is the quantity of energy available for redistribution throughout the system. Consequently, cultural climax represents the peculiar form of system coherence or 'maturity' found in cultures with super-elaborate economic organizations or alternatively superabundant natural resources. Under the former arrangement we have the urban states and empires – civilization; under the latter arrangement we have the climax of simpler systems under unusually advantageous conditions – the Magdalenian culture group of Palaeolithic Europe, or the famed Northwestern Indians of recent North America. Accordingly, culture climax follows the exponential burst of sociocultural variety identifying the formative phases of certain categories of cultural system and for this reason such phases are often organically described as the phase of cultural 'florescence'. However, all cultures have formative and coherent phases of integration but only under certain circumstances will these phases also attain cultural florescence and climax. There is of course a continuous gradation between poor economies and rich economies with a consequent gradation from non-climax, steady output cultures to climactic and amplified output cultures. The advantages of the climactic systems are their more effective capacity for the regulation and control of the environment insulating the individual and system, but against this capacity must be set the potential dangers of inflationary excess, overspecialization, overexploitation of resources, and the marked social inequalities of overorganization. The advantages of the non- or low-climax systems are their potential for a more egalitarian society with a less drastic and smoother development trajectory – the disdvantages being the vulnerability of the system to environmental fluctuation and the restricted range of its potential development.

On this basis it would appear that one might distinguish a general and widespread pattern of system development inherent in the structure of every material culture system as opposed to a restricted and special version of this development inherent only under certain economic conditions:

General system ontogeny	Climax system ontogeny
Threshold	Threshold/Archaic
Formative	Formative/Florescent
Coherent	Coherent/Classic climax
Post-coherent	Post-coherent/Post-classic
Threshold	Threshold/Archaic
The system may have several successive transformations each with a distinctive formative and coherent phase.	The system may have several successive transformations each with a distinctive florescent and classic climax phase.

It is patently obvious that these simple unimodal models can be multimodal – as in the case of the isolated Chinese and Egyptian civilizations, or the models may be truncated and substituted by external interference – as in the case of the Spanish destruction of the Meso-American cultures (Kroeber 1963).

So far we have suggested that cultural climax is a special and restricted manifestation of some cultural ontogenies but we have still not directly accounted for this special 'creativity' or explained its relationship with the formative phase of system development. It has been noted, however, that the florescence-climax sequence is restricted to systems so organized or situated that they may extract surplus quantities of energy from their resources and by concentrating it amplify the output of system variety. A first step is to find out how cultural systems can amplify variety and what sociocultural structures have this capacity.

Inasmuch as each newly formed cultural entity arises out of the elements of several pre-existing cultures and communities it is inevitable that the formative phase contains a wide diversity of contradictive and alternative variety. In such a phase the structure and coupling of the sociocultural system and subsystems have yet to be mutually stabilized and institutionalized within a unit system – the internal dislocation will thus be made severe by the contradictive wealth of diverse sociocultural information and discordant subsystem outputs. This state of formative growth invites vigorous experimentation to produce variety to stabilize the dislocations in a manner that is not found in communities in a more mature phase. As cumulative change progresses the possible developmental patterns and trajectories become further restricted as the attributes are increasingly integrated and institutionalized within a functional whole.

The formative system disequilibrium within and between the subsystems necessitates an optimal rate of generation of yet more fresh and newly comprehensive variety in order to minimize the maximum amount of dislocation in the system. This new variety can only come from the two customary sources:

internal generation by integrative inventions,
external generation and communication by diffusion.

The formative system phase is therefore characterized by a great diversity of intrinsic variety requiring a correspondingly large quantity of 'new' variety from internal integrative inventions and external diffusion. Consequently, as Kroeber has so admirably shown, the formative phase represents the ideal conditions for the roughly constant population of latent genius cumulatively to interact and produce a cluster of integrative inventions and discoveries – retrospectively marked by periods of clustered geniuses and threshold achievements (Kroeber 1963). This formative phase is also an unusually receptive and integrating phase for these same reasons. Such 'creativity' or burst of new variety in attributes and artefacts is thus a potential of formative 'youth' in a sociocultural system – not to be found in the same degree in later phases. It is not that the invention or acquisition of new variety ever ceases it is simply that the 'florescence' marks a greatly increased rate of new variety development.

However, if the above hypothesis is correct why is the florescence-climax phenomenon only observed in certain kinds and situations of systems? The answer is simply a matter of degree and is expressed in our previous contrast between satisficer sociocultural systems, organized towards the steady exploitation and release of energy and variety, as opposed to those optimizer systems with the amplifying release of bursts of energy and variety. The capacity for such energy and variety amplification resides in certain forms of sociocultural organization and structure, where these are the necessary but not sufficient prerequisites for climax potential. One such organization is the city. The city is a most peculiar and extremely sophisticated unit depending upon the organized population and resources of a local territory, which in turn may perhaps rest upon a similarly highly organized culture – a nation – and in the most powerful units this may in turn draw upon an organized and widespread extractive empire (fig. 69). The city is therefore an energy or variety amplifier in this context and the nation may perhaps be seen as an artificially organized culture and the empire as a similarly artificially optimized culture group. The alternative optimizer and therefore potentially climatic strategy is a smaller amplifying unit based upon a more flexible cultural system but equally highly organized in a situation of high resources and low population. This is the low florescence and climax category which may be seen in such hunting–fishing–gathering contexts as the Magdalenian and Kwakiutl tribes, with their highly specialized near-optimal subsistence strategies in abundant environments. Inevitably, the scope and stability of climax in such small unit systems must be less than that of the urban-agrarian technocomplexes.

In summary, then, we have carefully distinguished between the – formative, coherent, post-coherent – ontogeny which is repeated in all cultural systems, and the – florescent, classic-climax, post-classic – sequence which marks only the ontogeny of near-optimizer

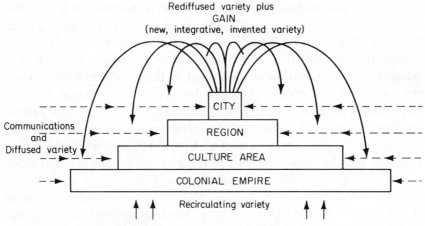

Rediffused variety plus
GAIN
(new, integrative, invented variety)

CITY

REGION

CULTURE AREA

COLONIAL EMPIRE

Communications
and
Diffused variety

Recirculating variety

Fig. 69   The city as an energy and variety amplifier plugged in the cultural network. Raw material and variety of all kinds are drawn from the city's region, culture, and perhaps imperial areas – this variety is integrated and recirculated from the city (to varying degrees) as powerful, new variety (complex machines, tools, etc., including social, religious, and conceptual artefacts as well as material ones).

economies, often in the wake of an economic boom. The European Renaissance provides a fine example of just this florescence and climax sequence, following and depending upon the economic boom immediately preceding it. It is important to note that northern Italy was a cultural unit with a cultural ontogeny and climax even though it was never a single political unit – it was a unit of which the components were as unaware but inseparably a part, as were the city states within Classical Greece or the organisms within a biotope.

Florescence, climax, and post-climax are therefore merely a matter of degree – the enormously amplified manifestation of variety changes found on a smaller scale in all formative, coherent, post-coherent transitions. All formative phases of cultural systems will have contained heterogeneous and diverse cultural variety momentarily integrated from many sources and only metastably balanced within the unit culture system. In all cases this will give rise to foci of dislocation and stimulate the invention and acquisition of new and comprehensive variety – but it is the severity, scope and amplified potential of these everyday developments which may chance to give rise to a florescence and climax in an economically advanced cultural system.

Kroeber has summarized and documented this process in terms of his hypothesis of 'pattern fulfilment' (1948, pp. 360–5; and 1963, pp. 825–46). He postulates that every cultural element, of every level, has a limited potential range of development or transformation which is quickly reached in outline in the formative florescence and then slowly filled-in from the climax through the post-climax phases. On this hypothesis the climax is the classic phase of outline or essential pattern fulfilment, which is thereafter conservatively filled with branching development. The interpretation and hypothesis offered here differs from the Kroeber model because although conceptually satisfying that expression is very difficult to support in detail. When is a pattern 'fulfilled' or 'filled-in', why does the pattern not continue its expansive development of new variety? The explanation offered here suggests that it is not that every cultural pattern has its fulfilment capacity but conversely that the cumulative growth developing the pattern is initially stimulated by formative dislocation and ceases, or rather decreases in its rate of development, when those dislocations are nearly stabilized. The florescence is brought about by large-scale stimulative dislocation in certain kinds of system and the climax is the arbitrary stabilization of that dislocation in a 'new', emergent cultural configuration integrated for the first time.

This variant of the Kroeber hypothesis can perhaps be most clearly expressed in the definition of the crucial terminology.

Florescence. The period of explosive growth in new and comprehensive variety in aspects of an optimizer cultural system or subsystem – thus defining the cumulative and catalytic development of variety necessary to stabilize foci of system dislocation, brought about by the system's development.

The term florescence, although only different in degree, is here separated from the small-scale version of the same process which is characteristic of the formative phase of all cultural systems.

Climax. The period following a variety florescence in a system or subsystem, in which the dislocating alternative and contradictive variety produced by integrative growth is first coherently stabilized in the newly emergent system format.

The term climax may be applied to the coherent emergence of a new format in any aspect of a climaxing system – pottery, painting, sculpture, architecture, drama, etc.

Cultural Climax. The period following a variety florescence in an optimizer cultural system – thus defining the first coherent configuration of the newly emergent cultural format, stabilizing the new variety generated in the various cultural aspects. The period commonly agreed as defining the phases in which the majority of a culture's arts and crafts reach their individual climax pattern. The process is cumulative and catalytic – the climax coincidentally of one or more components will often induce climax conditions in related aspects and if the conditions are suitable (metastable) these too will climax. The clustered individual aspect climaxes then provide a strong overall pattern and fresh system configuration – a renaissance transformation. Such conditions, as Kroeber pointed out, provide optimal preconditions for inventions and innovations on an integrative basis and thus retrospectively appear to cluster human genius (Kroeber 1963).

The archaeological record can therefore hope to detect the development of both cultural system formation and coherence and in special cases their florescence and climax manifestations. It should after all be possible to infer the general basis and character of the clustered geniuses of the Renaissance and Classical Greece from the material remains and the contrast with what went before and followed after. One very noticeable facet of these florescence-climax developments is their artistic investiture. This artistic development is very difficult to evaluate without recourse to contemporary value judgements although it should be noticed that it is usually restricted to only a selection of the available artistic fields. However, it is apparent that this artistic development is also part of the general stimulus to innovation to minimize the developing contradictions and ambiguities of the florescent diversity – creating new variety in order to reconcile or replace existing equivocal forms. Much of this dislocation may be social, religious, or psychological even though registered in artistic output and in this sense art and the artist are truly 'characteristic' of their period and context. Even this artistic output is very frequently functionally integrated within the contemporary culture as conveniently concentrated units of conspicuously wasted time – the essence of most prestige symbols and insignia.[2]

Notes

(1) The 'supra-cultural' nature of metal production and distribution in the European Bronze Age has been questioned by Rowlands (1971, pp. 213–15). In considering the ethnographic evidence for the position and status of smiths he points out that the 'detribalized' or 'itinerant' smith has been

298 Analytical Archaeology

encountered only very rarely. The existence of regional or industrial differences in metalwork as well as localized metalworking traditions in the European Middle and Late Bronze Ages also argue against the notion of supra-cultural production.

(2) The role of information processing and decision making in state formation have been discussed recently in a less abstract form by Johnson, who argues that 'primary state development involves overloading the decision making organization of a chiefdom. Since no single factor such as increasing irrigation, population, warfare, local exchange or whatever can be shown to have led to state development, it would appear that *multiple* sources of information input are required to force basic organizational changes at this level' (1973, p. 161). Flannery (1972) concurs with the key significance of decision-making through an increasingly centralized and segregated/hierarchical social organization in state formation. These processes of segregation and centralization, as well as the mechanisms by which they take place, are held to have occurred in the evolution of all state systems, but the 'socio-environmental stresses' (e.g. warfare/population growth/irrigation/trade) which brought them into play would have been localized in their particular configuration. The place of religion within the development of such climax state systems has been tentatively explored by Drennan (1976), who suggests that segregation and centralization increases the need for 'rituals of sanctification' to ensure acceptance and help maintain the new social order.

7 Culture and culture group

In the classification of relics perhaps the first step should
now be to assign them to their proper cultural group,
'Changing methods and aims in prehistory',
Proceedings of the Prehistoric Society for 1936, pp. 1–15
V. GORDON CHILDE 1936

1 Introduction

In an important sense the culture is the entity at the peak of the
hierarchical model of archaeological entities (fig. 49). The archaeological culture when properly defined represents the material culture
subsystem of a specific sociocultural system. The culture system and
the communities which generate it embody the largest unit with
internally the most richly cross-connected and mutually reinforcing
system of information variety, uniting and stabilizing every channel of
human intercommunication and behaviour. Social organizations of
greater size than the society and its culture are less richly networked
and consequently have less rich system 'behaviour'. The increasing
power and diversity of methods of communication have nevertheless
allowed a steady increase in the sustainable size of such sociocultural
systems.

The archaeological culture is therefore the entity category with the
biggest information content – to place an assemblage in a specific
culture is to attribute it with many general and specific characteristics.
To assign an assemblage or a culture to a culture group is to attribute
it to a larger entity but to one with a lower group information content
– a bigger entity in terms of area and population but less complex in
network organization and in the level of affinity between its
components. In precisely the same way the category 'species' in
biological classification carries more information than the categories
'order' or 'genus' although their populations are far greater. It is for
this reason that great care must be taken in archaeological terminology
in order to correctly isolate cultural entities from larger and less
informative entities. To designate Gravettian assemblages a culture,

for example, is to grossly mistake the size, nature and degree of organization of the entity under consideration – to attribute it with a false set of inherent properties. Our concern with the careful definition of the information levels of archaeological terminology and their more rigorous employment is directed at this very problem.

It must immediately be emphasized that of course all cultures are also part of culture groups and of such higher and increasingly general entities as technological complexes and socioeconomic groupings – in much the same way as a species necessarily falls within a genus and order. Component assemblages and cultural assemblages belong at one and the same time to the intersection of these several broad sets which are distinguished one from another as archaeological categories by the varying levels of complexity and necessary affinity uniting the assemblages in these sets. The relationship of the particular case or sample within these broad sets of collateral relatives conveys a great amount of latent information about the particular case. The more precise our definition of these sets the correspondingly more abundant our reward in precise information. Although it may prove impossible to allocate an assemblage to a precise culture it is usually much easier, requiring less information, to allocate the assemblage to a culture group – to one unknown culture of which the assemblage primarily belongs. In this way, although the individual cultures of Neolithic Europe remain myriad and ill-defined the culture groups offer a broadly simplified pattern of bundles of related transforms (fig. 70). By alternating between the minutiae of incisive analysis and the broad pattern of overall development orientation the archaeologist can grope his way forward to fresh information.

We might define a culture group as – *a group of affinally related, collateral cultures characterized by assemblages sharing a polythetic range, but differing states, of the same specific multistate artefact-types.* A low level affinity, perhaps 30 per cent or less, uniting the group in terms of shared sets of specific type states, but a residual high level affinity, perhaps 60 per cent or more, uniting the group in terms of sets of type families and multistate transform types. The essence of the culture group, so defined, then becomes the polythetic set of multistate artefact-types which are variously shared by the culture group's members and which together express the culture group's necessary identity.

The culture group essentially consists, then, of a group of closely related cultures often based on the regional subcultures of an expanding cultural tradition. In later prehistory, for example, Europe is

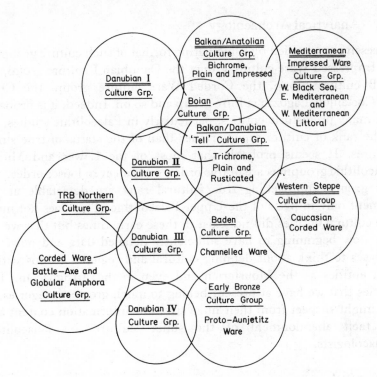

Fig. 70 A tentative Model of the main Culture Groups in Neolithic Europe *c.* 6000–2000 BC. Each Culture Group is a multidimensional football through time and space; the overlaps emphasize that as polythetic structures, and as an important factor in development, individual cultures may belong to and link several culture groups, without contradiction. Group content:

Balkan/Anatolian Group
Hacilar culture, Kremikovci and Karanovo I culture, Pre/Proto Sesklo, Starcevo-Koros-Cris

Danubian I Group
Eastern, Western and Northern Danubian I cultures, Bukk, Hinkelstein etc.

Boian Group
Boian, Dudesti, Vadastra, Butmir, and Marica cultures.

Balkan/Danubian Tell Group
Gumelnitza, Salcutza, Dimini, Petresti, Tripolye-Cucuteni, Thrace-Macedonian cultures.

Baden Group
Baden, Pecel, Kostolac, Bubanj, Vucedol, Mondsee, Zok, Laibach cultures.

Early Bronze Group
Periam-Mokrin, Glina, Foltesti, Kisapostag, Nagyrev, Perjamos, Unetice, cultures.

Corded Ware Group
Globular Amphora, Fatyanovo, Dniepr-Dniestr, Zlota/Vistula, Swedish, Danish, Haffküsten, Oder/Marschwitz, W. German, Dutch PFB, Swiss, Saxo-Thuringian cultures.

Mediterranean Impressed Ware Group
W. Black Sea cultures: Hamangia I, Burgas, Bug/Dniepr cultures. E. Mediterranean: Adriatic Smilcic, Molfetta, Sentinello I cultures. W. Mediterranean: Portuguese, Spanish, S. France, N. Africa, Sardinia, Malta, impressed ware cultures.

Danubian II Group
Vinca Tordos, Tisza, Lengyel, Stichband, and Rossen cultures.

Danubian III Group
Tiszapolgar, Ludanice, Bodrogkeresztur, Decea, Jordansmuhl, Baalberg cultures.

Danubian IV Group
Jevisovice, Aichbuhl, Schussenried, Altheim, Pfyn, Horgen cultures.

TRB Northern Group
Jordansmuhl, Baalberg, Salzmunde, Walternienberg, Wiorek, Lubon, Nosswitz, TRB A/B, C, Michelsberg, MN, TRB. Scandinavia and Netherlands.

Western Steppe Group
Caucasian Corded Ware, Usatova, Cernavoda, Cotofeni, Ochre Grave cultures.

These Culture Groups should be objectively delineated by clustering the cultural assemblages in terms of mutual affinity, by the standard taxonomic methods. However, in the absence of such studies this intuitive-subjective assessment can be used with caution.

successively occupied by a fluctuating format of such culture groups as the Impressed Ware culture group, the Danubian I culture group, the TRB culture group, the Corded Ware culture group, the Chassey/Cortaillod/Lagozza culture group and so on. Indeed, it is probable that many prehistoric entities, particularly in Palaeolithic studies, are of the rank of culture groups rather than of the status of true single cultures. It seems probable that most of the Lower and Middle Palaeolithic groupings are of this order, or of an even looser order, and that groups approaching true cultural rank are detectable at the moment only in parts of the Upper Palaeolithic. This does not mean that cultural entities did not exist in these early times but that we are only now beginning to have sufficiently detailed data and powerful analyses to think about defining cultural and regional groups within such entities as the Mousterian and even in the Aurignacian. The entities that we have at present belong to much grosser categories, as one might suspect from their huge size, low information content and the tacit abandonment of the suffix 'culture' by Palaeolithic archaeologists.

11 Culture group systems

Culture group systems are systems of interconnected cultural assemblages, varying in terms of their component assemblages, which in turn change as the integral of the changing artefact-types. The continued coherence of the culture group system depends on a low level of continuous intercommunication between the component regional assemblages. Any discontinuation of this limited diffusion of common cultural variety would gradually lead to the diminution and loss of the essential sets of shared multistate artefact-types and ultimately to the loss of the culture group's identity under the impact of divergent development. This is one way in which the 'death' of a culture group may come about.

The sociocultural basis of the culture group is particularly interesting and informative. The preceding chapter suggested that the culture and its cultural assemblage reflected a compact territory and society, providing an area of maximal internal intercommunication and diffusion. Two of the major means of diffusion linking such a cultural entity seemed to be the common social reticulation and a common language or group of dialects as a maximal means of intercommunication. Observation appears to support the approximate but rarely coincident equivalence of a language area with a culture area – at least the former set is usually larger than or equal to the latter set. It was further suggested that a deliberately organized culture with a common language formed the basis of the 'nation' as an entity. On these general lines we arrive at a rough equivalence and connection between the separate sets – culture, language, and nation (fig. 75).

Now, the culture group as a group of closely related cultures in adjacent but discontinuous territories should on this general basis reflect a group of closely related languages and societies – a language group and a sociocultural group. Furthermore, since one origin for culture groups seems to be the increasing divergence of an expanding culture with widespread regional subcultures, there is every reason to suspect that such a culture group would be marked by equally divergent languages forming a group with a once common background. One must hasten to add that since the culture group can also be formed in other ways this is not an automatic characteristic of culture groups and their language systems. Nevertheless, we can understand that it will frequently be the case that culture groups equate roughly and without exact coincidence with language groups and as such may provide the archaeologist with an invaluable but highly complex and dangerous clue to the development of such important phenomena as the Indo-European and other major language groups, with significantly greater success at the lower scale in such cases as the Celtic, Slav and Bantu linguistic and culture group entities. The complexity and danger in such studies lie in wait in the imprecise terminology, and the fact that linguistic and material culture sets are never simply equivalent to social sets. The time and space trajectories of language groups and culture groups are closely related but not identical, the complicating factor being the differing rates of change of the twin aspects.

The pre-existence of a common language group in a set of contiguous societies and territories necessarily constitutes an ideal precondition for the formation of a loose confederacy or tribal grouping. Such a confederacy is usually marked by a sufficient increase in mutual contact and interdiffusion of material culture as to mark out a roughly coincident material culture group. But to expect such a culture group to be exactly coincident with an absolutely homogeneous language group and tribal group would again be excessively naive. Nevertheless, the fact remains that such units as the Iroquois and Zulu confederations and the Scythian and Celtic tribal groupings have survived in the broad outline of their material culture, in the form of major culture groups defined in terms of artefacts (chapter 9). In some cases the deliberate organization of such a confederacy or grouping by a single culture may result in the formation of a focally organized and maximally implemented culture group – the colonial empire. There exists therefore a very loose but definite connection between the separate sets – culture group, language group, and social confederations, mainly as entities of roughly equivalent rank and occasionally as sequential consequences one of another.

In the case of the colonial empire as an artificially organized culture group, focused on an amplifying urban state, the sequence usually moves from the military occupation of a network of economically desirable colonies, followed by their partial acculturation into a culture group, sometimes with the temporary establishment of a shared language group. The risks of maintaining such an imperial territory have often resulted in a dramatic post-climax disintegration as the result of the cumulative effect of multiple factors reaching an historic threshold (chapter 2, III). Seen from outside the last factor in such a process and superficially the most powerful manifestation is often the military break-up of the system organization and the economic loss of the colonial territories. The destruction of the amplifier's input variety, however, robs the former colonial territories themselves of the optimized output of inventive and integrative variety, a reversion often characterized by contrast as a 'Dark Age' (fig. 69). Another alternative trajectory, out of the many possible, is the post-climax peaceful release of the former colonies and a transition to a network of independent cultures yet remaining within a single system organization. By avoiding the military and inflationary collapse of the system the amplifying units may still be preserved and continue to benefit the whole.

Even in this brief outline it has become apparent that culture groups may integrate and disintegrate in a number of different ways. Once formed, their trajectories may pursue a number of different general sequences with differing consequences. As systems, culture groups vary in their degree of system organization and structure, some are loosely organized or exist with no conscious harnessing of the organization, others are highly organized and deliberately structured systems. These and other factors considerably affect the ontogeny of the culture group and will be further examined in probing this aspect of these systems (section IV). It is sufficient for the time being to speculate that these diverse organizations, ontogenies and trajectories are not without constraint and therefore not without regularities.

III Phase pattern regularities

As we proceed through the hierarchy of archaeological entities from the culture onwards it becomes increasingly difficult to isolate the phase, time, and system regularities of these entities. This is partly because the units become increasingly large in size and numbers of components but mainly because there is insufficient analysed data to synthesize. Very few archaeologists have bothered about the detailed analysis of entities larger than the cultural assemblage, mainly perhaps because these larger entities still remain unclassified taxa – like the Palaeolithic units – or on the assumption that there is nothing to be gained by their definition. Those classificatory studies that have intelligently emphasized these larger groupings have been forced to document them in a general way, only broadly defined as – the Urnfield culture group, the Tumulus culture group or the Aunjetitz culture group, to give three European Bronze Age examples. What is required is a series of precise and detailed analyses of these entities and all aspects of their material culture and time and distribution trajectories. What are their shared polythetic sets of artefact-types, what is the size and nature of these sets, how does their development as an entity vary with this structure? It is impossible in so condensed a study as this to start to provide this missing detailed basis but before venturing into generalities it is essential that we sketch in a rapid and crude way some example and some model of what we intuit these entities to look like. In such circumstances the dangers are insuperable and the chances of a really penetrating insight almost negligible but at least the possibilities may make themselves apparent.

In an attempt to highlight the great potential of detailed studies at this level we will first develop a static phase model of a culture group and then compare it with a practical case – treated superficially. This basis will then allow us to illustrate the distribution and time regularities we might expect in other cases with a more fitting documentation.

STATIC MODEL

Let us take an imaginary culture group, 'G', defined by six contemporary regional cultures, 1, 2, 3, 4, 5, 6.

Each cultural assemblage in the group shares from amongst certain specific artefact-types, A, B, C, D, E... with certain variant type states, A_1, A_2, A_3; B_1, B_2; C_1, C_2, C_3; D_1, D_2; E_1, E_2; at different frequencies of occurrence per cultural assemblage (absent, infrequent and frequent/modal). Then, the static model of the structure of culture group unit – G, might be schematically represented by the polythetic relationships of the component cultural assemblages, in table 1.

Table 1   Schematic model of culture group 'G' illustrating the polythetic structure of the six regional cultures constituting the group

Specific artefact-type	Variant state	Cultural assemblages					
		1	2	3	4	5	6
Type	State						
A	A_1	X	x	—	X	—	X
	A_2	x	X	x	x	X	X
	A_3	x	—	X	X	x	—
B	B_1	X	—	—	—	x	X
	B_2	x	X	—	x	X	—
C	C_1	X	—	x	—	X	X
	C_2	—	X	x	X	X	—
	C_3	—	x	X	X	—	X
D	D_1	X	—	x	X	X	X
	D_2	x	X	—	X	x	X
E	E_1	X	—	X	—	X	x
	E_2	—	X	X	x	—	X

The simplified model in table 1 illustrates the expected polythetic structure of a culture group embracing several regional cultural assemblages. The entity of the unit is provided by the selective sharing of various states of a common set of multistate specific artefact-types – so that no one culture has all the types and each component culture has an independent structural identity. Although some types or type states may be shared by all the component cultures, this is an exception rather than the rule (Type A_2, table 1; flint axes, table 2). The essential system artefact-types in such a context are especially represented by those specific artefact-types existing in a multiplicity of states which are selectively preferred by the regional cultures. The key types from amongst this set would then include those specific types with a distinct chronological or regional correlation trend within the culture group. The inessential types are largely missing from this condensed model but would include those types or type states which were uniquely held by single cultural assemblages within the group – contributing nothing to the unity of the group but serving to differentiate members.

Example. The static phase model provides us with a particular way of looking at the artefact-types and assemblages constituting archaeological culture groups. When we attempt to analyse a known culture group in the same terms we immediately encounter certain difficulties. The first of these difficulties simply arises from the already stressed absence of sufficiently detailed studies of whole archaeological culture groups as taxonomic units; the model is difficult to test or modify because of the lack of analysed data. The second difficulty is also a consequence of lack of information – as a phase model the practical example should minimize time trends by taking contemporary cultural assemblages over only a short duration, perhaps a century or so. In practice, archaeological dating is so limited that the cultural assemblages of successive phases are rarely known for every culture within the group under analysis. The following example is characteristically imperfect in all these respects and in any case is intended merely as an illustrative sketch (table 2).

In the example, the well-known Corded Ware/Battle-axe culture group has been analysed into its components. This culture group may be set out as embracing twelve major regional cultural assemblages, each representing an homogeneous geographical area containing a concentration of interrelated assemblages within a unit culture –

Cultural assemblage in table 2: (p. 308)
    (1) The Middle Dniepr culture
    (2) The Upper Dniestr culture
    (3) The Fatyanovo culture
    (4) The Złota/Vistula culture
    (5) The Haffküstenkultur
    (6) The Swedish Boat-axe culture
    (7) The Oder/Marschwitz culture
    (8) The Saxo-Thuringian culture
    (9) The Danish Battle-axe culture
   (10) The North German/Dutch Protruding Foot Beaker culture
   (11) The West German Beaker culture
   (12) The Swiss Corded Ware culture

Table 2 The Corded Ware/Battle-axe culture group illustrating the polythetic structure of the twelve regional cultures constituting the group

Specific type	Variant state	Cultural assemblages											
		1	2	3	4	5	6	7	8	9	10	11	12
Beaker	Cord	X	x	x	X	x	—	X	X	X	x	x	x
	Herringbone	X	X	x	x	X	—	x	x	x	X	X	x
	Groove	—	—	—	x	x	—	x	x	x	X	x	x
	Maeander	—	—	—	x	x	x	—	—	—	—	—	—
	Round base	X	x	X	x	x	X	—	—	—	—	—	—
Globular amphora	Flat base	X	X	—	X	x	—	x	X	x	x	X	—
	Round base	x	—	X	—	—	x	—	—	—	—	—	—
Bowl	Flat base	X	X	—	X	X	x	X	X	x	x	x	—
	Round base	x	x	X	x	x	X	x	—	—	—	—	—
	Polypod	—	—	—	x	—	—	x	x	—	x	x	—
	Oval	—	—	x	X	x	x	x	x	—	—	—	—
Ovoid storage jar	Flat base	—	x	—	X	X	x	x	x	x	x	x	x
	Round base	x	x	X	—	x	x	—	—	—	—	—	—
Globular beaker	Flat base	—	—	—	x	—	x	x	x	x	X	x	x
	Round base	—	—	x	—	—	—	—	—	—	—	—	—
Flowerpot	Flat base	—	—	—	x	—	x	X	x	x	—	—	—
Battle-axe	Struve A	x	x	x	X	x	x	x	x	x	x	x	—
	M. Dniepr	X	X	x	x	—	—	x	—	—	—	—	—
	Fatyanovo	x	x	X	x	x	x	x	—	—	—	—	—
	Facetted	—	x	—	x	—	—	x	X	x	x	x	x
	Uckermark	—	—	—	—	—	—	X	x	—	—	—	—
Boat axe variant	Jutland	—	—	—	—	—	x	x	—	X	—	—	—
	Swedish	—	—	x	x	x	X	—	—	x	—	—	—
Axe	Flint	x	x	x	X	X	X	X	x	X	x	X	x
Trapezoid blades	Stone	x	x	x	X	x	x	X	X	—	x	X	x
	Flint	x	x	x	X	x	X	x	x	x	x	x	x
Dagger	Flint	x	x	x	x	x	X	X	x	X	x	X	—
Arrow heads	Hollow base	x	x	x	x	x	—	X	X	—	x	x	x
	Trapeze	—	x	x	x	x	—	x	—	—	—	—	—
Wrist Guard		x	x	x	x	—	—	x	x	—	—	—	—
'V' Buttons		—	x	x	x	x	x	x	x	—	—	—	—
Pins		x	x	—	x	—	x	x	x	—	—	—	—
Belt fasteners	Rings	X	x	x	x	x	x	x	x	x	—	x	—
	Plaques	x	x	X	x	x	—	x	—	—	—	—	—
Graves	Flat	x	x	X	X	X	X	X	X	x	x	x	x
	Barrow	X	X	—	x	x	x	x	X	X	X	X	x
	Shaft	X	X	—	x	x	—	x	x	x	x	x	—
	Catacomb	X	x	—	—	—	—	—	—	—	—	—	—
	Wood cist	X	X	—	x	x	x	x	x	x	x	x	x
	Stone cist	x	x	—	x	x	x	x	x	x	x	x	x

— absent. *x* – infrequent. *X* – frequent.

This culture group example therefore has twelve major cultural assemblage components whose regional distribution is suggested on the map (fig. 71). This culture group distribution map is already of great interest since it illustrates the broad linear correlation of the distribution with the European deciduous forest zone, barring the distorting influence of the Baltic Sea and important excursions into the mixed coniferous zone in Russia and Sweden (cultures 3, 6) and into the edge of the true Steppe zone in the Southeast (cultures 1, 2). Essentially the map suggests a linear distribution with radial distortions and emphasizes the discrete distribution of the cultures within the group – their concentrations are not continuous and it is doubtful if the total distribution was ever continuous.

Continuing the analysis, table 2 schematically illustrates something of the structure of the twelve cultures in terms of their shared specific artefact-types and their type states. In reality the Corded Ware/Battle-axe culture group list of artefact-types is very much more extensive and the structure of the whole group much more polythetic than is suggested in this table. For the purposes of condensation and convenience large numbers of types held by only one or two of the component cultures have been omitted and the types themselves are only crudely characterized by the headings used here. A final qualification must emphasize that this example is purely schematic and that contrary to our intentions the assemblages represented here probably stretch over a period of several hundred years, somewhere between 2500 and 2000 BC.

Nevertheless, even admitting the sketchy nature of this particular evidence and all its limitations, the resulting structure of the culture group does seem to reasonably approximate our tentative phase model (table 1). That the individual cultures are grouped within the culture group entity as a polythetic and not a monothetic group seems fully substantiated (table 2). In the same way the importance of the alternative states of the specific artefact-types in knitting together the cultural assemblages within a single group is also quite apparent. The very weakness of this real example shows how important it is that the individual specific artefact-types be defined accurately and in detail. In the same fashion it is apparent that the definition of the variant states within each multistate specific artefact-type is equally essential in order to appreciate the nuances of regional affinities and the structural integration of the group of cultural assemblages. It is particularly interesting to compare the structure of this culture group from

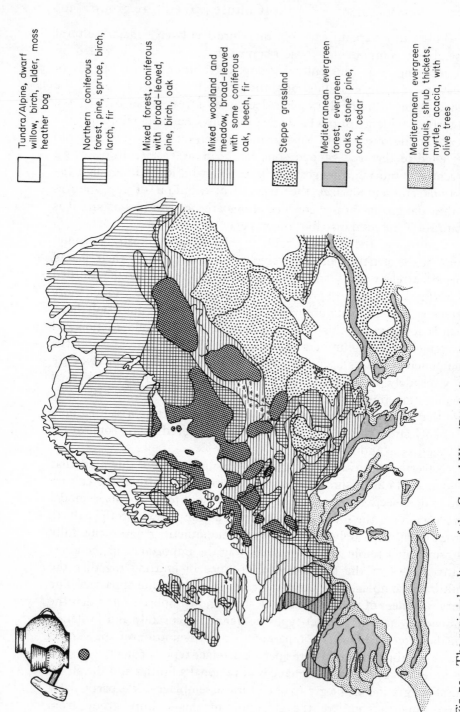

Tundra/Alpine, dwarf willow, birch, alder, moss heather bog

Northern coniferous forest, pine, spruce, birch, larch, fir

Mixed forest, coniferous with broad-leaved, pine, birch, oak

Mixed woodland and meadow, broad-leaved with some coniferous oak, beech, fir

Steppe grassland

Mediterranean evergreen forest, evergreen oaks, stone pine, cork, cedar

Mediterranean evergreen maquis, shrub thickets, myrtle, acacia, with olive trees

Fig. 71 The regional cultures of the Corded Ware/Battle-Axe culture group *c.* 2500–2000 BC. Note the linear constraint of distribution within the mixed deciduous forest zone, with radial modifications centred on the southeastern Baltic; compare fig. 73.

pre-history with the similar structuring of the material culture of historically related groups of North American Indian tribes (figs 77–86).

DISTRIBUTION AREA MODEL

If our previous discussion of the relative merits of the 'cultural brick', 'radial contour' and 'polythetic' models of cultural artefact-type distributions is accepted then it follows that a compound polythetic model should fit the culture group situation (figs 67, 72, chapter 6, III). In this case we have not one but several cultural areas defined by the reinforcing central tendencies of numerical distribution of the various multistate artefact-types, each rapidly falling away beyond the areas of mean, mode and median distribution – with types shared polythetically across the web (fig. 72). The culture areas of a culture group

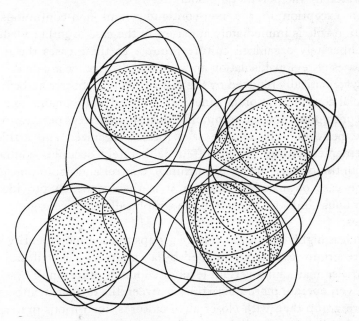

Fig. 72 A schematic model expressing the relationship between the distribution boundaries of the sets of cultural assemblage artefact-types and the boundaries of four cultures within a culture group. A much simplified extension of the polythetic distribution model (fig. 67iii) from the culture to the culture group. Clearly, the means and modes of the distribution sets are as relevant as their boundaries in this situation.

are rarely completely contiguous and continuous, partly because such a situation would more frequently mark the expanding culture with regional subcultures (the embryo culture group) and partly because there are usually attractive geographical foci which cluster primary settlement in density for socio-economic reasons. In addition, there is no reason to assume that cultures of the same culture group are necessarily less territorially defensive between themselves than independent cultures and consequently they will mutually repel one another into constantly readjusting but distinct culture areas. Although the human population may on rare occasions be semi-continuous over the entire area it will still reflect centres of density and uneven dispersion. The material effect of this arrangement is the clined distribution density patterns of the artefact-types which are a complex function of the human population distribution – the patterns illustrated by the polythetic model (fig. 72).

An exception to the non-contiguous and non-continuous distribution rule is immediately apparent in the case of military empires or deliberately organized culture groups. In these cases the normal processes of regional isolation and regional divergence are deliberately and systematically reduced by the institution of elaborate and effective artificial communication channels which incidentally maintain a large and continuous flow of commonly diffusing variety, permeating the whole network. The empire as a focally organized and artificially implemented culture group often deliberately occupies contiguous and continuous territories to maximize control and communications. In the case of maritime empires it is the sea which provides the continuous link between the geographically non-contiguous territories.

In less highly organized culture groups the common identity at the culture group level is maintained by a variety of sociocultural links which also maintain a certain level of common diffusion. These links may even operate more powerfully between the distant members of a culture group than with closer alien cultures, for various preferential reasons. Political, religious, historical, cultural and linguistic congruence probably help to maintain most of the culture group links that the archaeologist perceives in secondary material artefact terms.

It is already apparent that one process capable of generating culture group entities is the regional isolation and increasing divergence of the peripheral regional subcultures of an expanding culture. Indeed, the differentiation between a large culture with regional subcultures and a culture group with regional cultures is both arbitrary and difficult. One criterion we have already noted is the non-contiguous and discontinuous distribution of culture areas in a culture group – as opposed to the semi-continuous entity of the large culture with subcultures. This factor in itself gives the culture group a larger mean distribution area than the large culture, a factor normally endorsed by a larger absolute population in people and artefacts. It should be possible to characterize the separation of the range of culture and culture group sizes but here again little work has yet been done. A rough estimation would suggest that the range of prehistoric culture areas tends to cover territories of radius *c.* 20–200 miles, whereas culture groups usually spread across territory of radius *c.* 200–750 miles. On this basis alone one would see the European Michelsberg as an expansive Neolithic culture with a radius of *c.* 150–200 miles and six regional subcultures, as opposed to the Corded Ware culture group with its radius of *c.* 600 miles and twelve regional cultures (Scollar 1959). It would be foolish to use this size criterion alone but it is certainly one significant indicator. In all such studies one is unavoidably and therefore deliberately measuring the collapsed palimpsest of the fluctuating distribution of the culture group through time. It is once again preferable to come to terms with the realism of 'vertical' tradition taxa than with the largely illusory mosaic of 'horizontal' unit distributions.

One corollary of the development of an expanding culture with subcultures into a dispersed culture group is the regular pattern of dispersion of culture areas in the group. The constraints operating in this situation are first of all the peripheral and radial development of regional subcultures distant from one another and from the central areas, and secondly the geographic constraints peculiar to the territory. In practice two repetitive modes of culture group distribution are noticeable – the radial and the linear (fig. 73). The radial arrangement of cultures around a core of inner culture areas is the obvious unrestricted development of the ideal expansion, with interdiffusion weakening as a function of the distance from the original culture areas; it is however a dangerous simplification to simply postulate a single central 'ur-culture' and concentric expansion from it, as we shall see. The alternative linear model is appropriate when geographic zonation or constraint has channelled the expanding culture group. This is frequently the case with culture groups aligned on major river axes or following ecological zones (Danubian I,

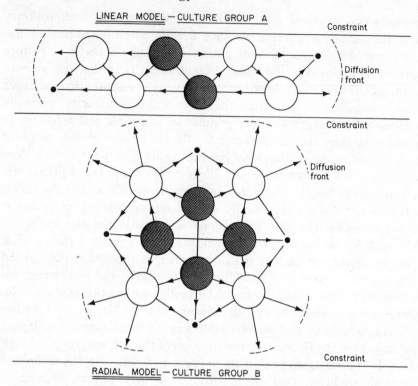

LINEAR MODEL — CULTURE GROUP A

RADIAL MODEL — CULTURE GROUP B

Fig. 73 Regularities in culture group distributions and expansions – the linear model (A) and the radial model (B). The linear model best fits culture group expansion within the constraints (ecological or otherwise) of a narrow zone. The radial model approximates culture group development within a relatively homogeneous field, only peripherally constrained (compare fig. 97). The 'primary' culture areas are shaded; the dots suggest the territories for 'induced' convergent development – other factors being equal.

Circumpolar or the Mediterranean Littoral culture groups). Although good examples of both radial and linear culture group patterns exist it is quite obvious that this bipolarization is artificial and that most real distributions have elements of both formats, e.g. the Corded Ware culture group (fig. 71). Nevertheless, it is similarly apparent that the dispersion pattern will have considerable effect upon the maintenace of the group identity and the culture group's subsequent time-trajectory. It follows that since most cultures are consciously or unconsciously part of a culture group the development of the specific culture cannot be meaningfully studied in isolation from the phenomenon in which it is set.

A striking example of this latter observation is the relationship between culture group networks and their subsequent transformation and reorientation at the hands of an infiltrating entity – sometimes a transform of one of the regional cultures. In its simplest aspect the pre-existing culture group network acts as a pre-stamped circuit into which the infiltrating culture can preferentially expand by acculturating the nodes within the net of ready constructed set of channels and information. If the infiltrating culture is simply a particularly expansive regional transform of a pre-existing culture group then there is every probability of pre-existing sociocultural and linguistic congruence to facilitate the penetration. Here again we have a preferential constraint likely to give rise to geographic pattern repetition in the successive phases of a territory's history. As examples it might be relevant to point to the western expansion of the Corded Ware culture group into the pre-existing format of the related TRB and Michelsberg culture, or the European Bell beakers into the Chassey/Cortaillod/Lagozza territories. Historically the same conditions seem to operate at the subcultural level in the Scythian interpenetration of the Slavs, the Swedish Varangian infiltration of the Rus and the earlier Goth movements down to the Black Sea. In some of these examples there is good reason to suppose pre-existing connections and in others it is certain that the process is simply one regional transform expanding within its former culture group network. On occasions this 'backspread' helps to conceal the former relationships between transform cultures so that a former peripheral area may later become important and axial and vice versa.

IV Time pattern regularities

Culture group systems are changing systems of cultures, assemblages and artefact-types – expanding, fluctuating and contracting with time. The time-trajectory of these large but loosely interconnected entities is a compound of the individual trajectories of the component cultures – commencing with the first appearance of the cultures as a related group, followed by their mosaic of interlinked successive transformations, and terminating with the reduction and disappearance of the affinity threshold linking the cultural assemblages at the culture group level.

The levels of change within these large systems grade from changes in attribute states to changes in cultural assemblages. The trending changes at all these diverse levels may act independently or they may variously correlate and co-ordinate to mark major and minor thresholds in the whole system's time-trajectory. These trends and their joint interaction have been discussed at length for the case of culture trajectories (chapter 6, IV) and we need only remind ourselves of the main frame of development at this different level:

   (i) The quantitative change and oscillation in numbers of arte-fact-types, especially those essential multistate types poly-thetically shared across the culture group

      (a) as variation in the number of different artefact-types defining the culture group's overall polythetic set in successive phases;

      (b) as variation in the number of different artefact-types per cultural assemblage in successive phases;

      (c) as variations in both of the above aspects jointly, in a variety of combining trends.

  (ii) The quantitative change and oscillation in numbers of the population of component assemblages forming the combined culture group assemblage in successive phases.

 (iii) The qualitative change and oscillation of the cultural group system as a structured system of specific artefact-types and their intercorrelation.

Each of these levels of system interaction can be characterized in the ambiguous terminology of ontogeny which only becomes meaningful when the particular level and factors of change are precisely specified. In addition the degree of organization of the particular culture group system can make a considerable difference in the variety of possible time-trajectories – varying from the unorganized and loosely controlled systems to deliberately and highly organized urban imperial systems with a climax potential.

The demographic relationships of culture group ontogeny are as unclear as those of cultures themselves but in the same way it is apparent that population trends are involved. The culture group certainly represents a far larger population of individuals than the average culture, and culture group formation by cultural expansion and subcultural divergence suggests that quantitative population expansion would be a powerful factor in this over-extension of a culture in terms of its internal communications. However, such factors as the peripheral exploration and exploitation of new ecological niches and economic stances would be equally involved.

The qualitative change and oscillation of the culture group as a structured system expresses the integration of all the varied levels of system interaction in a summary form. To review the general nature of the changes involved we must generate a dynamic version of our earlier static polythetic model (table 1). This can be simply accomplished by using the dynamic constellation trajectory model relating the intercorrelation of artefact-types within changing culture systems. The culture group as a system of cultures can be portrayed as a galaxy of nucleated constellations of artefact-types – the nucleated constellations representing the correlated types defining the component cultures. Such a model is, of course, multidimensional with many artefact-types webbing the space between particular cultural assemblage clusters and representing the types polythetically shared as the very basis of the affinity linking the group of cultures in the culture group. Nevertheless, each culture will still display a large number of idiosyncratic and less widely shared types, not to mention particularly structured complexes of types. In so far as the culture group is concerned it is the polythetically shared types which define the culture group and therefore represent that system's essential and key variables. The maintenance of this set, or some transform of this set, reflects the maintenance of the culture group; the fluctuation of this set of types conversely represents the weakening or strengthening of the group ties between thresholds defining the disintegration of the culture group or its assimilation into a single cultural entity.

The time-trajectory version of this correlation model consists of the cultural constellations of artefact-types moving through time – transforming the model into a complex interweaving bundle of trajectories. The types and the cultures move from state to state and transform to transform defined by the correlation of the changes involved. The cultural constellations of types may move closer together in interlinked affinity or further away in diverging dissimilarity. The essential set of shared multistate artefact-types defining the culture group may lose some types, gain others and together move through various type transformations and transitions. The relationships between the component cultures are never the same at any one time, neither are those between the artefact-types and the type states interlinking the group of cultures – they change constantly.

The degree of intercorrelation and the changing rates of change involved once again play a major part in defining the system thresholds.

The segments of the system trajectory that are particularly interesting are those reflecting the origin, development and disappearance of culture groups as unit material culture systems. We can examine these critical sections of culture group ontogeny first of all as abstract parts of the dynamic model and then as the material manifestation of certain sociocultural processes.

CULTURE GROUP ONTOGENY

The 'birth' of a culture group depends upon the coming into being of a relationship between a group of cultural assemblages that share a polythetic range but differing states of some specific multistate artefact-types. Now this relationship may be reached by two different categories of trajectory. In one category we have the possibility of the regional subcultural assemblages of an expanding culture gradually diverging and becoming decreasingly similar until they are reduced to this level of loose culture group affinity – the break-up of an expanding culture into a culture group. Alternatively, the other category of trajectory may start with quite separate and different cultural assemblages and then successively and cumulatively introduces into them a widely diffusing set of common artefact-types or type-states – the partial acculturation and convergence of a group of diverse independent cultures. The one category of culture group origins depends upon the reduction of the affinity of assemblages to a decreasingly similar but loosely united level; the other category depends upon the elevation of the assemblages' affinity to an increasingly similar but equally loosely united and identical level.

In more detail, the first category of culture group development arises from one cultural assemblage system trajectory. In this culture trajectory a post-coherent phase is reached in which more and more inessential artefact-types enter the system – at first as chance and sporadic introductions but increasingly in regular and increasingly ordered complexes connected with new activities and behaviour. These novel artefact-types, cumulatively and successively introduced, gradually establish several 'new' subsystem formats in which the novel types are essential and even key variables. Finally, these subsystems become substantially separate transform systems by virtue of the emergent properties of their coherent new formats; nevertheless, they still remain linked as transform cultures sharing differing states of the same multistate artefact-types in addition to their novel idiosyncratic types.

In the second category of culture group development the converse situation applies. We have several distinct cultural assemblage trajectories – they may be so distinct as to be quite independent culture systems or they may be very distantly related transforms with little in common. This group of cultures may share connection and communication with a common source of steady, strong variety output; a source of saturating diffusion. This common cultural source, or group of sources, successively and cumulatively introduces a variety of states of the same specific artefact-types into the group of independent cultures. The formerly diverse cultural assemblages increasingly share a small set of directively correlated multistate artefact-types giving rise to a low level affinity, which freshly unites the cultures at the culture group level. One interesting reflection arises from the point that although jointly subject to a common source of saturating diffusion the independent cultures could well have rejected the diffusing variety, or separately selected quite disparate sets of variety. The fact that the independent cultures simultaneously accepted similar sets of variety to stabilize their system dislocations suggests that they were motivated by a simultaneous and common stimulus or crisis. Such a common stimulus might be environmental, social, religious, political, or economic – or any combination of these factors. An artificial convergent directive might be the military colonization of diverse cultures by a single culture, the extinction of a major game animal and its substitution by another quarry – or one might cite the convergent effects of the introduction of the horse to the very diverse cultures of North American Indians. Whatever the particular situation, the joint acceptance of the same set of variety by formerly independent systems points to a joint dislocation affecting all of them.

We might summarize these alternative trajectories to culture group status as *divergent* and *convergent* categories (Childe 1956, p. 147), not forgetting that disregarding their approach the ultimate status is identical. Nevertheless, the subsequent alignment and direction of these inevitably continuous trajectories will certainly be affected by the line of approach up to culture group status – just as the subsequent position of the aeroplane is severely constrained by its past course (chapter 2, 1).

As an example of the divergent trajectory one could suggest the transition from Danubian I to the variegated cultures of the Danubian II culture group in Neolithic Europe. For the opposite case – increasingly convergent acculturation – examples might be sought in the condensation and formation of the primary TRB and Corded Ware cultures in northern Europe or, in America, the convergent trajectory of independent cultures into the stable format of the Pueblo culture group with cumulative homogeneity.

The particular interest of this convergent category is its inference that cultures may frequently not arise in or from a preceding single culture and its trajectory but may also arise from the condensation of a group of adjacent unstable cultures, by increasingly convergent development under saturating diffusion. The sequence in such a hypothetical case would move:

(a) A group of independent and unstable cultures, unstable by virtue of a new and shared system dislocation – encircled by or adjacent to a culture, or groups of cultures, emitting useful variety.

(b) The formerly diverse and independent cultures sharing the same 'needs', acculturate to culture group affinity – itself facilitating previously slight intergroup diffusion and communication; the independent cultures coalesce into a transient culture group.

(c) The acculturation continues but the new culture group orientation promotes more powerful variety interchange between the member cultures going beyond the culture group affinity threshold and moving into the status of a large culture with ethnic or regional subcultures; the condensation of the culture group into a large 'new' culture and cultural assemblage.

Such a 'new' culture is an independent not a transform culture because although drawing variety from a source of acculturation and drawing other variety from a group of diverse cultures, nevertheless, the 'new' culture is a freshly unique integration with newly emergent characteristics and potential. If such a large and newly stabilized culture has effected a new and highly successful sociocultural strategy – as it is likely to have achieved by feedback adjustment to the original source of joint dislocation – then, there is every likelihood of a subsequent expansion by the new culture into neighbouring and congruent regions. Once again the cases of the TRB and Corded Ware cultures' successive expansions across the whole of the North European and Baltic Plain, spring to mind. The whole sequence may then tend to repeat in an oscillating development:

(a) a group of unstable, possibly *independent cultures,*
(b) partial and joint acculturation into a *transient culture group,*
(c) further condensation into 'new' large *culture with regional sub-cultures,*
(d) expansion into congruent territories suitable for the 'new' stance – becoming a large *culture with divergent regional sub-cultures,*
(e) over-expansion, regional isolation and crystallization of a *stable culture group,*
(f) increasingly divergent development into *independent cultures* acculturating with disparate groups of peripheral cultures,
(a) a peripheral group of unstable, possibly *independent cultures* . . . (b) (c) (d) (e) (f) . . .

This is not the only possible or necessary culture group trajectory, as we should anticipate from our basic postulates (postulate 13) but it is one class from a limited set.

Example. As a brief example of this oscillation we can pursue the Neolithic Corded Ware case in terms of these phases:

(a) a group of unstable format cultures of Southeastern Poland – the Upper Vistula and Bug TRB cultures *c.* 3200–3000 BC,
(b) their convergent and joint acculturation (from the Pontic Steppe and Carpathian Chalcolithic culture groups) into the nuclear Vistula/Bug Corded Ware culture group *c.* 3000–2800 BC,
(c) condensation into a more homogeneous Złota/Vistula culture with Vistula, Bug, and Dniestr regional subcultures *c.* 2800–2600 BC,
(d) expansion into congruent territories and acculturation of inhabitants – becoming a large culture with regional subcultures; Złota culture with earliest Haffküstenkultur, Oder, and Saxo-Thuringian subcultures *c.* 2600–2400 BC,
(e) overexpansion, regional divergence into full Corded Ware culture group – Złota, Swedish, Fatyanovo, Oder, Marschwitz, Saxo-Thuringian, Danish, Dutch, and Swiss Corded Ware cultures *c.* 2400–2200 BC.

(f) increasingly divergent development into independent cultures acculturating with disparate groups of peripheral cultures; acculturating with TRB Middle Neolithic groups around the Baltic, Pit Ware groups in Russia, Bell Beaker groups in the West, and Early Bronze Age groups in Switzerland, *c.* 2200–2000 BC,

(a) forming peripheral groups of independent cultures within diverse culture groups of the Early Bronze Age *c.* 2000–1800 BC.

The trajectory conveyed in the scheme (a)–(c) is one possible course for the convergent category of culture group trajectories. For culture groups based on the converse divergent category – an expanding culture breaking up into regional cultures – one probable trajectory is equivalent to the segment (d)–(f). However, a more frequent class of culture group trajectory is neither convergent nor divergent but parallel – that is to say the development of one culture group into another 'new' culture group. This replacement of one culture group by another 'new' culture group with a related distribution is more than the simple transformation of the whole system into a new state. The basis for such parallel 'renewal' arises from the capacity of a culture group system to act as a pre-stamped circuit of congruent cultures linked by ready made communication channels. We have already noted that such a system is particularly susceptible to interpenetration by any of its own expansive transform cultures and only slightly less so by an alien independent culture. In this way one culture group may be infiltrated and repatterned by another culture group, so that culture group formats tend to perpetuate the same area components remapped into simple composites. These culture group areas are not so simple that they can be permanently defined for all time but their variations are based on a common set of territorial components until such time as the technology or the local ecology is so drastically changed that a new modal mosaic is defined. In this way it is noticeable that the culture group areas of Neolithic Europe repeatedly centre as units based on: the Balkans/Lower Danube, the Middle Danube Basin, the Pontic Prairies, the North European/Baltic Plain, the East Mediterranean Littoral, the West Mediterranean Littoral and other similar areas. Similar components for similar culture group mosaics have been mapped for several periods and areas of the Americas but have usually been terminologically confused by calling them 'culture areas'.

Thus far the 'birth' of archaeological culture groups has been studied in terms of convergent, divergent, or parallel cultural transformations leading to thresholds defining 'new' culture groupings. The subsequent development of these culture groups may then display the same set of component culture trajectory alignments – convergent, divergent, parallel – in which the group may continue the trends leading to their initial appearance or move in the alternative directions, or oscillate from one trend to another. These same trends ultimately mark the 'death' of the specific culture group system, as an identity, by moving across the fundamental threshold maintaining the culture group's essential and key set of artefact-types.

The 'death' of a culture group system can come about in the same general way as the 'death' of an individual culture – by transformation or by displacement.

Transformation. The successive and cumulative introduction of new artefact-types condenses a new set of essential and key types, accompanied by the decreasing correlation and gradual fragmentation of the former key artefact-type constellation. This transformation into a quite 'new' grouping may be accomplished by:

(a) Convergence. The acculturating convergence of a culture group with increasing inter-group communication and diffusion condensing into a single large culture.

(b) Divergence. The territorial expansion of the culture group, leading to regional divergence and regional isolation in response to regional adaptation. The component cultures become decreasingly similar with decreasing intercommunication, which together with their divergent development takes the group across the threshold to unrelated and diverse independent cultures.

(c) Parallel transformation. The pre-related cultures of the culture group are optimally interlinked for the successful infiltration of a 'new' cultural system. This new culture may be an expansive transform of one of the culture group cultures 'spreading-back' through the system, or it may reflect the interpenetration of the system by an alien culture system.

Displacement. The displacement of a culture group in a given area by another alien culture group, representing the disappearance of the group only at that locus. Displacement and substitution is rarely total and usually leads to joint transformation; even in its extreme form the 'death' of the culture group is local and merely reflects the territorial shift of the group under some external impact.

It is once again self-evident that, as with other entities, the processes of culture group 'death' are the same as the processes of culture group 'birth' – 'death/birth' marks but a single threshold. The culture group and culture system trajectories are marked by only two kinds of change – 'death/birth' transitions at major thresholds and developmental change through a series of successive states marked by minor thresholds. The time pattern regularities of culture group systems arise from this fundamental basis to culture and culture group time-trajectories, plus the additional constraints that operate on every culture as a member of a culture group – however diffuse the grouping. To echo a famous line – no culture is an isolate, it exists as a component of a whole cultural group, standing as one of a set of transform cultures amidst independent cultures linked within other culture groups. The setting of the part within the context of the whole must constrain the time-trajectory of that part. The constraint limiting culture group time-trajectories is in part inherent in the entity as a system of organized artefact-types, assemblages and cultures, and in part stems from the setting or coupling of such systems.

v System pattern regularities

The culture group is a system of cultures, assemblages and artefact-types, occupying a dispersed but interconnected group of territories over a certain period of time. The system is most richly networked within its component culture subsystems which are more loosely interconnected within the culture group entity. The 'looseness' or relative simplicity of these inter-cultural connections may vary from unconscious and unorganized linkage to artificial and optimally organized networking. However, even at its most elaborate the culture group remains more richly networked within the component culture subsystems than between culture and culture in the entity. It would, perhaps, in this light be more accurate to see the culture group as a circuit of linked systems rather than as a system with subsystems; the culture is a more complex entity than the culture group.

Nevertheless, the culture group as a system or circuit of cultural entities does affect the 'behaviour' of its components. The culture group is maintained and exists by virtue of a common set of variety and the continued circulation of incoming variety at a certain minimal level. Should this variety circulation cease, or rather fall below the minimal threshold, the cultures in the circuit will diverge independently. If the variety continues to circulate within the group then the time-trajectories of the component cultures are continuously interrelated by a shared constraint and a certain level of common regularity in their development. Since the local environments of the cultures within the group will not be identical, the culture group interconnection acts as a useful circulating pool of adaptive information – some of which may be useful against the background of changing circumstances. A successful strategy in one member of the group may induce similar stances in the other members.

Cultural systems as behavioural information units may also be treated in terms of information compatibility and their cultural interaction seen as variety interaction. In this way pairs of cultures interact either as new, alternative, contradictive, or redundant variety when brought into contact one with another. However, since the cultures within a culture group share many features in common these units are usually additional, alternative or redundant to the culture group circuit – only becoming mutually contradictive under conditions of territorial competition or by radical transformation. Culture groups as mutually adjusted components of a dispersed system are rather uninteresting from the point of view of system interaction between independent cultures at a confined locus. This aspect of major cultural interaction will be examined later in connection with larger and more diverse systems (chapter 8, v).

In general, each cultural assemblage within the culture group has a largely self-contained, self-stabilizing strategy, preserving the sociocultural system in its local environment. The set of artefact-types shared between the cultures of the culture group represent that system's key and essential variety which, if dispersed, reflects the disintegration of the system. These multistate artefact-types held in common may be part of a shared past trajectory or the diffused and widely adopted essentials of a freshly successful adjustment to widely operating conditions. The continuous adjustment to stability and equilibrium takes place in each component culture in the group; the group as a system merely circulates information on these adjustments which may be accepted and integrated or ignored by the individual cultures.

The peripheral cultures of culture groups often fulfil the very valuable role of probing the boundary conditions of the culture group area and developing 'new' integrative variety to stabilize consequent dislocation. The boundary cultures then act as the developmental foci within the culture group system, from which a stream of newly developed or acquired variety may flood back and circulate around the system. In this way new ecological niches and boundary territories can be successfully penetrated and exploited. The penetration of the polar and circumpolar regions document the gradual re-equipment of whole culture groups to the threshold beyond which they could explode across the territory of this format. Similarly, the Neolithic penetration of Europe shows ecological constraints damming the Balkan–Anatolian culture groups within the area of semi-Mediterranean ecology for half a millennium before the boundary adaptation of the first Danubian culture exploded into the environment of 'real' Europe.

We have seen that the culture group may come into existence as part of this process by the common re-equipment of a group of independent or transform cultures, or by the regional divergence of an expansive culture. Each of these processes relates to the continuous readjustment of sociocultural systems to environmental variety by adaptive feedback minimizing immediate system dislocation. As a culture builds up and expands so its spreading periphery is internally tessellated into an extending network of newly condensed and formalized subcultures, often repatterning components from former social and geographic formats. It is the artificially formalized and institutionalized recognition of this intersecting network that marks the beginnings of primitive government and the deliberate organization of simple confederacies of the kind developed by the Iroquois, Zulus, Celts, Teutons, and Scythians. These are steps towards larger optimal and climax organizations if urban units are developed but if dependent on simpler socioeconomic units then the ontogeny is inevitably less elaborate (Gluckman 1963, pp. 67–80).

Note

(1) There is clearly room for disagreement over the contents of some of the culture groups defined in this model. The validity of groups such as Danubian II, as well as the general use of the division into Danubian I–IV established in the 1920s by Gordon Childe, can also be debated. There are

also a number of notable gaps in the cultural and geographical coverage of the model: the later Neolithic cultures of France and the Italian and Iberian peninsulae are good examples here. In spite of all these reservations, it seems advisable to leave the model as originally published, since it forms an integral part of the arguments developed and illustrated in this chapter.

8 Culture group and technocomplex

> Conversely all cultures under identical environmental
> conditions are liable to exhibit quite a number of common
> traits – behaviour patterns and archaeological types
> expressing them are imposed on men by external natural
> conditions such as raw materials, or are at least
> adaptations peculiarly well fitted to securing survival in a
> particular environment,
>
> V. GORDON CHILDE, 1956, p. 137

1 Introduction

As we have hinted several times during the course of earlier chapters
there appear to be larger and grosser archaeological groupings than
even the culture group. These grosser entities involve groups of
cultures which are not related or collateral cultures but which do share
polythetic complexes of type families on the basis of common factors
in environment, economy and technology. Since it is extremely
difficult to discuss an entity without a name let us tentatively call these
gross groupings *technocomplexes*. A term intended to convey a certain
kind of gross artefact complex as the vector of particular sociocultural,
technological, economic and environmental stances. The technocomplex is a larger and looser entity than the culture group; an entity of
larger size but lower rank than either the culture, or culture group.

The need to define such an entity stems from the dangerously
loose application of 'culture' to quite disparate levels of archaeological
entity and the equally perverse neglect to qualify entity labels by
classificatory indicators. If the rank of the taxon is never stated it
becomes difficult to ensure that only entities of a comparable level are
being compared. We have already seen that the loose employment of
terms like Tardenoisian, Gravettian, Palaeo-Indian, and Mousterian
probably reflect no more than widely diffused technologies in use in
similar contexts, although undoubtedly subsuming true entities of
cultural status. The Acheulean and Chopper-chopping tool complexes
surely reflect huge and loose alignments of this gross rank, rather than

those smaller, higher rank entities that we have discussed in detail. It would seem that the Palaeolithic archaeologist is probably, with rare exceptions, conceptualizing entities of technocomplex and culture group status as against his later colleagues' preoccupation with entities of cultural and subcultural rank. The importance of comparative status is that these differences in rank carry quite different information and implications about the range of the ethnic, sociocultural and linguistic attributes to be inferred for the entity. To confuse entities of different ranks is to confuse and impair the information content of the classification. Clearly we need to know something of the characteristics of the technocomplex entities and their behaviour in space and time.

The first step must be a general statement of the negative and positive characteristics of the technocomplex entities, leading to some attempt at a condensed definition of the concept. From the negative aspect it is useful to emphasize that the technocomplex is a more specific and a higher rank system than those defined in terms of broad technology or subsistence economics alone. The technocomplex is not the same as the technological categories of the 'three ages' scheme – Palaeolithic, Mesolithic, Neolithic, Bronze Age etc. – neither is it equivalent to the hunter–fisher–gatherer, simple horticulture, pastoral, or plough agriculturalist subsistence strategies. The technocomplex represents the partly independent arrival of diverse developing culture systems at the same general equilibrium pattern based on a similar economic strategy, in similar environments with a similar technology and a similar past trajectory.

The group of cultural assemblages falling within a particular technocomplex will probably be ethnically and linguistically quite diverse – any smaller homogeneous groupings will form culture group subsets within the more comprehensive complex. Furthermore, the assemblages need not share any specific artefact-types or type states, suggesting at first sight a total lack of affinity between the assemblages within the complex. This dissimilarity may indeed be total at the type and type state levels but the affinity relationship uniting the group does appear at the type group or type family level. The technocomplex assemblages may not share the same specific type or state of backed blade, burin, end-scraper, point, or bone harpoon but they will share a polythetic range of differing specific types and states from the common set of artefact-type families. The technocomplex assemblages need only share a polythetic selection from a shared set of families of artefact-types – most of which are artefacts broadly grouped by common function and technology.

The technocomplex entity begins to emerge as a comprehensive and low level category uniting a complex of type complexes, widely diffused in space and time and linked together as the skeletal frame of a general sociocultural mixed strategy adapted to the mould of a broadly similar environmental context. A complex of types and a complex of type complexes associated with the implementation of a particular subsistence pattern in a particular set of niches. Without further elaboration we may attempt to define the technocomplex as – *a group of cultures characterized by assemblages sharing a polythetic range but differing specific types of the same general families of artefact-types, shared as a widely diffused and interlinked response to common factors in environment, economy and technology.* A negligible level of affinity, perhaps 5 per cent or less, uniting the group in terms of shared specific types but a residual medium level affinity, perhaps 30–60 per cent, uniting the group in terms of shared type families.

11 Technocomplex systems

The technocomplex is a huge system networking culture groups, cultures, assemblages and artefact-types. The richest reticulation in the network remains within the individual, self-adjusting culture units. The extra-culture network is less complex, uniting only the general structuring of parts of the otherwise elaborately diverse culture systems; the linkage at this low level depending upon widespread diffusion and convergent development. The technocomplex system is really an interlinked set of systems sharing a broadly similar material and technological substructure but probably quite varied in the rest of their sociocultural superstructure, within the operating constraints.

Particular technocomplex formats are metastable equilibrium basins into which a number of independent and variform culture trajectories have converged. The steady state of systems within a particular technocomplex basin is metastable in so far as certain changes or sequences of changes in the coupled sociocultural and environmental systems might initiate displacement out of the stable region (chapter 2, 1). The particular technocomplex basin is thus both a metastable region and a constrained set through which culture system trajectories must pass and momentarily pause, before they may move on to certain other technocomplex basins. The culture must, for example, move into the food-producing technocomplexes before its trajectory can move into the full urban, metallurgical or industrial technocomplex regions. Each technocomplex has a limited number of alternative trajectories into and out of its basin, each trajectory with differing potential in terms of its route through successive metastable formats. It is the serious constraint offered by successive technocomplex basins that gives rise to the most general and striking regularities in cultural trajectories – the regularities summarized in the modern versions of the 'three ages' scheme in which the categories are not rigidly successive levels but sequences of groups of technocomplex basins linked by various trajectories with various but limited 'goals' (chapter 2, examples 3–5).

The trajectories of culture systems approaching a state of equilibrium and a technocomplex basin 'behave' as if they were goal-seeking systems, the state or basin being the goal. This directive factor in system trajectories we have seen to stem from coupled feedback subsystems in the integrated system (chapter 2, 1; fig. 11). An interesting feature of the trajectories into such stable basins is the 'trial and error' adaptive hunting of the system and all its oscillating components, all effectively scanning the available variety for suitable mutually stabilizing attributes and components. The cultural systems, as Semi-Markovian systems with semi-stochastic transformations, move from one state to one of a possible set of states, the selection being based on the limited range of possible states and having certain differential probabilities. As systems of this general kind, cultural trajectories from basin to basin are not unique and consequently the cultures within a technocomplex set do not form a wholly homogeneous category, neither are their past or future trajectories necessarily identical.

A technocomplex basin is defined by an integrated strategy involving a certain set of artefact-type families, a certain technology, a specific environmental range, with a particular blend of subsistence and resource exploitation methods. To analyse an example already mentioned, one can take the loose Tardenoisian technocomplex when used for assemblages from the Balkans to Britain and from Spain to Poland – the specific Tardenoisian culture group of France being a detailed subset within this gross set. In the Tardenoisian technocomplex we have a certain set of geometric microlith and flint and antler

332 Analytical Archaeology

artefact families, a micro-blade and burin technology, in the forest zone of post-glacial Europe, hunting small forest game with the bow and only marginally exploiting marine resources. This set of traits united the various far-flung territories and diverse assemblages of many different sociocultural and linguistic units (for a criticism of this interpretation of the Tardenoisian as a technocomplex, see Tringham 1971, p. 38).

This example immediately points to the terminological and taxonomic difficulties at present confusing the archaeological scene. The term Tardenoisian, like the term Maglemosian, or Natufian and most archaeological terms has been simultaneously used for a quite specific, localized culture or culture group and at the same time by loose extension, for broadly similar Tardenoisian-like, Maglemose-like, Natufian-like assemblage groupings. Usually, the frame and level of reference is left totally inexplicit. The technocomplex entity is here defined to encompass the latter examples of 'like' cultures, to distinguish them from the more closely interrelated culture groups and culture entities, in an effort to disperse this fog of imprecision. Under this burden of old terminology it is inevitably the case that one name is used for a specific culture, for the culture group that it represents and for the technocomplex that it characterizes – confusing the gross set with its subsets. It is essential to specify whether one means the Natufian culture of Palestine, the Natufian culture group of the Levant, or the Natufian-like technocomplex operating from Cyrenaica to Kashmir.

A technocomplex system reflects a certain general mixed strategy in the game between culture and environment. The moves in the game represent the successive states of the culture and environment trajectory, the culture aims to play for successive satisficer or near-optimizer equilibria against the successive moves of the environment. On both sides the next move is constrained by the present position on the board and its past sequence of states (chapter 2, postulate 14). Therefore, there are for both sides only a limited number of moves, and a limited number of outcomes or pay offs. The advantage of the culture system in this game is that it can anticipate the environment's moves to a limited extent based on observing previous moves (lead, fig. 11). The environment might play – arctic conditions, tundra flora, tundra fauna; the culture may play – hunting–fishing–gathering, co-operative band society, shaman magic, and Upper Palaeolithic technology. The outcome is fed-back to successive generations of the society which will adjust its successive stances accordingly. The culture is playing for dynamic equilibrium in a changing situation – the culture will play within the stable technocomplex region until it can no longer achieve an equilibrium outcome therein. The flexibility of the culture's game and strategy depends on the culture system's capacity as a regulator/insulator and cannot exceed the culture system's variety and its capacity as a multichannelled communication system with a continuous existence. The environment in this developing game may be thought of as directing the culture system's 'search' or oscillating 'hunt and stick' trajectory from stable basin to stable basin; the environment is the vetoer of all states of equilibrium in the culture system save only those in a certain set.

If, in the course of the game, there should be a direct contradiction or equivocation between the culture system's variety and the environment variety then this dislocation is minimized by cultural moves towards a 'new' set of variety, a 'new' strategy. This 'new' variety, or set of variety, represents the integration or invention of a novel set of variety, broad enough to be alternative to the former cultural variety and sufficiently comprehensive to meet the new environmental strategy. The culture may generate this 'new', stabilizing variety by outright acquisition, by internal invention, or by adopting a 'new' blend of old elements. Severe environmental changes therefore play a large part in stimulating the adaptive development of new cultural variety and this is often based on a minimax blend of old components, which will minimize the maximum amount of immediate system dislocation. Technocomplexes represent just this momentary strategic blend of components of old and tried efficacy which form a skeletal framework within which many different individual formats may be accommodated.

EXAMPLES OF TECHNOCOMPLEXES

In most existing studies of material culture, entities of technocomplex rank are either unlabelled, mislabelled, or delitescent. In American archaeology, the term 'tradition' is sometimes used more consistently for entities of this general configuration (e.g. Palaeo-Indian Tradition). However, since the term 'tradition' is also widely and conveniently used for the time-depth or time-trajectory of every kind of archaeological entity it falls somewhat dangerously into the rag-bag multilevel, multipurpose category that robs a term of its possible information content, as we have seen in the case of the term 'culture'. For this reason the term tradition has here been used for the time-depth aspect of all archaeological entities and the term technocomplex suggested for a specific entity with a spatial as well as a time dimension. The situation is further complicated by the developmental sequence in which the artefacts and technology defining a technocomplex will often first appear in a single culture, become widespread in a culture group expansion, and only terminally express a gross technocomplex entity; this is but one trajectory of technocomplex ontogeny. In such a case a single term may unwittingly be used at all three levels for very different kinds of system, as we have already described.

The technocomplex units that we are about to list were previously designated, cultures, culture groups, traditions, phases, or horizons, or they simply remained anonymous. Their names variously refer to the first culture to show the technocomplex format, a 'typical' culture within the group, or they refer to a major aspect of the technological, economic, environmental, artefact equilibrium polygon. The technocomplexes are noticeably larger and clearer for Palaeolithic prehistory than for later times – the reasons for this reflect the sparse, unidimensional and even monotypic representation of Palaeolithic entities as opposed to the multifacetted representation of later entities, down to subcultural levels. If, in a similar context, the material culture of modern Australian Aborigines was reduced to their stone artefacts alone then we might detect at most, perhaps three or four contemporary technocomplexes without any apparent further subdivision. If one takes into account the basketry, wood and bone artefacts, and decorative motifs from cave paintings to body paint – then the monolithic technocomplexes would reveal much smaller entities of culture and culture group levels, with a greater degree of correlated linguistic and social information. One suspects that the same diversification would appear in the superficially monomorphous 'cultures' of Australian prehistory and in such Palaeolithic entities as the European Acheulean and Mousterian.

Like the culture group, the huge space-time dimensions of the technocomplex have the great advantage of providing a much simpler outline of prehistoric trajectories – expressing them not as individual culture system trajectories but clustered in successive bundles. The European Palaeolithic sequence, for example, largely reduces to the interaction of the Acheulean, Clactonian, Mousterian, Aurignacian and Gravettian, or Perigordian, technocomplexes; many of these entities integrate successive technocomplex transforms, like the many facies of the Acheulean industries, or some of the five groupings within the French Mousterian. Later Palaeolithic technocomplexes (e.g. the Tanged Point technocomplex) have also been distinguished in the North European Plain (Schild 1976). Strongly localized and smaller time-space entities like the Franco-Cantabrian Chatelperronian, Solutrean, or Magdalenian, *sensu stricto*, by contrast suggest culture group transforms in time depth. Characteristically, several of the gross technocomplexes are notably connected with specialized but mixed hunting strategies in certain limited ecosystems – centred on the cave bear, horse, reindeer, buffalo or mammoth, for example.

In the same general way New World prehistory exhibits the same order of groupings – starting with the Palaeo-Indian, Old Cordilleran, Desert, Archaic, Northwest Microblade, and Arctic Small-tool technocomplexes (Willey 1966, fig. 2.31). The so-called Palaeo-Indian industries, for example, are united by the possession of large flint projectile points, some of them noted for their connection with the hunting of specific species – the Clovis point with the mammoth and the Folsom point with the bison. Recent attempts to rename the Palaeo-Indian complexes as 'big-game hunting traditions' amount to a recognition of their loose technocomplex basis.

The Palaeolithic prehistory of Africa provides a similar breakdown into groups of many differing levels. The great technocomplexes provide the *in situ* transformation of the Oldowan and Acheulean groupings moving on multilinearly into the Sangoan, Fauresmith, Levalloiso-Mousterian, and Lupemban technocomplexes. Here again there are well-documented connections between the generalized artefact assemblages shared within the technocomplex and particular environmental factors met by a common mixed strategy – such links connect the Sangoan complex, with its heavy axe and pick-like tools, with its territories in the Congo forest lands.

In Southeast Asia the growth of archaeological research within the last decade (e.g. in Thailand) has led to considerable revision of our knowledge of this area's development in prehistory. Among such revisions has been Gorman's (1970, pp. 82–3) reinterpretation of the Hoabinhian assemblages as a technocomplex 'reflecting common ecological adaptations to the Southeast Asian humid tropics', from the late Pleistocene until *c.* 6500–5000 BC. The last part of this period witnesses the significant appearance of cord-marked pottery, plant domestication and edge ground stone tools.

The later prehistory of all these various areas continues to show technocomplex groupings which are usually broken-up by the more minute focus on cultures and subcultures. Mesolithic examples have already been cited – the gross Maglemose-like, Tardenoisian-like and Blade and Trapeze technocomplexes which respectively dominated the North European Plain from Britain to the Urals, the forests of France to Roumania, and the Mediterranean littoral. The Neolithic of America develops the Woodland, Meso-American, and Southwestern technocomplexes amongst many others. In Europe the Neolithic cultures fall within a succession of Mediterranean and Danubian technocomplexes – later developing Northern and Atlantic complexes and eventually, in the east, seeing the development of successive Mounted Nomad technocomplexes. With the appearance of bronze metallurgy, studies based purely on metallurgical aspects have tended to obscure the great technocomplex groupings by forcing them into chest-of-drawers divisions. The Carpathian, Caucasian and Alpine technocomplexes develop long traditions from Chalcolithic system states down to the great Alpine Late Bronze Age, and Atlantic Late Bronze Age complexes – vaguely anticipating the Common Market and European Free Trade Area format. These technocomplexes comprehensively contain the various great culture groups of the period – the successive Aunjetitiz, Tumulus, and Urnfield groupings – and loosely unite assemblages sharing certain families of tools, weapons and artefacts with economies based on varieties of mixed farming and ard agriculture strategies.

The sociocultural generalizations linked with the regularities of 'tribal-heroic', 'feudal', and 'industrial' Europe are related to the constraining characteristics of the great technocomplexes of Iron Age and historic times. It has even been noted that these pattern regularities are equally meaningful for the culture trajectories of Japan as they are for Atlantic Europe. This does not mean that completely uniform and gigantic technocomplexes succeeded one another from the Atlantic to the Pacific. On the contrary, there is little significant connection until the Urban and Industrial eras – the fourth and fifth ages of the three ages scheme. What these convergent sociocultural regularities do emphasize is the increasing scope of piecemeal intercommunication and diffusion and the parallel development of great quantities of similar regulatory variety. The technocomplexes define very similar stable basins for very similar but not identical reasons.

The technocomplex of early medieval Western Europe was a quite localized entity that one might loosely characterize as the Franko-Teutonic technocomplex based on heavy plough agriculture, Iron Age technology, urban and feudal society operating in a sub-Atlantic, forested European environment. The artefact assemblages typical of this complex from c. AD 900 to 1200 included the horse accoutrement type complex, the castle, the mail-coat, conical helm, lance and shield, together expressing the aristocratic subculture of the elite. An equivalent subcultural assemblage existed for the Church and the iron scythes, ploughshares, billhooks, clippers, chisels, axes, storage jars, bowls, jugs, timber houses sufficed for the peasants – elaborated only in the distinctive burghs. Between the Franko-Teutonic technocomplex of the West and the samurai of the East lay many intervening technocomplexes including those of the Byzantine Empire, the Slavo-Scandinavian, and the Asiatic Nomad technocomplexes. The technocomplex of early medieval Japan was localized in eastern Asia and Japan and shared a complex based on intensive rice agriculture, an equestrian elite, an Iron Age technology, urban and feudal society and a Pacific, forested environment: a sociocultural strategy generally similar to that operating in the far West and constrained by similar contextual factors.

The technocomplex unites heterogeneous groups of otherwise varied linguistic and sociocultural alignments. Inevitably the technocomplex will occupy semi-continuous and contiguous territories and must include separately homogeneous units of culture or culture group, language and language group rank. On occasions a large culture group with a strongly individual economy, technology and environment will also form a single technocomplex; in the limiting case the borders of the two entities may roughly coincide.

III **Phase pattern regularities**

The technocomplex is marked by the possession of types from the same type families, in a polythetic selection propagated by interlinked diffusion over the technocomplex area. Technocomplexes in different areas of space-time may be very similar indeed, as one might expect for such generalized artefact-technology-economy-environment strategies and stable basins. These are the similarities that one notices between feudal Japan and feudal Europe, between the Celts and the Zulus, the Magdalenians and the Kwakiutl, the multi-kiva nucleated defensive settlements of the recent Pueblo and that of Neolithic Çatal Hüyük. Nevertheless, these convergent similarities do not place the cultures in question within single technocomplexes because the entities are not directly interlinked and because the affinity even in terms of type families is too low. It may be useful to bring together similar entities of this kind in socioeconomic or sociocultural categories in the manner of Steward but they are socially orientated rather than artefact orientated in their regularities. However, it is still very useful to draw attention to the sociocultural regularities connected with similar technocomplexes in different times and places.

The technocomplex system is a system of artefact-type families expressed in varying combinations of varying specific types. The essential type families of a given technocomplex are those most widely and frequently shared across the complex and, of these, the key type families are those that are most idiosyncratically distinctive and exist together as a syntactic format throughout the integrated existence of the technocomplex. The inessential type families in such systems are the artefact-types restricted to the particular component cultures or culture groups and not extending further in the net. Since the technocomplex is united by strong affinity links between sets of type families, the system can once again be modelled by a static arrangement of type family intercorrelations expressed in multidimensional space – rather like the culture group galaxy but with specific types replaced by type families (fig. 50).

As a polythetic entity the technocomplex cannot be defined by a single artefact-type contour. Instead we again have a general polythetic distribution model of overlapping and intersecting sets defining a broad area bounded by steep fall-off gradients in the essential type families and containing the mean, mode and median points of all the type family distributions although not necessarily containing their centres of origin (fig. 67).

The distribution areas of such technocomplexes are in keeping with their huge time and content dimensions. One may compare the roughly estimated range of radius of culture areas of *c*. 20–200 miles, and culture groups of *c*. 200–750 miles with that of technocomplexes which range from the giant Acheulean, Gravettian, or Palaeo-Indian areas of up to 3,000 miles radius down to the later and smaller technocomplexes of expanded culture group size, greater than 750 miles radius. The very order of these dimensions should be quite sufficient to emphasize that these different entities are systems of very different rank, complexity and 'behaviour'.

IV Time pattern regularities

Technocomplex systems express huge, loosely interconnected systems of culture groups, cultural assemblages, and artefact-types. The specific frame of reference of these systems is not the totality of the components' traits but merely those essential families of artefact-types which define the common, integrated strategy towards the economy and the environment in which it must function. The technocomplex is a stable basin or set of strategies through which a number of diverse culture and culture group trajectories will pass. As a stable configuration, in a particular context, the technocomplex acts as a goal into which culture systems will oscillate by feed-back adjustment.

However, even stable basins or sets must change with changing circumstances and the stable stance of yesterday may become an unstable stance today. The technocomplex basin is a moving target with its own time-trajectory and a changing format. Consequently, technocomplexes can be said to have an ontogeny on the usual basis of their appearance, growth, development and disappearance as defined by:

(i) the quantitative change and oscillation in the numbers of different artefact-type families polythetically shared within the technocomplex.

(ii) the quantitative change and oscillation in numbers of assemblages within successive states of the technocomplex development.

(iii) the qualitative change and oscillation of the technocomplex system as a structured system.

The first appearance of a given technocomplex is retrospectively marked by the individual appearance of the system's essential and key type families, often in several cultures at several times and places. The widespread interdiffusion of these type families within a common environment marks the initial directive correlation of these types into an increasingly stereotyped assemblage, emphasizing widely shared but variously elaborated activities of a fundamental kind. Many of these activities and their distinctive artefact-types will be found individually outside the technocomplex area – indeed they may well originate beyond its bounds. But it is only within the technocomplex that these varied and scattered behaviours are regularly integrated into a generalized system of a polythetic kind. Some artefacts and activities will be widely spread by diffusion, others will be jointly developed by parallel invention based on common needs and common available variety. The more universal the opportunity and the simpler and more widespread the dislocation stimulus the more likely the repeated independent and partially independent integrative invention and innovation. As remarked earlier, the very acceptance of the same set of basic technocomplex variety, by formerly unrelated systems, points to a joint dislocation affecting all of them; a common convergent directive based on environmental, cultural, religious, political or economic stimuli, or any combination or permutation of these factors. The outcome is the increasing convergence of the various oscillating time-trajectories of different cultural systems, finally converging into the bounds of a temporarily stable technocomplex basin.

The formation of a new technocomplex system is therefore largely a matter of the general acquisitive integration of certain widespread variety and its augmentation by internal invention on convergent lines. The successive technocomplexes of the Arctic provide good examples of marked convergence in basic equipment based upon the wholesale borrowing of both Asiatic and American variety, further developed by ingenious local invention and skilfully integrated into a series of unique technocomplex formats in the face of extreme environmental and economic constraint. In this context the famed inventiveness of the Eskimo is more than matched by his system induced capacity for integrating diffusing elements from without.

The specific technocomplex therefore appears as a shared means of adjustment to a particular set of changing conditions. The growth and development of the technocomplex reflect the spread and successive transformations of the basic set of activities and artefacts. The tech-nocomplex can therefore be viewed as a system with successive trans-form states segmenting its time-trajectory, terminal thresholds mark-ing the first and last appearance of the system as this kind of system. These thresholds mark the system's birth and death respectively and therefore the passage of the component cultures out of or into other technocomplex strategies. Such major thresholds are marked by the appearance or disappearance of a whole structured set of essential and key artefact families, the minor thresholds by similar changes in the successive specific artefact-types and subtypes characterizing the system phase states.

The disappearance of a technocomplex system reflects changes in the cultures and/or in the environment such that the technocomplex is no longer a stable strategy, or that a strategy with a better pay-off is freshly possible. It is also probable that the common orientation shared by cultures within a single technocomplex may occasionally increase in mutual congruence to the point where the technocomplex might condense into one or more culture groups. An homogeneous economic, material and technological background may well provide a firm basis for further convergent sociocultural and linguistic acculturation.

TECHNOCOMPLEX CATEGORIES

In an earlier chapter we distinguished between the climax system ontogeny of systems with near-optimizer strategies as opposed to those with satisficer and minimax strategies (chapter 6, V). The systems with a climax potential were either very highly organized, employing urban, urban-state, or urban-imperial units, or they might arise in areas of unusually rich resources exploited by a simple but near-optimally effective strategy. The climax itself represents the exponential and simultaneous burst of 'new' variety accompanying the formative development phase of such systems. This burst of variety, a spate of innovation and invention, comes about because the formative phase of a system freshly incorporates a maximum amount of internal dislocation, yet to be minimized, and requiring the rapid integration or invention of new variety as a comprehensive and stabilizing form. The coherent phase then reflects the effective diminishment of these dislocations and consequently a slowing of the rates of change and rate of new developments, together with the increasing institutionalization of the stable format. In this respect, so-called 'pattern fulfilment' reflects the coherent and post-coherent states of a system when the maximum dislocation of the formative phase has largely been stabilized by the newly developed variety; thus minimal dislocation means minimal new developments.

Now different kinds of technocomplex system appear to have different kinds of detailed ontogenies and the immediate difference is between technocomplexes with climax and non-climax ontogenies.

Whilst not confusing the very specific technocomplexes with the broader taxa of subsistence economies it is often useful to group technocomplexes under these subsistence categories for comparative purposes. In this way it is possible to compare and contrast the variety within the hunter–fisher–gatherer, pastoral nomad, and agrarian technocomplexes as groups and compare and contrast variety between these groupings. Each of these subsistence categories has climax and non-climax forms found within particular technocomplexes. Indeed, each successive technocomplex or technocomplex state is usually repatterned by the output of new variety from climax cultures within its structure.

It may prove useful to discuss the characteristics and necessary conditions operating in climax and non-climax technocomplexes within these subsistence categories.

Hunter–fisher–gatherer technocomplexes

Each of the gross subsistence taxa conceals an enormous range of cultural variety and variation – none more so than the hunter–fisher–gatherer economies. This range of variation can be much more specifically dealt with in terms of the particular component technocomplex systems, thus emphasizing one of the contributions of this taxon. Hunter–fisher–gatherers have existed for the whole two and a half million year span of hominid development. As economic strategies they have varied in their differential emphasis on hunting, on fishing, or on gathering, even to the exclusion of some of these aspects; varying the combination of these staples, their degree of importance, their role organization and of course the groups of species exploited. Technologically, their material culture has ranged from the simplest stone and wood-working traditions up to iron-using and latterly the use of fire-arms. The social organization of hunter–fisher–gatherers has equally spanned almost every variation from matricentred to patricentred and from large composite bands down to small dispersed families. Indeed it is a frequent occurrence in this form of organization that the groups change their whole social configuration and stance as they move around the resources of their territories.

Nevertheless, in each specific case there appears to be a strong correlation between the social pattern and the efficient exploitation of economic resources. The exploitation of resources is rarely optimal, under these conditions, because the risks would also be optimal; in such contexts the exploitation of resources and their distribution through society is coupled to group continuity not to individual welfare. The greater the real or imagined economic contribution by one sex, and the more specific and restricted their method of operation, the greater their polarity in the kinship scheme. In one sense, and one sense only, the multipurpose kinship mechanisms are adapted to exploit the environment to advantage and to arrange an effective distribution of the society's main productive agents. The most productive agents tend to be evenly and effectively distributed through the dispersed group by clustering the less productive agents around them, as a penumbra to a nucleus. This arrangement helps to ensure an efficient and wise distribution of food and produce whilst at the same time the same social network also operates towards quite other ends.

The variety of social superstructures that a given technocomplex can sustain is very large and any social reconstruction is made doubly difficult by the missing record of agents and roles in these societies. Some hunting–fishing–gathering tribes may be strongly patrilineal and patrilocal – especially where hunting is a staple and game is small and scattered; here the emphasis is on male hunting, with young males brought up within and intimately acquainted with every niche of their future hunting terrain (Steward 1955). However, other hunter–fisher–gatherer tribes are matrilocal and matrilineal, especially in cases where female gathering and fishing is the basis; where the same conditions operate, but the males do the fishing and gathering, quite the opposite structures may prevail. Archaeological evidence may thus indicate an appropriate sociocultural set and its limits but it will not specify a single social arrangement for a technocomplex.

In the absence of variety amplifying units such as the city, hunter–fisher–gatherers' climax potential can only be achieved by a near-optimal strategy in an area of unusually rich resources. The technocomplexes that show a climax development on a hunting–fishing–gathering basis have two main features in common:

(i) a formalized sequence of resources that may be successively exploited in rotation throughout most of the year;
(ii) a socially focused and organized exploitation of one or more gregarious staples.
These features or tactics are found to some degree in most hunter–fisher–gatherer strategies but they are especially highly

developed and institutionalized in the cultures with climax potential.

The first of these requirements – an annual resource rota – can be achieved in several different ways. Under one strategy, advantage is taken of various kinds of ecological zonation to devise, by trial and error feedback, a schedule which will take the group from zone to zone and from resource to resource just as each resource reaches fruition. The group concentrating and dispersing in phased succession as the type of resource and its density constrain – a rhythmic, alternating stance through the annual cycle. Another climax strategy may take advantage of an exceptionally well situated territory astride several closely packed ecological zones and by successive exploitation of zones close at hand may achieve settlement stability. The favourite kind of territory in the latter case usually embraces a land and sea strip with deep-sea, marine shallows, littoral, estuary and river, inland forest and lakes, as ecological niches with a great variety of resources with a rotational harvest.

The second requirement for a climactic hunter–fisher–gatherer strategy depends upon the availability of one or more gregarious staples and its organized exploitation by focused social segments. A gregarious staple resource, regularly congregating in dense and nucleated profusion in a small area is more easily exploited than a solitary and dispersed resource. Sometimes the resource species may be dispersed for the greater part of the year and only swarm at certain times in certain areas. In such a case the group will also congregate at these times and places and disperse at others; in other cases the resource is permanently mustered. The gregarious species may be aquatic or terrestrial and faunal or floral. The gregarious aquatic species range from the whale and tunny fish through the various seals, sardines, salmon, oysters, down to periwinkles – all the shoal fish and shellfish. The gregarious land species embrace the flocks and herds of buffalo, reindeer, horse, deer, elephant, mammoth, ducks, geese – all the gregarious animals and birds. Last, but not least, we have the gregarious plants – the nettles, the trees, the grasses, above all others – the cereals. The organized exploitation of one or more of these gregarious resources ensures a near-optimal payoff.

It is under conditions such as these that climactic hunter–fisher–gatherer communities like the Magdalenians focused on reindeer or bison, the Folsom technocomplex on bison and the Clovis and Gravettian technocomplexes on mammoth. Some degree of climax was even possible amongst the Californian Indians with strategies based on acorns, seeds and pine nuts, and in the Everglades complex of Florida on the basis of wild rice and fish. The shell middens of the Ertebølle and Mediterranean Epi-Palaeolithic groups attest a similar achievement, as do the more recent American Indians of the North-west Coast and the Eskimo of the Arctic (Forde 1934), where the latter could even competitively displace the technocomplex of the twelfth-century Vikings of Greenland. Under climax conditions the hunter–fisher–gatherer economies and societies are more delicately poised and more precariously balanced than are the communities of the peasant farmer.

This brings us to the dangers of a climactic hunter–fisher–gatherer technocomplex and some characteristics of the time-trajectories of this kind of subsistence strategy. We have suggested that economic patterns are strategies based on mixed combinations of resource exploitation, continually adjusting by feed-back oscillation. Over-specialization gives a maximum-yield strategy linked to a single group of rich resources, or a single resource. However, the disappearance or severe population oscillation of this resource can cause dramatic feed-back oscillations in the coupled sociocultural system. There are many cases where the periodic or permanent disappearance of mammoth, whales, oysters, salmon, sardine, buffalo, caribou and seals have dras-tically repatterned the dependent technocomplex systems. One characteristic of hunter–fisher–gatherer subsistence strategies there-fore is their oscillating instability, arising from the simplicity and directness of their coupling with the environment. Climactic strategies in this group are thus especially vulnerable, by virtue of the intense specialization and organization which yields the climax potential in those technocomplexes. By contrast, the slow and steady exploitation of hunting–fishing–gathering resources in a less specialized, minimax and satisficer strategy yields less potential but offers less risk and more certain continuity. It is for this reason, amongst several others, that the climax hunter–fisher–gatherer technocomplexes represent the cul-de-sac areas or basins of overspecialized trajectory development, whereas the future potential lay in the system organization of the less elaborately constrained and less climactic technocomplexes.

Pastoral nomad technocomplexes

Pastoral nomad cultures are every bit as varied as those of the hunter–fisher–gatherers but in the same way exhibit a characteristic set of constraints and regularities in their structure and cultural ontogenies. The technocomplex taxa help to break down the apparent monolithic unity of the pastoral nomad societies into smaller and variously equipped units, without reducing the view to the overcrowded level of individual cultures. Before we move to examine some of these constraints and regularities it is important to dispel two common misconceptions. The term 'pastoralist' simply encompasses that set of economies that make use of animal herding within their compound strategy. It is necessary to distinguish the pastoral or mixed farming aspects of sedentary agrarian strategies from those mobile nomad societies almost entirely dependent on herding. The term 'pastoralist' does not necessarily mean 'nomad pastoralist' neither does it coincide with 'mounted nomad pastoralist'. The point of this diatribe is the frequent transference of the narrowly constrained characteristics of 'mounted nomad pastoralists' to all 'pastoralist' societies. Archaeologically this amounts to the automatic mental impression that cultures with large herds are 'pastoralist' and that 'pastoralist' societies are always 'mobile mounted nomads' – the Corded Ware/Battle-Axe culture group has been a notable casualty in this respect, a sad mirage of the first plough agriculturalists in Europe.

Once this misconception is erased the group of technocomplexes under discussion immediately assumes a more concise form. The mixed farming pastoralists with more sedentary settlement patterns and cereal staples fall outside this pastoral nomad group, they come within the various agrarian strategies. The true pastoral nomad set itself falls into two broad and important divisions – mounted and unmounted (Forde 1934). The steed of the mounted pastoralist may variously be the horse or camel, or on occasion even the donkey, reindeer, yak or ox. The basis of the unmounted nomad pastoralist's strategy is on the contrary severely limited by the range and endurance of his own feet. Not surprisingly, there is an interesting convergence between the technocomplexes of mounted pastoralists and mounted hunters, like the Plains Indians, and similarly between unmounted nomad pastoralists and nomad hunter–fisher–gatherers – the parallels are significant but should not confuse the separate identities of these groups.

Pastoral nomad technocomplexes emerge with a wide range of variation within the limitations of their compound strategy. This is centred on certain herd animals but freely and regularly backed by hunting, fishing and gathering further resources, and by buying and stealing yet others. The range of variation expresses a varying habitat, a varying emphasis and combination of staples, a contrast between mounted and unmounted herding, and a variation in the beasts ridden and herded. Nevertheless, this broad range operates within composite constraints (fig. 7) that arise from the historical trajectories of these societies and from their necessary conditions. The most important constraint is the inability of most recent pastoral nomad subsistence strategies to be fully self-supporting and fully independent of surrounding systems of different kinds. The pastoral nomad economy has been described as a highly specialized 'parasite' strategy but this may not always have been the case. The general trajectory of most of the technocomplexes associated with pastoral nomadism has been greatly clarified by recent archaeological and historical research and some attempt to sketch this development is now possible (Phillips 1965).

The present evidence everywhere suggests that pastoral nomadism arose independently in many areas and periods from the increasingly pressured expansion of mixed farmers from primary agrarian niches into more marginal, arid territories. The pressure operating in these circumstances mainly arose from the exponential population increase following intensive agriculture and urban settlement in the primary areas – particularly the narrow river valleys and littoral strips. The expanding network of urban settlements with their peripheral halo of towns and villages progressively extended into most of the easily exploited agrarian areas. However, when this expansion into the primary areas had been effectively fulfilled the population did not cease to increase. The marginal and in most cases increasingly arid altitudes and territories were slowly penetrated at the expense of a slow repatterning of the economic strategy. Initially these peripheral groups pursued a mixed strategy based upon simple hoe agriculture and small herds of hardy animals, carefully backed by rotational hunting, fishing and gathering. As the groups moved into more marginal agricultural land the herding element became more vital and the agrarian less feasible and reliable.

Eventually, in order better to exploit the vast areas of thinly grassed land a more fully mobile sociocultural system was developed. In many areas this early form of unmounted nomadism was based around small, hardy, slow travelling, easily herded animals like the sheep and goat, with the donkey or some other species of pack animal for tents and equipment and the dog as a very useful adjunct. The earliest evidence for this kind of unmounted nomadism convincingly appears in the mountain zones and along the desert flanks of the 'fertile crescent' before the fourth millennium BC and is beautifully documented in the specific traditions of the Semitic Hebrew. The Old Testament gives a vivid account of a group of tribes of tented sheep and goat-herding nomads, traditionally from the environs of Ur and gravitating across the pasture from the eastern fringe of the desert to the western edge, in the period between 3000–1500 BC. Similar unmounted nomadism and transhumance developed in many other steppe, desert and mountain areas.

This web of montane, desert and steppe areas was by no means devoid of previous communities. Indeed, in both the Old and New World these were the niches of many minutely adjusted and well-balanced hunter–fisher–gatherer technocomplexes – mainly based on gathering seeds, nuts, fruit, and roots and hunting the small sparse game animals of the deer, gazelle, goat group. The presence of these hunter–fisher–gatherers is often registered by the rock art which clusters around the rock shelters, waterholes and other territorial resources, vigorously recording their main game animals. Indeed these symbols may have unconsciously served a vital role in the mutual territorial adjustments of wandering bands roaming vast overlapping territories – serving much the same purpose as the territorial scent marks of many terrestrial mammals. The pastoral nomads borrowed, adapted and integrated many features and doubtless intermarried with individuals from these earlier groups. The unmounted pastoralist technocomplexes incorporated much of the strategy and many of the artefacts of these well-adapted aborigine groups. This convergent development is, for example, well documented for the penetration of the Sahara and the Arabian deserts after c. 3000 BC.

Climax situations under pastoral nomad conditions seem mainly to have arisen when mounted nomadism was introduced – allowing a much larger territory, a much more flexible strategy and the herding of large and fast herd herbivores like horses, camels, and cattle. The impetus, inventions and innovations for this ecological breakthrough seem to have arisen yet again within the pastoral-agrarian communities of the marginal agricultural areas. Herds of cattle, horses and camels are first noted for these more sedentary communities, where the herding element is often registered by specific subcultural complexes.

The horse is by far the most useful mount in temperate conditions, to the south the camel has the advantage and to the north and east the reindeer and yak predominate. The horse seems to have been in use as a herd animal in pastoral-agrarian communities from the Pontic Steppes to the Iranian plateau by 3000 BC. In this area an ox-wagon based pastoral nomad technocomplex seems to have operated between 2500–1500 BC and to have introduced the horse as a traction animal around 2000 BC and as a riding mount by *c.* 1400 BC. In this way horse-mounted nomads herding horses, cattle, or sheep first appear and spread after 1400 BC on the Eurasiatic steppe. The subsequent introduction of horse riding to the East seems to have acculturated to nomadism the marginal Mongolian farmers of the desiccating fringes of the Chinese Empire. In the North horse riding and pastoral nomad herding seem to have induced the development of reindeer herding and riding by blending the knowledge of the indigenous reindeer hunters with the new technocomplex skills. In the south the camel was in military and nomad use by 1000 BC in the Arabian and Syrian deserts (Yadin 1963, p. 361). Mounted pastoral nomadism became a fully evolved subsistence pattern with many local variations and several regional and successive technocomplex manifestations.

The requirements for climactic conditions within pastoral nomad technocomplexes are much the same as for hunter–fisher–gatherers. In the case of the pastoral nomad the strategy already involves the successive exploitation of a rotation of resources and the socially focused interest in one or more gregarious staples. The additional requirement in this strategy is an advantageous exchange relationship with nearby agricultural technocomplexes. The nomad is customarily dependent upon these system interchanges for supplies of cereals, fruit, vegetables, metalwork, skilled artisans, manufactured goods and luxury items. The fluctuating 'symbiotic/parasitic' role of this system interaction is discussed in a subsequent section (section V). In any event the inherent instability of this kind of relationship emphasizes the other precariously balanced factors operating in a pastoral nomad climax.

As an example of a climax system within the pastoral nomad technocomplexes one might take the Scythian culture of the Pontic Steppe (Phillips 1965). In fact we have here the Scythian subculture of the Royal Horde characterizing and climactically repatterning the Scythian culture and expanded culture group, within the less homogeneous Scythian technocomplex – the technocomplex of the mounted pastoral nomad societies from the Carpathians to the Mongolian Steppe, from 500–0 BC. Under the organization of the focal Royal

Horde the Scythian tribes displaced and assimilated the Cimmerian nomads of the Pontic Steppe in the seventh century BC. This territory at this time was ideally suited for a climactic exploitation – the steppe grasslands were bordered by the resources of the deciduous forests to the north and the pleasant shores of the Black Sea to the south. The Black Sea littoral was shortly settled by immensely rich Greek colonial trading cities, whilst to the east and west lay the metallurgical centres of the Caucasus and the Carpathians, and on the southern flanks lay the towns and cities of the Persian Empire. The Scythians were able to extract tribute from the urban Greeks and Persians as well as staple produce from the subjugated Cimmerians and the neighbouring Slav, Celt, Teuton and Balt agriculturalists and Finnish hunter–fisher–gatherers. The basis of this interchange being the formidable military advantage of the Scythian cavalry and archery units and the mutual advantages of trade in both directions.

The final collapse of the Scythian climax provides an excellent example of multiple factors and cumulative effect. Some of the factors include the political detachment of the Scythians around the Greek colonies, the increasing settlement in an urban and agricultural system, the aggressive stance gradually adopted by the Persians, Celts, and Teutons, followed by physical invasion by the Sarmatians around 250 BC with their superior heavy cavalry stirrup-hauberk-lance-sabre-helmet complex.

The instability of pastoral nomad systems in general and climactic examples in particular, stems primarily from the instability of the flora and fauna resources of such extra-sensitive boundary habitats, the instability of the essential extra-system sources of variety, and the vulnerable nature of any climax organization in such a context. The oscillating progress of postglacial dessication was particularly severely registered in precisely the staple areas of these technocomplexes and although it would be excessively naive to attribute nomad movements to climatic changes, such changes were nevertheless one of the more important elements in the cumulative interaction of factors.

The social organization commonly found within pastoral nomad technocomplexes is narrowly constrained by the inherent system conditions. These societies display almost exclusively patricentred organizations with a regularly developed emphasis on polygamy. This structure seems to be connected with the trajectories behind these systems in which male organized herding became increasingly important and increasingly corporate with a corresponding decline of significant female gathering and food collection. In the same fashion these societies share a segmentation into units such that the smallest may efficiently operate its herds, tents and equipment in a dispersed configuration suitable to hard conditions, and the largest may periodically operate as an integrated unit in good conditions. Hardly surprisingly, these societies also share elaborate hospitality and feuding systems which at one and the same time may ensure the safe conduct of essential supplies, artificers, traders and caravans and yet, beyond an invisible line, permitting wholesale piracy, looting, warfare and murder in pursuit of valued staples. In general, the whole nomad sociocultural system from social values to language structure is usually pervaded by the central role of the prime staple resource – whether it be camels, horses, cattle or reindeer.

These characteristics of pastoral nomad technocomplex trajectories differ from those of hunter–fisher–gatherers mainly in degree rather than in pattern. The same oscillating instability of the staple resources operates just as drastically and must induce lag and lead oscillations in the coupled sociocultural systems. However, the larger average complement of sociocultural variety and organization helps to regulate and control the severity of these fluctuations to a degree not usually matched in hunter–fisher–gatherer communities – the oscillations may be smoothed by a modicum of system control. Under ordinary conditions the amplitude of the fluctuating system variables is less than in the simpler technocomplexes. Under exceptional conditions a climax configuration and strategy may be developed, also commensurately greater than that of the hunter–fisher–gatherers. Nevertheless, the stability of such a climax is inevitably short-lived under the cumulative impact of the many factors that it induces.

Agrarian technocomplexes

The agrarian technocomplexes have existed as integrated strategies as long and probably longer than those of the pastoral nomads, perhaps a full ten thousand years. The variety and blend of components in agrarian strategies range from garden horticulture to plough agriculture and from emphasis on domestic herds to concentration on vegetable or cereal staples. The particular equilibrium polygon between domestic animals and crops often integrates hunting–fishing–gathering components on a seasonal basis. The difference between agrarian and hunter–fisher–gatherer strategies is less marked than one might be led to believe – except in the case of agrarian climax conditions. The segmentation of the annual cycle is as marked and necessary to the successful harvest in the one economy as in the other. The Eskimo hunter–fisher–gatherer may divide his year into the caribou season and the seal season but then the agrarian Temiar of Malaya equally move from a hunting season to an horticultural season. The same minutely adjusted and formalized sequence of successively exploited resources forms the basis of the rotational schedules. The same socially focused and organized exploitation of one or more gregarious staples provides a common denominator. The differences that exist between non-climax examples of both subsistence techniques reside in many individually trivial characteristics but it is the cumulative implications of these differences in attitude and preference that gradually led some agrarian technocomplex trajectories into metastable configurations of much greater potential.

The trivial characteristics which initially began to distinguish the post-glacial hunter–fisher–gatherers whose trajectories did move towards domestication and those hunter–fisher–gatherers whose trajectories did not move in that direction are not yet clearly understood. These characteristics form a cumulative system of interrelated and interacting factors in which it is difficult to sort the consequences from the causes. However, we can notice the difference between those Epi-Palaeolithic communities that were already highly involved and intimately integrated in systems exploiting climax hunting, fishing or gathering conditions, whilst others were less specialized. Such an intense formalization and institutionalization of a focal activity makes divergent development very difficult. Another factor may have been the location of societies in ecological boundary areas of the world, where some formerly exploited staple became extinct or migrated away under the pressures of intensive exploitation, postglacial desiccation and the inevitable cumulative cycles of existence. Here again, a retrospective condition can be seen to be the strongly localized habitats and territories of the domesticable flora and fauna. Yet other factors would isolate those cultural communities who repeatedly made attempts to protect and regenerate their staple resources and those again that preferred to stay in a single settlement for as long as possible. Evidence is even accumulating that suggests that the more static societies with widespread exchange systems, initially dealing in such raw materials as obsidian, stone, shells, woods, and bitumen, were also in an optimally placed position to integrate and directively correlate the dispersed and individually insignificant agrarian innovations of peripheral groups. All of these factors represent constraints with very broad boundaries, sets individually including large areas of the world, but taken as a composite restriction the joint intersect sets of such possible areas and societies is much reduced (fig. 7).

Whatever the pattern of events, it is now clear that even when accomplished the integrated innovation of a strategy using domestic plants and animals as one component was a change to an alternative and not necessarily to a 'better' subsistence pattern. Nevertheless, in certain advantageous circumstances the cumulative interaction of the premiums of a more static settlement and of an increasing and storable food surplus began to produce climax results – the rapidly expanding range of cultural variety providing a more stable sustenance for more people. The addition of domestic plants and domestic animals to the existing range of resource variety added to the flexibility and variety of possible subsistence strategies.

Climax conditions were reached by agrarian technocomplexes that had integrated a wide and nicely balanced range of domesticates and had gradually transferred these staples to new ecological niches, simultaneously removing natural predators and placing the staples in unusually advantageous contexts. This transition seems to have come about with the permanent settlement of alluvial soils and their intensive exploitation by organized communities with optimal sociocultural continuity and employing such techniques as ditch irrigation, soil replenishment, and careful control in plant and herd management.

Under such conditions as these, villages produced a continuing surplus, the surplus supported subcultural specialists and some of the specialists set about optimally organizing the source of their own well-being. Villages grew into towns, towns grew into cities and cities grew into urban states and urban empires. The introduction and development of the urban unit produced an entity with a potential as unforeseen as that of agriculture itself. The city as a centre for well-supported specialists and artificers became a fountainhead for the integrative invention, innovation, adaptation and redistribution of variety of every kind – with a continuous input of raw materials and a continuous output of manufactured variety. The city became as much a social engine for the generation of new social variety as it was an amplifier for material variety (fig. 69; Wrigley 1967).

The city manager, or managers, continually strove to optimally adjust the territory and resources of the city, in their own interests.

The advantage was the occasional climactic development of a near-optimal subsistence system with a hitherto unmatched stability in terms of input and output fluctuation. Nevertheless, the disadvantages of a near-optimal strategy also followed. Both resources and manpower still fluctuated to some extent although this could be regulated by the new variety. Trade and business cycles also appear as inherent system oscillations. The cumulative effect of these fluctuating and oscillating variables may then occasionally result in a superimposition of trends in an oscillation of drastic amplitude. The world still anxiously waits to see whether such inflationary oscillations can be fully regulated and controlled.

The regularities of the time-trajectory of agrarian climax systems are well-known and have been studied in some detail (Steward 1955). The individual systems, in optimal cases, moved through the states of – incipient agriculture, stable agriculture, urban formative/florescent, urban state coherent/classic, imperial expansion, and eventually to imperial collapse and repatterning. This trajectory is, however, only one of the many possible for agrarian systems, depending on the particular strategy or not.

v   System pattern regularities

The system under investigation is the technocomplex system of cultures, assemblages and artefact-type families. This technocomplex category embraces a set of interconnected, related and unrelated subsystems that happen to share some aspects of the same general strategy of resource exploitation, in the same general environment, and with a broadly similar equipment. It follows from this definition that cultures within the same technocomplex would represent contradictive variety in terms of subsistence strategy if concentrated at a single locus, since they would be competing for the same resources, at the same time and in the same way. This contradiction can be avoided if the cultures are from different technocomplexes and exploit complementary niches, or if from the same technocomplex they may use the same territory and resources in succession (fig. 19). These relationships reflect part of the basis of the interaction of one socio-cultural system with another. The nature of this relationship clearly depends on the nature of the variety exchanged between the interacting and coupled systems, within the context of their environing system. When several such systems are coupled together, the whole can be at a state of equilibrium only when each is in a state of equilibrium, in the conditions provided by the others (Ashby 1956, p. 233).

The main problem arising from the analysis of cultural system interaction is the multidimensional nature of the variety interchange. This variety can, as we have seen, be new, alternative, contradictive or redundant variety affecting the existing system variety concerning social, religious, psychological, linguistic, economic and material culture, or any combination and permutation of these factors. In the simplest case the interchange may affect only one of these subsystems but it would be most unusual for the exchange not to have repercussions in some of the other aspects. This complexity can be arbitrarily simplified by treating the culture system's variety as projections within three broad sets – the sociocultural, the socioeconomic and the technocomplex aspects. The interaction between separate culture systems can then be examined in terms of the impact within these three sets and the reaction between the sets.

The dissection of sociocultural and socioeconomic interaction is beyond the proper sphere of this work. However, following the admirable analysis by Steward (1955) we have already noted that much of this interaction occurs between subcultural segments and their type complexes – in such processes as the truncation and substitution of subcultural units. Steward distinguishes several categories of sociocultural configuration connected and constrained by certain socioeconomic conditions. In this scheme a broad separation into family, folk, and state configurations is further subdivided into those societies employing strategies based upon – hunting–fishing–gathering in nuclear family, patrilineal band, matrilineal band, or composite band units, pastoral nomad bands and lineage units, or agrarian strategies with localized lineage villages, multilineage-multiclan villages, multivillage nations, up to urban and conurban states. If arranged in order of ascending complexity it is assumed that the more complex structures may also incorporate simpler forms.

The advantage of this gross categorization, like that of the complementary technocomplex scheme, is the ease with which generalized system interaction may be studied in a crosscultural framework. The regularities of interaction between state/family systems, such as the American/Shoshoni Indian case, can be compared with similar cases and with state/state subculture interactions like the Inca/Conquistadores, or the state/folk interactions of the Roman/Saxon and Roman/Celtic system impacts. The archaeological advantage of this treatment is that whereas the archaeologist can never identify the specific social structure of his groups he can by noting the technocomplex constraints in his systems at least specify the limited range of sociocultural units that they could be coupled with (see chapter 3, III and note 2).

It is on this general basis that the archaeologist can suggest that the operative units amongst say the Acheulean and forest Mesolithic technocomplexes would range from nuclear family bands in hard conditions to matricentred and patricentred bands of moderate size in good conditions and depending on the productivity and role allocation between the sexes. Large composite bands are only likely under climax conditions with the co-operative concentration on gregarious staples, such as we recognize in the Aurignacian and Gravettian technocomplexes and in the Magdalenian culture group. Composite bands and composite lineage groups are also to be expected as optimal arrangements in such technocomplexes as the Maglemose-like and Ertebølle-like communities of postglacial Europe. In the case of the Ertebølle tribes the emphasis on shellfish collection under optimal conditions, will probably have led to localized lineages of considerable size and varying from matricentred to patricentred according to the allocation of the role of the collection of the major staple. In the same way, it is very probable that such towns as early Çatal Hüyük were based on multilineage and multiclan units, with perhaps a matricentred orientation if the agrarian trajectory had passed from female seed-gathering to agriculture, but a patricentred focus if the agricultural role was male and the male hunting pattern was still important. This kind of approach can only be tentatively employed but is likely to be far more realistic than the unfounded equations between long houses, female figurines, and matrilineality that archaeologists still employ.

The regularities in system interaction can therefore be usefully scrutinized in terms of the likely interaction of the sociocultural, socioeconomic and technocomplex configurations involved, on the basis of their variety content and within the frame of the environmental context. Unfortunately, under archaeological conditions the only reasonably dependable data relates to the technocomplex morphology – the outline of the technological, economic, environmental and artefact equilibrium strategy. From this and the system's distribution and dispersion pattern, a limited range of sociocultural and socioeconomic superstructures may be inferred but cannot be further specified on other than a probability basis. The outcome of such system interactions depends upon the sociocultural masses, the context of the interaction and the technocomplex categories involved. The sociocultural mass here reflects the number of individuals concerned in the interchange, the area of their territory and the pattern of their dispersion within the territory.

The archaeologist can therefore look at system interaction only from the technocomplex point of view and this view will conspicuously lack information about other sociocultural interchange which will certainly have operated as an important factor. The terminology that archaeologists employ for the description of cultural system interaction yet again leans heavily on biological and ecological analogy – using such terms as parasite and symbiosis, or co-operation, disoperation, competition and toleration (Allee *et al.* 1950, p. 348). The analogy rests on the isomorphic similarities between biological, ecological and cultural systems but as we have seen previously, this similarity does not amount to identity and it is the unspecified set of differences that help to blunt the incisive development of cultural analysis. A specific set of cultural terms should be devised to meet this need but until cultural anthropologists provide us with such tools we will have to make do with our own redefinition of other people's terms (fig. 74).

The terms that seem to have a useful equivalent in technocomplex system interchange may be reused in the following way:

Symbiosis – an interchange to mutual advantage; the variety exchanged being new, alternative, or redundant but not contradictive.

Disoperative – an interchange to the disadvantage of one or both systems, the variety exchanged being contradictive or ultimately contradictive.

Parasitic – an interchange to the advantage of one system only; the new, alternative, or redundant variety passes only one way, in the other direction there is either no passage of variety or the harmful passage of contradictive variety.

Tolerative – an interchange bringing about no immediate change; either no variety is exchanged, or the variety is new or redundant and neutral.

Competitive – an indirect interchange via a mutually coupled system inducing change in one or both the competitors; new alternative, contradictive or redundant variety is induced in the competitive systems.

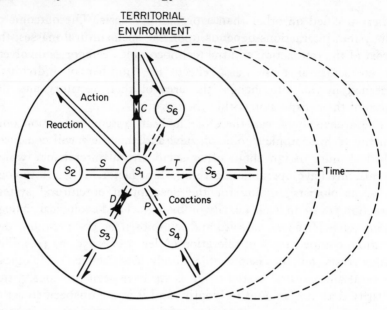

Fig. 74   A schematic diagram illustrating categories of cultural system interaction – at the technocomplex level, in a limited territory, in reference to the particular culture system S_1 and its relationships to other alien systems S_2–S_6: – S_1/Environment – Action/Reaction; S_1/S_2 – Symbiosis; S_1/S_3 – Disoperation; S_1/S_4 – Parasitic; S_1/S_5 – Tolerative; S_1/S_6 loop – Competitive.

These terms refer to the study of relationships between pairs of coupled technocomplex systems or rather cultural systems interacting at the technocomplex level, where all other levels are obscured. In reality a compound situation may involve two systems, three systems, four systems, and so on – giving a complex network of couplings and varied relationships in two, three or four phase systems. In this context it is useful to appropriate the term 'coaction' for the variously valued interactions between cultural systems and to restrict the terms 'action and reaction' for the interchange between the cultural systems and the environment. Although we can hardly develop a full discussion of cultural system interaction here, it may be useful to sketch the possibilities under the subsistence categories of technocomplexes.

Hunter–fisher–gatherer/pastoral nomad system coaction

The main feature of mixed two-phase coactions, such as that between a hunter–fisher–gatherer group and a pastoral nomad group, is that they offer some possibility of economic coexistence even in a single locus. A toleration which is usually impossible in coactions between groups of the same technocomplex or applying the same subsistence strategy in the same limited territory. However, it would be false to assume that such differently based economic coactions operate in a continuous state of tolerative or symbiotic harmony. Such a stable state may indeed be briefly established to mutual advantage but it would be quite exceptional if both systems had expanded and developed without at some stage impinging on one another's essential resources. In practice it is more frequently the case that mixed two-phase coactions go through a series of synchronous or semisynchronous oscillations involving both populations and their system attributes.

Let us take a hypothetical hunter–fisher–gatherer group in a territory gradually penetrated by an intrusive pastoral nomad system – assuming for convenience that neither is a climax system. Initially it may be possible for both systems to pursue their formalized and sequential exploitation of their particular selection of the area's resources. A tolerative interchange is possible, especially if the two systems mutually adjust their movement around the territory. In time, a symbiotic relationship may come into being so that the hunter–fisher–gatherer may desist from hunting the pastoralist's herds in return for an exchange of resources or services – an economic arrangement to mutual advantage. Nevertheless, in time the pastoral nomad system will expand at the expense of the resources of the hunter–fisher–gatherers who may be reduced to a parasitic, then a competitive and eventually to a disoperative interchange. If the hunter–fisher–gatherer system survives this coaction then the coupled systems may continue to fluctuate from state to state as their particular fortunes wax and wane – oscillating in any sequence through a succession of tolerative, symbiotic, parasitic, competitive or disoperative states.

The archaeologist may detect something of this economic interchange and possibly a little of the complementary coactions involving the whole of the rest of the sociocultural systems involved. Acculturation and integration, or subcultural truncation and substitution are likely to alter the system coaction into a totally new system situation.

In the particular case of hunter–fisher–gatherer and pastoral nomad coactions, conflicting interests are likely to arise very quickly in the interchange. The large herds of the nomad are just another resource to the hunter and furthermore they will certainly upset his game animal staples – competing both for fodder and for the water resources of the area. The interaction between the intrusive Bantu pastoralists and the hunting–gathering Bushmen is dramatically depicted in the territorial rock paintings of the Bushmen often showing their tribesmen stealing cattle, hotly pursued by the irate Bantu. The outcome in this case saw the gradual dominance of the Bantu groups modified by Bushmen acculturation, the appearance of 'new' hybrid Hottentot systems and the retreat of the remaining Bushmen groups into increasingly marginal territories. A somewhat similar interchange seems to have occurred between hunter–fisher–gatherers and pastoralists in the earlier pastoralist expansions into the Sahara, the Arabian deserts, and the Siberian plains. Gradually displacing the gazelle, deer, or reindeer hunters from the best grazing areas, leaving only their rock art as a reminder of their former presence and special interests.

Hunter–fisher–gatherer/agrarian system coaction

Once again we are concerned with a mixed two-phase coaction and once again we have sets of situations involving an oscillating relationship with the difference in this case being one of degree. The gulf separating the economy of the agrarian systems from those of the hunter–fisher–gatherer probably increases rather than decreases the possibility of brief periods of tolerative or symbiotic coexistence in a single area. Nevertheless, even these phases of mutual adjustment are likely to be dispelled when the agrarian system is expansive or climactic. The brief coexistence of the American Indian/European Settler system provides one tragic example and the deliberate extermination of the Tasmanian Aborigines and the Ona of Tierra del Fuego provide others. From the view of one technocomplex the hunter–fisher–gatherers are predatory vermin to be put down, from the other technocomplex view the fields and flocks of the agriculturalist are just a new set of resources to be exploited; this contradictive variety ensures severe dislocation in such a composite system.

Exceptions arise when the agrarian penetration is slight and not climactic – a situation likely to mark the early phase of the development in such a system. Alternatively, the hunter–fisher–gatherers may occupy a particular set of territorial niches or micro-environments such as not to impinge too heavily on the agriculturalists. Indeed, a symbiotic exchange may arise like the famous interchange between the Congo Forest Pygmies and contiguous Negro farmers, or the less laudable employment of hunter–fisher–gatherer aborigines as mercenary military specialists.

The recent settings for most hunter–fisher–gatherer/agrarian coactions have characteristically been in territories involving thick forest interspersed with cleared areas. In prehistoric times this inter-change must have been more frequently set in the lightly wooded grasslands that supported the big herbivore herds but which later supported domestic herds and crops. In this light, one wonders whether the defensive stance of such early 'towns' as Jericho and Çatal Hüyük was adopted against other agrarian settlements or against displaced pastoralists or hunter–fisher–gatherers.

Agrarian/pastoral nomad system coaction

Here again the juxtaposition of two differently based technocomplex systems will allow an oscillating coexistence. The distinctive feature in this interaction is the unusual stability of the periods of tolerative coexistence which depend upon the largely complementary resources and strategies of the two kinds of system. This tolerative or symbiotic relationship springs to mind in the cases of the Bedouin/Oasis Arab, Chukchi/Russian peasant, Lapps/Finnish peasant, Scythian/Slav peasant or Navaho/Pueblo coactions. Nevertheless, this kind of temporary stability may be distinctive but it is certainly not static or inevitable.

In the case of the changing relationships between the Lapp rein-deer herders and the Finnish peasants c. AD 1500–1900 we have a particularly well documented example (Whitaker 1955). This inter-action could be crudely summarized under three successive states in the interaction:

Phase I   Symbiosis, a few intrusive peasants learn from, and exchange with, the local nomad Lapps to mutual advantage.

Phase II   Tolerative, peasant communities become large and established and need the Lapps' output less and less; the Lapps have become semi-parasitic.

Phase III   Competitive, large peasant communities backed by an urban and industrial network expand into larger areas of land, fencing out the Lapps; the Lapps no longer able to obtain necessary resources, disoperative dislocation.

This case roughly sketches the fluctuating coaction between the two systems and in cases where the agrarian system is backed by urban technology and superior armament this is likely to be the broad sequence of events. However, the latter state of affairs only came into existence with the appearance of the firearm. It is therefore no accident that Central Europe was periodically ravaged by hordes of Pontic Steppe nomads – from the first appearance of mounted nomadism *c.* 1000 BC for almost every century until AD 1300. So long as the urban world's offensive armament remained the horse, the mounted warrior and the lance or bow, the mounted nomad was invincible unless surprised. The mounted nomad was a professional horseman, his units were optimally mobile and with the small compound bow, unmatchable in mobile firepower. Consequently, in pre-firearm times the fluctuating coaction trajectory did not always end to the advantage of the agrarian system. The Scythians decimated the eastern Slavs and settled amongst them first as predatory overlords and then as a substituted aristocratic subculture truncating the earlier social system. Somewhat similar sequences seem to have operated in the case of the later Sarmatians, Parthians, Huns, Turks and Mongols – seriously affecting marginal urban Europe, Asia and China. In the New World the interaction of the mounted Navaho and Apache nomads seems to have similarly proved a culminating factor in the dislocation of the Pueblo agrarian system. These examples may suffice to illustrate how technocomplex system interaction shows marked regularities and also how these coactions may be modified by changes in circumstances within the systems.

9 Group ethnology

The unit 'Iroquois culture' seems to have been shared by
tribes that were not only outside the famous confederacy
but in some cases not even affiliated linguistically,
G. R. WILLEY and P. PHILLIPS 1958, p. 53

1 Introduction

In the preceding chapters we have occupied ourselves with the
hierarchy of entities and patterns displayed by aggregates of cultural
artefacts. These artefacts have deliberately been treated in an abstract
and disembodied way in order that the regularities of their aggregate
'behaviour' in space and time might become apparent, without
prejudice from our feelings about the nature of hominid culture. The
result has been the gradual construction of an internally consistent
hierarchy of entities, each carefully defined and ranked in order of
complexity – from attribute to artefact, type, assemblage, culture,
culture group and technocomplex (fig. 49). Now, whether our purpose
is culture-historical and dominated by interest in sequence, or whether
it is cultural-ecology and dominated by system relationships – at some
stage a statement or hypothesis must be formulated to relate the ranks
of these artefact entities with the ranks of social, linguistic, and racial
entities. The range of connection of the archaeological entities must be
specified in human terms if their information value is to be maximized. Once this intermediate relationship has been outlined we can
return in the final chapter of this part to the overall implications of the
hierarchical model for archaeological theory.

Throughout historic and prehistoric time the individual man has
inherited a particular physique, acquired a particular linguistic dialect,
grown up within a particular social organization and used particular
artefacts in the pursuit of particular activities. The man has been the
node at the intersection of social, material, linguistic and genetic sets,
each operating in different attribute dimensions, categorizing different
aspects of the same populations. In each aspect or dimension the man

is connected in space and time to an ever-widening network of related individuals and items – some in a very remote and slight connection and others in a very direct and strong connection. For purely arbitrary reasons it has proved useful to distinguish in each particular plane or dimension the graded strength of connections relating a reference individual to successively larger and less similar sets of individuals. But since no two individuals ever possess completely identical groups of attributes even closely related individuals may be registered in different dimension sets and subsets, at least in respect of a few attributes. It then follows that the sets and subsets grading the interconnection of individuals' attributes will not be identical or equivalent in their content in the different planes or aspects. The contents and size of these aspect sets and subsets will be related however, because genetic make-up, language, social organization and material culture affect one another in constraints and consequent regularities. The relationship between the hierarchical sets racial group, race, subrace, or language group, language, dialect will be complex enough but the multidimensional relationships between the sets of differing aspects – race, language, social and material culture – will be vastly more intricate.

Unfortunately the intricacy of the connection between these taxonomic sets and subsets of different aspects has tended to lead to either a desperate over-simplification of the relationship or a denial of its existence. That a relationship does exist depends on our recognition of the constraints and regularities relating the individuals and their aspect attributes. Two kinds of connection are operating in these aspects – a genetic connection paramount in the physical aspect and sense communication connections dominant in the other aspects. Populations with a degree of communication and connection amongst their membership will inevitably tend to be more uniform within their boundaries than with unconnected individuals outside their set. The greater the degree of interconnection and intercommunication within the set the more uniform will be its characteristics. Consequently, it is the human family unit, in all its differing forms, that generates the basis of the taxa of race, language, social organization and material culture – the family representing the smallest population unit with optimal genetic and communication interconnection between its members. The time and space transformation of this unit immediately generates a widening network of kith and kin, uniting in a distant way a huge group of genetically related individuals and more localized clusters of individuals, segmented into sub-populations polythetically sharing common linguistic, social and material attributes. The taxonomic sets and subsets of race, language, social organization and material culture are thus related one to another as intersecting nested hierarchies with a variable but limited range of mutual relationships. The taxa of one aspect are related to the taxa of the other aspects as elaborate injective and surjective mappings, whose boundaries are always related and may sometimes coincide, with significant consequences.

The complexities of the problem of equating archaeological entities with social, linguistic and racial groupings rapidly becomes apparent. There is no *a priori* reason why the different ranks of groupings within the different aspects should equate exactly one with another – although much archaeological literature tacitly equates such entities as culture group and language group, particularly in relation to the Corded Ware/Battle-Axe and Indo-European problem. The opposing arguments over these problems take a very familiar course. On one hand we are presented with the simple equivalence of culture and language, culture group and language group, whilst on the other hand the argument emphasizes the lack of precise coincidence between cultural, tribal, linguistic and racial boundaries and consequently denies any correlation between these sets. We have already seen that simple and naive equation of these differently based entities is not possible and is demonstrably false, but lack of exact correlation between the entities does not mean that there is no correlation what-soever – it simply emphasizes the complexity of the relationship.

The statements that can be made relating these entities one to another, are once again conditional probability propositions, of the kind some *A*s are *B*s (chapter I, III) – 'most tribes are polythetically homogeneous in race, culture and language, with the tribe within the intersect of these differently bounded sets'. As statistical or probability propositions such statements have limits beyond which they are not necessarily accurate – the limits usually defining the precise level of racial, cultural, linguistic entities being equated and requiring a care-fully defined terminology. At the same time, probability propositions are not conclusively refuted by producing contrary examples from limiting cases; for example, although most language groups incorporate more than one culture, nevertheless in relict cases the language group may be equal to or smaller than a culture, as in the case of Basque. Against this difficult background, statements of useful predictive value can be made if it is accepted that they are of this nature and are true only within specified limits.

To proceed from the supposition that probability propositions linking social, cultural, linguistic, and racial entities can be made to actually making them is another matter. This problem is mainly set in the field of social, cultural and physical anthropology, and is not one for an archaeologist to answer. Nevertheless, we can perhaps look at the problem and consider how a solution may arise. We can note that the problem involves the old bugbear of dealing with different fields or aspects, each of which is internally divided into a series of levels of ranked entities. In such comparisons between the different hierarchical organizations the problem becomes one of knowing which rank of which field to compare with which? In material culture the choice ranges from the attribute, artefact, type, assemblage, culture, culture group, to the technocomplex, in linguistics we have the dialect, language, and language group levels and in social organization the family, family group, tribe, tribal group and so on (fig. 75). Add to

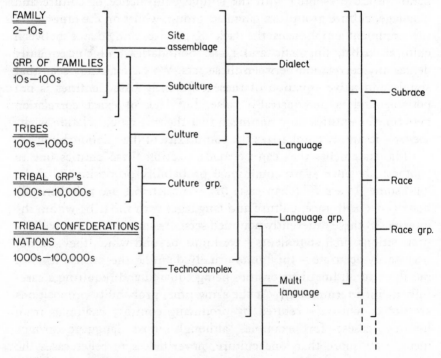

Fig. 75   A simplified attempt to illustrate the rough range of correlation between the hierarchical entity sets of four sociocultural dimensions – social, material, linguistic, genetic.

these the levels of race group, race and subrace and then add the proviso that all of these entities are arbitrary horizons of unspecified definition, and the difficulty of isolating significant mutual correlations is understandable. All that can be accomplished here is an intuitive assessment of the rough order of correlation between these entities, in the light of some practical observations of particular cases.

The aim in this inquiry is to try and assess the likely limits and implications of our archaeological taxa in human terms; an essential step if the application of these taxa to prehistoric assemblages is to yield the maximum amount of predictive information. In order to achieve this end, there seem to be three lines of approach the integration of which may lead to some success. The first of these is in a sense an internal method, in that having defined our hierarchy of entities with great care we may examine them to see whether their conditions naturally imply certain kinds of correlation. The second approach is ethnographic and depends upon the analysis of the relationship between the equivalents of the hierarchy of archaeological entities and their setting within recent primitive societies. The third approach is historical and rests upon the correlation, or lack of correlation, between archaeologically defined entities and historically documented peoples, wherever and whenever the prehistoric cultures cross the boundary separating the undocumented gloom from the historical sunlight. These three approaches will be tackled one by one and then some attempt will be made to integrate their implications (sections II, III, IV).

II   Internal evidence

Earlier discussion about the behavioural implications of our archaeological entities has already suggested the approximate equivalence between an archaeological attribute, artefact and artefact-type and a hominid action, sequence of actions, and a repeated sequence of actions (chapter 4). A specific artefact-type expresses the consistently regular recurrence of a specific range of attributes in a population of artefacts from a limited and continuous area of space and time. This regularity can only express a specific set of constraints – some of them functional and largely defining the artefact family – but many of them marking idiosyncratic requirements shared by the fabricators. If the artefact-type population expresses such shared idiosyncratic requirements it must represent the products of an inter-communicating human group. It now appears that we can say that the

makers of a specific artefact-type population were an intercommunicating and therefore connected human group from a limited and
contiguous area of space-time. Since the optimally interconnected and
intercommunicating human group is the family unit, it follows that
the artefact-type population would result from the handiwork of a
kernel representing the time and space transformation of a number of
these units generating a reticulated and widening network of kith and
kin and their associates. The characteristics of this specific artefact-
type would be optimally diffused amongst the appropriate operators of
this network by virtue of a common linguistic link and a repeatedly
intercommunicating social network. Almost by chance then, we can
perceive that the specific artefact-type will be largely contained within
an extended kith and kin network, within a common language area and
within a largely homogeneous breeding population.

However, we know very well that specific artefact-types diffuse
through trade, gift-exchange, warfare and many other forms of intercommunication, to neighbouring groups with an alien cultural, and
possibly linguistic and even racial background. This relationship
erases any simple 'one to one' equivalence between an artefact-type
and a social group, but is itself noticeably constrained by the pre-
requisite that the alien borrowers must be 'neighbouring' or at least in
communication with the originators. The frequency distribution of a
specific artefact-type in time and space is such that although artefacts
do travel beyond individual social webs, these diffusions are sporadic
and thinly represented by comparison with the repeated and sustained
interchange circulating within the web and mesh of a social unit, or
group of closely interconnected social units.

The distribution of a single artefact-type population in space and
time may in itself be a poor social marker. Fortunately however,
human families pursue a number of very different activities and
consequently manufacture a number of very different specific artefact-
types – an assemblage in fact. The compounded space and time
distribution of this polythetic ensemble, or assemblage of specific
types, produces the archaeological culture (fig. 67). The repeatedly
shared core area of these multidimensional and individual artefact-
type distributions should cumulatively define the common social unit
which is responsible for this regularity. A social unit greater than the
family but effectively intercommunicating in terms of codified actions,
sequences of actions, activities and general sociocultural behaviour,
requiring a common language, a common social organization and

therefore stipulating a largely homogeneous kith, kin and race group from a limited and contiguous area of space and time. The social unit that best accords with these specifications is that most richly networked, self-regulating, self-recognizing and variously constituted group of interrelated families – the tribe or tribal band.

These arguments suggest that a specific artefact-type population is mainly the product of the closely connected family units within a tribe or group of connected tribes. These larger groupings are better isolated by the compounded intersection of all the specific artefact-types shared between the assemblages produced by each person and family, thus partially eliminating the fringe effect of externally diffused variety inevitably stemming from the tribal group. The archaeological assemblage, especially a single site assemblage, can therefore usually be equated with a group of families; the archaeological culture polythetically incorporates the specific types from these assemblages in space and time. The preconditions for this sort of regularity infer that an archaeological culture is the time transform of an entity of roughly tribal level which would have been largely but not entirely homogeneous at the language and subrace level.

The nature of this partial equivalence is most important. An archaeological cultural assemblage is not identical in space or time distribution with a tribal group, a language, or a subrace and these sets themselves share different boundaries. Nevertheless, the archaeological culture is most likely to have been the product of a group of people with a largely homogeneous tribal organization, language system and breeding population – whether the people themselves recognized the set or not. The archaeological culture maps a real entity that really existed, marking real interconnection – that this entity is not identical to historical, political, linguistic or racial entities does not make it the less real or important. The archaeological entities reflect realities as important as those recognized by the traditional classifications of other disciplines; the entities in all these fields are equally real, equally arbitrary and simply different.

This general argument can be extended to the culture group and technocomplex entities. The culture group englobes a family of affinally related transform cultures, collateral cultures sharing a polythetic range but differing states of the same specific artefact-types. The fact that the individual cultures within a culture group are linked by still sharing specific types suggests that considerable interconnection exists, or previously existed, between the units of the group, although not as rich an interconnection as within a single tribe. These factors, taken with the connection between tribe and culture and the size and distribution pattern of the culture group, together suggest that the culture group reflects a large set of related tribes – a large tribal group or loose confederation. One would expect a linguistic diversity amongst such a grouping but probably within the bounds of a single language group if the basis of interconnection is to be explained, or at least sharing one common language. Finally, the technocomplex entity, characterized merely by a common strategy and only sharing generalized artefact families suggests no necessary social, linguistic, or racial linkage between its members, except in limiting cases. Nevertheless, the technocomplex is equivalent in size or smaller than the racial units with which it may in the past have occasionally converged – especially in those periods when some racial groups were marked by localized adaptation to severe conditions in a rigorously confined territory. On the whole, the technocomplex need reflect no social, linguistic, or cultural uniformity although it may occasionally do so and will necessarily incorporate numbers of such homogeneous groups.

The internal analysis of our definitions has suggested a very rough order of correlation between our archaeological entities and the main social, linguistic and racial entities. A correlation that is at least partly reinforced by the evidence of the time and space distribution patterns of these entities. It is noteworthy that even this rough correlation must collapse if a precise definition and a rigorous use of terminology do not underpin our taxonomy. The arbitrariness of the terms and definitions are immaterial so long as the arbitrariness is confined to an explicitly given pattern which is always followed. Nevertheless, even if we are only saying that single assemblages are usually the product of 10s–100s of people, cultures of 100s–1,000s, culture groups of 1,000s–10,000s and technocomplexes of 10,000s–100,000s then we are at least establishing some limits of correlation and saying something about the relative ranks of the entities concerned. In a discipline that is apt to treat the Acheulean as if it were equivalent to the Sioux, any categorization of entity, rank, and complexity is better than none.

III Recent ethnographic evidence

The ethnographic approach to the problem of assessing the limits and implications of archaeological taxa provides the most promising key to the information locked in archaeological data. Unfortunately, many attempts to release this information have resorted to a simple violence more in keeping with a gelignite or 'jemmy' approach than with that of making a delicate key for a complex lock. This ethnographic approach depends upon the analysis of the relationship between the material culture equivalents of our archaeological entities and their setting in relation to recent primitive societies. In this respect it is doubly unfortunate that anthropologists rarely study the material culture of their peoples in a way that can be related to this problem. Modern anthropology has momentarily turned away from ethnology and ethnography, to the embarrassment of the archaeologist and the detriment of both disciplines.

Luckily, a few superbly detailed and comprehensive ethnographic studies have been accomplished before the accelerating disappearance of the last primitive peoples and before fashionable indifference altered the trajectory of anthropology. These very few detailed studies, based upon the more recent methods of anthropology, are to be distinguished from the older, historical studies of ancient peoples. The pre-Renaissance accounts of primitive societies and their material equipment are extremely useful for their record of long-vanished tribal communities in what is now nationalist Europe, Africa and Asia. However, they are more valuable for their proximity to actual prehistoric societies than for the uneven and unreliable coverage of their ethnography. The evidence of these historical sources has its own special value which will be pursued in the section following this one. In the present section we will concentrate on the skeleton key provided by the few modern studies centred on this problem.

Most of the ethnographic studies that provide sufficient detail for archaeological comparison are based on African and American tribes. In Africa a wealth of information has been steadily gathered relating the oral traditions, anthropology, ethnology, history and archaeology of the indigenous Africans. Perhaps the most complete part of this record describes the Bantu peoples and their penetration into Southern Africa; a record which introduces all the characteristic difficulties and latent information concealed in the relationships between variously orientated hierarchies of taxa. It may prove useful to follow the Bantu example a little further.

The term 'Bantu' correctly designates a set of languages and dialects shared by many widely differing groups of people from Africa. The precise set 'Bantu' is a language group with perhaps about sixty major distinct component languages, comprising roughly 300 tribal dialects – in the recent phase of the Bantu entity trajectory. However, the Bantu as a set of interconnected and interrelated peoples have certain racial, anthropological, ethnographic and distribution regularities which follow from the constraints of their interwoven time-trajectories and shared language groupings. Most Bantu-speaking peoples constitute an interbreeding subrace within the set of the African, Negro race, itself a subset of the 'Black Skinned' racial group – a loose label for a huge group defined by a polythetic set of characteristics in addition to Black Skin. Some Bantu-speakers nevertheless reflect different subrace sets which have become acculturated minorities or subcultures within the Bantu milieu. Yet again, the Bantu-speakers also share certain social and ethnographic features which isolate them as a polythetic entity amongst their spatial and temporal neighbours. As a polythetic entity we would not expect any one of these features to be necessarily confined to the Bantu – most of them will be variously shared with non-Bantu-speakers from whom they may have been borrowed, or who may have been acculturated in respect of the particular characteristic. These polythetic attributes which secondarily centre around the Bantu-speaking tribes include a specific complex social organization and land tenure system based upon hoe agriculture, cattle and settled villages – as well as iron, copper and gold metallurgy. This largely Bantu-speaking complex is materially represented by a Bantu culture group of related and collateral cultural assemblage transforms, characterized by a polythetic assemblage of the same families but differing states of the same specific artefact-types. Politically, the Bantu-speakers have recently been represented by some 600 large tribes, some of which have periodically established transient dominance over local sectors to form impermanent 'nations' within the much larger set of Bantu-speakers.

Altogether, one can appreciate that the Bantu language group encompasses one set of people, the 'Bantu' culture group another somewhat equivalent set, the 'Bantu' technocomplex another much larger grouping, the ethnological 'Bantu' tribes another and the subrace 'Bantu' yet a fifth set (fig. 76). These sets are not identical. However, all of these sets share a large subset of people representing the intersect of all or most of these variously defined sets. It is this polythetically bounded common set with most of the variegated 'Bantu' essentials which we commonly designate 'the Bantu' – unless we are more narrowly concerned with the Bantu-proper, the set of

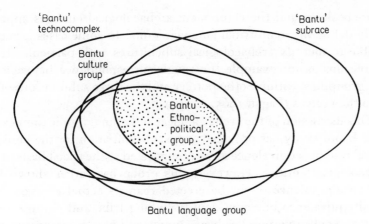

Fig. 76   A purely diagrammatic illustration of the kind of relationship operating and the kind of confusion endemic in the simultaneous use of a single taxonomic indicator 'Bantu' for several different sets of elements. The term could equally well be an archaeological one – the Aurignacian culture, the Aurignacian culture group, the Aurignacian technocomplex.

Bantu-speakers. The source for confusion is quite apparent in the variety of different sets that one can designate 'Bantu', a confusion of intent equally found in such similar terms as 'the Pueblo Indians' or the 'Iroquois Nation'.

Now if we were to take the recent Bantu-speaking entity and rot away its organic components then we must ask ourselves what we might archaeologically detect. There can be little doubt that the archaeologist would rapidly differentiate the technocomplex associated with the hoe agriculture/cattle/savannah/metallurgy strategy but this would include much of non-Bantu Africa. However, within this set it should be possible to detect the time and space transforms of a more specific culture group – a group of cultures not only within the same technocomplex but producing a closely related family of specific pot types, metal types, settlement types and human skeletal types. That this would indeed be possible is borne out by the present identification of five distinctive assemblages, mainly ceramic, which coincide with the principal Bantu languages – Sotho, Nguni, Venda, Lemba, Shangaan-Tonga – groupings that were still producing their characteristic artefact assemblages till recent times (Fagan 1965, p. 161; Schofield 1948). The archaeologist's culture group entity, in this case, roughly but not exactly isolates and identifies the

Bantu-speakers, and the component archaeological cultures approximately define the main tribal language units. In some cases it is even possible to identify archaeological subcultures with particular tribal subdivisions as for example the rough correspondence between the three groupings, within Sotho pottery and the three subdivisions of the Sotho themselves (Fagan 1965, p. 162).

This discussion of the archaeological and ethnographic dimensions of the Bantu entity has provided some substantiation for the kind and general ranking equivalence already suggested as the social basis of our archaeological entities. However, this probe has rather shown how such an equivalence might be erected than its actual erection. The partial equivalence but non-identity linking tribe and culture, tribal group and culture group has been supported but not demonstrated or clarified. Such a clarification can only come about if the material equipment of a large number of primitive tribes has been studied and published in terms of numbers of specific artefact-types and their distribution. One of the few extant studies of this level of adequacy is the series of quite remarkable analyses of Southwestern American Indian tribes, directed by Kroeber between 1930 and 1940 and executed by his pupils and colleagues from Berkeley University. These studies have already been subject to some skilful and enlightening analysis from the anthropological viewpoint but they can also provide us with an archaeological index of great value. To do this adequately would involve an elaborate programme of analysis and synthesis but some idea of the possibilities can be more rapidly extracted (Kroeber, Gifford, Driver, *et al.* 1935–50).

The original aim of these Californian studies was to attempt a record of the total list of cultural traits, reflecting material and social culture, for each of the hundred or so fast disappearing Indian tribes in the area. Most of these 'traits' equate with our artefact or artefact-type entities – including both material and social artefacts, or assemblages of attributes. Indeed, one of the ailments of this kind of treatment in anthropology has been the use of the term 'trait' or 'element' for entities varying from the level of a single action, to a sequence of actions or activity, to a sequence of activities or behaviour, making taxonomic assessment almost impossible. In archaeology we have the use of the terms – attribute, artefact, artefact-type, and assemblage to cover the material aspects of this same range. Consequently, although the original studies designate an 'animal head decoy', a 'circular subterranean house' and 'the rabbit dance' as 'elements' or 'traits' we will regard them as artefacts, artefact-types, or even assemblages of artefacts, respectively. Nevertheless, in these important studies we have an artefact by artefact comparison and analysis of tribes of known social structure, known language groupings and known history – a small but priceless mine of information.

It is impossible to summarize the huge amount of data contained in the Berkeley culture element lists, which eventually embraced tribes from Southern California to the Northwest Coast. However, most of the one hundred or so Californian tribes studied were hunter–fisher–gatherers or simple Pueblo maize-squash-beans farmers. The local terrain grades through parallel zones from the Gulf of California, through the littoral strip, the foothills, and then up into the high Cordillera mountains and the plateaux beyond, whence the rivers arise and run rapidly down to the sea, dissecting the zones with their valley systems. The climatic conditions vary with altitude but for the most part run from arid desert to pleasant Mediterranean conditions, with grassland and light forest in the more fertile river valleys. The area encompasses societies of incredible linguistic diversity making it a particularly suitable area for experimental observations (cf. Melanesia: Terrell 1977). The material equipment of the simple maize farmers is little different from that of their ancient Pueblo and Basketmaker ancestors; that of the hunter–fisher–gatherers is similarly archaic with the emphasis on collecting seeds, berries, acorns and pine-nuts, freshwater fishing, and communal hunting for deer, rabbit, birds, squirrels, bear and antelope – using their only domestic animal, the dog.

The total ascertainable culture of each tribe was recorded under a comprehensive series of headings; each heading covered a set of artefacts which were noted as present or absent (fig. 77). The authors discuss at length the problems of trait-levels and of forming exhaustive, unbiased lists of cultural equipment. Despite all the reservations, one is left convinced of the value and adequacy of the resulting lists as broad outlines. In order to convey their importance for our problems it may prove useful to condense and summarize some of the main points that emerge from these studies and then proceed to take some particular and more detailed examples of groups of tribes in a given area.

It was found that an artefact or element list of 1,000–2,000 artefacts sufficed to code the main cultural manifestations of each of these tribes. Since the tribal assemblages proved to come from a convincingly polythetic aggregate set and tribes shared some artefacts but not

Culture element distributions list

Symbols used in the element list

In the presentation of elements the following symbols are used: +, present; (+), probably present; −, absent; (−), probably absent; S, sometimes present; M, modern; I, imported; ?, inquired about but no satisfactory answer; blank, no inquiry made. M, modern, has been used only where the informant so stated.

Elements	WN	EN	NT	ST	SC	Ci	WM	WS	Hu	Me	Li	LI	OI	SU	Wa	Zu	SA	SI	KP	HP
HUNTING: *Individual (or small group) Hunting*																				
1 Stalking	+	+	+	+	+	+	+	+	+	+	+	+	+	+	+	+	+	+	+	+
2 Deer-mask decoy	+	+	+	+	+	+	+	+	+	+	+	+	−	+	+	+	+	+	+	+
3 Antelope-mask decoy	+	−	+	+	+	+	+	+	+	+	+	+	−	+	−	+	+	−	+	+
4 Buffalo-mask decoy	−	−	+	+	+	+	+	+	+	+	−	+	−	+	−	−	+	+	+	−
5 With hide	+	+	+	−	+	+	+	+	+	+	+	+	−	+	−	−	S	−	−	−
6 With fabric or painted material		−	+	−	+	+	−	M	+	+	−	−	−	+	−	S	S	−	−	−
7 Stick 'legs'		+	+	+	+	+	+	+	+	+	−	+	−	+	−	+	+	+	+	−
8 Bow and arrows as 'legs'	+	+	+	+	+	+	+													
9 Arms painted (antelope hunting)																				
10 Stations on trail	+	+	+	+	+	+	+	+	+	+	+	+	−	+	+	+	+	+	+	+
11 Game calls to decoy	+	+	+	+	+	+	+	+	+	+	+	+	−	+	−	+	+	+	+	+
12 With leaf in mouth	−	+	+	+	+	+					+		−	+	−	+	+	+	−	+
13 With tubular whistle	+	+	+			+														
14 Turkey or quail	+	+	+	+	+	+	+	+	+	+	+	+	−	+	−	+	+	+	−	+
Running down (wearing out):																				
15 Deer	−	+	+	+	+	+	+	+	+	+	+	+	−	+	−	+	+	+	+	+
16 Antelope	+	+	+	+	+	+	−	+	+	−	+	−	−	−	+	+	S	−	−	+
17 Buffalo	−	−	−	+	+	+	−	−	−	−	−	−	−	+	+	+	−	+	+	+
18 Rabbits	+	+	+	+	+	+	+	−	+	+	+	+	−	+	+	+	+	+	−	−
19 Deer	+	+	+	+	+	+	+	+	+	+	+	+	−	+	+	?	+	+	+	−
20 Elk	+	+	−	+	+	+	+	+	+	+	−	−	−	+	+	−	+	+	−	−
21 Bear	−	+	+	+	+	+	+	−	−	−	−	−	−	−	−	−	+	+	−	−
22 Other large game	−	−	−	+	+	+	+	−	−	−	−	−	−	−	−	−	+	+	−	−
23 Rabbits in snow	+	+	+	+	+	+	+	+	+	+	+	+	−	+	+	+	+	+	+	−
24 Quail (wet)	−	−	−	+	+	+	−	−	−	−	−	−	−	−	−	−	−	−	−	−
25 Deadfall, for rodents, etc.		+	+	+	+	S	+	−	+	+	+	−	−	+	+	+	+	+	−	+
26 Medium-sized game	+	+	+	+	+	+	+	+	+	+	+	+	−	+	+	+	+	+	+	+
27 Deer's legs broken by rolling logs		−	−	−	−	+	−	−	−	−	−	−	−	−	−	−	−	−	−	−
28 Trigger-bar trap	+	+	+	+	+	+	+	+	+	+	+	+	−	−	+	+	+	+	+	+
29 Baited trigger	+	+	+	+	+	+	−	−	−	−	+	+	−	−	+	−	+	−	+	+
30 Stone weight	−	−	+	+	+	+	+	−	−	−	+	+	−	−	+	−	+	+	+	+
31 Log	+	+	−	−	−	−	−	−	−	−	+	+	−	−	−	−	−	−	−	−
32 Stone side walls, collapsible	−	−	−	+	+	+	+	−	−	−	−	+	−	−	+	−	+	−	−	−
33 Cage trap	−		−	−	−	−	−	−	−	−	−	−	−	−	−	−	−	−	−	−
34 Pit trap, sprung by watcher	+	+	−			+	+	+	+	+	+	+	+	+	−	+	+	+	−	+
35 Pit trap, sprung by quarry																−		+		+

Fig. 77 Culture element list (fragment for twenty Apache-Pueblo tribes in the New Mexico region; for key to tribal name abbreviations see p. 389, chapter 9, III, example (2). Note the polythetic sharing pattern.

Source: Gifford 1940, p. 5.

others, the total artefact list for groups of tribes is not much greater, closer to 3,000–5,000 artefact-types per multitribal area. A test count showed that out of the 2,000 artefacts characterizing a group of tribes, only a maximum of *c.* 450 artefacts could be expected to survive under advantageous archaeological conditions – the remainder reflecting the intangible aspects concerning sociocultural structures. In this crude count we have the implication that even with optimal excavation and preservation the prehistorian is attempting to pronounce on less than 15 per cent of the basic culture. This observation confirms that it is on the basis of the microvariation of a very small sample of the cultural system that archaeological interpretations are based. This limitation must be squarely faced if archaeological interpretation is to be reliable.

The polythetic nature of the culture content variation is repeatedly and satisfactorily demonstrated in these lists (fig. 77). The variation is characteristically polythetic only in large part, with sometimes up to 2 per cent of simple, functional artefacts shared by all the heterogeneous tribes in one area, the percentage referring to the total artefact list for the group of tribes. Most tribes held 25–50 per cent of the total multitribal artefact list within their own particular polythetic selection. Significantly there is not a single tribe that does not share at least 30 per cent of its specific artefacts with some other tribe within a radius of several hundred miles. Conversely, a tribe can usually be optimally matched with a shared maximum of *c.* 90 per cent of its specific artefact list with a politically, historically, geographically, or linguistically related tribe in the vicinity – amounting to a virtual identity only unrecognized by the organizations of the tribes themselves. The absolute minimum number of artefacts shared by tribes of the same language group appears to be around *c.* 45 per cent but the average shared between language-linked tribes was much higher – *c.* 70 per cent. These crude figures are based on the element list consensus and are mainly intended to convey the complexity and general order of the relationships involved.

The archaeological implications of these figures are rather suggestive. The kind of situation recorded is not unlike the kind of information that one might expect from a well-studied area of Neolithic cultures within a common territory, except that the total number of different specific artefact-types recovered for each culture, the archaeological 100 per cent, is known to represent no more than 15 per cent of types that once existed to outline the culture systems. Given this limitation, the figures suggest that of this sample a background of

30 per cent of each culture list of artefact-types may be shared between assemblages from alien tribes lacking any significant political, ideological or linguistic relationship, given tribes of similar economic systems operating in similar environments. A 30 per cent affinity between cultural assemblages of specific artefact-types may not necessarily reflect any more than a common technocomplex background, accounting for perhaps the 30 per cent of specific types and maybe up to 60 per cent of the artefact-type families overall. However, a level around 70 per cent of shared specific artefact-types seems only to occur between very closely connected tribes, usually linguistically interlinked, and roughly united within an entity equivalent to our archaeological culture. Nevertheless, in exceptional cases some tribes sharing even 70 per cent of their artefact-types in one direction are not tribally or linguistically related but may represent proximate acculturation, in one case reaching 87 per cent of types shared with an 'unrelated' tribal culture. Unrelated politically or linguistically that is, since the 87 per cent behavioural affinity undoubtedly reflects a real 'relationship' which is encompassed and materialized by the archaeological culture but not in the tribal or linguistic sets. This example may serve once again to emphasize that the entities defined by archaeology, if properly defined, are not only less significant than the tribal, liguistic, or historical sets – they are simply different.

Perhaps, on average a 65 per cent linkage best coincides with the linkage between assemblages from tribal clusters. For example, a 60 per cent single linkage in one case clustered all the related tribes in a territory but unfortunately added 20 assemblages of unrelated tribes. Raising the level to 70 per cent linkage, based on matching specific artefact-types, eight tribal assemblages were clustered 'correctly', two assemblages were added 'incorrectly' and six tribal assemblages were not clustered although politically and linguistically affiliated to the group.

The figures outline the importance of a common language grouping as a factor capable of maintaining a residual level of cultural affinity – partly stemming from an interlinked past cultural trajectory, and partly from a continuing capacity for intercommunication. In this respect, the modal range of artefact-types shared by linguistically unrelated tribes was 0–30 per cent but if the tribes are linguistically akin this lower limit is centred around 50–80 per cent. Since it is the lower limit of shared artefact-types that is raised by a common linguistic background, it unfortunately follows that clustering tribal assemblages at the arbitrary 65 per cent level, whilst detecting the groups of tribes sharing common language ties, will also add to them some acculturated neighbouring tribal assemblages of quite different linguistic affiliation which may, on occasion, share up to 87 per cent of the crucial artefacts. These figures provide a clear warning that clustering assemblages in terms of overall affinity, whilst certainly isolating linguistically and tribally affiliated units, will nevertheless include some cultural assemblages of other language and tribal groups.

This discussion brings us back to the familiar situation that such propositions as 'all full La Tène assemblages were made by Celtic speaking tribes' are almost certainly incorrect, even if the total assemblages are properly defined by pottery, metalwork, settlement pattern and so on. What might be said with a fair degree of probability is that 'the majority of the tribes sharing the full La Tène assemblage were Celtic speaking but that, even so, some would belong to other language groups and some Celtic-speakers would possess other material culture'. A simple, one to one identification is impossible now and was impossible even at the time in the ancient past. Consequently, any sweeping general proposition or statement of identity is likely to be incorrect but this need not prevent the careful and skilful isolation of an underlying relationship between linguistic, historical and archaeological entities within the defined limits of a probability proposition.

The more important points of information arising from these complicated relationships might be summarized by saying that if we are clustering cultural assemblages on the basis of the degree of similarity of their specific artefact-type assemblages, then this investigation suggests that:

(1) A great deal depends on the nature of the index or coefficient of similarity used to measure the affinity between artefact assemblages (Doran and Hodson 1975, pp. 139–43).

(2) Up to *c.* 5 per cent of specific elements or artefact-types may be shared by *all* the alien cultural assemblages in a common technocomplex and ecosystem.

(3) Up to *c.* 30 per cent of specific elements or artefact-types may be shared between *some pairs* of assemblages without indicating anything more than a common technocomplex background.

(4) About 65 per cent of shared specific elements or artefact-types seems the best level to cluster cultural assemblages, probably interlinked by a common tribal and linguistic background – although this level will inevitably integrate some exceptions.

(5) All of these observations refer to an archaeological 100 per cent list of artefact-types which we know can only reflect less than c. 15 per cent of the former cultural contents.

Before illustrating some of these points with detailed examples, two kinds of observation can be made from the corpus of Californian material which concern matters vitally important for the prehistorian. The first of these observations registers something about the way in which the set of culture elements are polythetically shared between the settlements and assemblages within the culture area and tribal area (fig. 78). The second observation is complementary to this internal structuring but describes the manner in which sets of elements or types are externally shared between neighbouring tribes over a given area (fig. 79). These observations loosely based upon one hundred or so tribes in the Californian region cannot of course be sweepingly extended outside their frame of reference. In spite of this, the results are so consistent within the area and depend on such wide-spread constraints, that they present the possibility of a regularity of wider significance – to be tested in the light of new data from other areas.

The first kind of observation, registering variation within the culture area, is best illustrated by Gifford and Kroeber's study of the Pomo Indians (Gifford and Kroeber 1937; Kniffen 1939). The Pomo Indians have many tribelets with settlements dispersed with a mean mutual separation of about ten miles between sites. Careful study showed that c. 95 per cent of each Pomo element assemblage was variously shared between adjacent settlements, with 1 per cent of the elements or types being idiosyncratically local in distribution and the remaining 4 per cent of each site assemblage known elsewhere but not used or made outside its main locus. A transact across the culture area of the Pomo, from settlement to settlement, produces an irregularly fluctuating total of elements and types per site – with the total number of elements out of the total Pomo cultural assemblage represented at each site fluctuating slightly, and the actual polythetic selection of specific types at each site being slightly different.

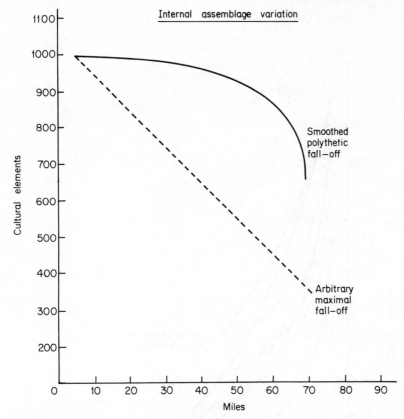

Fig. 78   Cultural assemblage variation *within* a culture area. The solid curve represents a smoothed transect from the centre to a periphery of the territory of the Pomo Indians – moving from nearest settlement to nearest settlement, registering the number of elements shared with central settlements.
Derived from Kniffen 1939; Gifford and Kroeber 1937.

Within the Pomo culture area therefore, the localized settlement assemblages produced a slightly fluctuating but roughly numerically stable individual site content – approximating a horizontal line. However, at the borders of the group, although the element content of each site remains approximately steady, an ever-increasing proportion of each assemblage content is made-up from non-Pomo artefacts whose distributions impinge upon the polythetic Pomo domain (fig. 78). Correspondingly, of course the proportion of Pomo artefacts begins to fall away slightly and then markedly, in the marginal areas –

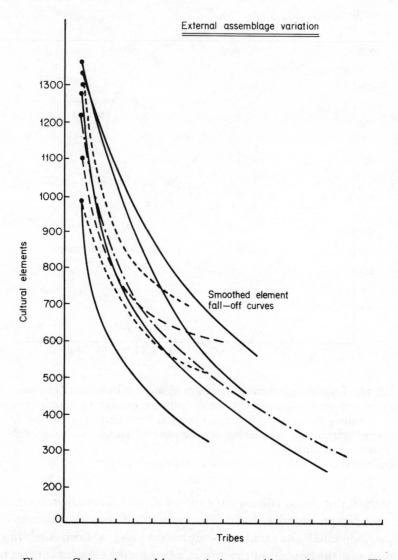

External assemblage variation

Fig. 79 Cultural assemblage variation *outside* a culture area. The set of curves represent smoothed transects from a chosen tribe to increasingly more distant tribes – moving from tribal area to tribal area, registering the number of elements shared with the arbitrarily chosen reference tribal assemblage. Eight separate transects are given here across various Southwestern American Indian tribes. Data from Anthropological Records, Berkeley, 1937–50.

registering the composite gradient fall-off at the edge of the Pomo polythetic distribution pattern (fig. 78). When this marginal fall-off of proportional content has reached the threshold of the cultural level *c*. 65–50 per cent the assemblages can no longer be regarded as ethnologically or archaeologically Pomo in character. The threshold is not quite a simple cline since the gradient suffers a comparatively abrupt descent to new cultural formats, belonging to neighbouring tribes whose margins are in turn saturated with shared Pomo elements. Such cultural divides are usually further marked by a break in the web of settlement pattern (fig. 80).

Let us take the hypothetical version of the Pomo case, in which each settlement fails to share 5 per cent of the artefact-types of its neighbour, and so on down a line of settlements at 10-mile intervals – assuming a continuous and maximal rate of loss at 5 per cent, rather than the demonstrated polythetic oscillation. Then it would require a culture area of 50 miles radius to achieve a drop to 75 per cent similarity between the central and the marginal site assemblages, or a 100 miles radius to achieve a 50 per cent affinity. Since we put our cultural/tribal boundaries at about the 65 per cent level, this would coincide with an area of about 70 miles radius – very close to the actual area of the Pomo tribe (fig. 78). In other words, the hypothetical maximum sustainable cultural area of the Pomo is closely approximated by reality and depends on the degree of linkage and communication between its component settlements. Once again we notice the broad coincidence between these hypothetical culture area limits, from 50 to 100 miles radius and those actually encountered in well-mapped prehistoric areas, under similar conditions.

This sketch of assemblage variation within the tribe or culture brings us logically to the assemblage variation between sets of neighbouring tribes. The method of study is similar to that adopted for the last analysis of internal variation. In this case a great deal more comparative data is available and we shall take several groups of neighbouring Californian tribes and draw arbitrary transects across them, each several hundred miles long and each passing through 10–20 contiguous tribal areas with known element lists. From this data the number of elements, or artefact-types, shared by tribe A with tribe B, tribe A with tribe C and so on, can be expressed down the entire length of the transect. One can then survey the decreasing degree of similarity between a given tribe and other tribes at increasing distances along the transect (fig. 79). The eight examples plotted on the diagram are the smoothed curves based on these transects for various areas and tribal sets. The general consistency of these curves is striking and informative.

Whereas the pattern of internal artefact assemblage variation produced a gentle convex curve, falling-away at the tribal boundary (fig.

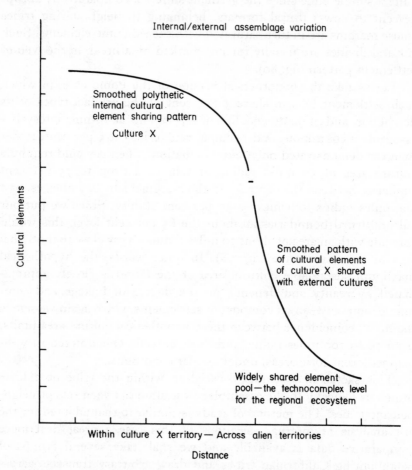

Fig. 80   Cultural assemblage variation within and without a culture area. A hypothetical transect from an arbitrarily selected central cultural assemblage – moving to the border of that culture area and then to increasingly more distant cultural assemblages. The curve plots the decline in assemblage elements shared with the arbitrary reference – it does not indicate an absolute decline in elements per assemblage, merely that a decline in the elements is shared with the reference.

78), the pattern outside the tribe falls extremely steeply from the 65 per cent to the 30 per cent level of shared elements; a fall from the cultural to the technocomplex level, at which it smooths out (fig. 79). The factors behind the combined curves express the contrast between the substantial polythetic affinity of assemblages within the tribe, falling-away slightly in the marginal areas exposed to optimal external diffusion, and then externally an abrupt gradient to a general background-level widely shared by heterogeneous societies sharing a territory with common constraints (fig. 80). This background level reflects a widely shared set of technocomplex elements polythetically dispersed among variegated tribes with similar economies, operating in similar environment and saturated by historical diffusion.

On this tiny sample of studies it can only be said that in several separate areas of the Southwestern United States several transects across different sets of contiguous tribes consistently show a pattern of minutely irregular but broadly exponential element loss beyond the tribal boundaries. Indeed, the ethnic definition of a tribe depends partly upon this external contrast with its own internally maintained pattern – this leads one to suspect that on occasions communities may be rather ambiguously oriented in tribal affiliation and this is in fact the case, allowing a disjunctive or contradictive social ambiguity which is of prime importance in the periodic recasting and repatterning of tribal formats. In any event, the internal and external affinity curves provide an interesting regularity and in the practical examples that follow it is possible to pick out significant departures from these curves which thus acquire a local predictive value in detecting abnormal links and barriers between tribes – sometimes linguistic, sometimes historical and political, and often topographical.

Examples. (1) This example is a sketch of the culture elements or artefacts of the Northwest Californian coast tribes, taken from Driver's comprehensive and detailed study (Anthropological Records, Berkeley, 1:6, 1939). The survey covers sixteen hunting–fishing–gathering tribes, including four pairs of confederate tribes, the whole representing four language groups, twelve languages and some sixteen dialects. The tribes occupy territories along 200 miles of Pacific coastline, half of them with a Northwest Coast culture, the remainder with a Californian Indian culture (fig. 81).

From north to south the tribes run:

Abbreviation	Tribe	Language group	Culture group
To.	Tolowa	Athabascan	Northwest Coast
Chim.	Chimariko	Hokan	Californian Indian
Kar. 1	Upper Karok	Hokan	Northwest Coast
Kar. 2	Lower Karok	Hokan	Northwest Coast
Yur. 1	Yurok (Y1)	Algonkin	Northwest Coast
Yur. 2	Yurok (Y2)	Algonkin	Northwest Coast
Wy.	Wiyot	Algonkin	Californian Indian
Hup. 1	Hupa (H1)	Athabascan	Northwest Coast
Hup. 2	Hupa (H2)	Athabascan	Northwest Coast
Chil.	Chilula	Athabascan	Northwest Coast
VD.	Nongatl	Athabascan	Californian Indian
Mat.	Mattole	Athabascan	Californian Indian
Sin. 1	Sinkyone (S1)	Athabascan	Californian Indian
Sin. 2	Sinkyone (S2)	Athabascan	Californian Indian
Ka.	Kato	Athabascan	Californian Indian
C. Yuk.	Coast Yuki	Yuki	Californian Indian

The first impression of these data is that no one set is identical with any other – the language groups do not exactly equate with the culture groups, and so on. Nevertheless, there is a measure of relationship in that the Northwest Coast culture group speak largely Hokan and Algonkin languages to the north but adopt Athabascan languages in the southern neighbourhood of the Athabascan speaking Californian Indians. One gets the impression that tribes of various language groups have divergently adopted the cultural equipment most suitable for their tribal territory and most widely diffused on their margins.

These data enable us to make three simple experiments which might illuminate the sharing and distribution of elements or artefact-types amongst neighbouring tribes of diverse languages and cultures.

(a) In the first experiment the broadly central tribe of the Yurok (Yur. 1 section) have been taken and the number of Yurok elements found in every other tribal assemblage noted on the map (fig. 81). The Yurok 1 have 1,376 elements in their own assemblage, they share most elements with their confederate tribe Yurok 2 which has 873 elements of Yurok 1 culture, and so on down the map. The contoured map confirms the way in which Yurok 1 elements fall away in an exponential and irregularly radial fashion. Significant distortion noticeably occurs to show surprisingly strong links with the geographically distant but linguistically akin Wiyot tribe, or to emphatically exclude the linguistically, geographically and culturally distant Coast Yuki. In other words the divergences from the idealized exponential and radial model of 'element fall-off' do reflect significant relationships – though these may be of many kinds.

(b) In the second experiment each tribe is connected with a line and a directional arrow to that other tribe with which it shares most elements or artefact-types – thereby linking tribes to other tribes with

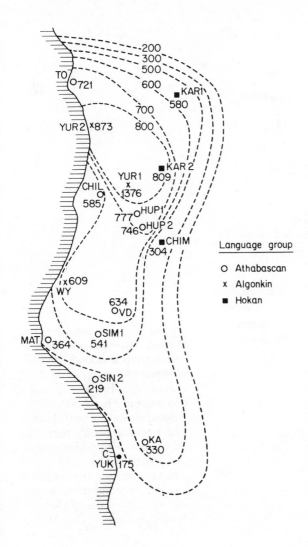

Language group

O Athabascan
x Algonkin
■ Hokan

Fig. 81 The assemblage sharing pattern of elements or artefact-types amongst neighbouring tribes of diverse languages and cultures (a). The map schematically illustrates the number of Yurok tribal elements (YUR. 1; an Algonkin language tribe) shared with neighbouring tribes of varying political, linguistic, and ethnic affiliations. Data from Driver 1939.

the most closely similar social and material culture (fig. 82). Once again language links appear stronger even than simple proximity links – the Algonkin-speakers, are clustered in one group, the Athabascan speakers in two, despite many Athabascan tribes being geographically closer to Algonkin tribes and vice versa. Of particular interest is the extraordinary link between the Tolowa and the Sinkyone 1, both speaking Athabascan but separated by a hundred miles and by ten tribes of two other language-groups. Most of the other surprising clusters reflect that the mountainous inland terrain may effectively

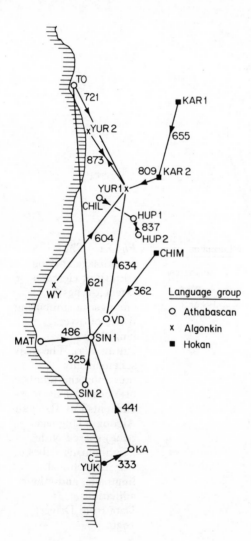

Fig. 82   The assemblage sharing pattern of elements or artefact-types amongst tribes of diverse languages and cultures (b). In this experiment a maximum linkage clustering with lines and arrows connects that other tribe with which every given tribe shares most elements in its assemblage. Area of map and data, as for fig. 81 – 200 miles of the Pacific Northwest Coast.

cut-off and re-orientate otherwise geographically and linguistically close tribes. Clustering tribal assemblages on the basis of linking assemblages with the most elements or types in common does clearly coincide with a reasonable cultural and linguistic grouping – for example the two affinity clusters focusing on the Yurok 1 and Sinkyone 1 tribal assemblages broadly equate with the Northwest Coast and Californian Indian culture groups respectively.

(c) The third experiment takes several representative tribes from this area and plots the exponential but fluctuating fall-off of their assemblage elements beyond their own borders (fig. 83). The transects move from nearest tribe to nearest tribe and graph the number of elements shared with the successively selected neighbours. The nature of the element fall-off beyond the tribal borders is well brought out, with the divergences from the model once again predicting unusual local, linguistic, or topographical ties or barriers. Much more precise and sophisticated analyses of the data are to be found in the original publication (Anthropological Records, Berkeley, 1:6 1939).

(2) As a comparative example we may take the similar study in the same series by Gifford of the Apache-Pueblo tribes (Anthropological

Abbreviations	Tribes	Language group	Culture group
WN	Western Navaho	Navaho	Apache/Navaho
EN	Eastern Navaho	Navaho	Apache/Navaho
NT	North Tonto Apache	Athabascan	Apache/Navaho
ST	South Tonto Apache	Athabascan	Apache/Navaho
SC	San Carlos Apache	Athabascan	Apache/Navaho
CI	Cibecue Apache	Athabascan	Apache/Navaho
WM	White Mt. Apache	Athabascan	Apache/Navaho
WS	Warm Springs Apache	Athabascan	Apache/Navaho
HU	Huachuca Mts. Apache	Athabascan	Apache/Navaho
ME	Mescalero Apache	Athabascan	Apache/Navaho
LI	Lipan	Athabascan	Plains Indian
LL	Llanero Apache	Llanero	Plains Indian
OL	Ollero Apache	Athabascan	Plains Indian
SU	Southern Ute	Llanero	Great Basin
WA	Walpi	Pueblo	Pueblo
ZU	Zuni	Pueblo	Pueblo
SA	Santa Ana	Pueblo	Pueblo
SI	San Ildefonso	Pueblo	Pueblo
KP	Kikimai Papago	Piman	Papago
HP	Huhula Papago	Piman	Papago

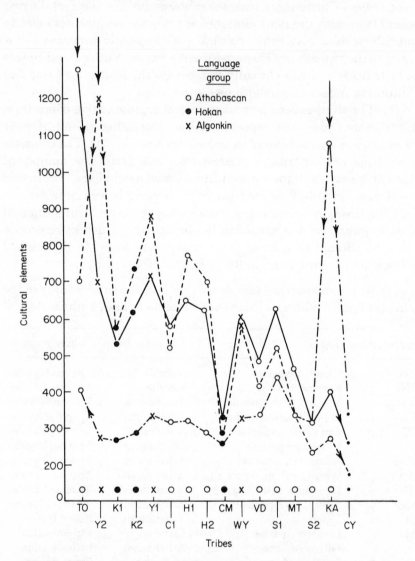

Fig. 83 The assemblage sharing pattern of elements or artefact-types amongst neighbouring tribes of diverse languages and cultures (c). Transects taken from three arbitrary reference tribal assemblages (arrows – Tolowa, Yurok 2, Kato) outwards across adjacent tribes at increasing distances across a single territory (area, figs 81, 82) – illustrating the real but fluctuating exponential fall-off of shared assemblage elements (smoothed in fig. 78).

Records, Berkeley, 4:1, 1940). In this study there are twenty tribes, some hunting–fishing–gathering others maize farmers, with five language groups and twenty languages; the main contrast is between the Pueblo tribes of ancient farming tradition and the Apache/Navaho tribes of a more nomadic character. The tribes are scattered over an inland plateau over a circle of *c.* 300 miles diameter.

Two simple experiments were carried out with these data which illustrate the unusually severe division in language group and culture group of the Apache/Navaho and the Pueblo block – a local case in which complementary technocomplexes have not accelerated convergent development.

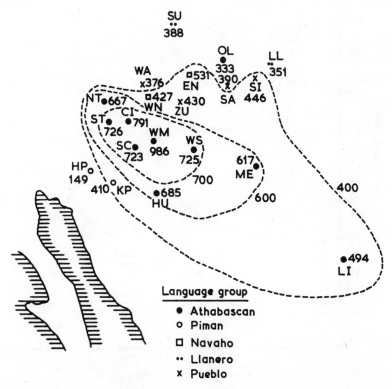

Fig. 84   The assemblage sharing pattern of elements or artefact-types amongst neighbouring tribes of diverse languages and cultures (a). A schematic map of the number of White Mountain Apache (WM) cultural elements shared with neighbouring tribes of varying political, linguistic, and ethnic affiliation – area, Colorado Plateau, USA.
Data from Gifford 1940.

(a) This map (fig. 84) again takes an arbitrary central-tribe – the White Mountain Apache (WM), and contours the assemblages of the remaining tribes according to the number of elements or types that their assemblages share with the referenced assemblage of 986 elements. Again, a broadly radial and exponential fall-off is suggested –

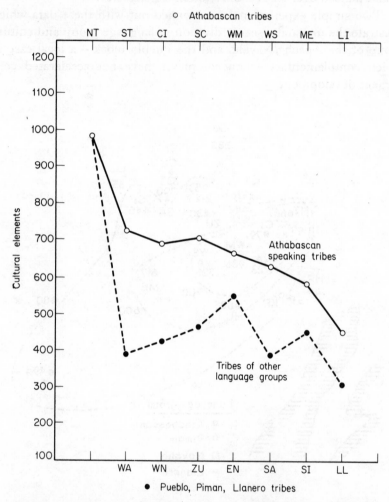

Fig. 85   A comparison between the rate of shared element fall-off along an homogeneous language group transect (Athabascan, North Tonto – Lipan assemblages, a 150-mile transect) and a heterogeneous language group transect (Athabascan, Piman, Navaho, Llanero, Pueblo; from North Tonto – Llanero assemblages, a 100-mile transect). The reference assemblage – North Tonto Apache (NT), area, fig. 84.

with a noticeably gentler gradient amongst the other Apache/Navaho tribes when compared with the culturally and linguistically alien Pueblo to the northeast.

(b) This unusually contrasting linguistic and cultural situation enables us to compare the rate of element fall-off amongst homogeneous and heterogeneous language sets. The North Tonto Apache (NT) at the extreme northwest were taken as a reference point and two transects drawn in different directions, one southeastwards through entirely Athabascan-speakers like the North Tonto themselves, the other transect goes due east, through variegated Piman, Pueblo, Llanero language groups (fig. 85). Each point on the transects plots the number of North Tonto elements shared by that particular tribal assemblage. The superimposition of the two graphs confirms the extra-tribal exponential decline in the two directions but greatly contrasts the severely rapid loss of elements in the alien language area despite the fact that its tribes are closer and the overall distance less. Thus the Athabascan-speaking Lipan tribe, over 150 miles away, still shares more North Tonto elements than does the Zuni Pueblo, only 50 miles away.

(c) Considerably more elaborate comparisons and clusterings of these tribes were prepared by Gifford and Kroeber (1937) using similarity coefficients and matrices (fig. 86).

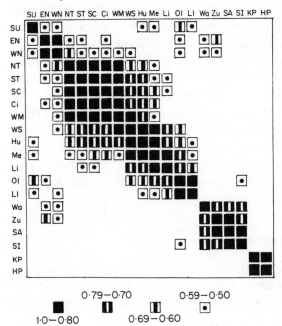

Fig. 86 Sorted matrix of coefficients of resemblance (Q_2) between the culture element assemblages of twenty Apache-Pueblo tribes, key, p. 389, chapter 9, III, example (2); also see fig. 77. This diagram isolates the Athabascan speaking tribes as a cultural group, although two portions of it have acquired considerable Pueblo material culture elements. Source: Gifford 1940, p. 201.

Before we move on to our third line of approach – the historical method – the tentative results of these ethnographic experiments might be restated. In the tiny sample of tribes studied, the evidence supported the view that individual site assemblages within a tribal area express polythetic variations on the total tribal assemblage, with a customary level of 65–95 per cent of shared elements or types linking pairs of assemblages from a single tribe. There does not appear to be any confirmation of the concept of a focal 'tribal hearth' within which all the tribal elements appear and thence decline radially in concentric zones (fig. 67). Beyond the tribal boundaries the tribal artefacts and elements still occur amongst other tribes but these fall-away in an approximately exponential decline in all directions from the tribal margins. Exceptions to this exponential decline do occur, with shared elements even reaching 87 per cent between tribally and linguistically unrelated assemblages in one exceptional case (Voegelin 1942, pp. 250–1). Such exceptions are clearly related to unusually good or bad lines of intercommunication and interconnection introduced by unusual topographic, linguistic, historic, or sociocultural ties and barriers.

In areas of fairly homogeneous environment, containing tribes of similar technology and economy the exponential decline defining each tribal entity tends to fall from the 95–65 per cent level down to a background level from *c.* 30 to 0 per cent of shared elements linking otherwise totally unrelated tribes, connected only by a common technocomplex strategy. All of the tribes studied have been within the same racial group at the American Indian level but, as one might expect in regionally interbreeding communities, subracial populations and characteristics are apparent and do partly coincide with kin-linked entities of tribal group level. The implications of the data make it clear that if element and artefact assemblages are clustered on the basis of overall affinity, then clusters of closely similar assemblages will usually unite tribally and linguistically linked units in a meaningful way although the entity will not exactly equate with either the one component factor or the other.

IV Historical ethnographic evidence

This brings us to our third method of inquiry which seeks to examine archaeological entities wherever and whenever they cross into the tinted light of history. The colouring of historical documentation arises from the inevitable filter effect of the individual author as a literate member of an elite literary subculture writing from the point of view and with the prejudices of his set, about selected matters of interest to that set. Once again it is possible to claim that historical evidence is more complete than the best archaeological evidence, but both have inherent bases and their information is intersecting and different, not merely better or worse. When the historian Bede tells of Jutes settling in Kent he means one thing; when the archaeologist notes the absence of Jutish assemblages from Kent, he is referring to another. To the historian, a group of heterogeneous North Germans politically united and connotatively symbolized by perhaps a single Jutish royal princeling may be designated Jutes. To the archaeologist an intrusive assemblage of Saxon and Frisian artefacts, lacking the key types of the Jutish assemblage, may not be designated an intrusion by Jutes. Many such historical and archaeological contradictions reside in the different frames of reference of the studies concerned – both may be right in their own way. It follows that in the contrast and comparison of archaeological and historical entities it cannot be assumed that the 'truth' is the prerogative of one discipline or the other; nor may it be assumed that the relationship between an archaeological and a historical entity is without complexity.

Historical ethnographic evidence cannot compete with the scope of recent ethnographic data. The historical evidence is too uneven and biased to provide the kind of information studied in the last section. However, selected historical evidence about ancient cultures and tribes may be a more equivalent base for comparison with ancient archaeological entities than that provided by modern ethnography. In the first place ancient documents often refer to the contemporary societies of which we have the archaeological skeleton and as a second consideration we cannot assume that the surviving primitive communities, driven into marginal niches, still provide a good model for prehistoric cultures.

The records of the best ancient historians are therefore invaluable in these respects. Indeed, the very basis of ethnographic identification and classification used by ancient authors was a polythetic and tacit blend of the distinctive attributes of dress and behaviour, peculiar aspects of material culture and social organization and secondarily the linguistic affiliation and tribal names of their barbarian neighbours. This basis closely resembles that underlying archaeological taxa, both integrating the diverse attributes materializing the pattern of many different cultural dimensions. In this respect the set of peoples identified by the ancient authors as recognizably Scythian, Celtic, German or Iberian are in all probability more closely coincident with the set of archaeological assemblages noted as Scythian, Celtic, German or Iberian than either group of sets is with the restricted linguistic sets of the same name. In these respects the tribal units and confederations discussed by the great Classical historians can usefully be sought in the archaeological record – from the hints of the Homeric sagas, to the detail of Herodotus on the Scythians, Tacitus on the Celts and Germans, or Ptolemy and Jordanes on the Balts, Slavs and Goths. These authors document the basic web of tribal Europe which survived and was transformed into the feudal nations of Medieval Europe and is still familiar from the territorial combinations and permutations that form the contries of Western Europe.

Example. As an example of particular significance, this kind of historical approach can be illustrated by the trajectory of the Urnfield culture group of Central Europe and its transitions from obscurity to limelight in the early centuries BC. The developments are registered in an equally fragmentary form in the archaeological and the historical record but they allow the broad comparison and evaluation of the evidence and entities involved.

The Urnfield culture group encompassed a group of related and collateral cultures characterized by assemblages sharing a polythetic range but differing states of the same specific artefact-types. In the archaeological record this assemblage is represented by settlements, pottery, bronze tools and weapons, together with various peculiar funerary and cult apparatus. The pottery assemblages vary upon cylinder-neck and biconical urns, elaborate dishes, plates and jugs and a fine-ware specializing in highly burnished, deliberately metallic fabrics and forms, with a decoration based upon corrugated grooving, circular and semi-circular bosses and turban effects. The large storage jars were also used for cremation burials, usually covered by a dish, and arranged with others in large cemeteries. Cult apparatus accompanying such burials often included theriomorphic models and clay rattles – with wildfowl, cattle and wild boar as favourites.

Differing regional variants on this pottery assemblage are found in the collateral cultures within the Urnfield culture grouping. The settlements included villages of substantial rectangular timber houses, often associated with large hill-top fortifications used as communal refuges for local communities. The economic background of the culture group centred around a mixed farming strategy with extensive ard agriculture and a complementary pastoral aspect with large herds of cattle and pigs. The rich bronze assemblage depended on an industrially mass-produced set of equipment distributed by a set of trade networks radiating from the large-scale exploitation of the Slovakian and Alpine deep copper mines. The characteristic weapons included the revolutionary flange-tanged leaf-shaped slashing sword, cavalry lances, javelins, the long oval shield and an occasional bronze version of the leather cuirass and crested helmet. The tool-kit ranged from plentiful palstaves, socketed axes, sickles, saws and hog-back knives, to dress pins and the sporadic bronze fibula. Beaten bronze sheet was increasingly used for cooking cauldrons and services of cups, buckets, basins and strainers for mixing liquor.

This assemblage made an integrated appearance as the result of the directive correlation of artefacts and elements formerly scattered through Central Europe but especially focused in the Middle Danube region. By the tenth century BC the culture group proper embraced not only the Middle Danube (Hungary) but also a northwestern territory in Poland (Lausitz culture), a southwestern area in the Western Alps (Hallstatt) and an Italian territory pointing into the Mediterranean; an overall distribution pattern resembling a hub with three radial spokes (figs 73b, 87).

By historical and archaeological accident we know far more about the sequence and identity of the Southwestern Urnfield spoke, involving the Alpine Hallstatt culture. In archaeological terms the Hallstatt time-trajectory has been segmented into broadly successive phases running from Hallstatt A down to Hallstatt D. These successive artefact modes map the fluctuating expansion of the assemblage distribution area to the south and the west. In the Hallstatt A phase, the full assemblage was confined to the western Alpine foothills and valleys in a territory including much of Austria. The Hallstatt B and C assemblages extend further southwest, until for a short period in the seventh to sixth centuries BC the advance down the Rhone valley was halted north of the classical city of Massilia – the Urnfield culture there sharing a boundary with an archaic Bronze Age culture which formerly extended along the Riviera coastline. By this time the Hallstatt Urnfield assemblage was re-equipping with iron weapons and tools, mostly copying the older bronze models. Early in the sixth century BC the

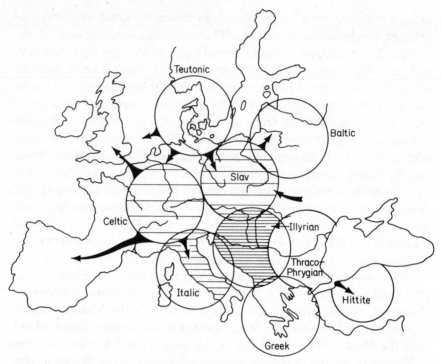

Fig. 87   A tentative map of the central areas of Indo-European languages *c.* 500 BC. The inner, shaded areas relate the emergent development of Celtic, Italic, Slav and Illyrian with the radial distribution of the Urnfield culture group *c.* 1200–700 BC, thus emphasizing the existence of an older, outer ring of non-Urnfield Indo-European areas – Teutonic and Baltic on one hand and Thraco-Phrygian, Greek, and Hittite on another.

Hallstatt assemblage overruns the Riviera coast and Hallstatt C and D assemblages freshly penetrate northern Spain.

The importance of this series of events is that they involve a total cultural assemblage on the move and each move can be roughly dated. Of yet greater significance is the fact that the Greek authors have preserved historic accounts of a series of movements in this region, in this period, and in this general pattern which match the changing archaeological configurations.

The ninth-century tradition of the Homeric poems tells us vaguely that the Riviera coast was then occupied by an indigenous tribe called the Ligyes, or Ligurians, and beyond them to the north lay the Cimmerians. In the seventh century the colonial Greek city of Massilia was established in the land of the Ligurians but in the sixth century Hecateus relates that beyond the Ligurians a powerful tribal confederation called the Celts had appeared. Herodotus, writing a little later, states that the Celts were centred in the Alps around the headwaters of the Danube but including much of Austria and the important town of Nyrax or Noricum, in Styria, also mentioned by Hecateus. Herodotus infers, and the later historian Eratosthenes confirms, that some Celts were occupying northern Spain. The large-scale trade between Massilia and the Celtic tribes on the headwaters of the Rhone and Danube distributed wine and luxury goods to the chieftains in return for organized supplies of raw materials, especially gold, tin, slaves and cereals. This interchange between the Celts and the Greek and Etruscan colonial cities gave rise to the aristocratic patronage of classically derived La Tène art in the fifth century Celtic area; a style which became the subcultural diagnostic of a cultural élite.

In the archaeological and the historical record of this area and period we have two outlines of events covering the ninth to fifth centuries BC. Both outlines coincide to a remarkable degree in pattern and sequence; taken together they produce a stereoscopic picture lacking only fine detail and uniform lighting. The coincidence between the historical and archaeological sets involved is of the kind suggested by recent ethnology and allows a reasonable identification of the Southwestern spoke of the Urnfield culture group, the West Alpine Hallstatt culture, as the material equipment of the Celtic group of tribes. This equation rests on the assumption that other languages were spoken in the group besides Celtic dialects and that many non-Celtic-speaking tribes, like the Ligurians, adopted Celtic material culture. The broad equivalence of some of the Celtic language group with some of the Alpine Urnfield culture and both with the ethnic Celtic tribes, remains satisfactory and convincing.

The ancient authors' identification of neighbouring barbarians focused on two levels of organization – 'peoples' and 'tribes'. The tribal unit was one which still underlay Classical society and one which could still be seen operating as politically autonomous units all around its borders. Over and above these small operational units could be recognized ethnic 'peoples' categorized by the broad intersect of subrace, language group and culture group sets. The historian Ephorus, for example, noted four major barbarian 'peoples' in the fourth century BC – the Celts, Scythians, Persians and Libyans.

(a) Celt (Avignon Museum)

(b) German (Marcus Agrippa's Basilica Neptuni, Rome)

(c) Scythian (Kul Oba vase)

(d) Dacian (Trajan's Column, Rome)

Fig. 88

Because these ancient identifications are ethnic and not purely linguistic the entities discerned equate quite well with archaeological assemblages with distinctive art styles, weapons, artefacts, and styles of dress. Weapons and dress especially impressed the ancient historians as characterizing and enshrining the essential differences between 'peoples'. Their perceptive and fortunate observation is supported by recent ethnographic situations, for example the identification of the various Red Indian tribes can be carried to a fine level purely on the basis of modal and idiosyncratic features of clothing (figs 88, 89). On this convenient but rough equivalence in the basis of ancient ethnic and archaeological taxa we may broadly equate the ancients' 'peoples' with culture groups or larger entities and the 'tribes' with archaeological cultures or smaller entities. It is still possible, after all, to

Fig. 89   Modal variations in tribal dress patterns among the Indians of the Western United States.
Source: Wissler 1923, p. 54.

distinguish a material culture group distinctively expressing Ephorus's – Celts, Scythians, Persians and Libyans.

We have momentarily strayed from the problem of the Urnfield culture group to study one of its three radial spokes – the Southwestern Celtic expansion. What do we know about the historical and linguistic identities of the other sections, the Central European Urnfields, the Northwestern Urnfields and the Italian Urnfields? These areas shared collateral developments of the same general Central European Urnfield assemblage. Furthermore, the movements which took the Urnfield cultures into France, Italy and Poland represent the last large-scale movements of total cultural assemblages before the record of Classical history scans the barbarian horizons and records its configurations. Surely, if the Celtic ethnic group makes such an impressive impact on the archaeological record, then something of the same order should correlate with the other Urnfield entities, of a similar size and dimension?

The Northwestern or Lausitz Urnfield group was connected with the Central European area continuously over a long period of prehistory – the formation of the Lausitz culture reflects more of a repatterning and reorientation than the other, later and more abrupt radial expansions. Unfortunately the area of the Lausitz Urnfields only emerges into history with the works of Tacitus in the first century AD. Nevertheless, Tacitus records that the lower Vistula valley, within the Lausitz territory, was in his time occupied by two tribal confederations, the Venedi and the Lugii – these are noted as resembling the Germans but differing from them in physical characteristics and in culture. The Venedi survived into early medieval Europe and are specifically identified by the Gothic author Jordanes as having split-up into the Antae and Sclavs – both historical Slav tribes, the latter naming the whole group. The Lugii, on the southern Vistula, was a confederation embracing the tribes of the Harii, Helvecones, Manimi, Helisii and Naharvali, according to Tacitus. These tribes also survived in the same general area, under scarcely changed names, until the tenth century AD at which time they are all Slav speaking. The conclusion would seem to be that the Venedi and Lugii tribes of the first century AD, occupying the lower Vistula basin, were ethnically Slavs. Therefore if the last preceding and surviving cultural assemblage tradition to move into this area was that of the Lausitz Urnfields, then this radial aspect of the Urnfield culture group was probably largely composed of Slav tribes and their ancestors (Jaźdżewski 1949).

Similar arguments seem unavoidably to connect the complex and lengthy Urnfield infiltration of Italy with the distribution of the historic Italic-speaking tribes; the last large-scale ethnic movement detectable in the peninsula before written history. The Central European area of the Urnfield culture group similarly emerges into Classical history as the area of the Thracian and Illyrian tribes.

Now, the Celtic, Slav, Italic and Illyrian languages are all part of the greater Indo-European language group, they are all fairly closely allied one to another. Consequently, it appears probable that the three main Urnfield cultures took the proto-Celtic, proto-Slav, and proto-Italic languages into their recent homelands. An additional implication is that western Celtic is the most recent language to detach itself, Italic the next, and Slav the earliest and most closely linked to the archaic Illyrian languages. This tentative identification has important corollaries.

If we look at a backdated linguistic map of Europe and accept the broad identification made above, we find that at least two prominent Indo-European languages are not dealt with in the Urnfield theory (fig. 87). These are the Teutonic group centred on Germany and Scandinavia and the Balt group centred on the Eastern Baltic. Now it is precisely in both of these closely related areas, in the East and West Baltic respectively, that archaeology records a surprisingly continuous and uninterrupted cultural and religious development throughout the Bronze Age and into the early Iron Age. In both areas, after a Middle Neolithic integration of Corded Ware/Battle-Axe and TRB culture groups an homogeneous local Late Neolithic tradition survives in essence until the Iron Age. We have therefore the suggestion that some of the Indo-European languages of Europe go back at least as far as the Middle Neolithic *c.* 2500 BC and involve the Corded Ware/Battle-Axe and TRB culture groups, and yet others – including the Celtic, Italic, Slav, Illyrian groups date from Late Bronze Age contexts *c.* 900 BC. Now, since the intervening phases of the European Early and Middle Bronze Age, *c.* 2000–1200 BC, contain numbers of cultural transforms from the TRB and Corded Ware culture groups, as well as proto-Urnfield cultures – we have the implication that the Indo-European language group has a long and complicated ancestry in Europe – going back into Neolithic cultures at least, with complex reticulated ramifications. A simple equation between the Corded Ware/Battle-Axe culture group and the Indo-European language group thus appears predictably impracticable, although few would deny the probability of that culture group playing some component role.

This section and its example may help to highlight some of the ways in which historical ethnic entities and archaeological entities are connected. The first point of importance is that archaeological data and its entities are not so much less accurate or less informative than historical data and entities, as differently focused. Artefacts provide different information and bias as behavioural documents to those provided by written documents. The difficulty of equating archaeological and historical entities resides in this difference; no simple or exact equivalence is possible but correlation does exist within limits. In this respect we have noted, for example, that the 'peoples' of the Classical historians usually broadly equate with the intersect of language group, culture group and subrace sets, whilst the smaller 'tribal' entities concern individual and specific language, culture and kinship sets.

Perhaps the final lessons of this section are the classificatory difficulties which arise in a time-trajectory in which entities may move from rank to rank and back again. The Celtic peoples first appear as an ethnic group of cultural status on the Middle Danube and Alpine borders of the Urnfield culture group, a group of tribes with a specific cultural assemblage and probably a specific group of dialects. In the course of time the culture expands into a large culture with regional cultures and then eventually becomes a culture group in its own right, with component cultures; linguistic development and diversification must accompany these developments but will not be a simple function of them, either in space or time distribution. By the first century BC the Celtic group has escalated to at least culture group status, with component cultures from Ireland to Spain and from France to Anatolia, with a comparable linguistic diversity. The same may be said of the Slavs and of the Scyths and many other major 'peoples'. Former populations are absorbed or acculturated and inject some of their attributes into the continuing system – often inessential attributes which will later play a crucial catalytic role in emergent repatterning. One is made aware of the rhythmical pulsating pattern of the repeated cycles of cultural 'birth', 'growth', expansion into culture groups, regional divergence, repatterning and realignment or 'death'; the archaeological entities are not static but move through many states and levels of organization.

Notes

The archaeological cultural assemblage is central to the discussion in this chapter and it has been a feature of British archaeology within the last decade that entities such as this and the culture group have been in declining usage. After Childe's (1929) pioneering systematization of European prehistory in which the 'culture' was the organizing unit of analysis, culture definition became one of the main foci of archaeological activity in the period up to the 1950s. Once defined in time and space, cultural similarities were interpreted in terms of their degree of social interaction: movement of people, diffusion and 'influences' were the processes most commonly suggested as being behind intercultural similarities. But now there are vociferous critics of this approach and it seems useful to summarize their positions, so that the arguments developed through chapters 6–9 can be put into perspective.

Daniel (1971, p. 149) has argued that the culture was merely a conceptual device for grouping together sites and artefacts in the absence of methods of independent absolute dating. With the explosion of dating methods in archaeology the culture concept has become redundant and should be abandoned in favour of description of 'the life and times of prehistoric people'. This 'descriptive' aim is open to vigorous debate but of more relevance here is the fact that Daniel gives insufficient attention to the *spatial* aspect of culture-definition: are there recognizable spatial patterns in the distribution of material culture which justify the creation of 'cultures' (as pursued in chapter 6) and their equation with human social groups (as argued in this chapter)?

One point of view here is that 'cultures' defined by material culture obscure the recognition of important variability in human behaviour. The ethnographic observations of Donald Thomson, published in the late 1930s (Thomson 1939), that the same group of Australian hunter–gatherers would use totally different material culture assemblages at different seasons of the year, have been stressed by the late Eric Higgs and his pupils at Cambridge (e.g. Higgs 1975, p. 77). The implication of these observations was that the archaeologist would identify four separate cultural assemblages from artefactual differences which simply reflected seasonal subsistence strategies. If this was the case with Thompson's Wik Monkan aborigines, could it not also be the case with other areas of the world where the archaeologist had distinguished different 'cultures'? Furthermore if the material culture assemblages from two or more sites were identical, did it follow necessarily that their subsistence practices were also similiar? Behind the monolithic façade of the 'culture' it was realized that a great range of economic variability might lie concealed and awaiting archaeological analysis (Higgs 1972, 1975).

A further source of variability lies in the increasing recognition of exchanged or traded items in the archaeological record. This has been a feature of research employing characterization studies of raw materials, using such methods as neutron activation analysis and optical emission spectroscopy (e.g. examples in Brothwell and Higgs 1969). In addition to studies of such materials as flint, igneous stone, obsidian and metal, the analysis of prehistoric pottery has been very thought-provoking. The often unwritten assumption that pottery was produced, used and discarded within the same social grouping, *in spite of* many ethnographic examples to the contrary, was widespread within European prehistoric studies. As pottery was also the most frequent artefact present on later prehistoric sites, it is not surprising that it became an important diagnostic feature in the definition of 'cultures'. Close similarities in forms, fabrics and particularly decoration were thought to represent the tradition of a common social group. The effect of trading and marketing patterns on British medieval pottery distributions (e.g. the wider distribution of fine wares compared with more localized everyday 'utility' wares) was stressed fifteen years ago by Jope (1963). But it was not until Peacock's petrological analysis of classes of Iron Age pottery in the Here-fordshire–Cotswold region of Western England that it was fully realized that 'study of the origins of (pottery) . . . styles . . . should lead to a greater under-standing of the cultural heritage or influences affecting the potters *and not necessarily the pot users*' (1968, p. 425, my emphasis).

With the recognition by British and European archaeologists of variability resulting from subsistence behaviour and trading or exchange patterns, there appeared an increasing reluctance to define and use 'cultures'. Cunliffe (1974), for example, preferred to define 'style zones' in the British Iron Age and Clark (1975) substituted 'social' and 'techno-' territories for 'cultures' in studying the late- and early post-glacial settlement of Scandinavia. There was also a revival of interest in ethnographic studies of trade, stimulated in Britain by Grahame Clark (1965). Spatial patterns in material culture were still recognized by archaeologists, but the pertinent question now was whether, they should be equated *necessarily* with social groups.

On an analytical level recent studies of individual artefact distribution patterns have used quantitative methods (e.g. regression and trend surface analyses) to define 'fall-off' curves of decreasing interaction with distance between communities (Hodder and Orton 1976, Hodder 1977a). The often implicit recognition of decreasing spatial similarity in artefact patterns has been the basis of 'culture' definition, but Hodder's work has demonstrated the parts played by communication (e.g. water, roads, topography), social and economic value (e.g. compare the distributions of low demand mosaic pro-duction centres and high demand roofing-tile kilns in Roman Britain), competing service centres (e.g. the results of the use of gravity models on the distributions of late Roman Oxford and New Forest pottery or British Neoli-thic stone axes) and settlement pattern density. It is further noted that individual artefact-types are not 'culturally-bound' – examples such as British Neolithic stone axes and French Grand Pressigny flint are known to be associated with more than one cultural assemblage. But if all these factors are admitted as affecting the precise forms of fall-off distribution patterns which we can observe in the archaeological record, what part if any did social and cultural factors play? In chapter 6 David Clarke argues that 'the number of specific types shared with other individual cultures will be small and the mutual boundaries fairly well defined by a band of exponential gradients marking the zones of 'most rapid fall-off' for the cultural artefacts in the boundary assemblages ... The central area or irregular plateau in which the mutual affinity between the polythetic assemblages remains high and roughly constant will then define the essential archaeological 'culture area' (above p. 266). This line of argument is supported by the ethnographic studies presented in chapter 9. The general point relating plateaux and distribution discontinuities to the existence of territoriality has been made by Soja (1971), but Hodder and Orton (1976, pp. 196–7) advocate caution in the automatic transfer of this to the interpretation of archaeological distribution patterns: their analysis of the distribution of coins of two pre-Roman tribes in Britain clearly does not reveal the predicted territorial pattern.

When turning to the associations between artefact distribution patterns, it is now argued that archaeologists should employ tests of association to distinguish between random and non-random patterns (Hodder and Orton 1976, p. 200) otherwise it may well be that 'cultures' could be defined on the basis of purely random 'association groups'. When association tests are applied to material of the North German Early Bronze Age and the Carpathian Basin Middle Bronze Age (op. cit., pp. 211–23), there emerges a range of distributions from localized groups based on ornament types to more widespread patterns formed by swords and axes. It is suggested that the localized ornaments reflect 'symbols of identity' (Hodder 1977a, p. 319) occurring in areas of higher settlement density, whilst swords and axes are in a much lower level of local demand and 'may relate to interaction at a high level in the social hierarchy' (Hodder and Orton op. cit., p. 221).

This distinction between distribution patterns and their significance in terms of human interaction has been pursued further by Hodder (1977b) in his work among three tribes in the Baringo district of West Kenya. Between two tribes, the Tugen and Njemps, there are clear distinctions in traits such as personal dress and compound plans and construction and there is little intertribal movement of traits. In the archaeological record this material culture evidence would be interpreted in terms of a *lack* of interaction between the two tribes. In actual fact there is well-documented data on contact *across* the tribal boundaries (e.g. markets, reciprocal exchange etc.). This observation runs contrary to one of the basic assumptions implicit in the use of the 'culture' concept: the degree of interaction between communities or social groups is *not* necessarily directly reflected in material culture patterns (cf. Binford 1972).

On the other hand Hodder notes that the methods of assemblage and culture definition presented in *Analytical Archaeology* would be capable of distinguishing the three tribes and assessing which are more closely interrelated. Here the archaeologist would be distinguishing artefactual patterns reflecting 'tribal identity', as Clarke does with the ethnographic data from

North America in this chapter. But three problems arise. Firstly there is the thorny question of the 'tribe' itself – how can one adequately define its spatial limits (Hodder 1977a, pp. 313–14)? Secondly, how can one distinguish fall-off patterns in artefact distribution which result from cultural diffusion from those which reflect declining interaction with distance from a central area (op. cit., pp. 314–15)? Thirdly many different 'cultures' could be defined in the Baringo district of West Kenya on the basis of the traits *selected* or *available* for study (i.e. on the basis of differential preservation and sample size).

What then are the main implications of this recent research for the 'culture' concept and its social interpretation as presented in chapters 6 and 9? Clearly there must be a more quantitative approach to the analysis of artefact distribution patterns, whether considered individually or in association with each other. There is a current feeling that the 'all-in' methods of 'culture' definition as proposed by Childe (1929) and developed by Clarke in this volume have left the archaeologist with rather coarse entities whose detailed structure needs closer examination – for example what *different* distribution patterns occur *within* cultural entities? Even when distribution patterns (e.g. localized vs. widespread types) and fall-off curves have been quantified, the archaeologist is still left with the problem of identifying the *processes* which gave rise to these patterns. Here we have to look through the filter imposed on us by the cultural and non-cultural factors that *distort* patterning in the archaeological record (Schiffer 1976) and recognize that the archaeologist may still be able to discern some signs of social groupings in material cultural patterns. But note must be taken of the other factors (e.g. cultural diffusion) which could give rise to similar or identical patterns. It is this linkage between *pattern* and *process* that is at the very heart of any attempt to interpret spatial patterning in material culture.

10 Entities and processes and procedure

Entitation is more important than quantitation,
'Intelligence, Information and Education',
Science, 148, pp. 762–5
DEAN R. W. GERARD 1965

1 Introduction

The material artefacts produced by hominid societies simultaneously fulfil a number of different roles – some consciously appreciated by their manufacturers but others functioning by unforeseen inter-actions. Material culture patterns are in the first place material behaviour patterns – patterns of socially acquired actions and activities condensed in solid form. Every artefact and assemblage expresses in its highly specialized structuring a particular set of behaviour direc-tively correlated towards its manufacture, in addition to another set of behaviour conveyed by the usage pattern anticipated in the design (fig. 26).

The obvious role of material artefacts, apart from their mani-festation of acquired behaviour, embraces material culture as an elaborate means of environmental regulation and control (figs 6, 9, 11). An increasingly elaborate material culture provides an increasingly powerful regulation and control mechanism networked within a particular sociocultural system. The greater the variety in the material culture, the more flexible may be the sociocultural strategy in blocking the destructive variety from the environment and the capacity to shield the system's essential format, enhancing the degree of system continuity. In this vital respect the material culture helps to sustain and insulate the sociocultural system and preserve the asset most precious to its generators – its continuity (figs 24, 25).

The least appreciated and most subtle role of material artefacts is their capacity for information communication, a symbolic and evocative role impinging on the psychological subsystem of the society itself in a continuous feedback loop. As an information communication system material culture is ancillary to all the other sociocultural communication techniques and like all such systems it has its own characteristics (chapter 3, II). Artefacts and assemblages constitute real messages because by definition they express consistently recurrent and ordered selections of attributes/artefacts from a limited set of possible components known to the agents concerned.

Of course other means of communication are far more important to society than material culture. Speech, writing, wireless, telephone and television compete and supplement individual gestures and social artefacts like ceremonies, customs, traditions, rituals and so on – all jostling one another in the continuing communication revolution. However, it is this continuous interchange of information of very many kinds, by numbers of very different channels each with varying characteristics, which jointly ensures the adequate transmission of an almost 'error-free' cultural message, despite the noise. Shannon's theorem shows that if the number of channels is greater than the equivocation then it is possible to get error-free transmission and sociocultural systems are networks with almost an infinity of such intercommunicating channels (Ashby 1956, p. 190).

The importance of the overall cultural message getting through from one generation to the next is that it expresses the model of the sociocultural survival system itself which, if received, is then capable of unfolding and generating the structure and transformations characterizing that system. The multiple channels consequently ensure the adequate communication of this message which is vital to sociocultural continuity but the inevitable ambiguity and distortion of the message fed-back into the younger generation allows an inevitable range for selective interpretation and progressive developmental change on that basis. Material culture is therefore just one channel for such communications and merely as one aspect of the whole sociocultural information system it too displays fluctuating attributes and assemblages and the selective development of successive formats in successive phases.

The role of material culture as an information communication system is particularly relevant to the task of the archaeologist. For, although the ancient societies are long since dead, the continuing existence of their material culture still conveys the weak coded messages which were intended for the culture's generators but which may yet be interpreted by us. The difficulty arises from the fragmentary nature of the surviving message, the obscurity of the material channel of its transmission and the complexity of the code. The archaeologist must try to separate the message from the noise, with especial care to minimize the interference from the variety inherent in his own acquired sociocultural receiving apparatus (fig. 111). One line of approach in the analysis of such coded information is to rely on the fundamental difference between the message variety and noise variety. Otherwise wholly similar, the message variety differs from the noise in having been structured or selectively ordered into a covarying and correlated set. Therefore, the archaeologist for a start can try to differentiate between the key variety amongst the attributes, artefacts and assemblages and the essential and inessential variety – the key variety being marked by its constraint and the consequent regularity of its joint trends and covarying intercorrelation patterns (chapter 2, 1).

The 'significant' system attribute and artefact variety trends and covaries in space and in time, whilst the 'inessential' attributes and artefacts vary irregularly, or not at all. Effectively, the message isolated by this approach should help differentiate those attributes and types which the generators were especially interested in controlling. The procedure, therefore, is to distinguish in the archaeological sample the controlled attributes and types from the uncontrolled or irregular aspects. Success in this respect then provides the archaeologist with the fragmentary and coded message 'cleansed' of its noise. The interpretation of this treated sample still poses the formidable problems of ascertaining the effect of the archaeological sampling as well as the necessity of attuning one's mind to receive the message in a way congruent with its transmission.

To summarize, it must be emphasized that material culture is but the network of a single dimension within a whole sociocultural behavioural information system and that no single aspect can be treated with reality alone or as a discrete part. Some part of the 'behaviour' of artefacts and assemblages expresses a peculiar manifestation of the inherent general behaviour characteristics of very complex sociocultural system entities. The material culture studied by the archaeologist may therefore be regarded as a material expression once fulfilling three main roles as:

(i) a communication channel of a wider behavioural information system;

(ii) a functional implementation of a particular material behaviour pattern;

(iii) a sociocultural system regulation and control subsystem.

The overwhelming aim of all three roles of material culture and indeed of all sociocultural variety is toward system continuity, with the great advantages which that constraint endows.

11   Entities

The opening chapter of this work suggested that a model or structured set of hypotheses gave birth to analytical archaeology with the 'three ages' scheme of Thomsen, in 1819. Such models remain the most powerful form of conceptual expression in archaeology today and hopeful signs suggest that the discipline is slowly moving away from iconic and simple analogue models towards symbolic models of greater scope and predictive power (chapter 1, VI; Clarke 1972). This movement gains momentum from the continuous and increasingly more powerful attempts to match archaeological perceptual experience with ever more accurate conceptual models. As an elementary step in the same direction, three low-level but general models were proposed as potentially useful in developing archaeological theory (chapter 1, VI):

(i) a model for archaeological *entities* – the hierarchical and polythetic model (figs 3, 49);

(ii) a model for archaeological *processes* – the general dynamic system model (fig. 11);

(iii) a model for archaeological *procedure* – the three sphere feedback model (fig. 2).

These three models have formed the frame of discussion throughout the preceding chapters and now we can summarize the main outcome from these deliberations under the same three models and headings – entities, processes, and procedure.

The model adopted for archaeological entities in this study has been a nested hierarchical model of individually polythetic entities arranged in ascending order of system complexity; where complexity is taken to register the degree of internal networking (figs 3, 49). Such an organization of archaeological data is a purely arbitrary conception adopted because: – it is concise – it suits polythetic entities – archaeological affinity distributions are appropriate to such a structuring – the field of inquiry is by this means broken down into successively smaller areas of uncertainty in an empirical manner – and as a 'natural' system it possesses a predictive capacity. Nevertheless, the fact that such a model is an arbitrary organization of data which in reality exist in dimensions of greater complexity should not be obscured. There are other kinds of model which might have been and could be adopted for the same data – branching dichotomous models or multidimensional models to name but two alternatives (Cherry 1957, pp. 227–8). Indeed, it has become increasingly clear in the course of discussion that archaeological entities do not really exist in simple hierarchical levels and that many of the most tantalizing problems are false problems arising from a model which is not entirely adequate. The problem of cross-correlating the 'hierarchical' sets of the social, cultural, linguistic and racial population dimensions is a case in point (fig. 75). The evidence rather more closely approximates with a continuous multidimensional system of elaborately networked multistate elements and the preceding chapters have sporadically attempted to outline alternative constellation models on these vague lines (figs 50, 51, 53, 54, 65, 66).

The hierarchical aspect of the model must therefore be taken as a temporarily acceptable expedient with some dangerous properties. In all probability a variety of more subtle multidimensional models will be developed for future archaeological classification. Similarly, we have repeatedly pointed out that although the polythetic interpretation is immensely more realistic and powerful than the old tacit monothetic models, the fit is still only approximate. In the first place most archaeological populations are not fully polythetic and in a second respect it is to be noted that there are very many different categories of polythetic relationship – varying in both numbers of elements and the range and nature of their 'sharing' pattern. It is to be expected that various categories of polythetic structure will variously and with varying accuracy model different archaeological entities. The nested hierarchical model of polythetic entities is to be taken only as a contemporary approximation.

Archaeological entities exist because there once existed networks of links between people which 'accidentally' generated links between their artefacts (fig. 48). These archaeological entities are for the most part compounded of many smaller entities clustered in certain ways and in this respect they are all 'populations'. Earlier discussion established that some of the most general regularities in archaeological taxa of all levels arise from this constraint and its consequences (chapter 4, I):

(1) The population entity is a unit system of components coupled in some environmental context such that the 'behaviour' of the whole is more complex than that of the elements and the successive states of the whole system influences the successive states of the parts.

(2) The population may therefore possess 'emergent' characteristics which are not found in its individual components.

(3) The population has a definite structure and composition, stipulated for any given moment but changing with space and time.

(4) The population entity is ontogenetic; it may exhibit a 'life cycle'
   (i) As the quantitative growth and oscillation in numbers of component elements;
   (ii) As the quantitative growth and oscillation in numbers of whole representative entities;
   (iii) As the qualitative change and oscillation of the system as a structured system.

(5) The population has a 'heredity' – an antecedent trajectory relating the population as a transform to other earlier populations.

(6) The population has the property of the numerical distribution of its elements in space, time and states. The clustering, central tendency, deviation, range and other statistical measures help define this important quality.

Technocomplexes, culture groups, cultures, assemblages, artefact-types and similar archaeological entities are all population systems, with the consequent population properties.

If we think of archaeological entities in terms of populations, then there are basically only two categories of archaeological variety and three levels of organization. All of the higher archaeological entities are populations of artefact-types and the lower entities are populations of attributes. Within these two categories of variety three broad levels of organization can be detected, based upon the necessary degree of affinity defining the items in the entity levels – varying from the highest degree of mutual similarity, through medium affinity, down to low affinity. Indeed, it was pointed out that the symmetry of the archaeological terminology underlined the symmetry of the affinity syntax relating these parallel entities (chapter 6, II):

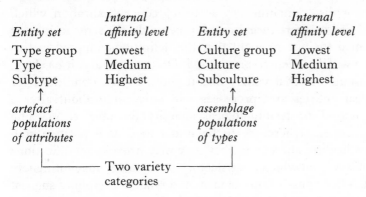

Entity set	Internal affinity level	Entity set	Internal affinity level
Type group	Lowest	Culture group	Lowest
Type	Medium	Culture	Medium
Subtype	Highest	Subculture	Highest
↑		↑	
artefact populations of attributes		*assemblage populations of types*	

— Two variety categories —

(In this context type is artefact-type, culture is cultural assemblage and subculture here represents local or regional subcultures.)

The general impression emerges that archaeological entities are categories of complex systems represented by populations of elements, generated by related categories of social units. The systems have a polythetic structure based on the constrained variation of sociocultural and environmental variety, a structure which is reflected in the distribution of elements within the entity categories and in geographic space (figs 67, 72). The time and space 'behaviour' of the complex systems representing archaeological entities can be separated into two aspects. One aspect reflects the regularities inherent in a particular system as a member of a class of similar systems with basically similar structures and limited by the constraints of that structure and in addition by similar contextual constraints. The other aspect of entity 'behaviour' reflects the idiosyncrasies arising from the particular and unique values and states of the elements in a specific system – which give rise to the peculiar behaviour of the particular entity within the constrained set of possible behaviours. One purpose of this study as a whole has been to try and isolate the 'inherent' regularities that might be expected from the various categories of archaeological entity systems in order that the unique and peculiar qualities of particular cases might be the more strongly emphasized. It may be argued that the time and space regularities isolated in this work are too general to be used in particular instances but in fact the isolation and separation of these very general regularities provides the best means of isolating and defining the residual specific peculiarities of given situations.

The nested hierarchical model of polythetic entities provides a convenient representation of the relationships governing archaeological entities, whilst remaining an arbitrary conceptualization which may be replaced by more recent developments. In the same fashion, it is not assumed for one moment that the definitions adopted in this work will be widely accepted or adopted. On the contrary, it has been assumed throughout that widely useful and accepted definitions for archaeological entities and processes will only come about after a prolonged period of terminological anarchy (chapter 1, V). The definitions suggested here are to be understood as a positive step towards this healthy anarchy in that they may provoke modifications and alternatives from which a satisfactory terminology may ultimately be selected. The history of the sciences and related disciplines suggest that such a period of clashing views and concepts is to be infinitely preferred to the prevailing complacency within archaeology.

III **Processes**

The major part of this book has been devoted to the discussion and definition of archaeological entities, or rather entity taxa, in the belief that the future of archaeology depends upon the further clarification of its concepts in order that powerful, modern techniques may be employed to the utmost capacity of their potential. These archaeological entities display constant change in a variety of dimensions and the operating vectors made apparent by these successive changes in state are usually called 'processes'. The first chapter suggested that one of the most useful models for archaeological processes of all levels would be a general dynamic system model and subsequently an attempt was made to develop such a model in terms of a system structure and a set of broad postulates about its inherent 'behaviour' (chapter 2, II, fig. 11, postulates 1–16).

The general dynamic system model provides a framework against which the particular changes of particular processes upon specific archaeological entities can be studied by postulating and separating the inherent general changes from the informative and unique circumstance changes, providing in addition a set of appropriate analytical procedures (chapter 2, III, fig. 12).

All archaeological entities are kinds of system and changing entities are dynamic systems. Since we are distinguishing archaeological entities or systems of varying levels of organization and complexity we should expect each kind of entity to have differing and appropriate kinds of process which may act upon them. We should not expect the processes that operate upon cultures or culture groups to be the same as those that operate upon artefact attributes, although since the former entities are compounds of the latter elements we might expect the processes appropriate to higher entities to integrate the simpler processes as well. Each level of the hierarchy of archaeological taxa has appropriate categories of processes which are relevant to that particular kind of entity. One of the purposes of the hierarchical classification is that the correct allocation of a particular archaeological entity to a particular rank should predict the appropriate category of processes which might be expected to operate upon the entity – providing a predictively useful classification.

Perhaps one useful initial step would be to distinguish three broad categories of 'general processes' which operate upon most sociocultural entities, with differing effects according to the system, the complexity of the entity and its levels of variety:

(1) Entity ontogeny
(2) Entity migration
(3) Entity interaction.

Entity ontogeny covers the quantitative appearance, growth, and disappearance of the entity population itself – the particular culture group, culture, artefact-type, or attribute, for example.

Entity migration simply expresses the capacity for the quantitatively growing and fluctuating entity population to have a fluctuating geographical distribution.

Entity interaction reflects those variety interchanges which must occur between any dynamic coupled systems and is usually marked by mutual element or variety fluctuation and adjustments by:

loss of variety
gain of variety
transformation of variety.

In sociocultural systems and therefore in archaeological systems it has been tentatively suggested that the equilibrium basis for dynamic adjustment in mutual variety is on the basis of the principle of continuity: sociocultural systems are continuously adjusting their variety in such a way as to minimize the maximum amount of immediate system dislocation, involving new, alternative, contradictive, or redundant variety. This moving equilibrium or stable format is continuously adjusted by the loss, gain or transformation of system variety at all levels. The gain or increase in system variety can usually be achieved either by development within the system, by internal invention, or it may be achieved by acquiring variety from outside the entity's own system, by acquisition from diffusing variety reaching the system's boundaries. In overall effects entity interaction, with its moving equilibrium, is marked by the qualitative change or gradual transformation of the entity population by virtue of the changing states of its component elements – the culture changes in terms of its changing artefact-type components, the artefact-type changes as the integration of its changing attribute states.

ARCHAEOLOGICAL PROCESSES

It has been suggested that archaeological processes mark the ontogeny, migration, or transformation of the various levels of archaeological entities in terms of their attribute or artefact loss, gain, and transformation. However, archaeological processes do not operate *in vacuo*; they are vectors of sociocultural factors and it is desirable to have a terminology which conveys the specific kinds of social processes which are likely to be connected with the categories of archaeological entities and processes. A process terminology is required which simultaneously implies various combinations of social and material culture changes. Such a terminology can conveniently follow the nested hierarchical model with the higher processes appropriate to the higher levels and subsuming the lower processes as components.

The hierarchy of archaeological processes therefore usefully links material culture changes in artefact-types and attributes to certain categories of social change which might bring them about. The precise interpretation of such an archaeological process depends upon the degree of deliberate organization involved in the particular case – differentiating between deliberately, optimally organized and comparatively unorganized processes. Organized diffusion, for example, is the counterpart of deliberate trade whereas ordinary diffusion may have no element of deliberate trade organization in its generation. In a similar way, culture group repatterning may come about simply by preferential diffusion around the pre-existing network of related cultures, or it may reflect the imperial colonization of the network by one of its members or by an alien culture. The classification of archaeological processes is socio-archaeological in much the same way that Steward's anthropological regularities are socio-cultural (Steward 1955).

The nested hierarchy of socio-archaeological processes may be sketched in the following way:

Technocomplex repatterning – the periodic repatterning of tech-nocomplexes, usually from successive climax centres; the wide-spread adoption of convergent strategies.

Organized form: the formation of international economic blocks or federations.

Culture group repatterning – the repatterning of the culture group by preferential diffusion around the pre-existing network of connec-ted cultures by a member culture or an alien culture.

Organized form: imperial colonization or unification by mili-tary conquest.

Cultural intrusion/substitution – the displacement of one culture by another in a specific territory and the occupation of unoccupied areas.

Organized form: military conquest followed by settlement; or mass migration.

Acculturation – the increased similarity of cultures consequent upon diffusion in one or both directions, convergent interaction.

Organized form: organized cultural intercommunication.

Cultural assimilation – the assimilation by one culture of another, which survives as an incorporated ethnic subculture.

Organized form: military conquest following acculturation.

Subcultural intrusion/substitution – the displacement of one subculture and its type complex by another of similar role.

Organized form: the substitution of one military, aristocratic, religious, or other class of subculture by another, by deliberate action.

Subcultural intrusion/insertion – the addition of a subcultural segment to an existing social structure, from without.

Organized form: the deliberate accumulative introduction of a new subcultural segment, e.g. slaves, workers, renegades, mercenaries, specialists etc.

Stimulus diffusion – the like response to like needs precipitated by a common outside stimulus which is not itself copied or adopted.

Organized form: deliberate derivative development by inter-action, e.g. from warfare, observation, or the transfer of knowl-edge.

Secondary diffusion – the process by which cultural elements spread beyond the limits of the culture area of origin.

Organized form: economic trade, gift exchanges, etc.

Primary diffusion – the process by which cultural elements spread within the limits of the culture area of origin, via the network of social interconnections; the recirculation of variety.

Organized form: internal trade.

Invention – the device of 'new' variety by the renetworking of existing components in a system with emergent characteristics – the stabil-ization of a sociocultural dislocation, either deliberately or by play, or accident.

Organized form: scientific experiment and research.

Loss – the loss of sociocultural variety by displacement by more comprehensive variety, by lack of raw materials, or by isolated drift.

Organized form: utilitarian displacement.[1]

These processes involve varying patterns of artefact-type and attribute trends, reflecting varying degrees of human movement and population reorganization. Most of these processes have been outlined, together with their characteristic pattern, in the successive chapters relating to the relevant entity levels. However, the outstand-ing omission from that discussion has been the ramifications involving diffusion and distribution models; it is therefore in that direction that we must now elaborate. The hypotheses developed throughout this section largely summarize or modify the fundamental deliberations of Kroeber, Dixon and Wissler wherein these matters are more fully explored (Kroeber 1948, Dixon 1928, Wissler 1923). Perhaps the only significant modifications are the substitution of a polythetic model of cultural structure and distribution for the older tacit monothetic model (figs 67, 72), and the addition of concepts and procedures derived from more recent work in geography (e.g. Gould 1969).[2]

DISTRIBUTION AND DIFFUSION MODELS

The process of diffusion of cultural traits and ideas operates upon entities of attribute, attribute complex, artefact-type, type-complex and assemblage levels. In this restricted sense archaeological entities of higher status cannot be said to 'diffuse', but geographical studies of diffusion have long included consideration of population movement and we will return to examples of these later. For the moment we are concerned with the processes by which cultural elements are spread through and beyond their area of origin. Following Dixon we will distinguish 'primary diffusion' and the spread within the culture area of origin, from 'secondary diffusion' beyond the originating area's boundaries (Dixon 1928, pp. 59–106). The term diffusion consequently conveys a set of related processes operating on a limited range of entity categories. The characteristics of diffusion will there- fore vary according to the entity level under consideration, the par- ticular kind of diffusion process operating upon it and the constraint of the plane of diffusion. The constraint in such cases is com- pounded from the permissive and limiting control of the physical environment and the state of the material, technological, economic, religious and psychological system variety and dislocation in the intervening communities, together with the latter's dispersion characteristics.

Primary diffusion occurs within the culture area of origin of the particular element, which is usually distributed the length and breadth of the territory by the continuously reinforcing and recycling of cultural variety within the reticulated kin and acquaintance network of the linguistically united cultural pool. The main mechanism of pri- mary diffusion is person to person contact, in the course of which the element will suffer cumulative modification and transformation. Within the culture area this element transformation will not usually be serious because of the constantly cross-referencing redundant information defining the cultural mode for that element.

Secondary diffusion denotes the processes by which cultural ele- ments are spread beyond the limits of the culture area of their origin. This external diffusion differs only in degree and capacity from pri- mary diffusion. The mechanisms are the same but less elaborately reinforcing, the degree of element modification and transformation during the diffusion are consequently the greater. The reticulated network of kin and acquaintance, webbed by common language, is here replaced by the more sporadic and less efficient traffic of cross- cultural marriage, warfare, slaving, trade and gift exchange. The capacity for element distortion increases with the diminishing efficiency of the person to person contact, which still remains the basis of the process.

The transfer of cultural elements by secondary diffusion clearly depends upon the successive acceptance and transference of the elements. This acceptance, modification and integration of the diffusing element itself, depends upon its congruence with the particular sociocultural system and the element's standing as novel, alternative, contradictive, or redundant variety in relation to the system and its foci of dislocation. If the element is not accepted by the sociocultural system then it does not diffuse in this particular direction (chapter 3, II).

The basis for the acceptance or rejection of the diffusing element depends on its capacity to minimize immediate system dislocation in the variety of intermediary cultures – it must satisfy a 'need'. The modification of the element in this cross-cultural passage is thus a vector of a number of factors – its relationship to existing cultural variety, the severity and location of the accepting system's dislocation foci, the extent and continuity of contact, the complexity of the element's structure, and the prestige of the bearers of the novelty. The changes in the diffusing element may involve changes in structure or status or both. Different elements will clearly be differently affected by diffusion processes depending upon their inherent characteristics and that of the intervening cultures – this gives rise to the effect of differential diffusion which selectively disperses elements from an array. The selective transmission of the compass, silk, gunpowder, and paper by medieval Islam and yet its conservative resistance to other Chinese variety had a marked effect upon the pattern of Oriental innovations reaching medieval Europe, for example.

The diffusion of cultural elements is quite apparently constrained by the nature of the elements being diffused and by the intervening sociocultural and environmental limitations. It follows that both primary and secondary diffusion patterns exhibit regularities consequent upon these general constraints – regularities which give rise to useful postulates and some tentative axioms.

The regularities may be summarized under the following propositions, wherein the term 'element' may mean attributes, attribute complexes, artefact-types, or type complexes:

Postulates

(1) Each specific cultural element has, or once had, a semi-continuous polythetic distribution pattern over a limited culture area.

(2) These overlapping areas contain the distribution mean, mode, and median of a large number of associated elements which together circumscribe the culture area within the wider dispersion pattern (fig. 67).

(3) The area of element origin need not be central nor need it be the source of later modifications and transformations of the element.

(4) On the contrary these later transformations are often peripheral innovations, where the diffusing elements encounter new environments and cultures – producing the phenomenon of 'frontier innovation and invention'.

(5) From the culture area in which it arises the diffusing element diffuses asymmetrically and erratically at varying rates, spreading outward in irregular but radial contours.

(6) Elements lost in the course of diffusion are permanently lost unless reintroduced from another source – hence seriation along a diffusion line is made possible.

(7) The widespread initial secondary diffusion of an element will frequently stimulate parallel developments and transformations, especially in contexts of similar conditions – stimulus diffusion and technocomplex convergence.

Tentative axioms

The axioms which may be developed from the preceding propositions have some general utility in the analysis of widely diffused assemblages and expanded culture groups. They might be stated as follows:

(1) Given a widely diffused assemblage of specific multistate cultural elements, then the specific element state or assemblage of element states with the largest area of distribution is likely to have been part of the earliest expansive assemblage.

(2) The assemblage with the greatest number of the early and widespread specific element states is likely to have constituted the earliest expansive assemblage.

(3) The internal affinity defining the culture group, culture and similar entities, despite their polythetic structure, depends upon a set of key specific artefact-types and cultural elements – the area of origin must provide a set of antecedent sources from which these key elements may have been integrated or developed.

(4) The final and total distribution area of a widely diffused assemblage may usefully be contracted by separating later expansions from the irreducible area of basic early distribution.

(5) The area of origin of a specific cultural element or entity is unlikely to be absolutely peripheral or absolutely central to its final and total distribution area but it is likely to have been within an area of concentration, not necessarily the area of densest concentration; the distortion of contextual constraints must be taken into account.

DISTRIBUTION MODELS

The analysis of element distributions in space usually produces two main categories of distribution pattern – a single continuous distribution area, or several discontinuous distribution areas. Now, if all known instances of a cultural element are plotted in time depth and the final distribution forms a single continuous area, then the inference is that the element originated in its integrated form somewhere within that unitary distribution. However, if the element distribution is nucleated within widely separated and discontinuous areas then the possibilities suggest either widespread diffusion followed by regional isolation, or independent invention in the separate areas or common stimulus followed by parallel regional development. Therefore, if a case for the diffusion of a particular cultural element complex is to be upheld then it is essential to demonstrate:

(1) That the elements are individuals in complexes or assemblages of similarly distributed elements.

(2) That the complexes being compared are really the same or are closely related transforms.

(3) That the components of the complex repeatedly occur together in more than chance aggregates, when compared with their total numbers and frequency of occurrence together.

(4) That the elements forming the complex must be shown to repeatedly occur together in a physical and chronological association, not merely repeatedly scattering over the same area.

(5) That the demonstrated complex cannot be more. easily explained as a general functional complex based on parallel development from a common basis.

These qualifications provide a simple and crude test for the relationship of apparent parallels between cultural elements which are suspicious by virtue of their discontinuous and distant location in relation to the distribution of the main body. The existence of similar or identical elements in widely separated and apparently unconnected areas must be checked by such tests before diffusion or intrusion can be invoked.

An excellent example is the superficially strong argument which would demand a connection between Southeast Asia and South America since these areas share the following elements: nut and lime chewing, pan pipes, tie-dying, terrace irrigation, plank extended dugouts, gauze weaving, the blow-gun, and bronze metallurgy. This ingenious argument for an intrusion or diffusion connection between the two areas can be countered on the basis of the simple tests already enumerated:

(1) The elements are not individuals in a single complex, they do not have the same distribution within their areas. The plank canoe is found in Chile, tie-dying in Peru, coca-chewing in the Andes, the blow-gun in the Amazon, and so on.

(2) The elements being compared are not more closely similar than parallel and functional constraints would require – they are not specific artefact-types.

(3) The components in the overall complex do not repeatedly occur together in more than chance aggregates of at the most two elements from the same assemblage.

(4) The component elements in this complex are from various areas and various chronological periods in Asia and America – not even repeatedly occurring within the same culture areas.

(5) The complex is not an association assemblage and can more easily be explained as an aggregate of elements separately developed for similar functional requirements in similar technocomplexes (Dixon 1928, pp. 180–226).

It is fairly clear from this and many other examples (e.g. Rowe 1965–6) that even having established the existence of similar complexes in separate areas it is essential to analyse their functional and idiosyncratic components before invoking diffusion. On the one hand one may distinguish largely functional complexes of elements linked together by their common association with a specific cultural activity which would necessarily require the presence of some or all of the elements – horse riding, chariotry, or cereal agriculture, for example. In contrast, there are those idiosyncratic accretions or adhesions, sets of elements linked together as an arbitrary and selective association of specific elements from a much wider possible vocabulary – an idiosyncratic complex. The elements gathered into these functional or idiosyncratic complexes may range from sets of attributes up to sets of specific artefact-types, or indeed complexes of type complexes. The importance of the contrast between the different categories of element complexes arises from the different implications and information which may be extracted from regularities in their distribution patterns. Specific idiosyncratic complexes shared by widely separated communities would point more firmly to some direct interconnection than would a shared functional complex, for example. Indeed, in a crude sense one might say that every cultural assemblage is composed of widely shared functional complexes relating to a common technocomplex background and less widely shared idiosyncratic complexes defining a limited cultural superstructure.[3]

DIFFUSION MODELS

Consideration of diffusion models and their relationship to distribution patterns takes us beyond Dixon's 'primary' and 'secondary' categories and into the work of modern geographers who have developed their own classification for diffusion processes. Their basic distinction is between *expansion diffusion*, by which information or cultural traits spread through an area while still remaining in their area of origin, and *relocation diffusion*, by which the carriers of the information or traits themselves move through new areas (migration). Expansion diffusion can in turn be divided into two subtypes, *contagious*, in which direct contact is the method of dispersal and increasing distance between individuals lessens the probability of contact, and *hierarchical*, in which dispersion occurs through a social, economic or political hierarchy (e.g. from large urban centres to small hamlets or vice versa). This classification is well presented and illustrated by Haggett (1972, pp. 348–9), and Gould (1969, pp. 3–8), who points out that these types of diffusion are not mutually exclusive. Barriers to diffusion may be physical, linguistic, religious, political or psychological, and normally they are *permeable*, 'allowing part of the energy of a diffusion pulse to go through, but generally slowing down the intensity of the process in the local area' (Gould 1969, p. 13). In rare cases the barriers may be either completely *absorbing* and stop a diffusion pulse from proceeding any further (e.g. swamps, high mountains) or completely *reflecting* and concentrate the energy of a diffusion pulse in a local area from which it will 'explode' forward with great force.

Archaeological studies of diffusion have (with a few exceptions) yet to approach the frequency or productive results of their geographical counterparts. But there have been a number of attempts to relate quantified archaeological distribution patterns to particular diffusion processes and we will outline their application here under the following general headings:

(1) distance-decay models
(2) wave of advance models
(3) stochastic simulation models
(4) trend models

In terms of the types defined above, (1) deals with cases of expansion diffusion, (2) with relocation diffusion and (3) and (4) with examples of both.

Distance decay models

The observation that human groups are characterized by a decreasing amount of interaction with the increase in distance between them has been the basis of much research into the processes behind cultural distribution patterns during the past decade. Models based on the distance decay principle have been stimulated from three different sources:

(a) the development of characterization studies (e.g. neutron activation analysis, optical emission spectroscopy) to trace the sources of different raw materials used to make prehistoric artefacts (e.g. for pottery see Peacock 1970);

(b) the introduction into archaeology of quantitative methods for analysing spatial patterns, largely drawn from contemporary geography (e.g. Hägerstrand 1953, Haggett 1965);

(c) an increased interest in the different types of trade or exchange and their operation and significance in small-scale societies (e.g. Sahlins 1972).

The characterization studies have provided the archaeologist with some reliable information on the types and quantities of raw materials (whether in that state or as finished artefacts) which were circulated or moved with their owners over sometimes large distances in the past. Whereas earlier discussions about cultural diffusion or trade in prehistory had rested almost solely on the criteria outlined above (distribution models, pp. 424–6), scientific source analysis now provided much needed independent evidence. Furthermore the increasing numbers of such analyses revealed the potential for the application of quantitative techniques (e.g. regression analysis, see below) to define their spatial distribution patterns.

The interpretation of these patterns depended upon the stimulus of developing 'substantivist' economic anthropology (e.g. Polanyi *et al.* 1957; Sahlins 1972), in which small-scale societies were viewed in terms of limited economic goals (non-optimizing, anti-surplus) and the operation of trade/exchange through social channels. Two types of economic transactions, reciprocity and redistribution, were distinguished (Sahlins 1972) and interest focused on the different types of social and political organization with which they were associated. The fundamental archaeological question which was raised was how these types of exchange patterns could be recognized within prehistoric societies.

It is important to realize that consideration of the spatial diffusion of cultural traits involves two key concepts: first the obvious one of movement of the traits themselves and secondly the human interaction with which this movement was associated. Here a strong analogy has been detected between trade/exchange and a communication system (Renfrew 1976), in which information may be transmitted by either the commodity exchanged or the concepts associated with that commodity or by direct communication between the people exchanging the commodity (op. cit. pp. 22–4). If the communication associated with exchange is to be fully investigated then it should be remembered that simply considering the whole problem under the general term 'diffusion' may conceal complex patterns and processes.

Early characterization analyses of prehistoric artefacts soon began to yield distribution patterns showing a general fall-off in frequency as distance from their raw material source increased. This property has been expressed as the 'Law of Monotonic Decrement': 'In circumstances of uniform loss or deposition and in the absence of highly organized directional (i.e. preferential, non-homogeneous) exchange, the curve of frequency or abundance of occurrence of an exchanged commodity against effective distance from a localized source will be a monotonic decreasing one' (Renfrew 1977, p. 72). Variations in the fall-off patterns shown by different types of artefact have been used to infer the operation of different models of trade. Three of these models are outlined briefly below.

(i) *Down the line exchange*: the successive reciprocal exchange of a commodity from its source, sometimes over very long distances.

Example. The exchange of obsidian in the Near East from known sources in the Levant, Anatolia and the Zagros area *c.* 7500–5500 BC (fig. 90a). Renfrew, Dixon and Cann (1968) distinguish a 'supply zone'

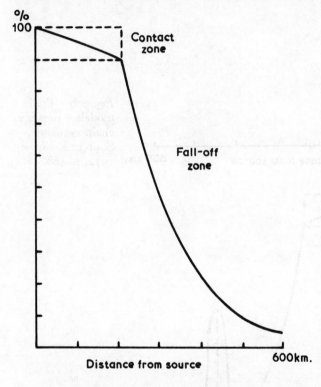

Fig. 90a   Trade models – down-the-line exchange. Source: Renfrew 1972, p. 466.

of *c.* 300 km radius from the sources in which the proportion of obsidian to other chipped stone fell very gradually and a 'contact zone' beyond this in which the obsidian frequency declined exponentially with increasing distance. Renfrew (1972, fig. 20.9 – reproduced here as fig. 90a) substitutes 'contact' for 'supply' zone and 'fall-off' for 'contact' zone.

(ii) *Prestige chain exchange*: the restricted transfer of prestige goods between people of higher social rank. The non-utilitarian nature

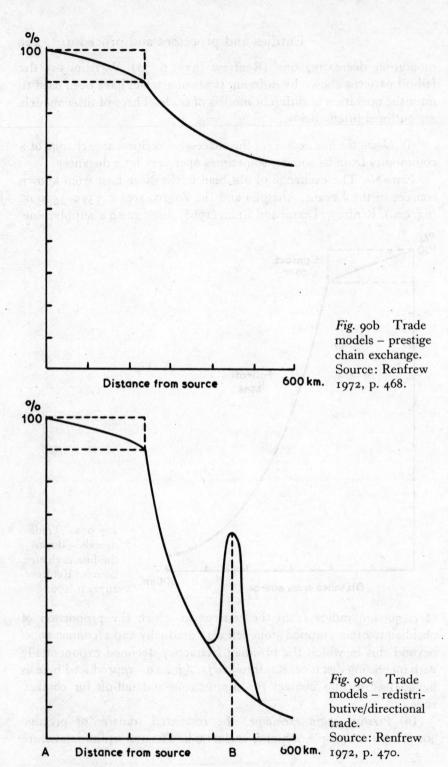

Fig. 90b Trade models – prestige chain exchange. Source: Renfrew 1972, p. 468.

Fig. 90c Trade models – redistributive/directional trade. Source: Renfrew 1972, p. 470.

of these goods and their subsequent further exchange increases the distances over which they travel and decreases their rate of fall-off (fig. 90b).

Example. The exchange of Spondylus shells of Aegean origin in Neolithic Europe (Shackleton and Renfrew 1970).

(iii) *Redistributive/directional trade* : either the existence of central places serves to concentrate the occurrence of exchangeable commodities for redistribution or in a related way there is a direct exchange of commodities between distant areas without involving any middlemen (fig. 90c). The latter type of trade was referred to as 'polarized diffusion' in the first edition of this volume (Clarke 1968, pp. 419–20).

Examples. Redistribution has been discussed by Renfrew (1972) in relation to the development of civilization in Bronze Age Greece. Examples of directional trade between discrete, distant areas have been increasingly recognized in the later prehistoric and early historic periods in Europe. The discrete inland concentration of Greek metalwork around Massalia and in the Rhine/Rhone/Danube head-waters of the Hallstatt mining technocomplex has been noted by Piggott (fig. 91). The distribution of Dressel type 1 amphorae pro-duced in southern Italy and shipped direct to southern England in the first century BC has been published by Peacock (1971, fig. 36). In Roman Britain there are good examples of directional trade in the occurrence of Severn Valley ware on Hadrian's Wall and the Antonine Frontier (Webster 1972, fig. 1; 1977), black-burnished pottery from southeast England in the Scottish frontier zone in the second to fourth centuries AD (Farrar 1973) and mortaria vessels from Col-chester in the same northern area AD 140–200 (Hartley 1973).

The analysis and interpretation of fall-off curves showing various types of decreasing interaction with increasing distance from a com-modity's source has been taken a step further by the use of regression analysis and gravity models (Hodder 1974). The fall-off curves of fifteen different types of commodity, ranging in date from the Neoli-thic down to the Roman period, were examined to find the regression line which gave the best fit to the varying frequencies of the data. All the regression gradients were plotted together (fig. 92) and were interpreted as showing two general patterns: first a group showing a small local distribution involving common, utilitarian and sometimes bulky commodities (fig. 92 – e.g. Roman tiles, Savernake pottery, Malvernian Roman pottery, Bronze Age palstaves) and secondly a

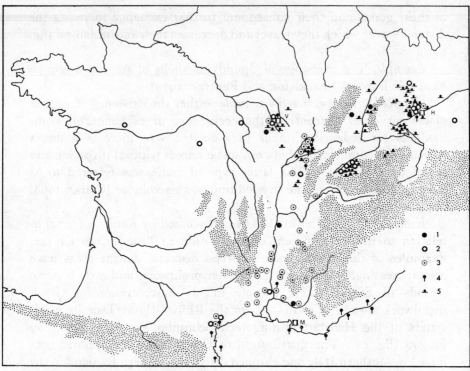

Fig. 91   An example of directional trade. The distribution of Hallstatt imports and luxuries, seventh-sixth centuries BC: 1 – imported Greek etc. bronzes, seventh century BC; 2 – imported bronzes and gold, sixth century BC; 3 – imported Greek pottery, seventh-sixth centuries BC; 4 – Massaliote amphorae, seventh-sixth centuries BC; 5 – Hallstatt C and D gold objects; M – Massalia; H – the Heuneberg; V – Vix.
Source: Piggott 1965, p. 188.

group of finer commodities produced in large numbers and exchanged or traded over larger distances (fig. 92: e.g. Oxford Roman pottery, Anatolian obsidian, Neolithic Cornish pottery). The analysis here enabled the archaeologist to make various inferences about the processes behind the distribution patterns of the different commodities. The use of a gravity model was designed to predict the boundaries between the service areas of two neighbouring towns and relates the interaction between them to their sizes and the distances separating them (Hodder 1974, pp. 183–5). The formula is expressed as follows:

$$D_{bj} = \frac{Dij}{1 + \sqrt{\dfrac{Pi}{Pj}}}$$

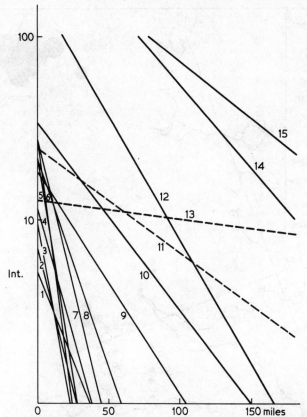

Fig. 92   A regression analysis of fifteen commodities:
1 – Rowlands Castle pottery; 2 – Dobunnic coins;
3 – Late Roman fine wares; 4 – Malvernian
Roman pottery; 5 – Roman tiles; 6 – Savernake
pottery (density); 7 – Savernake pottery (percentages);
8 – Neolithic picrite axe-hammers; 9 – New Forest
pottery; 10 – Bronze Age palstaves; 11 – Oxford
pottery; 12 – Neolithic Cornish pottery; 13 – Neolithic
Group I axes; 14 – Neolithic Group VI axes;
15 – Anatolian obsidian.
Source: Hodder 1974, p. 181.

where D_{bj} is the distance from the breaking point $_b$ to centre $_j$, i and j
are the two service centres, Pi and Pj are the respective population
sizes of the two centres.

This model was then applied to different types of Romano-British
pottery and to the distribution of British Neolithic stone axes of

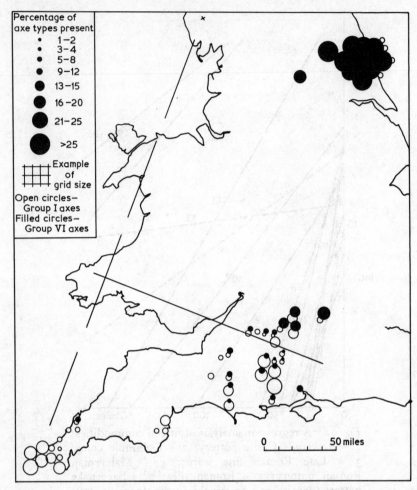

Fig. 93 Predicted 'breaking-point' based on a gravity model compared with the actual distribution of Group I and Group VI Neolithic stone axes. Source: Hodder 1974, p. 186.

petrological Groups I and VI. In the latter case (fig. 93) the predicted 'breaking-point' between the areas supplied by the two sources coincided very closely with the actual distribution boundaries in the Avebury district of southern England. The success of this model in this example and in predicting boundaries between Romano-British pottery distributions supports the hypothesis that competing service centres were responsible for the uneven spatial distributions of these commodities.

The assumption behind much of the research into distance-decay models has been that the differences in the shape of fall-off curves of various commodities could be related to differences in the processes by which they were moved between human communities. This can be seen quite clearly in the attempts to define different 'modes' of trade and their spatial correlates (e.g. Renfrew 1976 and recanted in Renfrew 1977, p. 88). But the problem raised by recent simulation studies (see below) is that the same general type of fall-off curve may be produced by different spatial processes (fig. 100). This complicates the interpretation of artefact distribution patterns, as does the recognition that 'barriers' to diffusion may not produce any major differences in these patterns (figs 100, 101). On the other hand it may still be possible to relate such factors as the degree of concavity of fall-off curves with close, frequent contacts with a production centre (Hodder and Orton 1976, pp. 142–5). It is reasonable to suggest that further consideration of the relationship between distribution patterns and the processes that produced them will help archaeologists to enter a new and stimulating phase in the analysis of trade and cultural diffusion in general.

Wave of advance models

The concept of a 'wave of advance' was initially developed in the field of genetics in the late 1930s and given mathematical definition a decade later. Its introduction into archaeology has been the work of Ammerman and Cavalli-Sforza (1971, 1973), who have attempted to measure the rate of diffusion of cereal agriculture into Europe from 6000 to 3000 BC. As an initial assumption they note the increasing frequency with which careful collection has yielded palaeobotanical remains on early Neolithic sites in Europe and conclude that 'it follows that the dates from the earliest known Neolithic sites in Europe can provide estimates of the spread of the cereals and with them of early farming' (1971, p. 675). They selected fifty-three sites in Europe with radiocarbon dated early Neolithic levels as their sample for a rate of diffusion analysis. This selection is governed by several criteria, including the use of dates with a standard deviation of 200 years or less and the deliberate exclusion of possible contaminated dates and of dates from areas where a retarded spread of agriculture was suspected.

Each date from the fifty-three sites was then plotted against the distance of each site from the diffusion centre in the Near East, and

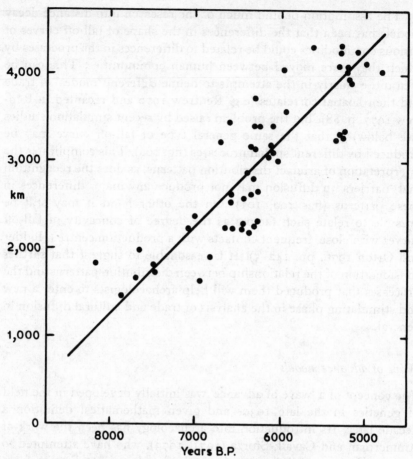

Fig. 94   The diffusion of farming into Europe. Points represent dated
Early Neolithic sites used in the analysis. The graph shows the linear
pattern of diffusion, with the solid line representing the principal axis which
gives an average rate of *c.* 1 km per year.
Source: Ammerman and Cavalli-Sforza 1973, fig. 1.

linear correlation coefficients used to see if the rate of diffusion was as
constant in time and space as the initial plot suggested. The
coefficients were all very high and confirmed the linear pattern seen in
fig. 94, in which the principal axis gives the average rate of diffusion as
nearly 1 km per year. The diffusion centre was taken as Jericho, but
tests on three other sites (Cayönu, Ali Kosh and Jarmo) confirmed
both the constant rate of diffusion and the general magnitude of the

average annual rate. As well as a couple of minor additional tests, the
same method was applied to the early Neolithic sites in north Africa
and central Asia and some degree of agreement with the European rate
and centre of diffusion obtained. Preliminary *regional* diffusion rates
were also calculated and confirmed, among other things, the expected
higher rate of spread of the Linearbandkeramik culture of central and
northwestern Europe. Some idea of the regional variation may be
gained from fig. 95, in which it is plotted alongside the general
diffusion at 500-year intervals.

Ammerman and Cavalli-Sforza then raise the important question
of *how* this early agriculture spread into Europe. Here they prefer an
explanation based upon population growth and movement (*demic*

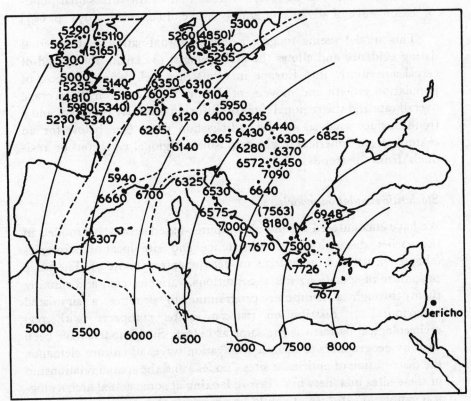

Fig. 95   The diffusion of farming into Europe. Dates in years BP. The arcs
show the expected pattern of spread at 500-year intervals with broken lines
indicating suggested regional variations.
Source: Ammerman and Cavalli-Sforza 1971, p. 685.

diffusion) to one which depends upon the spread of information and cultural traits (*cultural diffusion*). They point to the association of population growth with the adoption of cereal agriculture (and sedentism, see Binford and Chasko 1976) as the basis for this preference. This leads them to their main interpretative conclusion.

> It has been shown mathematically . . . that if such an increase in population coincides with a modest local migration activity, random in direction (comparable to a Brownian motion), a wave of population expansion will set in and progress at a constant radial rate. This is just what we have observed with the measured rate for the European data. There is good agreement between the measured rate and the constant rate of advance predicted by the model, which will be referred to as that of the diffusional population wave of advance or simply 'wave of advance'. (1971, p. 687)

This model seems to give a good approximation to the actual dating evidence and allows the archaeologist to explain the spread of cereal agriculture into Europe in terms of a well-defined process of population growth and movement. Future work on both the average overall rate and the regional rates of diffusion is clearly required, and a trend surface analysis of the radiocarbon dates (see below for an example from America) might help isolate regional variations or 'residuals' from the trends.

Stochastic simulation models

We have encountered the use of computer-based simulation models in the earlier discussions on subsistence and site location strategies (chapter 3, III) and on systems models (chapter 3, note 4). The basic procedure of specifying initial conditions, variables etc., and running them through a computer programme to produce a simulated behavioural or distribution pattern to be compared with real archaeological patterns is the same as before. Such models have been used by geographers to analyse innovation waves of culture elements, the distribution of entities at sites ('nodes') and the spatial relationship of these sites in a 'network'. Before looking at some actual archaeological simulation studies, it would be profitable to outline some of these geographical case-studies.

In studying innovation waves, the main impetus has come from the Swedish geographer Torsten Hägerstrand, who has developed the use of dynamic stochastic simulation models through Monte Carlo methods (1952, 1957). The stochastic element, or complex of random factors, arises from the very complicated interplay of minor factors in real diffusion situations – including the chance distribution of centres or nodes, the chance variation in output of the innovation at the different nodes, the chance aspect of the mechanisms of dispersal, and the chance mechanism of survival in the original situation and in the archaeological record sample. The procedure under these kinds of circumstance is in effect to say 'let us ignore the few obvious and easily ascertainable process factors and let us look at the same situation as a product of a multiplicity of unknown factors, acting in various directions – then we can compare the patterning from these kinds of factors with the real patterning involving additional essential variables'. The simulated spatial diffusion of a hypothetical innovation through successive time periods is shown in fig. 96 and is based on Hägerstrand's initial observation that the probability of contact between separate human groups or individuals will decrease in an exponential way as the distance between them increases (see above, distance-decay models). Given a pattern of contagious diffusion, the probability of

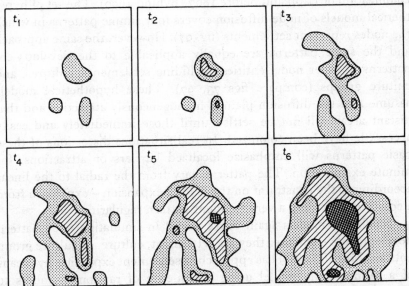

Fig. 96 Areal diffusion of a hypothetical innovation over successive time periods, $t_1, t_2 \ldots t_6$.
Source: Haggett, after Hägerstrand 1953; and Bunge 1962, p. 118.

acceptance of an innovation from any single point by other points in its neighbourhood can be predicted and the diffusion process can be analysed by a stochastic simulation model. Two interesting conclusions which Hägerstrand drew from this study are that initial innovation centres remain fairly stable through time (compare t1–6 in fig. 96) and that there may be chance long-distance spread of innovations at an early stage which themselves develop into secondary 'high acceptance' centres (cf. Jope 1973, figs 31a–c on the diffusion of the curving shaped gables in southern Britain *c*. AD 1500–1750). An important aspect of such simulation studies is their 'fit' to real geographical data and here the results inspire confidence in the general method: this is the case both for Hägerstrand's simulation of the diffusion of pasture subsidies in central Sweden in the 1920s–30s and for Bowden's study of the spread of wells for irrigation agriculture in eastern Colorado (Haggett 1972, pp. 360–1 and figs 15–11, 15–12).

Yuill (1965) has also used a Monte Carlo simulation model to study the effects of four different types of barriers on the diffusion of innovation waves.

The distribution of entities at sites or 'nodes', and their diffusion has been studied by Bylund as part of a historical study of the colonization of Lappland before 1867 (Bylund 1960). The set of hypothetical models of node diffusion covers four simple patterns in which the nodes represent settlements (fig. 97). However, the same approach and the same patterns are equally applicable to the development patterns of other nodal entities, including settlements, cultures, and culture groups (compare figs 73, 97). These hypothetical models assume that the diffusion plain is homogeneously attractive and that distant areas will not be settled until those immediately and easily accessible have been colonized. In real situations distortions of these basic patterns will emphasize localized barriers or attractions, for minute examination. The patterns vary from the radial to the linear according to the constraint on the field of expansion – expansion from a coastline providing a very frequent pattern regularity.

Stochastic models again prove useful in simulating node pattern developments – whether they are settlement, culture, or culture group entities. Morrill (1962) has approached settlement expansion by means of a Monte Carlo model using a sequence of random numbers to allocate each new settlement a direction and distance from a probability matrix derived from empirical studies generalizing a large number of real settlement expansions. These 'distance-and-direction-

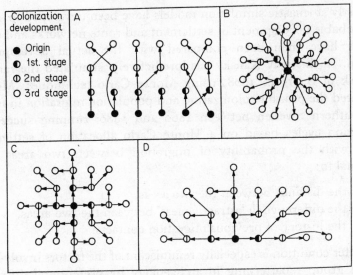

Fig. 97   Hypothetical models of entity diffusion.
Source: Haggett, after Bylund 1960, p. 226.

from-the-mother-settlement' rules are then combined with size growth rules to generate a realistic hierarchical development of the centres (fig. 98; Haggett 1965, pp. 97–8).

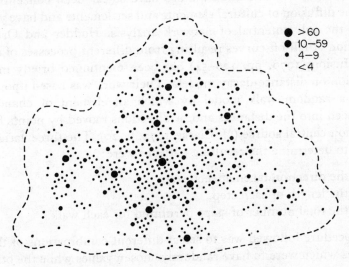

Fig. 98   Simulated settlement pattern generated by Monte Carlo methods.
Source: Haggett, after Morrill 1962, p. 119.

Lastly stochastic simulation models have been developed to study the probable development of settlement and route networks and these models have then been compared with the actual development pattern. In this way Kansky has 'predictively' simulated the railway network of Sicily in 1908, using Monte Carlo techniques. Morrill simulated the peasant colonization and population migration in forested southern Sweden between 1860 and 1980, running successive simulation cycles based on a Monte Carlo allocation of settlers to areas, with the probability of migration between two areas proportional to:

(a) the distance between the two areas,
(b) the difference in 'attractiveness' between the two areas,
(c) the history of previous migration contacts.

The latter condition is especially reminiscent of the factors involved in culture group repatterning in archaeology by preferential diffusion and infiltration around the pre-existing network of connected, collateral culture areas (chapter 7, chapter 10, III). In similar stochastic simulations, random walk processes have also been used to model the features of network development (see Haggett 1965, pp. 305–9; Haggett and Chorley 1969, pp. 294–302).

Archaeological simulation studies have so far been concentrated upon the diffusion of cultural elements and settlements and have yet to exploit the full potential of network analysis. Hodder and Orton's simulation of fall-off curves resulting from different processes of artefact diffusion (1976, pp. 126–54) has been mentioned briefly in the discussion on distance-decay models. Their work was based upon the use of a random walk model by which an element of chance is introduced into the distances and/or directions moved by points from a common central source (cf. Clarke 1972, p. 20). The three variables chosen to determine the resulting patterns were:

(a) the direction taken at each step,
(b) the length of each step,
(c) the total number of steps permitted for each walk.

The procedure followed was to select different combinations of these variables which were to have randomly chosen values while the others remained constant. Thus in initial random walks only *one* of the three variables was allowed to be random while in later studies this was extended to all of them. To take a simple example, if step length and

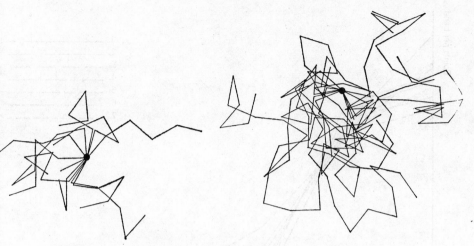

Fig. 99   Two examples of random walks from a central point.
Source: Hodder and Orton 1976, p. 128.

the total number of steps are both fixed, each point is allowed to 'walk' a certain step length in a randomly chosen direction for the number of steps stated. This is repeated 100 times. In spatial terms this results in an uneven but gradual dispersion of each point (fig. 99) which can be plotted on a fall-off curve in terms of the number of points reaching ten equally spaced concentric bands around the central source (fig. 100). Different shaped fall-off curves will result according to the values given to each of the three specified variables.

The initial results obtained from these simulations are of the greatest importance for the interpretation of the processes behind the archaeologically observed distribution patterns of prehistoric arte-facts. As we have already noted (above p. 435) the same concave fall-off curves can be produced by *different* combinations of variables (fig. 100) and the presence of variable 'barriers' to diffusion can only produce slight differences in distribution patterns as revealed in these fall-off curves (figs 100, 101). Any attempts to distinguish particular processes of trade or exchange (e.g. reciprocity vs. redistribution) as well as cultural boundaries on the basis of fall-off curves showing decreasing interaction with distance need to be made with great caution in the light of this simulation study.

In the first edition of this book, it was predicted that stochastic simulation studies of settlement expansion could release significant information to the archaeologist by their comparison with actual

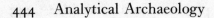

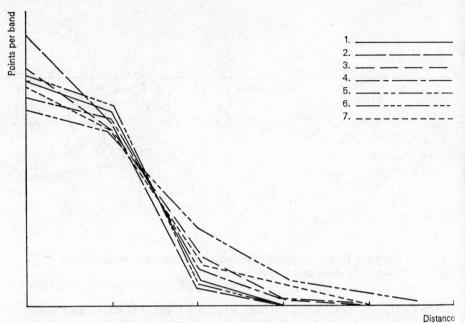

Fig. 100　A comparison of simulated fall-off curves for different combinations and values of the same variables. 1 – Number of steps chosen between 1 and 14. Step length fixed at 0·5 cm. 2 – Number of steps fixed at 18. Length fixed at 0·25 cm. 3 – Number of steps chosen between 1 and 8. Step length chosen between 0 and 1 cm. 4 – Number of steps fixed at 22. Step length fixed at 0·5 cm. 5 – Number of steps fixed at 6. Step length chosen from a negative exponential distribution with mean of 0·5 cm. 6 – Number of steps chosen between 1 and 14. Step length fixed at 0·5 cm. Barrier at 1·5 cm. 7 – Number of steps chosen between 1 and 4. Step length chosen between 0 and 1 cm. Only outward movement allowed.
Source: Hodder and Orton 1976, p. 140.

settlement distribution patterns (Clarke 1968, p. 472). Recent work is beginning to confirm this optimism. Zubrow's (1971, 1975) work in Arizona is one of the earliest publications dealing with this subject. His main concern is with the relationship between population and resources, for which he constructs a model of carrying capacity as a dynamic equilibrium system. This model incorporates such variables as population growth (i.e. a neo-Malthusian position by which population expands until limited by available resources), migration ('the development of populations in marginal resource zones is a function of optimal zone exploitation' 1975, p. 29), spatial and temporal variation in resources and climate. The model is expressed as a flow chart (1975, fig. 2.19) which is then used as the basis of a simulation of population growth and settlement expansion in the Hay Hollow valley from AD 200–1500. Eight simulations are run, starting from a single known settlement at AD 200 with an initial population of fifty: in these simulations the birth and death rates, the 'migration velocity' and the 'settlement longevity' are allowed to vary while the maximum settlement population, resource growth and consumption are kept constant (1975, p. 103, table 6.1). Zubrow's main interest is in the comparison of the simulated relationship between population growth and settlement in different microhabitats and the actual pattern revealed by

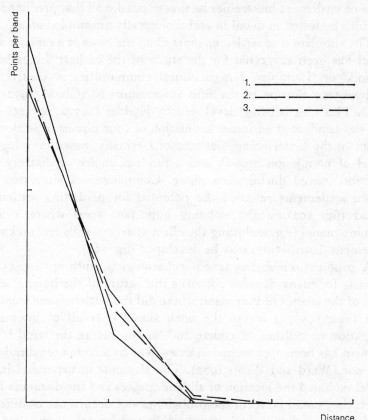

Fig. 101   A comparison of three simulated fall-off curves, two containing a differently located 'barrier' to diffusion. Number of steps chosen between 1 and 6. Step length fixed at 0·5 cm. 1 – Barrier at 0·75 cm; 2 – barrier at 1·5 cm; 3 – no barrier.
Source: Hodder and Orton 1976, p. 137.

archaeological research in the Hay Hollow valley. Here he concludes that there is a general degree of agreement between simulated and actual population figures, and that of the simulated site locations 50 per cent were in an unsampled area, 35 per cent where there are known archaeological sites and 15 per cent where there are no known sites. This predictive element is a vital part of any model and enables the archaeologist to ask new and relevant questions in his research. Zubrow suggests that further complexities (e.g. multiple initial settlement locations and multiple 'budding-off' settlements) can be built into the simulation and one could also suggest that the emergence of settlement hierarchies be investigated, and that predicted site locations be tested in detail in archaeologically unsampled areas.

The simulation of settlement spread on the basis of a random walk model has been suggested for the study of the earliest 'Linearband-keramik' or 'Danubian I' agricultural communities in central and northwestern Europe in the fifth millennium BC (Clarke 1972, pp. 20–4). This idea is being developed by Hodder (1977a, pp. 258–77), who has conducted an initial simulation of four phases of settlement spread in the Untermaingebiet area of Germany, based on a logistic model of population growth and a random choice of distance and direction moved during each phase. Comparison of simulated and known settlements revealed the potential for predicting settlement spread (fig. 102), whilst isolating important areas where a more complex model (e.g. including the effect of rivers, soils etc. on known settlement distribution) may be developed (fig. 103).

A problem which has taxed archaeologists, anthropologists and linguists for many decades concerns the nature of the human settlement of the islands of Polynesia: where did the settlers come from and were their voyages across the open seas the result of intentional navigation or drifting off course and 'sailing before the wind'? This problem has been approached in a new way by a computer simulation (Levison, Ward and Webb 1972). The elements incorporated in the model included the location of all land masses and the distances from which they could be seen, the probabilities of occurrence of different winds and currents in each 5° square in each month of the year, the speed of boats under these conditions, the chances of survival at sea, the risk of gales and the desired course. The simulation was set in motion as follows:

(a) select a starting island, a date and the voyage's maximum length,

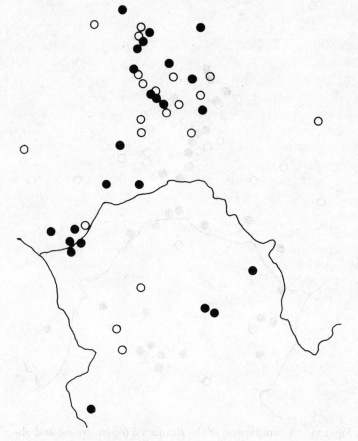

Fig. 102   A comparison of the simulated (open circles) and observed (filled circles) distribution of Linearbandkeramik phase 2 settlements in the Untermaingebiet.
Source: Hodder 1977a, p. 276.

(b) make a random selection of wind and current for that day,
(c) compute the position of the boat at the end of the day,
(d) if the boat has come within sighting distance of land, end the voyage,
(e) if the maximum length of the voyage has been reached, end the voyage, select the next date and start the simulation again at (b).

Following this procedure the authors used sixty-four starting islands to simulate 100,946 drift voyages and nine starting islands for 8,052

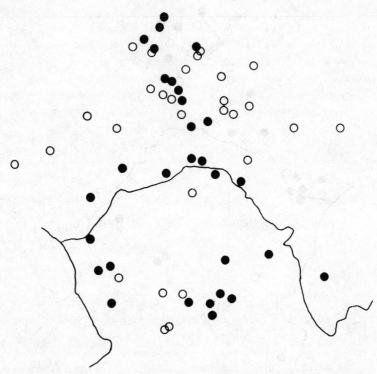

Fig. 103   A comparison of the simulated (open circles) and observed (filled circles) distribution of Linearbandkeramik phase 4
settlements. The visual fit is less good than in fig. 102 – note the
overrepresentation of simulated sites to the north of the river
compared with the underrepresentation to the south. A more
complex simulation should attempt to allow for these observed
patterns.
Source: Hodder 1977a, p. 277.

navigated voyages. On this basis they calculated the probabilities of
drift voyages from these starting points reaching other islands and
represented them on cartograms (e.g. fig. 104a–d). On this basis they
concluded:

- that drift voyages from the American continent and from New
  Zealand were extremely unlikely,
- that most of the major voyages involved in the Polynesian
  settlement required only elementary navigation systems,

– and that although drift was unlikely to be the sole process behind the settlement, once Fiji or Western Polynesia had been occupied, drift could easily have been responsible for the settlement of Tonga and Samoa.

Clearly such a simulation could be extended to other major island groups (e.g. the Caribbean) where similarly useful probabilistic conclusions on the earliest settlement might be drawn.

Trend models

One of the complications arising in archaeological distribution and diffusion maps is the transformation of the element plotted across the map: the element or complex changes as it spreads. This property means that the map of elements is not in fact a map of a single element state but is a map of a range of transform states of a multi-state element. Consequently, the elements dotted on one region of the map are usually closely similar but jointly rather different from the 'same' elements in another region. The full recognition of this complication emphasizes the fundamental basis of regional trends and their great importance for subsequent regional developments. The incipient trends and residuals of a particular distribution situation will frequently contain the key to later developing distribution patterns.

A very frequent archaeological phenomenon is the diffusion or intrusive spread of an assemblage in which, by an internal process, certain components are increasing and others are decreasing. This is a trending change, sometimes purely a fashion oscillation, sometimes possibly correlated with environmental stimuli. Let us consider an archaeological situation in which an assemblage or complex of elements is spreading in one main direction. As the assemblage spreads it gets later in date and element A increases markedly, whilst element B declines in frequency of occurrence at the same time (fig. 105). This is a situation in which the distribution map is a vector of four changing factors – time, space, percentage of A, percentage of B. Ordinarily it is almost impossible to perceive these trends and changing factors on a standard distribution map which plots multistate elements as single-state constants and maps geographical space but not chronological time. Trend maps provide the possibility of mapping and connecting such dynamic factors and expressing them as the surfaces of solid models.

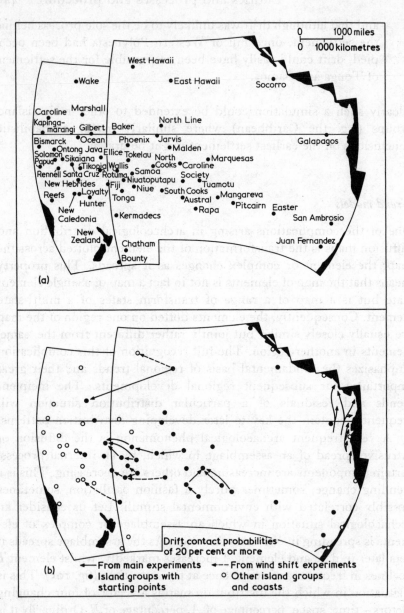

Fig. 104a–d   A computer simulation of the drift contact probabilities
for the setlement of the islands of Polynesia.
Source: Levison, Ward and Webb 1972, pp. 238, 240.

The following labels appear in the figure:

(a)

West Hawaii
Wake
East Hawaii
Socorro
Caroline   Marshall
Kapinga-
marangi   Gilbert   Baker
Bismarck   North Line
Solomon   Ontong Java   Phoenix   Jarvis   Galapagos
Papua   Ocean
Sikaiana   Ellice   Tokelau   Malden
Rennell   Tikopia   Wallis   North   Caroline   Marquesas
Santa Cruz   Rotuma   Samoa   Cooks   Society
New Hebrides   Niuatoputapu   Tuamotu
Reefs   Fiji   Niue   South Cooks   Mangareva
Hunter   Loyalty   Tonga   Austral   Pitcairn   Easter
New   Rapa   San Ambrosio
Caledonia   Kermadecs
New
Zealand   Juan Fernandez
Chatham
Bounty

(b)

Drift contact probabilities
of 20 per cent or more
→ From main experiments   ← - - From wind shift experiments
● Island groups with   ○ Other island groups
starting points   and coasts

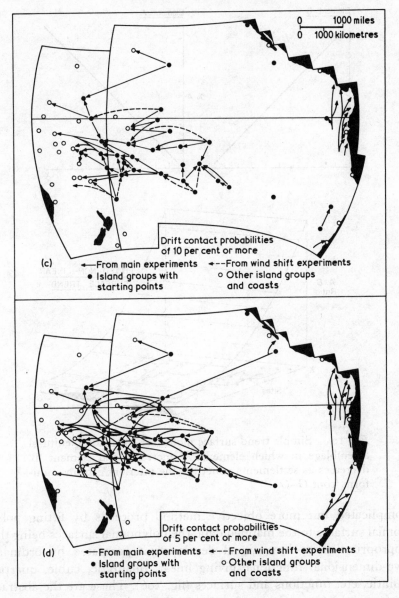

The simplest method of trend surface analysis consists of the construction of a generalized contoured map of data collected by gridded sampling methods. This 'grid generalization method' suffers from a lack of objectivity and depends heavily on the size of grid selected for data collection (Hodder and Orton 1976, p. 159). A more

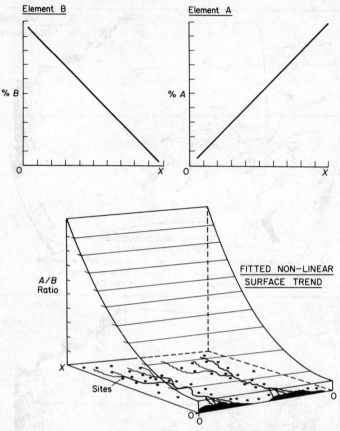

Fig. 105   Simple trend surface model for a spreading cultural assemblage in which element 'A' increases and element 'B' decreases as settlements penetrate the interior X from a uniform front O–O.

complicated but more objective method proceeds by fitting poly-nomial surfaces to the mapped data, the polynomial surfaces being the appropriate three-dimensional development generated by ordinary two-dimensional functions, giving linear, quadratic, cubic, quartic, quintic, etc. functions and surfaces (fig. 106). These are the abstract surfaces which may be used individually, or in a composite way, to model the complicated trends in the real mapped data. In modern practice the systematic trends in mapped variables may be separated from the local residuals by direct computer analysis of the map data. The residuals themselves, having been isolated, may display distinct trends in their own patterning, which themselves may then be

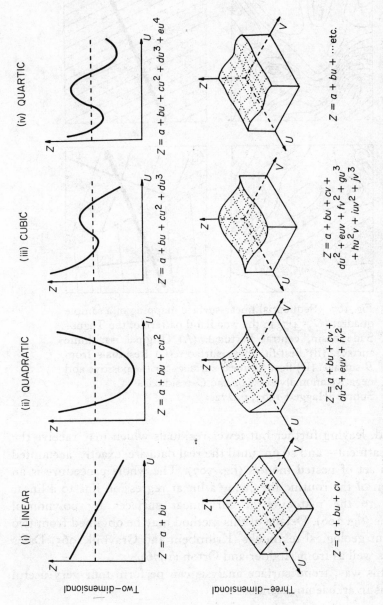

Fig. 106 Relations between two-dimensional functions and their appropriate three-dimensional surfaces.

Source: Haggett 1965, p. 273, after Chorley, Haggett and Krumbein.

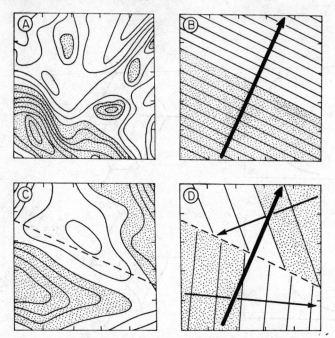

Fig. 107   Sequential linear-surface mapping of a sample
quadrat ($G = 4\cdot7$) in the woodland pattern of the Tagus–
Sado basin, central Portugal. (A) Original isarithmic
surface. (B) Best-fit linear surface. (C) Residuals from
B-surface. (D) Best-fit linear surfaces for the positive and
negative anomaly areas on the *C*-residuals.
Source: Haggett 1965, p. 272.

modelled, leaving further but fewer residuals which may receive the
same treatment – and so on, until the real data are 'exactly' accounted
for by a set of nested models (fig. 107). The whole procedure is an
extension of the routine for fitting a linear regression line to a linear
surface, to the matching of curvilinear surfaces by polynomial
functions (fig. 106). Details of this method may be obtained from two
important geological textbooks (Krumbein and Graybill 1965, Davis
1973), as well as from Hodder and Orton (1976).

In this way, trend surface analysis can perform four very useful
functions in archaeological research:

(i) for testing a conceptual distribution model against real data,
    in order to see whether the observed values or states are
    accurately met by the trend model predictions;

(ii) for the prediction of what may be expected to be found in assemblages from a certain area or locus, given certain trends;

(iii) for the reconstruction from a scatter of surviving data the pattern of variation as it must once have existed over a given territory: the reconstruction of 'ghost' surfaces (Haggett 1965, p. 274);

(iv) for the study of areal and spatial variation in a distribution pattern in order to develop a model for search and excavation procedure.

The first edition of this book contained the first applications of trend surface analysis in archaeology – a quadratic surface model of trends in the ratio of rusticated/painted pottery in the earliest Balkan Neolithic cultures (1968, fig. 82), a simplified trend map of the neck angle on southern British Beakers c. 1650–1500 BC (op. cit. fig. 100)

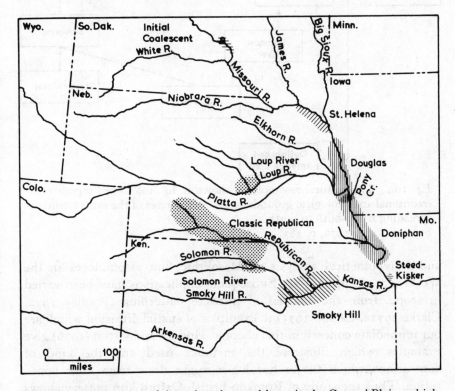

Fig. 108   The location of the cultural assemblages in the Central Plains which have been analysed by trend-surface analysis (see figs 109, 110).
Source: Roper 1976, p. 182.

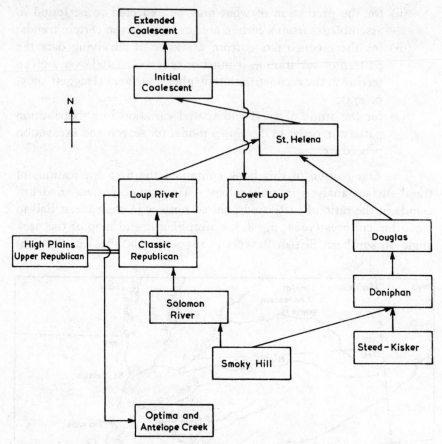

Fig. 109   The cultural assemblages shown in fig. 108 linked together on traditional archaeological grounds as different phases of the same tradition spreading from south to north.
Source: Roper 1976, p. 183.

and a hypothetical analysis of Mesolithic flint assemblages in the Weald (op. cit. pp. 485–9). Subsequent applications have been varied in scope, from the analysis of intrasite patterning (Bradley 1970, Clarke 1972a, Larson 1975) to examples of spatial diffusion which are our immediate concern in this chapter. Hodder and Orton (1976) give examples which illustrate the methods used and the kind of conclusions which the archaeologist might draw from their application. Thus the study of Romano-British Oxford kiln pottery shows the use made of successively more complex polynomial surfaces to reveal trends and residual patterns in the data (op. cit. figs 5.52–5.54), as well as the problems encountered in dealing with small numbers of irregularly scattered data points; the analysis of Bagterp spearheads in Scandinavia and north Germany confirms an earlier interpretation of the existence of workshop areas (op. cit. figs 5.55–56); and the mapping of the percentages of particular coins in the western Roman Empire has been interpreted as showing the north and westward spread of inflation from the first to the third centuries AD (op. cit. figs 5.58–5.65).

These examples fulfil various combinations of the functions of trend surface analysis in archaeological research which are outlined above (i–iv). This is also the case with a recent analysis of Central Plains radiocarbon dates published by Roper (1976). On traditional archaeological grounds it had been suggested that the various cultural assemblages in the American Central Plains represented the gradual

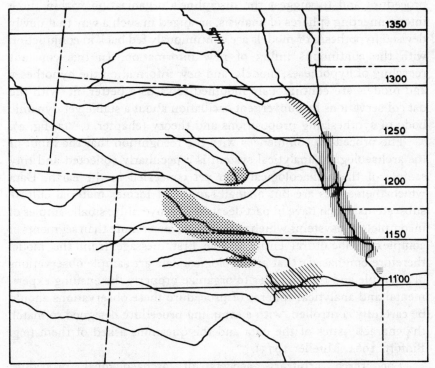

Fig. 110   Linear trend-surface contours showing the predicted south to north spread of cultural assemblages in the Central Plains (see fig. 109). Dates are in radiocarbon years BC.
Source: Roper 1976, p. 187.

south to north spread of agricultural villages with the same basic tradition (figs 108, 109). To test this hypothesis, Roper has gathered a sample of 112 radiocarbon dates from fifty-eight sites in this area and conducted a trend surface analysis. The results strongly support the hypothesis (fig. 110), showing a linear trend surface from south to north with no residuals which were too great to fit this general pattern. It is an interesting possibility that such a study would also be productive in analysing the initial Neolithic settlement of different parts of Europe (e.g. the Balkans, central Europe, Scandinavia).

IV **Procedure**

The last of the three elementary models developed in the opening chapter was a general model for archaeological procedure (fig. 2). This model attempted to sketch a general flow-chart for archaeological procedure and to suggest the discipline's organization within three interconnecting spheres of analysis, arranged in such a way that newly devised hypotheses or models are continuously fed back in conjunction with the continuous influx of new information. In this constant recycling of hypotheses, models, and new information the hypotheses and models are continuously modified towards a better 'fit' with the data observations by convergent oscillation about a stable yet dynamic body of synthesizing propositions and theory (chapter 1, VIa, fig. 2).

The procedure commences with the recognition that the input of the archaeological analytical system is a peculiarly collected and tiny sample of the archaeological data yet concealed in the earth. Data which themselves are but a small sample of former material culture subsystems which have in part decayed irrecoverably; small samples of incomplete subsystems which in turn were never more than segments of complex sociocultural entities. The first message from the model therefore emphasizes that archaeological data are sample observations of a sample and that in order to organize properly the ensuing experimental and analytical spheres of procedure these observations should be carefully controlled, with a sampling procedure designed to match the characteristics of the data and the questions asked of them (e.g. Binford 1964, Mueller 1975).

The three arbitrary aspects of archaeological procedure incorporate the sphere of contextual analysis, the sphere of specific analysis, and the central sphere of hypothesis and model construction – leading to interpretation (fig. 2) (contextual and specific attributes, see chapter I, III). Contextual analysis is here intended to convey the controlled sampling observation, and accumulation of archaeological data by excavation and collection. This sphere of archaeology is making very rapid progress towards a proper use of the experimental method and is gathering an increasing body of knowledge about how this technique may be applied in the field. At the same time, the coupled sphere of specific analysis has made similarly great advances by the increasing employment of feedback information from ecological and taxonomic models, as well as a growing use of statistical methodology and computer techniques. The contextual analysis provides data on distribution, stratification, association, and includes chronological and environmental data ranging from radio carbon dates to pollen horizons and animal bones. The specific analysis digests the specific attributes of the artefacts and assemblages recovered, experiments with their further analysis and searches for regularities in ordering, clustering, similarities, or correlations.

The information from both contextual and specific analysis is then centralized in the sphere of comparative analysis and integrated in building and rebuilding hypotheses and models. At this stage the data are a mass of contextual and specific attributes with varying degrees of already apparent regularities which may now be ordered to match an existing model simulating the particular archaeological situation, or if no such model exists then these data may suggest one for testing. The store of existing models in the central sphere of archaeology is enormously varied – some, as we have seen, are very old and rickety, others are brand-new but little tested. The majority of these models in the storage racks are iconic models for very specific situations – maps, graphs, histograms and so on. A more useful category includes the analogue models which range from historical and anthropological analogues to abstract analogues and simulations. The most recent shelf stores those very few and as yet rather limited symbolic models, including deterministic, statistical, and stochastic structures (chapter II, I).

One of the fundamental models in the central store is the archaeological classificatory model which enables the archaeologist to match his incoming observations and their regularities with the entities of the appropriate rank and order in the nested hierarchy. The careful and rigorous use of the model and the observations will enable the taxonomist to say something about the properties of the entities concerned and the processes which might act upon them, with various patterned results for which other models exist. A specific version of this hierarchical and polythetic model, relating to a particular region at a particular time, should contain sufficient information for the archaeologist to match his entities in terms of specific affinities and phylogeny. Such problems involve the continuous comparison, ordering, and reordering of assemblages until the new set of data and its attributes match transformations and trajectories from one set of developing cultural systems and differentiating that set from other systems, which are claimed as separate and parallel transformations. This procedure requires the clustering of time and space system transformations and the ever more accurate alignment of these clusters to those respective axes. In particular this process has to differentiate, assess and match the horizontal diffusion phase-system attributes of the new data from the socially inherited tradition-system attributes; a problem arising from the continuously interwebbed nature of cultural phylogeny (fig. 28). Numerical taxonomy is an essential tool in this procedure but does not of itself offer conclusive evidence of phylogeny but only of phenetic relationships.

When at last the particular set of new data has been analysed and re-analysed by the three operational spheres it may release a series of propositions, hypotheses, and models generated or modified by the particular information of the particular set of new data. These products represent the 'interpretation' of the new data and will now pass by different routes through the continuous recycling procedure. These products are channelled back to the input of the system where they are used to reframe and more accurately control the spheres of contextual and specific analysis, modifying their orientation and direction of search. Very occasionally, this constant recycling and re-comparison of theoretical output with practical input will precipitate a set of synthesizing propositions, or theories about the real world, as the data leave the central system. The output of such synthesizing propositions and theories depends entirely on the discipline of the procedural system, the energy devoted to its activities, the intelligent direction and channelling of those energies, and the quality of the components in the system. It should be noted that any analytical system which denies the existence of synthesizing propositions about its input data has a preconditioned orientation such that it is most unlikely to discover any, even should they exist.

So far, the only propositions about the archaeological world capable of use in interpretative procedures are:

(1) *The inherent space/time population regularities of archaeological entities* – those repeated regularities which can be made to appear when certain data are arbitrarily ordered in a certain way:

- the unimodal distribution of attribute states from a single multistate attribute within a unitary archaeological population (figs 29, 30);
- the double lenticular distribution of attribute states and type states in phase and tradition development (figs 55–60);
- the syntactical regularities of correlated attributes clustered within artefact-types and types clustered within cultural formats.

(2) *The inherent system regularities of archaeological entities as related kinds of special system* – those general regularities which arise because all archaeological entities are sets of elements which once formed part of sociocultural units:

(i) the general process model of archaeological systems as semi-Markovian systems coupled with environing or contextual systems; expressed by a dynamic model (fig. 11) and a set of sixteen postulates (postulates 1–16, chapter 2, II).
(ii) the hypothesis of multiple factors and cumulative effect (chapter 2, III, fig. 12).

(3) *The inherent system regularities of archaeological entities as parts of sociocultural information systems* – those repeated regularities which arise because archaeological variety is part of the stabilized variety in former sociocultural information systems:

the continuity hypothesis – sociocultural systems, and therefore archaeological systems, continuously adjusted their system variety in such a way as to repeatedly minimize the maximum amount of immediate system dislocation, in terms of new, alternative, contradictive, or redundant variety in relation to that system.

(4) *The inherent distribution and diffusion regularities of archaeological entities as parts of sociocultural population networks* – those crude postulates and tentative axioms which summarize and depend upon the regularities arising from constraints affecting diffusion processes (chapter 10, III, postulates 1–7, axioms 1–5).

Notes

(1) Sherratt (1972, pp. 528–9) distinguishes three further processes of change which he claims are reflected in the distribution of prehistoric cultural assemblages in southeast Europe. These are:

  (i) *boundary readjustment* – the acquisition or loss of small areas of advantageous land on the boundary of two neighbouring cultures;
 (ii) *unit reorientation* – the fluctuations in allegiance of small 'peripheral' population units between adjacent higher density 'core' areas;
(iii) *network linkage* – the merging of two previously separate cultures.

Another typology of non-seasonal human population movements has been proposed by Hill (n.d.). Arguing that such movements never occur without some form of ecological pressure which threatens the population's survival, he defines four types of process:

  (i) *range expansion* – the result of local population pressure. Human groups are compelled to expand into nearby areas (e.g. the Tiv of Nigeria);
 (ii) *range contraction* – the result of sometimes drastically decreasing food supply approaching a critical level (e.g. drought, competition, disease). The human groups are forced to contract their ranges into smaller favourable territories;
(iii) *range drift* – less severe than (1) and (2) and the result of such factors as the decreasing productivity of local resources; shifting cultivation is given as an example;
(iv) *range budding/migration* – the result of an increase in population pressure which cannot be offset by range expansion, of decreasing local productivity, of competition and of disease. Where types (1)–(3) may be equated with *continuous* distibutions of archaeological material, range budding results in a discontinuous pattern.

The relationship between population movement and the diffusion of cultural traits has been the subject of much debate in anthropological and archaeological circles during the present century. In some cases large-scale migrations were proposed by archaeologists on what now seem to be rather insubstantial grounds. Within European prehistoric studies the role of such population movement has declined in popularity while the part played in cultural change and distribution patterns by trade has received more profitable attention. Within American archaeology some brave attempts to relate migrations to archaeologically recoverable evidence were made in the 1950s (e.g. Willey 1953, Thompson 1958), but the complexities involved invite critical comment. The 'visibility' of a population movement in the archaeological record may often vary with the degree to which a distinctive cultural assemblage was preserved and diffused by the intrusive group. There is a distinct contrast, for example, between the archaeological evidence for the Roman conquest of Britain and for the rapid movement of the Philistines to the coastal Canaanite cities, where only a new tomb type and some artistic motifs distinguish them from the local population (Trigger 1968, p. 43). Further complications are introduced when one considers the usual sizes of samples of material culture or skeletal remains on which interpretations of migration have been based. This factor has been brought into focus by improved methods of data collection (e.g. fine sieving) and by the recognition that changes in the cultural assemblages of successive occupation phases in a single site may not be a representative reflection of total change at that site through time. Instead the archaeologist may be recording some compound of the changes in the spatial organization of that site during its occupation: what at one period may be the location for a domestic structure, may later become a livestock pen or a rubbish dump. On sites with shallow occupation deposits a complete excavation or a suitably designed sampling strategy may alleviate this problem, but on large, deeply stratified settlements (e.g. the prehistoric 'tells' of southeast Europe) examination of the spatial organization of early phases is made difficult by the constraints imposed by the excavator's limited resources. Even when we have taken such problems into account, there remains the question of chronology: are the site occupation 'phases' distinguished by the archaeologist of such a narrowly defined nature that changes in population over a period of five, ten or fifty years can be recognized in them? In many cases honesty and field experience require a negative answer. The compound nature of such 'phases' may often obscure significant local changes and mislead the unwary archaeologist. Schwerdtfeger (1972, pp. 555–6) has noted the change from round to rectangular structures within domestic compounds in Hauseland during the period 1928–68. This represents continuous change over a single generation, but to the archaeologist dealing with organic building materials such as mudbrick it may appear to represent a drastic break with previous tradition.

Thus any interpretation of changes in population as a result of migration has to be seen in terms of associated changes in material culture and then in relation to the effect of the formation processes of the archaeological record. Even if sufficiently fine control over these factors is established, it may still be that we are misleading ourselves in expecting cultural change to have proceeded by a continuous and regular rate in any particular site or region, so that 'breaks' in an occupation sequence necessarily have to indicate population discontinuity (chapter 5, n. 2).

(2) It should be noted here that the author's concern is with diffusion as a process by which cultural traits and ideas are spread through time and space. He is *not* involving himself in any general argument about the relative merits of 'diffusion' and 'evolution' as explanations of cultural change.

(3) Binford (1972, p. 239) has pursued this point even further in his study of mortuary practices. He argues that

it is only after we understand the organizational properties of cultural systems that we can meaningfully make comparisons among them in terms of culture content. The contemporary archaeologist's practice of making comparisons among cultural units in terms of inventories of culture content, while making no attempt to isolate and understand the variables affecting the frequency or distribution of content in the cultural units studied, is a fruitless and, I fear, meaningless pastime.

11 Discussion and speculation

Mind-like Behaviour in Artefacts,
Title of paper in *Brit. J. Phil. Sci.*, II, No. 6, pp. 105–21
D. M. MACKAY 1951

1 Theoretical background

This chapter will be used to cover a selective appraisal of the primary dispositions underpinning analytical archaeology and framing its orientation. Most of the contents, it is true, will have been covered in the preceding texts but the intention here is to draw together much that has only been obliquely discussed. Most of these primary dispositions represent the diffusion into archaeology of major developments in allied disciplines; a derivation, however, that does not necessarily make them peripheral to the organization of archaeology as a discipline in its own terms and dimensions. Certainly, scientific aids no more make archaeology a 'science' than a wooden leg makes a man into a tree – isotope dating, chemical analysis, and proton magnetometers remain adjuncts. By contrast, the primary attitudes which now permit tentative formulations in generalizing archaeological theory are central to the whole structure of the discipline – arising for the most part from cybernetics, information theory, behavioural studies, and not least from mathematics – symbolic logic, probability theory, set theory, game theory, inductive statistics, topology and numerical taxonomy (cf. Clarke, 1968, 1972, 1973; Doran and Hodson 1975).

The primary contributions to analytical archaeology are for the most part mathematical rather than scientific, symbolic and abstract rather than tangible. This simply emphasizes the important function of mathematical apparatus as symbolic machinery for modelling the central theory of organized disciplines in terms of structured deductive systems. At the same time these external contributions are possible because the relationship between analysts and their data may be as much enlightened by simple changes in viewpoint as by direct augmentation of the quantity of data. Archaeologists have concentrated far too much upon increasing the quantity of their data and far too little upon increasing the quality of their conceptual apparatus.

The main field of deployment for these primary contributions is in the field of systematization and generalization – the detection and organization of order, regularities, constraints and trends. The elementary advantage accruing from these activities being simply that such regularities can be used to predict behaviour and to highlight departure from expected behaviour patterns, with the consequent exposure of residual information. These primary attitudes stimulate the discovery of relationships which give order and regularity to otherwise heterogeneous material.

Such an approach immediately introduces the philosophical problem about the existence or absence of order in the extra-sensory 'real' world. Whether or not there is order or chaos in nature most philosophers agree that the order we perceive and use is in part an arbitrary order devised by man and extended by him into his interpretation of the environment – where arbitrary means 'selected to produce order in certain dimensions', not chance or random order. Thus, in its most elementary manifestations we have the psychological test drawings in which some subjects see only lines, others see faces, and others a goblet – the perception of order depending on the selective organization of the receiver rather than the geometry of the object studied (Haggett 1965, p. 2; Cherry 1957, pp. 256–302).

Without embroiling ourselves too deeply in the problem of order or chaos in the 'real' world we may notice that we have repeatedly employed such an arbitrary organization of data into an order which they need not necessarily possess.

(i) The normal distribution curve – with its unimodal and bilateral symmetry – has been much used as an expected model for the distribution of certain kinds of populations, with deviations from this persistent 'regularity' as an important source of information (figs 29, 30, 33–5; chapters 4, III; 5, III; 6, III). However, even with the appropriate categories of population it is only possible to extract this 'regularity' by selectively adopting a quite arbitrary ordering of the data – by frequency of occurrence in classes deliberately arranged in successive sequence on a certain scale. By using a different scale and a different sequence of class intervals the vertical frequency bars of the normal histogram could be redistributed in an irregular and non-normal outline. Indeed, the converse procedure – transformation – is often used to get a distribution 'regularity' out of 'irregular' data by trying out various scales (Haggett 1965, p. 288). The same kind of arbitrary requirements are equally necessary to obtain the 'regularities' of the other standard distribution curves – Log-Normal, Binomial, Poisson, Gamma, etc.

(ii) The unimodal distribution curves and trend 'regularities' of successive populations of archaeological entities may only be obtained by selectively employing certain scales and orders, and not by employing others (fig. 46; examine the effects of reordering the attribute classes (o), (a), (b), (c), (d), (e) in this figure).

(iii) It is only possible to model the 'regular behaviour' of the infinity of networks in a complex system by arbitrarily selecting a limited set of elements in the network – the strategic variables for the arbitrarily selected 'frame of reference', or system of interest.

These examples suffice to show that we are quite accustomed to getting 'regularities' out of data where they are not immediately apparent, by the deliberate manipulation of the observations involved and the arbitrary but consistent selection of certain dimensions but not others – the deliberate organization of the data into 'regularities' for our own predictive convenience. Indeed, it is towards the discovery of new relationships which consistently give order or regularity to our perception of the real world that much research effort is devoted. The accuracy and dependability with which a given 'regularity' may be obtained from the arbitrary but specified treatment of specified classes of data expresses the utility of that procedure as a model and tool. It is not so much a search for regularities in our data as the deliberate organization of our data into powerful regularities (chapter 1, IV).

Whether or not there is order in the external world is a topic that we can happily leave to the philosophers. We have seen that whether order exists beyond our outward organization of it or not, we draw great benefit from getting our perceptions into regularities and order, so long as those qualities dependably arise from a selected procedure upon selected aspects of the available data. Nevertheless, as archaeologists we are not so much concerned with the natural world as with the world of man and his artefacts and it is a characteristic of man, as we have just observed, that he deliberately introduces ordered relationships where none formerly existed. This is true of man's theorizing on the nature of the extra-sensory world and it is true of man's material handiwork – the artefacts.

All living organisms seem to introduce order into the world but man as a higher organism introduces a higher degree of order, extending from the material world to the intangible realms of thought. Whether or not there is order in the outside world is immaterial therefore to the deliberate orderliness brought into it by man and fossilized in his artefacts. This orderliness is the archaeologist's key to the material culture of ancient societies – the selectively ordered attributes, artefacts, and assemblages from the past enshrine the percepta and concepta of their fabricators – a message amidst the noise of disorder (fig. 111).

These deliberations suggest that the analytical archaeologist will be confronted by order and regularity within his data in two forms. Regularity and order which may be produced by certain standardized manipulations and procedures used by the analyst and certain other regularities and orders introduced by the deliberate activities of the people who made the artefacts. It is not entirely clear at the present time, how, and to what extent, the modern analyst can differentiate between these two categories of ordered information – between the message from the past and the characteristics of the receiver (fig. 111). In many respects the garbled information gained by archaeologists from the artefacts of ancient societies is disconcertingly similar to the garbled impression of the real world gained by a child from the artefacts of its own society. The analytical archaeologist's receiver may be more powerful and sensitive but at least the child has the advantage of redundant confirmations from other contemporary channels.

The archaeologist may therefore expect to both find regularities in his data and to be able so to rearrange his data as to produce yet other regularities. Many of these regularities will depend upon the constant or regular conjunction, association, or correlation of particular variables or even the association of lower-order regularities. If this repeated conjunction approaches a nearly constant relationship in all the observable data samples, such that all observed As are Bs, or all observed As have Bs, then these statements can be recognized as low-level laws – or rather accurate hypotheses. Even scientific laws rest upon no more extensive grounds than the assertion of the 'constant' conjunctions of specified properties within the tested sample of the real world. 'The world is not made up of empirical facts with the addition of the laws of nature: what we call the laws of nature are conceptual devices by which we organize our empirical knowledge and predict the future' (Braithwaite 1960, p. 339).

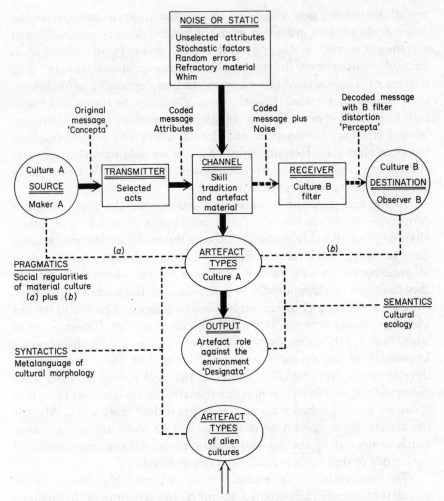

Fig. 111 Material culture as a communication system with three outputs – source A to the environment, source A to culture A, source A to culture B. By Shannon's theorem, effective communication may be established with the environment and culture A, in that errors due to noise may be sufficiently reduced by making the transmitter or receiver sufficiently complex. With culture B, communication via material culture is likely to be unreliable by virtue of the different tuning of receiver B.

The realization that 'Natural Laws' are not deterministic, but only statistical approximations of very high probability, has led to the abandonment of the old ideas of the 'Laws of Nature' as mechanistic controls beyond our senses. The replacement of normative laws by probabilistic laws now allows us to see that the raw material of the outer world shows a gradation from the 'near constant' conjunctions of certain properties in the physical world, down to the 'more than chance' conjunctions in the world of man-organized things. The degrees of 'conjunction' allow corresponding degrees of probabilistic laws – almost deterministic in the laws of science, to almost stochastic in the social sciences. Even in the physical sciences the gap between 'almost constant conjunction' and the old 'constant conjunction' laws has been shown by Heisenberg to be a serious field for uncertainty, if sufficiently large samples were employed (Heisenberg's Uncertainty Principle, 1927; see Haggett 1965, p. 25).

In the activities and fossilized actions of man the conjunction of properties is much less than constant but still much more than chance – thus allowing probabilistic laws but making them much more 'probabilistic', much more difficult to isolate, and with a broader field of uncertainty than the laws we organize for the physical world. On this basis we can confidently look forward to the increasingly more competent framing of increasingly more complex and powerful laws in sociology, social anthropology, and in related studies. These generalizing and synthesizing laws will so reorganize the archaeologist's knowledge of the sociocultural system that it is likely that parallel developments will rapidly follow in the archaeological field also. Nevertheless, one must not imagine that this step is imminent nor that it can be accomplished without a very great deal more work. All that the archaeologist need note is that he will be most unlikely to make much sense out of the sociocultural/material culture interface until both sides of that surface have been reorganized.

This impression of the world provides a reasonably close fit to the world that we are accustomed to move in – a world of free-choice within bounds but bounds severally hedged by variously ranged limits (fig. 7) and yet allowing stochastic choice within those bounds – a 'structured chaos' (Arbib 1967). One might broadly observe that for every locus or state that an entity or attribute takes, there is still a limited set of loci or states that the entity or attribute might have taken with equal probability, even given the constraints limiting that set. This permissible set becomes vanishingly small in the physical sciences but frustratingly large in the social sciences. Such is the case in the choice of a particular settlement site from among the many equally advantageous sites in an area, or in the selection and imposition of an artefact attribute state from among the many equally acceptable attribute states within the culturally accepted multistate set. In this light, much sociocultural information or tradition can be seen as providing a 'mind-making-up' procedure for narrowing the selection to a 'preferable set' and then providing an arbitrary procedure for selection within that set – whether by augury, oracle, or some other stochastic and cabalistic device. The first set is bounded by the functional and culturally induced constraints, producing regularities of one of our categories, and the second set is the range constraining the statistical regularities of our second category.

II Disciplined procedure

The part of the last section that informs us upon procedure might be summarized by saying that we should organize our data into regularities both for convenience and for information. Furthermore, it appears that by being selective, arbitrary, but consistent we can hope to learn about very complex systems by modelling the successive aspects which interest us, deliberately leaving out details which are irrelevant to that system aspect and separating the key, essential, and inessential variables. By starting with single aspect simulation models it should be possible to additively evolve more complex and increasingly comprehensive ensembles – although it is to be doubted whether sociocultural systems can ever be expressed by single model structures. In short, disciplined procedure in analytical archaeology may be adequately condensed in the words of Descartes – 'method consists entirely in properly ordering and arranging the things to which we should pay attention' (*Oeuvres*, vol. X, p. 379; Rules for the Direction of the Mind, rule V).

The general scaffolding for the procedure of archaeology as a 'learning' discipline has already been outlined in the recycling feedback model (fig. 2). In essence that procedure is based upon feeding a constant flow of contextual and specific observations into the 'analytical engine' in conjunction with the best available models appropriate to the particular data. Within the engine the aspects of the data satisfactorily accounted for by the models are redundantly used to reinforce and elaborate those structures of hypotheses; the residual data aspects not satisfactorily covered by the model are thus defined and may be used to modify or destroy the model, or develop new models. The output from this procedure is therefore – confirmed, modified, or new models which are then returned to the input of the procedural engine, to be fed in against appropriate new data. This procedure is effectively a multiple regression analysis system – an organized procedure employing John Stuart Mill's famous 'method of residues'.

However, the analytical engine is more richly networked than this schematic model suggests and there are several other internal flow patterns which may be employed successively or simultaneously to generate hypotheses and test models. Before we progress to the problems of the techniques for generating archaeological hypotheses and models it might be as well to run through an ordered procedural sequence.

UNILINEAR PROCEDURE

The sequential investigation of an archaeological problem may be approached as outlined below. The terminology specifically refers to a 'syntactical approach' to archaeological data, along the lines pursued in the discussion of archaeological entities (chapters 4–8). Nevertheless, the same procedure is immediately applicable to the 'pragmatic' and 'semantic' aspects of archaeological problems if the mathematical interpretation of the offending terms is replaced by the nearest subjective equivalent, so long as one is fully aware of the gap between the meanings of the two kinds of terms – they are usually overlapping but not identical sets. It is precisely this gap which in future we must seek to define in order that it may be diminished or allowed for. However, the outline procedure can be given by Chorofas (1965, pp. 25–30):

Initial cycle

(1) Choose and define the problem.
(2) Collect the appropriate data with the appropriate sampling procedure.
(3) Locate the strategic variables defining the arbitrary system aspect relevant to this problem – set up the system believed to contain the key, essential, and inessential variables.
(4) Set up analytical experiments to determine the relation of these variables to one another and to the parameters of the system:
   (a) Devise preliminary analytical experiments – to determine the dependence of the operational variables; analyse suc-

cessive examples of the system states to reveal the statistical dependence of the results on the various operational variables; employ analysis of relationships – contingency, variance, covariance, correlation and regression analysis, factor analysis, etc. – wherever appropriate, to define the key and essential variables.

(b) Devise further analytical experiments – for example, select various system states in which certain parameters are controlled, or may be held constant, in order to investigate the corresponding effect upon the other system variables.

(c) Narrow the operational variables to those key variables to which the results and behaviour of the system are most sensitive.

(5) Formulate a set of hypotheses, or construct a model, organizing the results of these experiments within the frame of the selected problems. Attempt to escalate any such model from an iconic to an analogue, or preferably symbolic status with deterministic, statistical, and stochastic components.

Recycle

(6) Design fresh experiments to test model or hypotheses, design appropriate sampling procedure, collection of data according to this plan, carry out these experiments.

(7) Test model or hypotheses against these new results, isolate any area of residuals unexplained or unsatisfactorily covered by the original model or hypotheses.

(8) Analyse residuals; accept, modify, or reject model or hypotheses according to outcome. Predict relevance to wider sphere of problems and data.

(9) Test the predictions by repeating the whole procedure in a new context: observe – hypothesize – predict – experiment – and, confirm, modify, or reject.

TECHNIQUES FOR GENERATING HYPOTHESES

Hypotheses are developed to relate observed properties to one another by means of a structural concept. In this way an hypothesis, or an hypothetical model, is constructed for the sake of predicting certain correlated regularities. Such hypotheses are consequently mere instruments in specific contexts and in this capacity they may be assessed as accurate, partially accurate, or inaccurate, rather than as true or false. A good model or hypothesis predicts more about a specific class of situations than does a less satisfactory alternative. The importance of this approach to hypotheses is that it removes the illusion of a unitary 'truth' and reveals that many hypotheses may all be partially 'true' at one and the same time but that they may be arranged in a scale of adequacy. The 'truth' about a given situation also depends upon the line of approach that we arbitrarily adopt in probing that situation. One situation therefore has many 'truths', some of which may be arranged to degrees of adequacy along particular approaches but the best of which can only be judged to be temporarily the most effective in different approaches to the same situation (Nagel 1958, pp. 74–5).

One of the problems of the model or hypothesis approach is therefore how to compare the effectiveness of alternative hypotheses and how to generate an adequate supply of replacements. The practical answer overall, seems to rely upon a 'shotgun' procedure, with a multiplicity of different researchers involved in a multilinear stochastic search. Nevertheless some individual procedures have proved capable of more explicit direction.

Method of total scrutiny

If there are no obvious hypotheses, or regularities which may be utilized in such hypotheses, then the data must be searched and reorganized in order to obtain such an organization. This process of scrutiny and transformation is described by Miller and Kahn (1962, pp. 315–24) as a 'shotgun' or 'Pleiades' method. Large quantities of data are assembled and then subjected to a study measuring the correlation between every aspect and every other aspect. The resulting matrix of relationships may then be scanned for any latent structure. This may be done rigorously and formally by matrix inversion and canonical analysis in the case of mathematical data (Haggett 1965, p. 285; Krumbein and Graybill, 1965, pp. 248–75).

Method of regularities

This method commences with the deliberate, intuitive, or accidental discovery of regularities relating properties within the data. The procedure is then concerned with the explicit formulation of as many examples of these regularities as is possible and a proof, by some null hypothesis procedure, that the observed relationships are not arising from chance factors. The correlated conjunction of properties which define the regularity may then be explicitly formulated as an hypothesis for testing.

Method of residues

This method employs the comprehensive regression procedure outlined earlier in this section (II, 1–9). The insufficiency of the conjectured factors to account for the observed effects allows the definition and isolation of residual properties requiring an alternative or a more extensive model. This procedure is formalized in residual and regression analysis (chapter 10, III).

Method of convergence and integration

In many studies there may already exist several hypotheses, each supporting the contributive effect of different factors but the factors and the hypotheses may prove not to be mutually exclusive. This situation then allows the employment of the hypothesis of multiple factors and cumulative effect and the Occam against Converse Occam procedure (chapter 2, III, fig. 12). If the individual factors are proved to play a part in the system under investigation then they may be integrated one at a time into the final model (Occam, too many→ sufficient). However, on many occasions, although the named factors and hypotheses may be operating and may indeed model much of the system behaviour, yet careful search should still be made to see if other unmentioned factors and hypotheses may not also be active (Converse Occam, too few→sufficient). The integration of the necessary factors into an interacting system then allows a more comprehensive hypothesis based on the system structure.

Such a complex hypothesis or model may then best be tested and further defined by the convergent integration of the separate evidence from as many differently based experiments and analyses as is possible. 'Variety in the kinds of positive instances for a theory is a generally acknowledged factor in estimating the weight of the evidence. Experiments which are conducted in qualitatively different domains ... control features of the theory whose relevance in any one domain may be in question' (Nagel 1958, p. 69). In an archaeological situation this might be represented by the convergent integration of separate evidence from each of the many domains constituting single cultural assemblages – artefact taxonomies, distributions, absolute dates, stratigraphies, ceramics, metalwork and so on. This method develops from the assumption that archaeological situations are likely to be many-factor rather than single-factor systems and that consequently the domain of each factor must be allowed for in the search for a comprehensive hypothesis.

Method of multiple alternative hypotheses

This approach is similar to the last in that both are designed to handle many factors or hypotheses relating to single situations. However, the preceding approach is only appropriate for the manipulation of factors and hypotheses which are not mutually exclusive. If a set of mutually exclusive, alternative hypotheses exist to explain a single situation then the method of 'multiple working hypotheses' may be usefully employed (Chamberlin 1897).

This technique suggests that if, at any one time, it is not possible on the existing evidence to decisively discriminate between alternative hypotheses, then these hypotheses should be continuously run in parallel through the regression procedure, until such time as the probabilities of one hypothesis have cumulatively increased and the probabilities of the alternatives have correspondingly diminished to vanishing point. This technique is a simultaneous and multiple version of the standard method of residues – multiple-regression analysis as opposed to simple regression analysis.

The different hypotheses are in this case processed in parallel with constant feedback of information between the channels providing a successive output on the comparative probability states of the alternatives. This comparative state can be estimated subjectively or objectively by using Bayes's theorem of inverse probability (Cherry 1957, p. 63) or Fisher's method of maximum likelihood (Nagel 1958, p. 36). Ideally, the individual probabilities of the alternative hypotheses will fluctuate as they more or less effectively minimize the residuals presented by the flow of fresh data, until the oscillating comparative output converges upon one or other hypothesis. This goal is reached when the cumulative modifications required to save the 'diminishing' hypotheses become more unplausible than the rejection of those hypotheses; hence one hypothesis should remain (Braithwaite 1960, p. 20). Care must however be taken to establish that the hypotheses or factors are really mutually exclusive, otherwise wasteful conflict will be generated between partially satisfactory models that should have been integrated by the method of convergence.

Method of isomorphism

This approach is potentially the most interesting and useful technique but in practice its abuse has tended to obscure its fundamental relevance. Crudely speaking it is the technique of borrowing and modifying models from other disciplines to suit a new context. The basis of the technique has only become explicit with the recent extension of system theory into diverse fields. This procedure has produced a crude taxonomy of system models which shows that many of the models or hypotheses of quite different disciplines are related in such a way that the homomorphism of a system model in one field is often isomorphic with the homomorphism of a similar model in a quite different field. Put more directly, it appears that models and hypotheses in various disciplines exhibit latent structural isomorphisms – they show surprisingly similar theoretical constructions operating as models for quite different data. 'Many scientific concepts in different fields have a logically equivalent structure. One can abstract from them a logical form which is quite general and takes on different peculiar meanings according to the context' (MacKay 1950).

Many examples of such inter-disciplinary isomorphisms may be collected – in some cases the isomorphisms have been brought about by deliberate borrowing between fields of study:

(a) *The exponential relationship laws* – in the physics of radioactive decay, in Malthusian population growth models, in economic production and consumption models, and in the various inverse square laws.

(b) *The mass action laws* – in physics, in chemistry, in population dynamics and mechanical dynamics (Lotka).

(c) *The minimum potential energy equilibrium laws* – in physics as Lagrange's principle, in geography as used by Lösch, and in the social sciences as Zipf's principle, in physical chemistry as Le Chatelier's principle, in electrodynamics as Lenz's law, and in demography as used by Volterra.

(d) *The Gaussian distribution laws* – in astronomy, in the physical
sciences, in geography, in empirical psychology, genetics, and
many other fields.

Archaeological models homomorphic with many of these
laws have been discussed in the course of this work (Haggett
1965, pp. 32–3).

This discovery of predictive isomorphisms has led to the optimistic pursuit of fundamental inter-disciplinary models, hypotheses, and
laws. However, a more productive development has been the increasingly systematic scrutiny and deliberate mutual scanning of the
deductive superstructures of the various disciplines, which has already
resulted in a most useful interchange of models and procedures. The
method of isomorphism must be used with the greatest care but if
properly controlled it offers primitive disciplines, such as archaeology,
the chance to borrow sophisticated, powerful, and beautiful pieces of
model machinery beyond their own temporarily limited powers of
fabrication. Where the disciplines are primitive and their fields excessively complex, as in archaeology, sociology, and social anthropology,
then such a borrowing procedure is likely to save a great deal of time.

To conclude this section on 'disciplined procedure' one might
scrutinize the phrase itself. Discipline, as Descartes emphasized,
consists of choosing a sphere of interest, defining the system involved,
and arranging and ordering the observations concerning that system.
Procedure, in this context, is conveyed by our model of the analytical
engine which may be constructed for disciplining archaeological data
(fig. 2). In its fully networked form this procedural machinery will
process many sets of data in parallel and by simultaneous but varied
techniques for generating orders, regularities, and hypotheses. These
methods for model and hypothesis construction may be expressed
either in ordinary language for subjective application, or in symbolic
form for mathematical manipulation and testing. Ordinary language
hypotheses and models are more readily conceived and understood
but tend to be very specific and restricted in scope, as well as rather
ambiguous and tacit in their implications. Symbolic hypotheses and
models are immediately capable of more general application and testing and are usually fully explicit, as well as offering the possibility of
development and transformation in a symbolic calculus. Both systems
of hypothesis and model construction should be employed but
wherever and whenever possible the ordinary language models should
be converted into symbolic forms.[1]

III   **Archaeological grammar**

Grammar comprises the organized and ordered body of the relationships of words as abstracted from a very large number of literary
contexts – the condensation of a large number of observed regularities.
It is clear that the outcome of the kinds of procedure that we have
been discussing should be some equivalent body of archaeological
grammar, similarly condensing a large number of observed regularities in archaeological data. Yet there seem to be not one archaeological
grammar but several 'rival archaeologies' based on what may appear to
be various incompatible basic propositions (Chang 1967, pp. 137–43).
These basic propositions of modern archaeology seem to exhort us to
take totally opposed views of the same data:

> Proposition 1. Archaeological data were formerly an integral part of
> sociocultural entities – whole systems in which the artefacts
> were elaborately networked. Archaeological data cannot there-
> fore be adequately studied as an artificially discrete subsystem
> separated from the whole circuitry of interaction which was its
> former context. Artefacts should be studied in a sociocultural
> and environmental context (e.g. Binford and Binford 1968).
> Proposition 2. Archaeological data are now detached from their
> contemporary sociocultural and environmental contexts.
> Archaeological data may therefore best be studied empirically as
> a material phenomenon with observable regularities. Artefacts
> should be studied in terms of their own attribute systems, away
> from the distortions of loose presuppositions about their former
> contexts.

The first proposition is found underlying the present activities of
the cultural ecology and cultural ethnology schools of archaeology.
The second proposition is the foundation of archaeological taxonomy
and morphology, employing the inductive statistics, numerical
taxonomy, and computer techniques which have been claimed to
'dehumanize' the discipline. The apparent conundrum is that both
propositions seem to be true and certainly the rival archaeologies that
they have given rise to have each made most useful contributions in
recent years. If this is the case, how are they to be reconciled and what
are the respective roles and mutual relationships of these rival
approaches, each with its own domain and its vociferous advocates?
    The answer to the conundrum of modern archaeology can best be
sought in the elementary structure of the discipline, in which the

isomorphism with the study of information and sign systems can be further extended. This is hardly surprising if we view language and sign systems themselves as artefacts like any other human fabrication. The initial step can best be taken by freely adapting some ideas from the theory of signs (Cherry 1957, pp. 8, 109–15). The terms we wish to use distinguish (fig. 48):

Designata – the set of roles or activities that a particular artefact was intended for.

Percepta – the information conveyed to an observer in the act of perceiving an object or artefact.

Concepta – the information contained in the abstract idea of an object or artefact conceived in the brain of a person or potential artificer, recalled from memory.

These terms make it clear that artefacts may be imagined as presenting three kinds of relationship at three interfaces with the outside world:

– relationships with other artefacts (involving their designata, percepta, and concepta)
– relationships with people (involving their percepta and concepta)
– relationships with the physical environment at the time of manufacture, involving their designata (see fig. 112).

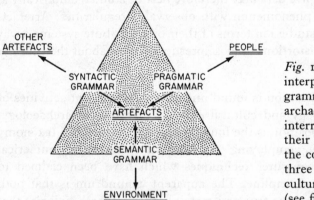

Fig. 112 Artefacts and interpretation. The three grammars of archaeological interrelationships and their three domains – the consequences of the three outputs of material culture communications (see fig. 111).

The relationships of artefacts at these three interfaces are in different domains – they are interrelated but they operate in different systems. These three classes of relationship will therefore have three different but related 'grammars' condensing their regularities. The grammars of these three relationship domains are usually called:

Syntactics – relations between artefacts and attributes at every level of their organization (designata, percepta, concepta).

Pragmatics – relations between artefacts and their users and observers (percepta, concepta).

Semantics – relations between artefacts and their roles in the physical world (designata).

It is therefore apparent that if the archaeologist is constructing an organized and ordered body of relationships that we might call archaeological grammar – then that corpus of relations involves not one but three separate and related grammars, those of archaeological syntactics, archaeological pragmatics, and archaeological semantics. The relationship between these separate grammars and their domains is perhaps best expressed by simple diagrams (figs 111, 112).

If we now return to the basic propositions of modern archaeology, with their different approaches, we will find that they are the complementary and interrelated approaches to the domains that have just been described. The first proposition requires that artefacts should be studied in terms of their sociocultural and environmental context; the appropriate grammars for this domain are archaeological pragmatics and semantics. The second proposition requires that artefacts should be studied in terms of their own attributes, as abstract systems; here the appropriate grammar is archaeological syntactics. In practice, the archaeologist wants to know and organize all these relationships of his data and to apply the integrated pragmatic and semantic approach as much as the abstracted syntactic approach in order that the evidence of all the domains might be brought together. However, this procedure is most efficiently accomplished if the archaeologist is aware of these separate sets of relationships and systematically sets about the independent construction of the different domain grammars. Otherwise the attempt at a single all-purpose grammar of archaeological relationships will promote confusion between procedures and introduce too many dimensions for effective analysis.

This section might close, therefore, with a brief outline of the appropriate roles and procedure of the three domains.

Syntactics

Archaeological syntactics is concerned with the domain of artefacts as phenomena suitable for empirical study in their own right; where the term artefact is intended to convey every level in the systems – from attribute state to technocomplex. The ideal is to organize and order syntactical observations into symbolic models of ascending capacity. The grammar developed from this approach may hope to achieve a calculus of relationships based upon observations of archaeological systems and the symbolic representation of such systems. This would allow the manipulation and transformation of these symbolic representations by means of a set of grammatical rules so that the consequences of a set of calculus operations would be isomorphic with the consequences of a parallel set of operations in the real world.

The ideal in syntactical archaeology is of course a very long way from being achieved. However, the possible beginnings of a grammar are nevertheless becoming apparent with the progressively more powerful use of symbolic models in archaeology and the increasing refinement of our knowledge of their relationships and trans-formations. These developments are very largely the result of the developing contributions of quantification, statistical procedure, and the impact of the computer. Indeed, it is a distinctive feature of syntactic grammar that it is much concerned with relative frequencies and statistical probabilities in the manipulation of its elements. The development of a symbolic and axiomatic representation of archaeological syntactics is at least possible – we have discussed the potential classification and transformation of general constellation models and a growing knowledge of the taxa of such systems in archaeological data will surely yield more lines for development.

Syntactic grammar in archaeology is therefore an abstract formu-lation, freely devised to enable a calculus of rules of formation, deduc-tion, and transformation to be developed. These rules are not neces-sarily inherent in the data, they are simply a formal and symbolic system devised to organize and exploit regularities in the data. A language system used by an observer to model and synthesize empiri-cal observations in a real world system.

Pragmatics

Archaeological pragmatics covers the domain of artefacts and their relations to the people who made them and the people who observe them. This observation immediately reveals an important dichotomy within this field of studies (fig. 111). On one hand artefacts convey certain tacit information to the person who made them and closely similar information to other persons of the same culture, since a shared sociocultural programming will ensure that within broad limits their filtering receivers are similarly interpreting the incoming information (fig. 111a). On the other hand the same artefacts will convey rather different but overlapping information to persons of other cultures, whose alien sociocultural programming will prevent them 'seeing' the artefact in the same 'light' as that received by the source group (fig. 111b). It is apparent that the archaeologist is firmly placed in the latter class of alien observers with a biased filter interpretation. The archaeologist parallels the New Guinea aboriginal in his cargo cult interpretation of the alien artefacts (chapter 3, III).

Archaeological pragmatics defines a field for the consideration, or attempted consideration, of artefacts within sociocultural contexts – in its recent aspect this constitutes cultural ethnology. The relations that archaeological pragmatics can hope to investigate are those which may suggest association between certain sociocultural organizations and certain sets of attribute or artefact regularities. Most of these pragmatic formulations have in the past been over naive – equating longhouses or female figurines with matricentred societies for example – but recently more sophisticated models have been erected and tested. These pragmatic models have largely been concerned with what archaeological configurations might be expected in connection with certain social organizations (e.g. Deetz 1965; Longacre 1968, 1970; Hill 1968, 1970; Whallon 1968; chapter 3, n. 2). At a broader level we have already considered some of the complex relationships in the grammar relating archaeological entities and group ethnology (chapter 9). At a minutely focused level archaeological pragmatics may be concerned with the symbolism of ceramic motifs, artistic conventions, heraldic codes, or written scripts. In all these levels the fundamental problems include the dichotomous implications of the archaeological data and the inevitable uncertainty about the actual nature of the specific sociocultural context.

Pragmatic grammar in archaeology may also in time come to be expressed in an abstract formulation. Although archaeological pragmatics must probe social/artefact relationships with the tools of frequency counts, correlation, and statistical probabilities it also deals with logical probabilities in the sense of Bayes, Bar-Hillel, and Carnap (Cherry 1957, p. 242). This facet is shared by archaeological semantics to a degree which distinguishes both semantics and pragmatics from syntactical grammar. Carnap has already succeeded in illustrating the way that a symbolic logic may be applied to kinship relations and this problem is congruous with those of relating the various levels of archaeological and sociocultural entities as well as to other pragmatic problems (chapter 9, fig. 75; Carnap 1958, pp. 220–5). From the opposite direction Steward (1955) has organized and defined significant regularities relating sociocultural categories and environmental constraints, which together control certain pragmatic regularities. However, it is quite apparent that in this field little or no archaeological progress can be made towards a symbolic and axiomatic expression until the sociologists and social anthropologists have themselves ordered their side of this interface.

Semantics

Archaeological semantics outlines the domain of relations between artefacts and their roles in activities in the physical world. These relationships are characteristically complex – the same roles may be filled by different but limited sets of artefact-type families, the same artefact will have many different roles within each culture (e.g. White and Thomas 1972) and many more within a set of cultures. It is this maze of intersecting sets and complex correlations that a semantic grammar must try and express.

In practice, artefacts are frequently used in polythetic sets which comprise an artefact-type complex relating to a specific activity, set of activities, or to a subcultural unit of some kind. The study of these kits, accoutrements, equipments and trappings offers a wider scope for the organization and detection of cross-cultural regularities. Such artefact-type complexes combine to make up much of the equipment defining the common ground of technocomplex entities – the complicated way in which this combination may be effected has been demonstrated by the Binfords' factor analysis of Mousterian technocomplex equipment (Binford and Binford 1966). It is therefore probable in terms of relating artefact complexes to certain roles in certain environmental contexts that a semantic grammar of technocomplex structure might be evolved.

An archaeological semantic grammar is therefore a systematization of observations in cultural ecology. Such a grammar would share with archaeological pragmatics a need for expression in terms of logical probability connecting the intersecting sets of conditions. This suggests the ultimate possibility of modelling the semantic 'behaviour' of archaeological data in terms of a symbolic calculus but this goal must lie in the distant future (Carnap 1958). In the meantime the archaeologist must press on with the accumulation of the necessary data. Technocomplexes must be explicitly defined in terms of their artefact-type complex structures and this configuration must be matched with the essential aspects of local ecology which induce the overall regularity.

IV Speculations

Analytical archaeology may perhaps be defined as the continuous elucidation of the relationships which permeate archaeological data by means of disciplined procedures directed towards the precipitation of a body of general theory. The temptation to see this aspect of archaeology as an archaeological science must be resisted. Analytical archaeology is not a science but it is a discipline, its primary machinery is mathematical rather than scientific. The archaeologist's pursuit of the scientific mirage has long obscured the point that a study may be based on empirical observation, experiment, induction and the formulation of hypotheses without necessarily being a science. The quality which distinguishes a science is the degree of certainty marking the recurrent conjunction of the properties which comprise the field of study and hence the degree of wide generality of its empirical propositions. The quality which distinguishes archaeology is the more than chance regularity marking the conjunction of certain archaeological properties which are restricted to limited regions by complex constraints and which may only be expressed in probabilistic propositions.

The relationships which analytical archaeology may hope to elucidate are those found in the separate but interconnected domains of archaeological syntactics, pragmatics, and semantics. These domains are the archaeological views of cultural systematics, cultural ethnology, and cultural ecology (the morphological anthropological and ecological paradigms – Clarke 1972). The relationships within each domain form independent grammars condensing the domain regularities. One of the more interesting possibilities arises from the chance that one or all of these separate grammars may eventually be expressed in a symbolic and axiomatic calculus. At the moment the abstract approach of archaeological syntactics, accelerated by its computer assisted take-off, displays the most promising potential for development in this way – perhaps employing a taxonomy of archaeological systems and constellation models and operating upon them by means of specified transformations. Nevertheless, archaeological pragmatics and semantics are also gaining impetus from computer studies and a combination of simulations with analogue computers and a symbolic logic using probabilities may ultimately model these grammars equally effectively. Unfortunately these thresholds can hardly be achieved until both sociology and social anthropology have fully reorganized and ordered their own grammars in these respects. For these reasons alone it looks as though the 'observer language' or meta-language of archaeological syntactics will be the first grammar to uncover a calculus of symbolic expression over the next few decades.

If the integrated 'wholeness' of sociocultural systems is accepted then the domain of archaeology as one arbitrary approach to these entities becomes complementary to the separate approaches and domains of social anthropology, social psychology, and the other social disciplines. In this view archaeology may have a very important role to play as the testing ground for complex techniques which may be sharpened against the artificially simplified data of archaeology before their more sophisticated employment against the further complexities of primary social data. It is already apparent that the statistical and mathematical methodology of both archaeology and anthropology could best be taught in a single course of lectures. A basic methodological link of this kind would go a long way to redress the short-sighted divergence of the specialized branches of these studies and simultaneously prevent the archaeologist from becoming too dilettante and the anthropologist from becoming too abstruse.

In any event archaeology is being subtly infiltrated by concepts from a multiplicity of disciplines and interstices between disciplines (see section I). Archaeology and these New Studies constitute a coupled system and therefore archaeology must adapt to the changing output of this context if it wishes to make the most use of these powerful arrivals. Archaeology must be rethought, reorientated, and rewritten in order to facilitate these developments and in order to reciprocally contribute to the modern context. It is too early and too dangerous to venture to attempt this reformation yet and it is certainly too great a task for any single author. Perversely therefore *Analytical Archaeology* is a personal attempt to do just this – 'anticipations, rash and premature' as Bacon's description of scientific hypothesis prescribes in the *Novum Organum*. To be justified only by the Preface to this work and by Bacon's further dictum – 'truth comes out of error more readily than out of confusion'. With these caveats it is still to be hoped that however transient its contents this work may be a homomorphic model of a future class of archaeological textbook which will repair these errors and elaborate analytical archaeology on a sound basis.

Notes

(1) The major thrust of this volume has been towards the analysis of models for archaeological entities and processes, while the author's views on procedure are expressed in less detail in this section and in earlier chapters (chapter 2, VI, A and fig. 2; chapter 10, IV). However, the last decade has seen a significant growth of interest in and debate about such matters as the formulation and testing of hypotheses and the existence of 'laws' of human behaviour. This matched the author's own interest in these subjects and it seems a useful exercise to direct the reader towards some of the primary sources.

Archaeologists have turned to other disciplines and in particular to the philosophy of science (e.g. Hempel 1966; Rudner 1966; Harvey 1969; Medawar 1969; Harré 1972; other useful references in Morgan 1973) for models of hypothesis testing and explanation. Apart from the need for a more disciplined approach to procedure, which is an aim shared by many archaeologists, there has been a more explicit commitment by younger American archaeologists to a model of explanation derived from the works of Carl Hempel: this is the 'covering law' model, and more specifically the 'deductive-nomological' method of explanation. This has been vigorously propounded by Lewis Binford (1972) and further expressed by Fritz and Plog (1970) and Watson, LeBlanc and Redman (1971). More practical considerations of how this procedure can be operationalized in archaeological research can be found in Hill (1972) and Plog (1974).

These views on procedure have not escaped criticism, both from archaeologists (e.g. Johnson 1972; Tuggle, Townsend and Riley 1972; Clarke 1972b) and by a philosopher of science (Morgan 1973). While much of the debate centres on detailed points of procedure, such as the deductive testing of hypotheses and the discovery and use of laws (Plog 1973; Stickel and Chartkoff 1973), two more general points have been emphasized by critics of the 'Hempel school'. First there is the question of the other different forms of explanation which have been discussed by philosophers of science and which should also be considered by archaeologists. Tuggle, Townsend and Riley criticize the Hempel school for treating the philosophy of science as a 'monolithic system of consensus on such problems in explanation as the place of laws, the symmetry of explanation and prediction, the nature of causation and the role of induction' (1972, pp. 3–4). This is expressed in a different but more forceful way by Morgan, who writes that 'there is no position so absurd that some philosopher has not propounded it at some time. Thus it makes little difference what doctrine you wish to support – you can always find some philosopher who, in his infinite wisdom, supports that doctrine' (1973, p. 259). The second general point concerns the validity of extracting the explanatory procedures of one discipline and imposing them on another.

> Any philosophy of science is thus merely a series of generalizations made by philosophers about the pattern of logical structures and concepts which relate the assumptions, observations, hypotheses, explanations and interpretations such as they observe in the work of natural scientists. It is therefore a fundamental mistake to impose any philosophy extracted from this limited set of disciplines upon a wider set of studies which were not included within the initial set from which the generalizations were made. (Clarke 1972b, pp. 237–8)

Definitions

ARTEFACT. Any object modified by a set of humanly imposed attributes.

ASSEMBLAGE. An associated set of contemporary artefact-types. To be distinguished rigorously from the loose physical or geographical aggregate.

ATTRIBUTE. General attribute; any logically irreducible character or property of a system, having two or more states (present/absent), acting as an independent variable and assumed by the observer to be of significance with reference to the frame of his study.

ATTRIBUTE. Artefact attribute; a logically irreducible character of two or more states, acting as an independent variable within a specific artefact system. An epistemically independent variable (Sommerhoff 1950, p. 86).

ATTRIBUTE COMPLEX. Artefact attribute complex; a polythetic set of different attributes repeatedly found together on individual artefacts within populations of artefacts.

CHANNEL. The behavioural relationships between two elements, or entities, conceptualized as a connection or coupling.

CLIMAX. The period following a variety florescence in a system, in which the dislocating alternative and contradictive variety produced by integrative growth is first coherently stabilized in the newly emergent system format.

COACTION. Cultural system interaction; the exchange of variety between coupled sociocultural systems of any rank.

COHERENCE. The overall level of element or entity intercorrelation within a system population from a given phase.

COMPLEX. A recurrent configuration of elements or entities within a larger system.

CONGRUENCE. In general usage, a concordant relationship between entities. In relation to sociocultural systems, a relationship between the sociocultural variety of separate systems such that no dislocation would arise from their coupling; their variety is mutually new, alternative or redundant but not contradictive.

CONSTRAINT. The relationship between two sets, when the variety that exists under one condition is less than the variety that exists under another.

CORRELATION. The average relationship between two or more variables, each of which is a series of measures on a quantitative character. More loosely – the interdependence between variables such that when one changes so does the other, in a manner similar to that denoted by a mathematical function but not as explicitly defined.

COVARIANCE. The covariance of two variables in a population of entities is the summation of the products of their deviations from their mean values divided by the number of entities summed.

CULTURAL CLIMAX. The period following a variety florescence in an optimizer cultural system – thus defining the first coherent configuration of the newly emergent cultural format, stabilizing the new variety generated in the various cultural aspects.

CULTURE. Specific cultural assemblage; an archaeological culture is a polythetic set of specific and comprehensive artefact-type categories which consistently recur together in assemblages within a limited geographical area.

CULTURE GROUP. A family of transform cultures; a group of affinally related, collateral cultures characterized by assemblages sharing a polythetic range but differing states of the same specific multistate artefact-types.
    A low-level affinity, perhaps 30 per cent or less, uniting the group in terms of shared sets of specific type states but a residual high-level affinity, perhaps 60 per cent or more, uniting the group in terms of sets of type families and specific multistate transform types.

DISJUNCTION. Alternative information variety in a given set – 'a or b' is a disjunction of variety *a*, *b* – 'alternative variety'.

DISLOCATION. The relationship existing between coupled systems or entities such that their output sets of information variety are in some part mutually contradictory and destructive – representing 'disequilibrium'.

ENTITY. An integrated ensemble of attributes forming a complex but coherent and unitary whole at a specific level of complexity. A special class of system.

EQUILIBRIUM. General equilibrium; the state of a system in which selectively specified velocities of transformation are zero – in which certain rates of change are minimized.

EQUILIBRIUM. Information equilibrium; those successive system states that minimize the maximum amount of information variety destroyed by system changes – minimizing immediate dislocation.

EQUIVOCATION. The receiver's uncertainty about a message containing contradictory information variety – 'contradictory variety'.

FLORESCENCE. The period of explosive rate of growth of new and comprehensive variety in many aspects of an optimizer cultural system – thus defining the cumulative and catalytic development of variety necessary to stabilize foci of system dislocation brought about by the system's development.

FUNCTION. Mathematical function; a quantity or dependent variable which takes on a definite value when a specified value is assigned to another quantity, quantities or independent variables; the mathematical expression of the dependent variable in terms of the independent variables so as to identify the relationship between them.

GAIN. The increase in information variety resulting from the receipt of a message – 'new variety'.

HOMOMORPHIC. A partial similarity in behaviour between systems such that the relationships between some of the system components remain the same. If two systems are so related that a many-one transformation can be found that, applied to one system gives a system that is isomorphic with the other, simpler system, then this is a homomorphism of the first (Ashby 1956, p. 103).

INDEPENDENT CULTURES. The relationship existing between cultural assemblages, or cultural states, which are not transforms from a single cultural assemblage system trajectory.

INDEPENDENT TYPES. The relationship existing between artefact-types or type-states which are not transforms from a single artefact-type trajectory.

INDUSTRY. A set of single-material artefact-type assemblages from a continuous space-time area, taxonomically linked by the mutual technological affinities.

    Frequently, a single material aspect from a technocomplex entity.

INFORMATION. The communication of constraint in variety between coupled systems or entities.

INTERACTION. System interaction; the exchange of variety between coupled systems of any kind.

ISOMORPHIC. Similarity in behaviour between systems such that the relationships between the system components remain the same. The canonical representations of two systems are isomorphic if a one-one transformation of the states of the one system into those of the other can convert the one representation to the other (Ashby 1956, p. 97).

MESSAGE. An ordered selection from a defined set of information variety.

MONOTHETIC. An aggregate of entities or systems are said to be monothetic if the possession of a unique set of attributes is both sufficient and necessary for membership of the aggregate (mono: 'one', thetos: 'arrangement'; discussed in Sokal and Sneath 1963, p. 13; fig. 3).

NOISE. Variety which does not represent part of the essential information from a source to a receiver; this variety is in no intrinsic way distinguishable from other categories of variety except in reference to the receiver.

ONTOGENY. The first appearance, development and disappearance of an entity system, or format.

PARAMETER. A numerical characteristic of a population; a statistical value distinct from a 'sample statistic' which refers only to a value derived from a sample of a population.

PHASE. An archaeological unit constituting the smallest taxonomically homogeneous set of entity states, having a higher affinity within the unit than across its borders, which may be distinguished within a minimal time-slice of that entity's system continuum.

PHENETIC RELATIONSHIPS. Relationship based on overall affinity assessed on the basis of the attributes of the entities concerned; without any necessary implication of relationship by ancestry.

PHENON. A quantitative and comparative estimate of the affinity between entities in a group, comparable only within the limits of a particular analysis.

PHYLOGENETIC RELATIONSHIP. Relationship by ancestry; transform entities from a single multilinear time-trajectory, or tradition.

POLYNOMIAL FUNCTION MODEL. Where the variable Y is not a linear function of X but a higher order function – a quadratic, cubic, quartic, etc., etc. polynomial; a kth-degree polynomial model being:

$$Y = \beta_0 + \beta_1 X + \beta_2 X^2 + \ldots + \beta_k X^k + e \quad \text{(see fig. 106)}$$

(Krumbein and Graybill 1965, pp. 299–301).

POLYTHETIC. An aggregate of entities or systems are said to be polythetic if each individual possesses a large but unspecified number of the attributes of the aggregate, if each attribute is possessed by large numbers of these individuals, and no single attribute is both sufficient and necessary to the aggregate membership (poly: 'many', thetos: 'arrangement'; discussed in Sokal and Sneath 1963, pp. 13–15; fig. 3).

POPULATION. Any finite or infinite collection of measurements, attributes, artefacts, assemblages, cultures, individuals or things defined by some common characteristic; does not refer only to living things (statistical and demographic populations).

PRAGMATICS. The study of signs and their relationships to their users and observers – especially to the users.

PROCESS. A vector which describes the series of states of an entity or system undergoing continuous change in space or time.

REDUNDANCY. The property of information variety in a message which presents an identical set of variety to that already held by the receiving system; the decrease in uncertainty brought about by the repeated reiteration of the same set of variety – 'confirmative variety'.

REGRESSION. A statistical method for investigating the relationships between variables by expressing the approximate functional relationship between them in an algebraic equation, or its graphic equivalent (fig. 106).

REGULARITY. The repeated relationship between two or more sets, when the same constraint in variety is operating.

SEMANTICS. The study of the imputed relations between signs and their designata – the 'meaning' of the signs.

SET. A collection of attributes, entities or vectors which are called the elements or members of the set.

SOCIOCULTURAL SYSTEM. The integrated equilibrium ensemble of variety forming the complex but unitary system generated by a successively regenerating network of intercommunicating individuals and communities. The polythetically homogeneous social culture, material culture, religious culture, psychological culture and economic culture of the largest, richly interconnected social unit.

STATE. General; a specific value of an attribute, or the specific values of a set of attributes, in a system.

STATE. Attribute state; alternative values or qualities of an attribute which may be found at that attribute's locus.

SUBCULTURE. A cultural assemblage subpopulation; an infra-cultural segment or activity alignment characterized by a specific artefact-type complex.

SUBTYPE. Artefact subtype or variant; an homogeneous subpopulation of artefacts which share a given subset within a specific artefact-type's polythetic set of attributes. A sub-population with a high level of affinity, perhaps 60–90 per cent, uniting the individuals as a whole.

SYNTACTICS. The study of signs and their relationships which may be summarized in a calculus of rules of formation and transformation – a freely invented language used by an observer for describing an observed system-language.

SYNTAX. Or syntactical format – the calculus or grammar expressing the canonical rules of formation and transformation governing a set of attributes and capable of modelling their behaviour.

SYSTEM. An intercommunicating network of attributes or entities forming a complex whole. An ensemble of attributes.

TECHNOCOMPLEX. A group of cultures characterized by assemblages sharing a polythetic range but differing specific types of the same general families of artefact-types, shared as a widely diffused and interlinked response to common factors in environment, economy and technology.

A negligible level of affinity, perhaps 5 per cent or less, uniting the group in terms of shared specific types but a residual medium level affinity, perhaps 30–60 per cent, uniting the group in terms of type families.

TRADITION. An archaeological unit constituting the overall system expressing the multilinear time-trajectory of an archaeological entity.

TRAJECTORY. The successive sequence of states of an attribute, entity or vector generated by successive transformations.

TRANSFORMATION. The set of changes or transitions brought about when an attribute, entity or vector is acted upon by some factor.

TRANSFORM CULTURES. The relationship existing between successive and collateral culture states from a single multistate cultural assemblage system trajectory.

TRANSFORM TYPES. The relationship existing between successive and collateral type-states from a single multistate artefact-type trajectory.

TRANSITION. The change that occurs when an attribute, entity or vector is acted upon by some factor.

TREND. A continuous consecutive movement in a series or sequence of states – whether they may be time series, spatial series or an abstract series involving archaeological data.

TYPE. Specific artefact-type; an homogeneous population of artefacts which share a consistently recurrent range of attribute states within a given polythetic set. An intermediate-level affinity, perhaps 30–60 per cent uniting the population as a whole.

TYPE COMPLEX. Artefact-type complex; a polythetic set of different specific artefact-types repeatedly found together in assemblages within populations of assemblages. Subcultural assemblages are always type complexes but some type complexes are not subcultures, e.g. the accretion or chance selection of types found diffusing from culture to culture may provide a selection not necessarily interlinked by an activity alignment.

TYPE GROUP. Artefact-type group or family; a group of affinally related, collateral artefact-types characterized by a common component subset of attributes forming a complex constraining their functional usage and raw material. A low-level affinity, perhaps 30 per cent or less, uniting the group as a whole.

VARIABLE. In general, any quantity or value which varies, or a quantity which may take any one of a specified set of values.

VARIANCE. The variance of a population is a measure of dispersion within the population, expressed by the mean-square deviation of the distribution – the arithmetic mean of the squares of the deviation from the distribution mean.

VARIETY. The number of distinguishable elements in a given set.

VECTOR. A compound entity, having a definite number of components.

Bibliography

ACKOFF, R. L., GUPTA, S. K. and MINAS, J. S. *Scientific Method: optimizing applied research decisions*. New York, 1962.

ALLEE, W. C. *et al. Principles of Animal Ecology*. Philadelphia and London, 1950.

ALLEN, W. L. and RICHARDSON, J. B. The reconstruction of kinship from archaeological data: the concepts, the methods and the feasibility. *American Antiquity*, 1971, 36, 41–53.

AMMERMAN, A. J. and CAVALLI-SFORZA, L. L. Measuring the rate of spread of early farming in Europe. *Man*, 1971, 6, 674–88.

AMMERMAN, A. J. and CAVALLI-SFORZA, L. L. A population model for the diffusion of early farming in Europe. In *The Explanation of Culture Change*, edited by Renfrew, C., 343–57, London, 1973.

ANASTASI, A. *Differential Psychology: individual and group differences in behaviour* (3rd edn). New York, 1965.

ARBIB, M. Models of the brain. *Science Journal*, 1967, 3, no. 5, 94–104.

ASHBY, W. R. *An Introduction to Cybernetics*. London, 1956.

AZOURY, I. and HODSON, F. R. Comparing Palaeolithic assemblages: Ksar Akil, a case study. *World Archaeology*, 1973, 4, 292–306.

BARKER, G. The conditions of cultural and economic growth in the Bronze Age of central Italy. *Proceedings of the Prehistoric Society*, 1972, XXXVIII, 170–208.

BARTH, F. The land use pattern of migratory tribes of South Persia. *Norsk Geografisk Tidsskrift*, XVII, 1959–60.

BENNETT, J. W. Ecosystem analogies in cultural ecology. In *Population, Ecology and Social Evolution*, edited by Polgar, S., 273–303, The Hague, 1975.

BENNETT, J. W. Anticipation, adaptation, and the concept of culture in anthropology. *Science*, 1976, 192, 847–53.

BERLYNE, D. E. Conflict and arousal. *Scientific American*, August 1966, 215, 82–7.

BERTALANFFY, L. von An outline of general systems theory. *British Journal of Philosophy of Science*, 1950, I, 134–65.

BERTALANFFY, L. von General system theory – A critical review. *General Systems*, 1962, 7, 1–20.

BERTALANFFY, L. von *General System Theory*, 1969.

BIBBY, G. *The Testimony of the Spade*. London, 1962.

BINFORD, L. R. Archaeology as Anthropology. *American Antiquity*, 1962, 28, 217–25.

BINFORD, L. R. 'Red ochre' caches from the Michigan area: a possible case of cultural drift. *South Western Journal of Anthropology*, 1963, 19, 89–107.

BINFORD, L. R. A consideration of archaeological research design. *American Antiquity*, 1964, 29, 425–41.

BINFORD, L. R. Archaeological systematics and the study of culture process. *American Antiquity*, 1965, 31, 203–10.

BINFORD, L. R. Archaeological perspectives. In *New Perspectives in Archeology*, edited by Binford, L. R. and S. R., 5–32, Chicago, 1968a.

BINFORD, L. R. Post-Pleistocene adaptations. In *New Perspectives in Archeology*, edited by Binford, L. R. and S. R., 313–41, Chicago, 1968b.

BINFORD, L. R. Mortuary practices: their study and potential. In *Approaches to the Social Dimensions of Mortuary Practices*, edited by Brown, J. A., Memoirs of the Society for American Archaeology, no. 25, 1971, 6–29.

BINFORD, L. R. *An Archaeological Perspective.* London and New York, 1972.

BINFORD, L. R. Interassemblage variability – the Mousterian and the 'functional' argument. In *The Explanation of Culture Change: models in prehistory*, edited by Renfrew, C., 227–54, London, 1973.

BINFORD, L. R. Forty-seven trips. In *Contributions to Anthropology: The Interior Peoples of Northern Alaska*, edited by Hall, E. S., Archaeological Survey of Canada, paper no. 49, Ottawa, 1976.

BINFORD, L. R. and S. R. A preliminary analysis of functional variability in the Mousterian of Levallois facies. *American Anthropologist*, April, 1966, 68 pt. 2, no. 2, 238–95; Special publication: *Recent Studies in Palaeoanthropology*, edited by J. D. Clark and F. Clark Howell.

BINFORD, L. R. and CHASKO, W. J. Nunamiut demographic history: a provocative case. In *Demographic Anthropology*, edited by Zubrow, E., 63–143, Albuquerque, 1976.

BIRMINGHAM, J. Traditional potters of the Katmandu Valley: an ethnoarchaeological study. *Man*, 1975, 10, 370–86.

BORDES, F. and DE SONNEVILLE-BORDES, D. The significance of variability in Palaeolithic assemblages. *World Archaeology*, 1970, 2, 61–73.

BOSERUP, E. *The Conditions of Agricultural Growth*. London, 1965.

BRADLEY, R. The excavation of a Beaker settlement at Belle Tout, East Sussex, England. *Proceedings of the Prehistoric Society*, 1970, XXXVI, 312–79.

BRAITHWAITE, R. B. *Scientific Explanation*. New York, 1960.

BRIARD, J. *Les dépôts Bretons et l'âge du bronze atlantique*. Rennes, 1965.

BROOM, L. and SELZNICK, P. *Sociology* (2nd edn). Evanston, Ill., 1958.

BROSE, D. S. Locational analysis in the prehistory of northeast Ohio. In *Cultural Change and Continuity*, edited by Cleland, C. E., 3–18, New York, 1976.

BROTHWELL, D. and HIGGS, E. S. *Science in Archaeology*. London, 1969.

BUCKLEY, W. F. *Sociology and Modern Systems Theory*. London, 1967.

BUCKLEY, W. (ed.) *Modern Systems Research for the Behavioural Scientist*. Chicago, 1968.

BUNGE, W. *Theoretical Geography*. Lund Studies in Geography, ser. C, General and Mathematical Geography, 1. Lund, 1962.

BURGESS, C. The bronze age. In *British Prehistory. A New Outline*, edited by Renfrew, C., 165–232, London, 1974.

BURNHAM, P. The explanatory value of the concept of adaptation in studies of culture change. In *The Explanation of Culture Change*, edited by Renfrew, C., 93–102, London, 1973.

BYLUND, E. Theoretical considerations regarding the distribution of settlement in inner north Sweden. *Geografiska Annaler*, 1960, 42, 225–31.

CAMPBELL, J. M. Territoriality among ancient hunters: interpretations from ethnography and nature. In *Anthropological Archaeology in the Americas*, edited by Meggers, B., 1–21, Washington, 1968.

CARNAP, R. *Introduction to Symbolic Logic and its Applications*. New York, 1958.

CASE, H. Irish Neolithic pottery: distribution and sequence. *Proceedings of the Prehistoric Society*, 1961, XXVII, 174–233.

CASSELS, R. Human ecology in the Prehistoric Waikato. *Journal of the Polynesian Society*, 1972a, 81, 196–247.

CASSELS, R. Locational Analysis of Prehistoric Settlement in New Zealand. *Mankind*, 1972b, 8, 212–22.

CHAMBERLIN, T. C. The method of multiple working hypotheses. *Journal of Geology*, 1897, 5, 837–48.

CHANG, K. C. *Rethinking Archaeology*. New York, 1967.

CHAPMAN, R. W. Burial practices: an area of mutual interest. In *Archaeology and Anthropology : Areas of Mutual Interest*, edited by Spriggs, M., 19–33, Oxford, 1977.

CHERRY, C. *On Human Communication*. New York and London, 1957.

CHEYNIER, A. *Jouannet – grand-père de la préhistoire*. Paris, 1936.

CHILDE, V. G. *The Danube in Prehistory*. Oxford, 1929.

CHILDE, V. G. *Piecing Together the Past : the interpretation of archaeological data*. London, 1956.

CHILDE, V. G. *Social Evolution*. London, 1963.

CHISHOLM, M. *Rural Settlement and Land Use : an essay in location*. London, 1962.

CHORLEY, R. J. Geography and analogue theory. *Annals of the Association of American Geographers*, 1964, 54, 127–37.

CHORLEY, R. J. and KENNEDY, B. A. *Physical Geography : a systems approach*. London, 1971.

CHOROFAS, D. N. *Systems and Simulation*. London, 1965.

CLARK, J. G. D. Excavations at the Neolithic Site at Hurst Fen, Mildenhall, Suffolk. *Proceedings of the Prehistoric Society*, 1960, XXVI, 202–45.

CLARK, J. G. D. Traffic in stone axe and adze blades. *Economic History Review*, 1965, 18, 1–28.

CLARK, J. G. D. *The Earlier Stone Age Settlement of Scandinavia*. Cambridge, 1975.

CLARKE, D. L. Matrix analysis and archaeology with particular reference to British Beaker pottery. *Proceedings of the Prehistoric Society*, 1962, XXVIII, 371–83.

CLARKE, D. L. *A Tentative Reclassification of British Beaker Pottery in the Light of Recent Research*. 2nd Atlantic Symposium, Groningen, April, 1964. Published 1967.

CLARKE, D. L. *Analytical Archaeology* (1st edn). London, 1968.

CLARKE, D. L. *Beaker Pottery of Great Britain and Ireland*. Cambridge, 1970.

CLARKE, D. L. Models and paradigms in contemporary archaeology. In *Models in Archaeology*, edited by Clarke, D. L., 1–60, London, 1972.

CLARKE, D. L. A provisional model of an Iron Age Society and its settlement system. In *Models in Archaeology*, edited by Clarke, D. L., 801–69, London, 1972a.

CLARKE, D. L. Review of Watson, Leblanc and Redman 1971. *Antiquity*, 1972b, XLVI, 237–9.

CLARKE, D. L. Archaeology: the loss of innocence. *Antiquity*, 1973, XLVII, 6–18.

CLARKE, D. L. The Beaker Network – social and economic models. In *Glockenbechersymposion Oberied 1974*, edited by Lanting, J. N. and van der Waals, J. D., Bussum and Haarlem, 1976.

COLLINS, D. M. Seriation of quantitative features in late Pleistocene stone technology. *Nature*, 1965, 205, 931–2.

CONKLIN, H. C. *Hanunóo Agriculture: a report on an integral system of shifting cultivation in the Philippines*. Rome, 1957.

COWEN, J. D. The origins of the flange-hilted sword of bronze in Continental Europe. *Proceedings of the Prehistoric Society*, 1966, XXXII, 262–312.

CUNLIFFE, B. W. *Iron Age Communities in Britain*. London, 1974.

DANIEL, G. E. The transepted gallery graves of Western France. *Proceedings of the Prehistoric Society*, 1939, V, 143–65.

DANIEL, G. E. From Worsaae to Childe: the models of prehistory. *Proceedings of the Prehistoric Society*, 1971, XXXVII, pt. II, 140–53.

DANIEL, G. E. Stone, bronze and iron. In *To Illustrate the Monuments*, edited by Megaw, J. V. S., 36–42, London, 1976.

DAVIS, J. C. *Statistics and Data Analysis in Geology*. New York, 1973.

DEETZ, J. *The Dynamics of Stylistic Change in Arikara Ceramics*. Illinois Studies in Anthropology, no. 4, Illinois, 1965.

DEETZ, J. The inference of residence and descent rules from archaeological data. In *New Perspectives in Archeology*, edited by Binford, L. R. and S. R., 41–8, Chicago, 1968.

DETHLEFSEN, E. and DEETZ, J. Death's heads, cherubs and willow trees: experimental archaeology in colonial cemeteries. *American Antiquity*, 1966, 31, 502–10.

DIXON, R. B. *The Building of Cultures*. London, 1928.

DORAN, J. E. Systems theory, computer simulations and archaeology. *World Archaeology*, 1970, 1, 289–98.

DORAN, J. E. and HODSON, F. R. A digital computer analysis of Palaeolithic flint assemblages. *Nature*, 1966, 210, 688–9.

DORAN, J. E. and HODSON, F. R. *Mathematics and Computers in Archaeology*. Edinburgh, 1975.

DRENNAN, R. D. Religion and social evolution in formative Mesoamerica. In *The Early Mesoamerican Village*, edited by Flannery, K. V., 345–68, New York and London, 1976.

ELLSWORTH HUNTINGTON. *Mainsprings of Civilization*. New York, 1964.

FAGAN, B. M. *Southern Africa during the Iron Age*. London, 1965.

FARRAR, R. A. H. The techniques and sources of Romano-British black-burnished ware. In *Current Research in Romano-British Coarse Pottery*, edited by Detsicas, A., 67–103, London, 1973.

FLANNERY, K. V. Archaeological systems theory and early Mesoamerica. In *Anthropological Archaeology in the Americas*, edited by Meggers, B., 67–87, Washington, 1968.

FLANNERY, K. V. The cultural evolution of civilization. *Annual Review of Ecology and Systematics*, 1972, 3, 399–426.

FLANNERY, K. V. *The Early Mesoamerican Village*. New York and London, 1976.

FOLEY, R. Space and energy: a method for analysing habitat value and utilization in relation to archaeological sites. In *Spatial Archaeology*, edited by Clarke, D. L., 163–87, London and New York, 1977.

FORD, J. A. and WEBB, C. H. Poverty Point, a late archaic site in Louisiana. *Anthropological Papers of the American Museum of Natural History*, 46, New York, 1956.

FORDE, C. D. *Habitat, Economy and Society*. London, 1934.

FOX, C. *The Personality of Britain: its influence on inhabitants and invaders in prehistoric and early historic times*. Cardiff, 1932.

FRANKEL, D. Inter-site relationships in the Middle Bronze Age of Cyprus. *World Archaeology*, 1974, 6, 190–208.

FREEMAN, J. D. *Iban Agriculture*. London, 1955.

FRIED, M. H. *The Evolution of Political Society: an essay in political anthropology*. New York, 1967.

FRIEDMAN, J. Marxism, structuralism and Vulgar Materialism. *Man*, 1974, 9, 444–69.

FRITZ, J. and PLOG, F. The nature of archaeological explanation. *American Antiquity*, 1970, 35, 405–12.

GIFFORD, E. W. Culture element distributions: XII, Apache-Pueblo. *Anthropological Records*, 1940, 4 : 1.

GIFFORD, E. W. and KROEBER, A. L. Culture element distributions: IV, Pomo. *University of California Publications in American Archaeology and Ethnology*, 1937, 37, no. 4, 117–254.

GIMBUTAS, M. *The Gods and Goddesses of Old Europe 7000–3500 BC*. London, 1974.

GLOVER, I. C. The use of factor analyses for the discovery of artefact-types. *Mankind*, 1969, 7, 36–51.

GLUCKMAN, M. Political institutions. In *The Institutions of Primitive Society* : *a series of broadcast talks*, Oxford, 1963.

GOODY, J. R. *Production and Reproduction*. Cambridge, 1976.

GORMAN, C. F. Excavations at Spirit Cave, North Thailand: some interim interpretations. *Asian Perspectives*, 1970, XIII, 79–107.

GOULD, P. R. Man against his environment: a game-theoretic framework. *Annals of the Association of American Geographers*, 1963, 53, 290–7.

GOULD, P. R. *Spatial Diffusion*. Washington, 1969.

GOULD, R. A. Some current problems in ethnoarchaeology. In *Ethnoarchaeology*, edited by Donnan, C. B. and Clewlow, C. W., 29–48, Los Angeles, 1974.

GREEN, E. L. Location analysis of prehistoric Maya sites in Northern British Honduras. *American Antiquity*, 1973, 38, 279–93.

GREEN, J. A. *Sets and Groups*. London, 1965.

GREEN, R. W. (ed.) *Protestantism and Capitalism* : *the Weber thesis and its critics*. London, 1959.

HÄGERSTRAND, T. *The Propagation of Innovation Waves*. Lund Studies in Geography, ser. B, Human Geography, 4, 3–19, Lund, 1952.

HÄGERSTRAND, T. *Innovationsförloppet ur korologisk synpunkt*. Lund, 1953.

HÄGERSTRAND, T. *Migration and Area* : *survey of a sample of Swedish migration fields and hypothetical considerations in their genesis*. Lund Studies in Geography, ser. B, Human Geography, 13, 27–158, Lund, 1957.

HAGGETT, P. *Locational Analysis in Human Geography*. London, 1965.

HAGGETT, P. *Geography* : *A Modern Synthesis*. New York, 1972.

HAGGETT, P. and CHORLEY, R. J. *Network Analysis in Geography*. London, 1969.

HALL, A. D. and FAGEN, R. E. Definition of system. *General Systems Yearbook*, 1956, 1, 18–28.

HARRÉ, R. *The Philosophies of Science*. Oxford, 1972.

HARTLEY, K. F. The marketing and distribution of mortaria. In *Current Research in Romano-British Coarse Pottery*, edited by Detsicas, A., 39–51, London, 1973.

HARVEY, D. *Explanation in Geography*. London, 1969.

HAWKES, C. The ABC of the British Iron Age. *Antiquity*, 1959, XXXIII, 170–82.

HAYDEN, B. Population control among hunter–gatherers. *World Archaeology*, 1972, 4, 205–21.

HEMPEL, C. *Philosophy of Natural Science*. New Jersey, 1966.

HENCKEN, H. Carp's tongue swords in Spain, France and Italy. *Zephyrus*, 1956, VII, 125–78.

HIGGS, E. S. (ed.) *Papers in Economic Prehistory*. Cambridge, 1972.

HIGGS, E. S. (ed.) *Palaeoeconomy*. Cambridge, 1975.

HIGGS, E. S. and JARMAN, M. R. Palaeoeconomy. In *Palaeoeconomy*, edited by Higgs, E. S., 1–7, Cambridge, 1975.

HIGGS, E. S. and VITA-FINZI, C. Prehistoric economies: a territorial approach. In *Papers in Economic Prehistory*, edited by Higgs, E. S., 27–36, Cambridge, 1972.

HILL, J. N. Broken K Pueblo: patterns of form and function. In *New Perspectives in Archeology*, edited by Binford, L. R. and S. R., 103–42, Chicago, 1968.

HILL, J. N. Broken K Pueblo: prehistoric social organisation in the American Southwest. *University of Arizona, Anthropological Papers*, no. 18, 1970.

HILL, J. N. Seminar on the explanation of prehistoric organizational change. *Current Anthropology*, 1971, 12, 406–8.

HILL, J. N. The methodological debate in contemporary archaeology: a model. In *Models in Archaeology*, edited by Clarke, D. L., 61–107, London, 1972.

HILL, J. N. A processual analysis of non-seasonal population movement in Man and other terrestrial animals. n.d.

HILL, J. N. and EVANS, R. K. A model for classification and typology. In *Models in Archaeology*, edited by Clarke, D. L., 231–73, London, 1972.

HODDER, I. Regression analysis of some trade and marketing patterns. *World Archaeology*, 1974, 6, 172–89.

HODDER, I. Some new directions in the spatial analysis of archaeological data at the regional scale. In *Spatial Archaeology*, edited by Clarke, D. L., 223–351, London and New York, 1977a.

HODDER, I. A study in ethnoarchaeology in western Kenya. In *Archaeology and Anthropology*, edited by Spriggs, M., 117–41, Oxford, 1977b.

HODDER, I. and ORTON, C. *Spatial Analysis in Archaeology*. Cambridge, 1976.

HODSON, F. R. Numerical typology and prehistoric archaeology. In *Mathematics in the Archaeological and Historical Sciences*, edited by Hodson, F. R., Kendall, D. G. and Tartu, P., 30–45, Edinburgh, 1971.

HODSON, F. R., SNEATH, P. H. A. and DORAN, J. E. Some experiments in the numerical analysis of archaeological data. *Biometrika*, 1966, 53, nos 3, 4, 311–24.

HUGHES, G. B. and T. *The Country Life Collector's Pocket Book.* London, 1963.

HYMES, D. (ed.) *The Use of Computers in Anthropology.* London, 1965.

ISAAC, G. Ll. Studies of early culture in East Africa. *World Archaeology*, 1969, 1, 1–28.

ISAAC, G. Ll. Chronology and the tempo of cultural change during the Pleistocene. In *Calibration of Hominoid Evolution*, edited by Bishop, W. W. and Miller, J. A., 381–430, Edinburgh, 1972a.

ISAAC, G. Ll. Early phases of human behaviour: models in Lower Palaeolithic archaeology. In *Models in Archaeology*, edited by Clarke, D. L., 167–99, London, 1972b.

ISAAC, G. Ll. Early stone tools – an adaptive threshold? In *Problems in Economic and Social Archaeology*, edited by Sieveking, G. de G., Longworth, I. H., and Wilson, K. E., 39–47, London, 1976.

JAŹDŻEWSKI, K. *Atlas to the Prehistory of the Slavs.* Łódź, 1949.

JOCHIM, M. A. *Hunter–Gatherer Subsistence and Settlement: a predictive model.* New York and London, 1976.

JOHNSON, G. A. *Local Exchange and Early State Development in Southwestern Iran.* Anthropological Papers, University of Michigan, no. 51, 1973.

JOHNSON, L. Problems in 'avant-garde' archaeology. *American Anthropologist*, 1972, LXXIV, 366–75.

JOPE, E. M. The regional cultures of Medieval Britain. In *Culture and Environment: essays in honour of Sir Cyril Fox*, edited by Foster, I. Ll. and Alcock, L., 327–50, London, 1963.

JOPE, E. M. The transmission of new ideas: archaeological evidence for implant and dispersal. *World Archaeology*, 1973, 4, 368–73.

JUDGE, W. J. Systems analysis and the Folsom-Midland question. *Southwestern Journal of Anthropology*, 1970, 26, 40–51.

KLINDT-JENSEN, O. *A History of Scandinavian Archaeology.* London, 1975.

KNIFFEN, F. B. Pomo geography. *University of California Publications in American Archaeology and Ethnology*, 1939, 36, no. 6.

KROEBER, A. L. *Anthropology.* London, 1948.

KROEBER, A. L. *The Configurations of Culture Growth* (new edn). Berkeley, 1963.

KROEBER, A. L., GIFFORD, E. W., DRIVER, H. L. *et al.* Culture element distributions, I–XXVI. I–IV = *University of California Publications in American Archaeology and Ethnology*, 1935–7, 37, nos 1–4; V–XXVI = *Anthropological Records*, 1937–50, 1, nos 1–7; 4, nos 1–3; 6, nos 1–4; 7, nos 1–2; 8, nos 1–5; 9, no. 3.

KROEBER, A. L. and RICHARDSON, J. Three centuries of women's dress fashions, a quantitative analysis. *Anthropological Records*, 1940, 5, no. 2.

KRUMBEIN, W. C. and GRAYBILL, F. A. *An Introduction to Statistical Models in Geology*. New York and London, 1965.

LAMING, A. (ed.) *La découverte du passé*. Paris, 1952.

LARSON, P. Trend surface analysis in archaeology: a preliminary study of intrasite patterning. *Norwegian Archaeological Review*, 1975, 8, 75–80.

LAWICK-GOODALL, H. and J. von *Innocent Killers*. London, 1971.

LAWICK-GOODALL, J. von *In the Shadow of Man*. Glasgow, 1970.

LEE, R. B. !Kung bushman subsistence: an input–output analysis. In *Environment and Cultural Behaviour*, edited by Vayda, A. P., 47–79, New York, 1969.

LÉVI-STRAUSS, C. L'Analyse structurale en linguistique et en anthropologie. *Word*, 1945, 1, 33–53.

LEVISON, M., WARD, R. G. and WEBB, J. The settlement of Polynesia: a report on a computer simulation. *Archaeology and Physical Anthropology in Oceania*, 1972, VII, 234–45.

LEWIN, K. *Principles of Topological Psychology*. New York, 1936.

LITVAK KING, J. and GARCÍA MOLL, R. Set theory models: an approach to taxonomic and locational relationships. In *Models in Archaeology*, edited by Clarke, D. L., 735–55, London, 1972.

LONGACRE, W. A. Some aspects of prehistoric society in east-central Arizona. In *New Perspectives in Archeology*, edited by Binford, L. R. and S. R., 89–102, Chicago, 1968.

LONGACRE, W. A. Archaeology as anthropology: a case study. *University of Arizona, Anthropological papers*, no. 17, 1970.

LOTKA, A. J. *Elements of Physical Biology*. Baltimore, 1925.

MACKAY, D. M. Quantal aspects of scientific information. *Philosophical Magazine*, 1950, 41, 289.

MALMER, M. P. Jungneolithische studien. *Acta Archaeologica Lundensia*, no. 2. Lund, 1962.

MANDER, A. E. *Clearer Thinking (Logic for Everyman)*. London, 1936.

MARUYAMA, M. The second cybernetics: deviation-amplifying mutual causal processes. *American Scientist*, 51, pp. 164–79.

McARTHUR, M. Pigs for the ancestors: a review article. *Oceania*, 1974, XLV, 87–123.

McBURNEY, C. B. M. The cave of Ali Tappeh and the Epi-Palaeolithic of Iran. *Proceedings of the Prehistoric Society*, 1968, XXXIV, 385–413.

MEDAWAR, P. *Induction and Intuition in Scientific Thought*. London, 1969.

MELLAART, J. *Çatal Hüyük: a Neolithic town in Anatolia*. London, 1967.

MELLARS, P. A. Some comments on the notion of 'functional variability' in stone-tool assemblages. *World Archaeology*, 1970, 2, 74–89.

MILLER, J. G. Living systems: basic concepts. *Behavioural Science*, 1965, 10, 193–237.

MILLER, R. L. and KAHN, R. S. *Statistical Analysis in the Geological Sciences*. New York, 1962.

MORGAN, C. G. Archaeology and explanation. *World Archaeology*, 1973, 4, 259–76.

MORONEY, M. J. *Facts from figures*. London, 1957.

MORRILL, R. L. *Simulation of Central Place Patterns over Time*. Lund Studies in Geography, ser. B, Human Geography, 24, 109–20, Lund, 1962.

MUELLER, J. W. (ed.) *Sampling in Archaeology*. Tucson, 1975.

MURDOCK, G. P. (ed.) *Social Structure*. New York and London, 1949.

NAGEL, E. *Principles of the Theory of Probability, I and II*. Foundations of the Unity of Science, I, no. 6, International Encyclopedia of Unified Science, Chicago, 1958.

NEEDHAM, R. Polythetic classification: convergence and consequences. *Man*, 1975, 10, 349–69.

NEUMANN, J. von and MORGENSTERN, O. *Theory of Games and Economic Behaviour*. Princeton, 1947.

PEACOCK, D. P. S. A petrological study of certain Iron Age pottery from western England. *Proceedings of the Prehistoric Society*, 1968, XXXIV, 414–27.

PEACOCK, D. P. S. The scientific analysis of ancient ceramics: a review. *World Archaeology*, 1970, 1, 375–89.

PEACOCK, D. P. S. Roman Amphorae in pre-Roman Britain. In *The Iron Age and its Hill-Forts*, edited by Jessen, M. and Hill, D., 161–88, Southampton, 1971.

PHILLIPS, E. D. *The Royal Hordes: nomad peoples of the steppes.* London, 1965.

PIGGOTT, S. The Early Bronze Age in Wessex. *Proceedings of the Prehistoric Society*, 1938, 4, 52–106.

PIGGOTT, S. *Ancient Europe: from the beginnings of agriculture to Classical antiquity.* Edinburgh, 1965.

PLOG, F. Laws, systems of law and the explanation of observed variation. In *The Explanation of Culture Change*, edited by Renfrew, C., London, 1973.

PLOG, F. *The Study of Prehistoric Change.* New York, 1974.

PLOG, F. Systems theory in archaeological research. *Annual Review of Anthropology*, 1975, 4, 207–24.

POLANYI, K., ARENSBERG, C. M. and PEARSON, H. W. (eds) *Trade and Market in the Early Empires.* New York, 1957.

RAPPAPORT, R. A. *Pigs for the Ancestors.* New Haven and London, 1968.

RAPPAPORT, R. A. Ritual, sanctity and cybernetics. *American Anthropologist*, 1971a, 73, 59–76.

RAPPAPORT, R. A. The sacred in human evolution. *Annual Review of Ecology and Systematics*, 1971b, vol. 2, 23–44.

RATHJE, W. L. Models for mobile Maya: a variety of constraints. In *The Explanation of Culture Change*, edited by Renfrew, C., 731–57, London, 1973.

REICHEL-DOLMATOFF, G. Cosmology as ecological analysis: a view from the rain forest. *Man*, 1976, 11, 307–18.

RENFREW C. *The Emergence of Civilisation.* London, 1972.

RENFREW C. Monuments, mobilisation and social organisation in Neolithic Wessex. In *The Explanation of Culture Change*, edited by Renfrew, C., 539–58, London, 1973a.

RENFREW C. *Before Civilisation.* London, 1973b.

RENFREW C. Beyond a subsistence economy: the evolution of social organisation in prehistoric Europe. In *Reconstructing Complex Societies*, edited by Moore, C. B., 69–95, Cambridge, Mass., 1974.

RENFREW C. Trade as action at a distance: questions of integration and communication. In *Ancient Civilisation and Trade*, edited by Sabloff, J. A. and Lamberg-Karlovsky, C. C., 3–59, Albuquerque, 1976.

RENFREW, C. Alternative models for exchange and spatial distribution. In *Exchange Systems in Prehistory*, edited by Earle, T. K. and Ericson, J. E., 71–90, New York and London, 1977.

RENFREW, C., DIXON, J. E. and CANN, J. R. Further analysis of Near Eastern Obsidians. *Proceedings of the Prehistoric Society*, 1968, 34, 319–31.

REYNOLDS, R. G. D. Linear settlement systems on the Upper Grijalva River: the application of a Markovian model. In *The Early Mesoamerican Village*, edited by Flannery, K. V., 180–93, New York and London, 1976.

ROBBINS, L. H. Turkana material culture viewed from an archaeological perspective. *World Archaeology*, 1973, 5, 209–14.

ROE, D. A. The British lower and middle Palaeolithic: some problems, methods of study and preliminary results. *Proceedings of the Prehistoric Society*, 1964, XXX, 245–67.

ROPER, D. C. A trend surface analysis of Central Plains radiocarbon dates. *American Antiquity*, 1976, 41, 181–9.

ROWE, J. H. Diffusionism and archaeology. *American Antiquity*, 1965–6, 31, 334–8.

ROWLANDS, M. J. The archaeological interpretation of prehistoric metalworking. *World Archaeology*, 1971, 3, 210–24.

RUDNER, R. S. *Philosophy of Social Science*. New Jersey, 1966.

SACKETT, J. R. Quantitative analysis of upper Palaeolithic stone tools. *American Anthropologist*, April 1966, 68, pt 2, no. 2, 356–92; Special publication: *Recent Studies in Palaeoanthropology*, edited by J. D. Clark and F. Clark Howell.

SAHLINS, M. D. *Stone Age Economics*. London, 1972.

SANDERS, W. T. and PRICE, B. J. *Mesoamerica: The evolution of a civilization*. New York, 1968.

SAXE, A. A. *Social Dimensions of Mortuary Practices*. Ph.D. dissertation, University of Michigan, 1970.

SCHIFFER, M. B. *Behavioural Archaeology*. New York and London, 1976.

SCHILD, R. The final Palaeolithic settlements of the European Plain. *Scientific American*, 1976, 234, no. 2, 88–99.

SCHOFIELD, J. F. *Primitive Pottery: an introduction to South African ceramics, prehistoric and protohistoric*. The South African Archaeological Society, Handbook Series no. 3, Cape Town, 1948.

SCHWERDTFEGER, F. W. Urban settlement patterns in northern Nigeria (Hausaland). In *Man, Settlement and Urbanism*, edited by Ucko, P. J., Tringham, R. and Dimbleby, G., 547–56, London, 1972.

SCOLLAR, I. Regional groups in the Michelsberg Culture. *Proceedings of the Prehistoric Society*, 1959, XXV, 52–134.

SERRA PUCHE, M. C. Los Diagramas de Venn en la Comparación De Tradiciones Culturales. *Anales de Antropología*, 1976, XIII, 55–75.

SERVICE, E. R. *Primitive Social Organisation: an evolutionary perspective*. New York, 1962.

SERVICE, E. R. *Cultural Evolutionism*. New York, 1971.

SHACKLETON, N. and RENFREW, C. Neolithic trade routes re-aligned by oxygen isotope analysis. *Nature*, 1970, 228, 1062–5.

SHAWCROSS, W. An archaeological assemblage of Maori combs. *Journal of the Polynesian Society*, 1964, 73, 382–98.

SHENNAN, S. The social organisation at Branc. *Antiquity*, 1975, XLIX, 279–88.

SHERRATT, A. G. Socio-economic and demographic models for the Neolithic and Bronze Ages of Europe. In *Models in Archaeology*, edited by Clarke, D. L., 477–542, London, 1972.

SIMON, H. A. *Models of Man*. New York, 1957.

SMITH, I. F. The neolithic. In *British Prehistory: a new outline*, edited by Renfrew, C., 100–36, London, 1974.

SOJA, E. W. The political organisation of space. *Association of American Geographers, Commission on College Geography*, Resource paper 8, 1971.

SOKAL, R. R. and SNEATH, P. H. A. *Principles of Numerical Taxonomy*. San Francisco and London, 1963.

SOMMERHOFF, G. *Analytical Biology*. London, 1950.

SPAULDING, A. C. Statistical techniques for the discovery of artifact-types. *American Antiquity*, 1953, 18, 305–13.

SPOEHR, A. Marianas prehistory; archaeological survey and excavations on Saipan, Tinian and Rota. *Fieldiana: Anthropology*, 1957, 48.

STANISLAWSKI, M. B. Review of 'Archaeology as Anthropology: A Case Study'. *American Antiquity*, 1973, 38, 117–22.

STANISLAWSKI, M. B. The relationships of ethnoarchaeology, traditional and systems archaeology. In *Ethnoarchaeology*, edited by Donnan, C. B. and Clewlow, C. W., 15–26, Los Angeles, 1974.

STEIGER, W. L. Analytical Archaeology? *Mankind*, 1971, 8, 67–70.

STEWARD, J. H. *Theory of Culture Change*. Illinois, 1955.

STICKEL, E. G. and CHARTKOFF, J. L. The nature of scientific laws and their relation to law-building in archaeology. In *The Explanation of Culture Change*, edited by Renfrew, C., 663–71, London, 1973.

STILES, D. Ethnoarchaeology: a discussion of methods and applications. *Man*, 1977, 12, 87–103.

SULLIVAN, M. E. Archaeological occupation site locations on the south coast of New South Wales. *Archaeology and Physical Anthropology in Oceania*, 1976, XI, 56–69.

TAINTER, J. A. Woodland social change in west-central Illinois. *Mid-Continental Journal of Archaeology*, 1977, 2, 67–98.

TAYLOR, W. W. *A Study of Archaeology*. Memoir no. 69, *American Anthropologist* 50, pt 2, 1948.

TERRELL, J. Geographic systems and human diversity in the North Solomons. *World Archaeology*, 1977, 9, 62–81.

THOMAS, D. H. Archaeology's operational imperative: Great Basin projectile points as a test case. *Archaeological Survey Annual Report*, 27–60, Los Angeles, 1970.

THOMAS, D. H. A computer simulation model of Great Basin Shoshonean subsistence and settlement patterns. In *Models in Archaeology*, edited by Clarke, D. L., 671–704, London, 1972.

THOMPSON, R. H. (ed.) *Migrations in New World Culture History*. Tucson, 1958.

THOMSON, D. F. The seasonal factor in human culture. *Proceedings of the Prehistoric Society*, 1939, X, 209–21.

TRIGGER, B. G. *Beyond History: The Methods of Prehistory*. New York, 1968.

TRIGGER, B. G. Archaeology and ecology. *World Archaeology*, 1971, 2, 321–36.

TRINGHAM, R. *Hunters, Fishers and Farmers of Eastern Europe 6000–3000 BC*. London, 1971.

TUGGLE, H. D., TOWNSEND, A. H. and RILEY, T. J. Laws, systems and research design: a discussion of explanation in archaeology. *American Antiquity*, 1972, 37, 3–12.

TUSTIN, A. *The Mechanism of Economics*. London, 1954.

UCKO, P. J. Ethnography and archaeological interpretation of funerary remains. *World Archaeology*, 1969, 1, 262–80.

VERTES, L. Observations on the technique of production of Szeletian flint implements. *Proceedings of the Prehistoric Society*, 1960, XXVI, 37–43.

VERTES, L. Das Jungpaläolithikum von Arka in Nord-Ungarn. *Quartär*, 1965, 15/16, 79–132.

VITA-FINZI, C. and HIGGS, E. S. Prehistoric economy in the Mount Carmel area of Palestine: site catchment analysis. *Proceedings of the Prehistoric Society*, 1970, 36, 1–37.

VOEGELIN, E. W. Culture element distributions: XX: Northeast California. *Anthropological Records*, 1942, 7, no. 2.

WASHBURN, D. K. Nearest neighbour analysis of Pueblo I–III settlement patterns along the Rio Puerco of the East, New Mexico. *American Antiquity*, 1974, 39, 315–35.

WATSON, P. J., LEBLANC, S. A. and REDMAN, C. L. *Explanation in Archaeology: an explicitly scientific approach*. New York and London, 1971.

WAUCHOPE, R. Archaeological survey of Northern Georgia, with a test of some cultural hypotheses. *Memoirs of the Society for American Archaeology*, no. 21; *American Antiquity*, 1966, 31, no. 5, pt. 2.

WEBSTER, P. V. Severn valley ware on Hadrian's Wall. *Archaeologia Aeliana*, 1972, 50, 191–203.

WEBSTER, P. V. Severn valley ware on the Antonine frontier. In *Roman Pottery Studies in Britain and Beyond*, edited by Dore, J. and Greene, K., 163–76, Oxford, 1977.

WHALLON, R. Investigations of late prehistoric social organization in New York State. In *New Perspectives in Archeology*, edited by Binford, L. R. and S. R., 223–44, Chicago, 1968.

WHALLON, R. *A Computer Program for Monothetic Subdivisive Classification in Archaeology*. Michigan, 1971.

WHALLON, R. A new approach to pottery typology. *American Antiquity*, 1972, 37, 13–33.

WHITAKER, I. *Social Relations in a Nomadic Lappish Community*, 97–104. Samiske Samlinger, Bind II. Oslo, 1955.

WHITE, J. P. and THOMAS, D. H. What mean these stones? Ethnotaxonomic models and archaeological interpretations in the New Guinea Highlands. In *Models in Archaeology*, edited by Clarke, D. L., 275–308, London, 1972.

WIENER, N. *Cybernetics*. New York, 1948.

WILLEY, G. R. A pattern of diffusion – acculturation. *Southwestern Journal of Anthropology*, 1953, 9, 369–84.

WILLEY, G. R. *An Introduction to American Archaeology*. New Jersey, 1966.

WILLEY, G. R. and PHILLIPS, P. *Method and Theory in American Archaeology*. Chicago, 1958.

WISSLER, C. *Man and Culture*. London, 1923.

WOBST, H. M. Boundary conditions for paleolithic social systems: a simulation approach. *American Antiquity*, 1974, 39, 147–78.

WOLPERT, J. The decision process in spatial context. *Annals of the Association of American Geographers*, 1964, 54, 537–58.

WOOD, J. J. and MATSON, R. G. Two models of sociocultural systems and their implications for the archaeological study of change. In *The Explanation of Culture Change*, edited by Renfrew, C., 673–83, London, 1973.

WRIGLEY, E. A. London and the great leap forward – II. *The Listener*, 6 July, 1967, 7–8.

WYNNE-EDWARDS, V. C. *Animal Dispersion in Relation to Social Behaviour*. Edinburgh, 1962.

YADIN, Y. *The Art of Warfare in Biblical Lands*. London, 1963.

YUILL, R. S. *A Simulation Study of Barrier Effects in Spatial Diffusion Problems*. Michigan Inter-University Community of Mathematical Geographers, Discussion Papers Vol. 5, Michigan, 1965.

ZARKY, A. Statistical analysis of site catchments at Ocós, Guatemala. In *The Early Mesoamerican Village*, edited by Flannery, K. V., 117–30, New York and London, 1976.

ZUBROW, E. B. W. Carrying capacity and dynamic equilibrium in the prehistoric Southwest. *American Antiquity*, 1971, 36, 127–38.

ZUBROW, E. B. W. *Prehistoric Carrying Capacity: A Model*. California, 1975.

Index

absorbing barriers to diffusion 427
acculturation 106, 320–3 *passim*, 341, 349, 360, 419
Ackoff, R. L. 31
activities as information 100
activity subcultures 254
adaptation 57, 76; cultural information system 89; culture and 142n; essential variables 57–8; religious subsystem 112
affinity relationships 165, 226–8, 249, 300, 317, 329, 330, 338, 379, 414–15, 490, 493, 495, 496; *see also* phenetic relationships
agrarian technocomplex 351–4, 360–2
agriculture: agrarian technocomplexes 351–4, 356; crop yields (q.v.); food production 144n, 435–8; pastoral nomads 345–51; productivity 94–5, 114, 127
Aldrovande U. 4, 5
Allee, W. C. 84, 152, 357
Allen, W. L. 61, 139n
alternative variety 89–92 *passim*, 105, 114, 115, 129, 196–8, 237, 286, 355, 418, 489, 490
American Central Plains 457–8
American Indians 374–7 *passim*, 380–94 *passim*
Ammerman, A. J. 435, 436, 437
analogue models 31, 33, 38, 180; in procedure model 32, 35, 459; social organization 139n
analytical archaeology, defined 485
Anastasi, A. 171, 172
animals *see* fauna
anthropology: effect on archaeology 142n–143n
Arbib, M. 470
archaeological culture *see* culture
archaeologists: prehistorians and 10–11, 22; varying aims of 19, 20–1; Victorian 26
archaeology: aims 19–23; complementary to other social disciplines 486; defined 10, 12; desiderata in xv, 486; effect on anthropology

archaeology—*continued*
142n–143n; external contributions to 465–6, 477–8, 486; general theory of xvi–xvii, 10, 13, 37, 143n, 149, 465; grammar of 479–86; history of 2–10, 25; nature of 10–13; nature of data 13–19, 479; new developments in xvi; re-design needed in xvi
archaic range 193, 195
artefacts: as data 13–19; Australian aboriginal 334; behaviour and 85–6, 153, 409, 411–12; celestial theory 4, 5, 6; classical theory 3–4, 5; coded messages and 100; de Jussieu on 6; defined 35, 152, 206, 489; distribution 406n–408n, 425–35, 443; distribution or dispersion in terms of each attribute 187–91; elaboration (q.v.); Goguet on 6; Mahudel on 6; Mercati on 5, 6, 8; Montfaucon on 6; oscillation (q.v.); patterning 139n; relationship 480–1; Renaissance theory 4–5; roles of 409–10, 480, 484; study of 479; system model for 39–40, 196; *see also* cultural elements
Ashby, W. R. 21, 42, 44, 45, 47, 52, 54, 59, 63, 88, 90, 113, 144n, 147n, 155, 355, 410, 491, 492
assemblages: American Indian 380–94 *passim*; changes in stone tools 242n–244n; characteristics of grouped assemblages 266–7; defined 35, 206, 245–6, 489; diffusion 264, 265, 368, 449, 452, 455, 456, 457; distribution 263–6, 368; equated with groups of families 369; in culture groups 306, 307–9; levels of similarity 249; subsystems 286; trends 277–8; Urnfield culture group 396–8 *passim*, 402; *see also* cultural assemblage systems, culture, material culture, sociocultural systems, systems
attributes: attribute complexes 153, 158, 160, 231, 489; behaviour and 15, 18, 156; contextual 13, 14, 15, 156; core 212, 215,

attributes—*continued*
217; correlation (q.v.); definition 154–6, 203n–204n, 206, 489; distribution or dispersion in terms of each artefact 182–7; essential *see* essential variables; exotic and occasional characters 210; functional and idiosyncratic freedom 160–1, 184, 186, 210, 215, 228, 229, 230; inessential *see* inessential variables; inter-communicating 43, 45–6; key *see* key variables; logically irreducible 155, 156, 203n–204n, 489; multidimensional constellation 210–17 *passim*, 226; multistate (q.v.); of individuals 113, 363–4; personality 113; regularities (q.v.); selection for use 14, 155, 156; social subsystem 103, 106, 107, 109; specific 13, 14, 15, 156; subjectivity in selection for study 14, 18, 19; variance in type populations 278; variation within artefacts 37, 157–60 *passim*, 165–80 *passim*
Australian aboriginal artefacts 334
axes 169, 172–5, 178, 179, 186, 232–4, 242n
Azoury, I. 258

Bacon, F. 486–7
Bantu entity 371–4
Bar-Hillel 483
Barker, G. 121, 125, 127
Barth, F. 120, 121, 122
Bayes 476, 483
beaker pottery *see* British beaker pottery
beaker subculture 252, 277
behaviour: artefacts and 85–6, 153, 409, 411–12; attributes and 15, 18, 156; early hominids 86; entity systems 415; patterns as survival code 87; systems 51–3, 59, 63, 64, 73, 86, 149–50; variability in 405n
Bennett, J. W. 147n
Berlyne, D. E. 114
Bertalanffy, L. von 42, 147n
bimodality 172–4
Binford, L. R. 16, 19, 42, 98, 140n, 142n, 143n, 144n, 146n, 148n, 178, 205, 242n, 243n, 255, 258, 279, 284, 407n, 438, 458, 463n, 479, 484, 487n
Binford, S. R. 19, 205, 243n, 255, 258, 279, 284, 479, 484
Birmingham, J. 203n
Black Box 58–62, 74, 94, 107
blending strategy 93, 94, 95, 124, 198, 218, 268, 333
Bordes, F. 19, 41n, 168
Boserup, E. 143n
Bowden 440
Bradley, R. 456
Braithwaite, R. B. 16, 17, 22, 31, 33, 34, 94, 95, 468, 476

Briard, J. 169
British beaker pottery 145n, 158, 193, 194, 211, 212, 213, 455; subculture 252, 277
Broom, L. 282
Brose, D. S. 116
Brothwell, D. 406n
Buckley, W. F. 42, 147n
buffers 135
Bunge, W. 439
Burgess, C. 256
burial practices 28–9, 140n, 256, 257–8, 396, 463n
Burnham, P. 148n
Bylund, E. 440

Campbell, J. M. 114, 122
Cann, J. R. 429
canonical models 44, 59, 63, 64, 66, 67, 474
Carnap, R. 483–4, 485
cascading system 145n
Case, H. 170
Cassels, R. 127, 128
catalytic values 49
Cavalli-Sforza, L. C. 435, 436, 437
celestial theory 4, 5, 6
Celts 396, 398, 399, 400, 402, 403, 404
centralization 144n, 146n, 298n
Chamberlin, T. C. 476
Chang, K. C. 479
Chapin, F. S. 282
characterization levels 109–10
characterization studies 405n, 427–8
Chartkoff, J. L. 487n
Chasko, W. J. 144n, 438
Cherry, C. 63, 88, 90, 413, 466, 476, 480, 483
Cheynier, A. 4–7 *passim*
Childe, V. G. 36, 40n, 41n, 203n, 205, 245, 299, 319, 326n, 328, 405n, 408n
Chisholm, M. M. 125
Chi-square 41n, 139n, 170
Chorley, R. J. 32, 35, 145n, 442, 453
Chorofas, D. N. 472
Christian, V. 7
circuits 46, 47, 56, 60, 61
Clark, J. G. D. 168, 406n
Clarke, D. L. 31, 122, 128, 138, 143n, 144n, 145n, 146n, 158, 203n, 239, 242n, 243n, 244n, 252, 255, 277, 407n, 408n, 412, 431, 442, 444, 456, 465, 485, 487n, 488n
classical theory 3–4, 5
classification: meanings of, 41n; model, 459–60; problems in, 163, 165, 305; tools, 203n
climate 132–5 *passim*, 375
climax 292–7 *passim*; agrarian technocomplexes 351–4 *passim*; defined 489; hunter-fisher-gatherer technocomplexes 343, 344, 345; pastoral nomad technocomplexes 348–

climax—*continued*
  51 *passim*; strategies 344–5, 349, 351, 354; system ontogeny 292, 341; technocomplex 341, 343, 344, 345, 348–54 *passim*
clothing 191–2, 400, 401
clusters: analysis 149; attribute complexes 153, 158, 160, 231, 489; attributes 153, 155, 161, 171, 174, 176–7, 212, 214, 217, 231, 461; core attributes 212; entities as 35; inventions 294; social and economic subsystem components 107, 109; tribal assemblages 378–9, 389,
  types 207, 208
Clyde/Carlingford tombs 28–9
coaction 358–62, 489
coherence 231–3, 236, 284, 291, 319, 341; defined 58, 231, 489; 'maturity' trends 289; measure of 232, 284
Collins, D. M. 224, 225
communication 84, 86–7, 88, 110, 406n, 410–12, 428
comprehensive interchange 357–60 *passim*, 362
complex systems 46–7, 52–3, 56, 57, 60–1, 79–81, 101, 138; adaptive systems 147n, 148n
composite bands 355, 356
computers: as isomorphic models 59–60; pragmatics and 486; semantics and 486; syntactics and 482, 485
concentric exploitation zones model 125
concepta 200, 468, 469, 480, 481
concepts, systems theory as source of 143n–144n
Conklin, H. C. 121
constellation analysis (inter-assemblage relationships) 258–60
constraint(s): compounded 55; constrained sets 70–1, 77; continuous systems 45, 75; correlated 69, 77, 107, 109, 139n; defined 490; range of 54–5; regularities and 21–2, 75, 77, 111, 415; religious 114
contagious subtype 426
contextual analysis 32, 34–5, 458, 459
contextual attributes 13, 14, 15, 156
continuous variables 158
contradictive variety 114, 115, 129, 131, 196–8, 200, 237, 286, 333, 354, 355, 418, 489, 491
control *see* regulation
convergence 318–23, 338, 340, 348; and integration method 475–6
Converse-Occam 79–81, 475
Corded Ware/Battle-axe culture group 307–10, 313, 314, 315, 321–2, 346, 365, 403
core attributes 212, 215, 217
correlation: between attributes 210–13 *passim*, 217, 224, 225, 226, 229–32 *passim*, 236, 239, 240, 461; between types 283–4, 289–90;

correlation—*continued*
  317; coefficients of attributes 210–13 *passim*; correlated constraint 69, 77, 107, 109, 139n; correlated regularities 109–10, 111; defined 490; directive (q.v.); hierarchical entities of sociocultural dimensions 366; rates of change of system components 285
coupled systems 49–50, 57, 76, 92, 130, 138, 354–5, 417, 486, 490
covariance 71, 140n, 201, 473, 490
'covering law' model 487n
Cowen, J. D. 197
crop yields 94–5, 114, 116–19 *passim*, 121, 122, 124, 127, 145n
cultural assemblage phases 272–8 *passim*, 288–90
cultural assemblage systems 249–61; emergent 282, 283; independent 280, 319–24 *passim*, 492; oscillation 272–83 *passim*; phase pattern regularities 261–72; system pattern regularities 285–7; termination of trajectory 281–3; time pattern regularities 272–97; *see also* assemblages, culture, material culture, sociocultural systems, systems
cultural assimilation 419
cultural brick theory 263–5
cultural change model 242n–244n
cultural diffusion 438
cultural ecology 84–5, 101, 133
cultural elements 374–7, 379–80, 383–7 *passim*, 389–94 *passim*, 421, 422–4; *see also* artefacts
cultural morphology 84–5, 101, 133
cultural networks 253, 270
cultural ontogeny 272–97 *passim*
cultural phylogeny 164, 165, 460
culture: adaptation and 142n; ambiguous use of term 30, 247–9, 299–300, 328; areas 267–9; as an information system 86–7, 88–101, 150, 410–12, 461; as system with subsystems 101–31; as temporal and spatial analytical unit 40n; declining use of concept 405n–408n; defined 490; differences 271; entity 279; infiltrating 315; information content 299; states 285; *see also* assemblages, cultural assemblage systems, material culture, sociocultural systems, systems
culture climax 290–7, 490
culture groups: American Indians 385–6, 389, 393; assemblages in 306, 307–9; Bantu 372, 373–4; convergent and divergent trajectories 318–23; Corded Ware/Battle-axe (q.v.); defined 35, 206, 300, 490; demographic relationships 316–17; displacement

culture—*continued*
323–4; distribution area model 311–15; dynamic model 317–18; in Europe 300–2, 326n–327n; language 302–4 *passim*, 312, 370; links 312, 369–70; non-contiguous and non-continuous distribution 312, 313; ontogeny 318–24; parallel trajectories 322, 323; peripheral cultures 326; phase pattern regularities 305–15; range of areas 313; repatterning 418–19; static model 305–10; system pattern regularities 324–6; systems 302–5; time pattern regularities 315–24; trajectories 304–5, 318–24 *passim*; transient 320, 321; TRB 315, 321–2, 403; Urnfield 396–9, 402–4

cumulative effect 49, 68–9, 76, 78–81 *passim*, 287, 461

Cunliffe, B. W. 406n

Cuvier, G., baron 15

cybernetics *see* systems theory

Daniel, G. E. 28, 40n, 405n

Darwin, C. 15, 24

data 13–19, 458, 466–7; collection 12–13, 32, 463n; *see also* excavation

dating 162, 307, 405n, 438, 457, 459

Davis, J. C. 454

De Perthes, Boucher 7

De Sonneville-Bordes, D. 19, 168

'deductive-nomological' explanation 487n

Deetz, J. 139n, 186, 199, 234, 244n, 483

demic diffusion 437–8

demography *see* population

descent groups 139n–140n

determinate systems 54, 59, 61, 63

Dethlefsen, E. 186, 199

diffusion: assemblages 264, 265, 449, 452, 455, 456, 457; axioms 423–4; barriers 426–7, 435, 443, 444, 445; cultural 438; demic 437–8; diffusing elements 422–3; exchange and 420, 428–31, 443; expansion 426; gain from 131, 196, 293, 319, 320, 418; information flow 89; models 426–58; organized 418, 420; postulates 422–3; preconditions for 424–6; preferential 419, 442; radial contour theory 264–5; regional rates 437; secondary 420, 421–2; social 106, 270; stimulus 420; technocomplex and 340; trade and 420, 428–35, 443

dimorphism 257–8

directional/redistributive trade 430–1, 432

directive correlation: agrarian technocomplexes 352–3; defined 58; essential variables 107, 131, 180, 202, 229; future conditions 58, 61; key variables 117, 131, 180, 202, 229, 230; processes model 77; trajectories 70,

directive correlation—*continued*
107, 117; types and 153, 229, 233, 238, 281, 282, 287, 339

disciplined procedure 471–8, 487n

discrete variables 157–8

dis-elaboration 99–100, 105

disjunction *see* alternative variety

dislocation 76, 96–8, 237–8; defined 491; economic subsystem 286; material culture subsystem 130, 286; psychological subsystem 113–14, 286; religious subsystem 110–11, 286

disoperative interchange 357, 358, 359, 362

dispersion: Late Bronze Age socketed axes 169; Mousterian flint leaf-points 167; of artefacts in terms of each attribute 187–91; of attributes in terms of each artefact 182–7; population entity characteristic 152, 414

displacement: culture groups 323–4; equilibrium 76; loss of sociocultural variety 420; termination of type system 230

distance decay models 427–35

distribution: artefacts 187–91, 406n–408n, 428–35, 443; assemblages 263–6, 368; attributes in terms of each artefact 182–7; cultural elements 422–3; curves 165–78 *passim*; entities at sites 440; fall-off (q.v.); models 263–6, 424–6; specific types 368

distribution areas 81–3, 165; culture group model 311–15; diffusion of cultural elements 422–4; technocomplexes 338–9

divergence 252, 253, 270–1, 318–23

Dixon, J. E. 429

Dixon, R. B. 263, 420, 421, 425, 426

Doran, J. E. 13, 23, 41n, 143n, 146n, 147n, 161, 168, 203n, 204n, 205, 212, 213, 214, 244n, 259, 379, 465

Drennan, R. D. 141n, 298n

Driver, H. L. 374, 387

dynamic equilibrium, 49–50, 75–6, 78, 93, 417–18, 444; between system and environment 134–5, 333; economic subsystem 115–16, 121; psychological subsystem 113–14; subsystems in 103, 104; three level debate 93-4, 113

economic subsystem 102, 114–29; dislocation 286; dynamic equilibrium 115–16, 121; environment and 116, 121–2; extractive source of system energy 291; gain 116; oscillation 116–17, 121

Einstein, A. 33

Ellsworth Huntington 116

entities 15, 20, 21; areas 81–2, 83; cultural 279; defined 22–3, 491; dispersion of 152, 414; distribution at sites 440; implications of polythetic nature 37; interaction 417;

entities—*continued*
    inter-communicating 43, 45–6; migration 417; model 35–7, 206, 412–16; ontogeny 151–2, 414, 417; properties and nature, 151–2, 180, 414, 415; structure and composition 151, 414
environment: as complex system in moving equilibrium 138; as system with subsystems 132–8; attributes of 133, 135; changes affecting land use 125; defined 132; economic subsystem and 116, 121–2; insulating system from 53–4, 90, 91, 135, 332–3, 409; processes model 74–5, 76; subsystems of, 133–5
equilibrium 47–51, 198; basin 50–1, 55, 75; definition of 78, 491; dislocation 76; displacement of 76; dynamic (q.v.); information 491; metastable 49, 68, 76, 330; problem of definition 47–8; stable 48, 68, 70, 76, 129; state of 75; statistical 50; steady state 49; types of 48–51; unstable 48
equivocation: defined 491; information flow 89–92 *passim*; social subsystem 105
essential types 262, 280, 285, 287, 306, 317, 323, 338, 339, 340–1
essential variables: adaptation 57–8; as information 88; as relevant attributes 56–7, 71; directive correlation (q.v.); dynamic system 230; environment 133; nature of 70–2, 145n, 155, 201, 210; ontogeny 99, 180, 202; processes model 72–3, 75; selection in Black Box problems 61; social subsystem 107; unilinear procedure 472–3; wide constraints and 54
ethnic subcultures 251–2, 261, 320
ethnographic studies 370–94; historical 394–404
Evans R. K. 203n, 204n
excavation 12–13, 32; *see also* data collection
exchange: communication and 428; diffusion and 420, 428–31, 443; exchanged items 405n–406n, 427
exponential relationship laws 477

Fagen, R. E. 42, 132
fall-off 381, 383–7 *passim*, 389, 390, 392–4 *passim*, 428–31 *passim*, 435, 442–3, 444, 445
families (artefacts) *see* type(s)
Farrer, R. A. H. 431
fauna 132–5 *passim*, 141n, 344–9 *passim*, 351, 352, 353, 360, 361
feedback: as system property 45–7
basis of control and regulation 76; information 91–2, 476; material culture subsystem 130; negative 47, 147n; networks and 46; positive 47, 144n, 146n; regulating subsystems 52–3; subsystems 46–7

Fisher's maximum likelihood method 476
Flannery, K. V. 98, 112, 125, 127, 128, 144n, 146n, 147n, 298n
flora 132–5 *passim*, 344, 345, 348, 350, 351, 352
flow charts 32, 34, 144n–145n, 444–5, 458
fluorescence 292–7 *passim*, 489, 491
Foley, R. 127
food production 144n, 435–8
Ford, J. A. 222
Forde, C. D. 345, 346
format: area 267; artefact 200, 201, 230; blending contradictive variety 200; cultural 75, 91, 93, 99, 279, 280, 282, 285, 286, 287, 461; culture group 318–19, 322; essential variables and 99, 201–2; information 91; integration of attributes into 229; social subsystem 105; stability 75; syntactical 93, 99; type 229
formative system phase 289, 292–4, 341
Fox, C. 269
Frankel, D. 258
Freeman, J. D. 121
Fried, M. H. 103, 139n
Friedman, J. 142n
Fritz, J. 487n
frontier innovation/invention 423

gain: continuity and 461; coupled systems 490; cultural assemblage subsystem 286; defined 491; economic subsystem 116; formative system phase 292–4, 341; from diffusion 131, 196, 293, 319, 320, 418; growth of new cultural format 285; information flow 89–93 *passim*, 97–8, 99; material culture subsystem 131, 196–7, 198; psychological subsystem 114; technocomplexes 333; *see also* fluorescence
game theory 66–72; strategy in 94–6, 117–21 *passim*
Gaussian distribution laws 478
general models 34; entities 35–7, 206, 412–16; procedural 32, 34–5, 458–60; processes (q.v.); social organization 139n
general system ontogeny 292
geographical models 266–9
geology 132–5 *passim*
Gerard, D. R. W. 409
Gifford, E. W..374, 376, 380, 381, 389, 391, 393
Gimbutas, M. 112
Glover, I. C. 212
Gluckman, M. 326
goal-seeking 51–2, 70, 76, 98; *see also* homeostasis
Goguet 6, 8
Goody, J. R. 16
Gorman, C. F. 335

Gould, P. R. 117, 118, 119, 122, 420, 426
Gould, R. A. 203n
gravity models 431–4
Graybill, F. A. 170, 454, 474, 493
Green, E. L. 127, 128
Green, J. A. 55, 83
Green, R. W. 111
grid generalization method 451
group ethnology 363–408
grouped trends 287–90
groups, networks of 104–5

Hägerstrand, T. 427, 438–40
Haggett, P. 118, 119, 426, 439–42 passim, 453, 454, 455, 466, 467, 470, 474, 478
Hall, A. D. 42, 132
Harré, R. 487n
Hartley, K. F. 431
Harvey, D. 487n
Hawkes, C. 268
Hempel, C. 487n
Hencken, H. 197
'heredity' of population entities 64, 65, 66, 88, 89, 152, 325, 414
hierarchical subtype 426
Higgs, E. S. 125, 146n, 405n, 406n
Hill, J. N. 16, 138, 139n, 140n, 147n, 203n, 204n, 462n, 483, 487
Hodder, I. 125, 128, 406n, 407n, 408n, 431–5 passim, 442–8 passim, 451, 454, 456
Hodson, F. R. 13, 23, 41n, 146n, 147n, 161, 168, 203n, 204n, 205, 212, 213, 214, 244n, 258, 259, 379, 465
homeostasis 51–2, 76, 147n–148n; see also goal-seeking
hominids 86–7
homomorphic 94, 491
Hughes, G. B. and T. 185
human group networks 104–5
hunt and stick 52, 76, 92, 105, 130, 200, 333
hunter-fisher-gatherers 98, 114, 121–4, 125, 128, 143n, 294; American Indians 375, 385–93 passim; coaction with agrarian systems 360–1; coaction with pastoral nomad group 358–60; technocomplex 342–5, 348, 352
hypothesis generation 473–8; convergence and integration 475–6; isomorphism 477–8; multiple alternative hypotheses 476–7; regularities 474–5; residues 475; total scrutiny 474
'hypothetico-deductive method' 16

iconic model 31, 32, 35, 459
illusory skewness 167
independent cultures 280, 319–24 passim, 492
independent systems 54, 56, 282, 283
independent types 228, 236, 492
individuals and attributes 363–4

induction 15, 16, 18, 112
inessential types 262, 281, 285, 307, 318, 338
inessential variables: as noise 88; defined 71, 145n, 155; dynamic system 230; environment 133; presence in all artefacts 210; processes model 75; unilinear procedure 472
information: acceptance of 97; activities as 100; defined 492; equilibrium 491; essential variables as 88; feedback 91–2, 476; noise and 58, 88, 410, 411; oscillation and 91–3; rejection of 97; state evolution and 298n; variety in 89–93 passim, 112, 113
information system 86–7, 88–101, 150, 410–12, 461
initial state 69–70
insulation of system from environment 53–4, 90, 91, 135, 332–3, 409
integral definition 58
intercommunicating attributes/entities 43, 45–6
invention 89, 97, 99, 130–1, 184, 196, 198, 230, 278, 293, 333, 340, 348, 418, 420, 423, 439–40
Isaac, G. Ll. 136, 137, 148n, 161, 178, 179, 198, 234, 242n, 243n
isomorphism 59–60, 73, 477–8, 480, 482, 492

Jarman, M. R. 146n
Jaźdźewski, K. 402
Jochim, M. A. 122, 123, 124, 128
Johnson, G. A. 298n
Johnson, L. 487n
Jope, E. M. 253, 406n, 440
Judge, W. J. 201
Jussieu, A. de 6

Kahn, R. S. 474
Kansky 442
Kemp 145n
Kennedy, B. A. 145n
key types 262, 280, 285, 287, 306–7, 323, 423
key variables: blending strategy and 198; covariance (q.v.); defined 71–2, 145n, 155; directive correlation (q.v.); dynamic system 230; economic subsystem 117; environment 133; ontogeny 180, 202, 240; processes model 75; social subsystem 106; system pattern regularities 238; unilinear procedure 472, 473
kinship 102, 103, 269–70, 343
Klindt-Jensen, O. 40n
Kroeber, A. L. 113, 164, 191, 192, 268, 293, 294, 296, 297, 374, 380, 381, 393, 420
Krumbein, W. C. 170, 453, 454, 474, 493
kurtosis 165, 289

lag and lead 73, 76, 92, 98; artefact system 198, 200; economic subsystem 115–16; social subsystem 105
Lagrange's principle 477
Laming, A. 6
language: American Indian 377, 385–94 passim; Bantu 371–4; culture groups 302, 303, 304, 312, 370; diffusion and 421; divergence 271; psychological subsystem 102, 113; technocomplexes 337, 341; Urnfield culture group 398, 399, 402, 403, 404
Larson, P. 456
Lawick-Goodall, H. and J. 18, 19
laws: exponential relationship 477; for social studies 470; Gaussian distribution 478; Lenz's law 477; mass action 477; minimum potential energy equilibrium 477; Monotonic Decrement 428–9; natural 468–9; requisite variety 54
Le Chatelier's principle 477
Leakey, M. 242n
Le Blanc, S. A. 487n
Lee, R. B. 122
lenticular patterns 190, 192–5 passim, 199, 220–5 passim, 236, 273, 461
Lenz's law, 477
Levison, M. 446, 450
Lévi-Strauss, C. 104
Lewin, K. 113
linear model, culture group distribution 313–14
Linearbandkeramik settlements 446, 447, 448
Loire tombs 28–9
long barrows 28–9
Longacre, W. A. 139n, 140n, 203n, 483
Lösch 477
Lotka, A. J. 49, 477

McArthur, M. 142n
McBurney, C. B. M. 138
Mackay, D. M. 465, 477
Malmer, M. P. 172–4, 175
Mander, A. E. 15
Markov, A. A. 63; chain 63–4, 145n, 146n
Maruyama, M. 147n
material culture 18, 40n; functions 409–12 passim; ontogeny 288–90; role of the subculture 250–61; social basis 269–72; subsystem 102, 115, 129–31, 286; see also cultural assemblage systems, culture, sociocultural systems, systems
matrilineal band 355, 356
matrix inversion 474
Matson, R. G. 147n
maximin strategy see minimax strategy
Medawar, P. 487n

Mellaart, J. 112
Mellars, P. A. 19
memory: incompletely observed Black Box system 61; processes model 74; semi-Markovian systems 65
Mercati, M., 4–5, 6, 7, 8, 40n
messages: coded 100; defined 492; information systems 88, 410–11; sociocultural systems 86, 89
metastable equilibrium 49, 68, 76, 330
micro-strategy 201
migration: entity 417; human populations 462n, 463n; South Persian nomads 120–2
Mill, J. S. 472
Miller, J. G. 42
Miller, R. L. 474
minimax: group size 137–8; strategy 95–6, 119, 120–1, 130, 198, 201, 333, 345
minimum potential energy equilibrium laws 477
mixed strategy 93, 94, 95, 116–19 passim, 124, 125, 131, 198, 218, 332, 335, 347
modal range 193, 195
models: analogue (q.v.); branching dichotomous 413; canonical (q.v.); cascading system 145n; classificatory 459–60; complex adaptive 147n, 148n; cultural change 242n–244n; culture group distribution area 311–15; culture groups 305–10, 317–18; dangers in model building 34; defined 31; diffusion 426–58; distance decay 427–35; distribution 263-6, 424–6; entities (q.v.); general (q.v.); geographical 266–9; gravity 431–4; homeostatic 147n–148n; iconic 31, 32, 35, 459; informative 20, 21–2; intuitive procedure 31; isomorphic see isomorphism; material culture system ontogeny 288–90; model building as archaeological activity 12–13; morphological system 145n; multidimensional 413; polynomial function 493; polythetic (q.v.); procedure 32, 34–5, 458–60; processes (q.v.); social organization 139n; stochastic 146n, 438–49; symbolic (q.v.); systems (q.v.); systems theory as source of 144n–146n; three ages 4–10 passim, 22, 30–1, 329, 331, 412; trend 449, 451–8; wave of advance 435–8; see also simulation
Moll, G. 83
monothetic, 35–6, 41nn, 492
Monte Carlo methods 145n, 439–42
Montelius, O. 10, 40n
Moore, G. E. 22
Morgan, C. G. 487n, 488n
Morgenstern, O. 67
Moroney, M. J. 27, 188
morphological system 145n

Morrill, R. L. 440, 441, 442
motifs 156, 160, 199, 255, 334, 463n, 483
Mousterian assemblages 167, 168, 260
Mueller, J. W. 278, 458
multidimensional analysis 258–60
multidimensional constellations 210–17 *passim*, 262
multilinear development 68, 76, 92, 94, 105, 117, 119, 193, 225–6, 229, 238
multimodality 165–6
multiple alternative hypothesis method 476–7
multiple factors and cumulative effect 78–81, 461
multiple regression analysis 476
multiple subcultural aspects 258
multiplier effect 146n
multistate attributes 156–9, 178, 187, 190, 191, 192, 197, 461
multistate types 228, 238, 280, 306, 309, 316, 317, 319, 325, 490
Murdock, G. P. 62, 106, 107, 108, 138n, 268

Nagel, E. 474, 476
Needham, R. 37, 138n
negative feedback 47, 147n
networks: cultural 253, 270; feedback and 46; human groups 104–5; network linkage 462n; oscillation and 77; quantity affecting regulatory potential 91; social 270; systems as 56
Neumann, J. von 67
neutron activation analysis 405n, 427–8
nodes 56–7
noise: attributes as 15; concept of 88, 492; inessential variables as 88; information and 58, 88, 410, 411; separated from information in models 31
nomads 345–51
normal probability curves 165, 166, 167, 170, 171, 176, 178, 466
numerical taxonomy 23, 33, 460
Nyerup, R. 8

Occam's Razor 79–81, 475
occupational subcultures 253–5, 261
Olduvai Gorge 232–3, 242n–244n
ontogeny 68, 69, 99, 151–2, 180ff, 202, 218–43 *passim*; cultural 272–97 *passim*; culture group 318–24; defined 492; entities 151–2, 414, 417; essential variables 99, 180, 202; key variables 180, 202, 240; material culture system model 288–90; systems 68, 69, 99, 292; technocomplex 339–41; type 218ff, 238–42
operational variables 472–3
optical emission spectroscopy 405n, 427–8
optimizer strategies 94, 198, 291, 332, 354

organic phylogeny 164
organized diffusion 418, 420
Orton, C. 125, 128, 406n, 407n, 435, 442–5 *passim*, 451, 454, 456
oscillation: artefact system 198, 200, 218, 219, 221, 224, 230, 236, 238; cultural assemblage systems 272–83 *passim*; economic subsystem 116–17, 121; elaboration and 184–7; goal-seeking 52, 98; information transmission 91–3; material culture subsystem 130; networks and 77; occurence of 76–7; population entity 151–2; psychological subsystem 113; religious subsystem 111; social subsystem 105; subsystems 77; time pattern regularities 180ff; trajectories 68; women's fashions 191–2; *see also* qualitative change and oscillation, quantitative change and oscillation

palaeolithic cultural systems 136–7
parallel trajectory 322, 323
parallel transformation 323
pastoral nomad technocomplex 345–51, 358–60, 361–2
patrilineal band 355, 356
patterning: artefactual 139n; assemblage 264, 266; burial practices 140n; distortion factors 408n
Peacock, D. P. S. 406n, 427, 431
perceived resources 115
percepta 102, 110, 153, 200, 202n–203n, 267, 468, 469, 480, 481
peripheral cultures 326
permeable barriers to diffusion 426
phase pattern regularities 162–80, 209–17, 261–72, 305–15, 337–9
phenetic relationships 164, 493; *see also* affinity relationships
Phillips, E. D. 347, 349
Phillips, P. 40n, 162, 363
phytogenetic relationship 493
phytogeny, cultural 164, 165, 460
Piggott, S. 256, 431, 432
'Pleiades' method 474
Plog. F. 143n, 144n, 145n, 146n, 148n, 487n
polarized diffusion 431; *see also* redistributive/directional trade
Polyani, K. 428
polynomial function model 493
polythetic groups: American views of 41n; attributes within artefacts 182, 183, 187, 201, 208; Bantu entity 372; cultural assemblage systems 246, 249; culture groups 306, 308, 309; defined 36–7, 493; intersecting sets 81–3; origin of concept 41n; systems transformation 68, 69; type ontogeny 239, 240

polythetic model 35–7, 206, 264, 266, 311–15, 338, 412–16
population: arrangement 124; defined 493; entity *see* entities; fluctuations 277–8; growth 444–5; movement 462n–463n; pleistocene 145n; resources and 444–5; size regulation 143n–144n
positive feedback 47, 144n, 146n
post-coherent—'decline' trends 289–90
pottery 26, 406n, 455–6
preferential diffusion 419, 442
prestige chain exchange 429–31
Price, B. J. 139n
primary diffusion 420, 421, 422
probabilistic laws 470
probability: alternative hypotheses 476; propositions 17–18, 365–6; transition 63–6 *passim*, 76, 107, 108
procedure: disciplined 471–8, 487n; models 32, 34–5, 458–60; unilinear 472–3
processes: defined 494; general processes categories 417; hierarchy 419–20, 462n; terminology 418
processes model 38–40, 72–81, 416–58 *passim*, 461
productivity, agricultural 94–5, 114, 127
prototypical range 193, 195
prudential strategy *see* minimax strategy
psychological field space 113
psychological subsystem 102, 103, 112–14, 286
Puche, S. 83

qualitative change and oscillation: cultural assemblage system as a structured system 272, 278–83; cultural group system as a structured system 316, 317–18; entity system as a structured system 152, 414; technocomplex system as a structured system 339; type system 224ff, 236, 237, 289–90
qualitative multistate attributes 157, 174
quantitative change and oscillation 151, 152, 276–8, 288–90, 316, 339, 414; attribute/artefact changes 182–91, 236; number of type families in technocomplex 339; number of types 272–6, 288–90, 316; type population 217–21, 223–4, 236, 288–90
quantitative multistate attributes 157

radial contour theory 263–5
radial model, culture group distribution 313–14
random walks 442–3, 444, 446
randomized strategy 93, 94, 95, 198
range expansion, contraction, drift, budding and migration 462n
Rappaport, R. A. 39, 140n, 141n, 142n

rates of change 51, 61, 99, 285, 289–90
Rathje, W. L. 144n
reciprocity and redistribution 428, 443
redistributive/directional trade 430–1, 432
Redman, C. L. 487n
redundant variety 89, 90, 91, 114, 115, 129, 196–8, 230, 237, 286, 355, 418, 490, 494
regression analysis 406n, 431–2, 433, 473, 475; defined 494
regularities: as tests for real data 150; Black Box investigation 59; constraints and 21–2, 75, 77, 111, 415; contrived 466–8; correlated 109–10, 111; correlated constraint and 69–70, 77, 107, 109; defined 494; hypothesis procedure 474–5; inherent 461; nature of 21, 461; phase pattern (q.v.); search for 20, 150; social organization 109, 139n; system pattern (q.v.); systems trajectories 45, 69–70, 77; time pattern (q.v.)
regulation: cultural assemblage systems 262, 333; economic subsystem 116, 117; goal-seeking 51–2; population size 143n–144n; processes model 76; ritual and 141n, 142n; simple system 65, 71; subsystems 48, 52–3, 65, 74, 412; types as measure of 135–7; variety and 53–4, 90, 91
Reichel-Dolmatoff, G. 141n
religious subsystem 102, 110–12, 140n–143n, 286, 298n
relocation diffusion 426
Renfrew, C. 102, 139n, 146n, 147n, 428–31 *passim*, 435
residence groups 139n–140n
residues method 475
resources: annual rota 344; exploitation 114–16, 343–5, 352, 354; perceived 115; population and 444–5; resource use schedule 124; unexploited 114
responses *see* transformation(s)
reversion 99–100, 105
Reynolds, R. G. D. 145n
Richardson, J. B. 61, 139n, 191, 192
Riemann, G. F. B. 33
Riley, T. J. 487n
rituals 102, 110, 112, 141n–142n
Roe, D. A. 156, 168
Roper, D. C. 455, 456, 457–8
route networks 442
Rowe, J. H. 425
Rowlands, M. J. 255, 297n
Rudner, R. S. 487n

Sackett, J. R. 149, 158, 159
sacrifices 141n, 142n
Sahlins, M. D. 427, 428
sampling 167–8, 458, 459, 463n
Sanders, W. T. 139n

satisficer strategies 94–6, 114, 119, 198, 291, 332, 345
saturating diffusion see acculturation
Saxe, A. A.. 140n
scanning 52, 93, 130
Schiffer, M. B. 40n, 145n, 408n
Schild, R., 335
Schwerdtfeger, F. W. 463n
scientific laws 468
Scollar, I. 313
Scythian climax system 349–50
seasonal variation 405n
secondary diffusion 420, 421–2
sedentism 144n
segregation 144n, 146n, 298n
self-regulation see regulation
Selznick, P. 282
semantics 469, 481, 484–5, 486, 494
semi-Markovian system 64–6, 74, 106, 138n, 331, 461
sequences see trajectories
Service, E. R. 103, 139n
sets: ambiguity and 27–9; boundaries of 55; constrained 70–1, 77; defined 494; intersecting 81–3; Linearbandkeramik 446, 447, 448
settlement 124, 352; patterns 128–9, 146n, 406n, 440–2, 443–9; Polynesia 446–9, 450–1; pre-classic settlements 145n; residence and descent groups 139n–140n
Severn/Cotswold tombs 28–9
sex: male/female role allocation 343, 350–1, 356; subcultures 256–8, 261
Shackleton, N. 431
Shawcross, W. 223
Shennan, S. 257
Sherratt, A. G. 462n
'shotgun' method 474
Simon, H. A. 94
simulation 145n–146n, 438–49; see also models
site-catchment analysis 125, 126–7
site location strategies 124–9; criticisms of 125, 127–8; multiple occupation and functions 463n; non-subsistence factors 128; specific location and resources 127–8
skewness 163, 165–70 passim, 178, 187, 188, 466, 467
Smith, I. F. 26
Sneath, P. H. A. 23, 36, 157, 164, 214, 216, 270, 271, 492, 493
social confederations 303–4
social diffusion 106, 270
social models 269–72
social networks 270
social organization 109, 139n–140n, 342, 350, 368, 372; model 139n

social structure 106–10 passim; burial practices and 140n
social subcultures 255–6, 261
social subsystem 102, 103–10; equivocation 105; nature of 103–5; oscillation in 105; structural sub-types 106–7, 108, 138n
sociocultural programming 483
sociocultural systems: collapse of 98–9; configuration categories 355–6; defined 42, 84, 494; elements as forms of information 100; environment and 133–5, 332–3; interchange 354–6; 'memories' 112, 130; messages 86, 89; model of change 242n–244n; nature of 85–8, 369; role of individual 96–7; see also assemblages, cultural assemblage systems, culture, material culture, systems
socioeconomic level 138
Soja, E. W. 407n
Sokal, R. R. 23, 36, 157, 164, 216, 270, 271, 492, 493
Sommerhoff, G. 58, 153, 155
Spaulding, A. C. 41n
specialist subcultures 254, 261
specific analysis 32, 34–5, 458, 459
specific attributes 13, 14, 15, 156
Spoehr, A. 221
stable equilibrium 48, 68, 70, 76, 129
stable region 50–1, 55, 75
standard deviation 187–90 passim
standard distribution curves 467
Stanislawski, M. B. 140n
staples 344–7 passim, 349, 351, 352, 353, 356, 360
state (community): configuration 355; evolution 144n, 298n
state (value), defined 494
statistical equilibrium 50
steady state equilibrium 49
Steiger, W. L. 147n, 203n, 204n
Stevens, S. S. 84
Steward, J. H. 62, 90, 107, 109, 138, 145n, 256, 291, 338, 343, 354, 355, 419, 484
Stickel, E. G. 487n
Stiles, D. 12
stimulus diffusion 420
stochastic sequence 52, 59, 63
stochastic simulation models 146n, 438–49
stone industries 136–7
strategy: blending (q.v.); climax, (q.v.); game theory 94–6, 117–21 passim; minimax (q.v.); mixed (q.v.)
stratigraphy 40n
subcultural kits see type complexes
subcultural segmentation 258
subcultures: activity 254; aristocratic 255–6; defined 250, 494; ethnic 251–2, 261, 320;

subcultures—*continued*
identified with tribal subdivision 374; intrusion/insertion 419; intrusion/substitution 419; occupational 253–5, 261; regional (q.v.); role of 250–61; varieties of 251

subsistence organization strategies 117–24, 145n, 405n

'substantivist' economic anthropology 428

subsystems 39, 42, 101–31; arbitrary choice of 101–2; cultural assemblage 286; dynamic equilibrium 103, 104; economic (q.v.); environmental 133–5; feedback 46–7; general postulates and 150; material culture (q.v.); oscillation and 77; psychological (q.v.); regulating 48, 52–3, 65, 74, 412; religious (q.v.); social (q.v.)

subtypes 213, 215–17 *passim*, 238, 426, 494

Sullivan, M. E. 128

supra-cultural metal trade 248, 297n–298n

supra-entity 235

symbiosis 268, 349, 357–61 *passim*

symbolic calculus 485

symbolic logic 484

symbolic models 32, 33, 35, 459, 482

syntactics 469, 481–2, 485–6, 495

synthesizing principles 20, 21–2

system pattern regularities: attributes within artefacts 195–202; cultural assemblage system 285–7; culture groups 324–6; key variables 238; technocomplex system 354–62; type system 237–42

systems: as networks 56; behaviour (q.v.); cascading 145n; circuits (q.v.); classification problem 44; common properties 45ff; complex (q.v.); coupled (q.v.); cultures as 101–31; defined 43, 495; described 43–4; determinate (q.v.); environment as system 132–8; independent 54, 56, 282, 283; insulation from environment 53–4, 90, 91, 135, 332–3, 409; isomorphic *see* isomorphism; model 39–40, 196; ontogeny 68, 69, 99, 292; simple 62–72 *passim*; simultaneous membership of multiple systems 56; synergy in 46–7, 56, 60, 101, 150; technocomplex (q.v.); *see also* assemblages, cultural assemblage systems, culture, material culture, sociocultural systems

systems theory 38, 143n–148n; approach to explanation 146n; burial data and 140n; outline of 42–72; reception in America and Britain 142n–143n; source of concepts 143n–144n; source of models 144n–146n; source of propositions/principles 146n; theory of archaeology 143n

Tainker, J. A. 140n, 146n

Tardenoisian technocomplex 331–2

taxonomy: as archaeological activity 12–13; numerical 23, 33, 460

Taylor, W. W. 40n

technocomplex: American Indian 385; Bantu 372; basin 330–1, 339, 340; categories 341–54; defined 495; diffusion and 340; distribution areas 338–9; ethnology and 370, 372, 385; examples 333–7; gain 333; nature of 206, 328–30; ontogeny 339–41; repatterning 419; system 330–62 *passim*; Tardenoisian 331–2

terminal state 69–70

terminology 23–30, 357, 370, 416; ambiguity 27–30, 247–9, 299–300, 328, 332; non-specific generalizations 17–18, 27; processes 418; value judgements 26–7

Terrell, J. 375

Thomas, D. H. 41n, 115, 145n, 178, 203n, 243n, 484

Thompson, R. H. 462n

Thomsen, C. 8–10, 22, 30, 40n, 412

Thomson, D. F. 405n

Thorlacius, S. 8

three ages system 4–10 *passim*, 22, 30–1, 329, 331, 412

three level debate 93–4, 113

thresholds; 'birth/death' trends 288–9; constrained sets as 70; cumulative effect and 49, 68–9, 76, 78–81 *passim*, 105–6, 287; 'death/birth' trends 290; definition of 201–2, 238; differentiating culture states 285; differentiating transform cultures 285; nature of 49; survival of information systems 91; systems transformation 68–9; technocomplex 340–1; type ontogeny 239–40

Thünen, von 125

time lag and lead 92

time pattern regularities 180–95, 217–37, 272–97, 315–24, 339–54

time-trajectories: cultural assemblage systems 52, 162, 278–83 *passim*, 283–4, 285, 325, 340; culture groups 315, 316, 317; models 73, 74, 189–91, 228–31; supra-entity 235; technocomplex 339, 340; type population 52, 162, 163, 182, 183, 184, 187, 191–5 *passim*, 218, 224, 236, 239, 241, 242n

tolerative interchange 357–61 *passim*

tools classifications 203n

total scrutiny method 474

Townsend, A. H. 487n

trade 420, 427, 428–35, 443

traits 374–5, 407n, 408n, 462n

trajectories: cultural assemblage systems 44, 45, 63, 64, 68, 69, 70, 74–7 *passim*, 281–3, 331; culture groups 304–5, 318–24 *passim*; definition 43, 495; directive correlation

trajectories—*continued*
(q.v.); divergent 318–23; economic subsystem 117; game theory 67–70 *passim*, 72; oscillating 68; parallel 322, 323; previous 64, 65, 66, 88, 89, 152, 325, 414; processes model 74–7 *passim*; regularities in 45, 69–70, 77; social subsystem 106–8 *passim*; technocomplex 331, 347; termination of cultural system trajectory 281–3; time- (q.v.); transition probabilities and 64

transform cultures 279–80, 282, 285, 319, 495
transform types 228, 229, 232, 236, 495
transformation(s): closed 62, 63; continuity and 45, 62, 63, 74, 75; convergent, divergent and parallel 323; defined 43–4, 495; game theory 67–72 *passim*; many-valued 63; matrix 62–7, 69, 74, 106, 238; processes model 76; simple system 62–6; single-valued 62–3; type system termination 230; *see also* qualitative change and oscillation, quantitative change and oscillation

transient culture groups 320, 321
transition 63–6 *passim*, 76, 107, 108, 495
TRB culture group 315, 321–2, 403
trend surface analysis 406n, 438, 451–8
trend(s): defined 495; material culture ontogeny 287–90; models 449, 451–8
tribes: American Indian 374–7 *passim*, 380–94 *passim*; as social units 369; Bantu 372, 374; character 113; fluctuations in tribal patterns 105–6; interaction 407n; spatial limits 408n; subdivisions identified with subcultures 374; Urnfield culture group 399, 402, 403, 404

Trigger, B. G. 132, 463n
Tringham, R. 139n, 332
Tuggle, H. D. 487n
Tustin, A. 116

type(s): 'aggregate' of 245–6; American Indian 377, 378, 380–94 *passim*; as measure of insulation 135; comparison of rank 216; complexes 250, 251, 252, 258, 261, 279, 284, 330, 355, 484, 496; concepts 203n, 207, 208; defined by attributes and their ranges 153, 200; definitions 35, 206, 208–9, 496; directive correlation (q.v.); dynamic system 225–30 *passim*; essential (q.v.); essential families 338, 339, 340–1; group 215–17 *passim*, 496; independent 228, 236, 492; inessential 262, 281, 285, 307, 318; inessential families 338; key (q.v.); key families 338, 339, 341; lack of analyses 209; material culture subsystem 129, 130, 131; multistate (q.v.); new type 234–6, 323; not 'culturally-bound' 406n; ontogeny 218ff, 238–42; phase pattern regularities (q.v.); population 130, 238; problems of definition 205–6; qualitative

type(s)—*continued*
change and oscillation 224ff, 236, 237, 289–90; quantitative change and oscillation in numbers of 272–6, 288–90, 316; quantitative change and oscillation in population of 217–21, 223–4, 236, 228–90; 'real' 203n; relationship categories 228; socioeconomic level 138; specific 213, 215, 217, 306, 309, 319, 367–8, 369; 'strength' of system 232; system pattern regularities 237–42; technocomplex system of families 338; termination of system 230, 241, 283; time pattern regularities 180–95, 217–37; transform (q.v.); two cultures compared 90–1; usage patterns 207; use of the term 214–15; variance of attributes within population 278; variation in attributes 37, 157–60 *passim*, 165–80 *passim*

Ucko, P. J. 140n
unilinear procedure 472–3
unimodal patterns 163, 165–70 *passim*, 178, 187, 188, 466, 467
unit reorientation 462n
unstable equilibrium 48
Urnfield culture group 396–9, 402–4

variables: continuous 158; defined 496; essential (q.v.); inessential (q.v.); key (q.v.)
variance: defined 496; of attributes in type populations 278
variation: of attributes within artefacts 37, 157–60 *passim*, 165–80 *passim*; one attribute/one type population 165–74 *passim*; one attribute/several type populations 177; seasonal 405n; several attributes/one type population 176–7; several attributes/several type populations 177–8
variety: alternative 89–92 *passim*, 105, 114, 115, 129, 196–8, 230, 237, 286, 355, 418, 489, 490; categories of 414–15; contradictive 114, 115, 129, 131, 196–8, 200, 237, 286–7, 333, 354, 355, 418, 489, 490, 491; cultural assemblages 250; culture groups 325; defined 496; economic strategies 115; fluctuations in 417–18; goal-seeking 51, 52; in information 89–93 *passim*, 112, 113; new *see* gain; noise as 492; redundant 89, 90, 91, 114, 115, 129, 196–8, 230, 237, 286, 355, 418, 490, 494; regulation and 53–4, 90, 91; technocomplex 340
vectors: defined 496; diffusing elements and 422; incompletely observed system 61; Markovian treatment of states as 64–5; node as systems vector 56
Venn diagrams 82–3
Vertes, L. 167, 170

Vita-Finzi, C. 125
Voegelin, E. W. 394

Ward, R. D. 446, 450
Washburn, D. K. 116
Watson, P. J. 16, 487n
Wauchope, R. 275
Webb, C. H. 222
Webb, J. 446, 450
Whallon, R. 41n, 139n, 483
Whitaker, I. 361
White, J. P. 178, 203n, 243n, 484
White, L. 142n, 148n
Wiener, N. 42
Willey, G. R. 40n, 162, 335, 363, 462n

Wissler, C. 263, 264, 268, 401, 420
Wobst, H. M. 145n
Wolpert, J. 94, 114
Wood, J. J. 147n
Worm, O. 7
Worsaae, J. J. A. 10
Wrigley, E. A. 353
Wynne–Edwards, V. C. 18, 143n

Yadin, Y. 129, 349
Yuill, R. S. 440

Zarky, A. 127
Zipf's principle 477
Zubrow, E. B. W. 146n, 444–6